The Correspondence of
the Dukes of
Richmond and Newcastle
1724–1750

SUSSEX RECORD SOCIETY
VOLUMES ISSUED BY THE SOCIETY

Volumes marked with an asterisk can be obtained from the Hon. Secretary, Sussex Record Society, Barbican House, Lewes, East Sussex BN7 1YE

Most of these Volumes have been photographed in Microfiche by Messrs. Chadwyck-Healey Ltd., 20 Newmarket Road, Cambridge, to whom enquiries should be made.

Frontispiece: Charles Lennox, 2nd Duke of Richmond by William Smith
Reproduced by permission of the County Archivist, West Sussex Record Office.

The Correspondence of the Dukes of Richmond and Newcastle 1724–1750

EDITED BY
TIMOTHY J. McCANN

SUSSEX RECORD SOCIETY
VOLUME 73

Issued to Members of the Society for the years
1982–1983

Published in 1984 by
Sussex Record Society
Barbican House, Lewes.
BN7 1YE

This volume has been published with the help of grants generously provided by the Marc
Fitch Fund, the Twenty Seven Foundation, East Sussex County Council and West Sussex
County Council.

ISBN 0 85445 032 7

Produced by Alan Sutton Publishing Limited
17a Brunswick Road, Gloucester

Printed in Great Britain by
Redwood Burn Limited, Trowbridge

CONTENTS

LIST OF LETTERS

THE CORRESPONDENCE OF THE DUKES OF
RICHMOND AND NEWCASTLE, 1724–1750

1.	Sep. 1724	Goodwood Ms. 1160 f. 120	Newcastle to Richmond
2.	8 Jun. 1732	Goodwood Ms. 1160 f. 1	Pelham to Richmond
3.	22 Jun. 1733	B.L. Add. Ms. 32,688 f. 13	Richmond to Newcastle
4.	30 Jun. 1733	Goodwood Ms. 1160 f. 4	Newcastle to Richmond
5.	2 Aug. 1733	B.L. Add. Ms. 32,688 f. 40	Richmond to Newcastle
6.	3 Aug. 1733	Goodwood Ms. 1160 f. 119	Newcastle to Richmond
7.	5 Aug. 1733	B.L. Add. Ms. 32,688 f. 46	Richmond to Newcastle
8.	6 Aug. 1733	Goodwood Ms. 1160 f. 5	Newcastle to Richmond
9.	6 Aug. 1733	Goodwood Ms. 1160 f. 121	Pelham to Richmond
10.	14 Aug. 1733	B.L. Add. Ms. 32,688 f. 88	Richmond to Newcastle
11.	15 Aug. 1733	B.L. Add. Ms. 32,688 f. 100	Richmond to Newcastle
12.	17 Oct. 1733	B.L. Add. Ms. 32,688 f. 518	Richmond to Newcastle
13.	26 Dec. 1733	B.L. Add. Ms. 32,689 f. 97	Richmond to Newcastle
14.	30 Dec. 1733	B.L. Add. Ms. 32,689 f. 116	Richmond to Newcastle
15.	31 Dec. 1733	Goodwood Ms. 1160 f. 115	Newcastle to Richmond
16.	11 Jan. 1734	B.L. Add. Ms. 32,689 f. 138	Richmond to Newcastle
17.	13 Jan. 1734	B.L. Add. Ms. 32,689 f. 140	Richmond to Newcastle
18.	11 Feb. 1734	Goodwood Ms. 1160 f. 2	Newcastle to Richmond
19.	20 Feb. 1734	B.L. Add. Ms. 32,689 f. 160	Richmond to Newcastle
20.	2 Jul. 1734	B.L. Add. Ms. 32,689 f. 280	Richmond to Newcastle
21.	24 Nov. 1734	B.L. Add. Ms. 32,689 f. 495	Richmond to Newcastle
22.	22 Nov. 1735	Goodwood Ms. 1160 f. 8	Newcastle to Richmond
23.	16 Dec. 1735	Goodwood Ms. 1160 f. 9	Newcastle to Richmond
24.	23 Dec. 1735	Goodwood Ms. 1160 f. 10	Newcastle to Richmond
25.	3 Feb. 1736	Goodwood Ms. 1160 f. 6	Newcastle to Richmond
26.	17 Feb. 1736	Goodwood Ms. 1160 f. 7	Newcastle to Richmond
27.	19 Jun. 1736	Goodwood Ms. 1160 f. 11	Newcastle to Richmond
28.	21 Sep. 1736	B.L. Add. Ms. 32,690 f. 166	Richmond to Newcastle
29.	21 Jun. 1737	Goodwood Ms. 1160 f. 12	Newcastle to Richmond
30.	27 Jun. 1738	Goodwood Ms. 1160 f. 15	Newcastle to Richmond
31.	18 Aug. 1738	B.L. Add. Ms. 32,691 f. 303	Richmond to Newcastle
32.	18 Aug. 1738	Goodwood Ms. 1160 f. 116	Newcastle to Richmond
33.	26 Aug. 1738	B.L. Add. Ms. 32,691 f. 307	Richmond to Newcastle
34.	8 Sep. 1738	B.L. Add. Ms. 32,691 f. 343	Richmond to Newcastle
35.	10 Sep. 1738	B.L. Add. Ms. 32,691 f. 349	Richmond to Newcastle
36.	19 Sep. 1738	B.L. Add. Ms. 32,691 f. 364	Richmond to Newcastle
37.	22 Sep. 1738	B.L. Add. Ms. 32,691 f. 372	Richmond to Newcastle
38.	29 Sep. 1738	B.L. Add. Ms. 32,691 f. 386	Richmond to Newcastle
39.	18 Oct. 1738	B.L. Add. Ms. 32,691 f. 415	Richmond to Newcastle
40.	24 Nov. 1738	B.L. Add. Ms. 32,691 f. 490	Richmond to Newcastle
41.	28 Nov. 1738	Goodwood Ms. 1160 f. 16	Newcastle to Richmond
42.	1 Dec. 1738	B.L. Add. Ms. 32,691 f. 497	Richmond to Newcastle
43.	2 Dec. 1738	Goodwood Ms. 1160 f. 17	Newcastle to Richmond
44.	20 Jul. 1739	B.L. Add. Ms. 32,692 f. 158	Richmond to Newcastle
45.	26 Jul. 1739	Goodwood Ms. 1160 f. 18	Newcastle to Richmond
46.	31 Jul. 1739	Goodwood Ms. 1160 f. 19	Stone to Richmond
47.	7 Aug. 1739	Goodwood Ms. 1160 f. 20	Stone to Richmond
48.	9 Aug. 1739	Goodwood Ms. 1160 f. 21	Newcastle to Richmond

49.	4 Sep. 1739	Goodwood Ms. 1160 f. 22	Pelham to Richmond
50.	25 Sep. 1739	Goodwood Ms. 1160 f. 23	Stone to Richmond
51.	14 Oct. 1739	B.L. Add. Ms. 32,692 f. 574	Richmond to Newcastle
52.	30 Nov. 1739	B.L. Add. Ms. 32,692 f. 488	Richmond to Newcastle
53.	13 Mch. 1740	Goodwood Ms. 1160 f. 3	Newcastle to Richmond
54.	17 Mch. 1740	Goodwood Ms. 107 f. 717	Pelham to Richmond
55.	3 Jul. 1740	Goodwood Ms. 1160 f. 25	Stone to Richmond
56.	10 Jul. 1740	B.L. Add. Ms. 32,693 f. 470	Richmond to Newcastle
57.	10 Jul. 1740	Goodwood Ms. 104 f. 251	Newcastle to Richmond
58.	16 Jul. 1740	B.L. Add. Ms. 32,694 f. 163	Richmond to Newcastle
59.	27 Jul. 1740	B.L. Add. Ms. 32,694 f. 325	Richmond to Newcastle
60.	30 Jul. 1740	B.L. Add. Ms. 32,694 f. 365	Richmond to Newcastle
61.	1 Aug. 1740	B.L. Add. Ms. 32,694 f. 385	Richmond to Newcastle
62.	11 Aug. 1740	B.L. Add. Ms. 32,694 f. 460	Richmond to Newcastle
63.	13 Aug. 1740	B.L. Add. Ms. 32,694 f. 469	Richmond to Newcastle
64.	31 Aug. 1740	B.L. Add. Ms. 32,694 f. 544	Richmond to Newcastle
65.	2 Sep. 1740	Goodwood Ms. 104 f. 252	Newcastle to Richmond
66.	2 Sep. 1740	B.L. Add. Ms. 32,694 f. 563	Richmond to Newcastle
67.	3 Sep. 1740	B.L. Add. Ms. 32,694 f. 567	Richmond to Newcastle
68.	4 Sep. 1740	Goodwood Ms. 1160 f. 26	Newcastle to Richmond
69.	5 Sep. 1740	B.L. Add. Ms. 32,694 f. 587	Richmond to Newcastle
70.	7 Sep. 1740	B.L. Add. Ms. 32,695 f. 22	Richmond to Newcastle
71.	8 Sep. 1740	Goodwood Ms. 1160 f. 27	Newcastle to Richmond
72.	19 Sep. 1740	B.L. Add. Ms. 32,695 f. 88	Richmond to Newcastle
73.	20 Sep. 1740	Goodwood Ms. 1160 f. 28	Newcastle to Richmond
74.	23 Sep. 1740	Goodwood Ms. 104 f. 253	Newcastle to Richmond
75.	29 Sep. 1740	Goodwood Ms. 1160 f. 101	Pelham to Richmond
76.	19 Oct. 1740	B.L. Add. Ms. 32,695 f. 290	Richmond to Newcastle
77.	2 Nov. 1740	B.L. Add. Ms. 32,695 f. 365	Richmond to Newcastle
		Goodwood Ms. 1160 f. 29	
78.	9 Nov. 1740	B.L. Add. Ms. 32,695 f. 381	Richmond to Newcastle
79.	27 Nov. 1740	Goodwood Ms. 1160 f. 30	Pelham to Richmond
80.	29 Nov. 1740	Goodwood Ms. 104 f. 254	Newcastle to Richmond
81.	25 Dec. 1740	Goodwood Ms. 1160 f. 31	Newcastle to Richmond
82.	26 Dec. 1740	B.L. Add. Ms. 32,695 f. 517	Richmond to Newcastle
83.	30 Dec. 1740	Goodwood Ms. 1160 f. 32	Newcastle to Richmond
84.	31 Dec. 1740	B.L. Add. Ms. 32,695 f. 542	Richmond to Newcastle
85.	2 Jan. 1741	B.L. Add. Ms. 32,696 f. 5	Richmond to Newcastle
86.	4 Jan. 1741	Goodwood Ms. 104 f. 255	Newcastle to Richmond
87.	6 Jan. 1741	B.L. Add. Ms. 32,696 f. 11	Richmond to Newcastle
88.	7 Jan. 1741	B.L. Add. Ms. 32,696 f. 19	Richmond to Newcastle
89.	10 Jan. 1741	Goodwood Ms. 1160 f. 24	Newcastle to Richmond
90.	7 Feb. 1741	Goodwood Ms. 104 f. 256	Newcastle to Richmond
91.	17 Feb. 1741	B.L. Add. Ms. 32,696 f. 178	Richmond to Newcastle
92.	21 Feb. 1741	Goodwood Ms. 104 f. 257	Newcastle to Richmond
93.	27 Mch. 1741	B.L. Add. Ms. 32,696 f. 265	Richmond to Newcastle
94.	30 Mch. 1741	Goodwood Ms. 1160 f. 34	Newcastle to Richmond
95.	11 Apr. 1741	Goodwood Ms. 1160 f. 35	Stone to Richmond
96.	30 Apr. 1741	B.L. Add. Ms. 32,696 f. 436	Richmond to Newcastle
97.	2 May. 1741	Goodwood Ms. 1160 f. 36	Pelham to Richmond
98.	17 May. 1741	Goodwood Ms. 1160 f. 37	Stone to Richmond
99.	11 Jun. 1741	Goodwood Ms. 1160 f. 38	Stone to Richmond
100.	14 Jun. 1741	B.L. Add. Ms. 32,697 f. 190	Richmond to Newcastle

101.	16 Jun. 1741	B.L. Add. Ms. 32,697 f. 202	Richmond to Newcastle
102.	19 Jun. 1741	B.L. Add. Ms. 32,697 f. 213	Richmond to Stone
103.	20 Jun. 1741	Goodwood Ms. 104 f. 319	Stone to Richmond
104.	21 Jun. 1741	B.L. Add. Ms. 32,697 f. 232	Richmond to Newcastle
105.	26 Jun. 1741	B.L. Add. Ms. 32,697 f. 247	Richmond to Newcastle
106.	15 Jul. 1741	B.L. Add. Ms. 32,697 f. 316	Richmond to Newcastle
107.	25 Jul. 1741	Goodwood Ms. 104 f. 260	Newcastle to Richmond
108.	28 Jul. 1741	Goodwood Ms. 104 f. 321	Stone to Richmond
109.	29 Jul. 1741	B.L. Add. Ms. 32,697 f. 363	Richmond to Newcastle
110.	1 Aug. 1741	Goodwood Ms. 1160 f. 39	Stone to Richmond
111.	4 Aug. 1741	B.L. Add. Ms. 32,697 f. 382	Richmond to Newcastle
112.	11 Aug. 1741	B.L. Add. Ms. 32,697 f. 409	Richmond to Newcastle
113.	23 Aug. 1741	B.L. Add. Ms. 32,697 f. 450	Richmond to Newcastle
114.	29 Aug. 1741	Goodwood Ms. 107 f. 718	Pelham to Richmond
115.	3 Sep. 1741	Goodwood Ms. 1160 f. 40	Pelham to Richmond
116.	7 Sep. 1741	B.L. Add. Ms. 32,698 f. 13	Richmond to Newcastle
117.	8 Sep. 1741	B.L. Add. Ms. 32,698 f. 15	Richmond to Newcastle
118.	11 Sep. 1741	B.L. Add. Ms. 32,698 f. 38	Richmond to Newcastle
119.	11 Sep. 1741	Goodwood Ms. 104 f. 261	Newcastle to Richmond
120.	15 Sep. 1741	B.L. Add. Ms. 32,698 f. 45	Richmond to Newcastle
121.	17 Sep. 1741	Goodwood Ms. 1160 f. 44	Stone to Richmond
122.	30 Sep. 1741	B.L. Add. Ms. 32,698 f. 86	Richmond to Newcastle
123.	2 Oct. 1741	B.L. Add. Ms. 32,698 f. 94	Richmond to Newcastle
124.	5 Oct. 1741	B.L. Add. Ms. 32,698 f. 102	Richmond to Newcastle
125.	6 Nov. 1741	B.L. Add. Ms. 32,698 f. 268	Richmond to Newcastle
126.	7 Nov. 1741	Goodwood Ms. 1160 f. 45	Newcastle to Richmond
127.	11 Nov. 1741	B.L. Add. Ms. 32,698 f. 306	Richmond to Newcastle
128.	12 Nov. 1741	Goodwood Ms. 1160 f. 46	Stone to Richmond
129.	18 Nov. 1741	B.L. Add. Ms. 32,698 f. 338	Richmond to Newcastle
130.	25 Nov. 1741	B.L. Add. Ms. 32,698 f. 377	Richmond to Newcastle
131.	2 Jan. 1742	Goodwood Ms. 104 f. 258	Newcastle to Richmond
132.	9 Jan. 1742	Goodwood Ms. 104 f. 259	Newcastle to Richmond
133.	7 Mch. 1742	Goodwood Ms. 1160 f. 33	Newcastle to Richmond
134.	9 Mch. 1742	Goodwood Ms. 1160 f. 47	Newcastle to Richmond
135.	14 Apr. 1742	B.L. Add. Ms. 32,699 f. 175	Richmond to Newcastle
136.	17 Apr. 1742	Goodwood Ms. 104 f. 322	Stone to Richmond
137.	1 Jul. 1742	Goodwood Ms. 1160 f. 41	Stone to Richmond
138.	10 Jul. 1742	Goodwood Ms. 1160 f. 42	Stone to Richmond
139.	28 Jul. 1742	B.L. Add. Ms. 32,699 f. 335	Richmond to Newcastle
140.	25 Aug. 1742	Goodwood Ms. 104 f. 262	Newcastle to Richmond
141.	28 Aug. 1742	Goodwood Ms. 1160 f. 43	Newcastle to Richmond
142.	29 Aug. 1742	B.L. Add. Ms. 32,699 f. 386	Richmond to Newcastle
143.	3 Oct. 1742	B.L. Add. Ms. 32,699 f. 430	Richmond to Newcastle
144.	16 Oct. 1742	B.L. Add. Ms. 32,99 f. 463	Richmond to Newcastle
145.	9 Nov. 1742	B.L. Add. Ms. 32,699 f. 521	Richmond to Newcastle
146.	10 Nov. 1742	B.L. Add. Ms. 32,699 f. 529	Richmond to Newcastle
147.	11 Nov. 1742	Goodwood Ms. 140 f. 263	Newcastle to Richmond
148.	28 Nov. 1742	B.L. Add. Ms. 32,699 f. 539	Richmond to Newcastle
149.	30 Nov. 1742	Goodwood Ms. 1160 f. 48	Newcastle to Richmond
150.	1 Dec. 1742	B.L. Add. Ms. 32,699 f. 549	Richmond to Newcastle
151.	3 Dec. 1742	B.L. Add. Ms. 32,699 f. 557	Richmond to Newcastle
152.	6 Dec. 1742	Goodwood Ms. 1160 f. 49	Newcastle to Richmond
153.	14 Dec. 1742	Goodwood Ms. 1160 f. 50	Newcastle to Richmond

204.	16 May. 1744	B.L. Add. Ms. 51,424 f. 25	Pelham to Richmond
205.	17 May. 1744	B.L. Add. Ms. 51,424 f. 27	Newcastle to Richmond
206.	20 May. 1744	B.L. Add. Ms. 51,424 f. 29	Richmond to Pelham
207.	20 May. 1744	B.L. Add. Ms. 32,703 f. 55	Richmond to Newcastle
208.	22 Jun. 1744	B.L. Add. Ms. 32,703 f. 146	Richmond to Newcastle
209.	23 Jun. 1744	Goodwood Ms. 1160 f. 57	Newcastle to Richmond
210.	26 Jun. 1744	Goodwood Ms. 1160 f. 58	Stone to Richmond
211.	30 Jun. 1744	Goodwood Ms. 1160 f. 59	Newcastle to Richmond
212.	30 Jun. 1744	Goodwood Ms. 1160 f. 60	Stone to Richmond
213.	4 Jul. 1744	B.L. Add. Ms. 32,703 f. 192	Richmond to Pelham
214.	8 Jul. 1744	B.L. Add. Ms. 32,703 f. 198	Richmond to Pelham
215.	10 Jul. 1744	Goodwood Ms. 1160 f. 61	Pelham to Richmond
216.	12 Jul. 1744	Goodwood Ms. 1160 f. 62	Newcastle to Richmond
217.	15 Jul. 1744	B.L. Add. Ms. 32,703 f. 223	Richmond to Newcastle
218.	17 Jul. 1744	Goodwood Ms. 1160 f. 63	Stone to Richmond
219.	9 Aug. 1744	Goodwood Ms. 1160 f. 64	Stone to Richmond
220.	25 Aug. 1744	Goodwood Ms. 1160 f. 65	Newcastle to Richmond
221.	30 Aug. 1744	Goodwood Ms. 104 f. 283	Newcastle to Richmond
222.	1 Sep. 1744	Goodwood Ms. 1160 f. 66	Pelham to Richmond
223.	1 Sep. 1744	Goodwood Ms. 104 f. 324	Stone to Richmond
224.	2 Sep. 1744	B.L. Add. Ms. 32,703 f. 299	Richmond to Newcastle
225.	4 Sep. 1744	Goodwood Ms. 104 f. 284	Newcastle to Richmond
226.	13 Sep. 1744	Goodwood Ms. 1160 f. 67	Newcastle to Richmond
227.	16 Sep. 1744	B.L. Add. Ms. 32,703 f. 309	Richmond to Newcastle
228.	18 Sep. 1744	Goodwood Ms. 1160 f. 68	Newcastle to Richmond
229.	6 Oct. 1744	Goodwood Ms. 107 f. 719	Pelham to Richmond
230.	6 Oct. 1744	Goodwood Ms. 1160 f. 69	Newcastle to Richmond
231.	7 Oct. 1744	B.L. Add. Ms. 32,703 f. 355	Richmond to Newcastle
232.	18 Oct. 1744	Goodwood Ms. 1160 f. 70	Stone to Richmond
233.	20 Oct. 1744	Goodwood Ms. 107 f. 720	Pelham to Richmond
234.	21 Oct. 1744	B.L. Add. Ms. 32,703 f. 374	Richmond to Newcastle
235.	8 Nov. 1744	Goodwood Ms. 104 f. 325	Stone to Richmond
236.	10 Nov. 1744	Goodwood Ms. 104 f. 285	Newcastle to Richmond
237.	4 Dec. 1744	Goodwood Ms. 1160 f. 71	Pelham to Richmond
238.	8 Dec. 1744	Goodwood Ms. 1160 f. 72	Newcastle to Richmond
239.	11 Dec. 1744	B.L. Add. Ms. 32,703 f. 464	Richmond to Newcastle
240.	17 Dec. 1744	Goodwood Ms. 104 f. 326	Stone to Richmond
241.	9 Jan. 1745	B.L. Add. Ms. 32,704 f. 4	Richmond to Newcastle
242.	12 Jan. 1745	Goodwood Ms. 104 f. 286	Newcastle to Richmond
243.	10 Feb. 1745	B.L. Add. Ms. 32,704 f. 64	Richmond to Newcastle
244.	14 Feb. 1745	B.L. Add. Ms. 32,704 f. 79	Richmond to Newcastle
245.	3 Mch. 1745	B.L. Add. Ms. 32,704 f. 111	Richmond to Newcastle
246.	5 Mch. 1745	Goodwood Ms. 1160 f. 56	Newcastle to Richmond
247.	8 May. 1745	B.L. Add. Ms. 32,704 f. 280	Richmond to Newcastle
248.	7 Jun. 1745	B.L. Add. Ms. 32,704 f. 356	Richmond to Newcastle
249.	8 Jun. 1745	Goodwood Ms. 1160 f. 73	Stone to Richmond
250.	18 Jul. 1745	Goodwood Ms. 1160 f. 74	Newcastle to Richmond
251.	23 Jul. 1745	B.L. Add. Ms. 32,704 f. 517	Richmond to Newcastle
252.	31 Jul. 1745	B.L. Add. Ms. 32,704 f. 551	Richmond to Newcastle
253.	3 Aug. 1745	Goodwood Ms. 104 f. 288	Newcastle to Richmond
254.	7 Aug. 1745	B.L. Add. Ms. 32,705 f. 20	Richmond to Newcastle
255.	10 Aug. 1745	Goodwood Ms. 1160 f. 75	Newcastle to Richmond
256.	11 Aug. 1745	B.L. Add. Ms. 32,705 f. 33	Richmond to Newcastle

257.	13 Aug. 1745	Goodwood Ms. 1160 f. 76	Newcastle to Richmond
258.	14 Aug. 1745	Goodwood Ms. 1160 f. 77	Newcastle to Richmond
259.	16 Aug. 1745	B.L. Add. Ms. 32,705 f. 57	Richmond to Newcastle
260.	25 Aug. 1745	B.L. Add. Ms. 32,705 f. 110	Richmond to Newcastle
261.	5 Sep. 1745	Goodwood Ms. 1160 f. 78	Stone to Richmond
262.	7 Sep. 1745	Goodwood Ms. 1160 f. 79	Stone to Richmond
263.	8 Sep. 1745	B.L. Add. Ms. 32,705 f. 147	Richmond to Newcastle
264.	12 Sep. 1745	Goodwood Ms. 1160 f. 80	Stone to Richmond
265.	14 Sep. 1745	Goodwood Ms. 1160 f. 81	Newcastle to Richmond
266.	15 Sep. 1745	B.L. Add. Ms. 32,705 f. 181	Richmond to Newcastle
267.	16 Sep. 1745	B.L. Add. Ms. 32,705 f. 187	Richmond to Newcastle
268.	17 Sep. 1745	Goodwood Ms. 1160 f. 82	Newcastle to Richmond
269.	17 Sep. 1745	B.L. Add. Ms. 32,705 f. 191	Richmond to Newcastle
270.	18 Sep. 1745	B.L. Add. Ms. 32,705 f. 194	Richmond to Newcastle
271.	21 Sep. 1745	Goodwood Ms. 1160 f. 83	Newcastle to Richmond
272.	21 Sep. 1745	Goodwood Ms. 1160 f. 85	Stone to Richmond
273.	24 Sep. 1745	Goodwood Ms. 1160 f. 84	Stone to Richmond
274.	25 Sep. 1745	B.L. Add. Ms. 32,705 f. 215	Richmond to Newcastle
275.	25 Sep. 1745	B.L. Add. Ms. 32,705 f. 217	Richmond to Stone
276.	21 Oct. 1745	B.L. Add. Ms. 32,705 f. 266	Richmond to Newcastle
277.	21 Nov. 1745	B.L. Add. Ms. 32,705 f. 338	Richmond to Newcastle
278.	22 Nov. 1745	B.L. Add. Ms. 32,705 f. 346	Newcastle to Richmond
279.	23 Nov. 1745	B.L. Add. Ms. 32,705 f. 354	Richmond to Newcastle
280.	23 Nov. 1745	B.L. Add. Ms. 32,705 f. 360	Richmond to Newcastle
281.	24 Nov. 1745	B.L. Add. Ms. 32,705 f. 362	Richmond to Newcastle
282.	24 Nov. 1745	B.L. Add. Ms. 32,705 f. 363	Newcastle to Richmond
283.	25 Nov. 1745	B.L. Add. Ms. 32,705 f. 365 Goodwood Ms. 1160 f. 86	Richmond to Newcastle
284.	28 Nov. 1745	B.L. Add. Ms. 32,705 f. 387	Richmond to Newcastle
285.	29 Nov. 1745	B.L. Add. Ms. 32,705 f. 395	Richmond to Newcastle
286.	30 Nov. 1745	Goodwood Ms. 104 f. 290	Newcastle to Richmond
287.	30 Nov. 1745	B.L. Add. Ms. 32,705, f. 399	Richmond to Newcastle
288.	1 Dec. 1745	Goodwood Ms. 104 f. 291	Newcastle to Richmond
289.	3 Dec. 1745	Goodwood Ms. 104 f. 292	Newcastle to Richmond
290.	4 Dec. 1745	B.L. Add. Ms. 32,705 f. 405	Richmond to Newcastle
291.	5 Dec. 1745	B.L. Add. Ms. 32,705 f. 409	Richmond to Newcastle
292.	6 Dec. 1745	B.L. Add. Ms. 32,705 f. 411	Newcastle to Richmond
293.	7 Dec. 1745	B.L. Add. Ms. 32,705 f. 421	Richmond to Newcastle
294.	11 Dec. 1745	B.L. Add. Ms. 32,705 f. 427	Richmond to Newcastle
295.	12 Dec. 1745	Goodwood Ms. 104 f. 293	Newcastle to Richmond
296.	15 Dec. 1745	B.L. Add. Ms. 32,705 f. 435	Richmond to Newcastle
297.	19 Dec. 1745	B.L. Add. Ms. 32,705 f. 445	Richmond to Newcastle
298.	24 Dec. 1745	B.L. Add. Ms. 32,705 f. 458	Richmond to Newcastle
299.	30 Dec. 1745	B.L. Add. Ms. 32,705 f. 468	Richmond to Newcastle
300.	17 Jan. 1746	Goodwood Ms. 1160 f. 87	Stone to Richmond
301.	29 Jan. 1746	B.L. Add. Ms. 32,706 f. 59	Richmond to Newcastle
302.	29 Jan. 1746	B.L. Add. Ms. 32,706 f. 63	Richmond to Stone
303.	31 Jan. 1746	B.L. Add. Ms. 32,706 f. 89	Richmond to Newcastle
304.	1 Feb. 1746	Goodwood Ms. 1160 f. 88	Stone to Richmond
305.	5 Feb. 1746	Goodwood Ms. 104 f. 295	Newcastle to Richmond
306.	5 Feb. 1746	B.L. Add. Ms. 32,706 f. 104	Richmond to Newcastle
307.	6 Feb. 1746	B.L. Add. Ms. 32,706 f. 114	Richmond to Newcastle
308.	(10 Feb. 1746)	Goodwood Ms. 104 f. 297	Newcastle to Richmond

309.	11 Feb. 1746	B.L. Add. Ms. 32,706 f. 140	Richmond to Newcastle
310.	18 Feb. 1746	B.L. Add. Ms. 32,706 f. 163	Richmond to Stone
311.	26 Feb. 1746	B.L. Add. Ms. 32,706 f. 219	Richmond to Newcastle
312.	28 Feb. 1746	B.L. Add. Ms. 32,706 f. 229	Richmond to Stone
313.	4 Mch. 1746	Goodwood Ms. 104 f. 327	Stone to Richmond
314.	4 Mch. 1746	B.L. Add. Ms. 32,706 f. 237	Richmond to Newcastle
315.	6 Mch. 1746	Goodwood Ms. 1160 f. 89	Newcastle to Richmond
316.	9 Mch. 1746	B.L. Add. Ms. 32,706 f. 278	Richmond to Newcastle
317.	20 Mch. 1746	Goodwood Ms. 104 f. 328	Stone to Richmond
318.	23 Apr. 1746	Goodwood Ms. 104 f. 329	Stone to Richmond
319.	24 Apr. 1746	Goodwood Ms. 104 f. 330	Stone to Richmond
320.	25 Apr. 1746	B.L. Add. Ms. 32,707 f. 98	Richmond to Newcastle
321.	25 Apr. 1746	B.L. Add. Ms. 32,707 f. 102	Richmond to Stone
322.	26 Apr. 1746	Goodwood Ms. 1160 f. 90	Stone to Richmond
323.	27 Apr. 1746	B.L. Add. Ms. 32,707 f. 110	Richmond to Stone
324.	6 May. 1746	Goodwood Ms. 1160 f. 91	Newcastle to Richmond
325.	7 May. 1746	B.L. Add. Ms. 32,707 f. 155	Richmond to Newcastle
		Goodwood Ms. 1160 f. 92	
326.	8 May 1746	Goodwood Ms. 1160 f. 93	Newcastle to Richmond
		B.L. Add. Ms. 32,707 f. 159	
327.	10 May. 1746	Goodwood Ms. 1160 f. 94	Pelham to Richmond
328.	11 May. 1746	B.L. Add. Ms. 32,707 f. 188	Richmond to Newcastle
		Goodwood Ms. 1160 f. 95	
329.	14 May. 1746	Goodwood Ms. 1160 f. 96	Richmond to Pelham
330.	18 May. 1746	B.L. Add. Ms. 32,707 f. 212	Richmond to Stone
331.	20 May. 1746	Goodwood Ms. 1160 f. 97	Stone to Richmond
332.	25 May. 1746	B.L. Add. Ms. 32,707 f. 245	Richmond to Newcastle
333.	31 May. 1746	Goodwood Ms. 1160 f. 98	Newcastle to Richmond
334.	4 Jun. 1746	B.L. Add. Ms. 32,707 f. 280	Richmond to Newcastle
335.	8 Jun. 1746	B.L. Add. Ms. 32,707 f. 294	Richmond to Newcastle
336.	17 Jun. 1746	Goodwood Ms. 1160 f. 99	Stone to Richmond
337.	24 Jun. 1746	B.L. Add. Ms. 32,707 f. 348	Richmond to Newcastle
338.	25 Jun. 1746	B.L. Add. Ms. 32,707 f. 352	Richmond to Newcastle
339.	28 Jun. 1746	Goodwood Ms. 104 f. 316	Newcastle to Richmond
340.	29 Jun. 1746	B.L. Add. Ms. 32,707 f. 378	Richmond to Newcastle
341.	1 Jul. 1746	Goodwood Ms. 1160 f. 100	Pelham to Richmond
342.	29 Jul. 1746	B.L. Add. Ms. 32,707 f. 503	Richmond to Newcastle
343.	12 Aug. 1746	B.L. Add. Ms. 32,708 f. 58	Richmond to Newcastle
344.	20 Aug. 1746	B.L. Add. Ms. 32,708 f. 108	Richmond to Newcastle
345.	21 Aug. 1746	Goodwood Ms. 104 f. 296	Newcastle to Richmond
346.	10 Sep. 1746	B.L. Add. Ms. 32,708 f. 249	Richmond to Newcastle
347.	12 Sep. 1746	B.L. Add. Ms. 32,708 f. 280	Richmond to Newcastle
348.	19 Sep. 1746	B.L. Add. Ms. 32,708 f. 338	Richmond to Newcastle
349.	21 Sep. 1746	B.L. Add. Ms. 32,708 f. 346	Richmond to Newcastle
350.	23 Sep. 1746	B.L. Add. Ms. 32,708 f. 362	Richmond to Stone
351.	12 Oct. 1746	B.L. Add. Ms. 32,709 f. 45	Richmond to Newcastle
352.	8 Nov. 1746	Goodwood Ms. 104 f. 298	Newcastle to Richmond
353.	8 Nov. 1746	Goodwood Ms. 104 f. 331	Stone to Richmond
354.	30 Nov. 1746	B.L. Add. Ms. 32,709 f. 283	Richmond to Newcastle
355.	4 Dec. 1746	Goodwood Ms. 104 f. 299	Newcastle to Richmond
356.	16 Dec. 1746	B.L. Add. Ms. 32,709 f. 332	Richmond to Newcastle
357.	1 Jan. 1747	Goodwood Ms. 104 f. 300	Newcastle to Richmond
358.	2 Jan. 1747	B.L. Add. Ms. 32,710 f. 5	Richmond to Newcastle

359.	4 Jan. 1747	Goodwood Ms. 104 f. 301	Newcastle to Richmond
360.	1 Feb. 1747	B.L. Add. Ms. 32,710 f. 134	Richmond to Newcastle
361.	13 Feb. 1747	B.L. Add. Ms. 32,710 f. 210	Richmond to Newcastle
362.	15 Feb. 1747	B.L. Add. Ms. 32,710 f. 203	Richmond to Newcastle
363.		B.L. Add. Ms. 32,710 f. 234	Richmond to Newcastle
364.	Mch. 1747	B.L. Add. Ms. 32,710 f. 404	Richmond to Newcastle
365.	7 Apr. 1747	B.L. Add. Ms. 32,710 f. 419	Richmond to Newcastle
366.	11 Apr. 1747	Goodwood Ms. 104 f. 302	Newcastle to Richmond
367.	12 May. 1747	B.L. Add. Ms. 32,711 f. 33	Richmond to Newcastle
368.	16 May. 1747	Goodwood Ms. 1160 f. 104	Stone to Richmond
369.	3 Jun. 1747	B.L. Add. Ms. 32,711 f. 196	Richmond to Newcastle
370.	7 Jun. 1747.	B.L. Add. Ms. 32,711 f. 254	Richmond to Newcastle
371.	20 (Jun.) 1747	B.L. Add. Ms. 32,713 f. 628	Richmond to Newcastle
372.	20 Jun. 1747	Goodwood Ms. 104 f. 303	Newcastle to Richmond
373.	(21 Jun.) 1747	B.L. Add. Ms. 32,713 f. 625	Richmond to Newcastle
374.	2 Jul. 1747	Goodwood Ms. 104 f. 304	Pelham to Richmond
375.	16 Jul. 1747	Goodwood Ms. 104 f. 305	Newcastle to Richmond
376.	16 Jul. 1747	Goodwood Ms. 107 f. 721	Pelham to Richmond
377.	17 Jul. 1747	B.L. Add. Ms. 32,712 f. 146	Richmond to Newcastle
378.	18 Jul. 1747	Goodwood Ms. 104 f. 306	Newcastle to Richmond
379.	19 Jul. 1747	B.L. Add. Ms. 32,712 f. 156	Richmond to Newcastle
380.	22 Jul. 1747	Goodwood Ms. 1160 f. 105	Stone to Richmond
381.	30 Jul. 1747	Goodwood Ms. 104 f. 307	Newcastle to Richmond
382.	12 Aug. 1747	Goodwood Ms. 104 f. 308	Newcastle to Richmond
383.	14 Aug. 1747	Goodwood Ms. 107 f. 722	Pelham to Richmond
384.	29 Aug. 1747	Goodwood Ms. 104 f. 309	Newcastle to Richmond
385.	5 Sep. 1747	Goodwood Ms. 104 f. 310	Newcastle to Richmond
386.	10 Sep. 1747	Goodwood Ms. 104 f. 332	Stone to Richmond
387.	12 Sep. 1747	Goodwood Ms. 104 f. 311	Newcastle to Richmond
388.	2 Oct. 1747	B.L. Add. Ms. 32,713 f. 205	Richmond to Newcastle
389.	18 Oct. 1747	B.L. Add. Ms. 32,713 f. 277	Richmond to Newcastle
390.	20 Oct. 1747	Goodwood Ms. 104 f. 312	Newcastle to Richmond
391.	26 Oct. 1747	Goodwood Ms. 104 f. 333	Stone to Richmond
392.	21 Nov. 1747	Goodwood Ms. 104 f. 313	Newcastle to Richmond
393.	1 Jan. 1748	Goodwood Ms. 1160 f. 102	Newcastle to Richmond
394.	3 Jan. 1748	B.L. Add. Ms. 32,714 f. 10	Richmond to Newcastle
395.	3 Jan. 1748	B.L. Add. Ms. 32,714 f. 14	Richmond to Newcastle
396.	26 Jan. 1748	B.L. Add. Ms. 32,714 f. 105	Richmond to Newcastle
397.	2 Feb. 1748	B.L. Add. Ms. 32,714 f. 172	Richmond to Newcastle
398.	6 Feb. 1748	Goodwood Ms. 1160 f. 103	Newcastle to Richmond
399.	7 Feb. 1748	B.L. Add. Ms. 32,714 f. 190	Richmond to Newcastle
400.	9 Feb. 1748	B.L. Add. Ms. 32,714 f. 200	Richmond to Newcastle
401.	12 Feb. 1748	B.L. Add. Ms. 32,714 f. 219	Richmond to Newcastle
402.	13 Feb. 1748	Goodwood Ms. 104 f. 314	Newcastle to Richmond
403.	13 Feb. 1748	B.L. Add. Ms. 32,714 f. 223	Richmond to Newcastle
404.	17 Feb. 1748	B.L. Add. Ms. 32,714 f. 235	Richmond to Newcastle
405.	2 Mch. 1748	B.L. Add. Ms. 32,714 f. 292	Richmond to Newcastle
406.	16 Apr. 1748	Goodwood Ms. 1160 f. 107	Stone to Richmond
407.	20 Apr. 1748	B.L. Add. Ms. 32,714 f. 504	Richmond to Newcastle
408.	25 Apr. 1748	B.L. Add. Ms. 32,714 f. 531	Richmond to Newcastle
409.	26 Apr. 1748	B.L. Add. Ms. 32,714 f. 538	Richmond to Newcastle
410.	2 May. 1748	Goodwood Ms. 1160 f. 108	Stone to Richmond
411.	May. 1748	Goodwood Ms. 1160 f. 118	Newcastle to Richmond

412.	24 May. 1748	Goodwood Ms. 1160 f. 109	Ramsden to Richmond
413.	17 Jun. 1748	B.L. Add. Ms. 32,715 f. 206	Richmond to Newcastle
414.	21 Jun. 1748	B.L. Add. Ms. 32,715 f. 222	Richmond to Newcastle
415.	28 Aug. 1748	B.L. Add. Ms. 32,716 f. 133	Richmond to Newcastle
416.	6 Sep. 1748	B.L. Add. Ms. 32,716 f. 188	Richmond to Newcastle
417.	21 Sep. 1748	Goodwood Ms. 1160 f. 110	Newcastle to Richmond
418.	12 Oct. 1748	B.L. Add. Ms. 32,717 f. 103	Richmond to Newcastle
		Goodwood Ms. 1160 f. 111	
419.	12 Nov. 1748	Goodwood Ms. 155 f. 18	Pelham to Richmond
420.	Nov. 1748	Goodwood Ms. 156 f. 24	Richmond to Pelham
421.	13 Nov. 1748	B.L. Add. Ms. 32,717 f. 308	Richmond to Newcastle
422.	11 Dec. 1748	B.L. Add. Ms. 32,717 f. 407	Richmond to Newcastle
423.	11 Dec. 1748	B.L. Add. Ms. 32,717 f. 409	Richmond to Newcastle
424.	18 Dec. 1748	B.L. Add. Ms. 32,717 f. 489	Richmond to Newcastle
425.	21 Feb. 1749	B.L. Add. Ms. 32,718 f. 98	Richmond to Newcastle
426.	21 Feb. 1749	Goodwood Ms. 155 f. 97	Pelham to Richmond
427.	26 Feb. 1749	B.L. Add. Ms. 32,718 f. 111	Richmond to Newcastle
428.	16 Mch. 1749	B.L. Add. Ms. 32,718 f. 127	Richmond to Newcastle
429.	17 Apr. 1749	B.L. Add. Ms. 32,718 f. 175	Richmond to Newcastle
430.	18 Jun. 1749	Goodwood Ms. 104 f. 287	Newcastle to Richmond
431.	14 Jul. 1749	B.L. Add. Ms. 32,718 f. 301	Richmond to Newcastle
432.	16 Jul. 1749	B.L. Add. Ms. 32,718 f. 309	Richmond to Newcastle
433.	19 Jul. 1749	B.L. Add. Ms. 32,718 f. 321	Richmond to Newcastle
434.	19 Jul. 1749	B.L. Add. Ms. 32,718 f. 322	Richmond to Newcastle
435.	23 Jul. 1749	B.L. Add. Ms. 32,718 f. 337	Richmond to Newcastle
436.	31 Aug. 1749	B.L. Add. Ms. 32,818 f. 155	Richmond to Newcastle
437.	7 Sep. 1749	Goodwood Ms. 1160 f. 113	Newcastle to Richmond
		B.L. Add. Ms. 32,818 f. 190	
438.	12 Sep. 1749	B.L. Add. Ms. 32,818 f. 214	Richmond to Newcastle
439.	24 Sep. 1749	B.L. Add. Ms. 32,719 f. 184	Richmond to Stone
440.	7 Oct. 1749	B.L. Add. Ms. 32,719 f. 225	Richmond to Stone
441.	(8 Nov. 1749)	Goodwood Ms. 104 f. 317	Newcastle to Richmond
442.	9 Nov. 1749	Goodwood Ms. 104 f. 318	Newcastle to Richmond
443.	24 Dec. 1749	B.L. Add. Ms. 32,719 f. 332	Richmond to Newcastle
444.	25 Dec. 1749	Goodwood Ms. 104 f. 294	Newcastle to Richmond
445.	22 Mch. 1750	B.L. Add. Ms. 32,720 f. 154	Richmond to Newcastle
446.	31 Mch. 1750	B.L. Add. Ms. 32,720 f. 182	Richmond to Newcastle
447.	9 Apr. 1750	B.L. Add. Ms. 32,720 f. 194	Richmond to Newcastle
448.	29 Apr. 1750	B.L. Add. Ms. 32,720 f. 253	Richmond to Newcastle
449.	3 May. 1750	B.L. Add. Ms. 32,720 f. 273	Richmond to Newcastle
450.	10 May. 1750	B.L. Add. Ms. 32,720 f. 307	Richmond to Newcastle
451.	18 May. 1750	B.L. Add. Ms. 32,720 f. 337	Richmond to Newcastle
452.	31 May. 1750	B.L. Add. Ms. 32,720 f. 431	Richmond to Newcastle
453.	6 Jun. 1750	B.L. Add. Ms. 32,721 f. 51	Richmond to Newcastle
454.	15 Jun. 1750	B.L. Add. Ms. 32,721 f. 111	Richmond to Newcastle
455.	18 Jun. 1750	B.L. Add. Ms. 32,721 f. 125	Richmond to Newcastle
456.	21 Jun. 1750	B.L. Add. Ms. 32,721 f. 139	Richmond to Newcastle
457.	17 Jul. 1750	Goodwood Ms. 1160 f. 114	Pelham to Richmond
458.	18 Jul. 1750	B.L. Add. Ms. 32,721 f. 400	Richmond to Newcastle
459.	27 Jul. 1750	B.L. Add. Ms. 32,721 f. 461	Richmond to Newcastle
460.	27 Jul. 1750	B.L. Add. Ms. 32,721 f. 465	Richmond to Newcastle
461.	3 Aug. 1750	B.L. Add. Ms. 32,722 f. 46	Newcastle to Richmond
462.		Goodwood Ms. 1160 f. 123	Stone to Richmond

ACKNOWLEDGEMENTS

I am grateful to the Trustees of the Goodwood Collections for permission to publish the letters of the Duke of Newcastle, Henry Pelham and Andrew Stone, which are among the Goodwood Archives in the West Sussex Record Office at Chichester. Lord March has given me every encouragement in the twelve years during which I have been responsible for the Goodwood Records. David Legg-Willis, the House Manager at Goodwood, has given me much assistance. Mrs. Patricia Gill, the County Archivist at Chichester, has been a constant source of advice and support. I am grateful to the Trustees of the British Library for permission to publish the letters of the Duke of Richmond, which are among the Newcastle Papers in their custody. Professor Mary Margaret Stewart kindly drew my attention to the letters, once at Goodwood, about the elopement of Henry Fox with Lady Caroline Lennox, which are now among the Holland House Papers now also in the British Library.

Several years ago, W.E. Thumwood transcribed a number of Newcastle's letters to Richmond, under my supervision, and gave me much help in deciphering Newcastle's unreadable handwriting. I am grateful to the Council of the Sussex Record Society for undertaking the publication of this volume. My friend and colleague, Peter Wilkinson, the Honorary Secretary of the Society, has read the typescript, and the volume has greatly benefited from his valuable suggestions and encouragement. Dr. Marie Clough, the Society's Literary Director, has been a wise and generous critic. Alan Dibben, formerly County Records Officer for East Sussex, and a member of the Council of the Society, has given this volume his wholehearted support. I am grateful to the Marc Fitch Fund, the Twenty Seven Foundation, East Sussex County Council and West County Council for generous grants towards the production of this volume.

Alison McCann, my wife and colleague, has given up much of the last few years to the 2nd. Duke of Richmond, time that she would rather have devoted to the 3rd. Earl of Egremont. She has read every word of this book, and it has benefited greatly from her paleographic skill, her knowledge of eighteenth century Chichester, and her constant encouragement. Without her advice, support and commitment the volume would never have been completed.

EDITORIAL PRINCIPLES

So far as is possible, the letters transcribed in this volume have been printed exactly as they were written. No doubt it would have been easier to read the correspondence had some of the spelling, punctuation, and the varied renderings of personal and place names been modernised, but something would have been lost in the process. Richmond, Newcastle and Henry Pelham all express their personalities in their style of writing.

The following principles have been used in the editing of the letters. Superscript letters and numbers have been silently lowered to the line. Neither they nor the frequent abbreviations have been expanded. The headings, salutations and conclusions of letters have usually been united into sentences, instead of being spread over much of the page, as in the original. They have not been standardised, as their subtle changes often reflect the emotions expressed in the letters. The few undated letters have been dated, usually from internal evidence, within square brackets. The only undatable letter is printed at the end of the series. Where letters are incorrectly dated by the writer, this is indicated within square brackets. My own spelling has always been poor, transcribing Richmond's letters has made it considerably worse: Richmond's spelling is eccentric, but consistently so, and I have chosen to follow his practice. All the writers, and both Newcastle and Andrew Stone in particular, use capital letters for proper nouns. They have been left as originally written. I have not altered the eccentric spellings of personal and place names (Richmond and Newcastle disagree about the spelling of Sir Thomas Prendergast's name for forty years) but they are in the correct forms in the index. I have tampered very little with the punctuation of any of the writers, except to supply end punctuation where it is omitted, or an occasional interior mark of punctuation where it is demanded by clarity. Very occasionally I have introduced a new paragraph to break up a particularly indigestible passage. All underlinings are those of the original writers.

The source of the text of the letters is indicated in the List of Letters on pp. ix–xvii, and manuscript sources have been used on all occasions. Some of Richmond and Newcastle's letters were printed by the Earl of March, in *A Duke and His Friends*, (1911). I have compared our respective transcripts only when in doubt about the reading of particular words or names. To have attempted to identify all the persons mentioned in the letters, would have required a wider knowledge than I possess, and would have made the book even longer than it already is. I have tried to identify all those who play a significant part in those affairs discussed by the two Dukes. Needless to say, I have not always succeeded. Once identified, persons are not identified again. I have minimised cross-references, but readers will normally find persons identified on the page where their name first appears, and this will be indicated in the index. An index of persons and places has been provided, and subjects are identified in the Chronology that preceeds the letters.

INTRODUCTION

In 1723, the Duke of Newcastle wrote to Bishop Bowers of Chichester, concerning the forthcoming election for the city seat, "all our friends here think we should espouse the Duke of Richmond's interest as being the most solid support of the Whig interest in Chichester. I therefore conclude you will give your interest to the young Duke's candidate for the City of Chichester, which certainly is right for us to do upon all accounts as the Duke of Richmond is a growing young man and may be very considerable in your parts"[1]. The two Dukes, whose relationships began with this mutual interest in politics, became firm friends as well as political allies for the rest of their lives, and their surviving correspondence consists of 462 letters, dating from 1724 until Richmond's death in 1750. 250 of these letters, which Professor Curtis in his *Chichester Towers*, described as "those wonderful unguarded letters to Newcastle, into which Richmond was wont to pack his horse sense, his sizing up of men, his humour, and so much of his affection"[2], are deposited among the Newcastle Papers in the British Library. The letters from Newcastle and his brother Henry Pelham to Richmond, which were once at Goodwood and Gordon Castle, are now among the Goodwood Archives in the West Sussex Record Office at Chichester.[3] Professor Reed Browning, in his recent biography of Newcastle, wrote that "the Newcastle Papers in the British Museum reveal Richmond as a racy correspondent, whose unblushing epistolary manner, in our own era of easier standards, need no longer be confined to the archives"[4]. The surviving correspondence between the two Dukes is here printed for the first time.

Horace Walpole claimed that Richmond "loved the Duke of Newcastle, the only man who ever did"[5], and Richmond's lifelong devotion to him does Newcastle great credit. "To you, and you only, I open my heart, knowing it is to the best and dearest friend I have in the world"[6], Richmond wrote to Newcastle, and their correspondence charts their relationship from electoral allies to affectionate and intimate friends. The characters of the two men come across vividly in their letters. Richmond's letters are a lively illustration of the life of a country magnate, as he writes of his 'Sussex caravan'; his friends and their hospitality; their dinners and their drinking bouts; their masques and their poetry; their hunting and their cricket; and, of course, their local politics. Richmond was very much Newcastle's agent in the western half of the county, and kept him informed of local opinion; advising him on the distribution of jobs and favours; and suggesting recipients for Newcastle's voluminous correspondence. He also gave dinners for Newcastle's supporters and arranged itineraries for his parliamentary candidates.

Although their relationship was founded on their mutual support for Whig principles, and their shared enthusiasm for Sussex politics, Richmond and Newcastle were also national figures,and their letters discuss the matters of concern of the day. Both were members of the Council, and Richmond gave willing support to his political friends in the various crises which befell the Whig administrations, and, particularly with Newcastle himself, offered cool and sensible advice to his often harrassed, sensitive and despairing friend. Although Newcastle kept him informed of all the discussions about politics and foreign affairs, Richmond took particular interest in military matters. He watched with

---

1. Newcastle to Bishop Bowers, 6 June 1723. B(ritish) L(ibrary). Add. Ms. 32,686, f.253.
2. L.P. Curtis, *Chichester Towers*, (1966), p.35.
3. See Francis W. Steer and J.E. Amanda Venables, *The Goodwood Estate Archives*, vols. I and II, (1970, 1972), and Timothy J. McCann, vol. III, (1984).
4. Reed Browning, *The Duke of Newcastle*, (1975), p.360.
5. Horace Walpole, *Memoirs of the Reign of King George the Second*, (1847), vol. 1, p.3.
6. Richmond to Newcastle, 10 September 1746. B.L., Add. Ms. 32,708, f.249.

dismay the pathetic attempts of the English fleet to sail to the West Indies in the war with Spain; he thirsted for news of the army during the War of Austrian Succeession; he stoutly defended the 'Blues' after the Battle of Dettingen; and gave sage advice during the long peace negotiations, which Newcastle discussed freely with him.

At the beginning of their friendship, much of Richmond's correspondence with Newcastle is taken up with the small round of local affairs, and jobs for local supporters, but Richmond becomes an altogether more considerable figure, when he takes a central role in international events. When he accompanied George II and Carteret to Hanover in 1743, Richmond was Newcastle's only trusted confidant at the royal court, and played a crucial role in keeping Newcastle informed of the policy for conducting the war, and of the intrigues surrounding the appointment of Henry Pelham to succeed Wilmington as First Lord of the Treasury. "Whenever I think of it, I shall ever remember with the utmost joy, & gratitude that friendly, unreserved, & confidential Correspondence, with which you have honoured me during the whole summer", Newcastle wrote to Richmond on his return to England, "& I hope you are assured, it has freed in me such a sense of your goodness, that no time or circumstances can alter". When, in 1745, Richmond was given command of the cavalry, and was leading the troops defending the capital against the southward march of Bonnie Prince Charlie and his Jacobite army, his descriptions of his own troops; the conditions in the camps; and the health and morale of the soldiers, are fascinating sidelights on that well documented campaign. Something of Richmond's attention to detail, and his strong leadership, can be seen in his single handed attempt to stamp out smuggling in Sussex, and in his letters about the destruction of the famous Hawkhurst Gang.

As their relationship deepened, something of the affection between the two men can be seen in Newcastle's understanding treatment of Richmond, when Henry Fox eloped with Lady Caroline Lennox, Richmond's eldest daughter in 1744, and in Richmond's painful misunderstanding with the Pelham brothers when he was later forced to work in government with Fox. It showed in their mutual interest in, and affection for, each others families, and in Newcastle's concern during Richmond's final illness.

Newcastle's letters, as befitted a man who was Secretary of State throughout the period of this correspondence, are, of necessity, weightier, and contain more detail of national rather than purely local affairs. Almost two hundred letters, whether in his own 'illegible hand', in the hand of his secretary, Andrew Stone, or written by Stone at his direction, reflect Newcastle's principle preoccupations:- his conduct of the war against France (the letters include descriptions of the battles of Dettingen and Fontenoy, as well as of the campaign in the West Indies against the Spaniards); his conduct of parliamentary elections, and particularly those in Sussex; his administration of the Whig government in London; and his consuming interest in places and patronage. Newcastle's letters tell the story of England's part in the War of Austrian Succession, and, while Richmond hunted in Sussex, Newcastle kept him informed of all the news, as well as of the views of other ministers, and consulted him regularly with regard to the various peace negotiations. With Richmond as his 'lieutenant in the west', Newcastle and Henry Pelham dominated Sussex elections, and the correspondence paints a graphic picture of the whole electioneering process, as well as fully documenting the stories of the General Elections of 1734, 1741 and 1748. Newcastle wrote openly about ministerial conflicts at Whitehall, and of the problems of dealing with George II. He candidly described the intrigues surrounding the moves to oust Walpole in 1742 and Carteret in 1744; was unable to hide from Richmond his frequent disagreements with his brother Henry Pelham, and his petty jealousies of his ministerial rivals; and revealed the considerable pressures under which the Pelham administration laboured before their mass resignation in February 1746, when they forced a reluctant monarch to realise the power of a ministry supported by a majority in Parliament.

The Jacobite Rebellion of 1745 and 1746 can be followed as a chronological narrative in these letters, for Richmond and Newcastle never wrote more frequently than during that campaign. From the first brief mention of the Pretender's landing in Scotland, until the final victory at Culloden, the two men wrote to each other almost daily. Newcastle's exciteable nature was fully revealed in his increasing panic as the Stuart army approached London. Richmond, scornful of the rebels, but acutely apprehensive of an invasion from France, steadies his friend, and takes to the field himself. Newcastle writes to Richmond imploring him to save London, adding "I must keep out the Pretender if I can"[7], just at the moment when the King's relationship with his ministers is at breaking point. Richmond leads the army until the Jacobites are driven out of England, and receives a letter of triumphant relief from Newcastle after the victory at Culloden.

But in all these letters, full of matters of great national importance, Newcastle cannot resist indulging in his favourite pastime of patronage, and the letters are full of the appointments of Sussex men to local positions in the church; in government departments; in the customs office; in Ireland; and in almost every walk of life.

"None can deny to Thomas Pelham Holles, Duke of Newcastle, a foremost place among the political artists and bosses of history", wrote Professor Curtis. "In English politics no less than in English government he played a significant role for over fifty years"[8]. He was born Thomas Pelham in 1693, the eldest son of Thomas Pelham, Ist. Lord Pelham, and Grace Holles, sister of John Holles, Duke of Newcastle. His younger brother, Henry Pelham, was born two years later. Thomas Pelham added the name of Holles, when he succeeded as adoptive heir to the estates of the Duke of Newcastle in 1711. In the following year, he succeeded his father as Lord Pelham. On the death of Queen Anne in 1714, he supported the Hanoverian succession and was rewarded with the title of Earl of Clare. He was created Duke of Newcastle in 1715, for his support against the Jacobite Rebellion in that year.

Because of his wealth and position, Newcastle was naturally destined for a political career. He was brother-in-law to Viscount Townshend, and, at first, gave his support to the Townshend and Walpole faction of the Whigs, but, when the party split in 1717, he went over to the Earl of Sunderland. He was connected to Sunderland by his marriage in that year to Lady Henrietta, daughter of the Earl of Godolphin. In April 1717, Newcastle was appointed Lord Chamberlain and a member of the Privy Council, and, in 1724, he succeeded Carteret as Secretary of State for the Southern Department. He was to be Secretary of State for an unparalleled thirty years, only exchanging the Southern Department for the Northern Department in February 1748, in order to be better placed to control the peace negotiations after the War of Austrian Succession.

Henry Pelham[9] began his political career when he was brought into Parliament for Seaford at a bye-election in 1717, but from 1722 until his death in 1754 he sat for the county seat of Sussex. In 1721 he was appointed a Lord of the Treasury; he was Secretary at War from 1724 to 1730; and was Paymaster General from 1730 to 1743. As Paymaster General he acted as deputy to Sir Robert Walpole in the House of Commons, and Walpole later adopted Pelham as his political heir. On Walpole's fall in 1742, Pelham succeeded to the leadership of the 'old corps' of Whigs in the Commons. He refused the Chancellorship of the Exchequer, against Walpole's advice, but became leader of the House of Commons when Pulteney accepted a peerage. In 1743, on the death of the Earl of Wilmington, Henry Pelham succeeded him as Ist. Lord of the Treasury, a position he held until his death eleven years later. Pelham was the 'premier', but his ministry was very much a triumvirate of Pelham, Newcastle and the Earl of Hardwicke[10].

7. Newcastle to Richmond, 12 December 1745. W(est) S(ussex) R(ecord) O(ffice), Goodwood Ms. 104, f.293.
8. L.P. Curtis, *ibid.*, p.29.
9. See John Wilkes, *A Whig in Power: The Political Career of Henry Pelham*, (1964).
10. See William Coxe, *Memoirs of the Administration of the Right Honorable Henry Pelham*, (2 vols. 1829), and John Owen, *The Rise of the Pelhams*, (1957).

More than two thirds of the correspondence between Richmond and the Pelhams took place at a time when they were the two leading figures in the government of the country. After Richmond's death in 1750, Newcastle himself twice became Ist. Lord of the Treasury. First, when Henry Pelham died in 1754, Newcastle succeeded his brother, and continued to hold the office until 1756. Then, he was 'premier' again from 1757 to 1762. He held office for the last time when he was Lord Privy Seal in Lord Rockingham's administration from July 1765 to August 1766. Thereafter he lived in retirement until his death in 1768.

Newcastle's inheritance included a great deal of land in the county of Sussex, and his scattered estates were spread over a good deal of the eastern half of the county, and stretched from Lewes to Hastings. The property included three residences in Sussex. Laughton Place, the traditional family seat of the Pelhams, he found too small, and soon mortgaged it. Bishopstone near Seaford, was used by Newcastle as a hunting lodge, but, as he grew older, it fell into disuse. Halland in East Hoathly was his favourite seat in the county. Newcastle felt secure in its secluded park, and collected an assemblage of suits of armour and tapestries to furnish his home. He leased Newcastle House in Lewes and turned it into a club to promote the Whig and Pelham interests in the borough and county town. But he needed a house nearer London, and, early in his life, he made Claremont near Esher in Surrey, his regular home in the country, and lavished his money and affection on beautifying the house and its grounds. When Henry Pelham married Katherine Manners, daughter of the Duke of Rutland, in 1726, Newcastle gave his brother much of the Pelham estates in the county, so that Pelham owned as much land in Sussex as Newcastle, but in Sussex, Newcastle was always 'the King'.

> Then fill your glass. Full let it be
> Newcastle drink while you can see.
> With heart and voice, all voters sing
> long live great Holles – Sussex King.[11]

Electioneering was Newcastle's favourite activity, and throughout his life he participated actively in Sussex elections. Sussex returned twenty eight members to Parliament in the eighteenth century. Newcastle was the most powerful electoral patron in England, and, of the fifteen or so members of Parliament who owed their seats directly to the Duke, at least seven came from Sussex – two each from Sussex, Lewes and Seaford and one from Hastings. The seven Sussex members included his brother Henry Pelham; James Butler, his brother's partner in the county seat; Andrew Stone, his private secretary; and four of his Pelham relatives. At the same time, Newcastle had a powerful influence in other seats in the county. Sir John Shelley, Newcastle's brother-in-law, sat for Arundel for 14 years, and the Duke had influential allies in Colonel Ingram at Horsham; the Duke of Dorset at East Grinstead; and the Duke of Richmond at Chichester. Newcastle saw the Duke of Richmond as a valuable political ally in Western Sussex, as soon as Richmond succeeded to the title, and, with the Duke of Somerset's influence declining as he grew older, Richmond was seen as the future dominant interest in that part of the county.

Newcastle's life and career have been widely studied, but less attention has been paid to Richmond. Charles Lennox, only son of the Ist. Duke of Richmond and Ann Brudenell, and grandson of King Charles II and Louise de Keroualle, Duchess of Portsmouth, was born at Goodwood on 18th May 1701. He was styled Earl of March until he succeeded his father in 1723. His early years were spent peacefully and happily with his family, and he was privately educated. His first public act was his marriage, which was solemnised at the Hague, where he was staying immediately before his departure on the Grand Tour. The marriage was apparently arranged to settle a

---

11. B.L., Add. Ms. 32,698, f.82.

gambling debt incurred by his father. The groom was 18 at the time of the wedding in December 1719, and his bride, Sarah, daughter of the Earl of Cadogan, only 13. Immediately after the ceremony, Lord March set out on the Grand Tour, travelling in Holland, France, Austria and Italy for the next three years in the company of his tutor and life long friend Tom Hill. His bride returned to her parents.

Lord March's career began on his return to England in 1722. He was reunited with his wife, and the marriage which had started so unpromisingly, turned out very happily, as is testified by the good selection of family letters that have survived to bear witness to the lifelong love of the couple[12], and by the twelve children that were the result of their union. He began his service in the army, and was made Captain in the Royal Regiment of Horse Guards in September 1722. In the same year, he was elected Member of Parliament for Chichester, being returned unopposed for the seat which the family had nursed for him while he was abroad. His parliamentary career was to be short lived, however, for, on 27 May 1723, his father died at Goodwood, and March succeeded him as 2nd. Duke of Richmond and Lennox.

Goodwood, which Richmond inherited from his father, was 'a mansion house', originally built by the Earl of Northumberland in the early seventeenth century, which his father had used as a hunting lodge and occasional residence, and a small estate, which consisted of the immediate park and farms in Boxgrove and Westhampnett. The 2nd. Duke purchased the Manors of Singleton and Charlton in 1730, thus extending the estate north to the Downs, and including the forests of Singleton and Charlton. He made other additions to the property, and when he died, he bequeathed his son an estate of some 1,100 acres, of which 200 acres was parkland.

Although Richmond had many ideas at different times in his life to rebuild or to enlarge Goodwood House, the fact that he was not a wealthy man, meant that his plans were never fulfilled. Nevertheless, for much of his life, Richmond was involved in building work at his various houses at Goodwood, Charlton, Greenwich and Richmond House in Whitehall, and, while doing so, he patronised such architects as Alessandro Galilei, Colen Campbell, Lord Burlington, Roger Morris and Matthew Brettingham. Richmond's tastes were Palladian, and for all his lack of resources, and his failure to build a new Goodwood House, he left his mark on the Sussex landscape and on the taste of his time.

Richmond's surviving Account Books[13] reveal a constant expenditure on work at Goodwood House, but surviving designs enable various rebuilding schemes to be identified. The Duke had met Galilei during his Grand Tour with Tom Hill, and persuaded the Florentine architect to produce striking plans for a house that he presumably intended to replace Goodwood[14]. In 1724, Richmond entertained Colen Campbell at Goodwood, where the architect apparently designed a new kitchen for the original house. The Duke commissioned from him an exact survey of the old house and a design for a new up to date mansion, both of which Campbell published in his *Vitruvius Britannicus*[15]. Again the project came to nothing, presumably due to lack of money. Little more was done at Goodwood House itself for almost twenty years, but it is clear from the accounts that Matthew Brettingham was employed on some new building work

12. W.S.R.O., Goodwood Ms. 102, ff.1-34.
13. W.S.R.O., Goodwood Mss. 117, 126 and 130.
14. I. Toesca, 'Alessandro Galilei in Inghilterra', in *English Miscellany III*, (1952), figs. 5 and 6 show the sketch plan and elevation of the house that Gallilei designed for Lord March.
15. Colen Campbell, *Vitruvius Britannicus III*, (1725), plates 51–54. Campbell and Roger Morris's original drawings of the original Goodwood House and the planned new house are on loan from the Goodwood Estate Archives to the Royal Institute of British Architects. See John Harris, *Catalogue of the Royal Institute of British Architects, Drawings Collection: Colen Campbell* (1973), pp.9, 10. Campbell's estimates for building the new house are in W.S.R.O., Goodwood Ms. 135.

at Goodwood towards the end of the Duke's life, after he had worked for him at Richmond House in 1745.[16]

Richmond House in Whitehall, from where Canaletto painted his famous views, was built by the 1st. Duke of Richmond, but in 1725, Tom Hill described it as "from top to bottom full of brick mortar dust"[17], and the 2nd. Duke commissioned a set of drawings for rebuilding the house from Lord Burlington[18]. It is not clear how much work was done on the house in accordance with Burlington's designs: Matthew Brettingham spoke of undertaking, "the work of several years in alterations and additions to the old and new part of the House, garden and Court Walls etc at Whitehall from the year 1744", but we know that Richmond was obliged to look elsewhere in London for accommodation. He rented a house in Pall Mall in 1733, and another in Arlington Street in 1734, and hired a room in Bell Alley and one in King Street in which to place his goods while Whitehall House was pulled down. Vanbrugh Castle at Greenwich, which the architect himself had built, was rented by Richmond throughout the 1730s. Even there, he was unable to resist making building alterations, this time employing Nicholas Hawksmoor.

In 1730, Richmond had a successful evening at the gambling tables, and wrote to Monsieur Labbe, his London secretary, "As I have had the good luck to win upwards of two hundred pounds at Tunbridge Wells, I send you a hundred and fifty of it, which I know will be welcome; butt you must take care to sett aside the same sume upon this Michaelmas quarter, to pay for the bricks & timber I have taken upp, for my building at Charlton"[19]. Richmond was now Master of the Charlton Hounds, and he invested his winnings in his hunting lodge at Charlton, the headquarters of the Charlton Hunt. The Historical Account of the Rise and Fall of the Charlton Congress[20] suggests that a building was already at Foxhall, when Richmond joined the Hunt. Richmond invited Lord Burlington to provide designs for rebuilding the house, which still survives, and has recently been restored by the Landmark Trust. It is tempting to think that Richmond himself was now contributing ideas for the designs of the many buildings that he was working on, as he had done in Ireland for his wife's relative Sir Thomas Prendergast.

Richmond used his architectural contacts when he wished to cement his political control over his neighbouring city. He was the largest contributor to the fund for rebuilding the city's Council House in North Street, Chichester, and again he commissioned a design from Lord Burlington[21]. The Council House, which was planned in 1729 and completed by 1732, in complete contrast with Richmond's other building projects, is rather different from Burlington's surviving design. Since the 1740s, it has generally been attributed to Roger Morris, who had succeeded Campbell in working for Richmond, on Campbell's death.

The 2nd. Duke also populated the park at Goodwood with buildings. First, there was the pedimented temple to house the Neptune and Minerva Stone[22], which had been dug up in Chichester, which survived near the house until the end of the last century. In 1743,

16. W.S.R.O., Goodwood Ms. 130. See also Brettingham's letters to the Duchess of Richmond, Goodwood Ms. 109, ff.847 and 863.
17. Hill to Richmond, 24 July 1725. W.S.R.O., Goodwood Ms. 103, f.200.
18. Lord Burlington's original drawings of Richmond House are on loan from the Goodwood Estate Archives to the Royal Institute of British Architects.
19. Richmond to Labbe, August 1730. W.S.R.O., Goodwood Ms. 102, f.110
20. W.S.R.O., Goodwood Ms. 151.
21. Lord Burlington's original designs for the Chichester Council House are on loan to the Royal Institute of British Architects. A front elevation is reproduced in T.P. Connor, 'Architecture and Planting at Goodwood, 1723–1750', in *Sussex Archaeological Collections*, vol. 117, (1979), pp.185–193, between pp.188 and 189. I am greatly indebted to Mr. Connor's article.
22. See Roger Gale, 'An Account of a Roman Inscription found at Chichester', in *Transactions of the Philosophical Society*, vol.32, no.379, pp.332–338. and M. Hills, 'Remarks on the Stone Bearing a Roman Inscription. Found at Chichester in 1723, and now at Goodwood', in *SAC*, Vol 7, (1854), pp.61–63.

he built on the site of a wooden cottage that had once been the home of Philip de Carne his servant, Carne's Seat, which was probably designed by Roger Morris[23]. This fine stone house, with its magnificent view over the Channel to the Isle of Wight, became Richmond's favourite spot on the estate. It was from here that he watched the fleet setting sail for the West Indies. Nearby, to the north, was constructed the delightful Shell House, decorated by the Duchess of Richmond and her daughters with shells sent from the West Indies. Finally, Richmond created the 'Catacombs', which Vertue described as, "stone cells under ground and dark recesses – or passages – subturane, which are as well contriv'd as curious, vast stone porpheryes sea pebbles &c varyously disposed"[24], to house his remarkable menagerie.

The Duke of Richmond collected strange animals, just as he collected strange plants, and the famous menagerie that he formed at Goodwood, was one of the most noted features of the estate in his time. The animals were collected from all parts of the world, many being sent to England by Richmond's friends with diplomatic appointments, and were housed in dens with iron barred gates. The meticulous Duke kept lists of the animals in his care, and, at one time, they consisted of, "5 wolves, 2 tygerrs, 1 lyon, 2 lepers, 1 sived cat, a tyger cat, 3 foxes, a Jack all, 2 Greenland Dogs, 3 vulturs, 2 eagles, 1 kite, 2 owls, 3 bears, 1 large monkey, a Woman tygerr, 3 Racoons, 3 small monkeys, armadilla, 1 pecaverre and 7 caseawarris"[25]. The menagerie quickly became a tourist attraction, so much so that Henry Foster, Richmond's steward, told him in 1730, "we are very much troubled with Rude Company to see ye animals. Sunday last we had 4 or 5 hundred good and bad".[26]

Much of Goodwood that we see today was the creation of the 3rd. Duke of Richmond. He carried out part of Wyatt's design for rebuilding Goodwood House itself as an octagon. He commissioned the celebrated stable block from William Chambers in 1759, which now houses the dressage horses for the international competitions at Goodwood. He was responsible for much of the planting in Goodwood Park that has survived today. However, just as the 2nd. Duke has left his mark on the buildings on the Goodwood Estate, so he has also left his mark on the landscaping of the park, and some of the planting was undoubtedly his. Colen Campbell described, "the Park, Gardens and Plantations, which, for the beautiful variety and extension of prospect, spacious lawns, sweetness of herbage, delicate venison, excellent fruit, thriving plantations, lofty and aweful trees, is inferior to none"[27], and published a plan of the estate in 1725.[28] The 2nd. Duke introduced the famous cedars of Lebanon, purchased plants and shrubs from his friend Peter Collinson, and, on the famous horticulturalists's advice, bought a number of specimens from Lord Petre's nursery at Thorndon in Essex. Sir John Miller, Richmond's friend and neighbour in Lavant, was a fellow planter, and Richmond's correspondence is littered with requests for unusual specimens and schemes for planting in the park. Dr. Richard Pococke, writing four years after the Duke's death, described, "thirty different kinds of oaks and four hundred different American trees and shrubs"[29], in the park.

Although Richmond did not hold any of the great offices of state, the posts that he did hold and the honours that he accepted were real responsibilities rather than mere

23. Original drawings of designs for work at Goodwood House attributed to Roger Morris are on loan from the Goodwood Estate Archives to the Royal Institute of British Architects.
24. Walpole Society, *Vertue's Notebooks V*, (1939), p.143.
25. W.S.R.O., Goodwood Ms. 134.
26. Foster to Richmond, 8 April 1730. W.S.R.O., Goodwood Ms. 108 f. 815.
27. Colen Campbell, *Vitruvius Britannicus III*, (1725), p.9.
28. For the estate plan, see Colen Campbell, *ibid.*, plates 51 and 52. The plan is reproduced in T.P. Connor, *ibid.*, between pp.188 and 189.
29. J.J. Cartwright, (ed.), *The Travels through England of Dr. Richard Pococke successively Bishop of Meath and Ossery during 1750, 1751, and later years.* Camden Society, (1889), p.111.

sinecures. In 1726 he was appointed a Lord of the Bedchamber to King George I, and he continued to hold the office under King George II until 1735. On 7 January of that year, he was appointed Master of the Horse, in succession to the aged Duke of Somerset, and held that office until his death. On 9 January he was sworn a member of the Privy Council, and, first as a supporter of Walpole's government, and later as a personal friend and supporter of the Pelhams, he was a staunch defender of the Whig party and the Hanoverian succession. He was a loyal and disinterested servant to the first two Georges, and was "thoroughly zealous for both the Government and the Administration". He described himself as "bred up from a child in Whig principles", and told Newcastle "I never can, nor never will vote against my principles".

Richmond was regarded as a figure of substance, and, when the hunting season permitted, he was a conscientious attender at meetings of the Council. He acted as Newcastle's agent when he accompanied the King to Europe in 1743, and Newcastle ensured that Richmond was involved in the great decisions of peace and war, during the general European war. Although he frequently complained to Newcastle in his letters that his advice was ignored, it is clear that Newcastle valued Richmond's advice and sheer common sense. Richmond was trusted as an intermediary during King George II's quarrel with his eldest son in 1738[30]; he was Lord High Constable of England for the Coronation of George II in October 1727; and he was chosen as one of the Lords Justices of the Realm during the King's absences in Hanover in 1740, 1745, 1748 and 1750. Finally, at the conclusion of the War of Austrian Succession, Richmond was asked to undertake a special Embassy at Paris.

In 1722 Richmond was returned unopposed as Member of Parliament for Chichester. His own parliamentary career was short lived, as he succeeded to the Dukedom in the following year, but after his election, it became the custom to pay Richmond's family the compliment of allowing them to recommend one member for the City, on condition that the inhabitants of Chichester were left free to choose the other. The system worked throughout the Duke's lifetime, and Richmond recommended successively: Lord William Beauclerk, his cousin and brother officer in the Royal Horse Guards; Sir Thomas Prendergast, an Irish relative of his Duchess; James Brudenell, his uncle; and, finally, Viscount Bury, his nephew. However, when Richmond tried briefly to gain control of the City's second seat, by encouraging his neighbouring friend and fellow planter Sir John Miller to stand against John Page, the local independent member, there arose "such a flame as was never seen there before", so that Sir John Miller was forced to withdraw, and Richmond to promise that he would never think of nominating both members.

Although Chichester was the only seat that Richmond controlled, he had influence in several neighbouring constituencies. In the 1734 election, he attempted to gain a seat at New Shoreham, a venal borough that Richmond described as "a new whore, that is anybody's for their money"[31]. He proposed Sir Thomas Prendergast for the seat, and obtained a promise from Sir Robert Walpole of the government interest, which was important because of the local customs officers, and because of the local men who were employed at Deptford and Woolwich. But Walpole's attitude was ambivalent, Prendergast failed to prevent the election of an unfavourable returning officer, the nominee of one of his opponents, whom Walpole had promised to find a seat elsewhere, and, in a field of four candidates, Richmond's nominee was defeated. In 1747 Richmond intervened at Arundel. There the predominant interest belonged to the Lumley family, Earls of Scarbrough. The family had inherited the estates of the Earls of Arundel, and one of their number had sat for the constituency from 1708 to 1747. In 1747 the Lumleys did not put up a candidate for Arundel, and Richmond stepped in and proposed Robert

30. See W.S.R.O., Goodwood Ms. 40 and 41.
31. Richmond to Newcastle, 5 August 1733. B.L., Add. Ms. 32, 688, f.46.

Brudenell and William Leaves as his candidates. However, they were both defeated by what Henry Pelham called "the bribery of Taaffe and Orme"[32], the successful candidates.

Despite these setbacks, Richmond was a figure of considerable political importance in Sussex. He was Mayor of Chichester in 1735, and he dominated the Common Council throughout his life, finally succeeding the Duke of Somerset as High Steward of the city in 1749. As the Duke of Somerset grew older, Richmond replaced him as the natural leader of the Government Whigs in the western half of the county. He was clearly the most active and the most powerful political magnate, and he delivered West Sussex to Newcastle as surely as Newcastle controlled East Sussex. Apart from the scare provided by the two opposition candidates put up in 1734, in an attempt to take advantage of the unpopularity of the Excise Bill, Richmond and Newcastle ensured that the County of Sussex returned two Government supporters unopposed throughout Richmond's life.

An example of the Duke's local power and influence was Richmond's campaign against the Sussex smugglers[33]. Sussex smuggling in the 1740s was described as, "a guerrilla war between the smugglers . . . and the officers of the government", a war, marked by "an organised resistance to the government, in which towns were beseiged, battles fought, Customs Houses burnt down, and the greatest atrocities committed"[34]. Richmond was roused to action by the infamous murder of Galley and Chater in 1748[35]. He made the capture and conviction of the murderers his personal responsibility, and determined to stop smuggling in Sussex altogether. To this end, he arranged a special Commisssion in Chichester to try the smugglers in 1749, and spent much of the last three years of his life tracking down the smugglers, and keeping a detailed record of his activities[36].

Although Richmond's active service life was relatively short compared with that of some of the later members of his family, his army career was important, and he played a significant part in some of the major campaigns of his time. His career began on his return to England from the Grand Tour, when in September 1722, he was made Captain in the Royal Regiment of Horse Guards, though he had been appointed Guidon of the 1st. Troop of Horse Grenadier Guards in March 1721[37], when he was still abroad. A fine series of papers has survived from Richmond's period of captaincy[38], and they show him to have been an unusually conscientious officer. On 8 April 1724, Richmond was appointed Aide-de-Camp to King George I, a position that was confirmed by King George II on his accession. He was made a Brigadier General in July 1739, and a Major General in June 1742. In 1743 he accompanied his Sovereign throughout the campaign in Europe, being responsible, as His Majesty's Master of the Horse, for a baggage train of 662 horses and a due complement of carriages and wagons[39]. He was present at the Battle of Dettingen, and his presence there enabled him to defend his regiment vehemently against an unjust charge of cowardice. When Charles Edward Stuart landed in Scotland in 1745, in an attempt to gain the throne for his father, Richmond immediately offered his services in support of the Hanoverian dynasty. He was created Lieutenant General in

32. Pelham to Richmond, 2 July 1747. W.S.R.O., Goodwood Ms. 104, f.304.
33. See Cal Winslow, 'Sussex Smugglers', in D. Hay, P. Linebaugh and E.P. Thompson, *Albion's Fatal Tree. Crime and Society in Eighteenth Century England*, (1975), pp.119–166.
34. Charles Fleet, *Glimpses of our Sussex Ancestors*, (1878), vol. 1, pp.74–75.
35. See a Gentleman of Chichester, *A Full and Genuine History of the Inhuman and Unparalleled Murders of Mr. William Galley, a Custom-House Officer, and Mr. Daniel Chater, a Shoemaker, by Fourteen Notorious Smugglers, with the Trials and Execution of Seven of the Bloody Criminals at Chichester . . .*, (1749).
36. Richmond's papers relating to his pursuit of the smugglers are now W.S.R.O. Goodwood Ms. 154–156.
37. For Richmond's military commissions, see W.S.R.O., Goodwood Mss. 62–68.
38. For Richmond's papers relating to the Royal Regiment of Horse Guards, see W.S.R.O., Goodwood Mss. 69–91.
39. M.M. Reese, *The Royal Office of Master of the Horse*, (1976), p.216.

June 1745, and full General in November of that year. He was put in command of the forces that awaited the Scottish Jacobites on their march south, and, when they finally turned back after reaching Derby, he chased the retreating army as far as Carlisle, before returning to his Sussex estate, safe in the knowledge that he had rid the country of invasion. The office that gave him most pleasure came to him late in life. In February 1750 he was appointed Colonel of the Royal Horse Guards, and was thus reunited with many of the officers with whom he had served as a young man.

Among Richmond's correspondents were some of the greatest wits of the day, such as Pulteney, Chesterfield and Lord Hervey[40]. He exchanged letters with Voltaire and Montesquieu[41]; exchanged courtesies with Colley Cibber and Henry Fielding[42]; and even hazarded a correction to Richardson's *Clarissa Harlowe*[43]. Among his Sussex circle, Richmond was addicted to verse, and his surviving papers include a multitude of poems written by Tom Hill, Alderman Samuel Chandler, Mr. Justice Bodens and the Rev. James Bramston[44]. There are also a number of prologues and epilogues to plays performed by Richmond's family and friends for their own amusement; though we know from Hogarth's picture of 'Dryden's *Conquest of Mexico* being acted at Mr. Conduitt's house in the Mint', and the surviving programme of a performance at St. James's in April 1732, that some of the Duke's family performed before the Royal Family.

Like many of the eighteenth century aristocracy, Richmond was a devotee of opera. On 30 November 1725, he was elected a Governor of the Royal Academy of Music[45]. Among his papers is an autograph list of persons willing to subscribe £200 to the Corporation of the Royal Academy of Music towards carrying on operas, to begin in 1728[46]. Opera was the chief link between Richmond and Owen MacSwiney, the impresario and art dealer, who was employed by the Academy from 1724. He toured Italy looking for singers and scores, and reported to Richmond on his discoveries and his progress[47].

MacSwiney had met the Duke of Richmond on his Grand Tour, and was to become a sufficiently good friend to be offered the job of Richmond's secretary, several years later. As early as 1726, MacSwiney had been involved in buying pictures in Italy for the Duke of Richmond. During the 1720s, MacSwiney commissioned the famous paintings of Allegorical Tombs of famous Englishmen, from contemporary Italian artists from Bologna and Venice, such as Canaletto, Piazzetta, Cimarola, Mirandolesi, Donato Creti, Francesco Monti, and Marco and Sebastiano Ricci[48]. A Goodwood Inventory of 1739[49] makes clear that twelve of the twenty four paintings that MacSwiney commis-

40. Some of Lord Hervey's letters to Richmond are printed in The Earl of Ilchester, *Lord Hervey and His Friends, 1726–1738*, (1950).
41. Montesquieu's letters to Richmond are printed in Robert Shackleton, 'Montesquieu's Correspondence', in *French Studies*, (1958), pp.324–345.
42. See Mary Margaret Stewart, 'Henry Fielding's Letter to the Duke of Richmond', in *Philological Quarterly*, vol. 50, no.1, (1971), pp.135–140.
43. W.S.R.O., Goodwood Ms. 109, f.891.
44. Examples of the poetry of the Goodwood caravan can be found in W.S.R.O., Goodwood Mss. 141, 146 and 2001.
45. W.S.R.O., Goodwood Ms. 105, f.393.
46. W.S.R.O., Goodwood Mss. 143 and 144.
47. Owen MacSwiney's letters to Richmond are now to be found in W.S.R.O., Goodwood Ms. 105, ff.384–440.
48. The Allegorical Tombs paintings are discussed in, Edward Croft Murray, *Decorative Painting in England II* (1970), pp.22–24, and 239–242; in Barbara Mazza, 'La Vecenda dei "Tombeaux des Princes". Matrici, storia e fortuna della serie Swiny tra Bologna e Venezia', in *Saggi e Memoria*, vol. 10, (1979), pp.79–102 and 141–151; and in George Knox, 'The present state and condition of twelve very elegant pictures painted or to be painted for His Grace the Duke of Richmond under the direction of that celebrated virtuoso Eugenio MacSwiney', in *Arte Veneta*, forthcoming.
49. W.S.R.O., Goodwood Ms. 99.

sioned, were framed in panels in the Great Dining Room at Goodwood, and Vertue's Notebooks[50] give precise descriptions of ten of them. The paintings were eventually sold by Christie's for the 4th. Duke of Richmond in 1814.

The 2nd. Duke of Richmond is also famous as the patron of Canaletto. Canaletto is first mentioned in MacSwiney's letter of 1726. Twenty years later, the faithful Tom Hill, writing to Richmond on 20 May 1746, remarked that, "Canales alias Canaletti, is come over with a letter from our old acquaintance [Joseph Smith] the Consul at Venice to Mac[Swiney] in order to his introduction to your Grace, as a patron of the politer parts, or what the Italians understand by the name of virtu. I told him the best service I thought you could do him wd be to let him draw a view of the river from your dining room, which in my opinion would give him as much reputation as any of his Venetian prospects"[51]. Thus were born the famous paintings of 'The Thames from Richmond House', and its companion view, 'Whitehall from Richmond House'[52], which still hang at Goodwood.

Richmond's intellectual pursuits were by no means confined to the arts, and he was particularly interested in the study of medicine, science and antiquity. In April 1728 he was awarded a doctorate in law at the University of Cambridge. In June of the same year, he was elected a Fellow of the Royal College of Physicians. Later in his life, in 1741, he was President of the London Hospital. He had always taken an interest in the hospital, subscribing 20 guineas, and five guineas on the occasions of the annual sermons. He was one of those responsible for the hospital's move to Whitechapel Mount. Richmond also took a personal interest in medical matters, and among his acquaintances in Chichester's medical fraternity were several of the early innoculators. Smith and Dymer, two local surgeons, had performed innoculations in the city within months of the introduction of the practice[53]. The Duke was a patron of Dr. George Bayley[54] and his brother Dr. Edward Bayley of Havant, and knew his neighbour Thomas Sanden, another doctor, and his friend Dr. William Guy. The well known List of the Population of Chichester in 1740, which is still preserved at Goodwood[55], was commissioned by the 2nd. Duke in an attempt to discover the effect of the smallpox epidemic in Chichester in the previous year.

The 2nd. Duke of Richmond was elected a Fellow of the Royal Society in February 1724. In September 1728 he was invited to attend a meeting of the Académie Royale de Sciences in Paris. These were by no means simply honours paid to his rank and station. Richmond was a friend of Abraham Trembley[56], and had watched some of Trembley's experiments on hydra at Sorgvliet, when he was staying with the Bentincks at the Hague in 1743. In January of that year, the Royal Society devoted two sessions to polyps and related subjects, and in 1744 a letter from Richmond was read to the Society, in which he confirmed Trembley's experiments, and described how he had personally witnessed them[57]. Richmond and Trembley became firm friends. The Duke obtained a diplomatic post for him at Aix-la-Chapelle, and later appointed him tutor to his son. The 3rd.

50. Walpole Society, *Vertue's Notebooks V*, (1939), pp.143–144.
51. Hill to Richmond, 10 May 1746. W.S.R.O., Goodwood Ms. 103, f.244.
52. See John Hayes, 'Parliament Street and Canaletto's Views of Whitehall', in The *Burlington Magazine*, (1958), pp.341–349.
53. N.J. Alldridge, 'the Mortality Pattern of Infectious Diseases in Chichester, 1720–1812', unpublished. A copy is in W.S.R.O., MP. 1674.
54. See Francis W. Steer, *Dr. John Bayley of Chichester*. Chichester Papers No.34, (1963), and Francis W. Steer and Richard R. Trail, 'Dr. John Bayley's Meteorological Records and Comments, with notes on some later records of sanitation in the Chichester area', in *Medical History*, vol.9 (1965), pp.267–272.
55. W.S.R.O., Goodwood Ms. 1998. The document is transcribed in Francis W. Steer, *The Number of Persons within the City of Chichester 31st. December 1740*. W.S.R.O., Lists and Indexes No.1, (1954).
56. See John R. Baker, *Abraham Trembley: Scientist and Philosopher, 1710–1784*. (1952), especially pp.39, 131–132, and 136–137.
57. Richmond's letter to the Royal Society is printed in *Philosophical Transactions*, vol.42, (1744), p.510.

Duke, under Trembley's tutelage, enjoyed a scientific education first at the University of Leyden, and then on the Grand Tour, which embraced meetings with such scholars as Allamand, Frisi, Donati, Haller and Reaumur. Like Trembley, the 2nd. Duke was interested in earthquakes, and when tremors were felt in Chichester in 1734, Richmond went to a great deal of trouble to collect written reports from witnesses in the city, as well as from Dr. Bayley in Havant, which he forwarded to Sir Hans Sloane and the Royal Society[58].

The Society of Antiquaries elected Richmond a Fellow in April 1736 on the proposal of Martin Folkes, and the Duke actively supported the investigation of antiquity. When the famous Neptune and Minerva Stone was dug up in Chichester by workmen building the new Council Chamber in North Street in 1732[59], it was presented to Richmond, and he had the stone transported to Goodwood, where it was preserved in a specially built temple, which survived until the stone was moved to its present resting place in the wall of the Assembly Rooms. He purchased, and re-erected at Goodwood a tall prehistoric monolith, well before such examples of the use of monuments became fashionable in eighteenth century landscapes. In April 1750, Richmond presented to the Society a drawing of a piece of Roman pavement found in the Bishop's Garden in Chichester in 1740[60]. The Duke paid for the restoration of the Market Cross in Chichester in 1746, and for the well-known engraving of it by George Vertue, and, in 1749, he presented a copy of the engraving to the Society[61]. Right at the end of his life, in March 1750, he was elected President of the Society of Antiquaries[62].

Notwithstanding his intellectual interests, Richmond's greatest enthusiasm was reserved for sport, and it is clear from his correspondence that hunting was the ruling passion of his life. The Hunt at Charlton was founded while Richmond was still a young man, but in 1728 the Duke of Bolton, the then Master of the Hunt, presented his hounds to Richmond. Richmond became joint Master with his neighbour the Earl of Tankerville from Uppark, and, in 1731, he became Master and sole proprietor of the Charlton Hounds. From that moment the Charlton Hunt became the most important hunt in the country, and remained so until the Duke's death in 1750[63]. Such was the importance of hunting at the time, that the Charlton Hunt was probably the most important sporting event, and possibly the most important social event in England outside the capital. The tiny Sussex village of Charlton was crowded with the peerage of England, many of whom owned small hunting boxes in the area. Richmond's detailed accounts show that 17 peers and their retainers and 143 horses were quartered in the village for one meeting in 1743[64]. The Duke started work on Foxhall, his own hunting lodge and the centre of the Hunt in 1731, and kept a detailed diary of his hunting[65], as well as accounts of keeping and feeding the hounds[66]. The Hunt was formed into a Society, and Richmond himself kept the Minute Book[67], which recorded the business of the Society, and the names of those

58. The papers that Richmond collected relating to the 1734 Earthquake are now in B.L., Sloane Ms. 4025, ff.224–238.
59. See J.E. Bogaers, 'King Cogidubnus in Chichester: another reading of RIB 91', in *Britannia*, vol.10, (1979), pp.243–254.
60. See A.E. Wilson, 'The Beginnings of Roman Chichester', in *SAC*, vol.94, (1956), pp.100–111, and the Society of Antiquaries, Minute Book Vol. VI, 1749–1751. 5 April 1750.
61. Society of Antiquaries, ibid., 23 November 1749.
62. Society of Antiquaries, ibid., 1 March 1749/50. For Richmond's Presidency of the Society, see Joan Evans, *History of the Society of Antiquaries*, (1956), pp.101–103.
63. The Earl of March, *Records of the Old Charlton Hunt*, (1910).
64. W.S.R.O., Goodwood Ms. 149. f.31.
65. Richmond's Hunting Diary, 1738–1746, is now W.S.R.O., Goodwood Ms. 152. Copious extracts from it are printed in *Records of the Old Charlton Hunt*.
66. W.S.R.O., Goodwood Ms. 149.
67. W.S.R.O., Goodwood Ms. 2003.

who had passed the rigorous requirements of membership. Richmond alone had the special privilege of bringing anyone he liked from Goodwood to dinner at Charlton.

The Dukes of Richmond and their families have been closely associated with cricket since the seventeenth century. The 2nd. Duke was, perhaps, the most famous cricketer in the family, and his exploits on the cricket field have been chronicled[68]. He pioneered organised cricket in Sussex by challenging Sir William Gage to cricket matches in 1725 and 1727[69]. In the latter year, when arranging two cricket matches with Mr. Broderick of Peper Harrow in Surrey, he drew up in conjunction with Mr. Broderick, the first formal laws of the game[70]. For the next twenty years the Duke's team played regular matches in London, Surrey and Kent, he employed several of the most famous players on his estates in Sussex or his houses in London, and, when his team began to disappear from the records, he acted as sponsor to the famous team which represented Slindon[71]. A few details of his expenditure on cricket equipment can be found among Richmond's personal accounts, while those of his Duchess show her expenditure in sponsoring matches. Among Richmond's papers can be found the earliest known scoresheets of cricket matches[72], and correspondence from Sir William Gage, Lord John Sackville and John Fuller of Uckfield about the game.

On the death of the Duchess of Portsmouth in Paris in November 1734, Richmond succeeded his paternal grandmother as Duke of Aubigny in France and to the Seignory of Aubigny, and he and his Duchess went to France for three months in 1735 to claim their inheritance. During the visit to Aubigny, the Duke and Duchess paid homage to the French King for their estate. Richmond became very fond of France, and enjoyed the hunting that the Aubigny estate provided. It became his custom to visit France in the autumn of each year, and he often combined these visits with a journey to the Hague, where he stayed with his friends and cousins the Bentincks or with his wife's family the Cadogans. Richmond's familiarity with these European Courts and his personal popularity made him an obvious choice for an Embassy to Paris after the Treaty of Aix-la-Chapelle had finally brought the War of Austrian Succession to an end.

A number of honours and lesser responsibilities were given to Richmond during his life. He was Grand Master of the Freemasons of the Grand Lodge of England in 1724[73], and there are numerous mentions of masonry in his correspondence, though few in his letters to Newcastle. He was nominated a Knight of the Bath in May 1725, and installed by proxy in June, as he suffered a mild attack of smallpox. In the following year he was invested a Knight of the Garter. He was appointed an Elder Brother of Trinity House in 1737, and served until his death, being Master from 1741 to 1745. After a long contest with the Earl of Pembroke, who earlier had been his rival for the Mastership of the Horse, he was elected a Governor of the Charterhouse in 1739[74].

Richmond was taken ill in the Summer of 1750, and was forced to postpone a proposed

68. John Marshall, *The Duke who was Cricket*, (1961).
69. W.S.R.O., Goodwood Ms. 1883. See also H.F. and A.P. Squire, *Henfield Cricket and its Sussex Cradle*, (1949), pp.33–34.
70. W.S.R.O., Goodwood Ms. 1884. See also Timothy J. McCann, *250th. Anniversary Cricket Match in the dress and under the laws of 1727. The Duke of Richmond's XII v. The Gentlemen of Pepper Harrowe*, (1977), which reproduces the agreement in facsimile.
71. See Edmund Esdaile, 'Their chivalry was cricket', in *Journal of the Cricket Society*, vol.4, no.2, (1969), pp.25–29, and vol.4, no.4, (1970), pp.45–49, and Timothy J. McCann, 'The Duke of Richmond, Slindon, and the 1741 Cricket Season in Sussex', in *Journal of the Cricket Society*, vol.11, no.1, (1982), pp.29–31.
72. W.S.R.O., Goodwood Ms. 1885. See also H.F. and A.P. Squire, *ibid.*, pp.40–43, which reproduces the scoresheet.
73. See E.A. Boerenbeker, 'The relations between Dutch and English Freemasonry from 1734 to 1771', in *Ars Quatuor Coronatorum*, vol.83, (1970), pp.149–192. I owe this reference to Professor G.S. Rousseau.
74. Charterhouse. Minutes of the Governors Assembly. 13 October 1738 and 16 February 1739/40. I owe these references to Jock Moss and R.L. Arrowsmith.

visit to Ireland to stay with his daughter Lady Emily Lennox, who had married the Earl of Kildare. He collapsed at his half way house in Godalming when returning from London to Goodwood, and survived long enough for his beloved Duchess to reach his bedside from Sussex, and died in her arms of cancer of the bladder on 8 August 1750. He was buried in Chichester Cathedral.

"The Duke of Richmond is dead, vastly lamented" wrote Horace Walpole to Sir Horace Mann[75], and, apart from Queen Caroline, who described him as "so half-witted, so bizarre, and so grandseigneur, and so mulish, that he is as troublesome from meaning well and comprehending so ill, as if he meant as ill as he comprehends"[76], Richmond was always spoken of with affection and respect by his contemporaries. "There never lived a man of more amiable composition; he was friendly, benevolent, generous, honourable, and thoroughly noble in his way of acting, talking and thinking", wrote Lord Hervey in his memoirs[77]. In a letter to Stephen Fox, Lord Hervey wrote that "the Duke of Richmond was cheerful and entertaining which he always is"[78], and, in a letter to Henry Fox, Richmond's son-in-law, he remarked of the Duke and Duchess, "I am quite at a loss to comprehend how so much indolence and agitation could ever meet"[79]. Henry Fielding, who had helped Richmond in his campaign against the Sussex smugglers, called him, "the noble Duke . . . one of the worthiest of magistrates, as well as the best of men", and wished that "his life, for the good of mankind had been prolonged"[80]. Abraham Trembley in his instructions to his son, described Richmond as "a man even more remarkable for the manner in which he lived in the distinguished rank he held in his country, than for the rank itself; an amiable, virtuous, affable man, endowed with that urbanity and frankness that give lustre even to virtue, and whose kindness I had often experienced"[81].

Among his biographers, Richmond was understood best by his successor the 8th. Duke, who wrote, "despite his comparative lack of landed and borough interest, Richmond's family, title, and loyalty to the Brunswick system rendered it easy enough for him to become a county riband and magnate. His affability, kindlier than was the wont of his species in good King George's golden days, his straightforward honesty, and transparent patriotism, singled him out as a plain man, abnormally trustworthy, and of a solid integrity, among the intriguing caballers and malignant time-servers who fluttered between Court and Cabinet. Richmond had, in short, the inestimable advantage of being a safe Whig without being a party man at all. Walpole, Townshend, Pulteney, Carteret, Hervey, Chesterfield and the rest evidently regarded him as a safe and creditable pawn, too simple and upright to be formidable to their combinations. The King believed in him, with tolerable correctness, as one of the few genuine disinterested adherents of the dynasty"[82].

75. Horace Walpole to Sir Horace Mann, 1 September 1750. *Horace Walpole's Letters*, (1906), vol. 2, p.223.
76. Lord Hervey, *Memoirs*, (1931), vol. III, p.828.
77. Lord Hervey, *ibid.*, p.12.
78. Lord Hervey to Stephen Fox, 3 October 1734. Earl of Ilchester, *Lord Hervey and His Friends, 1726-1738*, (1950), p.207.
79. Lord Hervey to Henry Fox, 6 October 1736. Earl of Ilchester, *ibid.*, p.252.
80. Henry Fielding, *An Enquiry into the Causes of the Late Increase of Robbers*, (1751), p.69.
81. Abraham Trembley, *Instructions d'un pere a sens enfans, sur la nature et sur la religion*, (1775), vol.1, p.viij.
82. Earl of March, *A Duke and His Friends*, (1911), pp.xiii–xiv.

CHRONOLOGY

1693 July	Thomas Pelham, later 1st. Duke of Newcastle, born.
1695	Henry Pelham born.
1701 May	Charles Lennox, Earl of March, later 2nd. Duke of Richmond, born at Goodwood.
1711 July	Thomas Pelham inherited the Holles estates and took the name of Holles
	Tom Hill appointed tutor to the Earl of March.
1715 August	Thomas Pelham Holles created 1st. Duke of Newcastle
	Newcastle appointed Vice-Admiral of Sussex.
	Jacobite Rebellion.
1717 February	Henry Pelham elected MP for Seaford.
April	Newcastle appointed Lord Chamberlain of the Household.
	Newcastle appointed a Privy Councillor.
1719 December	March married Lady Sarah Cadogan, daughter of the 1st. Earl of Cadogan.
	March embarked on the Grand Tour with Tom Hill. He did not return to England until 1722.
1720	Henry Pelham appointed Treasurer of the Chamber.
1721 April	Henry Pelham appointed a Lord of the Treasury
1722 March	General Election
	Henry Pelham elected MP for Sussex.
	March elected MP for Chichester.
	March entered Horse Grenadier Guards.
June	March returned to England.
September	March appointed Captain in the Royal Horse Guards.
1723 March	March's daughter, Lady Caroline Lennox, born.
May	March succeeded his father as 2nd. Duke of Richmond.
1724 April	Newcastle appointed Secretary of State for the Southern Department.
	Henry Pelham appointed Secretary at War
	Richmond appointed ADC to the King.
June	Richmond's son, the Earl of March lived for a few days.
	Richmond elected Grand Master of the Freemasons (Grand Lodge of England).
1725 May	Richmond created Knight of the Bath.
	Richmond had mild attack of smallpox.
June	Henry Pelham appointed a Privy Councillor.
October	Richmond visited Aubigny.
November	Richmond's daughter, Lady Louisa Margaret Lennox, born
1726 May	Richmond created Knight of the Garter.
	Richmond appointed Lord of the Bedchaamber to the King.
June	Richmond visited the Hague
1727 August	General Election
October	Richmond appointed Lord High Constable for the Coronation of King George II.
	Duchess of Richmond appointed Lady of the Queen's Bedchamber

1728 June	Richmond elected Fellow of the College of Physicians
	Richmond granted LlD at Cambridge University.
September	Richmond set out on continental tour, visiting Spa, the Hague, Aubigny, Spain, Portugal and Paris.
1729 May	Richmonds daughter, Lady Louisa Margaret Lennox, died.
October	Richmond returned to England
1730 May	Henry Pelham appointed Paymaster General.
September	Richmond's son, the Earl of March, lived for a few days.
1731	Richmond elected Master and sole proprietor of the Charlton Hounds.
October	Richmond's daughter, Lady Emily Lennox, born.
1732 January	Richmond broke his leg and was on crutches until November
August	Richmond ill.
1733	Outbreak of the War of Polish Succession
1734 April	General Election
May	Richmond visited the Hague
October	Richmond visited Holland and France.
November	Richmond succeeded as Duke of Aubigny on the death of his grandmother the Duchess of Portsmouth.
1735 January	Richmond appointed Master of the Horse.
	Richmond appointed a Privy Councillor
May	Richmond visited Aubigny.
September	Richmond visited Paris
	Richmond's son, the Earl of March, born.
1736 April	Richmond elected Fellow of the Society of Antiquaries.
October	Richmond visited Holland
1737	Richmond appointed Elder Brother of Trinity House.
December	Richmond's son, Lord George Lennox, born.
1738	
1739 July	Richmond appointed Brigadier General
	Outbreak of War of Jenkins's Ear.
November	Ádmiral Vernon captured Porto Bello.
	Richmond's daughter, Lady Margaret Lennox, born.
1740 February	Richmond appointed a Governor of Charterhouse.
October	Death of the Emperor Charles VI
	Outbreak of the War of Austrian Succession
1741 May	General Election
	Richmond appointed Master of Trinity House
November	Richmond appointed President of the London Hospital.
1742 January	Sussex County Bye-Election.
	Election of Charles VII as Emperor
February	Fall of Sir Robert Walpole
June	Richmond appointed Major General.
	Treaty of Breslau
November	Richmond's daughter, Lady Louisa Lennox, born.
1743 April	Richmond travelled to Hanover with King George II, the Duke of Cumberland and Lord Carteret.
June	Battle of Dettingen
August	Henry Pelham appointed 1st. Lord of the Treasury.

November	Richmond returned to England.
1744 February	Richmond's daughter, Lady Sarah Lennox, Born.
May	Richmond's daughter, Lady Caroline Lennox, eloped with Henry Fox.
November	Fall of Carteret.
1745 May	Battle of Fontenoy
June	Richmond appointed Lieutenant General
August	Charles Edward Stuart, the Young Pretender, landed in Scotland.
September	The Young Pretender captured Edinburgh. Battle of Prestonpans.
November	Richmond appointed General
December	The Jacobite army reached Derby.
1746 January	Battle of Falkirk
February	The Pelhams with Richmond and others resigned their offices
	Earl of Bath appointed 1st. Lord of the Treasury. The Pelhams returned to power two days later.
April	Battle of Culloden
1747 June	General Election
July	Battle of Lauffeld
1748 February	Newcastle appointed Secretary of State for the Northern Department.
	Newcastle appointed Chancellor of Cambridge University
October	Treaty of Aix-la-Chapelle ended the War of Austrian Succession
	Richmond appointed special Ambassador to Paris.
1749 January	Special Commission to try the Smugglers held at Chichester
	Richmond elected High Steward of Chichester
	Richmond elected President of the Society of Antiquaries
1750 February	Richmond appointed Colonel of the Royal Horse Guards
	Richmond's daughter, Lady Cecilia Lennox, born
August	Richmond died at Godalming.
1751 August	Duchess of Richmond died
1754 March	Henry Pelham died
	Newcastle appointed 1st. Lord of the Treasury
1756 November	Newcastle left office
1757 July	Newcastle appointed 1st. Lord of the Treasury
1761	Newcastle appointed Lord Lieutenant of Sussex.
1762 May	Newcastle left office
1765 July	Newcastle appointed Lord Privy Seal
1766 July	Newcastle left office for the last time
1768 November	Newcastle died.

The Correspondence of
the Dukes of
Richmond and Newcastle
1724–1750

THE LETTERS

1. NEWCASTLE TO RICHMOND

Tuesday morning [September 1724]

My Dear Ld Duke,

Last night I received your Graces command about Shepeard[1] & att ye same time a letter & petition from him to the King,[2] which I will not fail to give this morning tho' I believe it will be to no purpose, for he having committed several Robberies after he made His Escape both times, will not be thought a very fitt Object for Mercy.

I am with great Truth My Dear Duke Yrs most sincerely

Holles Newcastle

2. PELHAM TO RICHMOND

Esher
June ye 8th 1732

My Lord,

I should have thank'd your Grace sooner for the honour of your letter but I did not receive it till yesterday by the post. Since Cosby's[3] departure the dog is come with bitter temper and now his mal is remov'd Lady Katherine[4] is of opinion that she and her children may live safe here notwithstanding the former terror she had about this dog. I must humbly thank your Grace for the preferment you design'd him in sending him ambassador to so great a Prince as the Emperer of Morocco; but if he continues to behave well his friends here desire he may not be transported. I rejoice att your Graces growing better and hope these crutches you mention with pleasure, will soon after they are used, be laid aside for two of the stoutest legs in England.[5]

I am with great Respect My Lord yr Graces most obedient

H. Pelham

3. RICHMOND TO NEWCASTLE

Goodwood
June 22d 1733

My dear Lord,

I find by a letter I received last post from Sr Thomas Prendergast[6] that he has kissed the Kings hand for being Privy Councellor in Ireland which as it is entirely owing to your Graces Goodness, give me leave to return you my most sincere thankes for it, & to assure you that this & all other favours, shall ever be acknowledg'd with the utmost gratitude by, My Dear Lord, Your Graces most faithfull, & obliged humble servant

Richmond

will you give me leave to wait upon you, when you come into Sussex? When do you come?

1. John Sheppard, 1702–1724, the well known criminal. He was finally hanged at Tyburn, after twice escaping from the condemned cell.
2. Sheppard's petition to the King is now W.S.R.O. Goodwood Ms. 109 f. 886.
3. William Cosby, 1690–1736, an Irishman, was a placeman of Newcastle. Newcastle appointed him Governor of Minorca, and he was a controversial Governor of New York, 1731–1736.
4. Lady Katherine Pelham, daughter of John, 2nd Duke of Rutland. She married Henry Pelham on 29 October 1726.
5. Richmond broke his leg in an accident in London in the winter of 1732/3. On 7 February, Colley Cibber wrote to him, 'Heartily wishing that your leg may be able to run up and down stairs after my Lady Duchess as long as you live'. (Goodwood Ms. 110 f. 78).
6. Sir Thomas Prendergast, 1700–1760, MP for Chichester, 1733–1734, was described by King George II as 'an Irish blockhead'. A cousin of the Duchess, he bombarded Richmond with applications for seats in Parliament, or lucrative Irish sinecures. He was an Irish MP, 1733–1760, and Postmaster General of Ireland, 1754–1760.

4. NEWCASTLE TO RICHMOND

Claremont
June 30th 1733

My Dear Lord,
  I am infinitely obliged to your Grace for the honor of your letter. You take a great deal too much notice of the trifle I was able to do for Sr Thos. Pendergrass. It is, and always will be the greatest pleasure to me to have an opportunity of obliging your Graces commands and of showing you how sincerely I am your humble servant. The Honorable Harry[1] & I are very thankfull for your intended visit to us att ye Races.[2] The Assizes & Races are to be the same week, that when the gentlemen are together we may know their sentiments as to the next election. May I therefore begg yt you would honor us with your company. The assises will be att Lewes Monday ye 30th of July, the horse Races Thursday the 2d of August, & Tuesday the 31st of July. I shall begg the company of my good friends att Haland.[3] Dear Duke be so good as to spend a few days with us att this time, and you will add to the many obligations already conferred upon Your Graces Most affect, humble servant
Holles Newcastle

5. RICHMOND TO NEWCASTLE

Goodwood
August 2d 1733

My dear Lord,
  Last week my scheme & full intent was to have been here on Sunday, & on Tuesday to have waited on your Grace at dinner. butt my Lord Cowper,[4] who was to have releived me, was pleas'd to leave me in the lurch, & I could not gett a mortal to releive me, till yesterday, which Albemarle,[5] as he was out of staff waiting did, & last night wee arrived here. So Your Grace sees it is not my fault that I have not waited on you, for I assure you I was very desirous to do it. I beg my sincere compliments & good wishes of success to the two candidates Mr Pelham, & Mr Butler,[6] & I shall very gladly do them all the services that lye in my poor power.
  I hear Yates[7] is gon to the East, whether it is to waite upon your Grace, or his dear freind Sr Thomas Dyke,[8] I can't tell. I am sure he is very ungratefull, if he does not serve Sr Thomas to the utmost of his power. butt without jobeing, I beg of you not to serve Yates if he should attack you; & if your Grace does not approve of Page,[9] I

1. The Hon. Henry Pelham, 1695–1754, MP for Sussex 1722–1754, was Newcastle's brother. He was successively, Secretary at War, 1724–1730; Paymaster of the Forces, 1730–1743; 1st. Lord of the Treasury, 25 August 1743–1754; and Chancellor of the Exchequer, 12 December 1743–1754.
2. Lewes Races.
3. Halland at East Hoathly in Sussex was Newcastle's favourite seat in the county.
4. William Cowper, 2nd. Earl Cowper, 1709–1764, was a Lord of the Bedchamber 1733–1747.
5. William Keppel, 2nd. Earl of Albemarle, 1702–1754, married Richmond's sister, Lady Anne Lennox. A soldier of renown, he fought at Dettingen and Fontenoy, and became a general. He was present at Culloden. Ambassador Extraordinary and Plenipotentiary at Paris, 1749–1754, he was also created Commander in chief in North Britain in 1748.
6. James Butler, 1680–1741, of Worminghurst, MP for Arundel, 1705–1708, and for Sussex, 1715–1722, and again 1728–1741. He bought his estate from William Penn in 1702.
7. Thomas Yates, 1697–17 , of Chichester, MP for Chichester, 1734–1741, was the son of Henry Yates of Warnham, once MP for Horsham. He married Margaret, daughter of Sir John Miller. He stood unsuccessfully at Chichester as a Tory in 1733, on the death of Lord William Beauclerk, being defeated by Sir Thomas Prendergast.
8. Sir Thomas Dyke of Horeham in Waldron.
9. John Page, 1696–1779, of Watergate in Donnington, MP for Grimsby, 1727–1734, on the interest of his first wife. He married secondly one of the influential Soane family of Chichester. He stood unsuccessfully for Chichester with Richmond's support in 1734. In 1741 he was returned unopposed, rather against Richmond's wishes, and shared the representation with Richmond's nominees until he retired in 1768.

earnestly request of you, to procure the votes of all your freinds, single for Mr Brudenell.[1]

There is another affair, I must also beg your Grace's assistance in; that is what I mention'd to you at Hampton Court, about Shoreham, I find Ungle[2] has declined there, & nobody yett declared butt Gold,[3] now if you are not engaged for anybody else there, I shall take it as the greatest favour in the world, if you would give us your assistance for Sr Thomas Prendergast there. I would not have you putt yourself to any expence, only give us leave to make use of your name with those you can influence. If wee have your Graces favourable answer then wee must try what wee can do with Gold.

My Lord Hervey[4] is here, presents his service to your Grace, & is very sorry he could not also attend you at Halland.

Jemmy Brudenell kisses your hands, he is now hard at worke & deep in calculation. We are sure of 450, out of about 530. which is pretty well, & good hopes, of getting 30, or 40, more between this & the election.

I am My Dear Lord, with the utmost truth, & respect, your Graces, ever faithfull, & obliged.

Richmond

6. NEWCASTLE TO RICHMOND

Lewes
Fryday Morning [3 August 1733]

My Dear Lord,

I am infinitely obliged to you for your kind Letter, but am in such a Hurry, that it is impossible for me to answer it att present, but will be sure to write more fully before I leave the Countrey. We are attacked by the Tories, (amongst whom Sr Cecil Bishop[5] was yesterday) by Mr Garland[6] a Dissenter, & Mr Sergison[7] for this Town, & we hear we are to be attacked by two for the County, but who they are we don't yett know; yesterday we hear they could gett nobody to stand. What this day will produce, we shall soon see.

Notwithstanding all this, we don't in ye least fear Success. We have had greater Appearances of Friends than ever. We are just now going round this Town. Page & Yates have both spoke to me, & Sr Thos Miller[8] sent to me for Yates by his son Tom.

1. James Brudenell, 1687–1746, MP for Chichester, 1713–1715, and again 1734–1746, and for Andover, 1715–1734, was brother to Lord Cardigan, and Richmond's brother-in-law. He was master of the Jewell Office, 1716–1730, and Groom of the Bedchamber to King George II, 1733–1746. Richmond made him a Gentleman of the Horse, 1730–1746. He was Recorder of Chichester, 1730–1746.
2. Samuel Ongley, 1697–1747, of Old Warden, Bedfordshire, MP for New Shoreham, 1729–1734, and for Bedford, 1734–1747, was the wealthy heir of Sir Samuel Ongley, sometime MP for Maidstone and a Director of the South Sea Company.
3. John Gould, 1695–1740, of Woodford in Essex, MP for New Shoreham, 1729–1734. He was a Director in the East India Company, 1724–1735.
4. John Hervey, Lord Hervey, 1696–1743, the memoir writer, was a frequent guest of both Richmond and Newcastle. For some of his letters from Richmond, see The Earl of Ilchester, (ed.), *Lord Hervey and His Friends*, (1950).
5. Sir Cecil Bishopp, 1695–1778, of Parham, MP for Penrhyn, 1727–1734, and for Boroughbridge, 1755–1768. In 1734 he fought the Sussex seat against Pelham and Butler, but after the arrest of his brother for Jacobitism in 1746, he became a supporter of Newcastle.
6. Nathaniel Garland, 'a rigid dissenter', joined Thomas Sergison in standing against Thomas Pelham of Lewes and Thomas Pelham of Stanmer in Lewes in 1734, and came within 8 votes of defeating them.
7. Thomas Sergison, 1701–1766, of Cuckfield Park, MP for Lewes 1747–1766, inherited a large estate in Mid Sussex and much property in Lewes. He stood for Lewes against Newcastle's candidates in 1734, 1741 and 1743. He also canvassed the County seat against the Earl of Middlesex in the 1741 bye-election, but finally came to an agreement with Newcastle.
8. Sir Thomas Miller, 1688–1733, of Lavant, MP for Chichester, 1715–1727, married Jane, daughter of Francis Goater, Alderman of Chichester, and was the father of Sir John Miller.

5

Att present considering our County Affairs, we have declared of no Side between them two, wch was all Page desired, but I will write more fully upon that Subject.

As to Shoreham, I have a great deal to trouble you with upon the subject, having been often spoke to by Sr R. Walpole[1] upon ye Subject & he once named a Person to join with Gould. I wish you would lett me know, by a Line by ye post tomorrow, directed to Bishopstone,[2] whether you propose soon to be in Town. I return to Hampton Ct next Tuesday. & if you come soon there, I could better inform you as to Shoreham by Word of Mouth than Letter. My Compliments to Ld Harvey & J. Brudenell. If he wants us, we come to a Man

Ever yrs

Holles Newcastle

Honble Harry sends his Compliments & thanks

7. RICHMOND TO NEWCASTLE

Goodwood
August 5th 1733

My dear Lord,

I received your Graces letter from Lewis where I am sorry to find you will have an oposition. I do not att all wonder at Sr Cecyl Bishops apearing in the Tory cause, for he is pleas'd to do that at Chichester, for so I shall judge of everyman that gives his interest to Yates, for his whole strength is the Tory interest. However Sr Cecyl is hearty for Mr Brudenell, so indeed are four out of five, of Whigs, Torys, Jacobites, Presbyterians, Free Masons & Germogans, 'Tho I own the Whigs are our sheet Anchor, & always will be so. I conclude Mr Pelham & Mr Butler will come to visit, this end of the County, now if they have not already appointed the time, Mr Brudenell & I are of opinion the best would be at the Mayors election, which will be on Munday the 24th. of September, for then the town, I mean Chichester, will be full, & wee shall all be there; & 'till then wee shall not be there. Wee conclude the Honble Gentlemen will lye either at the Bishops, or my Lady Farringtons,[3] butt wee hope, they will none of them lye at an enemy of ours, 'tho it may happen to be a freind of your's. butt if they will take up with Country Quarters, I hope they will honor Goodwood. I shall not go to town or to Hampton Court this great while, butt I beleive I shall go to the Installation, where if your Grace goes, I'l meet you, if not, I will call on you at Hampton Court, or Claremont in my way. All I can say now of Shoreham is, that if it had been a Borough that your Grace had ever had anything to do in heretofore, I should never have had any thoughts of it. butt I look upon it as a new Whore, that is any bodys for their mony; however I hope, & beleive your Grace, & I shall never differ in anything. haveing, I assure you without any compliment, the utmost regard for your Grace & shall be glad of any oportunity to show you how sincerely I am, my Dear Lord, Your Grace's most faithfull, humble servant,

Richmond

My Lord Hervey, Jemmy Brudenell, Dr. Sherwin,[4] & all the company here, are very much your Graces humble servants.

<hr>

1. Sir Robert Walpole, 1676–1745, MP for Castle Rising, 1701–1702, and for King's Lynn, 1702–1742, was 1st. Lord of the Treasury and Chancellor of the Exchequer, 1715–1717, and 1721–1742.
2. Bishopstone near Seaford was Newcastle's hunting lodge, but it passed into disuse as he grew older.
3. Elizabeth, Lady Farrington, was the daughter of John Peachey of Eartham, and the widow of Sir Richard Farrington, MP for Chichester between 1680 and 1715. Her step son was married to Sir Thomas Miller's daughter Ann.
4. The Rev. William Sherwin, died 1735, a Canon Residentiary of Chichester Cathedral, was elected to the Cathedral Chapter in 1718. Richmond disliked Sherwin, and, in 1733, staged a mock hold up of the cleric, in order to frighten him.

My service to the Honble Harry who I expect at Goodwood, in Septr & as many people as he pleases to bring with him, & my house can hold.

8. NEWCASTLE TO RICHMOND

Bishopstone
Augt 6th 1733

My Dear Lord,

I had this morning the honer of your Graces letter. Battine[1] will acquaint you with every thing that has past here. You may imagine we are in no small hurry, dispatching our agents to the several parts of the County. All our accounts hitherto are good, & we don't in the least fear them. However, nothing must be omitted, & we depend upon our friends in the West for their care of us. Battine will give you a list of all the parishes in Chichester Rape. I begg My Dear Duke, you would immediately send your people, to secure all your folks att Chichester, and in the neighbouring parts. I conclude they will sett up somebody att Steyning Races to join Mr Fuller[2] or he will make nothing at all of it. My Brother & Mr. Butler don't think of going round the County, till they see what the enemy does. The first visit they will make will be to your parts. My brother will see your Grace at ye Installation, & then settle it with you. In ye meantime he thanks you for your kind invitation, & will not fail to come to Goodwood, if you will be so good as to lett him.

As to Shoreham, you are very obliging to me in wt you say about it. I have had several messages & offers from them but you judge I believe very right of the way of making interest there. When I see you at the installation, wch I will contrive to do, or if I don't go, to begg you would call att Claremont on your way, I will tell you very freely all I know of the matter, & will determine nothing 'till then, for you may be assured I have always the greatest inclination to do what is agreeable to you. I dare say you will then be quite satisfied with the account, I shall give you of what I have said both to Yates & Page. My compliments to Lord Harvey, Jemmy Broderick &c. and believe me ever wth great sincerity & Respect. My dear Duke Your most affect servt

Holles Newcastle

P.S. Honble Harry is by Interest & Inclination much yours.

9. PELHAM TO RICHMOND

Bishopstone
Aug 6th [1733]

My Dear Lord,

My brother has acquainted your Grace with what pass'd att Lewes. I have nothing therefore to trouble you with but thanks for all former favors, and humble requests for the continuance of them on this occasion. Till we hear who the Torys set up in your part of the country I conclude it will not be thought proper to visit your parts, but when we do, Mr Butler & your humble servt shall follow your Graces commands. I hope to have the honour of seeing you when you come to the Installment, and will then consult with you what is proper to be done. In the mean time if your Grace will have the

---

1. William Battine, 1684–1770, of East Marden, was married to Mary Peckham of Littlegreen in Compton. He was a local magistrate and a member of the Chichester Corporation. He was Mayor of Chichester in 1742.
2. John Fuller of Brightling was, with Sir Cecil Bishopp and Thomas Sergison, one of the leaders of the opposition to Newcastle in the county. He stood unsuccessfully for the County seat in 1734.

goodness to secure Mr George Parker. Mr Soane,[1] Mr Covert,[2] and such others as you have a particular influence over you will greatly oblige him who is and ever will be my Dear Lord Your Graces most obedient and obliged humble servt

H. Pelham

P.S. How will Berkeley[3] be. My best respects attend the Dutchesse of Richmond, Ld Hervey, Jemmy Brudenell and all att Goodwood.

10. RICHMOND TO NEWCASTLE

Goodwood
August 14th 1733

My dear Lord,

I beg pardon for being so troublesome about this affair of Shoreham. butt if I don't make my application this week, I shant be able to do it this six weeks, for from the Installation I shall not return here 'till just before Michss & those few chaps there that already know my design, are very impatient. & I own I should be very sorry to loose this oportunity of serving Sr Thomas Prendergast, & it would be a little hard, that my regard for your Grace should be the only obstacle to his comeing into Parliament, for by what I can find already, I am pretty confident of success there. Therefore dear Duke lett me beg an answer from you by Thursday's post, else it will be too late.

I hope when I see you to give you a good account of our freeholders hereabouts. I find every man hearty for the Honble Harry, butt Master Butler of Worminghurst, they say will be push'd. & you may depend upon it Fuller will have the votes of every Tory on this side the County, for I thinke it is now again the old cause, Whig & Tory. as I hope you are convinced it is at Chichester, by the Good Company Coll. Yates kept at the Starr at Lewis.

Sir Thomas Miller, Alderman Soane, Alderman Covert, & all my freinds are hearty for Pelham & Butler. Butt Captn Smith, demurs upon the latter, however I hope he may be gott off. By the Installation I shall be able to shew you a list of all my freinds names, & how they will vote.

I am my dear Lord your Graces, most faithfull humble servant

Richmond

11. RICHMOND TO NEWCASTLE

Goodwood
August 15th 1733

My dear Lord,

Altho I troubled your Grace with a letter butt yesterday, yett I must trouble you again now with this, to give you an account of an answer I had but last night from one Mr North[4] of Shopwick, to whom I had sent my Steward to aske his vote for Messrs Pelham & Butler, which was, that he was very sorry he could not oblige me, butt that he had promis'd to vote single for Mr Fuller, at Coll. Yates's earnest request & desire. – _qu'en dite vous_? I am impatient for your answer to what I writ to you about yesterday, & I hope it will be a favourable one, else I shall be much disappointed. Mr

1. Francis Soane of Chichester was an Alderman of the City, and had a considerable influence there. He was father-in-law of John Page of Watergate. He was Mayor of the city in 1730.
2. Benjamin Covert, citizen and Alderman of Chichester, had been Mayor of the city in 1726 and 1731.
3. James Berkeley, 3rd. Earl of Berkeley, 1680–1736, was married to Richmond's sister, Lady Louisa Lennox. After a naval career, he became Lord High Admiral and Commander-in-Chief in the Channel, 1719.
4. Richard North of Shopwhyke in Oving voted for Bishopp and Fuller in the 1734 Election.

No. 1 Goodwood House in 1746
Detail of John Wootton's painting of Sheldon, a favourite hunter of the 2nd Duke of Richmond.
Reproduced by courtesy of the Trustees of the Goodwood Collections.

No. 2   Thomas Pelham Holles, 1st Duke of Newcastle by Isaac Gosset
Reproduced by permission of the Trustees of the Meade-Fetherstonhaugh Family.

No. 3   The Right Honourable Henry Pelham by Isaac Gosset
Reproduced by kind permission of the Trustees of the Meade-Fetherstonhaugh Family.

No. 4   Halland in 1793. The West Front by Samuel H. Grimm
British Library, Add. Ms. 5671, f. 47 (no. 82). Reproduced by permission of the Trustees
of the British Library.

Gould is an intimate freind of Sr Thomas Prendergast's, & I believe would joyn with him & assist him.

I beg to know if you will be at the Installation. I am my Dear Lord, with the utmost truth & sincerity, Your Graces Most faithfull, & obedient humble servant

Richmond

I have just now received a letter from Mr Butler in which he tells me Sr Cecyl Bishop, has declared for the County, & joyns with Fuller so I conclude now that Mr North of Shopwick, will not be for Fuller single, butt for Fuller & Bishop. Sr Cecyl, has already sent me word that he will voate for Yates, so it would be very unhandsome in the Coll. not to vote for him.

12.   RICHMOND TO NEWCASTLE

Goodwood
October 17th 1733

My dear Lord,

   I must beg & intreat of your Grace to do Wilkinsons job for him as soon as possible, for he & his two sons are confounded surly about it, so it is of the utmost consequence to us that it should be done imediately. & if it is done I must beg that he may have his superanuation sallery from the 13th of November 1731, when he quitted. I know the difficultys, & at an other time they would be reasonable ones, butt at present wee must lay aside all reason with these chaps, else wee shall come off butt poorly. Dear Duke do this & you will add a great obligation, to a thousand others that shall ever be acknowledg'd by your ever faithful

Richmond

13.   RICHMOND TO NEWCASTLE

Charlton[1]
Decr 26th 1733

My Dear Lord,

   In the first place, ten thousand thankes to your Grace for all your polite entertainment at Bishopstone; If every freeholder in the County was as well pleased with it as myself, Sr Cecyl Bishop & Esqr Fuller might whistle for a vote.

   Now in the true freeholders stile I must aske two more favours of you tho you have granted me two thousand already. The first is, that as Mr Folliot that was a poor Knight of Windsor, liveing at Chichester, is dead, & that it was in his room that I recommended Monsr Grandmaison to you, I hope you will procure it for Grandmaison. The next is, that you would be so good as to intimate to Robert Smith at Shoreham, who I hear is your Graces house painter, to give Sr Thomas Prendergast a vote. Adieu My Dear Duke, I am, & eternally shall be Your sincerely devoted servant

Richmond

14.   RICHMOND TO NEWCASTLE

Goodwood
Decr 30 1733

My Dear Lord,

   I have writ by this post to Sr Robert about our Shoreham affairs. as to any agree-

1.   Charlton in Singleton near Chichester was the centre of the Charlton Hunt, of which Richmond was elected the Master and Proprietor in 1731. Richmond had a hunting lodge there. See The Earl of March, *Records of The Old Charlton Hunt,* (1910).

ment with Mr Gould, I can not talk of it 'till I have a direct answer from Mr Frederick.[1] I have beg'd Sr Robert to delay giveing the employments as long as he can. butt if he will dispose of them; that Mr Henry Crawley may have the Collectorship, & Mr William Foster, the Comptrolership.[2] now I beg your Grace would back these two to Sr Robert, they are both Freeholders & are as hearty in the County as in the town. I hope in God Sr Robert will make no difficulty about it; for if he does, he'l quite blow me up there; which I am sure I dont deserve from his hands; so I wont so much as suspect it. I am vastly obliged to you for your kind letter, & your continual goodness to me & my freinds, must ever inviolably attach me to your service.

I am <u>Dear Duke</u>, as Tommy Miller calls you: Your ever obliged,

Richmond

Jemmy is here, & presents his respects to your grace, & wee both joyn in our humle services to the Honble Harry. Wee gett at Chichester, & at least keep our Ground in the Country.

15. NEWCASTLE TO RICHMOND

Bishopstone
Monday Morning [31 December 1733]

My Dear Lord,

I had yesterday your Graces most kind Letter, & you may be assured will never make any Engagement about Shoreham but by your means. I give that Answer to all the Applications made to me. I had a Petition in favour of Clark, & there was one Foster here, who Martin[3] says will gett you three Votes for ye Town. I have also been spoke to by Sr Wm Gage[4] in favour of one Crawley, but they will all apply to you, & when we have the pleasure of seeing you here, whoever you think most for your Interest shall be my Man, but I think you had better not promise anybody 'till you have talk'd to our friend Martin, who shall meet you here. I am extreamly glad to hear your Chichester Friends design to attend you hither <u>de bonne foy</u>. They shall be most heartily welcome & I wish you could perswade Mr Covert to come with them. Mr Cheale[5] I hear intends to attend you also. Our County Affairs go as well as possible. I wish I could say ye same of Lewes. We go thither this Day, where I hear the Enemy have summon'd their whole <u>posse</u> to meet us. By the best Accounts we have now a certain Majority, & if so we shall keep it. The spirit of ye whole Opperation is there. I believe we shall give a pretty good Account of them when we see you. <u>bien des complimens aux fameux Chasseurs de Londres et de Paris; avec mes tres humbles conseils de ne fou en pas trop.</u>

My particular Service to Albemarle, who will give you an Account of our manner of living here. Our House is small, but we have good Neighbours where we can lodge all our Friends. I wish we could know certainly, what day you will come. You must not think of leaving us 'till Wensday morning. All imaginable Success attend your pleasures, & Business, & believe me as I am most sincerely & affectly yrs.

Holles Newcastle

1. Thomas Frederick, 1707–1740, of Burwood Park, Walton-on-Thames in Surrey, MP for New Shoreham, 1734–1740, was a wealthy merchant, he was succeeded in the seat by his two brothers.
2. The government interest in New Shoreham rested on these appointments, and on the Shoreham men employed at Woolwich and Deptford.
3. Edmund Martin was instituted Vicar of New Shoreham on 27 December 1728, and held the living until his death in 1766.
4. Sir William Gage, 1695–1744, of Firle, MP for Seaford, 1722–1744, looked after Newcastle's interests in the eastern half of the county, and reported to him regularly. He was a friend and a cricket rival of Richmond.
5. John Cheale of Findon, Norroy King of Arms, was a regular guest of Richmond. The Charlton Hounds were kennelled at Findon for part of the year.

P.S. The Honble Harry as in duty bound is much yours.

16. RICHMOND TO NEWCASTLE

Goodwood
Jan 11th 1733/4

My Dear Lord,
'Tho I hope to have the honor of kissing your hands in the House of Lords so soon as Thursday next, I can't help takeing this first oportunity of thankeing your Grace for Robin Smith's vote, & then also for haveing ordered Mr Paxton to bid for these three houses at Shoreham, which I am very desirous of, & which I hope he will gett for me. In short there is no end of your goodness. So I'l say no more, butt that I am with utmost gratitude, my Dear Lord Your ever faithfull, & obliged,

Richmond

Thus stands our present calculation at Chichester

The Recorder[1]	375	
Mr Page	296	
Mr Yates	269	
The Recorders majority on Page		79
on Yates		106
Pages majority on Yates		27

17. RICHMOND TO NEWCASTLE

Goodwood
Jan 13th 1733/4

The Duke of Newcastle himself cant wish better to the present administration than I do. c'est tout dire. & I will as certanly be at Westminster on Thursday the 17th as your Grace; when I dont doubt butt I shall concur with your Wednesdays nights resolutions; butt very likely I shall not be able to attend you there. If I could possibly be of any service to the cause in general or your Grace in particular, I would go from hence barefoot rather than not be there. Pray forgive the liberty I take in encloseing to you, a letter for Mr Pelham of Soissoons, I dont know his christian name; nor where or how to direct to him, which is the reason of my giveing your Grace this trouble. you will also the easyer excuse it when I tell you it is only to transmit the orders of Madame de Monconseil, one of the handsomest women in France to him. I have of late been so regular a plague to you that I fear you'l be quite sick when you see my scrawl upon the outside of a letter. I am sure this requires no answer; butt whenever you have any commands for me, be so good as to direct to Goodwood near Midhurst, instead of near Chichester; else I may very likely receive it a day later than the ordinary course.
I am My Dear Lord Duke for ever and ever Your's

Richmond

The Recorder is gon. Mr Lawrance is still with me, & ha-ha-ha-ha-ha presents his respects to the Duke of Newcastle.
The whole Family of the Drinkwaters are zealous for the Recorder at Chichester, & for Pelham & Butler in the County; old Drinkwater told me the other day these words; as

---

1. James Brudenell.

soon as I read in the Craftsman[1] that a popish king <u>might</u> govern in England as well as a protestant one, <u>my eyes were open</u>; <u>I see what they want</u>, & I will have nothing to do with them

18. NEWCASTLE TO RICHMOND

Newcastle House
Feby 11th 1733/4

My Dear Lord,

It is in obedience to your Graces Commands, that I give you this trouble, to acquaint you, that the enemy have this day given us notice, that we are to have Business of Consequence in our House on Wensday next. It is to be a surprise upon us, that is what they are to go upon. Sr R. Walpole has some notion that He is to be personally attacked, & by the secrecy it is to be sure some point they think material. I rather believe it is about the army, & to make the officers of the army, not removable but by Court Martial, whilst they are in either House of Parliament. This would either make an independant army or exclude all peers from having any new Commissions, since it is scarce to be supposed, that the King would give Commissions to those He can't turn out, when He might give them to others, that He could remove. But whatever the mine is, that is to be sprung, we are very desirous to have all our friends present, that they may judge whether we deserve Censure or not. I hope My Dear Duke you will be so good as to lett us have your company. Sr Robert Walpole I understand has wrote to Lord Cholmely[2] to come up. I dare not presume to ask the favour of ye Duke of St. Albans[3] to come up with you, but your Grace will be so good as to make my compliments to Him, & acquaint Him with the contents of this letter if you think proper.

I am My Dear Duke Ever most sincerely & faithfully yrs

Holles Newcastle

My complemts to Lord Cholmley and ye rest of your company

P.S. I don't know whether you have any other Lords with you or not. I begg you would be so good as to write a line to Ld Tankervile[4] and make my excuse for not writing to him, being in such a hurry.

19. RICHMOND TO NEWCASTLE

Charlton
Febr 20th 1733/4

My Dear Lord,

Your Grace gave me leave to be troublesome to you, & I am a going to be extreamly so, for I have a thousand Jobs for you to do for me. The first is, that, if His Majesty should be displeas'd at my not comeing nor giveing my proxy in the Pension bill, your

---

1. *The Craftsman* was the journal of the Opposition, and was established in 1726, under the patronage of Pulteney and Bolingbroke. After 1730, the Old Pretender authorised his supporters to co-operate with the opponents of the ministry.
2. George Cholmondeley, 3rd. Earl of Cholmondeley, 1703–1770, succeeded his father in 1733. He was the Master of the Horse to the Prince of Wales, 1728–1735; a Lord of the Treasury, 1735–1736; and Chancellor of the Duchy of Lancaster, 1736–1743. He was married to Walpole's daughter Mary.
3. Charles Beauclerk, 2nd. Duke of St. Albans, 1696–1751, hunted regularly with the Charlton Hunt. He was Lord Lieutenant of Berkshire, 1727–1751; Governor of Windsor Castle and Warden of Windsor Forest, 1730–1751; and a Lord of the Bedchamber, 1738–1751.
4. Charles Bennett, 2nd. Earl of Tankerville, 1697–1753, of Uppark in Harting, was, for a time, Joint Master of the Charlton Hunt with Richmond. He was a Lord of the Bedchamber to the Prince of Wales, 1729–1733; Master of the Buckhounds, 1733–1737; and a Lord of the Bedchamber to King George II, 1737–1738. He was Lord Lieutenant of Northumberland, 1740–1753.

Grace would extreamly oblige me in telling Him that the reason of my not voteing against the bill now is that I am determin'd never to give any vote that should be inconsistent with any other I have formerly given, & that for the very same reason I am ever bound as far as lyes in my poor power to do every thing that can be of service to his Majesty, unless it be of disservice to my country, butt that I look upon as a thing that will not nor can not ever happen as long as his majesty lives. If you thinke it right to say this, do, if not, lett it alone, just as you please.

The next thing I must beg of you to do, is to speake to Sr Robert not about my conscience, butt about my Borough,[1] where God knows that ugly word conscience is not known. What I want to have you say to Sr Robert is this, that I have great reason to suspect, that his enemy Mr Phillipson,[2] & his freind Mr Frederick are joyning, which I must beg of him to prevent if possible, for it would hurt us extreamly, hurt Gould extreamly, help Frederick a little, & be of great advantage to Phillipson. so I hope Sr Robert will putt a stop to it, which I am persuaded by Frederick he can do. As your Grace is so good, so sincere, & so great a freind to us in this affair I dont doubt butt you will use your best endeavours with Sr Robert. The next thing I must then beg of you is to gett this Comptrolership for William Foster. Sr Robert promis'd it me, & Sanden[3] our Comptroler at Chichester, has, (at my recommendation) sent him a deputation to act as Comptroler, so that it would be barbarous not to gett the warrant from the Treasury for him now that he acts as such. The next job, is that for Wilkinson, which is to gett a new warrant for him, that he may have his superanuation from the 13th of November 1731, which was the day that Johnston succeeded him; what encourages me the more to aske this is that he claims a promis of your Grace for it, & Major Battine sayes its true that you did promis him. The next (for I have not half done yett) is that you would be so good as to speake to our good freind Sr Wm Gage that he would press Haslegrove to be for us, for I am sure Sr Wm can make one vote of him, the other indeed is reasonable that he should keep to sell to the best bidder. The next is that you would not forget to speake to Glanville about his tenants in Selsea, where if he does not take care, three out of six or seven I thinke that are there, will be for Bishop. Now the last favour I have to beg of you in this letter, & what I have most at heart, is, that you would believe me, as I really and truely am, Your Graces ever faithfull, & obliged humble servant

Richmond

Tommy Miller gives up all thoughts of the <u>beef eaters</u> consequently he will turn water drinker, I suppose.

20.   RICHMOND TO NEWCASTLE

Hague[4]
Fryday. July 2d NS 1734

My Dear Lord,
    Pray dont thinke me troublesome in putting you in mind of what you promis'd me when I saw you last at Claremont. I mean about speaking to Sr Robert about

1.   New Shoreham.
2.   John Phillipson, 1698–1756, of Park Hall in Harwich, Essex, MP for New Shoreham, 1734–1741, and for Harwich, 1741–1756, was a director of the South Sea Company, 1733–1756; a clerk in the Navy Office; and a Lord of the Admiralty, 1743–1744. His daughter was married to Robert Bristow, a later MP for New Shoreham.
3.   Thomas Sanden, the Comptroller at Chichester, was probably the father of Dr. Thomas Sanden, the friend and confidant of Sylas Neville, (See B. Cozens-Hardy, *The Diary of Sylas Neville, 1767–1788,* (1950).), and the founder of the Chichester Infirmary.
4.   In the Spring and early Summer of 1734, the Duke and Duchess of Richmond paid one of their frequent visits to the Hague.

Chichester & Shoreham. I have it so much at heart that the disappointment would be excessive great to me. To pretend to send news to a secretary of State would be prigonometry; butt to tell you that the Princess Royal & The Prince of Orange[1] are adored here by 99 out of 100 will I am sure please you. The Ladys are indeed in some huff about not being saluted, butt that will soon be forgiven I beleive if she can gett leave to salute them at her return, & if that silly ceremony was once got over I am sure, her behaviour is such, that she would not have an enemy in the country, nor indeed has he except your Butzlaars[2] & your Opdam's; the latter is my neighbour here; & a strong mercator vituli, amicus intimus de Domini Renewoode. The Princess went Incognita to see the Pensioners[3] Garden, & he & Mevrouwe Slingerland his Lady, mett her there, & received her R:H: with the utmost respect & politeness. The mob is outragious for them, & Butzlaar dreams of the De Witts every night. They are now just going round the Voor haute, & most nobly attended, & with such hurras, that I have much ado to refrayn hallowing out. Pelham & Butler for ever. Their cry which is a little more to the purpose here is Oranie boven. Butzlaar onder. Anglice, Orange above, alias Orange for ever, Butzlaar under, alias down with the Butzlaars: the latter to tell you the truth I did not hear myself, distinctly, butt I heard them make a damn'd noise, & I was told that several of the mob had cry'd so. In short the truth is that the Anti Orange boys are ready to beshitt themselves, & I have tried you with a confounded long letter, so adieu Mon Cher Duc. Amo te, ut amo me ipsum

Richmond

dont thinke of answering this, imprimis, because there is nothing in it to answer, secundo I shall be in England before an answer could reach me, for I embarque next Fryday on board the Pacquet for Harwich. Madame La Duchesse est grosse & reste icy.

21. RICHMOND TO NEWCASTLE

Charlton
Novr 24th 1734

My Dear Lord,

I this day saw Alderman Soane, who insists more than ever on our promis that he should be excuse serving as Sherif, so lett me beg of you not to forget to gett him excused, & be so good as to write one line to me only to shew him, for he is confounded uneasy. if you are so kind, pray direct to me at Charlton near Midhurst. I return you ten thousand thanks for the Buffalo,[4] she arrived on Fryday in perfect health.

I am My Dear Lord for ever Your's

Richmond

22. NEWCASTLE TO RICHMOND

Claremont
Nov 22d 1735

My Dear Lord

I received by the last post your Grace's letter and one att the same time from Mr

---

1. The Princess Royal had married William Charles Henry, Prince of Orange on 14 March 1734.
2. M. Boetzelaer was later the Dutch envoy to England in the various negotiations of the war with France.
3. M. Simon van Slingelandt, the Grand Pensionary, and sometime Receiver General of Holland.
4. The buffalo was for Richmond's menagerie at Goodwood.

Orme[1] relating to the election att Midhurst, in case of Mr Knight's[2] Death. As I have no interest there, and there may not be a vacancy there for some time, I begg you would excuse my saying any thing upon the subject 'till I have the honor to see you in Sussex or in London. I have a very true Regard for Mr Orme, & am sensible I have obligations to Him, which I shall always be ready to acknowledge, but Mr Knight & His family might think, they had reason to take it amiss of me, if during Mr Knights Life, I should any ways meddle, or concern myself in a Town, where I have no intrest, upon a supposition of Mr Knight's Death. This being the case, I must begg my Dear Lord that you would make my excuses to Mr Orme, for not answering his letter, since it is impossible for me to say any thing upon the subject but what I have said to your Grace. I hope to go the week after next to Sussex, & to take a Hunt att Charlton before my Return to London. My compl nts to Lord Delawar[3] & believe me ever My Dear Duke Yrs most affect'ly & sincerely

Holles Newcastle

P.S. May I begg my compliments to my Lady Dutchess

23. NEWCASTLE TO RICHMOND

Bishopstone
Decr 16th 1735

My Dear Duke,

I am infinitely obliged to you for your kind Letter and Invitation, but am sorry to hear by Battine, that you are angry with me for not having answer'd it sooner. I have been so much out of Humour about the Weather & my motions were on that account so uncertain, that I really could not say 'till very lately, whether I should be able to come or not. But as the Weather seems sett in for Frost, I have determined to gett to London assoon as I can, & intend to be there on Thursday next. I will however keep my Word with you, & certainly wait upon you from Claremont, which indeed is nearer you than this place. When the Weather is open, & I shall hear you are most at leisure, I will write to you, and settle my Journey with you, & since you are so good as to desire it, you shall be troubled with me two nights att least. We have drank your health att the Head of our western friends every day, and as <u>we ought</u>.

I am informed that the living of Lavington in Mr Orme's Gift is now vacant[4] and that Arch Deacon Barker[5] has applied to Him for one of his sons, who has lived in our neighbourhood, and is a very sober deserving man. I would not trouble Mr Orme with a letter, to ask the favour of Him, but if you can serve Mr Barker by saying a word to Mr Orme for Him, if He is not otherwise engaged, I should be very much obliged to Mr Orme and you. But if you think it improper to mention it, I begg you would not do

1.   Garton Orme, 1696–1758, of Woolavington, MP for Arundel, 1739–1754, was a man of dubious reputation. He married the daughter of the Rev. Daniel Lafitte of Bordeaux and Vicar of Woolavington as his second wife, after his first wife died in suspicious circumstances. He was Gentleman Usher to the Princess of Wales, and voted with the Leicester House party. At first supported by Richmond, he defeated the Duke's candidates at Arundel in 1747.
2.   Bulstrode Peachey, 1681–1736, of West Dean, and Chawton in Hampshire, MP for Midhurst 1722–1736, married the widow of William Woodward Knight in 1730, and took the additional name of Knight. His wife was the heiress of the Lewkenors of West Dean, and brought him West Dean House, and an interest in the Midhurst constituency.
3.   John West, 1st. Earl de la Warr, 1693–1766, was a close neighbour and friend of Richmond. He was Treasurer of the Household, 1731–1736; was an active debater in the House of Lords, 1732–1754; and, as a soldier, fought as a Brigadier at Dettingen. Richmond refers to him always as 'Del'.
4.   The Rectory of Woolavington was vacant on the secession of Robert Smythe, who had been presented to the living by Garton Orme in October 1730.
5.   James Barker was Archdeacon of Chichester, 1708–1736. He was Prebendary of Sidlesham, 1700–1704, and of Sutton, 1704–1725.

it. My compliments to all the good company with you, & I must begg that Mr Mayor[1] would assure His Corporation that I am much their servant. I am glad to hear you do the Duty of your office so well. The Honble Harry, Capt. Elliot,[2] Tom Spencer desire to be remembered to you, & I am ever my Dear Duke. Your Grace's Most sincerely & affec.tly

Holles Newcastle

24.   NEWCASTLE TO RICHMOND

Bishopstone,
Dec 23rd 1735

My Dear Lord,

The thaw coming just as I intended to leave this place, I could not forbear altering my Resolution. We have had four Days very good sport, but as the frost is returned, & likely to continue. If it is so tomorrow morning I shall sett out towards London. I had had so little sport att home, & was so uncertain in my motions, that I hoped you would excuse my not attending you att Charlton before my Return to London; & ye Honble Harry having left us last week had I come, He could not have beeen of the party, but we will Both come, before this season is over from Claremont, as I acquainted you in my last letter.

As to the affair of the postmaster of Ireland,[3] it is impossible for me to say any thing to your Grace by letter upon it, except that it has given me very real & great concern. Had I had an opportunity of talking fully to you upon it, I should have taken the liberty to have told you my opinion, with that sincerity & affection that I shall always speak upon anything that concerns your Grace; and I hope, just as I should think for my self, were I in the same Case. Upon reading your letter a second time, I think you mean, why should you not have the place yourself? I did not when I received your letter, take it att all in that sense, but imagined you meant, as it was formerly intended. What alteration that would make, I cannot say; but am afraid it would be thought pretty much the same thing. Forgive me my Dear Lord, for having said thus much, and be assured that I shall always be glad to do every thing in my power to serve & please you, for nobody can be more sensible than I really am of your goodness to me, or be more sincerely Mr Dear Duke Your most affect. & humble servt

Holles Newcastle

P.S.My compl'nts to Lord John & Andrew, if they are with you.

25.   NEWCASTLE TO RICHMOND

Newcastle House
Feb ye 3d 1735/6

My Dear Lord

I return you according to your Commands the two enclosed letters, as to the Reversionary Grant in Ireland, I believe it cannot be sett aside, & in my opinion would be very wrong to attempt. I am much obliged to Mr Orme for the Regard he has had to your Grace's Request, tho' I am perswaded it was impossible for Him to make any thing of it. As to his Zeal for ye Government, I can assure you & Him, I never had any

---

1.   Richmond was Mayor of Chichester in 1735, and again in 1744.
2.   William Elliott, 1704–1764, MP for Calne, 1741–1754, was made Captain in the 10th. Dragoons in 1723. Later he became Lieutenant Colonel in the Horse Grenadier Guards. He was equerry to King George II, 1743–1760.
3.   Richmond was attempting to obtain the post of Postmaster General of Ireland for Sir Thomas Prendergast. It was almost twenty years before he finally succeeded.

16

Doubt of it, but am myself always against giving any opposition to those, who mean the same thing. I wish you all imaginable pleasure & Diversion. May I begg my Respectfull Compl'nts to ye Dutchess of Richmond, with love & service to John etc.

I am Dear Duke ever yrs

Holles Newcastle

26. NEWCASTLE TO RICHMOND

Newcastle House
Feb 17th 1735/6

My Dear Lord,

I had the favor of your letter & have obey'd your Commands. I spoke to Sr Robert, who desired me to let you know, that a member of parlia'nt had applied to Him, but that He told Him positively, that He was engaged to Charles Feilding,[1] since that He has heard nothing of it, 'till your Letter came to me, He does not know whether He has applied elsewhere, but thinks it is possible He may. When I have an opportunity I will speak to the Queen, you may be assured Sr Robert will be for Charles Feilding.

I am ever yrs

Holles Newcastle

27. NEWCASTLE TO RICHMOND

Claremont
June 19th 1736

Mr Dear Lord;

I receved the last post the Honor of your Graces letter, and hope you are perswaded, that I am too sensible of your goodness to me, not to be always ready to obey your commands in the best manner I am able, and to give you my opinion (when you order me) with the utmost sincerity, affection and regard. As to the present vacancy of a Commissioner of the Revenue in Ireland, Sr R. Walpole is determined (as He has declared to Every Body) to recommend the fittest person, that He can find out for it, and I know He has already offer'd it to one, who has been long in the Excise Office in England, & thinks of nobody, but some such person for it. I also know that some Engagements that have been made for that Employment, will be postponed, since Mr Harrison's Death has made it necessary, to send one thither, who is purely a man of Business, and if such a one can be found out, one, that has been acquainted with that particular sort of Business. This being the Case, it will I am afraid, be to no purpose, to make upon this occasion, the application your Grace mentions, which is however entirely submitted to you by My Dear Lord Your Graces most obedient & most affect. humble servt

Holles Newcastle

P.S. I begg my compliments to the Dutchess of Richmond

28. RICHMOND TO NEWCASTLE

Whitehall[2]
Sept 21st 1736

My Dear Lord,

The inclos'd is a list of what employments the late Lord Berkeley[3] had, & what in my

---

1. The Hon. Charles Fielding was Sir Robert Walpole's candidate for Postmaster General in Ireland.
2. Richmond House in Whitehall from which Canaletto painted his famous views. See John Hayes, 'Parliament Street and Canaletto's Views of Whitehall', in *The Burlington Magazine,* (1958), pp. 341–349.
3. James Berkeley, 3rd. Earl of Berkeley, died in August 1736, while on a visit to Aubigny, the home of Richmond's grandmother, Louise de Keroualle, Duchess of Portsmouth. Richmond was his trustee. See Goodwood Ms. 108 ff. 779–792.

opinion ought to be continued to this Lord, for if the ministry should begin by disobliging him at first, I nor no man can answer for him, they are old long worn family
feathers & would be hard to be taken from him. I expect him over in a week. I shall
meet your Grace on Saturday at Pettworth, & am My Dear Lord Your Grace's most
faithful humble servant

Richmond &c

29. NEWCASTLE TO RICHMOND

Hampton Court
July 21st 1737

My Dear Lord,
   I will begin with giving you the satisfaction of hearing, that this Day our Accounts
have been so good of poor Lord Scarborough,[1] that we begin to have good Hopes of
Him. He is certainly much better, & ye Doctors said at noon, that they had very good
Hopes. I have since had an Account from the same, that they thought him out of
Danger, but I doubt that is not to be depended on. However the change for ye better,
is certainly very great & I hope to God will continue. The chief Dependance is on the
Bank. As to Sussex, I am not at all fond of a weeks Drunkenness, & dont intend to
have it. The Days of our Races cannot be alter'd now, & must therefore remain for
Thursday & I hope you will not fail to be both att the Assizes, & Races, wth yr Friends
& Servants from your parts. Monday, the assize Day there is no Bustle, nor drinking, I
hope you will pass Tuesday & Wensday quietly with me at Bishopstone, & we will go
together on Thursday to Lewes for ye Races when you may be as sober as you please. I
depend upon seeing you att Lewes, Monday ye 1st & of having your good Company
'till ye Saturday's Races are over. There is not much politicks stirring. The Definitive
Treaty between ye Emperor, & France was the other day communicated to us by
Washer & Bussy[2] with a memm desiring we would declare whether we would take part
in it, & in what manner. We have returned a Civil answer that we must act in Concert
wth the Dutch, & consult wth them what we will jointly do. Our Great Friend &
Brother Mason[3] will, I hope have little or no Difficulty in Tuscany. If he has we must
call a Lodge & send our Succours. May I present my Duty to my Sussex Queen.[4]
   I am my Dear Duke Yrs most sincerely & affectly

Holles Newcastle

30. NEWCASTLE TO RICHMOND

Whitehall
June 27th 1738

My Dear Duke,
   Your commands for the Charter House should certainly have been obey'd by me,
had I not with the rest of my Brethen been engaged, long ago to "Mother Gin"; if she
either declines it on account of her age, & infirmities, or any other vacancy happens, I

---

1. Richard Lumley, 2nd. Earl of Scarbrough, 1688–1740, MP for East Grinstead, 1708–1710, and for
Arundel, 1710–1715, lived at Stansted. After a career in the army, he ended as a Major General. He was
Master of the Horse, 1727–1734, when he was succeeded by Richmond.
2. François de Bussy, 1669–1780, formerly secretary to the Duc de Richelieu, was the agent of the French
Court in England. In fact, he was in the pay of the English Government.
3. Hon. Charles Fane, 1708–1766, of Basildon near Reading in Berkshire, MP for Tavistock, 1734–1747,
and for Reading, 1754–1761, was Minister Plenipotentiary at Florence, 1734–1740.
4. Newcastle's pet name for the Duchess of Richmond.

am engaged to you, and will speak also to the Chancellor, who I doubt not will be so too. I begg my Compliments to my Queen, & love to her loving subjects,[1] & am always my Dear Duke most sincerely and affectly. Yrs.

Holles Newcastle

31. RICHMOND TO NEWCASTLE

Goodwood
Aug. 18 1738

My Dear Lord,

Charles Feilding, Jemmy Pelham,[2] Mr Trevor,[3] & Sr John <u>Cam</u> Peachy,[4] are to be here on Munday the 28th & are to be made free at Chichester on the Tuesday. if that time suites with your Graces conveniency, wee Western humble servants of your's should be glad of your Grace's good & facetious company.

If you come you will be welcome, & remember Goodwood is your Quarters, & your Queen as you call her will do the honors at breakfast. butt no farther for she can not smoke Tobacco.

I have received a letter from Goldsworthy[5] who is in great aprehensions of one man's being apointed to succeed Fane at Florence. I hope it is not true, for Sr Charles Wager[6] assured me long ago, that you had given him an absollute promis for Goldsworthy, not only to succeed Fane at Florence, butt also to keep his Consulship at Leghorn. This Sr Charles assured me, & consequently I cant doubt butt you will do it. If you had not promis'd it, I should have asked it as a favour of you, Butt as Sr Charles sayes you have, it would be wrong in me to aske it, & must beg pardon for even putting you in mind of it.

I wish Mr Stone[7] would let me know, (as far as is propper to trust by letter) what has been done with Fitzgerald.[8] Pardon my curiosity, & beleive me my Dear Lord, Your Grace's ever faithfull, & obedient humble servant

Richmond &c

Poor Tom Till[9] is dead; it gives me great concern, for he is a great loss to me & my freinds in this part of the Country. Peter Buck[10] is Mayor, & he is to ecquip the Gentlemen with their freedom.

---

1. Richmond's children.
2. James Pelham, 1683–1761, of Crowhurst, MP. for Newark, 1722–1741, and for Hastings, 1741–1761, was sometime Newcastle's secretary, and looked after his electoral interests in East Sussex. He was Secretary to the Prince of Wales, 1728–1737.
3. John Trevor, 1716–1743, of Glynde, MP for Lewes, 1738–1743, was related to the Pelhams. He was a Lord of the Admiralty, 1742–1743. Horace Walpole described him as 'much disliked because he is of no consequence for estate, and less for parts, but he is a relation of the Pelhams'. He went mad on the death of his wife.
4. Sir John Peachey, 1680–1744, of West Dean, was MP for Midhurst, 1738–1744.
5. Burrington Goldsworthy was British Consul at Leghorn.
6. Sir Charles Wager, 1666–1743, MP for Portsmouth, 1710–1711 and again, 1715–1734, for West Looe, 1713–1715, and again, 1741–1743, and for Westminster, 1734–1741, was 1st. Lord of the Admiralty, 1733–1742.
7. Andrew Stone, 1703–1773, MP for Hastings, 1741–1761, was brother-in-law of William Barnard, Newcastle's chaplain at Claremont, and became Newcastle's secretary in 1732. Thereafter he exercised great influence over Newcastle and Pelham. He was Undersecretary of State, 1734–1751; a Lord of Trade, 1749–1761; and Secretary to the Prince of Wales, 1756–1760.
8. Sir Thomas Fitzgerald, also known as Geraldino, was the Spanish envoy in London.
9. Tom Till died on 16 August 1733 while serving as Mayor of Chichester.
10. Peter Buck was elected Mayor of Chichester to serve out Tom Till's term. (See W.S.R.O Archives of the City of Chichester, C2, p. 3.) He had been the previous Mayor.

32. NEWCASTLE TO RICHMOND

Kensington
Fryday Noon [18 August 1738]

My Dear Lord,

On Wensday night the Messenger arrived from Spain, with the Answer of that Court. They disavow Fitzgerald, & make great Alterations in the plan. These dispatches are of such importance, that the King is very desirous to have as many Lords of the Cabinet Council present, when they are considered, as we can get together. The Council is appointed att my Office on Monday morning next att eleven o'clock, & I begg you will not fail to be there, indeed I have in some Measure answer'd for your coming, & we can return together to Lewes. My Duty to my Queen

I am most sincerely & affectly Ever Yrs
Holles Newcastle

33. RICHMOND TO NEWCASTLE

Goodwood
Aug. 26th 1738

My Lord,

I am very sorry wee can not have the pleasure of seeing your Grace this <u>bout</u> as wee call it in Sussex. I shall have about thirty or forty of your freinds at dinner on Tuesday & I am apt to thinke wee shall drinke your Graces health in a bumper. I am sorry for what Mr Stone tells me about Goldsworthy, for I am sure Sr Charles understood that he was to keep his consulship, and to succeed Mr Fane, for I beleive the Consulship, as it is attended with less expense, is the best of the two. I have received a letter from my Lord Berkeley, who expresses great thankfullness to his Majesty for the hopes that has been given him of the Green Ribbon.[1] & desires me to make the handsomest speech I can upon the ocasion; butt as I cant possibly bee at Kensington for some time, I must beg the favor of your Grace to make this speech for me, or rather for my Lord Berkeley. The foundation of it is that he is infinitely obligd to his Majesty, & is & ever will be most thoroughly attach'd to his service. his expressions to me are rather too strong, butt, if you will be so good as to undertake it, I am sure he will be safe in your hands, & that you will say as much, & not more than My Lord Berkeley ought to say. he begs also that he might have leave to stay abroad till January, butt that he will then be here without fail for the meeting of the Parliament, he has already gott my Lord Scarborough's consent, & now desires his Majesty's leave. Pray be so good as to do this, & lett me know the Kings answer by my freind Mr Stone. This is giveing a great deal of trouble, & takeing great libertys with a Secretary of State, butt when I consider it is to the Duke of Newcastle, who I look upon to be the best freind I have in the world, & for whom I have the truest value and regard, I am easy, so shall make no more excuses, only beg him to be assured that I am his ever faithfull, & Obliged humble servant

Richmond &c

Sr Robert has not been pleased to make me any answer about Sr Thomas Prendergast, altho I have seen him twice since I wrote to him. Its very odd, & not altogether so civil. I expect Jemmy Pelham, & Mr Trevor this day.

---

1. Augustus Berkeley, 4th. Earl of Berkeley, 1716–1755, was created a Knight of the Thistle on 9 June 1739.

34. RICHMOND TO NEWCASTLE

Goodwood
Fryday: Septr 8th 1738

My Dear Lord,

I am very sorry I cant possibly waite on your Grace at Bishopstone, butt to morrow I sett out for Dell's,[1] & from thence to Wilton. I go <u>en famille</u> & shall not return 'till to morrow sennight. You know how happy I am when I can waite upon you, butt now 'tis impossible. I thanke you for your Berkeley negotiation, I wish your other may succeed as well. The freedom of Commerce to be determin'd according to Treatys,[2] that is foregoing Treatys, I fear will never do; for the word <u>no search</u> is I beleive in no Treaty, & that now is become the single point, & what I fear we shant so easily obtain; espetially if the good old Cardinal[3] drops as is mighty likely he will. I have two or three affairs I must trouble you with, one is about Goldworthy; Sr Charles has the thing mightily at heart, & I own I wish it. Gashry[4] writes me word that Sr William Blacket[5] had both those places for many years together, & I own I dont see at all that they are inconsistent; that it would be a great favor is certain, butt I suppose Sr Charles askes it as such. I wish however if it is not to be done that you would be so good as to lett me know the reason that I may at least have something to say to Goldsworthy, who has writ to me about it. Fane has certainly acted a double part with, for Goldsworthy affirms he promis'd to recommend him to you, & I hear he recommended Man,[6] The next thing I am to trouble you about is aske your Graces vote & interest as a Governor of St Thomas's hospital, for Mr Baker to succeed upon the first vacancy as surgeon in that hospital. I have yett been able to gett butt one vote, however thats worth two, for it is Sr John Campechy's; butt I must seriously desire you to interest yourself for him with the other Governors, he is son to Tom Baker the Chandler at Chichester, who is the cheif pillar of the Dissenters in these parts, & has a most exceeding good interest both in town & County, & has always been with us. The son is really a very good Surgeon, & fitt for the business! When you are in town he will bring you a letter from me, & I hope you will countenance him. His father Tom Baker is now my Tom Till as to the Presbyterian branch. One more thing I must aske & then I have done, it is that you would refresh Custom Hills memory about the Shoreham's sloop being order'd to Chichester. Their delay is intolerable, & I am sure there is a trick in it; for Prattin has <u>reported</u> 'till he is hoarse again, & nothing is done. It is now so depended on at Chichester, & I have so often assured them that it would be done, that I must have done at Chichester if it should now fail. It is now become a point that I can not upon any account whatsoever give up, for it would be most infamous usage to me both from the Customs & Treasury. Youl curse me & thinke I never shall have done, butt I must say one more <u>last word</u>; which is that I beg that Clarke may be prosecuted by the Attorney Genll for he laughs at the opinion, <u>se fout de nous</u>, & sayes he shall never aske any favor from you or me. he is a most sad dog, & if possible he should be putt to some trouble.

1. The Earl de la Warr's house at Bolderwood in Hampshire, where the Charlton Hounds were kennelled for part of the year.
2. The provisional convention drafted in September, which, with only minor alterations, became the Convention of Pardo.
3. Cardinal André Hercule de Fleury, 1653–1743, Bishop of Frejus, tutor and advisor to King Louis XV since 1715, and Premier of France.
4. Francis Gashry, 1702–1762, MP for Aldeburgh, 1741, and for East Looe, 1741–1762, was Secretary to Sir Charles Wager, 1st. Lord of the Admiralty, 1732–1742; a Commissioner of the Navy, 1741–1747; and Treasurer and Paymaster of the Ordnance, 1751–1762. He was a Director of the South Sea Company.
5. Sir William Blackett, 1690–1728, of Newcastle, MP for Newcastle, 1710–1728, had been Consul at Leghorn and Minister at Florence.
6. Sir Horatio Mann, 1701–1786, Frane's assistant at Florence from 1737, succeeded him, 1740–1786.

Adieu my Dear Lord, I am for ever most truely Your's

Richmond &c

I have also aply'd to the Honble Harry, for Baker, & I hope he'l be for him.

35. RICHMOND TO NEWCASTLE

Goodwood
Septr 10th 1738

My Lord,

As your Grace is a Governor of St. Thomas's hospital, I hope you will give me leave to recommend Mr Baker to you, for your interest to succeed upon the first vacancy as a Surgeon in that hospital. he is extreamly fitt for the business, else I should not have recommended him: Your Grace knows his father Mr Tho Baker of Chichester who has ever been a stedfast man to the true cause.

I am my Lord, Your Grace's ever faithfull humble servant

Richmond &c.

36. RICHMOND TO NEWCASTLE

Goodwood
Septr 19: 1738

My Dear Lord,

Doctor Budgen of Dorking, a freind & brother medicus of myne has writ to me to desire I would aske My Lord Chancellor's interest for his nephew Mr Thomas Budgen, who stands for Rygate in the room of the late Master of the Rolls.[1] now I would fain know first how this young Budgen's polliticks are, whether the Speaker aproves of him, who is for him & who against him, & all this to be sure your Grace has fish'd out by this time; so I should take it kindly if you would communicate it to me; & then I shall know what answer to make, nay I desire to make him what answer you please to direct, butt something I must say to him. I hope you received Pems[2] petition & myne for the poor Bristol Buggerer;[3] it would be scandalous to hang the poor Devil upon the single evidence of the boy. Remember the Judgement Lovel[4] pronounced upon the late Lord Townshend upon such an ocasion.

I am My Dear Lord, for ever Yours

Richmond &c

37. RICHMOND TO NEWCASTLE

Goodwood
Fryday: Septr 22d 1738

I am actually asham'd, My Dear Lord, to thinke how troublesome I am to you; & I can't express my thankes for your bearing with it; every article of my former letter, you

1. Sir Joseph Jekyll, 1662–1738, MP for Eye, 1697–1713, for Lymington, 1713–1722, and for Dorking, 1722–1738, was Master of the Rolls till his death on 19 August 1738. Thomas Budgen, died 1772, MP for Surrey, 1751–1761, probably considered the seat, but John Hervey was brought in as a stop-gap for Hardwicke's son.
2. Henry Herbert, 9th. Earl of Pembroke, 1693–1751, the 'architect Earl', Master of Wilton, and long standing friend of Richmond.
3. David Reid was convicted of buggery with one William Evans, a youth aged 16, at Bristol Quarter Sessions on 29 August 1738, and sentenced to be hanged. He was finally reprieved by a Royal Pardon signified by Lord Harrington. I am indebted to Miss Judith Close of the Bristol Archives Office for identifying this case for me.
4. Sir Nathaniel Lovell, 1619–1713, was Recorder of London, 1692–1708, and a judge on the Welsh Circuit.

have fully answered, & I am vastly obliged to you. As a Sussex freeholder, I have a title to be troublesome, butt then I am so farr reasonable as to be always satisfy'd with an answer from my freind Mr Stone, so I beg you would always make use of his hand, unless you are seized with a sudden rage of writing, & in that case you may be assured your letters can never be more welcome to any body than to me. This the Duke of Grafton[1] would call Sussex flattery, butt I assure you it is not. Now as to the Charterhouse affair, I entirely agree with your Grace that it would be odd to have Pem & I drawn up against one an other,[2] 'tho I cant help being less serious & thinke it would be more ridiculous, than unfortunate, butt I must aske one thing of you, which is to know if you can give any one reason for my giving it up, that would not be to the full as strong a reason for Pem to give it up, as the calculation is not quite so voluminous, as that of our County Election, I have enclosed it to you. by which you will see we are even as to promises. Lord Dartmouth[3] & Bishop of London[4] have both writ me word they shall not be there, butt then comes Doctor <u>Butler</u> who assures me in a letter, he is for us both, butt does not say which way he will vote. butt I would venture some odds he will do as <u>the Master</u>, I mean Mr Mann.[5] If so I must submit, butt I own very freely if I had a majority I should not at all like to submit. for which reason I should thinke ('tho it's presuming in me to advise <u>les Grosses festes</u>.) the best way would be to aske one another in a genteel familic way, how you are engaged, & when you come to the Election, all agree to chuse him unanimously that you know would have had the most votes, if you had come to a poll. If it falls upon Pem I am satisfy'd, if it falls upon me, I am sure <u>he</u> ought to be so. Dr Butlers vote will decide it, so I thinke you had better at once aske him. I thinke this ought to make it easy, at least I can promis for myself that I shall be satisfy'd, however I entirely submit it to you, Dear Duke, to do just as you thinke propper, & whatever you determine for me I shall abide by; being with the utmost truth & gratitude my Dear Lord, Your Grace's ever faithfull, & obliged humble servant

Richmond &c

Queen Taw[6] presents her best services to you.

There is a dispute for the Kings plate at Nottingham between Lord Weymouth[7] & Jack Neale;[8] Your Grace is the person apointed by me to take care of that plate so I desire to know who are your Deputys there, & who by your or their appointment were judges.

38. RICHMOND TO NEWCASTLE

Goodwood
Fryday. Septr 29th 1738

My Dear Lord,
 I should not so soon have troubled your Grace with a letter again, butt that it is

---

1. Charles Fitzroy, 2nd. Duke of Grafton, 1683–1759, was Viceroy of Ireland, 1720–1724, and Lord Chamberlain, 1724–1757. He was passionately fond of hunting, and often hunted with the Charlton Hunt.
2. Pembroke and Richmond were competing for a Governorship of Charterhouse. Pembroke was elected on 13 October 1738, and Richmond succeeded at the next election on 16 February 1740. I am indebted to R.L. Arrowsmith for this information.
3. William Legge, 1st. Earl of Dartmouth, 1672–1750, was a Secretary of State, 1710–1713, and Lord Privy Seal, 1713–1714.
4. Edmund Gibson, 1669–1748, had been Walpole's ecclesiastical advisor until 1736. He was Bishop of London, 1723–1748.
5. Nicholas Mann, died 1753, scholar, antiquarian and author, was Master of the Charterhouse in 1737.
6. Richmond's pet name for the Duchess of Richmond.
7. Thomas Thynne, 2nd. Viscount Weymouth, 1710–1751, was a Tory in politics, and Grandmaster of the Freemasons, 1735–1736.
8. John Neale, 1687–1746, of Allesley Park in Warwickshire, was MP for Chipping Wycombe, 1722, and for Coventry, 1722–1741.

natural to open ones heart to a freind. I have received a most shocking answer, 'tho in civil terms, from Sr Robert Walpole in answer to one I writ to him to beg he would oblige me in makeing Sr Thomas Prendergast easy. It would be too tedious to repeat my arguments to him, you have often heard them, & I urged it on the softest terms I could to Sr Robert, & at last he has been pleas'd to tell me peremptorily that he can never give me any answer upon that subject that will be to my satisfaction. I leave you to guess how this answer must affect me. I reflect on one hand my former obligations to him; & on the other I find he uses me that have always loved him, worse, or at least as bad as he could his most bitter enemy. It's hard to be ill used & not resent it, butt still I find it (if possible) more hard to be ungratefull. I hope you know me enough to do me justice in thinkeing that what I say proceeds from an honest, butt not a fearfull heart. I have made no answer to the letter, & very likely I shall not, butt tis with great difficulty I refrain. However Sr Thomas Prendergast has no tyes of Gratitude, so I am sure I can never blame what he may be pleas'd to say or do upon the occasion. I have not yet acquainted him with it, butt I shall next post. All I shall insist upon with Sr Thomas is that both he & I must own that your Grace has done all in your power to accomodate the affair. I beleive he is sensible of it, & I am very sure I am, for which, as well as for a thousand more reasons, I shall ever be bound to love & honor you. I beg pardon for this long detail, butt I could not help opening my budget to you, knowing your goodness & freindship for me would forgive it.

I am for ever, my Dear Lord Your Graces most faithfull humble servant
Richmond &c.

As my brother Budgen is of the wrong side of the post I must have done with him, by the by I know very little of him, so its pretty indifferent to me. You are very good about the Charterhouse affair, & I am sure I shall thinke whatever you please to do in it right. The Commisioners of the Customs have now a design to send the Sloop to Chichester for six months, which is a dirty shufling trick, & if she is not station'd there for good, it will be of no manner of service to me.

39. RICHMOND TO NEWCASTLE

Goodwood
Oct: 18: 1738

My Dear Lord,
I am extreamly oblig'd to your Grace for your goodness to me at the Charterhouse Election, & I am pleas'd at loosing it with your vote, & should have been very sory to have carry'd it without your vote. I shall not aply for the next election to all the Governors 'till I have seen you. I must beg of you to give Sr Thomas Prendergast leave to waite on you, about his american affair, to thanke you for what you have done, & to desire you to putt the finishing stroke to it; which with one letter or two more you may easily do. I beg this as a favour; & I flatter myself you wont deny me. I shall be in town next munday; so you know more of me than John Del. & I hope you know, what I would have every man know, which is that I am most truely the Duke of Newcastle's most faithfull, & ever oblig'd humble servant
Richmond &c.

40. RICHMOND TO NEWCASTLE

Goodwood,
Fryday, 24 Nov. 1738

My dear Lord,
On Wednesday I received the favor of your Grace's letter, & I do assure you that if I could be of the least service in the world to you, I would attend you with pleasure. You

know very well that before it is long I must go to London, where besides duty I have some business, & I hope to contrive to do them both at the same time the week after next, & to be back again in about a fortnight, when I shall certainly quit my hounds no more till a week before the meeting of the Parliament, when I certainly will attend you at the Cockpit & help make the speech, this time 'tho I had little or no hand in it the last. The weather is now so fine, the hounds in such order, & such a plenty of foxes, that I really can spare no time from my sport butt what neccessity obliges me to. In answer to which your Grace may say how are they then to expect to see me at Goodwood or Charlton? I answer because you have promis'd it for these five years and have never once come, I mean to Charlton, for you have honor'd Goodwood, 'tho not so often as I could have wish'd, butt att this time I would beg if you do come westward it may be to Charlton, for this reason, because at Charlton you may be quiet & snug, whereas at Goodwood you know it must be what Jemy Pelham calls <u>rantum scantum</u>, which would not be propper at this time, for Mrs. Brudenell is now here, is so very ill she has kept her bed these six weeks, and I really am in some apprehensions she will not soon get out of it, if ever, for she is certanly in a very dangerous & lingering way. So noise & company here would not be so propper, butt at Charlton where you are a member, you would make us all vastly happy in your company. Wee could lodge about six of you very well. Yourself, Honorable Harry, and Sr Wm Gage are of the Club. Then as for Linky,[1] Coll Carpenter,[2] or any body else you please to bring, they must either be ballotted for, or come with me as my guests from Goodwood. I have not a horse that you will care to ride except Looby and old Ginn. However, they are all at your service, & I am sure Dell would with pleasure mount you, whilst you lett him ride New Yorke, but why can't you bring a couple of your own horses? All at Charlton are yours. The company consists in; the Duke of St. Albans, Lord Harry, Dell, Jemy Cavendish,[3] Hawley,[4] Pansford,[5] Mr. Watson Little Rock's brother, and Mr. Frauquiere.[6] Jemmy is gone this morning to Town, & returns on Tuesday. Wee expect Lord Harcourt,[7] Sir Harry Lyddel,[8] and the Honywoods[9] very soon, and at Christmas, Sir Cecyl, butt not 'till then for at all other times it's dearer living at Charlton then at home butt at Christmas, it is much dearer at home, so at that good time wee never fail of his company. If you do come, pray lett it be either this week next, or about the 11th of next month when I shall be back from London. I have writ a long letter a prospos de rien; so I shall have done as soon as I have assured you my dear Lord, that I am for ever Your's

Richmond &tc.

1. Henry Fiennes Clinton, 9th. Earl of Lincoln, 1720–1794, was Newcastle's nephew and heir, succeeding him in the title in 1768.
2. Colonel Benjamin Carpenter was a member of the Charlton Hunt, and appears regularly in the Minute Book.
3. Lord James Cavendish, 1673–1751, was MP for Derby, 1701–1742, when he became Auditor of foreign revenues.
.4. Henry Hawley, 1679–1759, had a long army career. He rose to the rank of General, and fought at Dettingen and Fontenoy. He was Commander-in-Chief in Scotland when defeated at Falkirk, and commanded the Cavalry at Culloden. He was known as a strict disciplinarian. A member of the Charlton Hunt, he was a regular guest of Richmond.
5. Edward Pauncefort of Earley Court, was one of the founders of the Charlton Hunt. He was described in a piece of verse preserved at Goodwood as, 'Paunceford discreet, well looking, modest and all that'. Goodwood Ms. 141 f. 12.
6. William Fauquiere was a member of the Charlton Hunt and was present at the first meeting after the regulating of the Society on 12 February 1738.
7. Simon Harcourt, 1st. Earl Harcourt, 1714–1777, was a member of the Charlton Hunt. He was a Lord of the Bedchamber, 1735–1751; became a General, 1772; and was Viceroy in Ireland, 1772–1777.
8. Sir Harry Liddell, 1694–1746, of Ravensworth Castle, was MP for Morpeth, 1734–1747.
9. Philip Honywood, had a long army career, and was Governor of Portsmouth, 1740–1752. An old friend of Richmond, he was a regular guest at Goodwood and a member of the Charlton Hunt. He lent Richmond a horse at Dettingen, so that he could watch the battle.

41. NEWCASTLE TO RICHMOND

Bishopstone
Nov 28th 1738

My Dear Lord,
We have this day had as fine a Chace, as our Downs can show. Above ten miles over the best part of our Countrey, as fast as Doggs can go, & faster than Horses went except the Huntsman's, Lincky's, your humble servant's, & his groom's, and one more. The Honble Harry who is just returned from Norfolk & Suffolk, (but has not been lately att Charlton) affirms he has seen nothing like this, (which by the by he would scarce see all). Flushed with our Chace, & being much wanted by a great number of good friends, to go to dinner, you must not expect a long letter, tho' I must send a milion of thanks for yours. As your Grace goes to London next week, it will be impossible for me to attend you, whilst I stay att Bishopstone, for I am obliged to be in London the week after, and Lincky gives a Ball to the Ladies of the Seaford Assembly[1] next Thursday, which makes it impossible for me to come this week. However as we courtiers generally do, I will pay the promise or rather ten promises with one more, & will endeavour after your Return to Charlton, to attend you from Claremont, & will contrive to send my own horses, if I can, otherwise I will ride <u>New York</u>. We constantly drink your health every day, sometimes as a fine gentleman with Mrs Davies, at other times at ye head of our friends in the west. The Hon'ble Harry and Lincky are much yrs. My compliments to all your good company & believe me in great haste.
Yrs most affect'ly

Holles Newcastle

42. RICHMOND TO NEWCASTLE

Charlton
Fryday, 1st Dec. 1738

My dear Lord,
I am heartily glad to hear your Grace has had so good sport. I could wish I might send you the same account from hence, butt wee have done nothing to brag of this week. Your cutting a figure with Linky does not surprise me, but, confound you, where was Sir Francis? Ten miles in a fine country is sport enough with any pack of fox hounds, if they behave well during the whole time. Myne are at present in perfect order, & I must now tell you, you may see them if you please to honor us with your company next week, for my journey to London is difer'd to the week after. Lynky's ball is a very good excuse for this week, & your going to town, for the week after next, butt you must invent one for next week, if you don't come. So pray putt us off no more, butt make us all happy in your company, & I promis you, you shall be perfectly well lodg'd, mounted, fed, and drench'd.
I am for ever Yours,

Richmond &tc.

My best services attend Lynky and the Honble Harry. I hope they, Sir Wm Gage, & Coll Carpenter will come with you.
Wee can't make room for, confound you, Sir Francis and one or two more.

---

1. Seaford, though technically a Cinque Port, was treated by Newcastle as a Sussex borough. The Duke's interest came from his estate at Bishopstone, and the nominations were largely his.

43. NEWCASTLE TO RICHMOND

Bishopstone
Dec. 2nd 1738

My Dear Lord,

As I cannot make a good excuse for not waiting upon you next week, & must make one, I must depend upon your goodness for allowing it. Every post brings us accounts that Ld Essex[1] thinks of coming down to Bishopstone, & therefore I might say, I cannot be absent least He should cøme at that time, but the truth is, if I come to Charlton next week, I cannot return hither, before I go to London, & then I shall loose almost the whole week here, which I should be very unwilling to do, considering how much real pleasure I take with my own friends, & how seldom I am able to see them. Don't reproach me, tho' you justly may, I will, if possible, contrive to come from Claremont, & will endeavour to settle ye time wth you, when you come to town the week after next. Pray my compliments to all the good company att Charlton. All here are your Humble servants.

I am My Dear Lord Your Graces Most affect humble Servant
Holles Newcastle

44. RICHMOND TO NEWCASTLE

Goodwood
20 July 1739

My dear Lord,

Like a true Patriot, not a modern one, I declare that I prefer the publick good, to my own private interest, so if the embargo upon the Colliers[2] is of real service, I have nothing to say, butt as I am very certain it is not, I do most humbly beg your Grace, & my wise brother councellors whose never failing wisdom I respect & venerate, to consider of it, for last post I received a letter from my farmer who tells me fairly, if it is not imediatly taken off, he must inevitably breake, & then your humble servant is f..k'd; for the least I should loose would be £3125 which is one quarter, & perhaps the double, so pray thinke of this, & procure me redress of my greivance, which if not done imediatly, that which I have told you will inevitably happen to, my dear Lord, Your Grace's ever faithfull, & obliged humble servant,

Richmond &tc.

45. NEWCASTLE TO RICHMOND

Newcastle House
July 26 1739

My Dear Lord,

I received your letter & as I always obey your commands, I immediately talked to our Brethren upon the subject. I had a letter from Newcastle to the same purpose, & the embargo will be taken off to day or att furthest next Tuesday, which I hope will answer your end. The War Council dines today att Sr Robert's. Every thing goes on mighty well. Haddock[3] came wth his whole squadron ye 3d Ins before Cadiz, & there

---

1. William Capel, 3rd. Earl of Essex, 1697–1743, was a Gentleman of the Bedchamber, and had been Envoy in Turin, 1731–1736.
2. Richmond inherited two-thirds of the total returns from the duty of one shilling on every chaldron of coal exported from Newcastle, a duty originally granted to Richmond's father by King Charles II in 1677. It was worth about £15,000 a year, and was sold to the Government by the 3rd. Duke of Richmond in 1800.
3. Nicholas Haddock, 1686–1746, MP for Rochester, 1734–1746, rose to the rank of Admiral of the Blue in 1744. Between 1738 and 1742, he was Commander-in-Chief in the Mediterranean.

intercepts every thing he meets with, he has stopt a French ship and taken out the Spanish letters wch has occasioned a strong complaint from France, but we all think Haddock has done right. The Cardinal still talks in the usual style, fears a general warr, seems to wish not to take part & yett will I am afraid do it, tho' by that means alone, he himself brings on the general warr he so much dreads. My compliments to my Queen & all your good company. I hope we shall see you all att Lewes. I wish you would employ somebody to gett as many of our friends in your parts to come, as you can. Pray speak particularly to Sr J. Miller,[1] & all your gentlemen of Chichester & in ye neighbourhood, for it will be right to have as many of our friends as we can gett.

I am My Dear Duke in great haste Ever yrs

Holles Newcastle

P.S. 10 o'clock

I am just coming from our war meeting. The Arch. B.[2] dined with us, but his Grace not perceiving we mett upon Business, slipt away after dinner, unknown to every body, before our Business began.

We are agreed extremely well, have very proper answers to be given ye French Court & I believe shall some day next week send orders to Keene[3] & Castres[4] to come away.

We have this day in Council taken off the embargo absolutely, but shall continue the press.

We are all in good spirits, & we think our affairs go very briskly & well.

46. STONE TO RICHMOND

Whitehall
July 31st 1739

My Lord,

I am order'd by my Lord Duke of Newcastle, to acquaint your Grace, that the King has appointed Saturday next (the 4th of August) to review Gore's Regiment of Dragoons;[5] and the Saturday following, his Majesty will review Sabine's Regiment,[6] if it can be got ready, by that time, which is not certain.

Your Grace will forgive me, for troubling you with the inclosed Gazette of this Evening, which contains the Account received from Mr Robinson[7] this day at noon, of an action between the Imperial Army & the Turks, in which the Emperor's Forces have sustain'd a great loss. There is, I think, very little material, in Mr Robinsons Dispatches, upon the Subject, more than what your Grace will find in the inclosed Paper,

1. Sir John Miller, died 1772, of West Lavant, son and heir of Sir Thomas Miller, was a member of Richmond's circle, a local magistrate, a member of Chichester Common Council, being Mayor of the city in 1748, and a member of the Charlton Hunt. His youngest daughter married Richmond's nephew Viscount Bury in 1770.
2. John Potter, 1674–1747, was Archbishop of Canterbury, 1737–1747.
3. Benjamin Keene, 1697–1757, MP for Maldon, 1740–1741, and for West Looe, 1741–1747, was Ambassador at Madrid, 1727–1739, and again, 1748–1757. He negotiated the Treaty of Seville, 1729, and the Commercial Treaty, 1750. He was Envoy to Portugal, 1746–1748. He was a member of the Board of Trade, 1742–1744.
4. Abraham Castres, died 1757, was secretary to Henry Davenant at Genoa, Modena, Parma and Tuscany, 1714–1722, he was Plenipotentiary to Spain with Benjamin Keene, 1739. Later he was Envoy Extraordinary to Portugal, 1749–1757.
5. Gore's Dragoons, later the Tenth Hussars, were originally raised in July 1715, as a result of the Jacobite Rebellion.
6. Joseph Sabine, 1661–1739, MP for Berwick on Tweed, 1727–1734, came over from Ireland to Scotland with his Regiment in 1715. He was Governor of Gibraltar, 1731–1739.
7. Sir Thomas Robinson, 1st. Lord Grantham, 1695–1770, was Ambassador at Vienna, 1730–1748. He represented England in the negotiations with Maria Theresa and Frederick the Great, and was joint Plenipotentiary in the peace negotiations at Aix-la-Chapelle in 1748.

except, that the Body of the Forces under General Neiperg,[1] having now joined the main army commanded by Marshall Wallis,[2] they flatter themselves at Vienna that something may still be done against the Turks. The number of the kill'd is not known, but, it is apprehended, cannot but be considerable. It is certain, that Wallis, & the troops with him, were in the utmost danger, 'till Prince Hildberghausen, who has gain'd great credit in this action, came to disengage them.

I am with greatest Respect My Lord Your Grace's Most obedient and most humble servant

Andrew Stone

47. STONE TO RICHMOND

Whitehall
Aug 7th 1739

My Lord,

I received yesterday the Honour of your Grace's letter, by Webster; and am directed by my Lord Duke of Newcastle, to assure your Grace that he will not fail to speak to the King, upon what you are pleased to mention with regard to the next Review, and that He will very soon write to you Himself upon that subject.

As your Grace is pleased to order me to send you an account of the news we have from Vienna, I take the liberty of inclosing the Gazette of this evening, which contains the substance of what came by the two last mails; The last account, your Grace will see, is dated the 5th N.S. and was received this day at noon. I have not had an opportunity of seeing Mr Robinson's letters, and consequently can add nothing to this Relation which is transmitted by Him, and may be depended upon as authentick. My Lord Crawford[3] is wounded, in the thigh, and, it is fear'd dangerously.

I am with the greatest Respect My Lord Your Graces most obedient and most humble servant

Andrew Stone.

48. NEWCASTLE TO RICHMOND

Whitehall
Augt 9, 1739

My Dear Lord,

I never obey'd any of your Grace's Commands with more pleasure, or with more success than this last, of procuring you the King's leave to attend the Lewes Horse Races & assizes, rather than His Majesty's person att the Review. The King was extreamly gracious & good, & order'd me to assure you that He was very desirous you should go to Lewes, where He knew you would be doing Him service, & yt it was not att all necessary for you to be att the Review. So that I shall expect you without fail on Thursday the 16th in the morning. I begg you would lodge att some friends, I will make it easy with Sam Wheatley. As to news, Stone has sent you word of the second skirmish with the Turks. We certainly had the advantage, open'd a communication with Belgrade, and as the term is, nous avons mis en deroute 30 m hommes, with little or no loss. They expect another battle. I heartily wish it may turn out well. By our letters this

1. Marshall Count Adam Neipperg, was second in command of the Austrian forces under General D'Arenberg.
2. General Count Georg von Wallis, an Austrian general, was defeated by the Turks at the Battle of Kroszka.
3. John Lindsay, 20th. Earl of Crawford, 1702–1749, joined the Imperial Army under Prince Eugene in 1735. From 1738–1741, he served in the Russian Army. He served later at Dettingen, Fontenoy and in suppressing the '45 Rebellion.

day from Spain, they are in the greatest fear & consternation for the Alognes. They were not arrived at the Groyne ye 30th of July, our style, and we have certainly a very good chance for them. Had Vernon[1] had fair winds, they could hardly have escaped. I hope they won't yett. Combis'[2] journey seems to be delay'd, perhaps 'till they know the fate of ye Alognes but that entre nous. I conclude we shall soon have letters from France, we have had none since I see you att the Review. I begg my Compliments to all the good Company at Goodwood, & particularly to my Queen, and Monsr Ossario.[3] We will endeavour to make Lewes as agreable as we can to the ladies. I hope they will dine at Bishopstone, the Sunday after ye Races.

I am my Dear Lord Ever most sincerely and affectly Yrs

Holles Newcastle

49. PELHAM TO RICHMOND

Esher
Sepbr 4, 1739

My Lord,

I had not forgot your Graces commands in relation to Lord Craven's[4] estate. I desir'd <u>Soissons</u> who went to that part of the county, to speak to the person that mention'd it to me, to get a particular, and I doubt not but I shall have one, as soon as any is given out. I conclude you have heard that your friend old Quimp[5] has delivered to the King a pretty extraordinary memorial complaining in the King his masters name, of our squadrons stopping and searching their ships, to the dishonour of the Pavillion Du Roy. The Cabinet met yesterday to consider of a proper answer; I doubt not but they determin'd right. I am a week Politician, but there seems to be a scene of great action opening. Hunting in New Park is now the Royal diversion. Your Grace is better entertained att Goodwood, I told my brother what you said as to weather etc, he desires his compliments to your Grace, and if you will give me leave to add my sincere good wishes to you and yours, you will do but justice to my Lord Your Grace's most obedient, humble servt

H. Pelham.

50. STONE TO RICHMOND

Whitehall
Sept 25 1739

My Lord,

I have receiv'd the Honour of your Grace's letter, and am order'd by my Lord Duke of Newcastle to return your Grace His thanks for your kind Concern for his Health. His Indisposition was a cold, & a swelling in His face, which kept him at home for about a week; but His Grace is now perfectly recover'd.

We have had very little from my Lord Waldegrave[6] since the answer to Mor Cambis's memorial was receiv'd in France; which after all His eagerness to have it, it appears, He did not send to His Court, 'till several Days after it was deliver'd to Him. My Lord Waldegrave has had some Conversation with the Cardinal upon it, who, in

---

1. Edward Vernon, 1684–1757, MP for Penryn, 1722–1734, for Portsmouth, 1741, and for Ipswich, 1741–1757, commander of the squadron at Spithead preparing to attack the Spaniards in the West Indies, had been sent to Finisterre to intercept 4 Spanish ships from Buenos Ayres and Azogue.
2. Louis Dominique Comte de Cambis was the French Ambassador in London.
3. The Chevalier Giuseppe d'Ossorio was the Sardinian Envoy in London.
4. William Craven, 3rd. Lord Craven, 1700–1739, had died on 10 August.
5. Cardinal Fleury.
6. James Waldegrave, 1st. Earl Waldegrave, 1685–1741, was Ambassador at Paris, 1730–1740.

general, seem'd moderate enough, and disposed to be satisfied with it, at least for the present. By the Accounts this last Week, or ten Days, the Preparations in the French Ports seem to be carried on in a slack, and indolent manner; and the Opinion of the People there is, that France does not intend to join openly with Spain. This notion is confirm'd by Mad'me Cambis's journy, who is expected very soon in England.

The late Transactions at Belgrade,[1] & the Behaviour of the Court of Vienna, in consequence of them, have been equally extraordinary. Your Grace, I conclude, has seen in the printed Papers, the Emperor's Disavowal, and even Condemnation of His Ministers, and, for some days, they talk'd of nothing less, at Vienna, than empaling Mor Neuperg. Mr Jahlman, The Emperor's[2] late minister at the Porte was dispatch'd to Belgrade, with Instructions, as it was supposed, to conclude the Treaty, in consequence of Neuperg's Preliminaries, who was beleiv'd to have been sent for home to answer for His Conduct. But the truth now appears to be, that Jahlman was only second Plenipotentiary, and that Neuperg was continued first in the Commission, for concluding the definitive Treaty, which Mr Robinson in His last letter, says it was generally believed, was, by that time actually sign'd tho' what the Conditions of this Treaty were, and in what they differ'd from the Preliminaries (It being supposed that the Emperor had insisted upon some alterations, or at least explanations, in his favour) was not yet known, nor whether they had been able to prevail with the Turks, to save appearances, by taking any notice, in this Treaty, of the Czarina.

There are letters from Mr Haddock, & Mr Vernon, which bring nothing material. Mr Vernon's letter was from the Maderas, so that He is probably, by this time, arrived in the West Indies.[3]

Your Grace's letter to my Lord Waldegrave, was sent by Raddon the messenger, to Paris, on the 6th of this month. (The same night, I think, that your Grace was at the Cabinet Council). Raddon came back some days ago, and I heard by him that it was safely deliver'd.

I have the honour to be with great Respect My Lord Your Grace's most obedient & most humble servant

Andrew Stone.

51. RICHMOND TO NEWCASTLE

Goodwood
14 Oct. 1739

My dear Lord,

I am desired to send the enclosed petition to your Grace. You see I have mark'd each name how they voted, half right, half wrong, 'tho they all assure us now they are friends. Those that are not mark'd did not pole last election, so I can not tell whether they are freeholders as they say or not. The favor they aske is a small one, so I thinke it would be right to gett it done, butt if it is done pray don't loose the petition which may be of use at the next election. Wee are quite quiet at Chichester & had butt one vote against us at the mayor's election; and that was George Oglander by mistake. Lisbon

---

1. By the Treaty of Belgrade, 18 September 1739, Austria abandoned all the gains she had made from the Turks at the Treaty of Passarowitz in 1718.
2. Emperor Charles VI, who succeeded his half brother Joseph I in 1711. He had no male heirs and established the Pragmatic Sanction to ensure undisputed succession on his death, whereby the lands of the Hapsburg Austrian Empire were to remain intact, and the succession should go to his daughters, the eldest of whom was Maria Theresa.
3. Admiral Vernon had left England for the West Indies with instructions to 'committ all sorts of hostilities against the Spaniards in such manner as you shall judge the most proper'. He reached Antigua on 28 September.

Peckham[1] was a secessor. Your good brother, Sir John,[2] is not so quiet at Arundell, where he has lost his mayor. He would fain draw me into an affair too long here to mention, butt till I have my Lord Scarbrough's consent, I shall do nothing in it. 'Tis beleived that Leeves[3] of Tortington will stand there. I promis you he is a good man, 'tho I should not like his oposeing Sir John or Lord Scarbrough.

I avoid, as much as I can, entering upon a subject that I am confident you must be heartily tired of, butt it workes upon my spirits more than ever. You was so good as to say once you would gett your brother, Mr. Pelham, to talke to Sir Robert about it. I can't thinke you forgott it, for I never knew you forgett me, Butt I suppose it had no effect; what makes me thinke so the more is that Lady Prendergast's poor little 300 pounds pension as haveing serv'd the late Queen is stop't. I can not in duty & respect to my master imagine he has done it without advice, & then I am sure the advice is poor, mean, and bass. The Dutchess of Richmond has writ to Sir Robert Walpole upon it. It will be a most cruel case if he does not do his best to stop it. I am vex'd to be so troublesome to you, butt it is naturall to aply to ones best freinds, which I hope you will always give me leave to call you, & at the same time to allow me to be, my dear Lord, your Grace's ever faithfull, & most obliged humble servant

Richmond &tc.

Lett Stone tell me what news from France. I shall be in town next week.

52. RICHMOND TO NEWCASTLE

Charlton
Fryday: Novr 30th 1739

My Dear Lord,
Enclosed is my proxy which I desire your Grace to dispose of as you thinke propper. I am My Dear Lord, for ever Your's

Richmond &c.

53. NEWCASTLE TO RICHMOND

Newcastle House
March 13, 1739/40

My Dear Lord,
Capt. Rentone in a Spanish Ship taken by Admiral Vernon is just arrived express from Portobello, with letters from Mr Vernon, that on the 22d of Novr He took posession of Portobello, demolished all the fortifications of ye place, which were very strong, carried off near seventy pieces of brass cannon with powder, ball, etc. & destroyed 80 pieces of iron cannon.[4] I congratulate you most heartily upon this great success, which

---

1. Henry Peckham, a Chichester merchant, nicknamed 'Lisbon' Peckham because of his interest in the wine trade, built Pallant House in Chichester in 1712, which has recently been re-opened as the New Pallant House Gallery. See David Coke, 'Pallant House Chichester: Part I: Henry Peckham', in *West Sussex History*, no. 23, (1982), pp. 3–6. He was Mayor of Chichester in 1722, 1728 and 1732, and was a regular supporter of the opposition.
2. Sir John Shelley, 1692–1771, MP for Arundel, 1727–1741, and for Lewes, 1743–1747, was Newcastle's brother in law. His interest came from his seat at Mitchelgrove in Clapham. He had lost control of the Arundel Corporation, and refused to attend the Court Leet to elect a new member hoping to make the election of the new Mayor invalid. See G.W. Eustace, *Arundel Borough and Castle*, (1922), pp. 209–215.
3. William Leaves of Tortington had voted for the Opposition candidates, Bishopp and Fuller in 1734. He did not stand in 1739. Sir John Shelley was defeated by Garton Orme and James Lumley in 1741, and Leaves was defeated when he did stand in 1747.
4. For the capture of Porto Bello in Panama, see H.W. Richmond, *The Navy in the War of 1739–1748*, (1920), vol. 1, pp. 45–49.

has putt an entire stop to the Return of the galeons, & has render'd the Spanish trade there very difficult for ye future. You know the pension bill is to be demolished on Tuesday next. His Majesty goes to the House on Wensday next to pass ye Meeting Bill. & we are to have the State of the Nation on Thursday, where we are to be strongly attacked. I hope you will not fail to be with us on Thursday. I conclude you will be in town on Wensday, to attend the King to ye House. He told me he supposed you would be in town that day, but does not expect you on Tuesday. Send away all your company to be with us on Tuesday. God bless Admiral Vernon, & prosper His Majesty's arms.

Ever yrs

Holles Newcastle

54. PELHAM TO RICHMOND

March ye 17, 1739/40

My Dear Lord,

I had not the honour of your Grace's letter 'till yesterday att Claremont, and should not now trouble you with an answer, but to give you less trouble, and to convince you that I have lost no time in obeying your commands. As to my worthy Brother <u>Sr John</u>, I spoke to him long agoe, who said you had been so good as to allow of the removal of Stokes, and further I could make nothing of him; I believe his Grace has rather more influence in that family than myself but yesterday, I showd your letter to my Brother, who tells me the person that is already appointed Deputy Comptroler att Newhaven, is nephew to Charles Harrison of Seaford, and he will order a letter to be wrote to him immediately for his consent to the exchanges with Stokes & I dare say Mr. Harrison will have no objection to the exchange, but I question much whether it will be an equivalent for your friend, The post att Newhaven I know is of very small value, but nothing shall be done in it, 'till your Grace sees your friends, and servants att London. I am sorry Edsaw[1] is angry with me, but I guess'd he would. The case was this, he wrote to me for a place in the gift of Mr. Poole, which I promised him my interest to obtain, but when Mr. Poole enquired into it, he found it was normally sold, and that he was offer'd 300 pounds for it. This, I told Edsaw's friend, who was not willing to give the money, and did not see why I could expect Poole to give it him. I hope your Grace will forgive my troubling you with this account, but as you are so good to interest yourself in what relates to our country affairs, I was more desirous that you might be enabled to justifie me if you heard any more of it. I will give the Butlers a hint, for I agree with the Western opinions, that Edsaw is of consequence. My Brother tells me, he sent your Grace a full account of Admiral Vernon's dispatches. It has put us all in great spirits, so much so, that Lord Carteret mov'd in the House of Lords this day an address of congratulation to the King, which the H. of C. were desired to concurr in, and was agreed to accordingly. As these Gentlemen cannot do a right thing without some allay, they worded their Address so as to carry with it as much reflection upon particular Persons, as it did justice to our great & successfull Commander, but all that was left out in the Committee, and every thing ended well. Your good friend and my good Brother behav'd manfully and well upon the occasion, and to his no small satisfaction met with the applause even of other authors of the Address whose performance was sufficiently mangled. Forgive my Dear Lord the trouble of this long letter, I have not many opportunitys, in my way of life, of assuring you of my sincere regard, which makes mee more eagerly lay hold of this to testifie to you, how truly and I may say affectionately I am your Graces most obedient and faithfull humble servt

H. Pelham

---

1. Thomas Edsaw of Fittleworth House in Fittleworth.

55. STONE TO RICHMOND

Whitehall
July 3d 1740

My Lord,

As I did not doubt, but your Grace would see, in the Gazette of Tuesday last, a particular account of Vice-Admiral Vernon's late success in taking and demolishing the castle of Chagre (about 7, or 8 Leagues, to westward of Portobello) I did not think it necessary to trouble you with a letter upon that subject, which would not have come sooner to your Grace's Hands, (nor have been fuller, as to that action) than the Relation, which was given to the Publick. As to other news, I think nothing has happen'd very material, since your Grace left London. There have been pretty large Dispatches from my Lord Waldegrave; But, in general, things seem to be going in the old way, at that Court. The Cardinal talks with great appearance of confidence to His Lordship; wishes for an accommodation, But despairs of being able to do anything, towards bringing it about; sometimes talks in a way, as if He meant to intimidate, and, at other times as if He intends to continue in His present state of inaction. In the meantime Monsr Rochelard[1] is gone to Toulon, to take upon him the Command of the Squadron there, and Mor D'Antin[2] is set out for Brest; and it is generally thought, that Both these Squadrons will be got out, into the <u>Road</u>; but Ld Waldegrave seems, at present, to be of opinion, that they will go no further. We have heard nothing of Sir Chaloner Ogle's[3] squadron since He left Port Mahon, above two months ago.

Your Grace will undoubtedly have heard that the King has been pleased, at his Royal Highness the Duke's request, to consent that his R.H. may serve, as a volunteer,[4] on board Sir John Norris's[5] ship: An express was dispatched to Portsmouth, on Tuesday night, with an account to Sir J. Norris of the great honour design'd him.

I am, with great respect My Lord Your Grace's most obedient and most humble servant

Andrew Stone

56. RICHMOND TO NEWCASTLE

Goodwood
July 10 1740

The bearer hereof Wm Faith, is son to Mr. William Faith of Boxgrove a freeholder and one always in our Interest; the lad begs a recommendation to be admitted into the Yard at Portsmouth as a Joiner, having servd his time to that business at Portsmouth.

Richmond &c.

57. NEWCASTLE TO RICHMOND

Whitehall
July 10th 1740

My Dear Lord,

I had the favour of your Letter, & you know I am always desirous of doing every

---

1. Admiral Rochalart was commander of the French fleet in Toulon.
2. Admiral the Marquis d'Antin was commander of the French fleet at Brest.
3. Sir Chaloner Ogle, 1680–1750, MP for Rochester, 1746–1750, joined Admiral Vernon with naval reinforcements and succeeded him in command after the attack on Cartagena. He was created Admiral of the Fleet, 1749.
4. The Duke of Cumberland joined 'Victory' on 5 July 1740, on the start of his naval career.
5. Sir John Norris, 1670–1749, MP for Rye, 1708–1722, and again, 1734–1749, and for Portsmouth, 1722–1734, was a Lord of the Admiralty, 1718–1730. He was made Admiral of the Fleet and Commander-in-Chief in 1734, and commanded the Channel Fleet, 1739–1744.

thing you wish. I doubt much whether any Consul should be at present appointed, 'till the Correspondence is renew'd with the Republick of Venice. Lord Ch. Justice has recommended a Relation of His very strenuously, & says He had some time ago a promise from me. If it was so, as I believe in some measure it was, I had absolutely forgot my previous promise to you. I have wrote fully to the Ch. Justice, & will do nothing 'till I have the pleasure of seeing you, which I hope will be next week. I can easily imagine what Discourse you have had at Portsmouth, from the Letters I have received from thence. The Complaints are in some Measure well grounded, as farr as they relate to what had been promised, but then they are to be answer'd, that it was not in their power to do it, & that possibly just at this time may be true. I have laboured, petted, solicited & teased to gett every thing done that could be, & I hope things will come out tolerably well. The two small ships are, & will be immediately ready & now Sr J.N is joined by all Ogle's squadron, viz nine large Ships. He has a noble Fleet, & I hope will soon be under Sail with it. Lord Cathcart[1] take His leave of ye Regency this day, & goes to ye Isle of Wight next Tuesday, & I hope will sail forthwith. We have ordered 2 50 gun Ships to be added to Cathcarts Squadron & A. Balchen[2] will certainly join Norris wth four large Ships, & 2 more great ones will go from hence. Vernon will have a most noble Fleet also, amounting to 17 large Ships of the Line, with Bomb Vessels, fire Ships, & other small Craft, so that I begin now to be very easy upon these Heads, and if I am, (tho' it may be vain to say it) I believe every Body else who wishes well, may be easy also. I hear our Opposers in Sussex, intend to have a Meeting att Lewes next Week, in order to consider what they shall do.[3] I think this will end in an Opposition, entirely owing to your friend Sr Cecil. I begg you would enquire what they really intend to do, & I doubt not, but you will take the necessary means to disappoint them in your parts. Your Grace like Vernon commands with success in the West, whilst your faithful servant like Norris does His best more northward. As I conclude you will think proper to be in Town next Week, we shall then settle our Meeting at Horsham, the 4th of August. Coll: Ingram[4] invites us all to Supper as usual, & we desire all our friends to be at Horsham, for I suppose we shall there declare the Honle Harry & James Butler, tho' you will not say if we intend a Declaration, but only wish to see our Friends, & therefore you will speak to our friends to be Monday the 4th of August att Horsham, & they will be sent to come to Hills, but don't make it more publick than is necessary.

I am my Dear Duke ever most sincerely yrs

Holles Newcastle

P.S. My Duty to my Queen.

58.   RICHMOND TO NEWCASTLE

Whitehall
July 16 1740

My Dear Lord,

I am extreamly sory to find that your Grace's engagement to me for Mr Smith, has

---

1.   Charles Cathcart, 8th. Lord Cathcart, 1686–1740, Commander-in-Chief of the forces sent to the West Indies against Spain, was to die on the voyage, on 20 December.
2.   Sir John Balchen, 1670–1744, was blockading the Ferrol fleet. Admiral Byng's second-in-command in the Mediterranean, 1718, he had served in the Baltic, 1719–1727. Created Vice-Admiral, 1734, he was Admiral of the White in 1743.
3.   Samuel Medley of Buxted Place was anxious to stand against Henry Pelham and James Butler, the sitting members for the County of Sussex, and hoped that Sir Cecil Bishopp or John Peachey of West Dean would stand with him.
4.   Colonel Charles Ingram, 1696–1748, MP for Horsham, 1737–1748, had a large interest in the borough, having bought out the Eversfields in 1736. He lived at Hills near Horsham.

layn you under so many difficultys, & do assure you that if nobody interest butt my own was concern'd I should with the greatest pleasure releas you from your promis, which you was so kind as to give me last August was two years at Lewis for Mr Smith to suceed Consul Brown whenever he should dye or be removed. butt the misfortune is that I imediately acquainted Mr Smith with your Graces promis, which is already so known at Venice that a disapointment would be of the utmost ill consequence to him. So you see how imposible it is for me to relinquish that promis which you was so kind as to make me so long ago, I own, that, altho I wish Mr Smith extreamly well, I could wish I had never ask'd it, since I see it has given your Grace so much trouble & uneasiness, being with the utmost value & esteem, My Dear Lord, Your Grace's most faithfull humble servant

Richmond &c.

59. RICHMOND TO NEWCASTLE

Goodwood,
27th July 1740

My dear Lord,

Nobody as yett have absolutely refused going to Horsham, butt when I asked Page yesterday, he told me he beleived he should not, & then talked of the Lyon, the Victory & a Cock & a Bull, by which you see how he'l be, & as (you may imagine) I did not press him. Sir John Miller will certanly go; that is, he has promis'd it, which I own was more than I expected. Hayly[1] says (as much as he sayes) he is with us butt thinkes he can't go to Horsham; however, he is to dine here to day, & I'l make him drunk & see what wee can do with him. He is a sort of a Ld Talbot man. He express'd himself civilly to me, & repeated ten time he would do anything to oblige the Duke of Richmond, & lay'd an emphasis upon my name, which is a sort of a compliment I don't at all like, for I would have every Sussex man at least love the Duke of Newcastle as well as me. I could say a great many fine things, butt the Duke of Grafton would call it flattery, so I shall only say that I like those Sussex people best that help us upon principle rather than those that have a personal freindship as they call it. Tonny Chardin sayes he loves me, butt for all that I would not trust the dog with a shilling. Tanky[2] is just come here & he certanly attends you. I shall carry Alderman Soane in my coach, & an agreeable companion he is. Cheal will also certanly go. Every body here seems to despise the Oposition, At what time would you have us be at Horsham on Munday? If it is not to be 'till seven o'clock, I shall dine with the soveraign in my way. So pray lett me know it by Tuesday's post. Besides the Gentry, I beleive I shall bring some of our top farmers, that wee call yeomanly men. In short, I will do the best I can & am and shall be, my Dear Lord. for ever your's

Richmond &tc.

I shall call upon Sir John Campeachy to day or to morrow. Sir John Miller has been here. Do you send a regnt after Sir F or no?.

60. RICHMOND TO NEWCASTLE

Goodwood,
30 July 1740

My dear Lord,

I can now give you some account of the state of our affairs here, and you know I am

---

1 Thomas Hayley, died 1739, the son of Dr. William Hayley, Dean of Chichester, 1699–1715, was elected to to the Chichester Chapter in 1712. He was Prebendary of Heathfield, 1705–1735, and himself was Dean of Chichester, 1735–1739.
2. Charles Bennett, 2nd. Earl of Tankerville.

not apt to flatter you. Green[1] & Buckner[2] have been pretty much about, & I can't find that wee have lost one vote as yett; that is, I except Mr. Orme, who you know wee sett down against us. His only answer to my letter was that he would waite upon me at Goodwood, butt I have not yett seen him. I have heard that he say'd publickly at Chichester he was determin'd to be zealously for my interest there, but say'd nothing as to the County, so I take for granted he will be against us. Sir John Miller is as zealous for you as I am, & I wish it may last as long. I shall not take the merit of it upon myself, for I assure you I thinke it is entirely your own doing, & particularly in this last recommendation of his freind Holmes.[3] I have been to see Williams[4] but he was not at home, so I have just now writ to him. He is a very silly, purse proud fellow, so I wish you would write to him by Thursday's post, for as he knows you have writ to Sir John Miller, you may depend upon it he won't go without a letter, & I really thinke he's with us in his heart, so a little flattery will be well bestow'd. Hayly has promis'd to go with me to Horsham & so has Alderman Soane & most of our top people from Chichester, & almost all the clergy, & several of our substantial yeomen, such as Frank Peachy of Bersted,[5] Cobden of Drought,[6] Sam Row the smugler, John Newland,[7] that you must remember, Burnand of Norton,[8] the two Chittys of Singleton, Hounsham of Funtington, Hill of Yapton. Besides these all the gentlemen that I know will come: Cheale, Leaves, Fowler, Nash, Tom Strickland, etc., Tanky & I propose dineing with the Duke of Somerset,[9] if seven o'clock is time enough for Horsham, butt not else. Burnand of Norton, who is one of our best people, has gott over Sturt of Sidlesham, & Haselar of Lidsey, with two or three dependents upon each of them, & they were zealously against us last election. Belchamber is also zealous for us & will do us all the service he can, 'tho he must give one vote as his masters, the governors of Christ's Hospital, direct him; it was last time for Fuller, & must always be for the Jacobite that stands whosoever he is. The governors, you know, are composed of Citty Patriots. I hope to hear from Berkeley to night. The carpenter heard him promis me possitevely that he would come. I am very, very sorry to find that Cathcart is not nigh going yett. I long to have him beyond the lands end as much as Cartaret can.

I am, my dear Lord Your Grace's ever faithfull humble servant
Richmond &c.

Sir Ian[10] gott most imoderately drunk here last Sunday & was as fond of you & me as ever the humerous lieutenant was of the King. Nay, it is our Polliticks that please him,

---

1. Richard Green, died 1775, was Richmond's Chaplain. He was Rector of Merston, 1728–1775, Vicar of Birdham, 1739–1775, Prebendary of Hampstead, 1730–1743, and Prebendary of Bury, 1743–1775. Richmond obtained the Chaplaincy of the Royal Hospital at Chelsea for him in 1742.
2. Richard Buckner was Richmond's steward at Goodwood, 1731–1777. He is thought to have come over from Germany, was Mayor of Chichester in 1753, and was the father of John Buckner, Bishop of Chichester, 1798–1824.
3. Richard Holmes of Arundel.
4. Either Peckham Williams, 1713–1777, who bought the John Edes House, now the County Record Office, from Mary Frankland, John Edes' grand-daughter, or Hutchings Williams of Chichester.
5. Francis Peachey of North Bersted and Rumboldswhyke, was second, but first surviving son of William Peachey of Chilgrove. He was married to Mary, the daughter of the Rev. Charles Randall Covert, Vicar of North Mundham.
6. Edward Cobden of Drought alias Drovers in Singleton.
7. John Newland, 1717–1800, one of the three brothers from Slindon who played cricket for England in 1744. See Edmund Esdaile, 'Their Chivalry was Cricket' in *Journal of the Cricket Society*, vol. 4, no. 2, (1969), pp. 25–29.
8. John Burnand of Norton in Aldingbourne.
9. Charles Seymour, 6th. Duke of Somerset, 1662–1748, known as 'The Proud Duke' had lived in retirement at Petworth for a number of years. He felt that James Butler should yield his seat to 'more ancient familys in our county'.
10. Sir John Miller.

of which you know he is a perfect good judge. Your Queen, as you are pleas'd to call her, is much your humble servant. She is to go to Hampnet church[1] to hear a sermon of two hours, & to comend it mightyly, in order to gett the parson over to us. His name is Lewis;[2] he is a mad Welch enthusiast, a sort of Whitfeild, & a violent church man. He is a very noisy fellow & vastly followed by the people here, so 'tho he is a bad dog, it would be right to have him, for he can be very serviceable. As this letter is all upon Sussex elections, I shall make no excuse for the length of it.

61. RICHMOND TO NEWCASTLE

Goodwood
The merry first of August 1740

My Dear Lord,

After joy to your Grace upon the day, I shall only thanke you for your very kind & obligeing letter, & assure you, that it is butt doing me a peice of justice to thinke that I love & value you. If I find you expect me at Horsham before seven o'clock, I shall not go by Petworth, butt the short way by Pulborough. for I am determined to be punctual. I hope to bring about twenty freinds of the best & most substantial people in this neighbourhood, & more than that would only be mobbing; which at present is not the scheme. I want by this to avoid mobbing, that is an oposition. Williams will certanly attend you, & he has given me a kind hint that it is upon your account & not myne. Hayley will also come, & he has hinted that it is upon my account only, & that as I have told you, I really like less than the other. Page will not come for either of us, however I thought it was right to send him your letter, that he might have no excuse, for I hate your doubtfull fellows; & those very evill people that want to be well with both partys. Orme has sent me word by Green that he cant go to Horsham, & sayes a great deal too much stuff to putt into this letter; butt I have some hopes of persuading him to be neuter; & that I thinke is all wee can expect. I wish you had not aply'd to Dr Combs[3] about Sr Ian, for he told me tother day that damt he did not care a fart for Dr. Combs, which is decent & dutifull, however you have his heart & soul I promis you. I am obliged to you for the Dyke intelligence it looks well, & I have a great notion it will all end in proposing to compound with you for one at Lewis, & in that case you your-self are the only judge, & except Mr Pelham, it would be impertinent in any man liveing to advise. I intended to have gon to the Isle of Wight, butt can not, for I find by my Lord Cathcart that he intends at all events to embarque one Brigade on Sunday, & t'other on Munday. butt he writ me this as a secret, I suppose for fear of desertion. he complains sadly of Balchen's slowness, that reigning Admiralty distemper. I must now tell you that your poor Queen has been very much out of order however she is much better this morning, & I hope will be quite well by Munday. I assure you nothing butt a thing of such consequence to me as her illness shall hinder me waiting on you; in that case I hope you would excuse it; butt I am in great hopes that she will be quite well again by that time, for I am never so happy as when I can do any thing you like, being most truely my Dear Lord Your's for ever

Richmond &c.

Lady Vane[4] wont lett Berkeley come to Goodwood, butt he has absollutely promis'd to

---

1. Westhampnett Church, the parish church for Goodwood House, though the family preferred to be baptised in London and buried in Boxgrove Priory.
2. The living of Westhampnett was sequestered during the eighteenth century, but Thomas Lewis signed the Bishop's Transcripts, as curate, between 1736 and 1745.
3. Sir John Miller was married to Susan, daughter of Dr. Matthew Combe of Winchester in 1735.
4. Lucy Vane, wife of William Vane, 1st. Viscount Vane, 1676–1742, and daughter of William Jolliffe of Caverswall Castle in Staffordshire.

meet us at Horsham; why should not you bring him with you. I beleive he would go if you would aske him.

62. RICHMOND TO NEWCASTLE

Goodwood
Munday morning. Aug: 11th 1740

My dear Lord,

Altho the Dutchess of Richmond is not ill, yett her health is so precarious at this time that I could have no ease or comfort from her; so I must beg the favor of your Grace to make my excuse to their Excellencys for not attending this week as I ought to do. you may be assured it is no excuse, for in the first place I am desirous of doing my duty, & in the next I could have wish'd of all things to have waited upon you to Lewis; however I am still in great hopes of meeting you there, for I do positively assure you that nothing butt the Dutchess of Richmond's being ill shall hinder me, & from thence I propose returning with you to London, in the mean while I am & ever shall be, my dear Lord, Your Grace's ever faithfull, & obliged humble servant,

Richmond &c.

Tutté[1] begs you would write a line to my Lord Cathcart to recommend his son to him. I hope Cathcart sail'd to day for the wind has been South East all day.

63. RICHMOND TO NEWCASTLE

Goodwood
Aug: 13th 1740. Wednesday morn

My dear Lord,

The Dutchess of Richmond is a great deal worse, so you may imagine I am in no small trouble at present, first upon her account, & then for fear I should not be able to wait upon you at Lewis. If she continues as she is I certainly cant, butt if she is better, or if she should miscarry & be quite safe between this & fryday, nay even between this & saturday, I will most certainly attend you. for upon my sincerest word I never am happyer than when I am employ'd in any thing that can be of service to you, being my dear Lord for ever Your's

Richmond &c.

Sr John Miller & Hayley & several more have absollutely promis'd to go.

64. RICHMOND TO NEWCASTLE

Goodwood
Aug: 31: 1740

My Dear Lord,

I cannot express my vexation at Sr John Norris's return to Torbay, surely all the cursed ill luck in the world attends us. If you should hear for certain that the ferrol squadron is gone to the West Indias, would not you thinke it most absollutely necessary to send still six more of Norris's squadron to strengthen Cathcart, & Norris then will be stronger than the Brest squadron which in that case would be the only thing to aprehend. butt God knows I expect no more from Norris this season than I do from the Victory that is lay'd up.

---

1. William Tutté was a member of the Corporation of Chichester. He was married to Barbara, sister of William Hay, MP for Seaford, 1734–1755.

Now as to our Sussex affairs, I am very sorry to tell you that my Lady Derby[1] is for Medley,[2] Sr Cecyl has dined with her last week, butt as it is her principle I fear she came too easily into it. I am horridly vex'd I did not go sooner, 'tho I beleive it would have been to no purpose. She told me she certanly should do Mr Pelham all the service she could, butt then she mumbled out Medleys damn'd name; & in short I find she will be for him. however 'tho it is a bad thing to have her against us, I cant find she has above ten votes. butt I'l do my best, et je lui couperai l'herbe sous le pied, I know you hate a French proverb, butt I had never an english one ready. To morrow we begin askeing votes, butt we could not sooner for the alterations are prodigious, & I have butt just gott the last of the Chichester freeholders, which I have sent to Mr. Pelham. Sr Cecyl askes only for Medley, butt I dont yet hear if he askes singly for him, or not, when I do I'l let you know it.

I am my Dear Lord, Your Grace's most faithfull, & affectionate humble servant
Richmond &c.

Tom Hill[3] recommends strongly the enclosed memorandum, & I earnestly join with him. I assure you the man is a good man, staunch for the government, & was a Westminster schollar, which crowns the recommendation. so pray give it attention.

As 'tis apprehended that the trade at Venice may suffer for want of a Consul,[4] & on the other hand that the apointing a Consul at present may be improper. It is proposed that some private intimation may be given to the person that is to be Consul, by which the merchants may acknowledge him as such, without directly apointing him, or taking any notice of the Government of Venice.

N.B. The Duke of Richmond hopes that Mr Joseph Smith[5] will be that Consul.

65. NEWCASTLE TO RICHMOND

Whitehall
Sepr 2d 1740

My Dear Lord,

I think entirely with you, both as to Norris & Cathcart, & have but one Comfort what I think of either, which is, that I have nothing to reproach myself with. I was single of opinion from the beginning, that the Ferrol Squadron would go to the W. Indies. I was almost single in wishing, that Sr Chaloner Ogle, had been gone thither, & was not forward in countermanding Him. Had Ogle been in ye W. Indies, the Ferrol Squadron would never have gone thither, nor rapidly stirred out of port, & Ld Cathcart's success would in great measure been sure. I always pressed more Ships wth Cathcart, & shall continue to do so. As to Sussex, I am every day more & more obliged to you. Medley goes about to Cricket Matches, Fairs, etc., & has been att some of our great Towns, but I don't hear he meets with any success. He asks votes singly for Himself. Sr Cecil, I hear, is very active for him, & where he can't gett a promise of receiving the second vote, asks it for my Brother. I hear His Grace of Somerset does

---

1. Mary Stanley, Countess of Derby, 1667–1752, of Halnaker, the neighbouring seat to Goodwood, was the daughter and heir of Sir William Morley of Halnaker, and the widow of James Stanley, 10th. Earl of Derby.
2. Samuel Medley of Buxted Place canvassed Sussex for the opposition in 1741, but his candidacy fizzled out, and he died of smallpox just before the election.
3. Tom Hill was appointed tutor to Richmond in July 1711, and remained the Duke's guide, philosopher and friend until the Duke's death. His entertaining letters to Richmond are Goodwood Ms. 103, ff. 194–250, and the Goodwood Collection contains much of his humorous verse.
4. Between 1737 and 1744 there was a break in diplomatic relations between England and Venice, because of the honours paid to the Pretender in Venice.
5. Joseph Smith, 1682–1770, art collector, was British Consul at Venice, until 1760. He was a friend of Owen McSwiney and others of Richmond's circle.

not approve two eastern Men & they say is much for another western Candidate, but hitherto none appears. Sr J. Peachey they talk of tho' I can't believe it. You saw his Letter to me. I have not heard of him since.

I wrote a long letter to Ball[1] on Saturday. I reckon He is the best Agent we have in your parts, & will do whatever you would have Him. I wish you would tell Dear[2] that I will take upon me to direct Him to speak to all who depend upon the Bishop,[3] for my Brother & Mr Butler. I begg you would send Mr Farhill[4] in Ld Berkeley's name to the Bossomites, & all that depend upon Ld Berkeley. He may have forgot to give directions but you know He is most zealous with us. As to Tom Hill's Memm, I hope He knows, whatever comes from Him, will have weight with me. I know the Case & take it to be, as it is stated, in ye Mem. But ye Misfortune is, my good old Master, the late King promised what was not in His Gift, and how far the present Chancellor will look upon Himself to be obliged to perform such a promise of 18 years standing, I cannot say. He is so good to me upon all Occasions, yt I cannot press Him in this Affair, but I will mention it to Him & if I find Him inclined, I will encourage Him in it. I begg my Duty to my Queen, & kind Compliments to Lady Albemarle & Ossorio, & T. Hill.

I am my Dear Ld Ever most affectly yrs

Holles Newcastle

66. RICHMOND TO NEWCASTLE

Goodwood
Tuesday noon. Sepr 2d 1740

My dear Lord,

The whole fleet is once more under sail, the wind North East, I hope in God it may continue, tho I can see they have butt very little of it; wee are very busy in askeing votes, & in a post or two I hope to be able to give your grace a very good account of this part of the Country. Altho my Lady Derby has promis'd Medley, yett wee are in hopes wee can worke upon her so as not to take it ill at least that I should aply to her tenants, & I dont doubt butt I shall gett most of them. her cheif tenant Farmer Burnand went with me to Horsham & there promis'd Mr Pelham & Mr Butler, & nothing can make that man break his word. In the main I can assure you wee shall do very well, which gives the greatest satisfaction to my dear Lord, Your Grace's most faithfull humble servant

Richmond &c.

Pray what becomes of Captn Knowles?[1]

67. RICHMOND TO NEWCASTLE

Goodwood
Sepr 3d 1740

My dear Lord,

I am very sorry to tell you that Ld Cathcart & all the Ships are again putt back to St

1. Thomas Ball, died 1770, was successively Prebendary of Hampstead, 1727–1734; Prebendary of Eartham, 1730–1754, Archdeacon of Chichester and a Canon Residentiary, 1736–1770; and Dean of Chichester, 1754–1770. He was a political agent for both Richmond and Newcastle, and was their representive with the clergy.
2. John Dear was a member of the Corporation of Chichester, and Mayor of the city in 1740.
3. Matthias Mawson, 1683–1770, was Bishop of Chichester, 1740–1754.
4. John Farhill, a Chichester attorney, had been apprenticed to John Halsey, the Chichester Chapter Clerk in 1718. He had an estate in Steep, and acted as agent to John Jolliffe, MP for Petersfield. He was Deputy Recorder of Chichester.
5. Captain Sir Charles Knowles, 1704–1777, MP for Gatton, 1749–1752, was charged with destroying the fortifications at Porto Bello. He was surveyor and engineer of the fleet against Cartagena. He was later Governor of Louisburg, 1746–1748, and of Jamaica, 1752–1756. He was appointed Admiral in 1760.

Helens. These disapointments are shocking.

Out of 182 Freeholders in Chichester wee have already gott the absollute promises of 90. & I don't doubt butt wee shall gett 50 more.

I am my dear Lord, Your Grace's ever faithfull humble servant.

Richmond &c.

68.   NEWCASTLE TO RICHMOND

Whitehall
Sept 4th 1740

My Dear Lord,

For once I will trouble you with nothing relating to Sussex, but to thank you for your goodness, and to desire a continuance of it. Il s'agit des affaires d'une plus grande importance. I am very sorry to acquaint you, that yesterday, I had an express from Lord Waldegrave, that the Cardinal had owned to Him, that both the Brest & Toulon Squadrons were sailed, the first the 22 of Augt, ye last ye 15, both our style, and by His Discourse, it is very plain that they are Both gone to the West Indies, to protect the French Commerce, & to prevent our growing too powerful there so that in a short time, almost the whole navy of France, & Spain will be in ye W. Indies. This being so, it is to be consider'd, what we are to do. We shall have an extraordinary Regency tomorrow, att which Ld Chancellor[1] will be present. I believe we shall all be of opinion, to send such a sea force to the West Indies as may be sufficient to enable Ld Cathcart to go on with his designs, notwithstanding any opposition He may meet with from any quarter. This may make it necessary to stop or recall Sr. J. Norris. I have always been, & am still of opinion that the West Indies must be our part, & I think it should not be less so from the great desire in others to defeat us there. You see in what confidence I write to you. I am sure I may depend upon it, that you will not say one word a ame vivante. If you are not with us next Tuesday, I will take care that you shall be informed of every thing that passes. My respects to all the good company att Goodwood.

I am my Dear Lord Yrs most affect'ly & sincerely

Holles Newcastle.

69.   RICHMOND TO NEWCASTLE

Goodwood
Fryday Septr 5th 1740

My dear Lord,

The fleet were again under sail yesterday with a fair wind at East, butt now it is again Westerly, & I fear much they will be oblig'd to putt back. I am quite tired with seeing them go out & come back again; however it is some comfort to see that they do their best. I thanke your Grace for your most obligeing letter. It is very true you have been in the right all along about the ferrol squadron, butt you are in the wrong to say you was almost single in wishing Sr Challenor Ogle had gone to the West Indias, for I declared myself of your graces opinion. There is one thought occurs to me that I thinke of consequence, Anson's[2] expedition, altho it ought to be a secret, you know is none.

1.   Philip Yorke, 1st. Lord Hardwicke, 1690–1764, MP for Lewes, 1719–1722, and for Seaford, 1722–1733, was Solicitor General, 1720–1724, Attorney General, 1724–1733, and Lord Chancellor, 1737–1756. He was . Newcastle's life-long friend and political ally.
2.   George Anson, 1697–1762, MP for Hedon, 1744–1747, was 1st. Lord of the Admiralty, 1751–1756, and again 1757–1762. He was ordered to sail to the South Seas and to distress the Spaniards by sea and land. In fact, he was about to set out on his famous voyage around the world.

They are certainly aprised of it, then at Madrid; what if upon that they should have sent part of their squadron to the South Seas? This is only a surmise of myne. I wish it may be without foundation; butt if other people should be of my opinion, would it not be worth while to strengthen Anson with two or three ships more?

Now as to our Sussex affairs wee are hard at worke, & I thinke are beforehand with Medley, who is expected next week at Knighton.[1] In Chichester it stands thus at present.

Absollutely promis'd	102
against	10
doubtfull	41
not yet spoke to	31
	184

& out of the last 72, I dont doubt of getting 40, at the least. Wee went through Pagham, Bersted, Felfam, Bognor & Climping yesterday, where wee had a majority of the whole, butt several not at home that were out at harvest, to day they are gon to Slyndon, Norton, Aldenbourn, Yapton & Arundel, to morrow they are to go northward, to Midhurst, Cocking, Fenhurst &c; & next week, they shall try westward Battines way. Fanil has I beleive received my Lord Berkeley's orders, I have wrote to Mr Pelham to tell him of some letters he must gett from Mr Burrell[2] & Mrs Spence. The old Countess is slow in here motions, so barring the Credit of the thing she will do you no great harm. Lewis the mad welch parson, is violent for Butler because he sayes he knows him to be a churchman, butt he looks upon Mr Pelham to be a presbyterian; & Preden[3] the presbyterian parson objects to Mr Pelham's too great attachment to the Church, however 'tho not one of the Presbyterians will yett promis, I am convinc'd that I shall gett every man of them. Tom Hill thankes you for your goodness. I have a great mind to write myself to the Chancellor, 'tho if he wont do it for half a word of yours, he wont for a letter of myne. Enclosed is a letter from Smith. Pray my dear Lord lett that affair[4] be done one way or other. You see Goldsworthy by a delay lost his affair, & I am sadly afraid of some unforseen accident hapning. I beg pardon for being so troublesome. I shant be in town till Munday sennight, haveing some business of my own, butt none of Pelham & Butlers, which I look upon as my own, being my dear Lord for ever & ever Your's

Richmond &c.

70. RICHMOND TO NEWCASTLE

Goodwood
Sunday: 7; Septr 1740

My Dear Lord,

When there is business of such consequence upon the tapis I thinke it my duty to attend, so shall consequently be in town to morrow night. If you should dine at Mr Stones & have no particular party I should be glad to dine with you there. do you forgive this liberty? & is it not trespasing upon your goodness? I have strictly obey'd your commands as to secrecy. butt I find that Osorio has pretty nigh the same account, he shew'd me a letter from Paris which sayes, <u>La Flotte est partie de Toulon vers le</u>

---

1. Nyton in Aldingbourne.
2. Peter Burrell, 1692–1756, MP for Haslemere, 1722–1754, and for Dover, 1755–1756, was a Director of the South Sea Company, 1724–1733, and sub-Governor, 1733–1756.
3. John Preddon was minister of the General Baptist Chapel at Baffins Lane in Chichester, 1730–1761.
4. The appointment of a Consul for Venice.

de'twits, et celle de Breste est ausii partie & trois de cette derniere esquadie est allez a l'amerique, so you see it will not long be a secret. I wish Vernon does not do misceif to our affairs, by some rash enterprise. It is now more evident that ever, how right it would have been to have sent Ogle to the West Indias. our affairs here go on pretty well tho not so well towards the seaside as I imagin'd. Butler is extreamly disliked there. however in the main it is pretty well, Medley has treated at Shoreham, Sr Cecyl askes for Medley single, if he can't gett that then for Medley & Pelham.

adieu my dear Lord Yours for ever,

Richmond &c.

71. NEWCASTLE TO RICHMOND

Newcastle House
Monday Night Septr 8th 1740

My Dear Lord,

I am very glad you are come to town, I am sure you will extreamly approve all we have done, and are doing; upon certain advice that Both the French Squadrons, & ye Spanish one are gone to Ferrol. We have order'd all Norris' Squadron, & ye 6 ships formerly designed to go with Cathcart making in all 33 vast great ships to ye West Indies, under ye command of Ogle, so that Vernon will have 43 vast ships of ye line, a strength sufficient to deal with Both French and Spaniards. I must begg my Dear Lord, you will excuse my not dining with you tomorrow, for tho' the Ds of Newcastle is better, she does not stirr out of her chamber, & I always dine with Her, if I am not forced by Business to ye contrary. This I am sure you will not think a putt off in.

Yr most faithful and obliged Servt

Holles Newcastle

72. RICHMOND TO NEWCASTLE

Goodwood
Sept: 19: 1740

My Dear Lord,

Wee have heard a great peice of news here, if it is true, which is that an express is arrived from Haddock, with an account of the two French Squadrons, being join'd with the Whole Spanish Fleet, & gone into Malaga & are there embarquing troops, if so I have not the least doubt butt that their design is to attack Gibralter, which, it they do, I conclude they will take it, for by sea it is certainly very pregnable, espetially by such a great force, surely then it would be right for our whole force to take Gibralter in their way, & if they are there, or still at Malaga to try either to fight them or block them up, butt still I mean that they should be victuall'd for the West Indias to follow directly if they find they are gon. the Wind is now Easterly, & I hope Anson is gon. I wish the whole fleet was so to. surely if this news is true, wee have strength enough with Haddock, to beat them & perhaps destroy them in the Mediterranean, which (if it could be effected) would be of more advantage than any thing wee could do in the West Indias, & at the same time would facillitate our expeditions. The arrival of our East India ships is a fine article. I have some gentlemen here that are come from Portsmouth, & entre nous they tell me that business seems to slacken there. I dont like that. I hope in God this easterly wind wont be lost.

Now as to Sussex our affairs go on pretty well, in some places extraordinary well particularly about Fernhurst. That vile fellow Sr John Peachey, is asking publickly for Medly single, & brags he has gott 150 single votes already for him. he had aply'd to all at Fernhurst butt to no purpose. The rascall has been telling Ogle Riggs[1] that he

---

1. Ogle Riggs of Buddington Farm, a detached portion of Midhurst parish.

beleives poor James Butler has a pension, for which I thinke Jack at least ought to breake his head. I have sent a list of memorandums to Mr Pelham. I beg I may know when the day is fixed for the Kings being in Holland, that I may give directions about the relays. I will certanly be in town by Monday sennight butt as my mayors election is next week, & that I have not yett finish'd sending round to all the Parishes, I would gladly stay here this week.

I am with the greatest truth, & sincerest love & friendship, my dear Lord, Yours for ever,

Richmond &c.

73. NEWCASTLE TO RICHMOND

Claremont
Sept 20th, 1740

My Dear Lord,

I have been so taken up in despatching to Hanover, France, etc. that I have really not had time to write to your Grace this week. I desired Mr Stone to acquaint you, that we had order'd the Yachts to go for the King. Admiral Butcher sailed with them last Wensday, so I suppose they are now in Holland, & we may have our Master here the beginning of the week after next. Monsr Bussy has att last made His Declaration, or rather Communication, for he would leave nothing in writing. What he said was to the following effect, 'That as the sailing of their squadrons from Brest & Toulon was now publick, He should s'expliquer avec le Duc de Newcastle la' dessus, that the King of France took this Resolution, but dons le dernier moment, which however could not surprise us, since it was not to be doubted, but yt Ld Wal. had constantly acquainted His court, wth the Declarations, the Cardinal had often repeated to Him, 'That France could not suffer England to make new establishm'ts in America (which fact by the by, is not so, as there related), that our late armaments had made the sending their ships necessary, au reste, they were eloignés de toute idée de Reception, & had order'd our commerce legatione not to be troubled. A most offensive and impertinent Declaration. Bussy asked me what I had to say. I told Him the affair was too important for me to say anything, but yt I would transmit it to ye King, & receive His orders upon it, which I accordingly did last night. We are making all haste wth our ships, which they still say, will be ready in this month, that is ye best answer to France. We have no letters or messenger yett from Hanover, which a little surprises me, the wind having been fair. As for Election affairs, your correspondent for them is now ye Honble Harry. He setts out for Haland next Wensday. My compliments to all att Goodwood.

I am ever most affecty yrs

Holles Newcastle

74. NEWCASTLE TO RICHMOND

Whitehall
Sepr 23rd 1740

My Dear Lord,

I acquainted your Grace on Saturday with Monr Bussy's extraordinary & impertinent Communication or Declaration. I had yesterday your most obliging Letter. I never can say enough to you, for your constant goodness to me. There is no foundation for the supposed Account from Haddock about Gibraltar. For Godsake don't lett us be diverted, from our most necessary resolution of sending our Ships to the West Indies. We are no nation, if we cannot be superiour to ye French in ye W. Indies, & therefore, I am unwilling to attend to any thing that may delay or hinder that. Every thing is going on, or is swore, is going on with the utmost expedition, & by what we are told, I really

45

should hope Ogle will be ready with the whole Fleet to sail for ye W. Indies, in a Week or ten days. Dunkirk is repairing, or at least, preparing to be repaired in all haste, & France is arming all their Ports, bringing down their Troops to the Coast, & repairing their Fortifications.

As to the King's coming, the certain time is not known. If He comes as soon as He hears of ye arrival of ye Yachts, He may be here ye beginning of next Week, but by a Messenger I have had from Hanover I find He then did not intend to be in Holland 'till next Sunday sennight the 5th of October, but in all events, if you are in Town next Monday, you will be time enough, tho' I can say nothing to the Relays to be laid on ye Road, for I cannot judge whether He will come away upon ye arrival of ye Yachts, or stay till ye day, He had fixed before He knew of ye Yachts being sent, whch was done by us in consequence of a discretionary power left with us. I have so much, you see, to say abt France & French, yt I must entirely leave to you, the care of Pelham & Butler. They cannot be in better hands.

I am every & unalterably yrs.

Holles Newcastle

75. PELHAM TO RICHMOND

Bishopstone
Septr 29 1740

My Dear Lord,

Your Grace will forgive me, that I take this opportunity of a messenger going into the West, to trouble you with a journal of my motions, and to send you as good an account, as I can, of the situation of our affairs in this part of the country. I din'd att Grinsted on Wednesday and lay att Abergavennys.[1] I am pretty sure we have not above two against us both in that town, and I believe they will not go. His Lordship has sent all round his hat which is a very large one, and has met with success beyond expectation. I din'd att Halland on Friday, where we had above 200 freeholders, most of 'em double votes; those that would not promise then, I am pretty sure we shall have before the Election. This day I expect as many here, but there being several fairs in the neighbourhood may perhaps prevent some of 'em from coming. Lord President, whom I saw in his way to London last Friday, gives a very good account of his neighbourhood; in several places two to one of what we had last time; I mean all along double votes. Wednesday, I shall be att Sr Wm Ashburnham's[2] and don't doubt but we shall meet with the same success there, and Friday with Mr Pelham of Crow hurst. I have ordered a dinner att Burnet's for Satturday, which will take in the remaining part of Hasting Rape and Pevensey. You see we choose rather to entertain att private houses than go to the towns ourselves; it is much easier and wholesomer, and what the freeholders amongst us are used to, and like, as well. The ale house keepers to be sure do not; they must therefore be fed before the Election, and I have order'd our Agents, from time to time to spend small sums as they see occasions. I am now coming to our last journey. Jewkes[3] and Mitford[4] have desired I would be with Butler att Petworth sessions, which I have sent them word I will. I could not therefore omit acquainting your Grace with it, hoping you will excuse my waiting on you att Goodwood, as I ought to do. I must be back att Lewes on thursday night in order to attend the sessions there on Friday; by that time I shall be pretty well tired, for I own I find myself not so fit for

1. William Nevill, 16th. Lord Abergavennay, died 1744, built Kidbrook in East Grinstead.
2. Sir William Ashburnham, 1677–1755, of Broomham near Hastings, MP for Hastings, 1710–1713, and again, 1722–1741, and for Seaford, 1715–1717.
3. John Jewkes, 1683–1743, of Petworth, MP for Bridport, 1730–1734, and for Aldborough, 1735–1743, was a lawyer, and Newcastle's election agent in the Petworth area.
4. William Mitford, 1699–1777, of Pitshill in Tillington.

46

these kind of exploits as I used to be. I propose therefore to go on satturday afterwards to London or Claremont, and take some rest. I hope your Grace will be so good as to send such Justices of the Peace as you think proper to Petworth, for I should be glad to face the worthy Sr John Peachey with as good an appearance as I could; he will certainly do us a good deal of mischief, but not equal to the good I hear of in other parts of the country. There is a talk here as if Medley was to stand att Steyning upon the Fagg[1] interest. Much good may it do him. He will certainly loose it, if he does, and I can't see it will do him much good for the County. I send you a remarkable circular of your friend Orme's. But since that I hear he has declared for Medley, and desires 'em to reserve their second votes. You are more likely to know the truth of this than I am. I beg my most humble respects to Lady Dutchesse and am with the greatest truth and Respect My Dear Lord your Grace most obedient humble servt

H. Pelham

76. RICHMOND TO NEWCASTLE

Goodwood
Octr: 19: Sund: 1740

My Dear Lord,

I had the vexation & mortification to see the fleet still at Spitthead on Fryday evening. however at ten o'Clock yesterday morning they were under sail; butt they had not gott clear of St. Helens by four, & to day it is so haisy that wee cant see them, however I hope they have gott out 'tho there is butt little wind butt what there is is South by East, which is very good, butt it is very warm & I am sadly afraid of a Westerly wind. This thing I own gives me the utmost concern. The answer as allways what can wee do? I own that I am for punishing those that wont obey orders; & if Sr Challenor Ogle will not thinke fitt to obey the Kings orders, he ought to be stop'd, try'd by a Court Martial, & some other good officer made a Flag & sent in his room. I do declare one thing, which is that if the house of Lords or Commons, nay the enemys in either should thinke fitt to call either Sr Challenor or whosoever may be in fault in this cruel national disapointment, to account, & that it should come to my vote, I shall give it for the enquiry. I would never be for distressing the innocent, butt can never be for screening the guilty. I beg pardon for troubling you with so much stuff, butt non-sensical as it is perhaps, yett it is the sincere opinion of my dear Lord, Your Grace's ever faithfull & obliged humble servant,

Richmond &c.

You bid me tell you when any thing vex'd me. This is therefore is consequence of your orders.
If you have any commands for me pray direct them to Whitehall. butt I expect no answer to this.

77. RICHMOND TO NEWCASTLE

Goodwood
Sunday night [Nov. 2 1740]

My Dear Lord,

Not haveing had an oportunity of speaking to you at the birthday, I must trouble you with some words, not of my own, butt of the person I was telling you of the other day, since which I have seen him, butt he had not seen the foreigner that wanted to speake with him. he strongly repeated his opinion he had given in his former discourse, & he is

---

1. Robert Fagg, 1704–1740, of Wiston had been MP for Steyning, 1734–1740. His family owned much property in the borough, but there was no predominant interest.

extreamly pleas'd to hear that other people are of his opinion. butt the very first step he sayes that ought to be taken, & that imediately, is to secure the King of Prussia, which he sayes the only way to do, is to begin by hireing troops of him, which (as it is also his interest) he thinkes may secure him, butt without him nothing can be done. he also sayes that if wee are in earnest in this affair no time ought to be lost, & he is for sending a propper person, (that was his expression) to Vienna directly, with offers of money in case it is necessary. however he did not know nor I neither 'till afterwards, that the Queen of Bohemia's letter is stop'd with Count d'orten. My Lord Chancellor told it me, & I thinke it a very odd thing, surely they cant carry their Austrian stupidity so far as to be makeing any private bargain with France. butt 'till that letter comes to be sure no step with them can be taken, butt that need not hinder overtures being made to the King of Prussia, perhaps it may be done already, & the person I mentioned as well as myself talke very ignorantly upon the subject, tho he is not apt to talke so. I told everything that had pas'd between us to my Lord Chancellor, except the message from the foreigner, which he desired me to mention to nobody butt your Grace. I own his scheme to me seems so sensible, well founded, practicable, & for the honor of the King, & this country, that I could not help giveing the utmost attention to it; & consequently I can't help wishing it had yours. I mention'd you a particular threat that he say'd upon ocassion might be used. I asked him an explanation of that. butt I dont find he could make out any grounds for it, farther than that by a general confusion in all countrys, people might loose their rights, & therefore 'tis always right to avoid those confusions, by takeing propper resolutions, propper steps & putting them in practice without delay. This is the substance of his discourse, to the best of my remembrance. I thought it right to lett you know it, & I own I thinke that when advice is good, it ought to be taken 'lett it come from whom it will. I had almost forgott to tell you that he sayes that if these things are done he shall be satisfy'd, if not, he gives you notice that he shall take the first oportunity in publick to aske why they were not done. Adieu my Dear Lord

Your's most affectionately

Richmond &c.

78. RICHMOND TO NEWCASTLE

Goodwood
Novr 9th 1740

I am extreamly obliged to your grace for your obligeing letter, by which I thinke things are en bon train, butt am sorry to find you thinke there would be difficulty in the most material point of all viz; the cash, which I fear (by what I have heard) will be so necessary that without it nothing can be done; I tremble at the thoughts of the Zarina's[1] death. I fear that would be a coup fatal to the Gd Duke.[2]

Since I have been here I have seen nobody that can give me any account about our affairs here except Buckner. he assures me all goes on well, & nobody has heard anything of Medley's coming here as yett, however I shall have more news perhaps to send you by Wednesday's post, for I have company to dine with me to day, amongst others Jemmy Lumley, & also Battine & Mr Palmer one of Lady Farrington's heirs, who as this is his second visit will I beleive be with us, 'tho he did not absolutely

1. Anne Ivanova, 1693–1740, was the daughter of Ivan V, the brother of Peter the Great. She became Czarina in 1730, and died on 28 October 1740.
2. Anton Ulric, Duke of Brunswick. His wife, the Grand Duchess Anna Leopoldovna was Regent of Russia from October 1740 until she was deposed by Elizabeth in December 1741.

promis me the first time he came. butt he say'd he wish'd extreamly well to the interest. butt as Tutte brings him, I take for granted he is with us. Sr John 'tho hunted with us yesterday, & sayes everything goes well, for <u>our Whig interest,</u> & <u>wee Whigs,</u> shall carry it. his neighbour Cobden is dead; which is a good thing for he was an enemy & a substantial man.

I am my dear Lord, Your Grace's most faithfull, humble servant,

Richmond &c.

79. PELHAM TO RICHMOND

Spring Garden
Nov 27 1740

My Dear Lord,

I should have return'd your Grace my sincere thanks for the honour of your letter, by the last post, had not the house of Commons sat so late, that I own I had not spirits to do any thing but eat and sleep afterwards. We had a pretty long day yesterday also, but both ended very well with us I think we have spirits and inclination of our side as well as truth and justice. The votes will shew you the business as well as I can tell it you, and therefore shan't trouble your Grace with a repetition of them. In the House of Lords, I conclude you have heard Chesterfield[1] and his <u>new friend</u> the late Marshel have made a parcel of ridiculous motions about the Commission given in the late service ranks of Generals, and ye Secretary att Wars Commission; which I believe most people think rather exposes the movers, than reflects on the Government. I am told by some of your friends that Monday will be a more serious day in your house; and I fancy it will be very agreable to see the faces, as well as have the consciences of the best men to appear of our side. This I write quite from myself, and you will have the goodness I hope to forgive the freedom I take. I can never sufficiently thank your Grace for your repeated favors to me, I hope you don't think my inactivity proceeds from neglect, att present it is impossible for me to do any thing, and I begin to think the assistance of my friends will make it unnecessary for me ever to do much. I will certainly speak to Sr Jacob Ackworth in favor of Woods, in a little time, but I should wish I could have a short Respit. Last week he promis'd me the building of a ship att Shoreham, even against Phillipson's intrest, tho' with his consent and I have had from Portsmouth the assurance of another man's being employ'd in the Dockyard, upon the first vacancy, which may possibly interfere with Wood's. However your Grace may venture to assure him we will amongst us, some how or other take care of him in the manner he desires, and that I hope before it is very long. John Newland I know deserves very well, but his case is more difficult to answer than another man's of less merit. He can't change his way of life and therefore must have, what is properly call'd a sine cure, if it ever is in my power to help him, in my own way, or by speaking to others, your Grace may command me. But it would not be acting fairly by him, to give him too great hopes, tho' perhaps an opportunity may happen sooner than we expect. I hear good accounts from all parts of the country, but none that I can depend upon more than those that come from your Graces kind protection. I receiv'd a letter from Mr Buckner by one Duke directed to your Grace, but to be open'd by me, if you were not in town. The man's son is releas'd, and the father very happy.

I am with the greatest respect Your Graces most obedient humble servant

H. Pelham

---

1.   Philip Stanhope, 4th. Earl of Chesterfield, 1694–1773, statesman and letter writer, though a leader of the opposition, entered the Pelham Ministry on the retirement of Cartaret. He was later Envoy to the Hague, 1745; Viceroy of Ireland, 1745–1746; and Secretary of State for the Northern Department, 1746–1748.

80. NEWCASTLE TO RICHMOND

Claremont
Novr 29. 1740

My Dear Lord,
    I received this afternoon the honour of your Letter. We seem so eager for Business in the House of Lords, that it will be more difficult to say, when there will not be Business, than, when there will. We had last Week several Accounts called for relating to the promotions in the army, which will be brought in next Tuesday. We shall receive on Monday the Report of a Committee appointed to search Precedents relating to the Method of calling for papers, whether by Address to the King, or by order on the respective Offices. I suppose you have seen the string of Orders for Accounts, & papers in ye votes of the H. of Commons. We expect the same on Monday in ye House of Lords. We are determined to grant every thing, that may tend to make the enquiry effectual, & not discover to the Enemy our Instructions to our Admirals, Generals, &c. As the principal question in ye H. of Commons for all orders for sailing, etc., was moved by my Brother, we intend to move the same in our House. In short we will defy them, for I think we may. Thus you see, we may have Business every day & so it is impossible to say, what particular time is the most likely. Our foreign affairs go pretty much as they did. The new Government in Russia, is very desirous of a Treaty with us. The King of Prussia seems very well disposed at present. The States of Holland, I hope, will agree to another Augmentation of 10,000 Men. We hear nothing yett of ye Court of Vienna, & France is just where it was. I hear we are to have an Augmentation of 10,000 Men, seven Regiments of Foot, & four of Marines of 1000 Men each. You see I am not a bad Correspondent, tho' I think you have cast me off, & gone to ye Honble Harry.
    I am ever yrs
Holles Newcastle

81. NEWCASTLE TO RICHMOND

Bishopstone
Dec 25th 1740

My Dear Lord,
    I conclude the thaw has brought you to Charlton, as it has done me here. I wish you would be so good as to honor me wh your company. You had a list of those I hoped to have with you, indeed it is material yt we should have some appearance from the west for it is strongly reported here, that Medley has a great interest there. If you could come only for one day, I should be obliged to you; if not, I begg you would send yr Chichester friends, & neighbours, under the Command of Green etc. You will forgive this liberty. Everything here goes, as you can wish.
    I am ever unalterably yrs
Holles Newcastle

82. RICHMOND TO NEWCASTLE

Goodwood
Fryday night. Decr 26 1740

My Dear Lord,
    I shall certainly waite upon you next Saturday at Bishopstone, & will stay with you on Sunday. Sr John Miller who is now with me, will also certainly attend you, & wee will pick up what freinds wee can; nobody of consequence in this part of the Country is against us, butt this is a time that they chuse to stay at home, however wee will do what wee can.

50

I am my dear Lord, Your Grace's most faithfull humble servant
Richmond &c.

on Thursday wee hunt by the way, & dine at Findon,[1] where wee stay till Saturday, hunt that morning, & after hunting go to Bishopstone, so very likely wee maynt arrive till night. <u>Sr John</u> will hunt with you on Saturday wee shall have no Charlton people butt Harcourt & Paunceford with us, & I shall certanly bring them. Sr John will be with you on Tuesday.

Wee have had a very fine chaise to day, nobody butt Dayrolle[2] with me, who will also attend you, with your leave. I shall employ Green to get what people I can.

83. NEWCASTLE TO RICHMOND

Bishopstone
Dec 30th 1740

My Dear Lord

I am very much obliged to you for your kind intention of coming to Bishopstone, but as you can't be with us 'till Saturday night, and we all decamp from hence on Sunday, in order to be in London on Monday, I must begg you would not give yourself the trouble to come this time, unless you can be here on Fryday, which I conclude, from ye Dispositions you have already made, will be disagreable to you. For the same reason, you will be so good as to stop <u>Green</u> & Company. We had yesterday twice as many people as this House would hold, all very zealous for ye County, & most of them so for Lewes also. We go to Lewes tomorrow, lie there tomorrow night, hunt on Thursday & dine here that day, & shall have a Ball for the Seaford ladies on Thursday night. On Fryday we all dine at Firle with Sir Wm Gage, & return hither at night, hunt on Saturday & go towards London on Sunday. I beg you would desire <u>Sr John</u> to meet us at Sr Wm Gages, on Fryday & he shall go home with us in my Coach. My Dear Duke we have been fully employ'd, & shall be so whilst we stay. The Town of Lewes is our <u>Plague</u>, but I think it safe. My Best Respects to Harcourt, & compliments to Pansford &c. The Honble Harry is much yours & I am always most sincerely so!
Holles Newcastle

P.S. Would Sr John come to dance wh our ladies on Thursday. Mr Mill & Mr Leaves are both here.

84. RICHMOND TO NEWCASTLE

Goodwood
Decr 31st 1740

My dear Lord,

My situation at present is very disagreeable, & uncertain: my youngest daughter is very ill,[3] that is she has a fever, & we don't know what the consequence may be. so if I go to Findon to morrow the Dss of Richmond stays here. from thence I can soon return if the poor child should be worse. butt if it should be better on Fryday I'l try to waite upon you at Bishopstone either Fryday or Saturday tho you do go away on Sunday. I assure you I always wish to be with you. however dont expect me, for fear it should not be in my power. There is only Ld Harcourt & Dayrolle with me. Sr Jn Miller can't go,

---

1. Findon was the seat of John Cheale, where the Charlton Hounds were kennelled for part of the year.
2. Soloman Dayrolles was secretary to Lord Chesterfield. A friend to Richmond, he was a Gentleman of the Privy Chamber to George II; Master of the Revels and Gentleman Usher of the Black Rod; and Resident at the Hague from 1747 to 1751.
3. Lady Margaret Lennox, born 16 November 1739.

for my Lady Miller is extreamly ill. In case I am not with you on Tuesday will you be so good as to lett me know by the post, when & what day you expect business in the house of Lords. & direct to me at Goodwood, for if I dont go to Bishopstone I shall return here on Saturday. If I come on Saturday it will be by dinner, butt will be with you if possible on Fryday. My best services attend Mr. Pelham. The profound dull quietness of this part of the Country, proves that there is no oposition stirring at present. I am glad to hear things go so well with you in your part. I shant bring above three or four people with me if I do go. the heartyest have excuses, & really it is not worth while to plaque & press them at this time.

    I am my dear Lord Your Grace's ever faithfull, humble servant
Richmond &c.

a most sad story of <u>Jack Butler's lasciviousness</u>[1] makes a great noise hereabouts. he is certainly form'd for love; butt he should use it with discretion.

85. RICHMOND TO NEWCASTLE

Findon
Fryday: Jan 2d 1740/1

Youl be at dinner, so I beg that Mr. Stone may answer this
My Dear Lord,

    My attending your grace to morrow at Bishopstone, or not, will depend upon two circumstances. the first whether my little girl is better or worse which I shall hear to night, that is butt too good an excuse, the other (which I hope you will be so good as to indulge me in) is hunting to morrow, butt if it should be so very bad a day, that wee cant hunt, I'l attend you, if you desire it, tho I should be wett to the Skin. I should certanly not thinke of so triflieing a thing as hunting, if my going to Bishopstone could be of the least real service to you, or if it was necessary to shew the world how sincerely I love & esteem you. butt I hope that is out of all doubt, since therefore it is very likely I shant go at all, I must beg you would be so good as to lett me know when you thinke there will be business in the house of Lords. our Freind Huske[2] told me from his freind that there certanly would be some soon, butt that there would be fair notice given. I therefore wish (if you dont know now) that you would lett Mr Stone write to me on Munday by what wee call the by post, & direct it to me at Goodwood by Midhurst bag, & I will contrive if any thing comes on next week to be in town by Wednesday, for unless you know it by this time, I take for granted it wont be before Thursday. butt if there should be nothing to be done this next week, I should be prodigiously glad to enjoy this fine weather here, in this most delightfull country for one week longer, & on Sunday sennight I should certanly go of course to town. Wee had a very fine chase yesterday & ran to ground. Sr Cecyl, Sr Charles Goreing & John Midleton were out with us. Wee ask'd them all to dinner, butt only John Midleton came. & delightfull company he was. he sayes whoreing lost Yates his first election,[3] a bad omen for the Butlers. I wish I could have talk'd to you about Sr Ian,[4] who now has a mind to stand at Chichester, in oposition to Page, & I thinke he might run him hard. I dont know how Sr Robert Walpole would like it, after what he told Mr Pelham to tell me, butt I am convinced Page must either deceive Sr Robert or be the vilest of men. for it is notorious how publickly he abuses Sr Robert every day, so in my poor opinion Sr John

1. James Butler's morals were the chief reason why the Duke of Somerset refused to support him.
2. General John Huske, 1692–1761, was a frequent guest at Goodwood. As a soldier, he fought at Dettingen; was second-in-Command at the Battle of Falkirk in 1746; and led the second line at Culloden.
3. Thomas Yates was defeated by Sir Thomas Prendergast in the Chichester bye-election in 1733, by 250 votes to 203.
4. Sir Ian was Sir John Miller.

Miller would be much the better of the two. butt whether he can throw out Page I dont know, as for myself I must be neuter, 'tho several of my people I know would vote for Sr John. I find Medley does no better here than in our part, which is nothing at all. I find Huske has not the thing he wanted, tiss butt a young Regiment & naturally an Irish one that he has, 'tho now in England. Bland[1] who is a younger Coll. a younger Lt Coll: & ('tho a man of service) has still seen less than Huske, I find has gott a Regt of Dragoons, which I thinke must hurt poor Huske. however that may be made up soon, for poor Kirke is dying or dead. Frederick & Brand have both been with me in town. I fain would give them some answer butt can not 'till I hear Colebrooks[2] positive answer whether he stands or no at Shoreham, so pray let me know it. I beg pardon for troubling you with so monstrous a long letter, & am my dear Lord for ever & unalterably Yours

Richmond &c.

My sincere services attend Mr Pelham. have you a blanc proxy or two in your pocket, as a Secretary of State ought to have, if you have pray send them for me & Harcourt who is yours.

86. NEWCASTLE TO RICHMOND

Bishopstone
Jany 4. 1740/1

My Dear Lord,

I am extreamly concerned for poor Lady Amelia. I hope however she will do well & that no ill consequence will happen to the Rest. I begg you would be easy as to your coming to Town. I will send you a Proxy by tomorrow or Tuesday's Post. Make your excuses, & be sure to lett you know, when any particular Business comes into our House. I have had no news from London. Things seem as ill as possible between, ye King of Prussia, & ye Court of Vienna.

Now as to Sussex & my Guests. I hope they all return satisfied with us. We had a great deal of Company to receive them here. I have assured <u>Dear</u> that I will join (as I sincerely shall) in applying to the Bishop for Him. I have done my best with honest Burnand & Mr Bridger. <u>Hibbins</u>[3] I don't take, but I have been very civil to Him. As to the Smuglers, their Petition comes in a sad time, just when the most barbarous Murder has been committed by a most desperate Gang in our part of ye County. However we will see, but I really think it so wrong that we should not engage to do it, & if we did, I must question whether we should succeed. Now as to Sr John Miller I am delighted (as we all are here) with His design of standing at Chichester, concluding it is not <u>against</u> your Interest & <u>inclinations</u> & no otherwise. Upon that supposition we drank, yesterday, the <u>Recorder</u> & <u>Sr John</u>. You know I like the <u>odd fellow</u>, & therefore if you like the enclosed to Him, seal it, & send it to Him; if not, burn it, for I will have nothing to do wth any Body but wth your approbation. <u>Carpenter</u> I will talk to. The living, I suppose He wants, He may sure of, when it falls. I am in great haste just setting out for Haland, & tomorrow for London.

I am ever & unalterably yrs

Holles Newcastle

My Compliments & good wishes to ye Ds of Richmond

1. Humphrey Bland, 1686–1763, general and military writer, was successively lieutenant-colonel and colonel in the Dragoons. He was Major General in the campaign in Scotland in 1745–1746; Governor of Gibraltar, 1749, and Edinburgh, 1752–1763; and Commander-in-Chief of the forces in Scotland, 1753.
2. Possibly Robert Colebrooke, 1718–1784, of Chilham, Kent, who was returned as MP for Maldon, 1741, and continued to hold that seat until 1761.
3. Rev. Lucius Henry Hibbins, on whose behalf Richmond wrote regularly to Newcastle seeking preferment until the end of his life.

87. RICHMOND TO NEWCASTLE

Goodwood
Jan: 6: 1740/1

My Dear Lord,

I must beg you would not go too farr in encouraging Sr John to stand at Chichester, for I begin to find it will hurt you in the County, & me in the town, for Page's interest which is a strong one is outragious, & would declare at once for Medley in the County, & Page single in Chichester. I own I never liked this scheme of Sr Johns, tho I should certanly like him better than Page, butt he cant be chose, & he will hurt us. upon which I have wrote the enclosed to the Mayor[1] & Green for them to shew, & Sr John has confirm'd the truth of it to Page. & Harris,[2] butt he sayes he will not tye himself up from standing, 'tho he thinkes he shant; butt I wish you could settle that affair at Grimsby for him which will make all easy.

My poor little girl has gott the confluent kind of small pox, which is very dangerous, 'tho no bad symptoms as yett appear, however 'tis butt the 5th. day, so nobody can tell yett how it will go with her. I hope you have been so good as to make my excuse to the King. butt ('tho I can do the poor child no good) it would be barbarous to leave the Duchess of Richmond in the cruel anxietys of mind that she is now in.

I am my dear Lord Your Grace's most faithfull, humble servant

Richmond &c.

Jack Wickliff has gott never a horse in Chichester, so he has taken care not to be able to vote for us there. I own I expected it, 'tho all our freinds were so ready to answer for him. I wish he had a better place some where else.

88. RICHMOND TO NEWCASTLE

Goodwood
Jan: 7: 1740/1

My dear Lord,

Your grace will forgive me, I hope, if I say your vivacity (upon the affair of Sr John Millers proposeing himself at Chichester) has been rather too great, at least anticipated; for I fear it will hurt your interest in the County a good deal, & myne at Chichester 'tho in a much less degree; because I have never seem'd to shew a publick aprobation of it, whereas you have publickly declared it in drinking the Recorder & Sr John. dont be allarm'd at my beginning my letter so gravely, I assure you my dear Duke I dont mean it by way of complaining, for it is much more upon account of the county election than that of the Citty, where (notwithstanding such a flame, as was never seen there before) I am sure Mr Brudenells election is safe, & so I hope is Pelham, & Butler, butt I assure you if this was to go on, it would give the greatest shock to them that could be from this corner, Soane who was the most zealous freind wee had for the County as well as for the town, is outragious, & sayes that if Page is oposed by the Duke of Newcastle he will do his utmost for Medley, & if I am concern'd in it he will quit Mr Brudenell. & several more talke in the same way, & I assure you they are a great many, & you know I always say'd Page had a great interest. for my Declaration or <u>Manifesto</u> which is a much greater name for my letter, they will absolve me, & (what I shall dislike as much) lay the whole blame upon you, for which reason I have suppres'd your last letter you enclos'd to me for Sr John, & if I may be allow'd to advise I could wish you would write to him & advise him to desist, that is declare he

---

1. Thomas Sanden was Mayor of Chichester from September 1739 to September 1740.
2. George Harris of Donnington, Page's neighbouring landowner.

will <u>not stand,</u> for he has not said he will; butt it would come with much greater weight if you could give him hopes of some other place, for I find he wants most excessively to be in what wee call <u>Parliament house.</u> butt the apprehensions of spending his money here, I thinke will stop his career. he sayes he should not grudge a thousand, butt for twice that summe I am very sure he would not come in for Chichester; you will say I have alter'd my opinion pretty quick, (tho I always told you that Page's interest was a strong one) butt it is within this four & twenty hours that I find it to be extreamly so, & the general cry at present I do assure you is Page for the Citty, & Medley for the County. I would therefore compound for the first, with all my heart & soul to throw out the other for the County. Now my dear Lord you will say, (& I own I fear with reason) that I drew you into this publick declaration for Sr John, by my letter from Findon to you in which I did express some pleasure in his standing. I own I had rather he should be chose than Page, because wee have a chance for him <u>gratis</u>, & I am sure we cant have Page without <u>buying</u> him, as I do Toys at Chenevix, for more than he is worth, butt as Sr John certanly has no chance & his standing, will as certanly hurt the common interest, I wish sincerely he may desist. he has already declared that he mett with no encouragement from me, which is really truth; & I'l try to gett him to declare also that he had none from you; which is also truth, <u>because</u> I have stop't it by burning your letter to him; and not letting you know you writ it. As this letter is of some consequence to us both, I will make no apology for the length of it. so shall only conclude with assureing you my dear Lord that I am for ever & ever Your's
Richmond &c.

If Albemarle has room for A proxy, I beg he may have the enclosed, if not, you will putt it into any safe hands you please, provideing they are decent hands such as the d: of Graftons, Lord Delawarr's &c. My poor little girl goes on butt slowly, she can't be out of danger before saturday, & happy it will be, if she is so then, for she has a very bad sort. I do my best to smother my anxiety, butt 'tis a most cruel scituation. T'is Margarett my youngest daughter not Emily. She with her two brothers are at Charlton, & as yett in perfect health. butt I dread what in all likelyhood may come.
Since I have writ this very long letter I have received one from Sr John[1] of which I send you a coppy enclos'd. It is so good, so reasonable, & really so much more than I expected, that I thinke he deserves the greatest of thanks from us both. so pray write to him. the first part of my letter is now of no consequence, so I am sorry to have troubled you with it.

89.   NEWCASTLE TO RICHMOND

Newcastle House
Jan 10th, 1740/1

My Dear Lord,
I never was so much concerned, & if you will allow me to say so, surprised, as I was at the Receipt of your last letter. By the first part, I apprehended you were really angry with me, for what had passed at Bishopstone abt Sr J. Miller, as thinking it might hurt Mr Brudenel, & by the whole that you was so much surprised at the satisfaction I had show'd at Sr John's Design of standing at Chichester. And, tho' it is now all happily over, give me leave my Dear Lord, to reason a little with you upon it. On Fryday I recd your letter at Firle, where you acquaint me, with Sr John's intentions, say indeed <u>you</u> must be <u>neuter</u>, think him a much better man that Page, & seem only to have some doubts about what passed formerly wth Sr R. Walpole. On Saturday comes to Bishop-

---

1. Sir John Miller's letter to Richmond announced his withdrawal from the contest.

stone your own man Mr Dear, publishes to every Body Sr John's Design of standing, seems vastly delighted with it, tells me Page has lost his Interest, that nobody of ye church but <u>Ball</u> would be for Him, that of the presbyterians he had only the parson and two others, & I think named Alderman Soane. Upon the whole that there was nothing in it & seemed a perfect agent for Sr John, that your Grace indeed was obliged to be neuter. Upon this, & from a real inclination to Sr J. Miller at 12 o'clock at night or rather one in the morning, I drank success to the Recorder, & Sr J. Miller, but was so cautious in every thing I said & did, as always with this salvo, that it did not hurt Mr Brudenel, & Dear will tell you, yt in the message I sent by Him to the Dean, I expressly told Him, I would have Him be for Sr J. Miller, if it was not <u>disagreable</u> to the D. of Richmond, & your Grace will remember, I sent my letter open to you for Sr J. Miller, which I am glad you have suppressed. I have not directly or indirectly said one word to Him any other way, that I would not tie up my hands, 'till I knew you liked I should. For a Drunken Toast, I look upon as nothing, & now my Dear Duke, I rejoice to find this ugly affair is over. we are both prodigiously obliged to Sr J. Miller. I shall write to Him to thank Him by this post, & if I can, will get Him thrust into parliament somewhere. but he must be kept up to his 1000 pds. I shall also write to Ball, to explain matters to Page & Soane. The D. of Grafton & Albemarle has two proxies each, & Ld. Delawar is not in town, so I have given yr proxy to ye D. of Montagu. We hear of Business every day, but it is very uncertain when, & what we shall have, they talk much of a personal attack on Sr Robert. Things go very well in Holland & no where else. The Dutch seem determined vigorously to join with us in support of ye P. Sanction.[1]

Ever yrs

Holles Newcastle

P.S. I hope all is well at Goodwood.

90. NEWCASTLE TO RICHMOND

Newcastle House
Feby. 7. 1740/1

My Dear Lord,

I send this Messenger on purpose to acquaint your Grace, that the personal question upon Sr Robert Walpole will certainly come on in our House on Fryday next the 13th inst. I therefore begg you would send this Messenger to my Lord Berkeley & write to Him in the most pressing terms to be in the House that Day, since Proxies upon this occasion will be of no use. I hope He will not refuse your Grace, for we are very desirous to have the appearance of all our friends upon this Occasion. We shall have Business on Tuesday, but it will not be of much consequence, being to call for papers relating to the Convention, which I believe (in the manner they call for them at least) will not be thought proper by the House, so I would not give you the trouble to come up for that, but hope you will not fail to be in Town on Thursday, the Day before our great Day. Sr R. Walpole writes to Lord Tankervile. I wish you would bring Him up with you.

I am my Dear Duke Ever most sincerely & afectly yrs

Holles Newcastle

---

1. The Pragmatic Sanction was the imperial document that specified the indivisibility of the Hapsburg dominions on the death of the Emperor Charles VI, and stated that in the absence of male heirs the succession should go to his daughters, the eldest of whom was Maria Theresa.

91. RICHMOND TO NEWCASTLE

Hampton Court
Tuesday morning [17 February 1740/1]

My Dear Lord,

I desired Mr Pelham to lett you know what pas'd between Jemmy Lumley & me yesterday; he insisted upon giveing up his place,[1] which he sayes he finds the King is determin'd to give to Bloomberg, & then sayes he very ingeniously, <u>I shall be at liberty when I have no place to vote as I please</u>. I told him, that was the same whether he had any place or no, that I had a place to, butt thought myself at liberty to do as I pleas'd notwithstanding. however he say'd that he did not give it up, upon any peake, & would lett all his acquaintance in Sussex know that he continued firm in the true Whig interest there. I told him that was kind & handsome, & that I could wish he would call upon me again on Thursday morning, which he has agreed to do between eleven & twelve, now I wish you could meet him at my house or see him between this & thursday. & advise him not to give up his place at all before the elections are over, for you may depend upon it, it will hurt our affairs in Sussex, lett the fool say what he will, they will insist upon it he is disobliged, & his people will not be so staunch as I could wish them. & ten to one (if the thing should happen) he may openly turn against us himself, so certanly it would be best to disswade him from resigning 'till the elections are over, & then lett him do what he will. 'Tis a strange Curr. you may have some influence over him, butt I am sure I have none.

Pray remember to dine with me on Thursday, with Truches, Lord Hyndford,[2] & Lord Harrington.[3] & pray thinke of six more, & lett Mr Stone write down their names, & give them to the bearer to invite them to dine with me on Thursday. would you have the Bavarian or not? tis equal to me; provideing I have butt the people <u>you</u> thinke propper. so I beg you would give your orders to the bearer, <u>Peter</u>, who has parts farr beyond your freind <u>Swiss</u>, & he will obey them.

I am my dearest Lord, most sincerely Your's
Richmond &c.

92. NEWCASTLE TO RICHMOND

Claremont
Feby 21st 1740/1

My Dear Lord,

I had the honor of your Grace's letter here this afternoon. I am extreamly sorry that my Brother & I are engaged to dine with Lord Burlington[4] next Fryday. I will endeavour to putt it off, but as that may not be practicable, I wish you could putt off

---

1. James Lumley, 1706–1766, MP for Chichester, 1729–1734, and for Arundel, 1741–1747, when he stood against Newcastle's brother in law, Sir John Shelley, resigned as Avenar and Clerk Marshall to the King, a post he had held since 1735. On the death of Lord Scarborough in 1740, he inherited the Lumley estates, and an important electoral influence in Arundel.
2. John Carmichael, 3rd. Earl of Hyndford, 1701–1767, was a diplomat. He was Envoy to the King of Prussia during the Invasion of Silesia, 1741; played an important part in the Treaty of Breslau, 1742; and was Envoy to Russia, 1744–1749. He took part in the negotiations for the Treaty of Aix-la-Chapelle.
3. William Stanhope, 1st. Earl of Harrington, 1690–1756, MP for Derby, 1715–1722, for Steyning, 1727, and for Derby again, 1727–1730, was Secretary of State for the Northern Department in succession to Townshend, 1730–1742, and again, 1744–1746, and Lord President of the Council, 1742–1745.
4. Richard Boyle, 3rd. Earl of Burlington, 1695–1753, statesman and architect. He provided a set of drawings for the rebuilding of Richmond House in Whitehall in the 1730s, but in the absence of evidence, apart from Canaletto's view from its window, it is difficult to know how far Burlington's designs were followed in the house. He also provided Richmond with drawings for the new Council House in Chichester, though the building is significantly different from Burlington's drawings.

the Charlton Meeting to some day in the week after, for I should be very unhappy, not to be able to attend you.

I was sure you would be extreamly concerned for poor Lord Cathcart. You will see in the Gazeet most of the news that came from Sr Ch: Ogle & Brig: Wentworth,[1] who has taken the Command upon Him, and as He is a very good man, & as the chief Business will probably be over, & we have not great variety of good & experienced Officers, tho' Wentworth has not seen much, it is determin'd not to send any Body over Him, but leave every thing to Vernon & Him.

We shall have a Meeting on Tuesday night about the place Bill. I wish you could be with us that night, tho' I conclude you will not. The protest is not quite so strong, as some have been, & I think it is rather the opinion of some of our most considerate friends, not to meddle with it, for fear of uniting the Opposers, who are all now broke to pieces. However, we shall probably talk about it on Tuesday night. The Men of War are all safe, & sailed for Jamaica ye 25th or 26th December; ten Transports were missing, but I think Ogle thought to meet them at St. Christopher's. They were all in good spirits, & the Land Forces in tolerable good Health. Our foreign Affairs go on, as they did, France rather more taking off the Mask every day; they desire or will grant the passage of ye Spaniards into Italy. We shall I hope soon, bring the Affair of Prussia to some point. My kindest Remembrance to ye Dukes of St Albans[2] & Kingston,[3] and all other friends.

I am every yrs

Holles Newcastle

P.S. Bring Tankey up wth you if you can.

93. RICHMOND TO NEWCASTLE

Ditton
March 27 1741

My Dear Lord,

The enclosed petition[4] was sent to me from Chichester, butt as it is in favor of the very man that Frank Whitworth,[5] say's is justly condemn'd I have nothing to say for it, only as it is subscrib'd by four Sussex freeholders I thought it right to send it to you, & I suppose you will thinke it right to send it to the Duke of Bolton.[6] I have sent them word that I will have nothing to do with it, & that I take for granted you will not neither; for that I believe the King will grant no pardon of that kind unless recommended by the Judge that try'd the man. have I answered right?

Your's most sincerely

Richmond &c.

1. Thomas Wentworth, 1693–1747, of Sunninghill in Berkshire, MP for Whitchurch, 1743–1747, succeeded Lord Cathcart in command of the land forces in the West Indies on Cathcart's death. He later served in Flanders, and accompanied Marshal Wade on his march to Newcastle in 1745. He was Ambassador in Turin, 1746–1747.
2. Charles Beauclerk, 2nd. Duke of St. Albans, 1696–1751, was Governor of Windsor Castle and Warden of Windsor Forest, 1730–1751. He was Lord Lieutenant of Berkshire, 1727–1751, and a Lord of the Bedchamber from 1738. He hunted regularly with the Charlton Hunt.
3. Evelyn Pierrepoint, 2nd. Duke of Kingston, 1711–1773, was a general, and was Colonel of Kingston's Light Horse in 1745 and 1746.
4. A petition to Newcastle and the Duke of Bolton in favour of Edward Smith of Hambledon in Hampshire, convicted at Hampshire Assizes of assaulting a servant of one of the Keepers of the Forest of East Bear.
5. Francis Whitworth, 1684–1742, MP for Minehead, 1723–1742, was Secretary for Barbados, 1719–1742, and Surveyor of Woods and Forests North and South of the Trent, 1732–1742.
6. Charles Paulet, 3rd. Duke of Bolton, 1685–1754, was the original Master of the Charlton Hunt. Richmond and the Earl of Tankerville took it over from him in 1730. He married, as his second wife, Lavinia Fenton.

I beg you would read the enclosed which I propose to send to Hibbins, I wish it dont make him fly off; & I am sure he can hurt us. butt I can not possibly tell him a lye, & I must make him some answer, which you see I have done as civilly as I can. I own I wish something could have been done for him, for I am very positive he might be of great use to us. however since nothing can be done for him 'tis butt honest to tell him so. Pray send me back the letter that I may send it, if you do not disaprove of it.

94. NEWCASTLE TO RICHMOND

Claremont
March 30th 1741

My Dear Lord,

I received yesterday your Graces letter, wth the enclosed petititon. I had before heard of the case. The fellow is so notorious a rogue that I am told the whole country desire to get rid of Him. so nothing can be done for Him, & I think it to no purpose to send the petition to the D. of Bolton. As to your letter to Mr Hibbins, I am farr from desiring to amuse Him, but I submit it to you, whether it is necessary at present, to tell Him so very directly, that we will do nothing for Him, but pray do in it just as you like.

I am my Dear Duke Ever most unalterably yrs.

Holles Newcastle

95. STONE TO RICHMOND

Claremont
April 11th 1741 Twelve at Night

My Lord,

A messenger, that came late this evening from Whitehall, brought me the Honour of your Grace's letter of yesterday's date from Godalmin; My Lord Duke receives an account from the office in the following words; "That there has been a Battle, between the Queen of Hungary's Forces, & the Prussians, in Silesia,[1] in which the latter had obtain'd a compleat victory; that Count Brown and M. Palfi were both kill'd, on the Austrian side; and Mons Shulembourgh who I think was brother to the Duchess of Kendall, on that of the Prussians.

This afternoon the Lords of the Admiralty receiv'd letters from a Lieutenant of the Lenox man of war, who had the Command of a Tender. He spoke with a Dutch ship off Folkstone on the 9th Inst., the Master of which inform'd him, that on the 4th He spoke with nine large French men of war, about 50 leagues from the Lands End, which were come from the West Indies, & steering for Brest. This account is confirm'd by a letter that I have this Day received from Mr Hall, at Dover, and I think there can be no Room to doubt but these ships were M D'Antin's Squadron returning home. I suppose we shall soon here that the Toulon squadron have been seen on their way to that Port.

There are letters from Jamaica which mention Mr Vernon's having sail'd, with the last Division of his Squadron, on the 26th of Janry; having sent out the two other Divisions some days before. My Lord Duke has a letter from Mr Wentworth dated Jan 20th which in general gives a good Account of the State of the Forces under his Command: we are in daily expectation of letters of a fresher Date. If they arrive before your returns to Town, I shall not fail to send you an immediate Account of the Contents of them.

I am with the greatest respect My Lord Your Grace's most obedient and most humble servant

Andrew Stone

---

1. Frederick the Great of Prussia had invaded Silesia on the death of the Emperor Charles VI. The Austrians launched a counter-invasion. The Battle of Mollwitz was fought on 10 April.

96. RICHMOND TO NEWCASTLE

Whitehall
30 April 1741

My Dear Lord,

When does the King go to Hanover? when do you go to Sussex? have you gott leave for me to be at Chichester, & to be excused waiting upon the King to Gravesend? & have you gott the King's leave & the sign manual for me to go to Holland in case it should be necessary this summer. short answers to these querys will extreamly oblige Your faithfull slave

Richmond &c.

97. PELHAM TO RICHMOND

Lewes
May ye 2nd 1741

My Dear Lord,

According to your Grace's commands I send you the earliest notice of our success att Lewes, Mr Pelham 156, Mr Trevor 154, Sergison 117, by which you see our majority was 39 and 37. They would have made some disturbance in the Court, but our Candidates acted with spirit and that put an end to all, and we finished the affair to the general satisfaction of our friends, and the Poll ended quietly. Jemmy's[1] election att Hastings will be the same day as yours att Chichester, which makes it impossible for him to attend your Grace, the other gentleman mentioned in your letter may possibly, tho' not probably be wanted here, they hope therefore your Grace will excuse them, unless some opposition should arise att Chichester, and then they will come att a moment's warning. There is not the least talk of an opposition for the County, your Grace will therefore do what is most easy and convenient to you. We take it for granted you will choose to meet us in the City, where we shall be on Thursday between twelve and one. James Butler meets us att eleven o'clock upon Slinden Heath, and after our kind salutations to each other he will seek refuge att Goodwood, and Jack, if he is in the country, represent his father haud passibus equis as Candidate for the County. My brother is now here, come from London yesterday, and returns thither tomorrow, will attend your Grace on Thursday to Goodwood, and from thence to the Seaford election, which now not be till the Monday following. All sucess attend you where you are, no one rejoyces more sincerely att the good state of your family, nor can be more truly and with greater respect your humble servt

H. Pelham

98. STONE TO RICHMOND

Claremont
Sunday Night May 17th 1741

My Lord,

My Lord Duke of Newcastle receiv'd this evening an account from Worminghurst, of the death of Mr Butler,[2] which happen'd this morning at eleven o'clock; and, as my lord Duke, and Mr Pelham, think it absolutely necessary, that some Resolution should be taken, without loss of time, with regard to the County Election, I am order'd to dispatch this messenger to your Grace, very early tomorrow morning, to beg, that you would be so good as to put off your going to Sussex, for a day or two, that His Grace

1. James Pelham was successfully returned for Hastings on 5 May.
2. James Butler of Worminghurst, MP for Sussex since 1728, died of smallpox on 17 May, thus necessitating a bye-election in the county seat, so delightfully described in L.P. Curtis, *Chichester Towers*, (1966).

and Mr Pelham, (who will be in town tomorrow before noon) may have an opportunity of concerting with your Grace what may be most proper to be done upon this melancholy incident.

I am to acquaint your Grace, that my Lord Duke receiv'd an Express, this afternoon, from Vice Admiral Vernon, with letters dated April 1st from Cartagena Harbour;[1] which give an account of our having taken the outworks, and fortifications of that place; and being in full possession of the Harbour. The troops were preparing to attack the town, which, it was thought, could not possibly hold out long. All the Men of War, that were in the Harbour, were sunk by the Spaniards, except Don Blas's own ship, which was taken by Mr Vernon. Poor Lord Aubrey Beauclerc,[2] and Colonel Douglas, of the Marines, were killed by cannon shot; The loss otherwise seems to have been inconsiderable. Captain Lawes of the Spence Sloop, which brought these Dispatches, says that the troops, in general, are in good health. Mr Vernon's letters are, as usual, very long: He seems extremely pleased with his success, and not to doubt of the continuance of it. My Lord Duke thought your Grace would not be displeased to have as early an account of it as possible, and as it will be necessary to consider what orders should be sent to the West Indies upon this event, his Grace hopes, that may be an additional motive with your Grace to defer your journey to Goodwood for a few days.

I am with the greatest respect My Lord Your Grace's Most obedient and most humble servant

Andrew Stone

P.S. Captain Knowles is made Governor of Bocca Chica Castle.[3]

99. STONE TO RICHMOND

Whitehall
June 11th 1741

My Lord,

The occasion of my giving your Grace this trouble is to acquaint you with the state of the affair of the Riding Officer for the Port of Chichester: The Person, recommended by your Grace for the Post, was, immediately upon the vacancy, appointed by the Lords of the Treasury, to succeed to it. Several days after this, Mr Colebrooke wrote to my Lord, Duke of Newcastle, & Mr Pelham, to desire, they would recommend a friend of his, whom they formerly promised. My Lord Duke, not knowing any thing of what had pass'd, accordingly did so; and, it not being remember'd at the Treasury, that the vacancy was already filled up, Mr Colebrookes friend was appointed. But, as soon as the case was understood, care was taken to set it right, and the Person whom your Grace recommended is left (as he ought to be), in quiet possession of the Place; and I must do Mr Colebrooke the justice, to acquaint your Grace, that he most readily withdrew his pretensions when he heard that it was your Grace's recommendation, that took place of his.

I am with the greatest respect My Lord Your Grace's most obedient and most humble servant

Andrew Stone

My Lord Duke orders me to make his compliments to your Grace, and hopes you will excuse his not writing himself.

There is no news from the West Indies and nothing material from any other parts.

---

1. The assault on Cartagena, in Colombia, was chosen as the next point of attacking the Spaniards by the Jamaican Council of War. The early optimistic reports were not fulfilled.
2. Lord Aubrey Beauclerk, 1710–1741, was killed in the attack on Bocca Chica.
3. Bocca Chica Castle in the Dominican Republic.

100. RICHMOND TO NEWCASTLE

Goodwood
14 June 1741

Ten thousand thankes to you My Dear Lord for the very kind & obligeing letter you was so good as to write to me. Sr John Miller is now with me, & in a great fuss he is, for he meets with strong & unexpected difficultys at home about his comeing into Parliament, I have advised him to take some time to consider of it. I own I should be very sorry that he should at last refuse it, 'tho he sayes at all events he will not if it is insisted upon, because he has given his word, butt in that case to be sure wee must excuse him, if he desires it. & you know it is only upon his own account that I would now have him stick to it. for if he should not wee have always Jack Butler ready for it. I am obliged to you for giveing way to my rideing officer at Pagham, which certanly belongs to Chichester where I always have recommended, & where I hope you will always thinke it is right for me to recommend. Sergison[1] was expected last night at Westdean,[2] & 'tis beleived he will go to a Great Crickett Match in Stansted Parke to morrow between Slyndon, & Portsmouth.[3] if he does I'l face him there with fifty staunch freeholders all engaged to us. & I hope Mr Moodie will help us. Lisbon Peckham is very busy in the Manhood,[4] & Dear is in London, tho he is expected here to morrow. The Bishop should be wrot to, to order his people to be a little more vigilant. I'l speake to Dear as soon as he comes to go directly into the Manhood.
    I am My dear Lord, Your Grace's ever faithfull
                                                        Richmond &c.

I have just now a certain account that Sergison is at Westdean, & Sr John Peachy askeing votes with him.

101. RICHMOND TO NEWCASTLE

Goodwood
16 June 1741

My Dear Lord,
    Your Grace's letters are so kind that I cant help answering them every post, so if you are troubled too often 'tis you own fault. Sr John Chardin[5] would say, why will you be so kind?
    I have wrote to the Duke of Dorsett[6] to know if Ld Middlesex[7] will be here on the 10th July to go his Western Circuit before the Lewis Races, or on the 25th which will be after them 'twill be the same to me.

---

1. Thomas Sergison, 1701–1766, later MP for Lewes, 1747–1766, had been put up by his supporters to oppose Richmond and Newcastle's candidate for the county bye-election, and was now canvassing the western half of the county.
2. West Dean was the seat of Sir John Peachey, one of the Opposition gentry.
3. Slindon v. Portsmouth at Stansted Park on 15 June 1741. See Timothy J. McCann, 'Cricket and the Sussex County Bye-Election of 1741', in *Sussex Archaeological Collections*, vol.114, (1976), pp.121–125, for the importance of cricket in the campaign.
4. The Hundred of Manhood includes the parishes of Birdham, Earnley, West Itchenor, Selsey, Sidlesham and East and West Wittering.
5. Sir John Chardin, 1643–1713, traveller and author.
6. Lionel Sackville, 1st. Duke of Dorset, 1688–1765, had an important interest in the eastern half of the county. He was Lord Lieutenant of Ireland, 1730–1737, and again, 1750–1755; Lord President of the Council, 1745; and Master of the Horse, 1755–1757. For much of his life he was Constable of Dover Castle, and Lord Warden of the Cinque Ports.
7. Charles Sackville, Earl of Middlesex, 1711–1769, eldest son of the Duke of Dorset, was MP for East Grinstead, 1734–1742, and again, 1761–1765, for Sussex, 1742–1747, and for Old Sarum, 1747–1754. He was Newcastle's candidate for the bye-election. He was a Lord of the Treasury, 1743–1747, and Master of the Horse to the Prince of Wales, 1747–1751.

Sergison was at the Cricket Match attended by Lisbon Peckham, old Eastgate the hatter, Ludgater & two or three more of the Chichester Torys. he did not venture to aske a vote, nor could he have gott one I do really beleive. Tanky was there ready to puff his cheeks at him, butt he never appear'd before us, butt quietly stole away, as soon as wee came. all our freinds seem'd mighty hearty, & were in great spirits espetially as Slyndon beat Portsmouth, & had nine men to go in. the Duke of Somersets Chaplain[1] told Jemmy Bramston[2] this morning that he was sure the Duke would be neuter. I am glad to hear every thing goes so extraordinary well in Hastins Rape. wee shant do quite so well here, butt I beleive better than ever 'tho, which will be pretty well you know. Aprospos to my Lord Cheif Justice Wills,[3] I beg you would be so good as to appoint Smith Consul, before you come to Lewis, else the hottheaded old fellow will throw more rubs in the way, & may make it more difficult for you, so I earnestly desire it of you my dear Lord, which I assure you I should not do, had I not pas'd my word upon your promis, which upon my word I am very sorry for, & as for the form, I cant butt thinke its a mighty easy matter for Your Grace to appoint Smith Consul by letter; without takeing any notice of the Republick. I beg therefore that you would do it now & gett rid at once, of my importunity which I am sorry for tho not asham'd of, & the passionate old judge will have time to cool before the assizes. I beg pardon, & am My Dear Lord, for ever & unalterably yours

Richmond &c.

Your Queen is your servant.
ten thousand thankes to you & my freind Mr Stone for your news. I am asham'd to give him so much trouble

102. RICHMOND TO STONE

Goodwood
June: 19: 1741

Dear Sir,

I am most extreamly obliged to you for the news you sent me. I hope it was only in obedience to the Duke of Newcastle that you gave yourself so much trouble, & not from imagining that I could be so unreasonable as to expect it from you, who I know have so much business of farr greater consequence upon your hands. however as I took the liberty to desire you to write to me incase you had any news from Carthagena I imagine I shall hear from you to night, for I know a Sloop is arrived from thence at Portsmouth, butt by their secrecy there I am sadly afraid there is no good news. I must also thanke you for the explanation of the rideing officers affair, in which I am sure I have all the reason in the world to be satisfy'd, espetially as my man has gott the thing.

I must beg one favor more of you which is gett the Duke of Newcastle's leave for you to write once more to Governor Shirley[4] to recommend Sr Thomas Prendergast affair to him, for altho two terms of different payments are elaps'd he has heard nothing from thence of any sort.

I am dear Sir, Your faithfull humble servant
Richmond &c.

---

1. Possibly the Rev. Thomas Frampton, tutor at Petworth in the time of the Proud Duke, who held livings in Salisbury Diocese, and died in 1753
2. James Bramston, 1694–1744, poet and Vicar of Harting and Lurgashall, was one of the Goodwood circle. Some manuscript verse of his survives in Richmond's papers. His best known works were, *The Art of Politics*, (1729), and *The Man of Taste*, (1733).
3. John Willes, 1685–1761, MP for Launceston, 1724–1726, for Weymouth and Melcombe Regis, 1726–1727, and for West Looe, 1727–1737, was Lord Chief Justice, 1737–1761.
4. William Shirley, 1694–1771, was Governor of Massachusetts, 1741–1756, and of the Bahamas, 1759–1770.

My sincere service to the Duke of Newcastle who I shall not trouble with a letter this post. Mr Sergison is now about the parishes in this neighbourhood, butt Buckner has been before him, & I am very sure he will meet with ten negatives to one promis, except only at Midhurst & West Dean, where to be sure he must have a very great majority by Sr John Peachy's interest. I dont know whether His Grace will like it, butt I fear Lord Middlesex will poll 30 more at Chichester than even Mr Pelham did; he poll'd 119. there are 201 freeholders now in the Citty, & I can not possibly see above 40 that will vote for Sergison.

103.   STONE TO RICHMOND

Whitehall
June 20th 1741

My Lord,
    Last night, Mr. Wentworth's Packet was brought from Portsmouth. There is only one Letter from Him, (and that a short one) dated in Cartagene Harbour, April 26th. He gives an Account of their Landing, on the 5th of that Month, that He advanced with 1500 Men, through a long narrow Defile in a Wood. Upon coming out of the Defile, He was opposed by a Body of 600 Men, but advanced upon them, and obliged them to retire with Precipitation. His Camp was form'd within a Mile of the Castle of St Lazar; the same Day, & the following, the rest of the Troops landed, making, in the whole, about 4000 Men; But unfortunately they were obliged to lie upon their Arms, three Nights, for want of Tents, which must have been one great Occasion of the Sickness, that so soon got amongst the Men. Before they proceeded any further, it was thought absolutely necessary to make themselves Masters of the Castle of St Lazar. It was at first intended to raise a Canon Battery; But as the Men grew every day more & more sickly, and the Rainy Season coming on; and as they had lost most of their Engineers, it was at last Resolved at a Council of War to storm the Fort; which was accordingly attempted on the 9th, at Break of Day.
    The Attack was made by 1200 Men, under the Command of Brigr Guise,[1] in two different Places; But, (as Mr Wentworth says) not directly in the Places where it was intended. The Grenadiers immediately enter'd the Enemy's Works; But, not being properly sustain'd, on one of the Attacks, by the Officer, who commanded the Grenadiers; and, on the other Col Grant being mortally wounded, the most forward of them were almost all kill'd; and they were at last obliged to retire, with the Loss of about 640 Men, (Officers included,) either kill'd, or wounded. The American Troops had some share in this Attack; but gained no credit by their Behaviour on this Occasion.
    After this, the Sickness increased so much, amongst the Troops, that, by the 15th, near 500 Men sicken'd, or died; amongst the former, were almost all the principal Officers of the Army. Mr. Wentworth called a Council of War, who came to a Resolution to lay before the Admiral the bad Condition they were in, and that they could proceed no further if he could not furnish them with a considerable Number of Men; and, as that could not be done, it was Resolved, at a General Council of War of Sea & Land Officers, to reimbark the Remainder of the Troops, which was accordingly done on the 16th. Mr. Wentworth adds, that, since their embarking, the Sickness had not only increased amongst the Troops but spread in the Fleet; that Colonels Blakeney, Wolfe, Lowther, Wyngard & Gooch, were not able to do much Service, from their ill State of Health; and that Cols Moreton, & Grant were dead; as were also Lieutent Colonels Thompson, Blagrave, Johnston, & Harding, (The two last were of the

---

1.   John Guise, died 1765, brigadier and colonel commanding the 6th. foot at Cartagena. He became a General in 1762.

American Regiments), Major Dawson, and several other Officers of inferior Rank. Brigr Wentworth says that the Troops are so shatter'd, that He is persuaded, it would be difficult to find a thousand Men, fit to land against an Enemy, (tho' the Returns do not make the Number of the kill'd, sick, & wounded, very considerable), and that He is persuaded the Sickly Season, upon which they were then only entering, would make a great Havock amongst the Officers, & Soldiers, remaining.

This is the melancholy Account, that Mr. Wentworth gives of the Condition of the Troops under His Command; He seems so much dispirited, that I am almost tempted to hope, He represents things in the very worst Light, they can be seen in. Mr. Vernon, on the contrary, appears to be less affected with the Disappointment, than could be imagined; He says nothing, in his Dispatch, of Mr. Wentworth's Conduct; But from the Letters & Papers that pass'd between them, before & after the fatal Attack of St. Lazar, it is very plain, that He had but an indifferent Opinion of it. He complains from the very Beginning, of Mr. Wentworth's Delays, and tells him, that he is of Opinion, the Castle of St. Lazar might be taken by surprise; which probably was a great Inducement to Mr. Wentworth, to hazard that Attack; which (whatever might have been the Event, if He had proceeded in another manner) was certainly the immediate Cause of the Miscarriage of the Expedition, and, (it is to be fear'd, in the Consequences) of the Ruin of the Army.

I am extremely concerned to be obliged to send your Grace so disagreable an Account as this must be; But as I had your Command to send you the particulars of this most unfortunate Affair, I have endeavoured to do it, in the best Manner that the very great Hurry of Business would permit me.

I am with the greatest Respect My Lord Your Grace's most obedient & most humble servant

Andrew Stone

104. RICHMOND TO NEWCASTLE

Goodwood
June: 21: 1741

My Dear Lord,

I am vex'd to a degree that I can't express upon our misfortune in the West Indias. I hope to hear the particulars of it from somebody this post. butt am extreamly sorry to find at least by the Portsmouth tittletatle that Vernon & Wentworth disagree & they one & all there throw the whole blame upon Wentworth, butt whether he is to blame or no, if he is not well with Vernon, I am very clearly of opinion that Wentworth should be recal'd, & some good officer sent in his place, Legonier,[1] Hawley, or in short somebody above Guises rank, & that is fitt to command, ought to go. I would also draught one thousand only at present & send them imediately to reinforce those corps, butt then, I thinke a good body of men, I mean six more regiments should be raised to replace six already rais'd that I would send to them. two of which should be old corps from Ireland with good officers to command them, such as Irwin's & Bligh's, & those two regiments to be replaced by two of the new ones from hence. I beg pardon for takeing upon me to form schemes, butt a fools bolt is soon shot, & you give me leave to speake my opinion such as it is to you, & I do verily thinke this Nation undone if we dont repair this misfortune by giveing a great stroke in the West indias, as soon as possible. you will say to me why dont you come up & give your opinion at Whitehall, I will certanly be in town on Sunday, butt I know very well of how very little weight my

---

1. John Ligonier, 1680- 1770, MP for Bath, 1748–1763, had a long military career, joining the army in 1702. He was captured at Lauffeld; commanded the British foot at Fontenoy, and was Commander-in-Chief in the Austrian Netherlands, 1746–1747.

opinion is at that bord. I see how bad it is that the officers abroad should have disputes & I am sure that disputes amongst the Kinges servants at home would be fatal to His Government, which stops my mouth upon several ocasions; for I have nothing so much at heart as the Kings service because I am sure this Country is undone if that cant be cary'd on. I need not say any more, you know my meaning, & no mortal liveing butt yourself knows these my sentiments for the reasons I have given you. I beg pardon for troubleing you with so much serious stuff. I am melancholy but not dejected. Our misfortune is a great one, butt I am very sure it can be repair'd, & if your advice is follow'd I dare swear it will, forgive me for troubling you so much & beleive, my dear Lord, Your ever faithfull & most affect humble servant,

Richmond &c.

every thing here goes on very well.

105. RICHMOND TO NEWCASTLE

Goodwood
June: 26; 1741

My Dear Lord,
     I am not vain enough to say I am glad you thinke as I do, butt I may with modesty say that I am very happy that my thoughts agree so well with yours, tho I can hardly thinke four regiments are enough upon this ocassion. I shall have the pleasure of seeing your Grace next tuesday, & could wish that you would appoint any time on Tuesday Wednesday or Thursday, & any place, where your Grace, the Duke of Dorset, Mr Pelham & my self may meet to settle finally my Lord Middlesex's western tour.[1] Sergison has been at every Freeholders house at Chichester & entertain'd his freinds at the Dolphin,[2] they say they had thirty, butt wee can make out butt 27, of which only 23 were Chichester Freeholders. I am sure he wont poll 40, out of the 203, that are there, which will be the greatest majority wee ever had there; wee shall have above thirty that never voted for us before, & I can find butt two that wee have lost, & those very scrub fellows.
     I am my Dear Lord, Your Graces ever faithfull & most sincerely affectionate
Richmond &c.

Mr Sergison was very kindly entertain'd by that good Whig, Mr Joliff[3] of Petersfield. Wee are all going to dine with Sr Ian, whose encreases in zeal every day but absolutely declines comeing in to parliament. surely wee can have no difficulty with the Duke of Dorset. I'l mention nothing of it, butt Sr Ian has told it himself to several people, so pray settle it for Jack Butler with the Duke of Dorset as soon as you can.

106. RICHMOND TO NEWCASTLE

Goodwood
Wed: 15: July 1741

My Dear Lord,
     In the first place I shall begin regularly at Petworth, where I dined with the Duke of Somerset, who was very particularly civil to me butt stiff in his resollutions of being for neither Middlesex nor Sergison, alltho all the country say he is for the latter, however

---

1. The Earl of Middlesex's itinerary is detailed in a letter Richmond wrote to the Earl of Dorset, 4 July 1741. Kent Archives Office, Sackville Ms. U269 c.150/10.
2. The Dolphin Inn in West Street, Chichester.
3. John Jolliffe, 1697–1771, MP for Petersfield, 1741–1754, and again, 1761–1768, bought the Manor of Petersfield from Edward Gibbon in 1739. In 1738 he was Receiver General of the Duchy of Lancaster.

he assured me he was not. after dinner wee saw about 100 freeholders in the town, butt a vast many kept away by the Duke of Somerset's desire. wee find by Ward the messenger that both Jewks's, Nash,[1] & Mittford, are displeased with my Lord Middlesex's not staying there longer, which was my fault if anybodys, butt Mr Pelham particularly desired me not to stay with John Jewks, because of his bad health. for I had first design'd to have layn there. On Munday, wee had a very poor meeting here, not half as many as when you was here. there were just 253 freeholders that promis'd their votes. The reasons for the thinness of this meeting were, a Great Cricket Match at Green,[2] the Sessions, at Horsham, & the assizes at Winchester all happening upon that day which was very unlucky for me, else I am very sure I should have had 100 more, & almost double that number that have absollutely promis'd me. at Chichester also yesterday wee had a very bad meeting, not above 100 altho I have had 156 absollute promises that may be depended on. wee had a good deal of Sergison among the mob at night butt I know that signifys nothing there for I am still sure he can not possibly have 40, out of the 204, that are there. you know our root & where wee go, & now Port Down fair will keep away a great many from Tanky, & Jemmy Lumley, & Sr Ian. & Magdalen Hill fair will also hinder numbers of people from comeing to the assizes & races at Lewis. I have done all I can butt very few will go; my hand shakes & I am not sober at this time so excuse both what I have write & what I shall write. in the main I dont find that Sergison getts upon us at all; butt wee certanly have not seen so many people as I could have wish'd, which has fretted me not a little, adieu my Dear Ld, every body here is much your humble servants, butt none liveing more so than your for ever attach'd

Richmond &c.

107. NEWCASTLE TO RICHMOND

Bishopstone
July 25th 1741

My Dear Lord,

I am very sorry to acquaint your Grace that the melancholy News we heard yesterday, of the Death of poor Lord Augustus,[3] was confirmed this morning by a Messenger, who brought me an Account of what was come from Admiral Vernon. I send you enclosed, all that Mr Vernon says upon that unhappy subject, & do most sincerely condole with you, upon a Loss which is not only very great to those whom I esteem & love, but is indeed a great one to His King & Country. If poor Lady Fitzroy is at Goodwood, I begg you would say what is proper to Her from me. There is not one Word from Mr Wentworth, but I find from Vernon, that they are determined not to be idle, & that they to go about the 10th of last June, to attack St Iago de Cuba[4]. They had their Council of War at Govr Trelawney's[5] in which they all agreed but Trelawney, who was for going to Panama, & not to St Iago de Cuba. They have taken a Spanish Ship, with Letters of the greatest importance in which it appears, that D'Antin had not only Orders to join the Spaniards, and assist them in falling upon us, but even to assist in making an attempt upon Jamaica. This discovery may be of some service. The Sickness wch had been very bad, was abated, the great Ships are coming

---

1. Probably Gawen Harris Nash of Petworth, a correspondent of Newcastle.
2. A Cricket Match at Wisborough Green on 13 July 1741.
3. Lord Augustus Fitzroy, 1716–1741, MP for Thetford, 1739–1741, died 28 May 1741 of a disease contracted at Cartagena.
4. Santiago de Cuba was selected as the next target of the British forces in the West Indies at a meeting in Jamaica on 26 May 1741.
5. Edward Trelawny, 1699–1754, MP. for West Looe, 1724–1732, was Governor of Jamaica, 1738–1752.

home, & there is a great want of Seamen, & reinforcements of both sorts. Thus much for Vernon. I am sorry I could not stay to attend you longer at ye Cricket Match, tho' I hear you went away immediately. My Brother would go. I had 15 long miles home, & if I had once got in, I should perhaps have been more unwilling to go afterwards. The Enemy went away immediately. I saw a Letter from Arundel, that the D. of Somerset's Man had been with all the Freeholders there, so I find His Grace would engage all the West, but thank God, that is not in His power.

I am my Dear Duke Ever yrs

Holles Newcastle

P.S. My compliments to ye Ds of Rd Paunceford, Bodens[1] ambo &c.

108.   STONE TO RICHMOND

Whitehall
July 28th 1741

My Lord,
I should not have fail'd sending your Grace, by Saturday's Post, an Account of the News we had received from the West Indies, if I had not imagined, that the Messenger, I sent to my Lord Duke of Newcastle on Friday last, would have found your Grace at Bishopstone.

The Account, published in the Gazette, and from thence transfer'd into the other Papers, contains very near all, that is material in Mr. Vernon's Letters; except that the Expedition, they were going upon, (and which Mr. Vernon hoped to be ready for about the Middle of June), was intended against St Iago de Cuba. This Resolution was taken at a private Council of War, held at Mr. Trelawny's House at Jamaica, in which Mr. Vernon, Mr. Wentworth, Sr Ch. Ogle, & Mr. Guise, were unanimous; but Governor Trelawny dissented.

Your Grace will be surprised to hear, that there are no Letters received by this Express from Mr. Wentworth; so that we should be entirely ignorant of the Conditions of the Land Forces, were it not for Lord Elibank,[2] who is returned to England. His Lordship reports, that there are about 1500, or 2,000 Men, fit for Service.

Mr. Vernon is sending home the seven 80 Gun Ships, that are not sheath'd; and about four others. Great Numbers of Seamen, as well as Soldiers, have been lost by Sickness; But Mr. Vernon says that it was abated; and that He hoped the Sick Men were upon the Recovery.

It is generally reported, that Colonel Daniel is dead; and that Cottrel has the Regiment; But I cannot answer for the Truth of it.

We are in daily expectation of Letters from Mr. Wentworth; which it is supposed, are coming by the Torrington, that sail'd from Jamaica about the same time as the Kennington.

All out letters from France, Holland, & Germany, are full of the Military Preparations of France; which, it is confidently reported, will have very soon four Armies on Foot,: and the Accommodation between the Courts of Vienna, & Berlin,[3] seems almost desperate.

1. Mr. Justice Bodens, a Goodwood regular, versifier and bon viveur. With Samuel Chandler he compiled a volume of verse in the Goodwood Archives. In another volume, he is described as, 'Bodens genteel good natur'd merry wise and fat'. Another poem in the collection includes the lines,
"When Bodens shall a Haricot refuse
And fast himself to feed a hungry muse
When Ducal Dinners he shall once neglect
And a hot pastry treat with cold respect."
2. Patrick Murray, 5th. Lord Elibank, 1703–1778, advocate and lieutenant colonel in the army. His account of the attempt on Cartagena is in the Hardwicke Papers (B.L. Add. Ms. 35,898.)
3. Maria Theresa was induced by Walpole to make a truce with Prussia in July 1741.

I am with the greatest Respect My Lord, your Graces most obedient & most humble servt

Andrew Stone

P.S. I will be sure to take care of the petition your Grace sent me.

109. RICHMOND TO NEWCASTLE

Goodwood
July: 29: 1741

My Dear Lord,

I received your Grace's most obliging letter from Bishopstone, & am very sorry to find that the bad news wee heard of poor Lord Augustus's death is butt too true. I most sincerely pitty the Duke of Grafton. I find as your Grace sayes that the Duke of Somersett is sending to every body, in the West; mais je lui couperai l'herbe sous la pied, if I can, & I dont doubt butt I shall in some degree. I must now tell you that I had a most ridiculous visit yesterday from Sr John Peachy, in the afternoon. butt not one word of polliticks, which I carefully avoided, for fear of the beasts comeing out with some impertinence. wee toasted Ladys only, Mrs Trevor was myne, butt he fitted me I assure, you with toasting of my Lady Bishop. I design to return the agreeable visit in a day or two.

Have you heard that Sergison treated his people the night of the Crickett Match at Portslade[1] & that there was a bloody Battle between them & Slyndenors? butt the last came off victorious tho with some broken heads. enclosed are a couple of petitions that I beg may be delivered to the Treasury. I assure you thay are of consequence to the interest, else I should not presume to send them to you. so I hope you'l pardon the liberty I take, & order them to be lay'd before the treasury, & lett Mr Stone lett me know the answers. The beautifull Countess of Pembroke[2] is just arrived, so I must have done & am my Dear Lord, most truely & sincerely Yours

Richmond &c.

The intelligence that is taken surely must be of great use. Your Queen as you call her is very much your humble servant.

110. STONE TO RICHMOND

Claremont
August 1st 1741

My Lord,

My Lord Duke of Newcastle has received the honour of your Grace's letter, inclosing two Petitions to the Lords of the Treasury, which his Grace orders me to assure you, He will take the best care of, He is able; tho' He cannot pretend to answer for the success they will meet with.

His Grace also directs me to acquaint you, that the final Resolution will probably be taken, by the Lords Justices, either on Tuesday, or Thursday next, and the Orders given, with regard to the Reinforcement, which is proposed to be sent to the West Indies. My Lord Duke thought it proper to give your Grace this Notice, in case you should be disposed to be present at the meeting of the Lords Justices, when this matter comes finally under consideration.

---

1. Slindon v. Portslade at Portslade, 28 July 1741. The Cricket Match is described in letters from Sir William Gage to Newcastle (B.L. Add. Ms. 32,697 f.388.)
2. Mary, Countess of Pembroke, was the daughter of Richard, 5th. Viscount Fitzwilliam, and Frances, daughter of Sir John Shelley.

My Lord Duke bids me tell your Grace, that things abroad continue much in the same situation, (which is not the most agreable one), that they have lately been in.

I am with the greatest respect My Lord Your Grace's most obedient and most humble servant

Andrew Stone

111. RICHMOND TO NEWCASTLE

Goodwood
Aug: 4: 1741

My Dear Lord,

I only trouble your Grace with this to send you the enclosed petition[1] which was sent me by Mr Leeves, & sign'd by him & several other Arundell freeholders. I know nothing of the man myself, butt I find Leeves presses it very hard, so I could not do less than send it to you. I have just obtain'd the same thing for a Chichester man, also a freeholder, so I could not apply for it myself, else I should not have troubled your Grace about it. I am most truely & affectionately, my dear Lord,

Your faithfull humble servant,

Richmond &c.

every thing is very quiet hereabouts. Sr Cecyl Bishop dined with my Lady Derby to day. for no good to be sure, butt she is safe.

112. RICHMOND TO NEWCASTLE

Goodwood
Aug. 11th. 1741

My Dear Lord,

Nothing butt the Duchess of Richmond's illness would have hinder'd me being in town this week. however I will certanly be at the Cock Pitt on Tuesday next. I wish I could dine with you at Mr. Stones or any where that day. however If I'm troublesome I can dine at Whites. I can not express the distress I have been in for your poor Queen was most dangerously ill for two dayes, however she is now thanke God, as well as possible in her condtion, & gives her service to you. The Bishop was here yesterday, & told me a secret in which he begs his name may not be mention'd, which I hope your grace will observe, he sayes that the Duke of Somersett press'd Sr Cecil to stand & offer'd to be at the whole expense himself. butt he declining it, & Sergison sending the Duke word that he only stood to support the Duke of Somersett's interest, & to oppose yours, & as a proof of it he was willing to give it up to any body His Grace would desire, which won the old fools vain heart, & twas upon that he declared imediately for Sergison. This the Bishop sayes he knows to be true. butt begs his name may not be mention'd.

I wish you would back Jack Butler's request to Sr Charles Wager.

I am My Dear Lord, Your Graces ever faithfull & affectte servant

Richmond &c.

113. RICHMOND TO NEWCASTLE

Goodwood
Sunday. Aug: 23d: 1741

My Dear Lord,

Genll Hawley is now with me, & I have had a great deal of discourse with him, & he

---

1. A Petition to Richmond from Thomas Briggs of Arundel, an unemployed joiner, requesting a place as joiner in Portsmouth Dockyard.

speaks just in the same handsome manner he writ, that he has no notion of hesitateing a moment where he shall go if it is for the Kings service, butt he still insists upon it that it is not for the Kings service to send him upon this great command for the reasons he mentions in his letter to me which your Grace saw. Then he owns (butt that is only in his private conversation with me) that he should dislike it extreamly, firstly from the great uncertainty of getting any honor, & the great danger of loosing it by ill success which may not be his fault, secondly the difficulty that there must be in Agreeing with Mr. Vernon, & the impossibility of doing anything right in concert with Mr. Wentworth; in short I find he thinkes of Mr. Wentworth as wee all do. I then consulted with him who would be a propper person to send, & he is clearly of opinion that there are butt three. Clayton,[1] Hargrave,[2] & Dalzeel.[3] the two first you know can not go, as for the latter he acknowledges that the man is an officer, & has seen more than most of them; butt as to his private caracter he entirely agrees with the generall voice of mankind he also added as to himself that he had not the least aprehension of any dangers of sickness, sea, or anything else, that he would as soon go to the West Indias as to any other part of the world, & should have no difficultys butt the publick one he has mention'd in his letter to me, & the private ones I have now communicated to your Grace, which as they are in private conversation to me he hopes they may be kept so. he also hopes that the excuse he has made may not hurt him with the King, or in any bodys opinion. I have ventured to assure him that the Lords Justices seemd perfectly satisfy'd with it, & that in my own opinion the King would not be displeas'd at it; I did not see why the King should know anything of it butt if he did I did not see why he should dislike it; at least if he did know it I hoped & beleived it would be represented in a right light to his Majesty, as to be sure it ought to be in justice to Mr. Hawley. I also ask'd his opinion of Sinclair,[4] he sayes he is certanly a good officer in his sphere, a brave man, & always served in the foot, butt that he never served butt as a Captain. This is the substance of our discourse, & I thought it right to acquaint your Grace with it. & am my Dear Lord for ever & most sincerely Your's

Richmond &c.

Have you never heard that Dalzeel's personal courage has been call'd in question very much? I have. butt this is only between you & I: I should not chuse to fight with any body, much less with an old weatherbeaten Scotch man, 'tho if what I've heard is true I should be safe. lett this letter be dockitted <u>most private</u> or what is safer wipe your a..e with it.

114. PELHAM TO RICHMOND

Claremont
Augt 29, 1741

My Dear Lord,

Your Grace will easily excuse my not answering your letter, which I received on Wednesday, when I tell you that I have been kept here ever since that day, in the most melancholy scituation of seeing the Dutchesse of Newcastle in great danger, and my Brother absolutely dispairing of her life 'till yesterday morning. She has been attended

---

1. Brigadier General Jasper Clayton, had been Commander of land forces in the Mediterranean, 1731, and Lieutenant Governor of Gibraltar.
2. Lieutenant General William Hargrave.
3. General Robert Dalzell, 1662–1758, had fought as Lieutenant Colonel under the Duke of Marlborough. He was Commander of the forces in North Britain, 1732.
4. Major General James St. Clair, 1668–1762, MP for Dysart Burghs, 1722–1734, and again, 1747–1754, for Sutherland, 1736–1747, and for Fifeshire, 1754–1762, served under Cumberland in Flanders, and was Commander-in-Chief of the expedition against Canada in 1746.

by Mead,[1] Broxholme[2] and Wilmot;[3] the two former went to London this day, but the latter is here still. Her complaint has been a fever with a violent inflamation in her bowels; I don't think the symptoms were ever of the most desperate kind, but the long continuance of her disorder, and nothing giving a turn to the distemper 'till the third or fourth bleeding put us all into frights, and made His Grace next to a distracted man. This day we have had ups and downs, but upon the whole Dr Wilmot thinks the disease is got the better of, and that, without some unforseen accident, she will certainly do well. I am the longer upon this subject, knowing your Grace's good nature, and particular concern for whatever affects the Duke of Newcastle. He desires me to make you his best compliments, and as you did design to call here on Monday, has directed me to acquaint your Grace wth the circumstances of his family. I am a well wisher to our friend Sam: Chandler;[4] Mr. Maunsher[5] has no obligations to me, but is almost every post desiring to have one, If it is not disagreable to Sr Charles I will write to him with all my heart, and if it is, your Grace would not have me. I hope to have the honour of seeing your Grace in Town next Tuesday. If I do, I will or will not write that post as your Grace shall direct. I beg my compliments to the Dutchesse of Richmond and service to all friends

I am my Dear Lord Your Grace's most obedient, humble servt

H. Pelham

115. PELHAM TO RICHMOND

Whitehall
Sep 3rd 1741

My Dear Lord,

I have the pleasure, according to your Grace's commands, to acquaint you that the Dutchesse of Newcastle continues in as good a way as can be expected; she had some small return of her disorder yesterday morning, but it went off without any ill consequences, and the Dr thinks she is rather the better for it. I design therefore to set out tomorrow morning for Sr Robert Walpole's, and shall not be back unless called for, in ten days. I spoke to Sr Charles, who has some expedient to propose for our friend Sam: Chandler tho' he tells me the governing people of Portsmouth are not so fond him, as they ought to be. I have a small piece of good news to tell you, as you are a good natural man, that poor Harry, after having been given over to a violent fever, is in a mending way and likely to do well. Publick affairs are in the same state of disagreableness you left 'em. I hope Lady Dutchesse and all your Grace's family are well.

I am with great respect Your Graces most obedient servt

H. Pelham

116. RICHMOND TO NEWCASTLE

Godalming
Septr: 7th: 1741

My Dear Lord,

As I most sincerely hope the Duchess of Newcastle is perfectly recover'd, I should be

1. Richard Mead, 1673–1754, was Physician to King George II from 1727.
2. Noel Broxholme, 1689–1748, was a physician who practiced in London. He was Radcliffe travelling fellow in 1715.
3. Sir Edward Wilmot, 1693–1786, was Physician General to the Army in 1740; later he was Physician to Frederick, Prince of Wales, and to King George II.
4. Samuel Chandler was an attorney with a penchant for light verse, and the author of the Goodwood Miscellany 1744. He was one of the Goodwood circle and acted as Richmond's election agent. He was an Alderman of Portsmouth; was Mayor of the City in 1746; and a Justice and Deputy Mayor in 1750.
5. John Mounsher, 1692–1762, one of a large family, many of whom sat on Portsmouth Corporation, was a rope-maker, a postman and a Turnpike Commissioner. Admitted to the Corporation in 1728, he became an Alderman in 1732.

glad to waite upon your Grace to night at Clairmont, butt I hope, if you have any particular business or company, that would make myne the least troublesome, you would be so good, as to send my friend Hallobone to Cobham to lett me know it; that I may go on to London. I have nobody with me butt Swiny;[1] who if I go to Claremont I will leave at Cobham unless you command to the contrary, & I can't be with you till late, because I shall see a Crickett Match I have made of poor little Slyndon, against almost your whole County of Surry, it is to be play'd at the basin upon Merroe down.[2] I shall expect you commands at Cobham, & am My Dear Lord for ever Your's
Richmond &c.

117.   RICHMOND TO NEWCASTLE

[September 8 1741]

My Dear Lord,
   I am extreamly sorry to hear the Duchess is not so perfectly recover'd as I wish'd. butt am very truely obliged to you for stopping me, for it would have been troublesome to you, & it can never be agreeable to me to see you in concern being for ever Your's
Richmond &c.

I'l with pleasure attend you to morrow at Mr. Stones
Wee have beat Surrey almost in one innings.

118.   RICHMOND TO NEWCASTLE

Septr 11th 1741

My Dear Lord,
   as I am going to Goodwood, & shall see Hibbins, I beg you will tell me whether you'l recommend him to the Duke of Devonshire or no. the man has certanly some merit with us for he has bestir'd himself, & has really done service both in the last election & this: & I really never heard any farther harm of the man, than that he was a little troublesome with his Law, butt he wont make the worse person for that. I would write myself to the Duke of Devonshire, butt that his Grace has difficultys & I thinke quere ones about giving this Government of Gallway to Sr Tho. Prendergast, altho Sr Robert express'd himself so kindly about it; he sayes he thinkes it should be an officer, because of so many papist's being there, now I would fain know if an officer who can't reside there, would do better than Sr Thomas, who if he had it would almost always live there, his house & estate being so near Gallway. you see therefore 'till this is clear'd up, I can't so well write to the Duke of Devonshire, butt if you would I should be obliged to you. & you see he claims a promis of you to the Duke of Ancaster. you may be satisfy'd as to the mans morals, for the Duke of Ancaster[3] & Lord Monson[4] both say he is a very honest man, & I really never heard anything to the contrary tho I own he's odd, butt certanly a clever fellow, & I beleive an honest man; so whatever you'l do be so good as to lett me know it by the bearer; & pray lett me know how the Duchess of Newcastle does, being most truely her, & my Dear Lord,
Your Grace's ever faithfull humble servant,
Richmond &c.

1.   Owen MacSwiney, died 1754, had been Manager of the Haymarket Theatre, but was forced to live abroad for a time. He acted for Richmond as agent in Italy for the Royal Academy of Music, collecting singers and scores for performances in London. He also acted as agent for the paintings of the Allegorical Tombs that once hung at Goodwood.
2.   Merrow Down. Slindon v. Surrey, 7 September 1741.
3.   Peregrine Bertie, 2nd. Duke of Ancaster, 1686–1742.
4.   Sir John Monson, 1st. Lord Monson, 1693–1748, was Commissioner for Trade and Plantations, and a Privy Councillor from 1737.

pray send me back Hibbin's letter.

I know you'l curse me for this long letter, butt you'l forgive me again.

119. NEWCASTLE TO RICHMOND

Claremont
Sept 11th 1741

My Dear Lord,

I will begin with telling you, becuase I am sure you will be glad to hear it, that the Dutchess of Newcastle is so well, that she is now actually abroad in the Coach, for the first time, to take the air. In the next I will certainly write to the D. of Devonshire but more for Sr T. Pendergrass, who, I think, should have this Government, & I will therefore press it, than for your troublesome friend Hibbins, who is either Lawyer, Parson, or anything else, that serves his interest. I must keep your letter from Him, to know wt to write to ye D. of Devonshire. My Duty to my Queen. Send me some Sussex news. Sergison says He shall have a Majority in ye West.

I am in haste ever yrs

Holles Newcastle

120. RICHMOND TO NEWCASTLE

Goodwood
Septr 15th 1741

Surely My Dear Lord you are the best of men & best of freinds, I never before wrote or spoke to you in a stile that look'd like flattery, this may look like it, butt upon my honor it is not so, for 'tis the true sentiments of the heart of your ever faithfull, & ever oblig'd humble servant

Richmond &c.

Pray be so good as to lett me know the Duke of Devonshire's[1] answer when you have it.

Not a word have I heard of Sergison since I came down. that he will have a majority in the west is a most stinking lye of his.

121. STONE TO RICHMOND

Whitehall
Sept 17th 1741

My Lord,

I am directed by my Lord Duke of Newcastle, to send your Grace, with His sincerest thanks for the favour of your last letter, an extract of one, which he has wrote by this night's Post, to the Duke of Devonshire; which He heartily wishes may have the desired effect. I hear, the Duke of Devonshire was to set out, as this day, from Chatsworth, for Dublin.

Your Grace will have seen the printed Accounts of the great success of the Russian Army, under Felt. Marshal Lacy,[2] against the Swedes, in Finland; The Russian Army is said to have consisted of 18,000 men; and the Swedes were 12,000: But the latter were so advantageously posted, with a strong Intrenchment, and under the Cannon of a Fort, that the attack must have been very hazardous.

1. William Cavendish, 3rd. Duke of Devonshire, 1699–1755, was Lord Lieutenant of Ireland, 1737–1745.
2. Peter Lacy, 1678–1751, was an Irish soldier who joined the Russian Army and was made a Field Marshall in 1736.

Our letters from Mr Trevor[1] on Saturday last brought an Account that a Courier was arrived from Mr Vanhoey,[2] with positive Assurances, that a Treaty of Neutrality was signed between His Majesty, as Elector, & the Court of France:[3] which Mr Trevor says, occasion'd a great Consternation at the Hague: But Mr Trevor has since receiv'd a Letter from my Lord Harrington, which contradicts that Report: However, as all the foreign Ministers here have had this Piece of News from their Correspondents at Paris, or at the Hague, the Town has been full of it, for two or three days past; and it seems to have gain'd a general Belief.

There is nothing particular with regard to the progress of the French Armies in Germany. The last letters from Hanover, dated about ten days ago, say that Mr Maillebois,[4] if He continued his March, might be upon the Frontiers of that Country in about three weeks from that time. The Danes, after making some Difficulties, at last, agreed to pass the Elbe; – But I am afraid the Body of Saxons, that was expected, will hardly march. The affairs of the Queen of Hungary are in a most desperate condition; By the last Letters from Mr Robinson,[5] they seem'd to be thinking of fortifying Vienna against a Siege; and Mr Robinson thought it probable, the Court might winter, at Bude. It is not doubted but the Elector of Bavaria[6] will be chosen Emperor; probably in the next month; and, as some say, unanimously: But this last particular, your Grace will easily believe, is by no means certain; and I must beg, you would be pleased not to take any Notice of my having mention'd it to you.

Sir John Norris is (I conclude), gone down to Portsmouth; but is to wait for further orders from hence, before He sails; and I beleive, it is not yet finally determined, whether the Squadron shall go on the Service, that was intended, when your Grace left London.

I am with the greatest respect My Lord Your Grace's and obedient and most humble servt

Andrew Stone

I inclose to your Grace Mr Hibbin's letter, which you desired might be returned to you.

122. RICHMOND TO NEWCASTLE

Goodwood
Septr 30th 1741

My Dear Lord,

I received his Majesty's orders by my Lord Harrington to have all the relays at their stations by the 12th <u>& not before</u> particularly specify'd, so if his majesty arrives sooner,[7] he must pick a post horse or come afoot; for I will punctually obey his orders. & I shall be in town myself on the eleventh, & not 'till then, since I shall remain there 'till after the birth day. As to our Sussex affairs every thing is very quiet here, & I have hardly heard Sergison named since I came down, only Green sayes he is treating in the wild. Last Munday wee had the Election of Mayor[8] & other Magistrates at Chichester,

1. Robert Trevor, 1706–1783, later 1st. Viscount Hampden, was the British Minister at the Hague, 1739–1746.
2. Abraham van Hoey was the Dutch Ambassador to France.
3. King George II's declaration of the neutrality of Hanover gradually leaked out during September 1741.
4. Jean Baptiste François Desmarets, Marquis de Maillebois, 1682–1762, was a Marshall in the French Army. He conquered Corsica in 1739, and defeated Charles Emmanuel of Saxony in 1745.
5. Thomas Robinson, 1695–1770.
6. Charles Albert, Elector of Bavaria, was declared Emperor Charles VII, in succession to Charles VI, who had died in October 1740, in defiance of the Pragmatic Sanction.
7. King George II was returning from his annual sojourn in Hanover.
8. Thomas Wall was elected Mayor of Chichester at the meeting of the City Corporation on 28 September 1741.

& every thing went as usual, nem. con. Costellow[1] the only man of their side with us, & that was for the dinner & drinke. however wee made him drinke to your Grace, & to Pelham & Middlesex in Bumpers which seem'd to sett very easy upon him. The Great Mr. Williams went to take the air in his <u>coach & six</u>. Orme was with us, & seem'd very hearty in the common cause. I am sorry to tell you that Sr John Norris is still at Spitthead I wish the French fleet would attack him, for I am confident he would beat them, & that at least would secure us, 'tho wee could do no good to the rest of Europe.

I am My Dear Lord, Your ever faithfull, & most affectte humble servant

Richmond &c.

on saturday I go to Wilton & shall stay there 'till saturday sennight, so if you have any commands for me you may direct them there, butt if you have not dont give yourself the trouble of writeing. I should not have troubled you with this butt in obedience to your commands.

123. RICHMOND TO NEWCASTLE

Goodwood
Octr 2d 1741

My Dear Lord,

The poor Dean[2] is in so bad a way that 'tis thought he can't hold it out long. if he should dye, I hope you will not forgett Ball, for I assure you it would be of very great service to the interest in general to have him, & it would very much hurt myne to have any body else there whilst he's alive. then I must beg your interest for poor Green to be residentiary. there can be no objection to him butt his <u>small talke</u>, there can be none against his actions, for he is incapable of <u>doing</u> a bad thing, & I assure you his talke is mended, nay he's grown almost quite good; if you would speake to Clarke,[3] I thinke I could gett Ball & Bagshall[4]. to morrow wee go to Wilton.

I am my Dear Lord for ever Your's

Richmond &c.

124. RICHMOND TO NEWCASTLE

Wilton
Oct: 5th: 1741

My Dear Lord,

Since I wrote last to your Grace, I have again heard that the poor Dean is certanly dying, if so, pray remember the contents of my last letter. 'tis what I have greatly at heart, so I hope I need say no more upon it to you. If the Archdeacon[5] was not in the way I do assure you that I should like Mr. Clarke preferably to anybody, firstly because he belongs to you, & secondly because wee could not have a better man.

1. John Costellow, 1677–1744, citizen and alderman of Chichester, was Mayor of the City in 1720. He was a gold and silversmith and a clockmaker, and some of his work can be found among the Cathedral Plate. He voted for the opposition candidates — Bishopp and Fuller — in 1734.
2. James Hargraves, a protégé of Newcastle, had been Prebendary of Thorney in Chichester Cathedral, 1723–1732, and Dean of Chichester since 1739, on Newcastle's recommendation. His illness precipitated the action described in L.P. Curtis, *Chichester Towers*, (1966).
3. William Clarke, died 1771, Prebendary of Hova Villa in Chichester Cathedral 1728–1771, Canon Residentiary, 1739–1771, and Chancellor of the Cathedral, 1770–1771, was Vicar of Buxted, and was described as, 'a man of unaffected piety, and evangelical singleness of heart'.
4. John Backshell, died 1750, was Prebendary of Hova Ecclesia, 1720–1750, and Canon Residentiary, 1736–1750. By his marriage to a daughter of Sir John Miller, he became brother-in-law to Thomas Gooch, Prebendary of Somerley and Canon Residentiary, 1719–1738.
5. Thomas Ball was Archdeacon of Chichester, 1736–1770.

I am my Dear Lord for ever & most affectly Your's
Richmond &c.

I shall certanly be in town next sunday night.

125. RICHMOND TO NEWCASTLE

Goodwood
Novr 6 1741

My Dear Lord,

I have seen the Archdeacon who is perfectly well satisfy'd & pleas'd with the scheme incase of the Dean's death, which I beleive is near, for he is very bad. butt he sayes that as the Chancellor[1] is butt a little older than himself he shall have butt a very distant prospect of that, so he should be glad to have a promis of the Bishop for the liveing of Selsea, or the Chancellorship whichever should first become vacant, not both. Manningham[2] has Selsea, also an other liveing, & a good prebend, so the Bishop will have that to dispose of to any body else; as also the Chancellorship, if Selsea is first vacant. now really & truelly I thinke this is an exceeding reasonable request in a man that you have offer'd the Deanery to you. as for Green he sayes that the Chaplaincy of Chelsea College is the thing upon Earth that he has all his life wish'd most for, & that, he will never more trouble your Grace, Mr. Pelham, or me, & indeed I am extreamly oblig'd to you both for it. so much for the Church.

Wee hear nothing of Sergison here, Parson Hancock[3] told me yesterday, that Lisbon Peckham told him that he doubted if he should go so farr as Lewes for the Election, that it was a lost game, & that he wonder'd Mr. Sergison would give himself so much trouble, for a thing in which 'twas impossible for him to succeed. all this wee know very well, butt I am glad to hear that Lisbon Peckham say'd it. If you have any news, pray lett Mr. Stone write it to me.

I am my Dear Lord, for ever Your's
Richmond &c.

Fine weather & glorious sport.
King Henry will waite upon your Grace next week. pray see him. he is the happyest man in the world, & talks of nothing butt his obligation to your Grace.

126. NEWCASTLE TO RICHMOND

Claremont
Novr 7th, 1741

My Dear Lord,

I have this moment received your kind letter, I will be sure to speak to the Bishop about our friend the Archdeacon, I dare say the Bishop will do any thing, that can reasonably be expected of Him. I think the present scheme makes every thing easy. I find my Brother was under some sort of Engagement, or rather has had some very strong application for the Chaplainship at Chelsea, tho' He very readily agrees to give it Green. He wishes, I believe to have it to say, that you had applied to Him for it, which is with Him an excuse to every Body, so that a strong application from you, does the Business. I am heartily glad Green likes it so well, & indeed it is the best, &

1. Robert Rawlinson was Prebendary of Waltham, 1719–1747, and Chancellor of the Cathedral, 1719–1747.
2. Thomas Manningham was Rector of Selsey, 1712–1750. He was Prebendary of Ipthorne, 1711–1750, and Treasurer of the Cathedral, 1712–1750.
3. John Hancock had been Vicar of South Bersted since 1723. He was later Prebendary of Hampstead, 1744–1745, and Prebendary of Selsey, 1745–1761.

properest thing for Him. I am mightily happy in having concurred with you in serving our friend Cheale, Had we been sooner, Lord Effingham told me yesterday, he would have given Him, Clarenceux. I shall be glad always to see Norroy, but a Herald, enters, whether I will or no.

As for publick news; to be short, we send five of our largest Ships to Haddock, with the best of orders. Sr John Norris is come to Spitehead. Our Master told me yesterday, the Elector of Bavaria, had retired, the Duke of Lorrain[1] & his Brother are gone to Neuperg's Army, which is now stronger than the French Bavarian Army in Bohemia, but then there is a French Saxon army on the other side of Bohemia. Quant de Prusse, parait a present assez bien dispose, Dieu siait comment cela finira. Things certainly in general, look better, than they did, I hope we shall make the right use of it. Pray tell Sr J. Miller, that tho' I have not answer'd His Letter, I have already spoke for His friend Capt. Holmes, & hope I shall succeed. I am glad you have good Sport. The news of Lisbon Peckham, looks very well. My Duty to my Queen, & compliments to all friends.

I am my Dear Duke ever yrs

Holles Newcastle

P.S. What relates to Prussia is the greatest of Secrets.

127. RICHMOND TO NEWCASTLE

Goodwood
Nov: 11: 1741

My Dear Lord,

I am vastly obliged to your Grace for your very kind letter, butt wish you had told me what Sr Charles & the learned seamen say of the danger of Anson's fleet; for by the account in the Gazette I own I can't butt thinke allmost all the chances are against them. tho' my freind Legge's account is butt a very blind one. I really am in a prodigious anxiety for that dear boy Keppel,[2] who next to my own family is as dear to me as anything can be. however I have desired Gashry to send mee the best accounts they have. I have delivered your message to Sr John Miller who is extreamly obliged to your grace, as I doe swear the archdeacon will be when I tell him how good you are to him. You will see Cheale before you receive this, he is gon up richly freighted with high spirits & obligations to your grace which he will proclaim with a loud as well as sincere voice. Now as to Green Mr Pelham is certanly most extreamly good to me in giveing him this Chaplainship: butt how to make a strong application to him for it, as you call it I can't tell; for I have already writ to him to thanke him for it, as you yourself told me I should do when I mett you at the Duke of St Alban's at dinner. so an application after thankes would be somewhat awkward. however if you thinke it's propper I will do it with great pleasure, & I at first thought as I told you that it was decent to begin that way, butt you told me that t'was his own thought & proposal & consequently I had nothing to do butt to thanke him, & that I have done most sincerely; for I really am most exceedingly obliged to him for it. I am glad Haddock's squadron is reenforc'd, I wish Mr Stone would be so good as to send me a list only of his fleet as it will be when these ships gett to him. I hope he'l have a touch with whoever transports the spanish troops, if that's their design. Your french article about Monsr — &c., pleases me much. before I have done I must aske you if you have heard from the Duke of Devonshire about the Government of Gallway for Sr Thomas Prendergast. Mr Pelham has also been very kind in opening his affair of his bill in parliament to Sr Robert. to repeat my

1. Grand Duke Francis of Lorraine was Maria Theresa's consort.
2. Augustus Keppel, 1725–1786, second son of the 2nd. Earl of Albermarle, entered the navy in 1735, and accompanied Anson on his voyage around the world. He later became an Admiral.

obligations to you both too often would look like flattery so I shall only say that I shall ever be his, & Your faithfull, & obliged humble servant

Richmond &c.

128.   STONE TO RICHMOND

Whitehall
Nov 12th 1741

My Lord,

My Lord Duke of Newcastle received, this day, the Honour of your Grace's Letter; and orders me to acquaint you, that we have had nothing more particular, with regard to Mr Anson's Squadron, than what your Grace will have been already acquainted with; Sir Charles Wager continues to hope, that Mr Anson, & the other ships may be safe; as He knows the Ships were in good condition; and it does not often happen, that Men of War founder at Sea: I heartily wish the event may justify his Hopes; But I must confess, I think, there is the greatest Reason to fear the worst. I send your Grace inclosed a List of Mr Haddock's Squadron. I cannot acquaint you with the names of the five ships, that are going out, to reinforce him; But your Grace will see their Rates; and that, when they are joined, they will be able to look any enemy in the Face. The last news we had of the Toulon Squadron was that they were cruizing off of Cape Gata, and extending themselves, in a Line from thence to the Coast of Barbary; But I think it most probable, that, after making a Parade there for some time, they will return into Port.

My Lord Duke is much obliged to your Grace for what you say upon Mr Green's Affairs. If your Grace will be pleased to write a Letter to Mr Pelham, desiring the Chaplainship of Chelsea College for Mr Green, without taking notice of any thing that has pass'd, in that Affair, your Grace's Application will, at once, determine it.

My Lord Duke has not heard from the Duke of Devonshire, upon the Government of Galway, since the letter, which your Grace saw, when you was in Town.

I am with the greatest respect My Lord Your Grace's most obedient and most humble servant

Andrew Stone

129.   RICHMOND TO NEWCASTLE

Goodwood
Nov: 18: 1741

My Dear Lord,

The poor Dean is dead,[1] & every thing will be I suppose as settled, which I am sure I shall have great reason to like, I wrote on Saturday as you desired to Mr Pelham, & would have done it sooner, if you had not told me at the Duke of St Alban's that it was not necessary. Enclosed is a letter from the archdeacon to me.[2] I hope you will press that affair with the Bishop, which is really very reasonable. I need not tell you that he is a fast freind, a man of great Weight in this part of the Country, to be absollutely depended upon, & of an unexceptionable character.

I am my dear Lord, Your Grace's ever faithfull & obliged

Richmond &c.

1.   Dean Hargraves died on the morning of 16 November 1741.
2.   Thomas Ball wrote to Richmond (B.L. Add. Ms. 32,698 f.323) requesting him to use his good offices with Newcastle, Pelham and the Bishop, in relation to the promise of the living of Selsey or the Chancellorship rather than the Deanery.

79

130. RICHMOND TO NEWCASTLE

Goodwood
Nov: 25: 1741

My Dear Lord,

Parliament or no Parliament I shall be in town on Sunday night next, for I have a week's business of my own in town, butt should be glad to know if the Parliament does meet or not on the first of December, because upon that the Dss of Richmond's comeing to town or not will depend. I dont mean to trouble your Grace upon so trifleing an occasion, butt should be glad of two words from Mr Stone. I hope wee shall soon have our new Dean.[1] I never reveal'd this secret nor any other, butt every body either knew it, or gues'd it here; & seem mightily pleas'd with it. Old Ashburnham talkes of nothing butt alterations in the Deans gardens, of about ¼ of an acre as you know. Sr Ian sayes Dam't I shall like a young Dean. Enclosed is a letter from Sam; I sent one of his last post to Mr Pelham. this encloses some intelligence tho rather bad than good, for Mr Medleys interest of this time seven years to come is not of great moment. Pray don't forget Ball, for that is really of consequence.

I am my dear Lord, for ever Your's most faithfully

Richmond &c.

131. NEWCASTLE TO RICHMOND

Claremont
Jany 2nd 1741/2

My Dear Lord,

I had the honor of your two most kind Letters, which like all yours, are full of goodness to me. We dined yesterday at the Duke of Dorset's, & I plainly see His Grace is not desirous of much Company at Lewes, tho' Entertainment will be prepared for as many as come. For this Reason, I would by no means have you bring a number with you, but I own I am very desirous, that you yourself, & all the gentlemen and friends should appear at the Election, that the County may see, who would have espoused our Cause, if there had been occasion, & Every Body may know where the Interest of the County is. I don't mean this singly with regard to myself, but as to the solid, established, joint Whig Interest in the East & West. We shall come, I believe, a good many of the better sort from the East, but as we are near home, it will be less inconvenient to us. I find our Petworth Friends will be backwards in coming. Jack Butler will be certainly there, & the Horsham Gentlemen. & I wish you would contrive to come in wth them, as we shall make but one party from the East, so I should think there should be but one from ye West. I reckon we shall be coming into Lewes about twelve o'clock. Pray don't bring any but Gentlemen or very topping Famers wth you, for if you do, it will all be laid at my door. Do what you can to bring Jemmy Lumley. I am glad to find Sr Ian will come. As to Mr Williams, if I was to send Him, I must send to every Body, which I fancy would not be liked, but I should think, Green or somebody might sound, whether He would not come with you. Pray gett what Gentlemen you can. You see the freedom I take, wch your own goodness brings upon you. Publick affairs are much as you left them. There is a Report (and I believe it) that Haddock, has fallen in with French & Spanish Squadrons, & I suppose finding them too strong, sheer'd off; There are three more large Ships order'd to go to Him immediately. The Affair of the second Regiment still is in suspense, tho' the D. of M.[2] has had very good hopes given Him

1. William Ashburnham, died 1797, was Dean of Chichester, 1741–1754, and Bishop of Chichester, 1754–1797.
2. John Montagu, 2nd. Duke of Montagu, 1690–1749, Master General of the Ordnance, 1740–1742, and again, 1742–1749, was Colonel of the 3rd. Regiment of Horse Guards, 1740–1749. He was made a General in 1746.

from Sr R.W. & told to be easy & go into ye Country. I am most heartily sorry for this Incident, and the more as I find it affects you, as well as my good friend Alb: for no man can love two people, better than I do you two, if you will allow me to say so. I have tryed with the D. of M. if an expedient could be found out, by making Him Brigr to make Him easy in Albe having the Regiment, but that won't do. You know at present, I am not in a situation to advise Sr R. & consequently can be of very little use to my Friends, in any thing but my sincerest wishes. Ld Harcourt & <u>Linky</u> meet you at Findon tomorrow. I begg you would not lett <u>Linky</u> drink. He has not been well, & is a poor tender creature, but don't lett Him know, I have given you this Hint. My service to all your good Company & believe me ever my Dear Duke most affectly yrs

Holles Newcastle

132.   NEWCASTLE TO RICHMOND

Claremont
Jany 9th 1741/2

My Dear Lord,

I thank you for your kind Letter, & the good news you sent me of our enemies difference in Sussex. I am sorry I cannot give you any hopes of the like in London, where I see nothing comfortable, or likely to turn out well. Some amongst us, are very sanguine in their Hopes, and are determined to act upon that foundation, But this is not the general Opinion, which is full of fears, for which, I am afraid, there is but too much Ground. God knows, how this will end; for my own part, I fear and dread the worst. We have Letters from Haddock, & Vernon; the former gives an Account, that just as He was preparing to attack the Spaniards, wth 13 ships of ye Line & 3 forty Gun Ships, against 17 large Ships of theirs, the French Squadron of eleven Sail appeared, & there being a certainty of their joining, a Council of War was held, & resolved, that we were too weak to attack them joined. Mr Haddock is gone to Port Mahon to wait for the Reinforcements viz Cornwal wth three large Ships from Lisbon, two more fifty G. Ships & Lestock wth the five large Ships from hence.[1] So (if it is not too late) when they are all together, we shall be a match for them. I believe you will believe me, when I assure you, it is a great Concern to me, that I begin to fear, that I shall not be able to come down to the Election. The letters from Vernon & Wentworth bring nothing new. They are where they have been for some time, & where I think, they intend to stay. On Monday night we meet the Admirals, to consider what should be done, & on Tuesday there is a Cabinet Council to determine what orders, in the present circumstances, should be sent to Haddock & Vernon. Nothing is yet thought of, or at least, determined for us to do in the House of Lords, on the State of the Nation, and as the King has so formally in His Speech, required our advice, His Ministers at least, should have some advice to give, which at present, they have not. A Cart Load of papers from my office are to be given in on Thursday, which are not yett copied & revised. Some material transactions, not to be committed to history have lately, <u>as I have been told</u>, passed at Court. All these Circumstances together, make it almost impossible for me, to come down to Sussex next week. My Brother however will be at Haland, on Wensday next, to attend Ld Middlesex to Lewes on Thursday, & I hope you will be so good, as to continue yr kind intention of coming to Lewes on Thursday, and excuse me, if I don't meet you there. I conclude this Frost has drove you back to Goodwood. My love to <u>Linky</u> if He is with you. I have heard nothing from Him. I hope His Cough is well. My service to all friends, particularly Sr Ian.

I am my Dear Lord Ever yrs

Holles Newcastle

1.   Commodore Richard Lestock, 1679–1746, arrived at Gibraltar with reinforcements on 1 January 1742.

133. NEWCASTLE TO RICHMOND

Claremont
March 7th, 1741/2

My Dear Lord,

I am extreamly sorry to find by My Brother that Sr Harry Lyddel declines coming into the Admiralty. Should he continue to refuse, it would be of very bad consequence, to what we are now contending for. I therefore begg your Grace would be so good, as to desire Him to be at your House tomorrow morning at eleven o'clock. I will meet him there, & I hope we may together perswade Him. If you think, it would be of service, you may desire Lord Harcourt to meet us, who, I am sure, will join in perswading Sr Harry to accept.

I am my Dear Duke, ever yrs.

Holles Newcastle

134. NEWCASTLE TO RICHMOND

Tuesday Night. March the 9th 1742

Joy, Joy, ten thousand Joys to you my Dear Duke, we have flung out the Secret Committee by two. Noes 244. Ayes 242. The 244 all old friends, but our new ones prevailed upon <u>some</u> to be absent. The King of Himself, without my speaking after the victory, said, "Now I will make Dr Ashburnham Dean of Chichester.

Ever yrs

Holles Newcastle

P.S. I will carry the warrt for your new Dean tomorrow.
Our master said, The Dear Whiggs, there is now an end of broad Bottom.

135. RICHMOND TO NEWCASTLE

Bolderwood Lodge in the New Forest
April, 14th 1742

My Dear Lord,

Parson West is dead, & your Grace may remember that wee both apply'd to the Chancellor two years ago, when wee dined together at the Duke of Grafton's, for Mr Carpenter to have the liveing of Bignor;[1] & I have just writ to my Lord Chancellor to remind him of it. so I beg your Grace would do the same, which I don't doubt of, since really wee are both engaged in it. & be so good as to lett Mr Stone acquaint the archdeacon of the success of our application, by Saturday's post as this is the last fox-hunting I can possibly have this whole season, that is 'till Novr next, & that the weather is excessive fine, I would fain stay out next week, & I imagine if I am in town on Tuesday sennight in the morning that is the 27th it will be time enough for any business in the House of Lords. As to polliticks you know my opinion, & you know I can do no good, I wish you or any other Whig could. & if it is butt in your power I know every thing that's right will be done.

I am My Dear Lord, Your Grace's ever faithfull, humble servant

Richmond &c.

---

1. John Carpenter was finally instituted to the Rectory of Bignor on the death of Edward West, on 1 February 1743, on the presentation of the King.

136. STONE TO RICHMOND

Whitehall
April 17th 1742

My Lord,

My Lord Duke of Newcastle had yesterday the Honour of your Grace's Letter; and hopes, you will excuse him for not answering it Himself. My Lord Duke thinks, there can be no Necessity for your Grace to be in Town, before Tuesday Sennight, (the Day, to which the House of Lords stands adjourn'd), when He hopes for the Pleasure of seeing you there; and I believe, it is intended, that His Royal Highness, the Duke, should be introduced that Day. Your Grace will have seen, that my Lord Fitzwilliam,[1] & Mr. Edgecumbe,[2] are created Peers. My Lord Duke orders me to acquaint your Grace, that some Steps have been taken, with regard to the great affair, and that he is not without Hopes, that it may succeed. If any thing material should happen, relating to it, before your Grace's return to Town, my Lord Duke will not fail to send you an Account of it.

I am not certain, whether your Grace may have heard, that the Expedition in which the Forces from Jamaica, are now gone, is against Panama.[3] It was first proposed by Mr. Wentworth, & Governor Trelawny; the Admiral barely acquiesced in it. They have received repeated Accounts at Jamaica, from Porto bello (which are here generally beleived to be true) that Mr. Anson was got safe into the South Sea & had taken some rich Prizes; But some of the Letters say, that he had been forced to sink two of His Ships for want of Men to navigate them; so that He had only two remaining with Him; and even those weakly man'd; and that He was besides, in want of Provisions. They add, that the Spanish Admiral, Pizaro, was at Lima, with four Ships, which He was refitting with all possible expedition, in order to go in pursuit of Mr. Anson's small Squadron.

The last Accounts from the Armies in Moravia, & Bohemia, are very favourable to the Queen of Hungary; the Austrian Troops having obtain'd some pretty considerable Advantages against the Prussians, and Saxons. But as the French & Bavarians are now joind, and are not far distant from Marshal Kevenhuller with the main Army, it is probable we shall soon have an Account of a general Action, which will decide the Fate of that War & indeed of the House of Austria.

My Lord Stair[4] has not been long enough at the Hague, to have done a great deal there, as yet; the Quarters are order'd in Flanders, for the English Troops that are to be sent thither; and I believe, it will not be long before they embark.

I am with the greatest Respect My Lord Your Grace's most obedient humble servant
Andrew Stone

P.S. My Lord Chancellor has given the Living of Bignor, to the Gentleman recommended by your Grace, & my Lord Duke.

---

1. William Fitzwilliam, 2nd. Earl Fitzwilliam, 1720–1756, was created Lord Fitzwilliam, Baron of Milton, on Walpole's fall, on 19 April 1742.
2. Richard Edgcumbe, 1680–1758, MP for Cornwall, 1701, for St. Germans, 1701–1702, for Plympton Erle, 1702–1734, and again, 1741–1742, and for Lostwithiel, 1734–1741, was created Baron Edgcumbe of Mount Edgcumbe, on Walpole's fall, on 20 April 1742, to prevent him being examined by the Secret Committee. He was appointed Vice-Treasurer and Paymaster General of Ireland at the same time.
3. In fact, the decision to attack Panama had already been abandoned.
4. John Dalrymple, 2nd. Earl of Stair, 1673–1747, Ambassador Extraordinary to France 1715–1720, was Commander-in-Chief of the Pragmatic Army.

137. STONE TO RICHMOND

Whitehall
July 1st 1742

My Lord,

As my Lord Duke of Newcastle imagines, your Grace might be glad to know, what passed yesterday in the House of Commons upon receiving the Report of the Secret Committee, He has directed me to send you an Account of it; together with what is material in the News, that has been received from abroad, since your Grace went out of Town.

My Lord Limerick[1] made the Report from the Committee yesterday: It took up above two Hours, in reading, tho' it was confined to three points only; viz; the contract with Mr Burrel & Mr Bristow,[2] for remitting the Pay of the American Troops;– the Weymouth election[3];– and the Secret Service Money. At the close of the Report, it is said, that the Committee are going through the Papers, relating to the Convention, which was refer'd by them; and will make their Report upon them, with all possible Dispatch.

When the Report had been read, a second time, by the Clerk, the House was silent, for some time, in expectation of a Motion from some Member of the Committee; but it soon appear'd, that they did not intend to make any. At last Mr Velters Cornwal[4] moved, that the Report might be printed; which was opposed; and, after a very short Debate, in which none of the Committee spoke, the previous Question was put; and pass'd in the Negative without a Division; and then the House adjourn'd. We met again this morning; and there being no Business to do, adjourn'd (upon a Division of 109, against 51), 'till Tuesday next; And I find, it is generally thought that, if the Committee should not make their final Report, within a reasonable Time, (which it is supposed, they will not do), the Parliament will be prorogued; so that I may be probably be able, some day in the next week, (if your Grace shall stay so long in the Country) at least to let you know the Day fix'd, for the Prorogation.

As to any Alterations with regard to Employments, tho' none are yet made, I am authorised by my Lord Duke to acquaint your Grace, that He thinks it probable, something of that kind may be done, in a day or two; and that He hopes in general, things will go well.

As to foreign affairs, our Accounts both from Italy & Germany, continue very favourable. The Citadel of Modena, the very day, the large Canon from Mantua were brought before it, surrender'd upon such Articles, as they could obtain;[5] one of which was, that the Garrison consisting of 4,000 men, should remain Prisoners of War. The Desertion and Want of Provisions continued in Ms Montemar's[6] Army; and as the King of Sardinia, & Count Trann,[7] are now at Liberty, to push their Advantage, they will in all Probability, be able to drive the Spaniards out of Italy, this Campaign.

1. James Hamilton, Viscount Limerick, 1691–1758, MP for Wendover, 1727–1734, and again, 1735–1741, for Tavistock, 1742–1747, and for Morpeth, 1747–1754, was chairman of the Secret Committee to enquire into the conduct of Sir Robert Walpole as Prime Minister.
2. John Bristow, 1701–1768, MP for Bere Alston, 1734–1741, and again, 1754–1761, for St. Ives, 1741–1754, and for Arundel, 1761–1768, and Peter Burrell, had secured extremely favourable contracts from Walpole for remitting money for the forces.
3. Four opposition candidates had been returned for Weymouth, hitherto a government borough, when Bubb Dodington broke with Walpole. The dispute centred on the removal of the Mayor, the returning officer, shortly before the election.
4. Velters Cornwall, 1697–1768, MP for Herefordshire, 1722–1768.
5. Modena surrendered on 28 June 1742.
6. The Duke of Montemar, the conquerer of Naples, had been forced to retreat after the capture of Modena and Mirandola.
7. Marshal Otto von Traun, the Austrian general, and Viceroy in the Milanese.

From Germany, we have a Confirmation of M. Broglio's[1] precipitate flight to Prague, having lost a great Number of Men in his March thither. Prince Charles, with the Austrian Army, were incamp'd very near that Place; and, by some letters from Vienna, it looks, as if they had thoughts of attacking it. The Great Duke had join'd the Army. They seem'd also, at Vienna, seem to think, that Marshal Keven huller[2] would have attack'd the French army in Bavaria, under the Duke D'Harcourt: So that a few Days will probably bring news of consequence from both the Armies. In the mean time, the King of Prussia is losing no time, to execute His Treaty with the Queen of Hungary, having divided His Army into three Parts; one of which he leaves in Silesia; another returns into Brandenburg; and the third Body is to go into the Duchy of Cleves. The King of Poland seems to have no other thought, than to take the benefit of the Article, relating to Him, in the Preliminaries; having immediately countermanded His Troops, that had been order'd to join the French; and sent a minister, (One Ms. Saul) to Vienna: He also sent an Officer to Prince Charles, to propose an Armistice, etc.

This great turn of affairs in Germany, and the strong Representations of our Ministers at the Hague, have so far animated the Dutch, that, on Friday last, the Province of Holland came to a unanimous Resolution to put 50 Battalions, (amounting to 40,000 men) & 50 squadrons, (amounting to 7,500 horse) into a Readiness to march, by issuing Money to the Officers, for that Purpose. What Difficulty, or Delay, there may be, in obtaining the Consent of the other Provinces, I know not; But it is gaining a great Point, to have the leading Province on our side; and it is more than probable, that, sooner or later, the rest must follow. My Lord Stair, & Mr Trevor have presented their Memorial, in answer to the famous Resolution of the States, which made so much Noise, here five or six weeks ago.

We are this evening dispatching a Courier to Turin, with the second Payment of the King of Sardinia's Subsidy and the Project of a Definitive Treaty, between His Majesty, the Queen of Hungary and the King of Sardinia.

We have no Letters from Mr Mathews[3] since He join'd the Fleet; But M. Ossorio greatly commends His Conduct, in giving assistance to the Governor of Nice, in order to oppose the Spaniards, if they should attempt to force a passage through that country.

Our accounts from France are very short; they affect there to appear as unconcern'd as possible; But it is certain, they are thunderstruck at the Loss of the King of Prussia; and the bad situation of their troops in Germany.

I wish I could conclude my letter here, without adding the disagreable news, we received on Monday last, from Jamaica, of the Fleet, & Transports being return'd thither from Portobello, after having lost a great number of men by sickness, and finding it impracticable to proceed any further, on their intended Expedition against Panama. We had however the comfort, to receive, with these Letters, a Confirmation of Mr Anson's having certainly been in the South Sea, and taken several valuable Prizes there. I believe, it is intended to advise the sending orders to the Land Forces at Jamaica, to return to England, there being very little Hopes, that they will be able to do any great Matter in those Parts.

I beg pardon for troubling your Grace with so tedious a Letter and am with the

---

1. Duke François de Broglie, 1671–1745, Marshal of the French Army, had been virtually beseiged in Prague by Prince Charles of Lorraine. He shared the command of the French forces in the War of Austrian Succession with Marshal Belle-Isle.
2. Marshal Count Ludwig von Khevenhuller, the commander of the principal Austrian army, had invaded Bavaria and captured Munich at the turn of the year.
3. Thomas Matthews, 1676–1751, MP for Glamorgan, 1745–1747, and for Carmarthen, 1747–1751, had been a Commissioner at Chatham since 1736, when he was appointed to relieve Admiral Haddock in charge of the Mediterranean fleet. He was made Admiral in 1743.

greatest Respect. My Lord Your Grace's most obedient and most humble servant
Andrew Stone

I have receiv'd from Govr Shirley a Packet for Sr Thomas Prendergast, inclosing, (as Mr Shirley informs me), Bills of Exchange; and I should be much obliged to your Grace for Directions in what manner to convey it to Sr Thomas.

138. STONE TO RICHMOND

Claremont
July 10th 1742

My Lord,
    I am directed by my Lord Duke of Newcastle to acquaint your Grace, that Thursday next is fix'd for the rising of the Parliament; and that He hopes to have the Pleasure of seeing your Grace in Town, before that time. My Lord Cartaret wrote, this day, to Lord Hervey,[1] to bring the Privy Seal to Kensington, on Monday next, which is to be given to Lord Gower,[2] on Tuesday; Lord Bathurst[3] will, at the same time, be appointed Captain of the Band of Pensioners; Lord Cobham[4] has a Commission of Field-Marshall, and succeeds General Dormer,[5] in the Command of the troop of Horse Grenadiers. An absolute Agreement is upon the Point of being concluded with Mr P,[6] who, in that case, will immediately go up into the House or Lords. If this scheme takes Place, Mr Vane[7] will succeed Lord Edgecombe, in his Irish Employment; the only Difficulty is what relates to Mr Furnese,[8] who has been named for Mr Legg's[9] place of Secretary to the Treasury. If this should be refused, the whole Scheme may fall to the Ground. If Legge quits the Treasury, He is to succeed Mr Whitworth as Surveyor of the Woods. My Lord Duke bids me to tell your Grace, that He thinks, in the whole House of Commons, there will be only Sr Robert Brown[10] removed.
    As to our foreign affairs; we have nothing new from Prague, but confirmation of

1. John Hervey, 1st. Lord Hervey, 1696–1743, was Lord Privy Seal, 1740–1742.
2. John Leveson-Gower, 1st. Earl Gower, died 1754, one of the Lords Justices of the Kingdom, 1740, 1743, 1745, 1748, 1750 and 1752, was Lord Privy Seal, in succession to Lord Hervey, 1742–1743, and again, 1744.
3. Allen Bathurst, 1st. Earl Bathurst, 1684–1775, MP for Cirencester, 1705–1712, was Captain of the Band of Pensioners, 1742–1744, and a Privy Councillor.
4. Richard Temple, Viscount Cobham, 1669–1749, MP for Buckinghamshire, 1704, 1705, and for Buckingham, 1708, 1710, had served with the Duke of Marlborough. He was created a Field Marshal and appointed Colonel of the Horse Guards, 1742, but later resigned in protest against the Hanoverian policy.
5. James Dormer, 1679–1741, had been Colonel of the Horse Guards since 1737.
6. William Pulteney, 1684–1764, MP for Hedon, 1705–1734, and for Middlesex, 1734–1742, had been Secretary at War, 1714–1717, and Cofferer of the Household, 1723–1725. Having failed to form an administration on the fall of Walpole, he was created Earl of Bath, merely stipulating that he should be a member of the cabinet under the Earl of Wilmington. In the Cabinet Council, 1742–1746; he was 1st. Lord of the Treasury, 10–12 February 1746.
7. Hon. Henry Vane, 1705–1758, of Raby Castle, MP for Launceston, 1726–1727, St. Mawes, 1727–1741, Ripon, 1741–1747, and for Durham, 1747–1753, was joint Vice-Treasurer and Paymaster General of Ireland, 1742–1744, on Pulteney's recommendation.
8. Henry Furnese, 1688–1756, MP for Dover, 1720–1734, for Morpeth, 1738–1741, and for New Romney, 1741–1756, a supporter of Pulteney, succeeded Henry Legge as Secretary to the Treasury, 1742.
9. Henry Legge 1706–1764, MP for East Looe, 1740–1741, for Orford, 1741–1759, and for Hampshire, 1759–1764, was Secretary to Walpole, 1735–1739; Secretary to the Treasury, 1741–1742; Surveyor of Woods and Forests north and south of the Trent, 1742–1745; a Lord of the Admiralty, 1745–1746, and of the Treasury, 1746–1749; Treasurer of the Navy, 1749–1754; and Chancellor of the Exchequer, 1754–1755, 1756–1757, and again, 1757–1761.
10. Sir Robert Brown, died 1760, MP for Ilchester, 1734–1747, was Paymaster of Works, 1741–12 July 1742.

Konigsey, and Belisle's[1] having had two Conferences, without having come to any Agreement. The Cardinal has made Overtures to the Court of Vienna for an Accommodation; But has been answer'd, that they will do nothing without England: and the Duke of Lorraine has declared, in a strong manner, that to be the Resolution of the Queen of Hungary. The Elector of Saxony has refused Permission to any of the French Troops to take Refuge in his Country, and has declared, that He will oppose by force any that shall attempt it: The Saxon Troops have, before this time, entirely evacuated Bohemia.

M. Maillebois'[2] Army has receiv'd Orders to retire from Westphalia, and is actually on its March towards the Frontiers of Flanders. The States General have agreed to put a considerable Body of their Troops, (tho' I think not so many, as was proposed by the Province of Holland) into a condition to march immediately. I should have mention'd before, that Bussy has made some insinuations here, that seem'd to lead to a Negotiation; But has been told that nothing would be done, without the Queen of Hungary, and the King of Prussia.

I am not certain, whether I acquainted your Grace in my last, that an Account was come from V.A. Mathew, of the burning of five Spanish Gallies in the Bay, or Harbour, of Tropes. Capt. Norris, who commanded in the execution of this Service says, the Gallies fired first upon Him. We have as yet no complaints from the French, upon the Incident.

I have only to add, that the Difficulties about transporting Lord Pembroke's Regiment are, in a great measure, removed; and that Captain Hervey has obtain'd leave, to sell his Commission.

I am with the greatest respect My Lord Your Grace's most obedient and humble sert

Andrew Stone

139. RICHMOND TO NEWCASTLE

Goodwood
July: 28th: 1742

My Dear Lord,

As I am likely to be out of town 'till after the Lewes races, would it be propper for your Grace to aske a favor of his Majesty for me, & relating to an employment under me. pray consider of it, & if you thinke it is not wrong, I beg you would do it, if you thinke it is not agreeable to my duty to the King, pray lett me know it, that I may go up myself. The case is this, poor old Froubert is litterally starving, & I have formerly recommended him to the King, begging a pension for him, butt <u>na</u> was the word, however if any thing could be found out without putting his Majesty to expence, he seem'd not to be against it. Now you must know that besides the six Equerrys, there are two others upon the Establishment that are call'd the Equerrys of the Crown Stable viz; Froubert & La Richausseè. now the latter is just dead, & I would recommend poor Froubert to His Majesty, that this employment may be joyn'd to Froubert's for his life only. for after his death I should chuse by all means to have them seperated again. Now what makes this the more reasonable is that the first intent of haveing two Equerrys of the Crown Stable was to have two accademys, & that they should have the government of each accademy, butt as one God knows is more than sufficient for this polite Country, I could wish poor Froubert to enjoy the advantage of the sallery of both. I

1. Marshal Duke Charles Belle-Isle, commander of the French forces who had entered negotiations with Konigsegg, the Austrian general, after the Treaty of Breslau, which had detached Saxony and Prussia from the coalition against Maria Theresa, had forced the French to retreat from Prague.
2. Marshal Jean Maillebois, who after an abortive demonstration towards Prague later in the year, was replaced by Broglie.

beg pardon for telling you this long story, butt it is neccesary if you thinke it is not wrong for you to speake to the King for me about it, & that you will be so good as to do it, for which I ought to make you ten thousand apologys, & would do it, butt that I know you love to oblige your freinds. for fear of mistakes I don't mean to aske whether it is right for me to aske this of the King, because I am sure it is, butt I desire only to know whether you thinke it is right for you to mention it to him from me. I own it would be right for me to speake to him myself about it, & so I shall when I have the honor to waite upon him, butt as that wont be soon, some of the lower appoitements may be recommending somebody else in the mean time, which I should be very sorry for. pray don't shew this letter, because of the <u>na</u> which had better not been in it, butt I can't be prudent enough to write an other letter & leave it out, tho perhaps your Grace may dislike the familiarity of my stile in that respect, & you would be in the right, & in that particular I own myself in the wrong, butt in another I shall never thinke myself so, which is in ever professing myself, my Dear Lord, Your Grace's most faithfull humble servant,

Richmond &c.

Pray lett me know how the Cabinet council went of upon that affair you mention'd. tho I dont like to trouble either your Grace or Mr Stone who I am very sorry to hear is not well. Tanky is here & much your's.

140.   NEWCASTLE TO RICHMOND

Lincolns Inn,
Aug 26th 1742
from Mr Perkins Chambers
Where there is no gilt paper

My Dear Lord,
   You have made me very Happy, in letting me know that my Queen & Her charming Daughters were pleased to receive generously our poor Endeavours to show our real Respect & Duty. Every thing with relation to the foreign Journey[1] stands just as it did, at least it does not advance, & till we hear from Genl Legonier, who went to ye Hague last Thursday, with the proposal I mentioned to you, nothing will be resolved further. It seems the general opinion that it will not take place. I will take upon me to say, there is no occasion for your coming to Town, on Monday, & I will watch for you, & send you word, as soon as you can possibly be wanted. There is no news. We hope soon to hear good from Prague. The Enemy has made a sally, but the particulars are not known. The King of Sardinia begins to boggle. I wish ye Court of Vienna may not stand out too long. You shall soon hear further. My love to <u>Linky</u> & Respectful Compliments to ye Ladies, Paunceford & Dayrolles & O.
   I am every yrs

Holles Newcastle

141.   NEWCASTLE TO RICHMOND

Newcastle House
Augt 28th 1742

My Dear Lord,
   I was this afternoon very unexpectedly, sent for to town, to meet my Lord Stair, who was as unexpectedly, come from the Hague. There are great things in agitation. My Lord Stair is still of opinion that his project on D — is practicable. I can say no more. I

---

1.   The King's annual visit to Hanover.

think you should come to Town, but say nothing to any Body, that I have given you this hint.

I am my Dear Duke, ever yrs

Holles Newcastle

P.S. My Duty to my Queen and compliments to the rest of ye good Company.

142. RICHMOND TO NEWCASTLE

Goodwood
Aug: 29: 1742

My Dear Lord,

I am extreamly obliged to your Grace for your most obligeing letter. butt my difficulty is this, The King order'd me to be ready, butt at the same time commanded me to secrecy, now it is impossible for me to be ready, & to keep his going a secret, so I wish you could contrive to aske him whether I am to order things or no, for it is impossible wee can be ready under a fortnight from the time wee have our orders. & the green cloth will be longer. so if I don't hear by Munday or Tuesdays post from your Grace that it is lay'd aside I must at all events be in town on Thursday. so pray lett me hear from you if you can by Mundays post, butt send your letter to the Genll post office, else I shan't have it 'till Wednesday. I beg pardon for being so troublesome. Linky leaves us to morrow which wee are all sorry for, for he is really the best boy that ever lived. pray aske him how Tanky received him, & you will have entertainment. twas come un chien dans un jeu de de quilles. & Linky up & testy about it.

I am my dear Lord for ever, Your's

Richmond &c.

143. RICHMOND TO NEWCASTLE

Whitehall
Sunday night Octr 3: 1742

My Dear Lord,

Your goodness to me upon all occasions is great, butt upon this, you touch the tenderest strings of my heart. The dear boy,[1] I really thinke out of all danger, butt, as he had two strong convulsion fitts on Fryday night, he certanly has been in danger, butt he has had none since, & little or no fever, 'tho his purgeing continues, butt in that article also he is better. he for some time would take neither medecines nor common nourishment, however 'tho he is still averse to the former, he takes the latter, so I have the comfort to tell you that I thinke him now really out of danger. a thousand thankes for your kindness to, my dearest Duke, Your ever faithfull & affectionate

Richmond &c.

The Dss Of Richmond & I joyn in our most sincere thanks for the Dss of Newcastle's kind concern for us, & our dear boy. I am engaged to dine with Linky to morrow.
N.B. the Prince & Princess came to town on purpose this day to receive my Lord Lincoln.

144. RICHMOND TO NEWCASTLE

Whitehall
Octr 16. 1742

My Dear Lord,

Since I saw your Grace this morning I have had another letter from the Arch

1. Probably Charles Lennox, Earl of March.

Deacon, in which he presses much for a peremtory promis of the Chancellorship when vacant, so I must beg of you when you see the Bishop to gett this promis of him which I am confident he will give you at the first word, & it will make my freind easy. so pray do it, & be so good as to lett me hear that it is done, by two words directed to Goodwood.

Your's my dear Lord for ever

Richmond &c.

I hope you found my Lady Duchess perfectly recover'd.

145.   RICHMOND TO NEWCASTLE

Goodwood
Novr: 9th: 1742

My Dear Lord,

I have nothing to trouble your Grace with butt to tell you wee have had no sport, & to aske whether the Bridge Club meets as usual at the Bridge tavern in Pallace yard on Tuesday next. If you like it should be so, the Duke of St. Albans & I will attend you, butt then you must be so good as to send to the man to summon the other members of the Club for that day, & I take for granted if you do it in time you will have a pretty full Club. butt if you don't care for it, 'tis very easily lett alone. I shall be in town early enough on Munday to receive his Majesty's orders for Tuesday, unless the meeting I mean of the Parliament should be putt off, if it is, you'l be so good, I hope, as to lett me know it, by a <u>Stone</u>, if not, I expect no answer of any kind.

I am, my dear Lord, for ever & most cordially Your's

Richmond &c.

I have received a most impertinent letter from Orme; such a one as none butt a true, ungratefull, country gentleman could indite.

146.   RICHMOND TO NEWCASTLE

Goodwood
Novr: 10th: 1742

My Dear Lord,

When I wrote to your Grace I thought I had nothing more to say to you 'till I should have the pleasure of seeing you in town, butt since that I have seen Mr Leeves, who is in a most violent fuss for fear of being Sherif. I told him that I thought he might be excused for this year, butt then it would really hard upon his freinds, if he would not accept of it an other time, butt he is so prodigiously averse to it that it must be contrived to excuse him for ever, or very likely wee may lose him for ever, & that I assure you would be a loss, for he has an exceeding good interest, & really I beleive a hearty freind, tho to be sure a touchy one. he desires of all things to be Gentleman of the Privy Chamber, meerly as he sayes to be excused from serving as Sherif, tho I thinke he would like the title, which to be sure is a pretty one, as Dayrolle has it, however for this year he must be excused & I take for granted you mean that Dennet of Bolney[1] should be Sherif, for William Peachy of Chilgrove, who is return'd, can not possibly serve, because he is <u>dead</u>. this therefore must fix it upon Dennet, unless you have a pocket Sherif. I wish I could have some answer by Thursday's post about Leeves, two words will be sufficient to shew him. I desired him to write to you himself, that the obligation upon him may be the stronger if he is excused.

I am my dear Lord for ever Your's

Richmond &c.

1.   John Dennett of Bolney was Sheriff of Sussex in 1743.

Francis Peachy of Bersted, who is son & heir to William Peachy of Chilgrove deceased, is in great apprehension for fear it should be sadled upon him, butt as it now stands I have told him 'tis impossible, as it really is.

147. NEWCASTLE TO RICHMOND

Newcastle House
Novr 11th 1742

My Dear Lord,

Tho' I am just going to the Cabinet Council to settle the Speech, I could not avoid returning you my Thanks for your two kind Letters. I had a Letter from Leeves, & I have order'd Mr Stone to answer it, that He was in the Judges List, & so put on, that He should certainly be excused, & yt I would very readily join with you, in recommending Him to ye D. of Grafton, for a Gentleman of ye Privy Chamber. I had this day a Letter from Albermarle, wth a blank Proxy, wch I have ordered to be filled up with your Grace's name. We have succeeded in our wishes about the March of ye Troops into Germany, for which, orders are sent to Lord Stair, so yt D d'Arenbergh,[1] went away quite satisfied. There has appeared an odd Incident this day. Lord Gowers & Ld Cobham, who was summon'd to ye Cabinet Council this evening, have Both declined coming, not being yett determined, 'till they have seen their Friends, what they shall do, upon ye great point of the Hanover Troops,[2] which is the principal article of the Speech, & consequently must be of the Address. The great Meeting is to be at Lord Carteret's House on Monday night. If you have no where better to dine, & will dine with me, you shall be very welcome, & we will go to ye Meeting together. Lord Twedale[3] I believe will move our Address, & Lord Mountford[4] second it. Both speech & Address are admirable in their way. Things go well in Germany. The French are certainly in great Distress, & ye March of our Troops will probably compleat their suffering. Pray my Duty to my good Queen & compliments etc. to Goodwood House & Charlton.

Ever yrs

Holles Newcastle

Tankey is prodigiously good.

148. RICHMOND TO NEWCASTLE

Goodwood
Novr: 28th: 1742

My dear Lord,

I must trouble your Grace in favor of as worthy & as honest a man as any in the world; he has a thousand merits, butt I do assure you, that of being a relation as well as a servant of your grace's, is a very great one with me. tis Mr Hutcheson. he has apply'd to me to gett him to be one of the Commisioners of the State Lottery, which I most certanly would have try'd for without troubleing you, butt that I could not in decency aske for two, & upon every lottery I have always recommended one Mr George

1. The Duc d'Arenberg was commander of the allied army on the Rhine.
2. Careret's policy on succeeding Walpole was to raise the subsidy to Maria Theresa; to abandon the neutrality of Hanover; and to take the Hanover Troops into English pay.
.3. John Hay, 4th. Marquis of Tweeddale, 1695–1762, was made Principal Secretary of State for Scotland, Keeper of the Signet (Scotland), and a member of the Cabinet Council, on 20 February 1742, as part of the changes on the resignation of Walpole. He was married to Carteret's daughter, Frances.
4. Henry Bromley, 1705–1755, MP. for Cambridgeshire, 1727–1741, had been created Lord Montfort on 9 May 1741, on the influence of George II's mistress, the Countess of Yarmouth.

Payne,[1] an old acquaintance of myne in Westminster; for whom as yett I have always succeeded. Now very likely my dear Lord you may have an engagement as well as myself, perhaps two, butt then surely a Secretary of State may recommend three, where I certanly ought to be satisfy'd with one. I say this sincerely, without any joke, so pray recommend him, if you really do not thinke it impropper. & consider another merit of this poor mans, which is that he was lay'd aside for our King Cheale. I have been as long upon this topick as ever the Archdeacon was upon his Chancellorship. butt I must trouble you a little about myself. In the first place I am delighted to see things go so well in the house of Commons. Then as to the house of Lords I take for granted any attendance will be unneccessary. & as for Cabinet Counsels they are quite out of fashion, so that all the business I can possibly have in town, is waiting upon my Royal Master which I ever was & ever shall be ready to do, when there is any real Duty that calls me, as for example this last summer, when I was three months as attach'd as ever Schutts was. butt I own I cant help preferring foxhunting, & being with my family, to what may be called fiddle-faddle waiting. so I could wish to be excused going up 'till after Christmass. now I know you'l be in a passion, butt dont be really angry with me, for rather than suffer that I will go up at any time. you see I am as submissive to you as ever you was to Tanky. I had certanly rather not go up at all, however if I am to go, I should chuse it about next Sunday or Munday; that is if the King should go to the house any day that week, so pray be so good as to lett me know whether you thinke he will go that week or no.

Harcourt is to come down or not, according to the sentence you pronounce. so pray lett him know your resollutions, which must ever be the guide of my dear Lord, Your Grace's most faithfull, humble servant,

Richmond &c.

I am sincerely concern'd for poor Clutterbuck.[2] if Sr Charles Wager has his employment, the King & his administration will act like themselves, & I'l be bound to say that there is not one honest man in the kingdome, will disapprove of it. Can this talke of Impeachment come to anything; pray lett Mr Stone give your answer, to Mr Hutcheson.

149. NEWCASTLE TO RICHMOND

Newcastle House
Nov 30th 1742

My Dear Lord,
    Tho' it is a very busy time with us, I would not omit returning you my thanks for your kind letter. I believe it is yett very uncertain, whether there will be a Lottery this year. I should be very glad to serve Mr Hutchison, both on his own account, & as you recommend Him, but as I do not yett know, wt applications my Brother & I may have, which may not be to be withstood, I cannot make any certain promise. Tho' I am always glad to have you with me, or near me, If you will forgive the familiarity of the expression, I must own I would not now interrupt your country sports, when there is no absolute necessity. As we carry every thing by such Majorities in the House of Commons, & bring on Tory elections, & postpone Whig ones as we please, by great Majorities, I conclude we shall have nothing to do in ye H. of Lords, at least for some time, & most likely, not till after Christmas, so you and all your good Company, (To

---

1. Possibly George Payne, 1703–1762, the uncle of William Collins, the poet.
2. Thomas Clutterbuck, 1697–1742, MP for Liskeard, 1722–1734, and for Plympton, 1734–1742, a Lord of the Admiralty, 1732–1741, and of the Treasury, 1741–1742, was Treasurer of the Navy, May to November 1742. He died on 23 November 1742.

whom pray my kindest compliments) may hunt at your ease, & I wish you better Sport than I am afraid you have yett had. The Land Tax etc., will pass before Christmas, so ye King must come to the House, but I conclude a day or two's Notice for that will be enough to bring you up at any time. Indeed the Whig cause seems now as strong or stronger, than it has been for many years. Our new Whig friends Sandys,[1] etc., act a most thorough, strong & resolute part, & succeed accordingly, by entirely pleasing us, & provoking to the last degree the Tories. I hope you will not think the Advancement of Murray[2] a prejudice to ye Whig cause, If it is, the Blame must fall absolutely upon my Brother & I.

I can give you but a very imperfect account of foreign affairs, for indeed we have no other. The Armies are very near one another in Bavaria; which is strongest, we know not; ours, I hope, & believe. The Emperor is in great distress, The French army at Prague, effectively blocked up there, The Queen of Hungary calling out for assistance, Holland showing more disposition to do well, than they have hitherto done, tho' as yett nothing certain. Sweden in the height of their good humour with us, declaring the D. of Holstein[3] successor to their Crown, whilst Denmark lately sold to France, is arming against this French step in Sweden, and the Czarina setting up another candidate to the Crown of Sweden, & on that condition offering us her friendship. This I conclude will be scarce understood by you, but I can't explain more by letter, & I begg you would not attempt to explain it to any Body else. In short, all Affairs abroad, are in great uncertainty, & may turn out very well, or very much otherwise. Genl Clayton is this day gone to Flanders, to consult with Ld Stair, etc. upon the intended March into Germany. I hear it is generally thought by our Officers, to be impracticable. If it is, as it may be, for I cannot pretend to be any judge, I am very sorry for it, for, had it been practicable, it would have very much pleased the Court of Vienna, & have had a good effect on our Affairs at home. I conclude you will not be able to read my letter. My duty to my Queen and compliments to Goodwood and Charlton.

I am my Dear Duke Ever yrs

Holles Newcastle

150. RICHMOND TO NEWCASTLE

Goodwood
Wednesday 'Dec' 1st 1742

My Dear Lord,

After so long a letter as I troubled you with last post I ought to be ashamed to trouble you again, butt it is uppon a publick concern. you must know then Kemp[4] has two liveings to dispose of viz; Slyndon & Binsted; so I wish that they might fall into Whig hands. I have not mony enough to purchase them myself, nor do I suppose that your Grace or Mr Pelham care to purchase any thing of that kind; butt I wish you would gett some of our freinds to enquire among themselves, if any body has a mind to lay out their mony in that way. The particulars are in the enclosed. it is in a corner of the County where a clever Jacobite parson might do us a great deal of mischeif. The present incumbent,[5] to give him his due is a Jacobite, butt he is so eternally drunke

---

1.   Samuel Sandys, 1st. Lord Sandys, 1695–1770, MP for Worcester, 1718–1743, was a Privy Councillor and Chancellor of the Exchequer, 1742–1743.
2.   William Murray, later 1st. Earl of Mansfield, 1705–1793, was Solicitor General, 1742–1754, on the influence of Newcastle and Carteret, and Attorney General, 1754–1756. He was Lord Chief Justice, 1756–1788.
3.   Adolphus Frederick, Duke of Holstein was heir-presumptive to the throne of Sweden.
4.   Anthony Kempe, 1672–1753, the Catholic Squire of Slindon House in Slindon.
5.   Robert Styles Launce was instituted to the Rectory of Slindon on the death of William Groome on 25 January 1739.

with rum brandy that he does us no harm. Kemp put him in at the recommendation of Parke.[1] I have now the refusall of these liveings, so I should be glad to have an answer, by about Sunday next, for as I can't buye them myself, it would be wrong to keep Mr Kemp in suspence, espetially as he sayes other people have made offers, & as they wont tell me who, I fear 'tis no freind.

I am My dear Lord, Your Grace's most faithfull humble servant,
Richmond &c.

I am very impatient to hear what becomes of the impeachment.[2]

151. RICHMOND TO NEWCASTLE

Goodwood
Decr 3d 1742

My Dear Lord,
Why would you give yourself the trouble of writeing so long a letter to me? since <u>a Stone</u> would have done as well. however I am extreamly obliged to you, & shall give you no further trouble than to assure you, I am for ever, Your's
Richmond &c.

Surely every body must approve of Mr Murray's advancement, since he has all the acquired qualifications that's possible for a man to have. The only objection that can be made to him; is what he cant help, which is that he is a Scotch man, which (as I have a great regard for him) I am extreamly sorry for. Pray what becomes of Strange?[3] I thanke you for what you say of Hutcheson, & you are in the right not to promis. butt pray dont forgett him.

152. NEWCASTLE TO RICHMOND

Newcastle House
Dec. 6th, 1742

My Dear Lord,
I make use of my friend Harcourt to send you an Excuse for not answering your two letters, by last Saturday's post. You are very good in sending me the account of the sale of the Living of Slindon, etc. You say very truly, that neither Mr Pelham or I, are purchasers, & the present time is too much taken up, for us to be looking out for other people to purchase, at least I dare not mention it, to the Honble Harry, who is fighting every Day in the House of Commons, at the Head of a victorious Army. You have heard by what Majorities, we have demolished Watkin Williams,[4] flung out the Revival of the Secret Committee, & rejected the place Bill. They are now hard at work in defending the Army, which our opposers are opposing, upon a principle this day laid down in the H. of Commons, that we should support the Q. of Hungary no way, but by money; so that the last year Sr R. Walpole was to be hanged, for not carrying on the war wth vigour in defence of the K. of Austria, and this year, we are to undergo the

1. John Parke, died 1753, was Prebendary of Middleton in Chichester Cathedral, 1720–1753, and a Canon Residentiary, 1723–1753. He supported Bishopp and Fuller in the 1734 Election, and was a thorn in the side of Richmond and Newcastle.
2. The proposed impeachment of Sir Robert Walpole, on grounds of corruption.
3. John Strange, 1696–1754, MP for West Looe, 1737–1741, and for Totnes, 1742–1754, was Solicitor General, 1737–1742, when he was succeeded by William Murray. He was Recorder of London, 1739–1742, and Master of the Rolls, 1750–1754.
4. Watkin Williams, 1693–1749, MP for Denbighshire, 1716–1741, and again, 1742–1749, and for Montgomeryshire, 1741–1742, moved for the revival of the secret committee on Walpole, seconded a place bill, and voted against the Hanoverian Troops at the opening of the session.

same fate, for having acted in support of ye Q. of Hungary, & in pursuance of the Addresses of Both Houses of Parliament. The present age, abounds so in scandal, that what relates to Persons only, is too familiar to be reckoned at all extraordinary but there is a Book lately published, called "The Case of the Hanover Troops",[1] which endeavours to prove that from Queen Ann's Death to this day, the late King, & the present King have had no view in all their Measures, but to serve & aggrandize the Electorate of Hanover, at the expense of Great Britain, & concludes, that the only Distinction is, Englishman, or Hanoverian or in other words, King George or ye Pretender. Since this will open the Eyes, of all who are not really Jacobites, the thorough attack that is made, in Print, & in Parliament, upon our New Friends, is a proof of their acting sincerely with us, & how necessary it is for us, to act thoroughly with them, and indeed, if we see the Majorities we have this year, & remember our Minorities last Session, we must own that the Whig Cause, has not been deserted. You are very good, in approving, the step about Mr Murray. My Brother, my Chancr, & I did it, upon ye most mature Consideration. Pray assure our Whig friends and Harcourt particularly, that it is our doing, & that we will be responsible, for Mr Murray's Behaviour, in every thing. I begg my compliments to Sr Ian, Tell Him I spoke considerately to Ld Chancellor, about His friend, & yt I shall certainly succeed, if the Case is not such, that Sr John himself, shall think it not reasonable to ask. Ld Ch has promised to enquire into it and as soon as I have the answer, I will write to Sr John. There is no foreign news, except yt the D. of Holstein is declared successor to ye Czarina, which setts aside His succession to Sweden. My duty to my Queen and service to all the Hunt.
   I am my Dear Duke Ever yrs

Holles Newcastle

P.S. I wish you could think of a Sheriff for us.

153. NEWCASTLE TO RICHMOND

Newcastle House
Decr 14th 1742

My Dear Lord,
   I thought I should have troubled your Grace last night with a letter to fetch you up to town immediately, we having had an alarm yesterday that the opposers intended to bring the affair of the Hanover troops into our House this week, but as we had no such proposal yesterday, & our House adjourned over Thursday, if they make such a Motion tomorrow, we shall only appoint next Tuesday to take it into Consideration, & I will be sure to give you Notice time enough to be here that day. We had also some thoughts of taking that most scandalous Pamphlet into Consideration in our House, in order to censure it in a proper manner, but we are not yet determined about it, or at least, when to do it. Nothing can come up to the warmth with which the opposers talked against the Hanover Troops in ye H. of Commons last Fryday. Hanover passed its time very ill, and my Brother Cartaret met with very severe & unjust Reproaches, & Treatment, such as Sr R. W. scarce ever had, but thank God, our majority is very staunch. We had upon ye Question of our English Army a majority of 120, on ye Hanover Troops in ye Committee 67, & upon ye Report 53, & I think I may venture to say, that if it is right to support ye Queen of Hungary, which you & I, have always thought, there was no way of doing it effectively but by these Hanover Troops. There is not much news from abroad. My compliments to my Queen, etc.
   I am ever yrs

Holles Newcastle

---

1. The famous pamphlet of 1742, *The Case of the Hanover Troops*, was attributed among others to Chesterfield and to Pitt.

154. NEWCASTLE TO RICHMOND

Claremont
Decr 18th 1742

My Dear Lord,

If I had not received your Grace's Letter this afternoon, I intended to have acquainted you with the King's going to the House next Tuesday to pass the Land & Malt Tax. I suppose you will not come to Town, & indeed I see no necessity for it. The Opposers have called for all the estimates of the Forces in our House, & have given Notice yt they intend after the Holydays to oppose wth the utmost vehemence, violence, & warmth imaginable the Hanover Troops, which your friend the Duke of Bedford[1] called in his Speech a <u>pernicious & Detestable Measure</u>, so I hope we shall have all our Friends up, to hear whether it was so or not. I will venture to affirm, if it was right, as the Opposers always said, and I always & you thought, to support the Queen of Hungary, that could not be done effectually any other way. There is little news from abroad, except that things in Holland really look better than ever. Trevor[2] thinks so, but perhaps He is now more partial to them, being soon to be Happy with Miss Cryning. I suppose our little friend's sister. The French are making great Augmentations of their Troops, amounting, milice included, to 80,000 men, great part of which however, will be wanted to recruit their Army. Our Army in Flanders will soon march, but how far I cannot yett tell. Pray my Duty to my Queen, & love to Lord March. Tell them, I received their Commands. I wish they were more reasonable, & more practicable, but however, I will speak to Yonge,[3] & see what can be done, & then will write to my Queen. You don't say, whether you have ever given my answer to <u>Sr Ian</u>. I hope & believe ye Chancellor will do it.

I am my dear Duke. Ever yrs

Holles Newcastle

155. STONE TO RICHMOND

Whitehall
Jany 6th 1742/3

My Lord,

I should have troubled your Grace with a Letter by the last Post; but defer'd it, 'till now, in hopes to have been able to send you some satisfactory Account of the late extraordinary event of the King of Sardinia's withdrawing His Troops, & suffering the Spaniards to take Possession of Chambey, & the neighbouring Places in Savoy, without the least Opposition; which, as your Grace will easily imagine could not but give great suspicion of some private negotiation between the Court of Turin, & those of Madrid & Versailles; especially, as the utmost endeavours that could possibly be used, have not induced the Court of Vienna to come to a final Agreement with the King of Sardinia. To our great surprise, we have not yet had one Word from Mr. Villettes,[4] relating to this extraordinary Transaction; but conclude, there is a Courier on the Road. Mor

---

1. John Russell, 4th. Duke of Bedford, 1710–1771, joined the opposition to Walpole, but was later 1st. Lord of the Admiralty, 1744–1748; Secretary of State for the Southern Department, 1748–1751; Lord Lieutenant of Ireland, 1756–1761; Lord Privy Seal, 1761; and Lord President of the Council, 1763–1767.
2. Robert Trevor, Envoy Extraordinary and Minister Plenipotentiary to the Hague, 1739–1746, married Constantia, daughter of Peter de Huybert, Lord van Kruyningen on 6 February 1743.
3. William Yonge, 1693–1755, MP for Honiton, 1715–1754, and for Tiverton, 1754–1755, was Secretary at War, 1735–1746. He hoped to succeed Pelham as Paymaster General in 1743, but his wife was granted an Irish pension of £600 per annum instead.
4. Arthur Villettes was Secretary at Turin, 1734–1741, and British Resident there, 1741–1749. He was later Minister to Switzerland, 1749–1762.

Ossorio, who seem'd extremely struck at the first News of the King of Sardinia's retiring before the Spaniards, has now received Letters from His Court; & in some measure seems to have recover'd his Spirits; so far, at least, as to be fully persuaded, that what has been done, was not in Consequence of any Negotiation.

Your Grace will have seen in the Gazette a full Account of Belisle's escape,[1] & the subsequent Capitulation of Prague. They affect at Vienna to be displeased with the Conduct of Prince Lobiowitz[2] in granting such Conditions to the Garrison, and Konigseg said, that He might have had the Town on those Terms, four months ago, & have been now, in the Heart of the Empire. The Queen of Hungary, being congratulated by the Cirile, by the Pope's Nuntio, & the Venetian Ambassador, on the Evacuation of Bohemia, & the Recovery of the Capital of that kingdom, answer'd in these Words : "Vous vous trompés: J'ai la coeur trop anglois pour y prendre plaisir". The French Army, (tho' the Accounts differ widely, as to Numbers) certainly sufferd greatly in their March to Egra, & are in Garrison there, at present, in a miserable Condition. Lobiowitz is to follow them, & if they remain at Egra, to cantoon his Army, eastward of that Town; But if they shall have left Egra, He is then to take his Quarters in the upper Palatinate. The appearances in Holland are extreamly good, but, as yet, only appearances.

I am with the greatest Respect My Lord Yr Grace's most obedt & most humble sert
Andrew Stone

156.   NEWCASTLE TO RICHMOND

Kensington
3 o'clock
[Spring 1743]

My Dear Lord,
I am in greatest Confidence, to acquaint your Grace, that a Letter I received last night from Lord Carteret, has created some Doubt in the King, with relation to His journey, but your Grace must not on any Account take the least Notice of it. I am however to lett your Grace know, that you are as from yourself to find some pretence to stop the Baggage, & the Horses. The Wind is now contrary & the Weather very bad, so you may order them not to go abroad on that Account, but stopt they must be, & you must take it upon yourself. Nothing must go 'til Carteret returns, who is expected tomorrow or Fryday. Lett me see you this evening at Stone's, or tomorrow morning
I am ever yrs

Holles Newcastle

157.   NEWCASTLE TO RICHMOND

Newcastle House
May 20th 1743

My Dear Lord,
I am infinitely obliged to you for your letter from Helvoetsluys, I heartily congratulate you upon your safe arrival,[3] but infinitely more upon dear Lord

1. Marshal Belle-Isle withdrew from Bohemia in December 1742, leaving a garrison in Prague under General François de Chevert.
2. Prince Johann G. Lobkowitz, Austrian general and diplomatist, was beseiging Prague. His son later courted Lady Emily Lennox, the second surviving daughter of Richmond, when she was a young girl.
3. Richmond accompanied King George II to the continent in his capacity of Master of the Horse in May 1743, and stayed for a time with the Bentincks in Holland.

March's[1] Recovery, who, I hope is now out of danger. You may easily imagine we have not much news to send you from hence. A great number of the Highland Regiment has mutinied, on going abroad, a party of near 100, marched back towards Scotland, 50 more were gone, but are returned to their Duty, & we have sent some troops after the rest, who, I believe, will bring them back. I am my dear Duke in great haste.

Ever & unalterably yrs

Holles Newcastle

158. RICHMOND TO NEWCASTLE

Utrecht
Fryday Night 27 May/7 June 1743

My Dear Lord,

I had not time to write to your Grace by the Messager this morning, & have now butt little to spare, for I have actually more business than I ever imagin'd I could have had in any whole life. our first division march'd off this morning, our second goes to morrow, our Third (which I belong to) goes on Sunday, & My Lord Chamberlayne's on Munday, if they have mony, from England, if not I go on without them, for Sr Thos Wynn[2] & I have each sufficient. I fear wee shall be three weeks getting to the army. If you see Taw she can give you an account of several difficultys too ridiculous to mention to you, butt my resollution is to admit of none. St Paul has advised me to use a Beemshire ore leffel, anglica, a Bohemian ear picker. butt in the vulgar, an oaken towel. & I dont thinke the advice a bad one when wee are in Germany. I shall write to you again during our route. all our horses are astonishingly well.

I am, my dear Lord, Your Grace's most faithfull, & affectte humble servant,

Richmond &c.

Pray putt the Honble Harry, (who I both love & honor) in mind of Brereton. that is, I wish he would putt the great Sr Wm Young in mind of him, for I hear subaltern commissions are expected from Hanover. Enclosed is a short list of our equipages.

159. RICHMOND TO NEWCASTLE

Utrecht
May 30/June 10 1743

My Dear Lord,

Wee are this moment setting out with our last division, & by next post I'l send your Grace our route & march; as I shall fix it with Howard's Major at Emerick. all has gon on hitherto very well butt it has been almost an endless peice of worke to gett up the baggage, however now that is done, I thinke our journey half over. if you write to me by the return of the post you may direct your letter to Mr Trevor, & he will send it

1. Charles Lennox, Earl of March, 1735–1806, was the third, but first surviving son of Richmond, and succeeded his father in 1750. During a long career in the army, during which he distinguished himself at Minden, he became a colonel. He was appointed Ambassador Extraordinary and Minister Plenipotentiary at Paris, 1765. He was later Secretary of State for the Southern Department, 1766–1767, and Master General of the Ordnance with a seat in the Cabinet, 1782–1795. Having once been an enthusiastic supporter of parliamentary reform, he later became unpopular for opposing all reform. See Alison Gilbert Olson, *The Radical Duke: Career and Correspondence of Charles Lennox, Third Duke of Richmond,* (1961).
2. Sir Thomas Wynn, 1677–1749, MP for Caernarvon Boroughs, 1713–1749, was Equerry to King George II, 1727–1749.

after me, butt as wee shall be at the army about the three or four & twenyth of June, OS; you will know best when & how to direct to me there.

I am my Dear Lord for ever & most affectly Your's

Richmond &c.

My best services attend Mr. Pelham. have you been so good as to speake to Lovel about Sr Tho: if you have not, I wish you would write to him about it.

160. NEWCASTLE TO RICHMOND

Newcastle House
June 7th 1743

My Dear Lord,

I am extreamly obliged to your Grace for all your kind letters, & hope you will be so good, as to continue your kind Correspondance after your arrival at the army. I conclude, I can send you no news from hence, either wth relation to the armies on the Rhine & Mayn, or of those in Bavaria. The French & Bavarians in Bavaria, I think, hardly give the Queen's Troops time to attack them, they retiring every where, upon their approach, by which Bavaria is now almost all subdued, & in the hands of the Austrians. Brunau[1] I conclude can't hold out long. The King will now soon be at the head of His Army. I doubt not but He will find as fine Troops, & as eager to be employ'd as ever were brought into the Field, & I as little doubt of their being well lead on, & commanded by his Majesty. We have had here a bland account from Holland that Lord Stair had sent the Duke of Marlborough,[2] wth 2000 men to intercept a party of French, that were gone to possess themselves of all the forage, between the Rhine & Darmstadt. Things go very well in Holland, & I hope you will soon have their 4000 or 5000 men with you in the army. Tomorrow, I think, the Rebel Highlanders are to be tried. Genl Folliott is president of the Court Martial & I don't perceive any inclination to favour them, in any instance. Some examples will certainly be made. I had a letter from my Queen about Goldsworthy. The place then promised, is since given to Sr John Shelley's Brother. Tom Hill has been with me, about His friend Blomer.[3] I spoke to the Arch Bp about Him. He must set it forward, & then, (when Cornwallis has a prebend) I can come, & support the Archbishop, but it must arise first from Him. There is a vacancy of a Riding Officer at Felpham. I did not intend ever to interfere. The Ds of Richmond has wrote to Ld Wilmington,[4] & Her man is to have it. I suppose you have left directions, as to any Vacancies of this kind, that may happen. I shall be very glad to write to Lovel. I think I have not yet spoke to Him & ye reason was, least my interfering, might hurt it, but now, I will be sure to do it, & I hope effectually. We have no news here. In times of War, nothing is talked of, but Motions & Operations of armies. I hope in God we shall soon hear good news from ours. There is an account from Holland, that Monr de Lequis Detachment to Monr Broglio is countermanded. I beg my dear Duke, you would be assured, nobody can wish you, & yours better than I do. I shall be very impatient to hear from you after your arrival in the army. Pray my kindest love & service to Albemarle. He has quite forgot me. I have wrote Him two very confidential letters, & have had no answer. My best compliments also to Lord

1. Marshall Khevenhuller had defeated Seckendorff at the Battle of Brunau in May 1743, and the French and Bavarian armies withdrew westward from Bavaria.
2. Charles Spencer, 3rd. Duke of Marlborough, 1706–1758, grandson of the great general, became Brigadier General after an army career, and distinguished himself at Dettingen.
3. Dr. Thomas Blomer was Chaplain to King George II.
4. Spencer Compton, 1st. Earl of Wilmington, 1674–1743, MP for East Grinstead, 1713–1715, and for Sussex, 1715–1728, was Speaker, 1715–1727; Lord President of the Council, 1730–1742; and 1st. Lord of the Treasury from 1742 until his death.

Holdernesse[1] & Harcourt, not forgetting the Revd Coll: Hay[2] & Coll Ld Bury[3] when you see Him.

I am ever, most affectly & unalterably yrs

Holles Newcastle

161.   RICHMOND TO NEWCASTLE

Kings Quarters at Hanau
Sunday June 19/30 1743

My Dear Lord,

As to be sure your Grace will have a very particular account of the Battle of Dettingen[4] from My Lord Cartaret, I shall say nothing to you upon it, only that our brave troops are in high spirits, & long to be at it again. Poor Clayton is a great loss, to give you any particular account of the wounded would be too disagreeable a subject to trouble you upon. Poor young Honeywood if he survives is the worst case I beleive of all haveing nine or ten wounds. H:R:H: the Duke[5] thanke God is in a very fair way of doing well, if they can butt keep him quiet, butt his spirits are so high & his tongue runs so fast that wee are in eternal fears that he will talke himself into a fever. Huske will do well tho the wound is a bad one the ball being gon quote through his heel. Albemarle is very well, & I assure you that the Horse gardes did remarkably well. Poor Bury was unluckily in the rear with the foot gardes that never were engaged. I must now thanke you for your very kind & obligeing letter which I received here. butt as the messager is just going I have only time to assure you my dear Lord that I am & ever shall be your Grace's most faithfull, obliged, & ever affectte humble servant,

Richmond &c.

The Revnd Coll Hay perform'd his Te deum very well & propperly to day. I have orderd a little entertainment for my freinds at Chichester for the victory.

162.   NEWCASTLE TO RICHMOND

Newcastle House
June 24th, 1743

My Dear Duke,

I could not let this Messenger go, without sending you a line of Congratulation on the best publick news, I have ever yet had, and on your own safety, which is always ye most agreable private one to me. I went yesterday & sent, ye moment I saw Jack Parker, to the Ds of Richmond, to acquaint Her with what had passed. I found she knew much more than I, and indeed, you would pity me, if you knew, how little I hear of what passes in the army. I have wrote to Albemarle, who, I think I may still call my

1.   Robert Darcy, 6th. Earl of Holdernesse, 1718–1778, was successively Lord of the Bedchamber, 1741–1751; Ambassador to Venice, 1744–1746; Minister to the Hague, 1749–1751; Secretary of State for the Southern Department, 1751–1754; and for the Northern Department, 1754–1761.
2.   Lord Charles Hay, 1700–1760, MP for Haddingtonshire, 1741–1747, was Lieutenant Colonel in the 1st. Foot Guards, 1743, fought in the campaigns of 1743, and was at Fontenoy in 1745. He was later ADC to King George II, 1749, and Colonel of the 33rd. Foot, 1753–1760.
3.   George Keppel, Lord Bury, 1724–1772, Richmond's nephew, was MP for Chichester, 1746–1754, when he succeeded his father as 3rd. Earl of Albemarle. A Lord of the Bedchamber to the Duke of Cumberland, he was his ADC at Dettingen, Fontenoy and Culloden. After a long army career, he ended as a General in 1772. He married Sir John Miller's daughter Ann.
4.   The Battle of Dettingen was fought on June 16/27 1743.
5.   William Augustus, Duke of Cumberland, 1721–1765, second son of King George II, and a military commander, was wounded at Dettingen. Later he commanded the allied army at the battle of Fontenoy and at Culloden in 1746, before being defeated at Lauffeld in 1747.

friend, tho' I have not had one Word from Him these four months. Upon the subject of His correspondence, Pray desire to see my letter to Him. I do depend upon you, that I shall now be informed of all that passes at the army. I hope you will remember your kind promise as to a Constant Correspondence, during your stay abroad. You may imagine, I shall be very impatient to hear what shall be undertaken in consequence of our Victory. I conclude we shall not stop here. Pray let me know how my Brother Secretary stands disposed towards us here, and how He acts towards you there. You see this is in ye utmost confidence, but I know to whom I write. I can't forbear observing yt the glorious part our Master has had in his own person in this great Action, adds much to the merit and advantage of it with me. Pray my kind compliments to Holdernesse, Harcourt, & Del, not forgetting Sr Tho: Wynne when He arrives. I saw a short letter from Del upon this occasion, which put me in mind, of the Duke of Marlborough's, when he had Marshall Tallard[1] in His Coach. I had yesterday the pleasure to see, the Ds of Richmond, dear Ld March, Lord George,[2] & Lady Amely,[3] Swinny and Sam Chaundler altogether, and in good Health.

My dear Duke, pray God preserve you I am ever most affectly yrs
Holles Newcastle

P.S. I have wrote to Lovel about Sr Tho: Pendergrass, secured Maddox's Prebend for Green, and done all your jobbs.

163. RICHMOND TO NEWCASTLE

King's quarters at Hanau
Fryday 24 June/5 May 1743

My Dear Lord,
     Is there nothing to be done for Blomer upon Maddox's translation?[4] the Arch Bishop has sent me word that he has not only mention'd him to the King, butt has likewise given in his names in writing to His Majesty, as a worthy clergyman & a hearty freind to the Government, & if his Majesty thought propper, very deserving of his Royal favour. These are his Grace's very words to a freind of myne. so your Grace sees you have a very good foundation to worke upon; & I dare swear you will, as you was so kind as to tell me you would, so pray thinke of it, you say when Cornwallis has a Prebend you will, so then pray take the lead since the Arch Bishop has laid the foundation as I told you. As to Chichester vacancys I have left propper instructions with Jemmy Brudenell, butt I have recommended an Arundel man for an Arundel vacancy to Mr Pelham, & the man is a freind both of Lumley's & our's, has a freehold, desires to be a freind of ours, & is recommended by Cheale, Leaves &c. Pray when will the Duke of Grafton make Leaves a Gentleman of the Privy Chamber, he promis'd him the first, butt I hear nothing of yett yett. I thanke you my dear Lord for your intending

1. Marshal Count Camille de Tallard was defeated and captured by the Duke of Marlborough at the Battle of Blenheim in August 1704.
2. Lord George Lennox, 1737–1805, second surviving son of Richmond, was made a General after a long army career in 1793. He was Secretary to the legation to the Court of France, 1765; Constable of the Tower of London, 1783; and a Privy Councillor, 1784.
3. Lady Emily Lennox, 1731–1814, Richmond's daughter, married James, Earl of Kildare and later 1st. Duke of Leinster. See Brian Fitzgerald, *Emily, Duchess of Leinster, 1731–1814. A Study of her Life and Times*, (1949), and his three volumed edition of her correspondence published by the Irish Manuscripts Commission.
4. Isaac Maddox, 1697–1759, had been Prebendary of Eartham in Chichester Cathedral, 1725–1730, and Prebendary of Hampstead, 1730–1743. Bishop of St. Asaph, 1736, he was translated Bishop of Worcester in 1743.

to speake to Lovel, about Sr Thomas Prendergast, & I take for granted you have secured the thing by this time, & I do assure you I shall be most particularly obliged to you for it, butt I long to hear what Lovel sayes to it. As I had half an hours leasure I ventured to trouble you with these requests, which I hope you will forgive from a man that loves you so sincerely as I do. Albemarle is gon with a Genll I dont know who, a Hanoverian, to take a strong post upon the River Nidda, near Hochts. he has been gon these two dayes so as wee hear nothing of him, suppose he has done the thing & all is quiet. butt I'l tell him what you say when I see him; butt I do assure you that nobody in this army has time to write, nay hardly even to eat or sleep. Poor Holderness is very much out of order with violent Head aches, Harcourt is in high spirits; is now in waiting; he was sent yesterday by his Majesty with a compliment to the Emperor at Frankfort who received him gratiously, & sends an other in return to his Majesty to day. Harcourt I find has allready hinted some things in a letter to you. I will tell it more plain, since I have not any fear of this letters being open'd by the enemy, butt if by accident the King himself sees it, I shall not be sorry for it, it is that, as really & truely wee All love him here as it is undoubtedly our duty so to do, it hurts us upon his account more than our own to see his great partiallity to the Hanover troops, of which there are butt too many instances, however as the officers only know it, I hope they will do their best to keep it from the men's ears, for really after their brave and gallant behaviour at Dettingen twould be a pitty to have them mortify'd, tho they grumble very much at one thing which 'tho a seeming trifle, as they in general dislike it, is of consequence, it is that of his wearing a yellow sash upon the Day of the Battle, which is the Hanoverian sash, & ours you know is red. I told my Lord Cartaret of it, & I hope he will persuade him to putt on a red one another time. Most people had a notion he putt himself at the head of a Hanover Regiment of foot at the Battle, butt the real truth was, that he was sometimes at the head of them, butt indeed as often at the head of Pulteneys,[1] & sometimes at the head of Onslow's[2] brigade, so if you hear him accused of that, you may say I vouch the contrary. I have troubled you with a long letter, I am sensible the latter part of it is on tender points & such as I have not, nor would not mention to any soul in England butt yourself, butt I thinke it my duty to your station & to the freindship you honor mee with, to tell you every thing I know, so I hope you wont thinke it from love of tittle tattle, that I say it, for I beleive you know that is not my turn. My Lord Cartaret[3] has promis'd to speake to him about it, & I hope he has, & that his advise will be follow'd. As for my own part I am sure I have no reason to complain, for His Majesty has always been extreamly kind & good to me, & I should be the most ungratefull of men, if I did not love & honor him with all the affection & duty that is due from a servant & subject to a kind & good master, butt tis for these very reasons that my heart is greived to see & hear some things, & I am sure it will hurt you as much, for I know your duty & affection for him & his family, butt I hope it will mend. I must now tell you that Monsieur de Piosasque[4] who came here this morning with a compliment from the Emperor to his Majesty; told me that His Imperial Majesty was so good as to aske kindly, after me & Albemarle, & to say that he should be glad

---

1. Harry Pulteney, 1686–1767, MP for Hedon, 1722–1734, and again, 1739–1741, and for Kingston-upon-Hull, 1767, was Colonel of the 13th. Foot, 1739, and Major General and Equerry to the King, 1743.
2. Richard Onslow, 1697–1760, MP for Guildford, 1727–1760, was Colonel of the 8th. Foot, 1739. He was made Brigadier General in 1742.
3. John Carteret, 2nd. Lord Carteret, 1690–1763, had been Secretary of State under Walpole, 1721–1724, and Lord Lieutenant of Ireland, 1724–1730. He then vigorously opposed Walpole, until he became Secretary of State for the Northern Department on Walpole's fall in 1742. He accompanied King George II in the campaign of 1743. He succeeded as Earl Granville in 1744. He failed to form a ministry in February 1746, and was Lord President of the Council, 1751–1763.
4. Le Comte Charles Piosassque, was Envoy of the Emperor Charles VII.

to see us, upon which I have asked the King's leave, when he changes his quarters, & is nearer Frankfort, to lett me waite upon His Imperial Majesty, which he readily consented to. Our troops are really in fine spirits, & I am sure will <u>redoubler leurs coups</u> if we come to blows again. Bury is much your humble servant, & is in perfect health, tho he lay three nights upon the bare ground; & the night of the battle he lay not only on the wett ground, butt litterally in the mud, & nothing to cover him butt his Cloake, from the most violent rain I ever saw, & which lasted all night, so that now I fancy he will not be in a fuss to see that his bed is air'd. Adieu My Dear Lord, forgive this long letter, you desired me to write to you, & you see I thinke I can never obey your commands too much.

I am with the utmost truth & gratitude, Your Grace's ever faithfull & most affectte humble servant,

Richmond &c.

164. RICHMOND TO NEWCASTLE

King's quarters at Hanau
Wednesday 29 June/10 July 1743

My Dear Lord,

As this goes by Lord Harcourt, I can venture to write with the utmost confidence to you, he will tell you his own story; butt as I know you love me, I beleive I need not aske your pardon for telling you myne. I wrote to Lord Cartaret long before I sett out from England to beg to be inform'd whether as Hanoverian horses were to come to the army, it was understood they as well as the whole stable should be under my direction, he answer'd me that I need not be in any doubt about it, for that he had no notion of any bodys interfering with me, for I had told him if that was the case, I certanly should not come. upon my arrival here I found 80 Hanover Horses, & I plainly saw they were not to be under my command, upon which I desired my Lord Cartaret to tell the King that if they were not I could not possibly serve his Majesty, butt that I desired he would give me leave to stay as a volluntier, for that I was very desirous to see out the campagne, which I am resolv'd to do at all events, butt between freinds I beleive my Lord Cartaret deliver'd butt half what I had said to him, for he told me the King was determin'd to keep his Hanover establishment of his stables seperate from the English. I had told him I only desired the appearances, for that as to really medling with his horses I certanly did not desire to do it, butt that I desired only that all orders might go through my hands, butt even that is deny'd me. he has a puppy of a <u>Vice Grand Ecuyer</u> here as he calls him; young Freechappell;[1] who in effect is Grand Ecuyer. can you imagine then my dear Lord that I can bear this ? can you thinke I ought to bear it ? no, I am sure you cant, & I most certanly will not. My Lord Cartaret very obligeingly sayes that my leaving his service at this time will have a very bad effect; & that with the Duke's illness, which has certanly very justly given the King great concern, I am determin'd for a few dayes to remain quiet; butt indeed it is impossible for me to go on in this way; the Duke has had a violent attack of a fever, & Ranby[2] thought him in very great danger the night before last, butt he has given him so much barke that he hopes he will have no return; he is very easy to day 'tho very low with the severe fitt he has had. however wee are in great hopes he is now in no danger, it has not only given concern to the King, butt I really beleive to every man in the whole army; for by his

1. M. Freechappell, Vice Grand Ecuyer, and a thorn in Richmond's flesh throughout the campaign.
2. John Ranby, 1703–1773, was surgeon in ordinary to the King's household in 1738, and became principal sergeant surgeon in 1743. He induced the government to found a corporation of surgeons separate from the barbers.

brave behaviour upon the day of the Battle, by his love of the service, by his generosity & compassion to prisoners, & by all the good qualitys that ever a young Prince was endow'd with; he has justly gott the love & esteem of every body. I know your attachment to the King so well that I will not vex you with a detail of the cruel partiallitys he shows to his Hanoverian troops & servants at our expence, butt if you care to hear them Lord Harcourt can give you a full account of them. butt the discontentedness of all his English subjects from the highest down to the lowest man in his army is not to be express'd. it greives me to the heart & soul to see it; you know my duty, & you know my affection to him; I was bred up from a child in whig principles, & consequently my attachment to him & his family, is so fix'd in my mind & heart, that not even ill usage can efface it, butt to serve him in my present station is impossible. however I am determin'd to remain some dayes as I am,; for great events are soon expected, as Prince Charles is so near Broglio's army certanly with upwards of 80,000 men; & wee imagine that Broglio's army will join Noalles[1] in a day or two at farthest. I own I should be glad to see the event, which I thinke can not butt turn out well; & then whenever I do quit his Majesty's service, I am determin'd to do it in the most dutifull, & respectfull manner I can. I would have this private discontentment of myne talked of as little as possible in England, so I hope you will mention it to nobody butt my two dear freinds the Duke of Grafton, & Mr Pelham. I must add indeed the Dutchess of Richmond, who (tho I give you my honor I never trusted with the few polliticall secrets I have known) yett as this concerns me & only me, I thought it butt right & reasonable to acquaint her with it. I am & ever shall be in all times, & upon all occasions, with the utmost truth, freindship, & attachment, my Dear Lord, Your Grace's most faithfull & affectionate humble servant

Richmond &c.

Fryd morn.
The French are all decamp'd butt wee are very quiet here. The King has been very much out of order, he kept his bed yesterday. butt is much better thanke God now, & so is the Duke.
Coll: Mordaunt[2] has desired the King's leave not to serve him during the Campagne as Equerry, so I look upon him as already out of employment. butt I look upon that as a trifle, but what's of more consequence is that there is not a general, nor a common soldier in the whole army that is not in some degree discontented; it is butt too true & it is with a most deep concern that I say it. pray burn this letter.

165. NEWCASTLE TO RICHMOND

Newcastle House
July 1st, 1743

My Dear Lord,
  I must return you my most sincere thanks for your very kind letter of ye 19/30 June and for your goodness in desiring the Dutchess of Richmond to communicate Her letter to me, which she did yesterday in the most obliging manner. I cannot sufficiently express to you, the sense I have of this mark of your favour and confidence. I must own the Relation of the Battle in your letter, was very welcome, for between you and I, that sent by my Lord Carteret, is universally thought here a very lame one, and if it was not for private Letters, we should scarce have known any particulars, and have been totally

---

1. Marshal Duke Adrien M. Noailles commanded the French army that had been defeated by the Pragmatic Army under King George II at Dettingen.
2. John Mordaunt, 1697–1780, MP for Pontefract, 1730–1734, for Whitchurch, 1735–1741, and for Cockermouth, 1742–1768. A nephew of the 3rd Earl of Peterborough, he became Colonel in 1741 and General in 1770.

ignorant of the Bravery of our English Foot, to which the Success of the Day is entirely owing. My Lord Carteret's saying nothing of the English in His first letter, raised a great outcry against Him, and as there was not one word of the English, particularly in the second Account sent by the Court messenger, we were forced to make a little addition to the paper printed authority, or there would have been a Clamour against my Lord Carteret not to be withstood. You see in short what confidence I write to your Grace. I know you will mention it to nobody but to <u>Albemarle</u>. We are here much in the dark about everything; we neither know the Numbers, nor situation of our Army, nor that of the enemy; nor have any Accounts of the intended Motions & Operations of our own Army, nor Conjectures about the probable Views & Designs of Marl Noailles. As to the Emperor's having abandoned France, & separated His army from the French, upon which I find you think, that the Peace between Him & ye Queen of Hungary is actually made, & yt the Emperor is to join us. My good <u>Brother</u>,[1] has been pleased to send me only Copies of a few Letters that have passed, which show a general Disposition in the Emporer to make up wth ye Q. of Hungary, & that His Impl Majesty, had separated His Army from ye French; that Monr Broglio, was coming to join Noailles, & that Pr Charles had been sent to, to follow Him, etc.; & this is the substance of what I know. You may therefore be assured, that almost any particulars, that come to your knowledge will be acceptable news to me. We have wrote a Letter to Lord Carteret, which perhaps may produce some further information. Your letter to ye Ds of R. gave me both Joy and Concern. Joy, for the great & glorious Victory obtained over the French; for your own safety, Albemarle's & that of all my particular friends; for the gallant Behaviour of all our English Officers, & the never to be forgotten Bravery of the English Foot, concern, for the Behaviour of the English Horse, and for some other <u>particulars</u>, which I am afraid are more to be lamented, than cured. I had a very kind, & confidential letter from Harcourt, which I take as a great Mark of his Goodness to me. I am heartily sorry for the subject of it, & have by this Messenger returned Him my thanks in the best manner, I can. And now my dear Duke, I must trouble you with an affair which mistifies and concerns me more than any thing of that kind ever did, and which I am sure from your good nature, and sincere love and affection for us Both, You will feel. You are no stranger to my friendship and affection for Lord Albemarle, of which I have endeavoured to give, all possible Proofs, for now upwards of twelve years, without any interruption. I will leave it to His friends & family to judge, whether I have succeeded in my endeavour to serve Him or not. This I will say, that I never in my life thought, the having done Him any service, was a Reason, not to do Him more the Day after, if it was in my power. All the Return I ever expected was His friendship & affection, and I have thought & do believe, I have had it most sincerely. But since he has been abroad, I have very seldom heard from Him, and it is now near four or five months ago since I have had one Word from Him. Notwithstanding, I have wrote three Letters most earnestly desiring it, & two sent by particular messengers, two or three months ago, the last of which was sent by Bowie, who broke His leg, & in that I most earnestly desired an answer. Since that, a Battle has been fought by our Army. He was in great danger, & has distinguished Himself, which He must know would, as indeed it has done, give me the greatest satisfaction. I have not only, not had one Word from Him, but not so much as a kind Compliment from Him by you, or any Body, so that I must think, He has taken something most strongly amiss of me, & has quite altered His opinion & affection towards me, and that is what, my dear Duke, I desire you would find out. I can declare upon my honor, that I not only, never intended to offend Him, but have always had, & have still the greatest friendship & affection for Him. I can think of but one thing, which can possibly be the occasion of

1. Carteret.

it, & that is, a Letter of affectionate concern & advice, that I wrote Him, upon his private affairs. If that be it, I am sure he is in the wrong. I love Him as a Brother, and I thought I could not show it better, than by advising Him as a Brother. I beg you would find out what is the Cause of this Change. When all the World have letters from their friends in the army, could any one Man alive think, I should not have had one single Letter from Lord Albemarle. It Hurts me to the greatest Degree, when I repeat it. If, as I really still hope is ye case, He has forbore writing so long, that now he does not well know what to say, I beg you would remove that difficulty at once, & assure Him that I shall receive a kind Letter from Him, with greater pleasure than ever, I did in my life, & <u>can I say more?</u> I beg you would give Him the enclosed letter, which I leave open for your Perusal, & you may read this letter to Him, if you think proper. I must again repeat my Desire, to have constant Accounts from you or Him, of the Motions of our Army. You see by what I have wrote, that I stand in need of them, & shall now do so the more, as the Ds of Rd goes next week to Holland. I thank God, she and all ye children are well. I dined with Her yesterday at Linkey's who is ever your most affect servant. I beg my most respectful Compliments to the Duke. We have been here a little uneasy about Him, his R.H. not having wrote by ye last Messenger, but I hope there is no foundation for it, & that we shall soon hear he is quite well. I intend to write a <u>Laconic</u> to Huske.

I am my Dear Lord, with the best wishes of Health & Happiness to you Your most affect, humble servt

Holles Newcastle

166. NEWCASTLE TO RICHMOND

Newcastle House
July 5, 1743

My dear Lord,

I troubled you with so long a letter, by the last Messenger, that you shall have a very short one by this, which is chiefly to thank you for your very kind letter of ye 24th June, July 5th & to assure you, that I shall ever obey all your Commands, as far as my power goes. I have had a very good answer from Lovel. He never promises, but Sr Thomas Pendergrass will certainly have it, if it is vacant in Lovel's time. Sr Marmaduke He says is better. As to Dr Blomer, there is nothing new vacant that He can have. I think the Arch Bishop plays off a little, but I will endeavour to settle things a little with his Grace. Cornwallis is promised the first, & I will see what can be done for Blomer afterwards, tho' really Dr. Middleton[1] who is three score years old, should be considered, but no Dr. Middleton with me, can be in Competition with a friend of yours. You will hear by this Messenger, & perhaps sooner, of the death of Lord Wilmington. It is said he has left no will, & in that case all his Land estate goes to ye Earl of Northampton.[2] As to the Treasury we have persuaded your friend Harry[3] to take it, (if the King pleases), without making at present any other alteration in ye Treasury, tho' to be sure, that must be, when ye King comes back. Harry writes to His Majesty, & I doubt not but we shall have a favourable answer. Ld Bath & His friends, have, as we hear dispatched a Messenger to Carteret three days ago, offering I suppose Ld Bath's service. I fancy our Master will not relish that. Pray lett us know what you can pick up about it. Harry & I have Both wrote to Ld Carteret upon the Subject. If the King does

---

1. Conyers Middleton, 1683–1750, divine and fellow of Trinity College, Cambridge.
2. James Compton, 5th. Earl of Northampton, 1687–1754, succeeded his uncle, the Earl of Wilmington, in 1743.
3. Henry Pelham.

not immediately determine for my Brother, it will have very bad Consequences here at home. Lord Carteret sends us Word, we may expect soon to hear of an action, but whether before the junction wh Pr. Charles army, is to us uncertain. The French Letters also mention Monsr de Noailles design to make another attempt. I hope in God it will be as unsuccessful as the last. In all these Dangers, I pray God preserve His Majesty, the Duke, my dear Duke of Richmond, Albemarle & Bury, with many others my very good friends. My Respects to Harcourt and Holderness & John Delawar, of whom we hear nothing of late. Lord March has been ill, but the Ds of Richmond sends me Word this evening, that He is much better. I hope you will hear by next post, that he is quite well. Pray make no excuse for ye length of your letters. They are always most welcome, & I hope to have them very frequently. My Brother sends his Compliments to you & Albemarle. Pray mine to Him, (when you see Him), and Bury. My letter is longer, than I first intended, but I know you will forgive it.

I am my dear Duke Ever most sincerely and affectly yrs

Holles Newcastle

P.S. I must beg you would not say one word to any Body whatsoever, of what I write you about the Treasury, & my Brother.

167. RICHMOND TO NEWCASTLE

King's head Quarters at Hanau
Wed: 6/17 July 1743

My Dearest Lord,

I have had many obligations to you in my life, very great ones, & such as I shall never forgett, butt this last, trifling as it may appear to your generous & good heart, I mean that very kind attention of putting good news upon the outside of my letter to the Duchess of Richmond, has gain'd my heart to such a degree that I really am at a loss for words to express my sincere gratitude to you for it. & also for the kind visit you & dear Mr Pelham were so good as to make her the very day you receiv'd the good news. I had the pleasure of your's of the 24th June, & also saw that which you wrote to Lord Albemarle, & as to what you desire of me, I have obey'd your commands as far as it lay in my power, & have wrote a long letter to you by Lord Harcourt.

You did well to rejoice at our Victory, it was certanly a great one, butt might have been the most compleat one that ever was gain'd. however 'tis now too late to reflect upon past mistakes, butt our inaction now must surprise all those that are not in the secrets of the Closet. I am very sure I am not, not do I desire to be, so you can really expect no news from me, for I do assure you Bury & Southby know as much as I do. I name the last because what I am going to tell you I had from him, it is what a french officer say'd to an English one at Frankfort. Parbleu Monsr vous est bien pollis apres nous avoir rosse a Dettingen de nous laisser partir en desordre sans nous suivre, et puis de nous laisser decamper come cela a vostre barbe avec plus de desordre mesme qu'apres la bataille, sans nous incomoder d'aucune facon. butt he was a pert talkative French Puppy, so nobody minded him. butt indeed I am afraid the generallity of people begin to talke very idly here, & I fear the longer wee stay here the more twill be. you say you are impatient to know what will be undertaken in consequence of the Victory. I cant tell you what will be undertaken, butt I can assure you nothing has been done; & it is just now twenty days since the action. The French army are march'd quite off, & wee conclude them pas'd the Rhine at Openheim; & Broglio is also running away for the Rhine as fast as he can, so to be sure the first great point is gained; that is you may safely say the French are drove out of Germany; & twas as surely owing to our Victory at Dettingen. I have nothing more to say to you at present, I wish I had, so I shall only

107

add that I am, & ever shall be, my dear Lord, Your Grace's ever faithfull, & most affectionate humble servant,

Richmond &c.

My best services attend Mr Pelham. you say you wrote to Lovel, butt dont tell me his answer. I thanke you extreamly for all my Jobs, as you call them.

168.   RICHMOND TO NEWCASTLE

King's quarters at Hanau
Wednesday July 13/24 1743

My Dear Lord,

I must beg leave to trouble your Grace with a affair that is of the greatest consequence to a Corps that I shall ever love & value, I mean the Blews. They have been cruelly, falsly & scandalously aspers'd in England, and we have traced it to the spreader of the lye, & find it to be Over the Messager. The enclosed is a coppy of part of a letter from a Gentleman in London to Coll. Beake,[1] which as soon as the Coll; received he lay'd before my Lord Stair, who publickly declared that the whole was a lye, as did also his gentleman of the horse Mr Drummond, who is quoted in the letter. & this has obliged the officers, in vindication of their own honors, to publish a fact, which otherwise they never would have mention'd, it was that they were not broke by the enemy butt by the King's own regiment of horse commanded by Generall Honywood, who, that is the Regiment, turning from the enemy rid full in amongst them, & broke their Rankes, which was the very time they were accused of giving way themselves. butt they afterwards formed & I saw them myself in perfect order, & before this accident hapned every body agrees they stood the strongest cannonading, with as good a countenance & with as much intrepidity as any regiment of them all in the King's service, as you may easily imagine, when I tell your Grace their loss by cannon shott.

Kill'd	Wounded
8 men	1 Cornet
22 horses	11 men
	14 horses

besides Sr James Chamberlayn's[2] horse who commanded a squadron that had his jaw broke & was kill'd. I only mention this to show your Grace that the cannonading was hott, & every body was witness to their standing it like brave men. I must therefore joyn with them in desiring that an example may be made of the Messager. enclosed is a letter to your Grace sign'd by the Commanding Officer of each Squadron.[3] I hope you will give attention to it, as it really comes from injured men of honor that claim your protection.

I am my Dear Lord, Your Grace's most faithfull & obedient humble servant
Richmond &c.

1.   Colonel Gregory Beake, died 1749, MP for St. Ives, 1741–1747, a lieutenant colonel in the Royal Horse Guards, fought at Dettingen and Fontenoy. Nearly forty years earlier, he had distinguished himself at Malplaquet.
2.   Sir James Chamberlayn was a loyal servant to Richmond in the Royal Horse Guards, and commanded a squadron.
3.   The letter signed by Gregory Beake, Charles Jenkinson and Sir James Chamberlayn is B.L. Add. Ms. 32,700 f.295.

169. RICHMOND TO NEWCASTLE

King's quarters at Hanau
Wednesday July 13/24 1743

My Dear Lord,

I must return your grace my most sincere thankes for your very kind, & obligeing letter of the 1st instant, which I will answer as fully as I can, butt I must first of all say or rather add something to the letter herein enclosed that I have troubled you with in relation to the blews. here has been an outcry against them here, & I find the same in England spread first of all by Over the Messager, as Sharpe has writ word to Beake, in which I hope or rather beleive your Grace & the Duke of Grafton will do them Justice, for I can never doubt of the contrary of either of you. butt now I apprehend you will say how came you to be obliged to go to them yourself, as I fear you saw I did by my letter to the Duchess of Richmond, to which I answer that I really then had heard they had turn'd tale, as every body in their rear thought by seeing them broke to pieces, 'tho they were quite form'd again by the time I came up to them, butt that is now fully explain'd in my enclosed letter, not butt that I own, & so do their own officers, that the men did not show the spirit they should have done, & what was expected of them on such an occasion; that is they did not rally so fast as they should, nor did they go on with that chearfulness that the foot & some of the dragoons did. butt to say that they ever run away, or even <u>gave</u> way, is absollutely false, & to do justice to the officers they have in this affair behaved like men of honor; whilst nothing was said they accused nobody, butt when their reputations was call'd in question they declared the truth & sadled the right horse.

I beg pardon for giving you so much trouble, butt could not avoid it, as it is in vindication of a sett of honest & brave men that I have always loved & esteemed. Now as to other affairs there is one which at present in my opinion is of the highest consequence to us all, I mean My Lord Wilmington's death, which I find hapned the day after the date of all your letters, & My Lord Cartaret knew it here only by a private Messager from Sr John Rushout,[1] who arrived at the same time with your Messager. I hope My Lord Cartaret will write openly to you upon it, by this Messager, butt I own in such an affair as this in which he must know my sentiments, I dont like his saying nothing to me about it, further than <u>that it was an event of great consequence & that he was sorry it hapned at this time</u>. butt I could have wish'd that he would have said he was in the same mind now that he openly declared himself in some time ago in London. I wont so much as suppose he is not, & I am willing to thinke he means that Mr Pelham can meet with no oposition butt from My Lord Bath. I say I hope & beleive he means so & I also hope that My Lord Bath, (who has always peak'd himself upon preferring the love of his Country to <u>all</u> other considerations whatsoever), will now shew it by giving up all pretentions to Mr Pelham; who I am very sure has the good wishes of every true lover of his King & Country in England, & what's more I'l venture to say that it is impossible the King's affairs can go on well without it. You'l say that's speaking very big for one's freind, butt, bad as my judgement may be in other points, I am sure wee have all learnt great experience within these two years. Pray make me easy upon this affair when you know anything, for I doubt much if I shall learn anything here. butt as Huske sayes secrecy is commendable, & I am very glad I know none of them. Now as to that part of your Grace's letter, which relates to Lord Albemarle, I shall say butt very little, only that he protests solemnly he never took any thing ill of you in all his life, that he loves you as much as you can love him, that he wrot to you a

---

1. Sir John Rushout, 1684–1775, MP for Malmesbury, 1713 and 1715, and for Evesham, 1722–1768, was Lord Commissioner of the Navy, 1742; Treasurer of the Navy, 1743; and a Privy Councillor, 1744.

fortnight ago, & write to you again by this Messager to tell you how asham'd he is of his neglect, so that I hope all is made up & I shall say no more about it. I am glad you gott something out of my letters to the Duchess of Richmond, & am sorry you had not more from other people; tho I told My Lord Cartaret you complain'd of his not sending you particulars enough, butt he sayes there were Messagers upon the road loaded with particulars. I hope you was so good as to report none out of my letters, butt such as were propper to be reported; butt the stile of a fond husband, for I wont say a foolish one, in that respect, to his wife, is not propper to be made publick to any butt such a freind as yourself.

Now as to further particulars of the battle I can recollect none to send you, as to our Numbers they have always been a secret, & as to the scituation of our army in the feild of Battle, I can say no more than what I have said, because hitherto I can learn no more, nay I have not been able yett to gett only the Names of the Battallions of the first line that were engaged; butt hope to do that with some trouble by the next post. Wee have at last gott a pretty exact list of the kill'd, wounded, & stray'd, which My Lord Cartaret indeed sayes he has sent you. Observe that amongst the stray'd are no english, butt 31 hanoverians, & 253 austrians, their 'tho I must do them justice that by stray'd or missing as they call it in returns, I dont apprehend them run away, but Prisoners or deserted, they would have you thinke it, butt I am apt to thinke the non effectives are included; whereas I fear our non effective are returned as kill'd men. as for intended motions & operations I have already often told your Grace that it was impossible & indeed impropper for me to know them, & as little do I know of the enemy's operations. I short I can only tell you two matters of fact; one is that the two french armys have gott safe to the other side of the Rhine, & wee have all been here as quiet as lambs for near a month. as to other particulars which you say are more to be lamented than cured, they go well enough at present as every thing is so quiet: I have fully enough explained myself upon that subject, particularly as to what relates to my self, by the letter I sent by Lord Harcourt. This very moment my old freind Jack Parker,[1] has just brought me yours of the 5th which has set my mind at rest about the Treasury, & I hope as Mr Pelham has no difficultys of his side he will meet with none from any other quarter. why should not Sandys be made a peer? he is immensly rich, & surely that would be to him a good equivalent for the Chanclrsp of the Exr & then you have the paymasters place for some better & more usefull man. My zeal often times runs me into ridiculous advice, butt as you know I mean well you will forgive it. I will certanly not mention what your Grace is so kind as to say to me about Mr Pelham to any mortal living, butt I hope the king will determine it immediately. What My Lord Cartaret meant by telling you that wee expected an other action soon I cant tell; butt I am sure nothing has look'd like it since Dettingen. You bid me make no excuses for the length of my letters, so I shall not, butt whenever I do write a long letter, I always thinke that it might have been shorter by haveing omitted several trifles, & that I am sure is the case now. I am very much obliged to Mr Pelham for his kind remembrance of me; I shall tell all your freinds how good you are in remembring of them, 'tho I must tell you that some of them thinke it a little hard you mention your services to Sr Thos Wynn at the same time. Surely 'tis the dirtyest dog that ever lived. I must now thanke you My Dear Lord for your kind concern for my poor boy March. I own I am a good deal uneasy about him, for I find the Duchess of Richmond is extreamly so. I am also obliged to you for your goodness in writing to Lovel, & thinkeing of poor Bloomer. I am my Dear Lord with the greatest truth & affection, Your Grace's ever faithfull, & obliged humble servant

Richmond &c.

1. Jack Parker, the messenger.

110

Wee hear poor Broglio is strip'd of every thing even the government of Strasbourg, & relequez a ses terres. wee have also heard that some of Prince Charles's hussars have pick'd up three squadrons of Le Royal, Cavallerie, before they could pass the Rhine. I had like to have forgott what you would with reason have been very angry with me for; it is that I obey'd your Grace's commands to his Royal Highness the Duke, who commands me to return you his compliments with his thankes for your great concern for him; he mends prodigiously fast. Huske answers your letter to day, he also grows better butt it will I fear be a long affair. Major Honeywood with his nine wounds will do well; I saw his brains the other day when he was dres'd. Poor Major Johnson is in a very bad way.

	Killed	Wounded	Lost	Total
English	263	557		820
Hanoverians	177	345	31	553
Austrians	315	409	253	977
	755	1311	284	2350

170. NEWCASTLE TO RICHMOND

Newcastle House
July 15th 1743

My Dear Lord,

Tho' I have no letters from your Grace to acknowledge, & nothing new to send you from hence, I could not let this Messenger go without congratulating you upon the Recovery of Dear March, who, Wilmot says is in a very good way, & has been often abroad to take the air. Perhaps I may differ in my politicks from all my friends in the army, but I own I am sorry your late neighbours, the French, have left you, & that you had not an opportunity of following them, & preventing their Return home. They must have fallen in all human probability to the neutral army, after Pr Charles had joined, & now, when, & where you will seek them, I know not. The last Messenger from the army did not bring very agreable accounts to us, & I am afraid our answers will not be better rellished at the army, but then I say, to you, and to you only in the greatest confidence. I am heartily sorry for poor Harcourt, for Godsake tell me the truth of the case. I think, it is impossible for Him to be in the right, in going away, & leaving the King. I will talk to Him in the best, & most friendly manner I can, when I see Him. My kind love to Albemarle & Bury. The Honble Harry is always yours. tho' at present not in good spirits. The town says, you are returning to Hanover. My duty to ye Dear Duke. I love & honor Him, as much as you do, & rejoice to hear He is so well.

I am ever yrs

Holles Newcastle

171. NEWCASTLE TO RICHMOND

Newcastle House
July 22d, 1743

My Dearest Lord,

As I do not dispatch a Messenger today, I cannot write so fully as I intend to do by the first Messenger that goes. I would not however omit returning you thanks, even by the post, for your two most kind and obliging letters of ye 10 and 17 N.S. which I received on Saturday last, the one by Harcourt, the other by the Messenger. You are too good to take notice of the little attention, I could not but show them to one I esteem so much, on her own as well as your account, as the Dutchess of Richmond. I was surprised to hear on my coming to town on Wensday night, that she went early the

111

next morning, wh dear Ld March, Ld George and Lady Emely to Holland. They were set out, before my Messenger was wh them in ye morning. I conclude all in good Health, & hope to hear when they are got safe in Holland. As I intend to write fully to your Grace in two or three days, I will enter no further into the Contents of your kind letters, than to assure you, you have not in ye world, one, who more sincerely loves & esteems you than my self. I shall open my Heart to you by the Messenger, & suppose I shall be able to say something, by a Messenger, that I have been expecting every hour for some days from ye army.

I am my dearest Duke ever most affectly and unalterable yrs

Holles Newcastle

P.S. Has Albemarle quite disguarded me, & for what

172. NEWCASTLE TO RICHMOND

Newcastle House
July 26th, 1743

My Dear Lord,

I write this only to excuse my sending the enclosed in Stone's Hand, but indeed, I have been so taken up this day, that I had not time to write it myself, so as you could read it. We are here extremely angry, and with reason, at the neglect shewed us, by my Bro' Secretary. What is this Scheme. Does He intend to make Lord Bath, or put in Winchelsea,[1] as His own Deputy; or keep the Treasury open to do as He shall think proper upon His Return to England; & will our Master lett Him do all this. As to the affair of the Blews, I will only add some of the Stories about them here in Town, before the arrival of Over, but I beg you would not mention me for having said any thing about them, but what I wrote in my ostensible letter to you. I know I have troubled you a vast deal upon this subject, but that arises from my concern at not being able to do just what you wish of me. I must beg yt the enclosed letter may be seen by nobody. You may tell Albemarle what you please of ye contents of it. I hope to hear soon of ye Ds of Richmond's safe arrival in Holland. Tom Hill had no account of it this morning. You may be sure, I am incapable of mentioning any thing, yt she was so good as to shew me in your letter, that was to be kept secret. I had an opportunity of telling Genl Wade,[2] ye secretary at war, this evening, of what I had heard of Ld Stairs Declaration relating to ye Behaviour of the Blues.

I am my dear Duke Ever Yrs

Holles Newcastle

173. NEWCASTLE TO RICHMOND

Whitehall
July 26th, 1743

Private

My Dear Lord,

I hope you will be satisfied with what I have wrote in my other Letter, which is an ostensible one, in answer to your Letter, and that from the Officers of the Blue Regiment. There can be no Commands from your Grace, which I shall not take

1. Daniel Finch, 8th. Earl of Winchelsea and 3rd. Earl of Nottingham, 1689–1769, MP for Rutland, 1710–1730, was 1st. Lord of the Admiralty, 1742–1744, and again, 1757, and Lord President of the Council, 1765–1766.
2. George Wade, 1673–1748, MP for Hindon, 1715–1722, and for Bath, 1722–1748, was Lieutenant General of Ordnance, 1742–1748. He was created a Field Marshall, 1743, and was Commander-in-Chief in Flanders, 1743–1745. He was Commander-in-Chief for Northern England, 1745.

Pleasure to obey; But, otherwise, I must own, this is not a very agreable Commission; and indeed I have nothing to do, (nor can have) with the Punishment, or Removal of Messengers; and therefore, if the Gentlemen did think the Regiment injured by this Fellow, and would have him punish'd for it, they should first have complain'd of him to Lord Carteret, who was upon the spot; and desired him, to take the King's Orders, to write to my Lord Chamberlain upon it. Your Friends here, (by whom I mean only Lord Chancellor, the Duke of Grafton, and my Brother,) are all of opinion, that the Certificate, given by Lord Stair, and your Grace, is the best justification, that can be, of the Behaviour of the Regiment; and that the turning out this poor Devil of an impertinent, ignorant Messenger, would not have the effect intended; and therefore it would be better to drop it. However, as you can never desire anything of me, that I will not do, as far as depends on me, I will be entirely guided by you, if you still wish, I should do anything in it; tho' I don't well see what I can do.

And now, My Dear Lord, I must thank you, for your most kind, and affectionate Letters, by Lord Harcourt; by the messenger, Harte, and by Webster; which arrived here last Saturday. I cannot sufficiently express my most sincere Concern for the melancholy Contents of your Letter, by Harcourt. Those accounts are but too much confirmed by all private Letters, that come, or Persons, that arrive, from the Army. What relates particularly to yourself, is indeed the most extraordinary, and unjustifiable, of the whole. Such Treatment of one of your Grace's high Quality, Station, and above all, your most distinguished Zeal for His Majesty, and for His family, and constant, & powerful Endeavours for his Majesty's service, is amazing. These Considerations must make the deepest impression upon me, and upon all, who have a Duty to the King, and Concern for his Service, as well, as are desirous to be thought Friends to their Country: and my most particular Friendship, and Love for you, must make that most disagreable Incident the more sensible to me. But the Conduct of every thing abroad is so unaccountable, as well with regard to the motions, & Operations, (or rather, no motions, or Operations) of the Army, as to the schemes, and negotiations for Peace; and the usage of all mankind is such, whether they are in the Army abroad, or intrusted with His Majesty's affairs here at home, that I neither wonder at any thing; nor can answer for any thing. The only thing, I think, we have to do; and therefore all I can advise my best friends, is, to be as cautious, as possible, in the Steps to be taken, in these difficult times, and, in these most disagreable Circumstances. I am most heartily glad to see, My Dear Duke, you do not want this advice. Your Conduct has been the most prudent imaginable, in a most provoking Situation; and I doubt not, but you will continue the same Prudence; and bear, as long, and as much, as can be born, considering what must be the Consequences of your leaving the King's Service, at this time, and for so good, or rather so bad a Reason. As to Ourselves, you will be surprised to hear, that my Lord Cartaret has not yet vouchsafed to answer, or even to acknowledge the Receipt of our Letters, of the 5th, upon the Subject of the Treasury; tho' they were arrived, on the 13th. O.S. which is now fourteen Days ago and before Webster, the Messenger, came away with Lord Carteret's last <u>Nothing</u> letters. In short, it is the most contemptuous usage, that ever was, towards Men of some Consideration, (and perhaps, one time, or other, his Lordship may find them so,) in this Country. He has great Schemes on foot. I don't know what to call them; they are neither for Peace, nor War: for France, nor against it. They tend to gain the Emperor; but at a dear Rate.

My Brother begs His most affectionate Compliments to your Grace. He is truly sensible of your goodness to Him, and joins with me, in earnestly desiring a Continuance of your most invaluable Friendship to us.

You see, My Dear Duke, with what Confidence, I write to you, which I am sure, you will pardon. My best Compliments to Albemarle; I write to Him by this Messenger, to thank him for his kind Letter. Pray remember me to all Friends. I am far from putting Sr Thomas Wynne, upon a Foot with them; and do not think, He would be much

obliged to me, for mentioning Him, at the Tail of my Letter in the Manner, I did.
I am my Dear Lord Your Grace's most affect. humble servt

Holles Newcastle

174. RICHMOND TO NEWCASTLE

King's quarters at Hanau
Wednesday July 27/ Aug. 7 1743

My Dear Lord,

It is now a fortnight since I last wrote to your Grace, butt I hope you received Dell's letter with my excuses. I was gon from hence a Week to Prince Charles's army, when I have the vanity to say he did just for me what the King did for him here, that is he turn'd out his whole army for me, after which I need say nothing more of his politeness to me. It is a most glorious army, the Horse prodigious fine, & so are the Dragoons, the horses good, & what's extraordinary is good order. butt nothing nigh the size or beauty of ours, that all look miserably now tho for want of their tails to drive away the flys. Their foot are short, thick strong well sett fellows, butt I do assure you Jemmy Pelham would cutt a figure in the front rank of their Grenadiers; butt these are the men that have beat the French, & have done it as you all know, de bonne grace & often, & I am persuaded, & they entirely so, that they will do it again. Altogether they make a good show, their whiskers indeed are not black'd with Jappan, their hair is not powder'd, nor do any of them wear false calves, under milk white Jessamy garters, butt still they are good troops, & as I have already said i'm sure they'l beat the French. They have not neither that excessive strickt discipline I had always heard of, for I saw some twenty sutlers tents (after the Watch was sett & Tatoo beat) full of soldiers & whores, singing, waving, & dancing. I ask'd Prince Charles if that was suffer'd. he answered oui suremont j'aime que me gens le divertisement, & sils aime mieux danser et chanter que dormir, ils sont toujours le maistre chez moy. Some troops are taught to look big & bluff, these laugh & smile, & dont look half as feirce, yett they look as if they had a mind to fight the foe, & not frighten the freind. I left them in full march for the Rhine, & wee are to march on Fryday or Saturday. our austrians are already march'd, butt I own I dont understand our operations, 'tho to be sure they are right, butt by what I can find wee are to cross below Mayence, & Prince Charles by Basle, or thereabouts which aboove two hundred english miles distant the place I left them at in their march was Rastat, which is above 120 english miles from hence, & wee are to march downwards & they upwards. however as this to be sure has been concerted, I take for granted it is right. I find your answers are not very well relish'd as you observe you dont promis support enough. butt how can you promis it without being sure of the House of Commons, & how can you be sure of that if you disoblige two hundred & odd, of your old Whig freinds, by putting the man in the world they dislike the most at the head of the Treasury. I told your brother Secretary so, he fell in a violent passion, & swore he had a better personal interest than any body in the House of Commons, & whilst in a passion talk'd in my poor opinion as weak as ever Ratt did, butt that did not last a minute, & then he was the man of sense again. he bewail'd the difficultys of the circumstances that is as to this particular point of the Treasury, & then he show'd me in great confidence both Ld Bath & Mr Pelhams letters. butt before I go on I must tell you that he began by telling me he had writ to you to lay our difficultys as to the warr before you, & that your answer was not relish'd, not meaning personally, butt that the answer of the Regency was not full enough, he promis'd to show it me, butt I had not time yesterday. Then I told him a lye, which was that you had said nothing to me about the Treasury, so desired he would acquaint me with it as every thing that regarded a Pelham, was a matter of concern to me, & then he shew'd me the letters & spoke with kindness & I really beleive with sincere confidence to me. he swears he wishes Mr

Pelham at the head of the Treasury, butt that as My Lord Bath contrary to his expectations desires it, he is engaged as far as in him lyes to him, as Mr Pelham & you know, & indeed Mr Pelham in his letter to him acknowledges it. I told him I was very sorry for it, for it was an affair of the utmost consequence. he agreed with me in that butt he said if Mr Pelham would give way now, he was sure it must naturally fall into his hands in six, butt his Lordship did not make that out at all clear to me, nor indeed did he attempt it, butt was satisfy'd with laying it down as a fact, which I cant say satisf'd me. his argument was that if My Lord Bath's people fly off wee are undone. Myne was that if our old Whigs fly off the being undone would be more certain. Jack Parker waits for my letter so I must have done & have not time to read it over so excuse the nonsense.

I am My Dear Lord, Your's for ever

Richmond &c.

175.   RICHMOND TO NEWCASTLE

King's quarters at Bibrick
Wednesday 3/14 June 1743
[dated August by Newcastle]

My Dear Lord,

I received your grace's three letters all of the same date the 26 July, by Carrington the messenger; as to that which I am to shew to the blews, of which I have not yett had an oportunity, I own you have explain'd it very plainly that the turning out of the Messager Over, would be too great a thing to undertake as it can't be done without the King's order, butt then my Dear Lord, I wish your Grace had desired the Duke of Grafton to have given him a severe reprimand, & to have given him orders to have asked their pardons whenever he return'd hither which may still be done, if the Duke of Grafton pleases, & as he very much depends upon your Grace, you might give him another reprimand yourself, & that I am very sure would satisfy the officers. butt really I must say if no notice at all is taken of the fellow, the will have great reason to complain, for as they can never see him without his grey hound, his person is sacred, else he would certanly gett a most hearty drubbing. so I hope both your Grace & the Duke of Grafton will be so good as to give him such a reprimand as you thinke propper, with orders to aske pardon of the officers. This will not only satisfy the whole regiment butt oblige them; & I assure you that it will particularly oblige me. & now I must return you my most sincere & gratefull acknowledgements for your two other very kind letters; by which I am very sorry to find you are under so much uneasiness. I hope it may be without reason, & that my Lord Cartaret will with that freindship he always has, & does to this day, & every day to me, profess to you, & Mr Pelham. butt one part of your letter I own surpris'd me which was that where you seem'd to mistrust his having a scheme of bringing in My Lord Winchelsea, because as the Dss of Richmond had writ me word before that was talked of in London, I asked My Lord Cartaret if there was anything in it, & he protested to me he never thought of it, that his sole wishes were for Mr Pelham, butt that he was engaged to support My Lord Bath if he insisted upon it, as now to his great concern he did. I find by him & our freind Huske who you know is his ecco, that their argument is that if my Lord Bath had it, he could not keep it six months & then Mr Pelham of course must have it, butt my answer to that is in the first place, that I would never trust to that, & in the next, that the majority of our best freinds would leave even Mr Pelham, if ever he submitted to it; & then Mr Pelham, your Grace & all of us should be upon a pretty footing, that of haveing no dependance butt upon my Lord Bath's freinds. My Lord Cartaret sayes that the King's affairs at home will be ruin'd & all our schemes, & success abroad destroy'd, if wee are quarrelling for Places at home, I grant it & am entirely of his mind. butt who is it owing to? & who are the quarrellers for Places, butt my Lord Bath & his freinds.

as to not answering Mr Pelham's letter, it is certanly abominable, 'tho perhaps he may answer it by this messager; butt I know he had not a few days ago, for he told me he did not know what to answer either to Mr Pelham or my Lord Bath; if he has answer'd the latter & not the former, it is unpardonable, & unjustifyable, if he has answer'd neither, which I am apt to thinke might be the case, 'tis not quite so bad, 'tho at the same time not at all excusable.

Now I must tell you that Albemarle tells me that the Duke of Marlborough told him, that my Lord Cartaret had recommended Lord Winchelsea, which after what I had heard I own astonish'd me, for tho I am turn'd of forty, I own I cant help still being surpris'd at double dealing, I shall learn better in time. butt I cant nor wont beleive this yett, & I am persuaded the Duke of Marlborough must have mistaken. however the event will shew it. His Lordship seems to be extreamly well with the King, & so I would have him as long as he is well with you, & that his schemes are right; & really now wee all thinke, wee are doing the right thing, for wee are now crossing the Rhine, Neiperg with his Austrians are over, & wee are all encamp'd upon a fine hill, just above, & commanding our bridge, which I now look upon out of my window, & a most glorious sight it is. from whence I hope our schemes here are alter'd something from what you describe them; & that they are now entirely against France. As for gaining the Emperor, it is entirely an Allemanick scheme, as well as my Lord Cartaret's, I find all the Germans here & in Prince Charles's army very desirous of it, butt then it is to gett him to act offensively against France, not for the assistance they say of his troops butt for the sanction of the empire. the messager waits so I must again leave off abruptly. Yours for ever I have not time to read my letter.

Richmond &c.

[Endorsed August 3/14]

176. RICHMOND TO NEWCASTLE

King's quarters at Biberick
Wednesday 10/21 August 1743

My Dear Lord,

I wrote a very long letter to your Grace by the last Messager, butt as he call'd upon me in a hurry I was forced to leave off very abruptly, which was very lucky for you, as the letter was at least long enough as it was. I thinke the last toppick was that of Mr Pelham's having had no answer, from your brother Secretary here, & I dont find he has sent any yett; I asked him the other day if he had, he said <u>no</u>, nor to My Lord Bath neither, I then ask'd him <u>why</u> he had not, his answer was, why what can I say to them? to which I answered he knew best, 'tho I should have no difficulty if I were in his case. butt I find it's very plain he intends to putt it off as long as he can. he sayes these things might be presently setled in England, butt at this distance tis not so easy. Now as to what relates to myself, I have taken my resollution to acquiesce in any thing till the campagne is over, for 'tho my freind Harcourt has gon off in that hasty manner, I never approved of it, & consequently shall certanly not follow his example, I have not vanity enough to thinke that my leaving his Majesty's service now or at any other time can have the least effect upon his affairs, butt upon my own private account, I mean plainly for my reputation I would not upon any account quit him during a campagne. I must also say that things are rather mended, Monsr Freechappel does nothing now butt the part of a head groom, that is in taking care of all his Hanover horses, & I do all the <u>functions</u> of the Master of the Horse, that is of helping him into his voiture, & setting in it by him & so forth, butt have nothing to do with his Hanover horses, nor voitures, only the privilege of going in them, butt the greasing the wheels & all that is entirely under Monsr Freechappell, so you see I have Cloake enough to cover my discontents;

butt between your Grace & I, I can never forgett what I thinke litterally was a barbarous & cruel usage, which was that of not even letting this Freechappel so much as offer me a horse, upon a day of such consequence as that of the Battle; I thinke I should have some merit with him in my private station, butt then thinke of that day, & that the King of England's Master of the Horse, must have been that day on foot, if Generall Honeywood had not been so kind as to lend him a horse. I own the reflection of it shocks me. butt I never have mention'd it to any body butt the Dss of Richmond & yourself, the two best freinds I thinke I have in the world, there can be no excuse for it butt the <u>yellow sash</u>, however without bragging I beleive I may say that it was the King of England & not the Elector of Hanover that beat the French that day. I had one peice of luck by it 'tho, for had I attended him, I should not have seen what was done beyond one Brigade, whereas, as I found butt too plainly I had nothing to do by him, I attended My Lord Stair the whole day, I had the advantage to see as much as any one man could of the whole affair. after it was over I went up to his Majesty, had the honor to dine with him, upon the feild of Battle, & after he had gott into his Voiture, & Monsr le Baron Lunenberg his Chambellan, (very like Clavering by the by, tho not by a great deal so lively) was seated by him, he did me the honor to aske me if I would go in his chaise; upon which not a little in the Falstaf stile I rub'd my face, & said I was so hott with the heat of the day that I rather chose to ride, I own I thought of <u>there lyes Percy kill the next yourself</u>, for God knows I was as cool as a coucumber, butt my pride would not lett me sett backwards. this is the truth of my story & too long & too silly a one it is to trouble you with, so I shall say no more on't. I must now tell you with a most sincere concern, that he has been very much out of order, his old complaint of the piles has been stop'd, which threw him into a violent purging, that weekn'd him to a terrible degree, then when that was stop'd, he had a swell'd & painefull leg, which must not be call'd the gout, that's gon off, & now it is in his eyes, one of them particularly extreamly bad. however he goes out every day & looks pretty well, butt you see here is a very ugly humour flying about him; & I own I wish Willmott was here, 'tho my Lord Cartaret sayes that Dr Werloffe[1] is the greatest Phisician, & man of best sense he ever talk'd with.

You will hear by this post at least of our scituation, if not 'tis soon told. The austrians are on the other side, haveing pass'd over our own bridge, The Hanoverians, I beleive march to day, & all the rest that is English & Hessians tomorrow. then wee encamp a little beyond Mayence, & my own private notion is, stay there 'till wee hear what success Prince Charles has had, & 'till the Dutch come up, who are expected in less than a fortnight, & surely then wee may go where wee please that is if it is right to go where wee please. Prince Charles has collected his whole army together between Frybourg & Brisack, in order to make a push a cross the Rhine, butt Monsr de Saxe[2] with 8 or 9000 men has <u>Cottoyed</u> him all the way from before Strasbourg, so there certanly will be some bloody noses there. I am quite in love with Prince Charles, he is to the full as agreeable as his brother & surely he has great millitary merit. I presented your Duty to the Duke, & he returns his sincere compliments to you, he is prodogiously mended within these few dayes, & yesterday he gott on horseback for the first time; poor Huske is in no danger of loosing his life or limb, butt Ranby sayes it is impossible he can do any service this year, so that wee are all trying to persuade him to gett to England before the cold weather comes in. this is a tedious letter, butt its your own fault, for haveing given me so much encouragement. My love to Dear Mr Pelham, & be assured my Dearest Lord, that I am for ever your Grace's faithfull & obliged
Richmond, &c.

1. Paul Gottlieb Werlhof was physician to King George II at Hanover.
2. Count Maurice de Saxe, illegitimate son of Augustus II of Saxony, was a successful French general who defeated the Pragmatic armies at Fontenoy and Lauffeld.

Is the Deanery of Peterborough too good for Bloomer? I know its a great trust, butt I'l be answerable he'l be honest.

177.   NEWCASTLE TO RICHMOND

Newcastle House
Augt 12th, 1743

My dear Lord,

I thank you for your very kind letter by Jack Parker. I did indeed expect that, considering what Letters He carried, & of what importance, He would not have returned to England without some answers, but hitherto we have none; & the private letters relating to the Treasury, not so much as acknowledg'd. I believe such a treatment, was never before heard of, from one Gentleman to another. You are extreamly good, to give me an account of what passed with Lord Carteret upon this subject. I could have wished, you had taken some notice of the Contents of Lord Bath's letter to His Lordship, & also, that you had asked Him, what answers, He had sent to those two letters, for I really think even He must have been embarassed what to answer. It is very true that my Brother does say in His letter to Lord Carteret, yt He told Ld. B. that Ld C. always declared, He must be for Him, if he desired it, & it is true in words, that Lord Carteret did say so, but all our Measures, all our Discourses, & Schemes have gone for some Months past, upon a Supposition, that my Brother was to be on ye Treasury, and Ld. Carteret even proposed to us, the doing it before the King went. But what is said on this side of the Water, if it was even intended then, is quite forgot now; & I conclude, as Ld. C. has no other view but his own absolute, sole power; and as He thinks by his attendance abroad, & <u>complaisance</u> there, He has an opportunity of getting his end, He is resolved to strike now, least when they come back, things may revert into their old Channel. Tho' it is easy to see that all His Schemes are founded upon one principle of <u>Power</u>, I own we are much at a loss here, how He intends finally to act in this great point. By his discourse to your Grace, He declares for Lord Bath. He has not yet sent back Rushout's servant, & by what we hear, He writes as little to them, as he does to us. All His Rants of P.ys promised credit in ye H. of Commons, of my Brother's coming in, in six months, etc, are nonsense. Does He think that we are now to acquiesce and take their leavings. I beg His pardon; we are not yet drove so low; & if we would, the party would not let us, for I do in my Conscience believe, my Brother could not, if He would, support Lord Bath's Treasury in this House of Commons. For Godsake my dear Lord, get His Scheme out of Him, if you can, & see whether there is Common Sense in it. He may think we make a mean figure here at being thus treated by our Brother minister abroad; but I can assure you, the Ridicule and Reproach fall upon Him. I wish you could let me know, how far He has got the K. into His way of thinking upon this Head; & whether any thing from the K. transpires relating to it. Lord C. tells you our answer was not relished, <u>we don't promise support enough</u>. I wish He would shew you His Letter, to which ours was an answer, & his Reply, & I will submit the whole, to the Determination of any one Intelligent, Impartial Englishman whatever. I might say, to any one Man, that understands, the interest of England, and the cause of the Q. of Hungary, & all Europe which we are now supporting; & my Reputation, shall stand & fall by that Determination.

As we have nothing from His Lordship, relating to Domestick Affairs, we have little, or nothing, relating to foreign ones, at least the most material ones. I mean the Motions & Operations of our two great armies. We don't yet know one word of what passed, & was settled wth Pr. Charles, etc. when He was at the army; where our army is gone; or what it is to do. Sure no ministers, or Country was ever used in such a manner. It is therefore charity in you, to send me whatever news you can pick up. I am most obliged to you, for the very entertaining Description, you give of the Austrian army, & am glad to find it is upon the whole so fine a one. I hope we shall soon hear, of something being done, we think it here, a great while since Dettingen Battle was fought, & expect a fresh Victory every Day. We are told the French are to have 200m men from Strassburgh to Dunkirk, & that they think themselves in no Danger in Alsace, but are not so clear about Lorrain. Pray let me know if the King has any thoughts of returning soon to Hanover or England. My best Compliments to ye D. of Marl. Ld Alble, Bury, Huske, & <u>Del</u>. I will thank Him by ye next Messenger for His long and instructive letter.

I am my dear Duke Ever most affectly Yrs

Holles Newcastle

P.S. Pray shew this letter to no mortal.

Newcastle House
Fryday Morning 10 o'clock

I have this moment received your Grace's kind letter of Aug. 3/17 by Crew. I will take care to have Over reprimanded, etc.

I must own my dear Duke, I am much surprised, that your Grace can give any attention to Lord Carteret's professions of friendship to us, after the most offensive, & unpardonable Behaviour, that ever was known. This is the light we see it in. Ld Carteret writes nothing to us, & we as little to Him. I beg you would keep the whole Contents of this letter entirely to yourself. I write in ye utmost confidence to your Grace, but hope yt nobody will know what I say to you upon this subject.

Ever Yrs

Holles Newcastle

178.   RICHMOND TO NEWCASTLE

King's quarters at the Chartreuse de Mayence.
Munday 15/26 Aug. 1743

My Dear Lord,

I am overjoy'd at a word My Lord Cartaret drop't to me to day; he say'd Mr Pelham is at the head of the Treasury,[1] & the thing is fix'd. I leave you to guess whether this gave me pleasure or not. Wee are now marching to Oppenheim to morrow, & the next day to Worms, & then I suppose over to Speir, tho at least the <u>Speir back</u> I fear wee must halt for some time at least, for wee take for granted the French are entrench'd up to their eyes there. however lines have been forc'd, & I'l answer for the Johns that they are ready to do any thing, butt then I hope in God they will have bread, for without that they can not fight. You'l see Poor Huske in a few dayes. he can inform you a good deal of the state of our affairs here. The King thanke God is very well, & the Duke is well enough to do duty, & march as Ld Genll with his Collum to morrow.

I am, My Dear Lord, Your Grace's ever faithfull, humble servant

Richmond, &c.

179.   RICHMOND TO NEWCASTLE

King's quarters at Worms
Tuesday 23 Aug./3 Sept. 1743

My Dear Lord,

I have received your grace's most obligeing letter of the 12th Augst, butt tho your

---

1. Henry Pelham became 1st. Lord of the Treasury on 25 August 1743.

complaints against our Minister here were then very justly founded, they are now at least palliated by his haveing answered the letters some time ago, & the thing (all the good part of mankind in England, so much desired) being done. I mean Mr Pelham's being putt at the head of the Treasury. you desired to know if I could fish out what answer he made to Lord Bath. I am butt a bad fisher, nay I can not even angle with John Delawarr, butt I ask'd him directly what answer he made him, he told me a propper one, & such as he hoped would do, butt he sayd he was not at all sure it would. so you see I am well as now as I was before I ask'd the question. I see by your postscript you are peevish with me for my too great credulity, I beleive it is a fault, butt I own I can't help beleiving the better sort of mankind honest 'till I know them other-ways & at the same time I beleive it's a great weakness in me. I know I am easily imposed upon, yett in this affair, & in this man, as to this particular affair I still thinke I am not, on the other hand I know very well that much less art than he is master of can impose upon me, & it is necessary in this affair & every other that relates to you, if he is not sincerely your freind, he should impose upon me., if he expects I should shew him common civillity. Butt I acknowledge he has been greatly wanting in that in not answering Mr Pelham's letter, however at last I hope he has made up for all. I say I hope because I thinke it for the interest of the whole that you should be well together. I long to hear how my Lord Bath & his freinds take his refusal. So pray tell me what you know of it. Now as to your being trusted with the future operations of warr, I must say, 'tho to be sure you ought to know every thing of that kind, yett surely they are so liable to alterations every day & every hour, & at the same time the danger of a messagers being taken that it may sometimes be improrner to putt them down upon paper, & in that case, I imagine it may possibly be right not to send them even to you. this do you see is only my own surmise, & very likely not a just one. butt I must lett you into one secret I have learn'd by accident, which was that your brother secretary knew nothing of the march to this place till a day or two before wee left Hanau, 'tho it was resolv'd on some time before. This I have heard as a truth, butt then remember that I don't answer for it. Our present scheme seems to be march into Alcace, & at the Speirback I imagine wee shall have a brush, Tho Neuberg & others say not. our men are brave & if they have bread & forrage they will undertake anything & do as much as men can do, butt our misfortune is that our Commanders are all ill together. Stairs I hear is resolved to quit, he is certanly used like a dog, & too hardly I thinke, 'tho to be sure he is sadly to blame for a great many things, Legonier is certanly our best & almost only man, Prince George is liked & esteem'd by every body, butt then he & the Duke D'aremberg hate one another personnally, & to give Neuberg his due every body hates him, 'tho notwithstanding that he has merit I do assure you, butt you see, & I see with concern that things can not go on in this way, & then the cruel partiality that is shew'n to that cursed nation that will be the ruin of us all, breaks the heart of all those that truely love the king.

You are so good as to say you write confidentialy to me, butt I thinke I do more to you, for I thinke I am offering my neck to the halter, butt my comfort is, I thinke you wont lay your hand upon your heart, & pronounce me quilty. as to what pass'd & was settled with Prince Charles, it is a most profound secret here, & so it ought to be 'tho I dont mean by that, that you ought not to know it, butt I am very sure except your brother secretary, nobody here ought to know it, butt it is imagin'd all this march is in consequence of it. As to the French's 200m men, that is too ridiculous to give credit to, butt it is impossible they should have near half that number in Alcace, & two thirds of that half is milice, I wish without Gasconade wee could see them once more in the feild, butt they are sensible of their own weakness, & I'm persuaded wee shall never see them butt behind lines, & I thinke most likely butt from the walls of Loudun, & there I fear they may laugh at us. for you know wee have no artillery with us. I fear there was once a sort of inclination towards Hanover, butt thanke God all that is certanly over, it would have wiped out all our honor at Dettingen. as for England nobody so much as mentions it; I shall certanly keep your Grace's letter secret, as I hope you will mine, tho if you thinke propper you are heartily wellcome to communicate the contents of it to any <u>good</u> man you love & confide in.

I am my Dear Lord Your Grace's ever faithfull, & most affectte humble servant
Richmond &c.

I am most extreamly concern'd for poor Tom Pelham, & Trevor,[1] pray what do you do about Lewes?

My Lord Cartaret has proposed that if my Lord Stairs quits to give the nominal command to the Duke & to make him a Mareschal, butt the King won't hear of it, & has a mind to give it to Prince George of Hesse, who is undoubtedly the most fitt man for it here; butt then the command of our troops to a stranger that can never be call'd to any account, is what you know would not be relish'd with us, so really I thinke my Lord Cartaret judges extreamly right in proposing the Duke, butt that H:R:H: should understand that in all great points he should have a propper regard for Prince George's advice, & of Lt: Genll Legonier's in every thing that relates to our national troops. I have gott an order of Battle of Prince Charles's army, & it is there

Ordre de Battaille &c.

Commande par S:A:S: Le Prince Charles &c.

a latere, Field Marescall Kevenhuller.

& so I would have it here, a latere Prince George. My Lord Cartaret told me all this in confidence, so you'l be so good as not to mention it to anybody, if he has not mention'd it to you, butt I take for granted he has.

180. NEWCASTLE TO RICHMOND

Newcastle House
August 26th 1743

My Dear Lord,

Moss the Messenger brought me your Grace's most kind letter of ye 16,27th of Augt on Tuesday last. I cannot say, whether my joy, or my surprise was the greatest, at receiving a Warrant from the King putting my Brother at the Head of the Treasury. That affair had depended so long, and been attended with so many disagreable Circumstances with regard to my Brother Secretary, that I must own, I concluded nothing, or nothing good, would be done in it, till the King's Return to England; and what is the immediate occasion of dispatching it now, I am at a loss to guess. Lord Carteret has wrote two private Letters to my Brother, & I, in answer to ours of the 5th of July last. That to my Brother, is a frank, open, manly letter with some expressions, that may be interpreted to carry with them something like an air of superiority, but not offensive. He owns he was for Lord Bath, but that the King had decided it for my Brother; By which it looks, as if the doing it now, arose purely from our Master, whose steadiness upon this occasion, must be owned, admired, & applauded by us. Ld Carteret's letter to me, had an air of affection & cordiality, wth a mixture of some dark expressions, which would admit, of disagreable interpretation. However, we have returned kind & friendly answers to both. I wish you could find out, what was the true Cause of finishing the affair of the Treasury at this time, & how my Brother Secretary is really pleased wth it, but I beg it may not be known, that this comes from me. My Brother desires his kindest thanks for your goodness upon this occasion. I am sure you

---

1. Both Thomas Pelham and John Trevor, the members for Newcastle's pocket borough at Lewes, died in 1743. It was a troublesome borough and Thomas Sergison regularly stood against Newcastle's candidates there.

will be glad to hear, that his Majesty's choice gives universal satisfaction, & that our friends have received a courage from it, which has been damped for some time. I am sure you will be persuaded that we shall have no other view, but the being the better enabled to serve the King, faithfully & affectly & to support our friends, & the good old Cause. I shall long to hear of your further Motions, & Operations. I pray God grant you success in all of them. My best love to Albemarle. Won't He write one Word upon this great Occasion. My compliments to the D. of Marl., Bury, & John Delawar. I am ashamed I have not yet wrote to Him, but it will take up time to answer so long, & so explicite a Letter

I am my dear Duke Ever Yrs

Holles Newcastle

P.S. The Deanery of Peterborough, has been engaged these three years to the Master of St John's Coll:, Cambridge and if it was not, must be given to a friend of Ld Fitzwilliam, who, you know, is the Person there to be considered, and is much displeased yt the Deanery is engaged.

181. RICHMOND TO NEWCASTLE

King's quarters at Worms
Tuesday 30 Aug./10 Sept. 1743

My Dear Lord,

Our affairs here are in a very ticklish way I fear. My Lord Cartaret will undoubtedly have sent you an account wee had of Prince Charles's scituation, however for fear he should not, I'l tell you what I can remember of it, which was that he pass'd the Rhine over his bridge on the night from the 4th to the 5th butt when he had gott over the River as he thought he found himself in a sort of Island encompass'd by a bog & an other small branch of the Rhine. There he was still on the 7th with 14 battalions entrenching & covering themselves as well as they could from the French Batterys that were playing briskly upon them from Fort Mortier, & several other Batterys they had erected, I must tell you this was just above Alt Brisack. every body here thinkes his scituation a bad one, however he & Kevenhuller both say they make no doubt butt they shall still carry their point, butt people here are of so different an opinion that they even doubt how he'l be able to retreat.

Prince Waldeck[1] with an other part of the army has try'd the Passage at an other place four or fives leagues higher it's call'd Rhineweiller, butt was imediately repuls'd for of five companys of Grenadiers, & 200 pandours, that had gott over, hardly a man escaped. he sayes he kill'd 800 French butt how he can tell that I cant possibly conceive, he sayes he lost 400 of his own, & that I fear he knows butt too well; & I also fear that as many thousands may & will be lost before they can gett over. As for us wee are waiting the slow motions of the Duch, whose first collone however arrived yesterday, an other is expected to morrow & they will all be here on Munday, Count Maurice arrived here yesterday. The French have abandon'd the Speir back, butt entrench'd themselves up to the noses from Landau to Germesheim, & have mined all the glacis of their entrenchments, so that I fear also will be a tough affair, so much so that in my opinion wee shan't attempt it. You see here our present scituation is rather doubtfull than good, I wont call it bad for I really thinke tis not so yett, butt my Dear Lord I fear wee have had opportunitys & mis'd them. however I find it's high Treason to say so, 'tho My Lord Stair I beleive will make no scruple of telling it. My Lord Cartaret assures me he has wrote you a full account of every thing relating to My Lord

---

1. The Prince of Waldeck was appointed to command the Dutch troops, under the Duke of Cumberland and Konigsegg.

122

Stair, so I shall say nothing of it, only that I fear there are faults of all sides. you will also have seen my freind Huske, who can put you au fait, of all our affairs here better than any body. so I have nothing more of polliticks to say to you, butt I must now trouble you with an affair that as it relates entirely to Tom Hill, you know must nearly concern me. he has wrote me a very long letter, which give him his due he is not apt to do. he expresses himself very handsomely, & with great gratitude to your Grace, for your goodness in giving him so good an employment in so handsome a manner, therefore his desiring an other espetially a better, he apprehends may seem too unreasonable. however he has left the whole with me, & if what wee aske is unreasonable I beg the whole fault may lye upon me. Inshort what I desire & beg for him is that he may give up this employment for a better & for one where there is less business. I could name one, butt I fear you will say that is farr above Tom Hill, at least in our present situation it is a thing for a member of Parliament, I mean that he may have a place at the board where he now acts as secretary. that there is not a man in all England that is fitter for it I beleive you will allow, & I beleive you will own that it is not very unreasonable in me once in my life to aske an employment of that Ranke for a freind, who I own has no Parliamentary merit of his own; which is certanly the only thing that can be said against him, & now I really must beg pardon for being so troublesome a solliciter to you. this I know is a thing to aske not only of you, butt of my Lord Cartaret & Mr. Pelham particularly, as it is a commoners employment, butt applying to your Grace, is applying to him. & to be sure you three are & ought to be under the King, the principall disposers of these employments; butt 'tho I am here with my Lord Cartaret, yett I thinke I should do most extreamly wrong if I apply'd to him before you. so unless you tell me to mention it to him I shall not. I beg now my Dear Lord your Grace would consider this affair with Mr Pelham, & whatever you thinke upon it, you would communicate to me, & if my request is ridiculous, tell me so plainly. butt one more thing I must most earnestly desire you to do, which is, after you have consider'd it, to send to Tom Hill to come to you, & that you would then plainly tell him what you thinke of it. I beleive I need not recommend to you to speake kindly to him, for I dare swear you love & value him, besides that I am sure you have some regard for him upon my account.

What do you intend to do at Lewis? I fear you will be putt to it to find out two propper people. I wish Sr Cecyl would be reasonable & come in heartily to you, if he would 'twould give you great ease there. your worthy Brother Shelley I fear will never do. have you any thoughts of Sr Ian, I fear he would do butt awkwardly. if you was distress'd, so as to be obliged to bring in an entire stranger for one, I wish you could persuade Tom Hill to it, my word persuade seems strong, & odd, butt I do assure you that before I recommended & chose Sr Thomas Prendergast at Chichester, I did all I could to persuade Tom to come in there, butt to no purpose, & meerly from a nice point of honor, which was that he would not swear to a borrow'd qualification, & as that would be the case now, I dont thinke you could persuade him, if you had a mind to it. butt I do assure you he is the man upon earth who you might the most trust to upon such an occasion, for his principles in polliticks as well as gratitude would for ever attach him to you & the good old cause. I beg pardon for troubleing your Grace with so tedious a letter, & am most truelly & affectionately, my Dear Lord, your ever faithfull & most obliged humble servant

Richmond &c.

Hughes[1] has wrote to me for the Chaplainship of Hull, butt I find it's engaged to my Lord Bath's freind.

---

1. Rev. Simon Hughes, Vicar of Donnington, 1733–1750.

Pray dont forgett poor Bloomer.
are you a little better satisfy'd with the correspondence of your brother secretary? I hope you are.

Thurd 12

The messager being kept here two dayes, I have just time to tell you it's reported here, the campagne is up, & that wee all go off next week. God knows if there is any truth in it; I hope not. Pray dont say it comes from me

182.   NEWCASTLE TO RICHMOND

Newcastle House
Sepr 2nd, 1743

My Dear Lord,
  Of the many kind letters, which I have received from your Grace, since you left England, none has been more so, than that of 23 Aug/3 Sep which Hammond the Messenger brought me on Wensday last. Your goodness in overlooking what you very rightly call, a little peevishness in me, upon the Subject of the Treasury, & the kind reason you give, for being disposed to believe, what has been said to you upon the Occasion, are such Marks of your friendship, as I shall always remember with the greatest gratitude. I acquainted you in my last with the general turn of Ld Carteret's Letters to my Brother & me, & of our answers. It is very possible He may think, they did not quite come up to some pretty strong Professions contained in His Letter to my Brother, but besides, that those Professions were mixed with some Intimations in both Letters that admitted of a Construction of a different Nature, we rather chose to confine ourselves to general expressions of Civility & good Humour than make professions before we knew how things stood, & what part Lord Carteret would really act in conjunction with us. For I may in confidence say more to your Grace, than we have yet done to Him, which is, that it is not only <u>our</u> Intention, that is, my Ld Chancellor's, my Brother's & mine, but our Inclination to act with Lord Carteret, with confidence & friendship, provided He really acts in the same manner towards us; but it must be upon the foot of Equality and not Superiority, of mutual Confidence & Communication, in all things, as well foreign, as Domestick. This is the only way for the King's Business to be carried on with ease and success to ourselves and the publick. A Contrary Behaviour must create Coolness and Diffidence amongst us, tend to division, and the forming separate parties, the consequence of which, must prove the Ruin of the one or ye other, & be the Destruction of the King's affairs. But this, as I said, can be only upon ye foot of Equality. We are willing Lord C. should fully have His share of power, but those He cannot have with safety to our old friends, or with security to ourselves, & upon this foot we are willing to agree with Him, tho' we have not told him so, 'till we see a little further into his own Disposition. Separate, or secret Measures and <u>separate court</u> will make this impracticable. You see with what freedom I write to you. I pour out my Heart, and this, you may be assured is our Scheme. Lord C. seems to have claimed some merit to you, in dispatching this affair at present. He may have it, but we are quite ignorant of it. He rather says otherwise to us, & indeed we are at a loss to know what was the Reason of its being done now, which we attribute singly to the King's firmness and adherence to his own Measure and Resolution. I will say one word only, as to the Communication of what you are doing in the army. I never was so absurd, as to think some particulars ought not to be kept an absolute secret, but the general Scheme and Plan, sure may as well be communicated here, as sent from all armies in ye world, to their respective Courts. You desire to know how Ld B. & his friends take this Refusal. Lord C letter to Ld Bath was I hear short, telling Him, that he had been for Him, but that the King had decided it for my Brother. Ld Bath has

been at my Brother's Door, made Him a civil Compliment at the Regency, but has said not one word to me upon the subject. I hear His Conversation is, that, as he never desired it for Himself, if His friends are taken proper care of, he shall be very well satisfied; but I beg you would not mention this, for that proper care, must depend upon their own Behaviour, & the Assurances they shall give of acting thoroughly, & cordially with us.

I thank you for the Accounts you send me relating to the Army, tho' I am truly sorry for some part of them. We conclude the Dutch have joined you before this time, & therefore shall be impatient to know what will be ye consequence of it. We don't like Pr. Charles not having yet passed the Rhine, & it has been surmised that he may be obliged to come down as far as Worms, in order to pass under the protection of your army. In the mean time, I think I see the Court of Vienna out of Humour, & the Negotiations with the King of Sardinia far from being concluded. But what is the greatest concern of all, is the Division amongst the Generals, & the probability that Lord Stairs may quit, of which I dread the consequence, for tho' He may be, and I suppose, has been to blame in some things, yet he must be Master of so many disagreable incidents that have passed in the army, that it may be unfortunate for the whole, that He should be disobliged. To be sure, the King will be at a loss, for a successor to Him. I like the scheme of ye Duke, if H.R.H. could have a proper & experienced officer attending Him a Latere, but that officer should be an Englishman, for the unanswerable Reasons which you give against Pr. George. Lord Carteret, has not said one Word to me, on this subject, nor on any other confidential one, but for the Remainder of this Campaign (after what has passed), I don't expect it. You say my dear Duke, yt you write with ever more confidence to me, & that you risk your Head. It can never be in safer Hands, for I would sooner hurt myself ten thousand times than be the cause of any to you. I have more reason to love you than I can express. I am not apt to be ungrateful, or unmindful of those who have really a goodness for me. Albemarle continues his usual silence. My kind service however to Him and the Duke of Marlborough. The Treasurer is yours most faithfully, & hopes for your Interest upon this Re-election[1]

I am ever most unalterably Yrs

Holles Newcastle

P.S. I beg you would not say one Word of ye Contents of this Letter to Lord C.

183.   NEWCASTLE TO RICHMOND

Newcastle House
Sep 16th 1743

My Dear Lord,

I received your Grace's most kind letters of the 10th & 12th N.S. and hope you are assured, that I have more real pleasure in obeying your commands, when I can do it, than in doing any thing to oblige almost any other man whatever. After this preamble, to come to the point. Tom Hill was with me, & came to tell me, that He most readily desisted from His Request, as he found it was not practicable, which He had learnt from ye Duke of Montagu's Discourse wth my Brother. I told Him very truly, I never could wish to oblige any Body so much as yourself, & never you so much as for Him, that my Brother & I had talked it over, that it would be impossible to give the Board of Trade to one not now in parliament. I think the first vacancy, was partly promised upon

---

1.   Henry Pelham had to seek re-election for the County of Sussex, 15 Dec 1743, on his appointment as 1st. Lord of the Treasury.

Sr R. Walpole's going out, to one, Sr Charles Gilmore,[1] a Scotch member. But my Brother has of Himself promised to find out, whenever He can, some employment for Tom Hill, which will be agreable to Him. What think you of Excise or Customs? My Brother has never mentioned it, & I know has some engagements. They are very good things, but then, they require great attendance. In short, we will take care to serve Tom Hill, in something He shall perfectly like.

As to Lewes, a stranger will be impracticable. Sr Jn Poole[2] is to come in for one and I think, at present, in order to unite the Whigs, & the Dissenters, we shall take Garland,[3] or His Son, on promise of acting wth us, both in Town, viz. Parliament & Country, viz. Elections. This is our present Scheme, but it may vary.

We have received the Treaty concluded with the Q. of Hungary, & ye Kg of Sardinia. There are some strong Articles, but it is a pure English Treaty, & I am heartily glad it is finished. It has cost us much time, & pains and was very near being quite lost. I suppose we shall soon hear, what the army is to do, & where to take your Winter Quarters. My Brother Carteret, writes freindly letters to us, is not very communicative in what is to be done, & quite silent as to the March of, the Operations, & the Command of our Army, but the King's Return to England, which, tho' by ye way of Hanover, I hope will be pretty soon, must put an end to all that

I am my Dear Duke Ever unalterably yrs
Holles Newcastle

My compliments to ye D. of Marlborough. Huske is very good but more cautious & wise than ever He was.

Ask Albemarle whether, He is not ashamed, to let you run away with all My Grace and Favour.

184. RICHMOND TO NEWCASTLE

King's quarters at Worms
Tuesday night 23 Septr 1743

My Dear Lord,

I wrote a short letter to your Grace by the post; which I know is an unfashionable way of writing, yett by that I am sure you will receive the news sooner than any body, that the French have left the lines of Landau, & retired to those of Lauterbourg, & that our whole army marches to morrow morning, butt as this goes by a messenger, I must tell you that in most people's opinion here this army of Noalles is gon to the aid of Coigny[4] to hinder Prince Charles from crossing, which I hear they will effectually do, then as wee advance, the lines of Lauterbourg, (tho but slenderly garded) will be impracticable to us, by their great strength; there are pollriticians here who say wee shall march to Speir & no farther because (besides those redoutable limits of their lines) wee have that polliticall limit of the Empire, & it is thought wee shan't pass it. butt that wee shall present ourselves to the enemy, & if they have a mind to come out to us, wee are ready to receive them, butt they will be too wise, & keep within their bounds, & by the Rhine & those lines keep us both at a bay. if so, what's to be done,

1. Sir Charles Gilmour, died 1750, MP for Edinburghshire, 1737–1750, was Paymaster of Works, July 1742 to December 1743, and a Lord of Trade from December 1743, until he was dismissed in December 1744 on the fall of Carteret.
2. Sir Francis Poole, 1682–1763, was MP for Lewes from 6 December 1743–1763. He owed his position to his marriage to Frances Pelham, a first cousin of Newcastle.
3. Nathaniel Garland had opposed Newcastle's candidates at Lewes in 1734. In fact Newcastle chose his brother-in-law Sir John Shelley instead.
4. Marshal François Coigny, the French general, in command of an army on the middle Rhine against Prince Charles.

wee must return to Winter quarters, <u>where</u> the Lord above knows, & Prince Charles must return to Bavaria, for he has no mony to subsist his troops, so he must winter in an enemys country. These are all the poor polliticks I can pick up, & such as they are I send them to you.

I must now thanke you my Dear Duke for your two kind letters. all I can find by your brother Cartaret is that he seems glad Mr. Pelham is at the head of the Treasury, 'tho he sayes his only apprehensions are from some disquiet that my Lord Bath may have taken at it. as to it's being done now, I could gett nothing from him butt that the King from the beginning was for Mr. Pelham, so as he found him determin'd, he thought it was right it should be done now, that the treasury business should go on. he had spoke for Lord Bath as he was engaged to do, & he could do no more, all this I thinke looks well & then I do assure you he always expresses himself to me with the utmost cordially & freinship for you & Mr. Pelham, owning he cant go on without you, tho he takes great care to say often you cant go on without him. The first I am sure is true, & the last I wont contradict, 'tho I cant quite admit it. he shew'd me both your letters & seems extreamly pleas'd with Mr. Pelhams, & not displeas'd with yours, 'tho he sayes you accuse him of some expressions in his, which he vows & swears he does not remember, as he keeps no coppys of private letters; butt by what you mention to me I know what you meant, <u>those expressions of superiority</u>, you said he had in his letter to you, & I fancy he was a little suspitious it was that because he said you often had jealousys of things he never meant, yett in the main he knew you loved him, & he loved you. In short by all I could see he seem'd to like the thing that's done, & he sayes if my Lord Bath is butt quiet all will go well. he then talked polliticks to me more openly than ever he did before, he said what a fine scituation wee were in from this late alliance of the King of Sardinia, & is for pushing the warr in Ittaly, for here he gives it up for this campagne as really most reasonable people do. butt then he dropt one expression, which I own I did not like, <u>all this will be patch'd up some how or other</u> <u>'tho this winter</u>. I told him <u>patching</u> was dangerous, & I hoped he that used to dislike <u>patch</u> worke would take care. upon which he said <u>a good peace to be sure or none at</u> <u>all</u>, <u>butt will Mr. Pelham & all our freinds find the 6 millions</u>? upon which I told him Mr. Pelham I beleive could sooner than any other. My Lord Cartaret is to be sure a man of great parts, but surely some times his talke is so incoherent, that (if one did not know him to be the man he is) I should not take him to be what he is; butt I take for granted <u>il se marque de moy</u>, which god knows he need not muster up half his parts to do.

Now as to your resollution of your manner of acting with him, 'tis right & manly, & I hope you'l stick to it, & I am sure all your freinds will approve of it. by your account Ld Bath seems cool to you, I am sorry for it, butt in my poor opinion he will breake with Ld Cartaret sooner than with you, for as Popularity is his Idol, he can have nothing of that kind against you, whereas I take for granted he'l quarrel with my Lord Cartaret if wee dont beat the French once more, which I fear is not in his, nor no <u>armys</u> power as wee are now scituated. Our Dear Master goes on with his usual partiallitys to those damn'd Hanoverian troops, which by the by you'l never carry an other year, for the hatred this weake partiallity has created in our troops, will never be gott the better of, our men not only hate them butt despise them to a degree you cant conceive, & every march it grows worse & worse. they have continually disputes together, & John always thrashes the <u>Hanover</u> for John always calls him so, not a Hanoverian. butt for all that the Hanover getts bread & forage, whilst John & his horse starves. 'tho I must own since My Lord Stair is gon, wee are better in that respect. Stair I suppose will cry out loudly, at the fine opportunity wee have lost, & I fear will mention some unanswere-able ones, that is, as to the reasonableness of the measure, butt then it may be say'd the project may be good, butt wee had not the means, that is bread & forage, the want of which was mostly his Lordsps fault. butt his projects surely were good. that is till

Prince Charles came to Hanau, butt what has been wrong from that day to this, has been in consequence of the scheme then taken, which has been singly follow'd, so nobody butt Prince Charles & Kevenhuller are to be blamed.

This is a tedious long letter so I shall have done. Adieu My Dear Lord, I hope you forgive the last long one I wrote to you about my freind Tom Hill. I am for ever & most affectionately, Your's

Richmond &c.

Spire. Sunday 6 Oct. 1743

This letter you see has layn a fortnight in Jack Parker's hands, butt at last I find he is going to day. You'l hear wee have been at Germercham & destroy'd the lines, & not a dog or a catt to oppose us. The campagne is now certanly over, & in about ten or twelve dayes the King goes to Hanover, & your humble servant to England. I shall have a great deal to say to you when I see you, butt nothing I fear that can please you, so 'till then My Dear Lord adieu.

I am for ever, & most affectly Your's

R

Pray lett me know what you do about the County election.
My best services attend Mr. Pelham.

185. RICHMOND TO NEWCASTLE

Spire
Munday night [30 Sep]/7 Oct 1743

My Dear Lord,

As I have wrote a long & I beleive very nonsensical letter to you already by the messager, I should be unwilling to trouble you any more, if it was not to return you my most sincere thankes for your very kind & obligeing letter of the 16 which I received this morning by Chalke the messager, & I do most sincerely thanke you for all your goodnes to me in your kind intentions for Tom Hill. you have fully satisfy'd both him & me. as to the impracticability of what I mention'd for him; & as to Lewis I really only threw it out in case you had wanted somebody, & even in that case I dont know whether he would have liked it. Excise & Customs are fine things, & I thinke he ought to be glad of either, however it's time enough to talke of either when I see you, which will now be soon for our army is actually under marching orders & that as it is presumed back to Mayence, &c. I have time to say no more only that I am for ever Your obliged, & most faithfull servant,

Richmond &c.

186. RICHMOND TO NEWCASTLE

Head quarters at Worms.
Sunday. 2/13 Octr 1743

My Dear Lord,

My Lord Cartaret assures me that by this messager, he sends you a very particular account, of all our past, present, & future measures, so I shall have butt little to say, only that wee left Spires de bonne grace, for His Majesty in person commanded the Rear Garde, which in a Retreat you know is the post of honor. & really as to everything of that kind nobody can possibly behave better; butt in that cruel partiallity to his Electle troops, it is really worse than ever, for he now almost constantly marches with them, & never takes the least notice of ours, to, I do assure you, the allmost generall dissatisfaction, of our whole English army. I have told several of his Hanoverian servants of it; & even they are sorry for it; it vexes me I declare more than I thought any thing of that kind ever could, for I actually tremble at the consequences, that may, butt I hope in God will not happen. His Majesty setts out in two or three dayes for Hanover, & as soon as I have settled all my business, which will take me up two or three dayes at Mayence I shall make the best of my way to England, butt whether straite by land to Ostend, or down the Rhine by Holland, I can not yett tell. I can't finish this without thanking you again, & again, for your very kind letter in regard to Tom Hill, & I also am not less obliged to Mr. Pelham, for the same kind favor from him.

I am My Dear Lord for ever Your most affectte & obliged
Richmond &c.

187. NEWCASTLE TO RICHMOND

Newcastle House
Oct. 4th 1743

My Dear Lord,
Tho' your Grace may possibly be gone, before this Messenger arrives, I could not however, omit this opportunity of returning you my thanks for your two most kind letters by Jack Parker. Lord Carteret has been pleased to send us, copies of Councils of war, etc, near three weeks after they were held, & the Resolutions partly known both here, & in many places abroad, but however, in that, he is incorrigible & will sooner or later feel the effect of it. I find you are preparing for Winter Quarters, some say on the Rhine, others in Flanders. Whatever disagreable thoughts or incidents this last Campaign may bring into my mind, whenever I think of it, I shall ever remember with the utmost joy, & gratitude that friendly, unreserved, & confidential Correspondence, with which you have honoured me during the whole Summer, & I hope you are assured, it has freed in me such a sense of your goodness, that no time or circumstances can alter. We shall now soon have our Master amongst us, I hope in God, in good Health. He will find here as faithful, honest, and affectionate servants as those that have attended Him in the Wars, tho' perhaps He may think, we have not had those Opportunities of showing it. The Ds of Richmond, & all ye good family are in perfect health. I have not yet been able to wait upon them. My dear Duke, I long for the pleasure of seeing you. I must beg my Compliments to Lord Albemarle, tho' He has quite forgot me.

I am with the most unalterable and sincere affection ever Yrs
Holles Newcastle

188. RICHMOND TO NEWCASTLE

Goodwood
Fryd 9 Decr [1743]

My Dear Lord,
I thanke your Grace for your most kind freindly & obligeing letter of the 6th & am very sorry to find how things go, I own you & your brother have a hard taske. you are both too honest men to hurt or to sacrifice the good of your Country to private resentment, therefore I conclude you will not breake now, that is immediately, butt then what will be the consequence of that ? My Lord Cartaret will have gott all he wants, & then can & will do without you at least for this sessions, & next summer. I therefore thinke it is your duty to yourselves & your freinds, to turn him out if you can. you see I speake plainly, & should not care if this letter was stuck up at Charing Cross. butt then the Quomodo. I thinke you have the fairest opportunity in the world, that is if Cartaret still persists in employing the Hanoverian troops. Oppose butt that point, which, (pray forgive the expression) as honest men you ought to do, & then either he or you must

129

retire. I own much more likely the latter, butt then you will retire like men, with dignity, honor, & deserving poppularity; & in my poor opinion, he cant hold it a month if you go out in such a way. & I shall be glad on such an occasion to aske my Conge of his Majesty with the utmost duty to him, which I shall ever retain as long as I live. I have said enough to you when I was in town about the Hanoverians & I am stronger than ever in the same opinion. I thinke you will hardly carry it in the house of Commons, & I am very sure our troops never will, nor never can serve with them, & moreover I myself am convinced they are bad troops, so I hope in God you will not aske me to be for them; if you do, you will lay me under the greatest difficulty. Pray pardon what I have said to you & thinke of it seriously, & if you should be of my opinion, I hope no time will be lost in applying for others, Prussians would be the best of all, butt Saxons are better than Hanoverians. You must be sensible no time should be lost in this, & an other affair of the utmost consequence is recruiting the army, & fixing upon your plan of operations, & providing your magazines, if you are determined to carry on the warr, nay these things should be done if you are not determin'd to make peace, even in a state of uncertainty. I take a great deal too much upon me, butt I am sure my advice is well meant.

I am My Dear Lord, with the utmost truth, Your Graces ever faithfull, & most obliged humble servant,

Richmond &c.

I am sorry to hear of your Whitlow. I have a cursed pain in my right arm, occasion'd I beleive by too much drinke. Joy upon your success at Lewis.[1]

189. RICHMOND TO NEWCASTLE

Goodwood
Sunday, morning 11. Decr. 1743

My Dear Lord,

Linky arrived here safe last night & I am exceedingly concern'd to find by him that things go so ill. however I expected it, & if you dont or cant gett rid of your collegue they will & must go worse. This last stroke of his of making Chomley Privy Seal, is in my opinion a strong one, butt what gives me most concern of all is that I fear Mr. Pelham gives a little into the only thing, which if he had opposed, in my poor opinion would have enabled him & all of us to have made a stand against this new Minister, who I thinke is drawing our Master & Country into destruction. I dont say I have butt little for I do assure you I have no concern for myself, only as I am a small part of the whole, butt upon my word I tremble at the thought of what will certainly happen, if wee are to be solely govern'd by my Lord Cartaret, & most particularly upon this point of the Hanoverian troops, which can not be carry'd by such a majority as the last question was in the house of Commons. & I am sure & very certain that our troops never will serve with them. I beg pardon butt I own I am glad you had a little gout the day of our division, butt I fear your heart suffer'd more than your foot. When will this cursed affair come in again in our house? I own my anxietys about it are great. For I see now plainly it will be cram'd down our throats, as for my employment I am heartily tired of it, & you know my kind Master has taken care all last campagne, that it should not be over agreeable to me, & I give you my word that nothing butt my regard to you & Mr. Pelham should have persuaded me to keep it a day after I return'd to England. So if affairs dont very soon mend, I hope you will not be against my following my own

---

1. Newcastle's candidates, Sir John Shelley and Sir Francis Poole, were elected unopposed for Lewes on 6 December 1743. Thomas Sergison, the perennial rival to Newcastle's interest in the borough, withdrew before the election.

inclinations, the first of which will be at all times be to prove myself the Dear Duke of Newcastle's & Mr. Pelham's faithfull, humble servant,

Richmond &c.

When you can go out, I am sure Taw would be glad to see you, & pray tell her what I have said to you, particularly about myself, for I hardly ever write upon Polliticks to her, by the common post.

190.   NEWCASTLE TO RICHMOND

Newcastle House
Decr 13th 1743

My Dear Lord,

I have received both your kind letters, & have read and considered them with great attention. Your Grace knows, my opinion has long been pretty much the same with yours, as to the great point, which is the subject of both your letters. We have lately talked the affair over very seriously amongst <u>ourselves</u>, and I find every body, except myself, is of another opinion. They all think, it will be impracticable to get any other troops to replace them, & if so, that the Discharging these, is at once putting an end to the War, & submitting to France. I own I don't see the impracticability of getting Saxons, or perhaps Munster troops, for Prussians, will more likely be of the other side, but, if our friends, who really judge cooly, & without prejudice in this affair are in the right, that no other troops can be got, the Question would then be much altered. Every Body agreed that some expedients, or <u>Temperamens</u> must be endeavour'd to be procured; that H.M. should not go abroad, in that the troops should act separately, for it was admitted amongst us, that as things stood, it would be impossible for them to act together. Turn it, in whatever shape they please, it will go very hardly down in ye H. of Commons, notwithstanding the great Majority's in both Houses, On the last question. I wish you would talk to my Brother. He will tell you His Opinion, as well as the Opinion of those (<u>our friends</u>) with whom we have talked. You are extreamly good, in desiring me not to press you upon this subject. I hope you don't think me capable of doing it. Your goodness to me, & particularly to my way of thinking, & acting, is such, that I shall never abuse it. My Brother will tell you, how things stand. They don't seem to mend, & I am afraid will not, as long as my Bror Secy remains where He is; Master almost of every thing, and every Body. My chief view at present, is; first, to do nothing wrong to ye King, & the publick; 2dly, to endeavour, to deserve the friendship, & good opinion of my friends. I have not yet been abroad, but will very soon wait on the Dutchess of Richmond, & obey your commands with pleasure. My kind Compliments to Linky, the Chanr of the Exchequer, & all my good western friends, to whom, I am a most faithful servant for ever, most affectly & unalterably Yrs

Holles Newcastle

191.   NEWCASTLE TO RICHMOND

Newcastle House
Decr 14th 1743

My Dear Lord,

I hope to have the honor & pleasure of seeing you at Claremont on Saturday, & yt you will take a Bed, with us. How can you think, you are ever troublesome to me. I must be a strange Creature, if that could be so. I thank you for your Proxy. I have room for it myself, & will never let any Body else have it, when I can help it. I had last night, as you see, yr Letter, & Ld Berkeley's. I waited on His Majesty this day for the first time since the Gvt. Lord Carteret was in with me. The King began addressing

Himself to Lord Carteret. 'What! the Duke of Roxborough,[1] won't take Lord of the Bedchamber; & then turned to me & said, I will make my Lord Waldegrave;[2] upon which I said, I had last night received a Letter from your Grace requesting it, for Lord Berkeley. He said, He would give it to Lord Waldegrave, and as there could be no objection to Him, & ye king was determined, I said no more. I must observe in the first place that my Brother Carteret had asked it for ye Duke of Roxburgh, unknown to us, notwithstanding his daily professions, which I will never mind: & in the next, yt when I named Lord Berkeley's Request, Lord Carteret said not one Word, nor indeed opened his lips the whole time. I didn't know yt any body has named Waldegrave to ye King. It looks as if it was His Majesty's own doing. This is the truth of ye case. I know you love truth, & I hope you think, I do so too. I send you a pretty Motion, that was made this day in ye H. of Commons. The Gentlemen in the Opposition, are afraid, I conclude, of carrying a Question, by the pains they take to propose such absurd ones. When we meet at Claremont on Saturday, I will give you a full account, how things stand, tho' there is little or no alteration, since the Chan. of the Excheqr left us. Pray my Compliments to all the good Compy with you, & be so good, as to give the enclosed to Ld Berkeley, if He is still wth you; if not, pray send it to Him.

I am my Dear Lord ever & unalterably Yrs

Holles Newcastle

192. RICHMOND TO NEWCASTLE

Goodwood
Sunday. 15. Jany. 1743/4

My Dear Lord,

If you apprehend anything of consequence comeing into our house on Thursday next I wish you would be so good as to lett me know it by to morrow Munday night's post, that I may be in town by two O'clock on Thursday, butt if you expect nothing it would be much more convenient to me not to be there till Thursday night. our election went off very well at Lewis, & the Duke of Dorset did extreamly well, butt our Knight of the Shire's silence is incorrigable. however as they know it is his way I am in hopes it offended nobody, butt several would not go from hence, particularly Leaves, because he would not speake to them last time. butt in Generall every body seem'd in great good humour.

I am my Dear Lord, Your Grace's ever faithfull, humble servant.

Richmond &c.

193. NEWCASTLE TO RICHMOND

Newcastle House
Jany 16th 1743/4

My Dear Lord,

I must thank you for your great Goodness to us, in going to Lewes. You cannot imagine how much our friends in our parts, are pleased to see, that real & sincere friendship that is between us. We are to have some Motion in ye House tomorrow, I don't know what it is, but I believe calling for papers, or some thing of that kind. I don't fancy we shall have any business on Thursday, so you need not give yourself the trouble to come sooner than is convenient for you. I am sorry to tell you, things go but ill in Italy, the Queen of Hungary is not pleased either wth the K. of Sardinia, or with

1.   Robert Ker, 2nd. Duke of Roxburghe, 1709–1753.
2.   James Waldegrave, 2nd. Earl Waldegrave, 1715–1763, was a Lord of the Bedchamber, December 1743–1752.

us, she wants us, to be attempting the Conquest of Naples, when there are scarce Ships and Troops enough, to defend us, against the French & Spaniards by Sea and Land. This has produced a modest Request, that we would furnish them 9000 men for Italy, & 12 more large Ships, neither of which is practicable. There is a tolerable answer come from Holland, The Preliminary Scheme, is to send ye 20,000 men to the Q. of Hungary, & to be under Her Orders, & to keep a Corps de Reserve of 20,000 more, to be ready to March upon ye first notice. They don't think of any operation in Flanders, but rather, on ye side of Lorraine, & on the Mosell. My Brother Secretary continues in his usual way, sometimes up, sometimes down, but I think is rather more dejected than usual.

I am my Dear Duke Ever most affectly yrs

Holles Newcastle

194. STONE TO RICHMOND

Whitehall
Febry 1st 1743/4

My Lord,

Late this Evening the Lords of the Admiralty received a letter from Captain Broderick,[1] of the Phoenix, with an Account that the Brest Fleet, consisting of 21 Sail, came out of Brest Water, on Thursday last, the 26 Janry. Captain Broderick kept sight of them, till Friday Evening, and then made for Plymouth, leaving them about half way over the Channel. Your Grace will easily beleive, this Intelligence has given some Alarm here: and it is thought not improbable, that the French Fleet is gone for Ireland. What makes it most to be apprehended, that they are designed against some Part of His Mtys Dominions, is, the certain Intelligence we have that the Pretender's Eldest Son arrived from Rome at Antibes on the 17th past; and it is thought probable, that He may have cross'd France, & gone on board the squadron at Brest: We have not indeed heard, that they had any Troops on board that Squadron; but it is certain, that a great quantity of small arms, (not less than 15,000 muskets) were put on board, some time ago.

My Lord Duke has wrote to the Lord Lieutt of Ireland, to stop the Draughts that were ordered to embark for Flanders: and the same Orders are sent to Scotland; and a Cabinet Council is summon'd to meet tomorrow morning to consider what further Precautions should be taken, or Orders given, in this critical Conjuncture.

I am with great Respect My Lord Your Grace's most obedient and humble servt

Andrew Stone

Some are of opinion that the French Fleet is gone to the Mediterranean.

195. RICHMOND TO NEWCASTLE

Goodwood
Fryday morning 3d Febry 1743/4

My Dear Lord,

I thanke your Grace for sending me the news bad as it was. I cant conceive butt that they are going to Ireland, if Captn Broderick's intelligence is true, which is that they were half way over the Channell when he left them & the wind was East I suppose, unless they were bound for the West Indias, for then they might with a N.E. wind steer near the South of Ireland I beleive. butt this course is quite contrary to the Mediter-

---

1. Thomas Broderick, died 1769, after a long career in the navy, during which he served at Porto Bello in 1739, and was in command at Cartagena in 1741, ended as a Vice-Admiral.

ranean, butt it's a fine fleet wherever they are gone I wish ours may be able to deal with them. I own I tremble at one thing which is entirely owing to such honest men as Archy Hamilton[1] who you know has been a favourite & has had three regiments & others, which is that half our army in Ireland are at this time Papists. I did not apprehend by Mr. Stone's letter that you would have me go up, nor can I see why I should, however if you thinke so now or at any other time lett me know it & I shall with great pleasure attend you, for I am most truely & sincerely My Dear Lord, Your Grace's most faithfull, humble servant

Richmond &c.

besides the Popery I'm afray'd of, I wish the army had been in better humour, & I wish other people dont now repent of what they have & what they have not done.

196.   NEWCASTLE TO RICHMOND

Newcastle House
Feby 4th, 1743/4

My Dear Lord,
I have just received your Grace's most obliging Letter, and do not see any Occasion for your coming to Town at present. The moment I do, I will send you word. The Brest Fleet still continues at the <u>Chops</u> of the Channel. They chaced last Sunday, two Men of War, & some Merchant Men, which however luckily got clear of them. Sr J. Norris is gone this day to Portsmouth & the moment he has a tolerable strength, (which, by the by, if he Has not, is most abominable), He will go after them and I hope demolish them. I hardly think now, they will go to Ireland. I believe they will remain in our Channel as long as they dare, insulting us, taking or disturbing our trade, and endeavouring to prevent our sending succours to the Mediterranean, or West Indies; & when Norris appears, they will fight if they are strong enough; if not, go before us, to the Mediterranean. These are my thoughts. We have wrote to France, to demand the sending the Pretender's Son out of their Dominions etc, pursuant to treaties, which we say, we don't doubt, but they do. <u>Reste a scavoir</u>, etc. Gen Chanel is come to concert Operations, they would have us attack with two armies, one in Flanders, the other on ye Moselle. These things are more easily proposed, than executed. This Brest Fleet has hindered my hunting, & going this day to Claremont.
I am my dear Duke Ever most unalterably Yrs

Holles Newcastle

P.S. My duty to my Queen.

197.   RICHMOND TO NEWCASTLE

Goodwood
12 Feb. 1743/4

My Dear Lord,
I thanke your Grace for your last kind letter, butt am sorry you should putt yourself to the trouble of writing, for I should be very well satisfy'd with <u>a Stone</u> when their is any curious news. I am very sorry to tell you that Sr John Norris is still at Spitthead. I

---

1. Lord Archibald Hamilton, 1673-1754, MP for Lanarkshire, 1708-1710, and again, 1718-1734, for Queenborough, 1735-1741, and for Dartmouth, 1742-1747, was a Lord of the Admiralty, 1729-1738, and from 1742-1746, and Cofferer and Surveyor General to the Prince of Wales, 1738-1747. His wife was mistress of the Prince of Wales. He was the only Lord of the Admiralty not to resign with the Pelhams in 1746.

hear the Regiments are soon to be disposed of, & that Beake is to have one, if so, I most earnestly wish my two good freinds may succeed in their ranke, I mean Major Jenkinson succeed to the Lnt Collcy, & Sr James Chamberlayn, to the Majority, he being eldest Captn. I own I have this so much at heart that I could wish the Duke of Newcastle would tell the King how earnestly his freind & humble servant the Duke of Richmond wishes for this regular promotion, & that I do declare upon the honor of an honest man that I did see them both behave particularly bravely & like good officers at Dettingen, & whatever may have been said of the Regiment, (which I insist upon was false, as I had the honor to tell his Majesty) nobody ever pretended to accuse the officers; & (as I have said) I was an eye witness of the officers particularly those two doing all that men could do. this, added to an acquaintance & intimacy of many years standing, makes me so very anxious for them. butt for all I love them so much & that the happiness of their lives depends upon it, I love you so much better, that if you thinke it will draw a sour answer upon you, & that it is anyways inconvenient for you to speake, I beg you'l thinke no more of it, & I beg you will be assured that I am upon all occasions My Dear Lord, Your Grace's ever faithfull & most affectionate humble servant,

Richmond &c.

Major Jenkinson has been one & thirty years in that regiment, & came in Lieutenant haveing been an Ensign before.
Sr James Chamberlayn has been a Captain seven & thirty years, & served under the Duke of Marlborough as Captain of foot in Flanders.

198. NEWCASTLE TO RICHMOND

Newcastle House
Feb 12th, 5 o'clock 1743/4

My Dear Lord,
   All Reasonings about the Brest Squadron are now over, for last night, in the night, there came a certain account that they were all come into the Dunkirk Road, where there had been an Embargo for some Days on all ships, etc. At three o'clock this morning, I sent a positive order to Sr J. Norris to proceed wth the whole force, with ye utmost expedition to Dunkirk to attack them, and this Day the Cabinet Council met, & gave the necessary Orders for the troops to march towards London. We meet again this evening, I own I am fool enough not to like all this. I conclude their Intention is, to take the troops now at Dunkirk, about 10,000 men, on board & make a push up the River. If Norris can get time enough, to put himself, between Dunkirk, & us, all is safe, but if our heavy arsed sailor does not come up, till after the French squadron is got into ye River, God knows what will become of this affair. A Message will be sent to Parliament on Tuesday to acquaint them with it, & I suppose your Grace, & the Rest of our friends will think proper to be in Town by that time. This is certainly a scheme of Cardinal Tencin's,[1] & I conclude ye little gentleman, is now at Dunkirk to come wth the Fleet. Thomson has delivered His Message to Monsr Amelot,[2] who has told Him, He must receive the King of France's Commands, before he can give an answer. My Dear Duke, things are in great Crisis, tho' most people are more easy than I am. Can Sr J.N. sail with this wind, S.S.W. I have wrote to Him, as pressing as possible. I sent

1. Cardinal Pierre Guerin Tencin succeeded as director of French policy on the death of Cardinal Fleury. He invited Charles Edward Stuart, the son of the Old Pretender, to Paris in the beginning of 1744.
2. Jean Jacques Amelot de Chaillon was the French Secretary of State.

to Linkey this morning, but he was gone. My kind Respects to the D. of St. Albans, & all ye good Company. I beg you would give the enclosed from Ld Loudoun[1] to Ld Home.[2]

I am ever most affectly Yrs.

Holles Newcastle

P.S. My Duty to my Queen.

199. RICHMOND TO NEWCASTLE

Charlton:
Munday [12 February 1744]

My Dear Lord,

I shall certainly be in town to morrow by noon. the D. of St. Albans, Linky, & Harcourt go with me.

Yours most truely

Richmond &c.

Pray lett me dine with you tomorrow, else I shall be upon the Parish.

200. RICHMOND TO NEWCASTLE

19 Aprill 1744

I received this letter[3] by the post from Portsmouth, I can't so much as guess who it comes from, butt I really beleive the contents of it to be butt too true.

I am My dr Lord, Your Grace's most faithfull, humble servant,

Richmond &c.

201. NEWCASTLE TO RICHMOND

Newcastle House
Tuesday morning [8 May 1744]

My Dearest Lord,

I cannot express the Concern that your letter has given me,[4] I should be unworthy the Friendship, I so much value, did I not most sincerely feel for you, & the poor Dutchess of Richmond, Opero is waiting in the outward Room, & ye moment He has done with me, I will dress, & come to you.

I am more than I can say, My Dear Duke Ever most affectly Yrs
Holles Newcastle

202. PELHAM TO RICHMOND

Arlington Street
Tuesday 8 O'Clock [8 May 1744]

My Dear Lord,

When the Duke of Newcastle told me att the House of Lords, what had happen'd in your family, I was as much surpris'd and concern'd as the nearest friend or relation you

1. John Campbell, 4th. Earl of Loudoun, 1705–1782, was ADC to the King, 1743–1745. He was defeated by the Jacobites at Prestonpans, 1745, and at Dornoch Firth, 1746.
2. William Home, 8th. Earl of Home, died 1761, was a Captain Lieutenant in the 3rd. Regiment of Foot Guards. He fought at Prestonpans. He was a Scottish Representative Peer, 1741–1761.
3. An anonymous letter to Richmond complaining of the weakness of the manning of the defences at Portsmouth.
4. Richmond had written to tell Newcastle that his daughter, Lady Caroline Lennox, had eloped with Henry Fox. They were married clandestinely on 2 May 1744.

have in the World. I could not let you go into the country without telling you so; Be assured, nothing that belongs to me shall ever countenance, what you so justly call the highest disobedience. I have too much of the <u>father</u> not to feel for you, and too much of the freind, to dwell long upon a subject that must give you the greatest uneasiness for whom, My Dear Lord Duke, no one can have a more sincere freindship love and Regard than your faithfull and affectionate

H. Pelham

203. PELHAM TO RICHMOND

May ye 15. 1744

My Dear Lord,

I am very sorry, that the hurry of business here prevented me from waiting on your Grace before you went out of town, I came to your house soon after you were gone. I can't give you any particular answer to what you mention in your letter concerning Dayrolles information, not having as yet seen Mr. Fox[1]. you may be assured nothing has transpired from me; when I am better inform'd how that affair stands, I will certainly let your Grace know. next thursday the Treasury meets, and I understand Mr. Fox will call upon me, before he goes to the Board, you may depend on my managing your delicacy in the way you would wish, I shall say nothing to you upon so tender a subject, but only this, that I hope and beleive, the one wrong step will not be made worse by another.

All your freinds here feel for your Grace and Lady Dutchess as you could wish, time and proper behaviour may produce that, which no one ought to mention to your Grace att present. As no man loves your Grace better, nor can honour your family more, I shall not officiously meddle with what I can have no pretence to interfere in, but from that affection which I shall ever have to you and yours. When I am upon this subject, I can't help saying that it is from a long observation that I have made of your own honest intentions in every thing, as well as the reguard you have always shewn to virtue and virtuous men that has gaind you my esteem, not unsensible of the many instances of freindship and good nature which you have always shewn towards me. This may look a little pedantick, the subject makes me serious, and when I am so I must say that I am, with the greatest truth and affection My Lord your Graces most obedient humble servt

H. Pelham

P.S. I must trouble your Grace with my most humble respects to ye Dutchess of Richmond

204. PELHAM TO RICHMOND

Arlington Street
May 16 1744

My Dear Lord,

I had the honour of your Graces letter this morning, I don't wonder that you forgot to mention what relates to the business of your office only, when you were writing to me upon a subject of so different a nature. I am told the King's horses were included in the account of forage deliver'd to the Troops last year, But nothing of that apeears in

1. Henry Fox, 1705–1774, MP for Hindon, 1735–1741, for Windsor, 1741–1761, and for Dunwich, 1761–1763, was a Lord of the Treasury, 1743–1746; Secretary at War, 1746–1755, Secretary of State for the Southern Department, 1755–1756, and Paymaster General, 1757–1765. Fox and Lady Caroline were totally estranged from The Duke and Duchess of Richmond and their family for four years, until the birth of their eldest son.

the papers deliver'd into my office. I beleive Mr. Hunter or Mr. Hume the Commissary of stores and provisions are the proper persons to give your Grace full satisfaction on this head. I must now, in some degree, return to the former subject; The King intending to make some Knights of the Bath, and having formerly promis'd Mr. Hanbury Williams[1] that he should be one, was apply'd to, before the late accident happen'd, to renew that promis to him, which His Majesty did, but out of reguard to your Grace and the Dutchesse of Richmond, and least it should appear to the World that he was shewing countenance to any one that had the least share in the late transaction, the King determined to keep some vacant, and not to nominate him as one att this time. Upon this he wrote a very handsome letter to the King, not taking any notice of the suppos'd reason why it was suspended, but very earnestly desiring the King to fulfill his intended favor to him. The only expedient therefore I could think of was to trouble your Grace with this letter, giving you a true account of this transaction, and how it stands att present, in which I must do my Master justice, for I verily beleive he will be govern'd in this affair as he finds it more or less affects you. I judge therefore, you will freely give me your thoughts upon it; and consider it in all its lights. The sooner I hear from you the better, and be assured whatever you think right will be agreeable to your most faithfull and affectionate

H. Pelham

205. NEWCASTLE TO RICHMOND

Newcastle House
May 17th. 1744

My Dear Lord,

I should have troubled your Grace sooner with a Letter, but as I had no publick news to send you, I did flatter myself it was unnecessary for me, to repeat to your Grace My most sincere professions of an unalterable attachment to you, and all yours, who behave dutifully to you, and if I don't act up to these professions I must go contrary to the Dictates, & Sentiments of my own Heart. Lord Lincoln tells me, He has wrote to you, upon His own, & His Sisters subject, & He has shew'd me His most obliging Letters from you, & ye Ds of Richmond. The Ds. of Newcastle sent immediately to Lady Lucy, deliver'd the Ds. of Richmond's Message, & accompanied it, wth ye best & strongest advice to Her, & I dare say she will exactly follow it. As for Lincky, you know Him, almost as well as I do, & I think he ought to love you, almost as much, as He should love me. The poor Boy, has really been vastly concerned, but your Letter has set him at ease, & I told Him before, what you had said to me upon the Subject. The King continues to think, & act most perfectly right, upon this occasion. I can never leave the Subject without begging you to assure the Dutchess of Richmond, of the Continuance of My concern, Regard, & if she will allow me to say it, Affection for Her, & every thing that relates to you, or any ways affects you.

As to publick affairs, there has happen'd an event yesterday, which surprises us all. The Accounts from Flanders are as bad as possible. Menin, I suppose beseiged, & by this time half taken, the pensionary in the utmost concern, full of Camplaint of us, & wth Reason seems almost to give half Flanders. viz. all their Barrier Towns forgone, Reproaches us with having no Concert, no Plan etc.

I have been preparing a paper, for an answer in writing to Boutslaer, upon the

---

1. Charles Hanbury Williams, 1708–1759, MP for Monmouthshire, 1735–1747, and for Leominster, 1754–1759, was Paymaster of Marines, 1739–1746. He later had a diplomatic career, being Envoy at Dresden, 1747–1749, and again, 1751–1755, and at Berlin, 1750–1751. He was Ambassador at St. Petersburg, 1755–1757. The King hesitated to make him a Knight of the Bath out of deference to Richmond, as Henry Fox and Lady Caroline Lennox had been married at his house.

principles which we have always talked, upon Declaring our Resolution to act in concert, acquainting Them with the conditions on which we would make peace, proposing a plan for carrying on ye War, and lastly proposing a Treaty between the King, the Queen of Hungary, the Kg of Sarda, & ye States General, wherein the views, & objects of the War, & the respective proportions, to be furnished by each power should be settled. I sent yesterday a line to the King; made this proposal to Him. He agreed to every part of it, order'd me to see, yt there was a Conference wth Boutslaer, & to send Him the Minutes of what I proposed. Ld Carteret went in afterwards. The King told Him what had passed, I this night communicated the paper to His Lordship at Ld Hardwickes. He approved, with great Readiness & Cheerfulness, & it will be given in writing to M. Boutslaer on Monday. What has occasioned this sudden turn, in King or Minister, we yet know not. We suspect some back game, but don't yet send it out. Ld Carteret must be mortified tho' He does not shew it. This answer if well pressed will have the best publick effect, if not, it will remain a justification of us in all events. I beg you would say nothing of this. I don't mean, that the Dutchess of Rd, may not see the Letter

I am My Dearest Duke more than I can express, Affectly
Holles Newcastle

Ps The Ds of Newcl begs Her Compliments to the Dutchess of Richmond

206. RICHMOND TO PELHAM

Goodwood
20 [May 1744]

Dear Sir,
  I do assure you that since my misfortune nothing has given me [so] much pleasure as the account you sent [me of] his Majesty's great goodness to the Duchess of Richmond & me upon this last melancholy occasion, & wee both beg of you to let [his] Majesty know, how truely sensible wee [both] are of it, & that wee shall ever rem[ember] it with the utmost duty & gratitude. as I would sacrifice my life & interest [in] his service, so I shall very readily sacrifice my resentment of private injury to the good cause, & if I did not, I should then [be] as bad a man as Mr. Hanbury Will[iams] notwithstanding which, as he may be [a] member of Parliament, I would not by [   ] have him disobliged upon my account as that would be makeing use of his goodness to hurt his service, I hope you [will do] me the justice, to beleive me incap[able of] it, & that I am most sincerely & a[ffectly] My Dear Sir Your ever faithfull humble servant
Richmond

207. RICHMOND TO NEWCASTLE

Goodwood
20: May: 1744

My Dear Lord,
  I am most extreamly obliged to your Grace for your very kind letter which I received last fryday, & I also received one from Mr. Pelham with the most kind instance of his Majesty's favor that I ever received, & I hope I have made him a propper answer upon the subject, at least I am very sure it is a sincere one. it is certanly a very great satisfaction to me to find so much goodness from my Master, & kindness from all my freinds upon this unhappy occasion, & I shall always own my very particular obligations to your grace & Mr. Pelham, butt that is not extraordinary, as you have both of you ever been such sincere freinds to me & my family.
  I am very sorry to find things go so bad in Flanders, & you may remember that I told

139

you three months ago that Huske foretold all this that has now hapned, & more that I fear will happen, which is that they will gett Ghent & Bruges, & so cutt off all communication with us, butt round by Holland & that consequently all Flanders must soon drop into their hands & perhaps our army. As to what you have done it is a prudent, a wise step, & I take for granted will be your last effort, for if this wont do, nothing will. butt pray dont be angry with me for saying, I wish you had done it two months ago. The Duke of St Albans is here & sends his love to you, the Duchess of Richmond also presents her kindest services to your Grace & wee both joyn in the same to the Duchess of Newcastle.

I am My Dear Dear Lord for ever & most affectly Your's

Richmond &c.

208.   RICHMOND TO NEWCASTLE

Goodwood
Fryday: 22d June 1744

My Dear Lord,
'Tis by your Grace's own desire that I trouble you with this, to lett you know that wee found our dear little George extreamly well, tho had Smith[1] not been sent for, he had certanly had a mortification in his arm, which must have been his death, butt thanke God 'twas timely stop'd, & as I have already told you he is perfectly well. I must now beg two lines from you My Dear Lord, or Mr. Stone, if there should be the least alteration in the King's going abroad. upon my word the more I thinke of it the more I am shock'd at it, it being not only a rash undertaking, butt what I know & am sure must be attended with very bad consequences abroad, & in all likelyhood fatal at home. for I am very sure we shall have all the old Hanoverian quarrells over again, gett or rather improve the ill will of the army, which is at present the only thing wee have to trust to, be beat very likely by the French abroad, & what is still more likely be invaded by them at home. for which considerations I really thinke no measures can be too strong or even violent to stop it, if entreatys wont prevail. & if the Parliament had been sitting, I think he would, & ought to have been address'd in the strongest terms, aprospos to Parliament. I would fain know what Whig, that ever consented to any of our troops at this time going abroad, can opose, (if a peace should come) the breaking of the whole army except the Gards; for if during a warr with France, & the Pretender's son at Dunkirke, wee are to laugh at an invasion, I am very sure wee need not fear one in time of Peace. however, I shall vote for them with a safe consceince whenever that time happens, haveing declared my opinion that it is madness to send a single man out of England at this time, & if I may be allow'd to say it much more so for the King to go. I beg pardon for troubleing you with so long a letter, butt when my heart is full, I thinke it incumbent upon me to tell you all I thinke, so pray forgive it, & be assured that I am for ever, & most affectionately your's

Richmond &c.

209.   NEWCASTLE TO RICHMOND

Claremont
June 23rd 1744

My Dear Lord,
Your Grace's extream Goodness to me, would make me inexcusable, if I should not inform you, of any Material Event, that concerns either the publick or ourselves. You

---

1.   Thomas Smith, the surgeon.

know what has been long my Thoughts, with regard to the present situation of the Administration, & the King's intended Journey, & I have ye pleasure to think they agree entirely with yours. We had a Meeting the other night, Lord Chancellor, Ld Harrington, my Brother & myself, to consider what to do upon the King's present Resolution to go abroad. We talked the thing over very fully, & at last unanimously agreed, first, to represent in the strongest manner to the King against the Journey, as very improper with regard to the circumstances of affairs abroad, viz. the inequality of our Army with that of the Enemy, the possibility of all Communication being cut off, between His Majesty, & His kingdom, when abroad, the little Disposition in either Austrians or Dutch, to approve what our Army does, or may do, & lastly, the figure His Majesty would make, as the Head of an Army, when the Dutch were actually negotiating a peace, to which He has in some measure consented, & when that Negotiation may affect the operations of ye King's Army. 2dly with regard to this kingdom, that the King's going at this time, when there would be so few Troops left in England, would create great Discontent, fear, and apprehension amongst the King's best Friends, who would think the Country abandon'd, & lastly that the present situation of ye Administration was such, that it would be almost impossible to carry Business on in ye King's absence, when His Ministry was so divided; that there could be no Confidence, etc., and when all these Arguments had been strongly used by us all, If the King still persisted in His Intention, we four unanimously agreed, not to accept the Regency, that is, in other Words to resign our Employments, and to acquaint our Friends of the Cabinet Council, with our Intentions. It has already come to my share to begin the Attack. I was yesterday an Hour alone with the King. I talked the whole affair over with ye utmost strength with Him. I said all that was decent, & could be said against His going; to which His Answer was, that we wanted to keep Him at home, to govern Him, that by His going we should be rid of the man we disliked so much (viz. Carteret). I can assure you, I spared no Thing, & indeed no Man. I set the danger of ye kingdom, in that light, yt He said of Himself. The two regiments, Price's and Mordaunt's, might be countermanded, that He had given you His orders, yt He must pay 6000 S.C., to all wch, you may imagine, I gave the obvious answers. We then came upon Lord C— conduct of His Administration which His Majesty defended in every Article, reproached us, with obstructing every Thing C— did, and yt it was enough for us to oppose, a Measure that my Lord C— proposed it. I did not spare my Master one jot. I told Him my Objection to Ld C, was not his going into ye War, but His not carrying it on, his Having no Scheme, no Plan, no Concert with the Dutch, or Plan to bring them into, yt H.My would see, C— would run, as hastily into a Peace as he had done into a War. I did not blame Him, for I feared he could not carry on ye War etc. Upon the whole we disputed most thoroughly. He said he left the Home Affairs to us, but as to the other Business, He Himself understood it, as well or better, He thought, than any body and then Carteret gets Him, by making Him think yt it is all the King, & He only follows, & indeed He is in the right, for he never dares contradict. Upon ye whole his Majesty heard me, & that is all I can say. I think, I have stager'd the Journey, & that is a good thing. I have done my Duty, I have acted as an Honest Man, & I hope I shall have your Approbation. It was agreed, we should not at first give the Kg reason to think, we intended not to take ye Regency, least that might look like a Menace, but we are determined, & His Majesty might perceive by my Discourse, I thought it was impracticable for things to continue as they are. In our Conference amongst our selves every body did extreamly well, but Ld Chancellor like an angel with all possible Courage, Resolution and Unconcernedness. Lord Chancellor, will I hope attack tomorrow, my Brother on Monday, & Harrington after that, so yt in ye course of next week, you will know how things are like to be settled. Since beginning my Letter, I have received your most kind Letter, & rejoice to hear Dear Ld George is so well. I flatter myself by your Letter, you will approve all that I have done, & wrote.

The D. of Dorset has talked strongly to ye King against his Journey, His Majesty says, it is only the Jealousy of the <u>Pelhams</u>. Ypres is taken, Nimes invested, Giroles corps reduced to little above 6000 Foot, & they to act as a separate Corps to defend the Barrier. It is an abominable, shameful Pact wh distressed ye Dutch. Pr. Charles is (as last year) on ye other side of ye Rhine.

I am ever yrs

Holles Newcastle

My kindest Respects to the Ds of Richmond

210. STONE TO RICHMOND

Whitehall
June 26th 1744

My Lord,

My Lord Duke of Newcastle has received the Favour of your Grace's Letter of yesterday's Date; and intended to have answer'd it Himself; but, being unexpectedly summoned to a Meeting of Business, at my Lord Carteret's, has directed me to make His excuse to your Grace. You was acquainted by His Grace's Letter of Saturday last, with what had passed, the day before, at Kensington. The Duke of Dorset had an opportunity, the same day, of speaking to His Majesty, and <u>Elsewhere</u>, upon the subject of the intended Journey, which He did in a very proper & judicious manner. Nothing was known, 'till Sunday, when His Majesty directed the Lord of the Bed Chamber to send my Lord Carteret to Him; and order'd His Lordship to send your Grace the Directions, which you received yesterday by the Messenger. My Lord Duke bids me acquaint your Grace, that He apprehends the Change in His Majesty's Resolution to have proceeded from the Representations made by Himself, & the Duke of Dorset. There was a Letter received on Saturday or Sunday morning, from Major General Read, which mentions a Report prevailing at Ostend, that a great Number of Transport Ships were got together at Dunkirk; which might possibly have some share in it; But my Lord Duke does not apprehend, that that had any great Weight. My Lord Carteret does not take any Part of it to Himself, tho' He professes (I think) to be pleased with it. His Behaviour towards your Grace's friends is remarkably easy, within these few Days past. We had an Account this day, from Sir Chaloner Ogle, that Admiral Torres was returning to Europe with an immense Treasure: It is under Consideration whether any ships should be sent out, to endeavour to intercept the Spanish Squadron; But I am very much afraid, it will not be practicable to send out a sufficient strength: and it is very probable that the Brest Squadron, which we have heard but little of, for some time past, may be gone to meet the Spanish Ships; and if so, it would be in vain to attempt any thing against them. There is other Intelligence, besides that sent by M. Genl Read, of a great number of Ships at Dunkirk. I beleive Admiral Martin[1] will be sent with six Ships, to block up the Harbour.

I am, with the greatest Respect My Lord Your Grace's most obedient & most humble servant

Andrew Stone

211. NEWCASTLE TO RICHMOND

Claremont
June 30th 1744

My Dear Lord,

Your Grace, I hope, will have the Goodness to forgive me for having directed Mr

---

1. William Martin, 1696–1756, commanded the squadron which enforced the neutrality of Naples, 1742. A Vice-Admiral, 1744, he commanded the fleet at Lisbon and in the North Sea.

Stone to send you an Account by Tuesday's Post, of what had passed, subsequent to my Audience on the Friday preceeding; and for making use of His Hand in this Letter, which may save you some trouble in reading, as it does me, in writing it. I should have sent you, last night, an Account of the great News,[1] we received yesterday morning, but, upon enquiry, found, that no Post went on Friday, to Chichester. Your Grace will now find an ample Relation of the whole, in the inclosed Paper, which was, this day, published by Authority. The Passage of the Rhine is a great event; and we flatter ourselves, will be attended with the most happy Consequences. M. Coigny's army, your Grace will see, is cut off from any Communication with Alsace, and left between two Fires: So that there is great Reason to hope, that both that Army, & the Imperialists under Seckendorf,[2] (who quitted their strong Camp at Philipsbourg, and passed the Rhine) will be destroy'd by Prince Charles, who it is not doubted, will push on His Operations with the greatest vigour. We have nothing new from Flanders, but that Major General Read was safely arrived at Ghent, with three of the four Regiments last sent from England. Ld Harry's Beauclerck's[3] being left at Ostend, to reinforce that Garrison. The Transports with the Dutch Troops were to sail last night, for Ostend; and to proceed from thence to join the Army, unless it should be absolutely necessary to keep them there for the Defence of that Place. Mr Wade, in his last Letter says, that He was of Opinion to have passed the Schelde, when the French first invested Ypres, in order to cover Ghent; But that, as the Austrian Generals did not think fit to consent to it, at that time, it would be rash to think of doing it now, when Count Saxe has been so considerably reinforced: But that, if the Enemy should pass the Schelde, the Allied Army have a strong Camp to assemble at, where they will be ready to receive them. But as M. Wade will be Himself greatly reinforced, by the three Regiments from hence, by the Six Thousand Dutch from England, & by General Ginkel's Corps, which consists of near 12,000 men, & will very shortly join the Army, it is to be hoped, He will be able to do something more, than remain barely upon the Defensive, especially as the Austrian Army is now on this side of the Rhine.

Your Grace will see the important Article from Muscovy. Prince Scherbatow[4] communicated it yesterday, by Order of His Court, to Ld Carteret. Chetardie, upon some Discovery made from his Letters, was actually under arrest, & examined by the Inquisitor General; and, it is said, under apprehension of being put to the Torture. His fall puts an End, at once, to the French Faction at that Court: and fixes the Administration in the hands of the vice-chancellor Bestuchaf.[5] This Incident and the necessary Consequences of it, will keep the King of Prussia in awe, and probably deter Him from the Execution of some Schemes, He may have form'd. I wish, I could give entire Credit to the Article from Turin; But I cannot but apprehend, the Loss of the Spaniards is a little aggravated in this Account; However, they have certainly abandoned Oneglia.

I met my Lord Carteret yesterday at Court, soon after the Arrival of this good News. His Behaviour was very extraordinary; When I wished him Joy, He put on an affected Gravity, and Solemnity; Harangued the Company, upon the greatness of our present Situation, with an Air (tho' He did not do so in words) that shew'd plainly He took the whole Merit of it to Himself. The little, He said to me upon the Subject, plainly shew'd the same; and that He thought this great Alteration for the better in our Circumstances abroad gave Him the Superiority at home; In which however, His Lordship may find himself mistaken.

1. Prince Charles crossed the Rhine with his army near Philippsburg and advancing on Weissenburg, cut Coigny off from his base in Alsace.
2. Count Friederich Seckendorff was Commander of the Imperial Bavarian army.
3. Lord Henry Beauclerk, 1701–1761, MP for Plymouth, 1740–1741, and for Thetford, 1741–1761, was Colonel of the 48th. Foot, 1743–1745, and later of the 31st. Foot, 1745–1749.
4. Prince Scherbatow was the Russian envoy in England.
5. Alexis Bestuzhev was the Russian Chancellor.

We went into the Closet together. The King was, as you may imagine, in very good Humour: We did not stay with Him very long; and as we were going out of the Room, (Ld Carteret, I think was actually out of it) He said, speaking of the Army abroad. "I wish, I was with them" or Words to that effect. Ld Carteret, who heard him imperfectly, said to me, immediately: What! Does He say, He will go abroad? To which I answered No. And this is all that passed on that Subject. It was easy to foresee, that some Reflection of that kind might arise, on this Occasion. This might be only a transient Thought: But should the serious Design of the Journey be resumed, I should be as forward, & as firm, in offering my Opinion, & Advice against it, as I was, when it was first proposed; and so, I dare say, will the rest of my Brethren.

I am my Dear Lord Ever yrs

Holles Newcastle

Pray my compliments to ye Dutchess of Richmond

212. STONE TO RICHMOND

Claremont
June 30th, 1744

My Lord,

I take this Opportunity of acknowledging the Honour of your Grace's Letter. My Lord Duke thinks the Archbishop of Bourges's scruple about the passport not to have much Foundation, but as He is not quite satisfied with the form of it, His Grace will get one signed by His Majesty, with a particular mention of the Servants that are to attend the Baggage. When it is sign'd, I will take care to transmit it to your Grace.

My Lord Duke orders me to return your Grace His best Thanks for what you are pleased to mention about your coming to Town: He bids me assure you, He will take care to keep you constantly inform'd of every thing material that passes abroad, & at home; by which your Grace will judge, when your presence in Town may be necessary. My Lord Duke thinks there is nothing to call your Grace immediately from Goodwood.

I am with the greatest Respect My Lord Your Grace's most obedient and most humble servant

Andrew Stone

213. RICHMOND TO PELHAM

Goodwood
4 July 1744

Dear Sir,

I hear a new Commission of the Peace for our County is comeing out, so I take the liberty to recommend

Thos Ridge Esqr of Milland.

Wm Peckham[1] Esqr of Nyton, or Knigton.

To be putt into the new Commission. butt I must take the liberty to recommend one thing to your consideration, which is whether you will listen to any application, for any of the Clergy, I hope not, for if you do admitt one, I assure you there will be above a hundred will be displeas'd, & the Archdeacon, & I hear the Dean, is entirely of my mind.

I am Dear Sir, for ever & most affectly Your's

Richmond &c.

---

1. William Peckham, died 1770, succeeded to Nyton in Aldingbourne on the death of Richard Peckham in 1742, under the will of his cousin Sir Thomas Peckham.

214. RICHMOND TO PELHAM

Goodwood
8 July 1744

Dear Sir,

Since I wrote to you last I have recollected two more of my neighbours that may be propper to putt into the new Commission of the Peace. one is the youngest Turner, of Bignor Parke, who is very desirous of it, & is often here, & I beleive really means to be hearty with us, & you know he has a very pretty fortune, & if <u>Mr. Orme</u> does not object to him, I beleive nobody else will, the other is Nash of Walberton who you know much more of than I do, he has not ask'd it, as least of me. I know nothing of his polliticks, & very little of him, he is to dine here to day; & he seems to be an odd cub, however if other Gentn are putt in, & he left out, might not he complain? so you are as good a judge as anybody whether it is propper to putt him into this Commission or not. all our freinds hereabouts are overjoy'd at the King's not going. They talke more than I could wish of Polliticks, however to do them justice they lay all that is wrong at the right door.

I am dear Sir, for ever, Your's

Richmond &c.

215. PELHAM TO RICHMOND

July ye 10, 1744

My Dear Lord,

I had the honour of your Grace's two letters, and if there is a new Commission of the Peace, I conclude the Gentlemen you name will be thought by every body, proper persons to be in that Commission; but I understand by my Brother, that there are so many difficultys, who to put in and who to omit, in our part of the country that he does not think of any alteration by the next Assizes. We shall have the honour to see your Grace, I conclude, about that time, and we can then talk together, and fix what shall be done, against the winter. There are so many different accounts since Prince Charles passed the Rhine that we don't know what to think here. Upon the whole, Marshal Coigny has certainly shown himself a great General by getting the bulk of his Army between the Prince and Alsace. Time will show how these things will end; I wish for the best, and am with great truth. Your Grace's most obedient servt

H. Pelham

216. NEWCASTLE TO RICHMOND

Newcastle House
July 12, 1744

My Dear Lord,

Tho' I have not heard from you since my last Letter, I would not omit sending you an Account of any thing material that happens, at home, or abroad. As to the Motions of Prince Charles' Army, & M. Coigny's, you have in the publick Prints all the certain Advices, that we have yet received about them. There are Reports, that P. Charles's Army is got to Haguenau; but I do not know, that they are to be depended upon. Surely, Coigny, or Seckendorf have shew'd themselves good Generals. Pr. Charles's passing the Rhine has already had the good Effect to occasion a great Reinforcement being sent from Flanders to the Rhine, under Duke d'Harcourt. There is news from Calais, that the French King, with 25,000 Men, & M. Noailles, is gone to join Coigny, but I do not beleive it. As M. Wade's army will now soon be as strong, as it will be this Campaign, by the Dutch Reinforcements, and Ours, that went from hence; and as the

145

French Army will be greatly weaken'd, by the Detachments they have made, we have agreed to send Orders to M. Wade, to remain no longer upon the Defensive; But, in Concert with D. D'Aremberg, & C. Nassau, to march to the Enemy.

Yesterday, in the Closet, the King treated our part of the Administration, for having forced him to stay at home, in such a manner, that we were obliged to make him strong answers upon it; and even to desire him to make choice of more able, & more honest ministers. In short, the Alienation of His Affections from his old Servants was so evident, that we met last night, Lord Chancellor, my Lord Harrington, the Duke of Dorset, the Duke of Grafton, the Duke of Devonshire, my Brother & I, and resolved unanimously, not to go on with my Lord Carteret; and to take our measures accordingly; without however determining when to begin the Attack. I flatter myself, that you will approve this Resolution.

Now as to Sussex; the Assizes come on so soon, that we shall have no new Commission of the Peace, till afterwards; that we may have time to consult with you, & our Friends, who may be proper persons to be put in. Those you have named, are certainly so. I hope you will not fail to meet us, at the Assizes at Horsham on Monday, the 23 inst. My Brother, & I, intend to make J. Butler[1] a visit at Warminghurst Park; to be there on Saturday, the 21st & to go from thence on Monday morning to Horsham. I am sure J. Butler would be extremely glad of your Company; and it would be infinitely good in you to meet us there: However, you will do as is most agreable to you.

I beg my compliments to the Dutchess of Richmond and Lady Emely; and am My Dear Duke Ever most affectly yrs

Holles Newcastle

P.S. I need not desire that the contents of this letter may be secret.

217.   RICHMOND TO NEWCASTLE

Goodwood
Sunday. 15. July. 1744

My Dear Lord,

It is very true that I have not answer'd your letters regularly, butt why should I trouble you when I have nothing of consequence to say? & when you know my way of thinking upon the present disagreeable scituation of affairs, as well as I do my self. You know I have been entirely of your opinion all along, & you know my resollution of quitting my employment as soon as you are out of yours, & before, if you & my freinds thinke it will be of any service to the common cause; I mean by the common cause carrying on the King's affairs & the affairs of the nation, in a fair honest & justifyable way; & no longer than that can any man that means well continue to serve. This has always been my opinion, & so it ever will be. I shall certanly attend you at Worminghurst on Saturday, & so on to Horsham. butt pray lett me know at what time you will be at Worminghurst, that I may not have too long a teste a teste with my honest freind Jack, who is the best man in the world, butt his whispers encrease daily in length & numbers. do you thinke you shall wante me to go to London with you from Horsham? if you do, lett me know it, & I shall readly attend you, if not, I shall be glad to return here. The Duchess of Richmond & Emily are much your humble servants, & I am my Dear Lord for ever & most affectly Your's

Richmond &c.

1. John Butler of Worminghurst, 1707–1767, succeeded to the family estate there on the death of James Butler, the MP for Sussex on 20 May 1741.

I always loved Lord Orford, butt I own my esteem for him is vastly diminish'd upon this last grant[1] he has gott. I did not know it till tother day, & could hardly beleive it. 'tis actually the most mean & avaritious thing I ever heard of in a man of his sense, figure & circumstances.

218.   STONE TO RICHMOND

Whitehall
July 17th 1744

My Lord,

I am by my Lord Dukes order, to return your Grace His thanks for the Honour of your Letter, which he received yesterday, and to acquaint you, that He, & Mr Pelham, having promised Mr Foliot to dine with him at his house in Surrey on Saturday next, shall not reach Worminghurst 'till towards night, where they promise themselves the pleasure of meeting your Grace. My Lord Duke bids me say, that He always wishes for your Grace in Town, when He is there Himself; that He does not at present know of any thing, that particularly requires your presence here; But that, when He sees you in Sussex, He shall lay before you the situation of affairs, from whence your Grace will be best able to judge what to do in that respect.

We are without any particular Accounts from the Armies on the Rhine, & in Flanders. By all that we have heard, there is great Reason to hope, that Prince Charles is going on successfully; and, as great Detachments are gone, or going, from the French Army in Flanders towards the Rhine, it is generally beleived, that the Allied Army there will soon be able to enter upon Action.

I am with the greatest respect My Lord Your Grace's most obedient and most humble servant

Andrew Stone

219.   STONE TO RICHMOND

Whitehall
August 9th, 1744

My Lord,

I have received the Honour of your Grace's Letter, with one enclosed for Consul Goldsworthy, which I will take care to have forwarded to him by the next Mail. We had yesterday the Letters, that were due from Holland, & Flanders; but nothing very material from the Armies, either on the Rhine, or in the Low Countries. Prince Charles was posted on the 6th inst. N.S. at Hochfelder: General Nadasti, with a Detachment, had taken possession of the Port of Sabern, whilst M. Coigny was supposed to be incamped behind the Moltzen. The Allied Army in Flanders was, on the 11th inst. N.S. very near Lisle: General Ligonier, with 50 horse, was at two Villages in the neighbourhood of that Place, and was fired at by two or three Canon. The very day before Our Army came to Pont à Tressine, from whence the last Letters were dated, the Garrison of Lisle consisted only of one Batallion of Swiss, and four of Militia; and it is wished by many, that our Generals had taken the Resolution to invest it immediately, tho' they had no heavy Artillery with them for carrying on a Siege. Counte Saxe, being sensible of the weakness of the Garrison, sent a considerable Reinforcement into the Town, the Evening before our Army came up. Duke d'Aremberg has given His Opinion, that C. Saxe cannot be forced in his present Camp behind the

---

1.   Robert Walpole, 1st. Earl of Orford, 1676–1745, received a pension of £4000 per annum, as from 24 June 1744.

Lys; so that, if we cannot undertake a Siege, it is to be fear'd, our present avow'd superiority in the Low Countries will not produce any thing of great éclat.

I have been longer upon this Subject, than I intended, or ought to have been, having an Affair of such infinite Consequence to acquaint your Grace with, as the open Declaration of the King of Prussia against the Queen of Hungary. An Express from my Lord Hyndford has brought a manifesto, printed at Berlin, containing the King of Prussia's Reasons, for giving Auxiliary Troops to the Emperor; and it is in the Quality of an Auxiliary to the Emperor, that He declares He will act against the Queen of Hungary, as England & Holland act, in the Quality of Her Auxiliaries.

On the 4th of this Month, He sent requisitorial Letters to the Regency of Saxony, (the King being at Warsaw) to demand a Passage for His Troops thro' Saxony to Bohemia. The Regency excused themselves from granting it without Orders from the King of Poland: upon which, the King of Prussia has declared that He would, in all Events, pass thro' Saxony; and that He would not defer His March, 'till they could send to Warsaw, & have an Answer from thence: and He proposes to go by the way of Dresden. The Body of Troops design'd for Bohemia consists of 50,000 men. The Court of Dresden is greatly alarm'd. They have not a sufficient Strength to oppose the passage of the Prussian Troops: But seem very well disposed towards it; and some Accounts say, that the Duke of Weissenfeldt is drawing together as great a Number of Saxon Troops, as He can, in order to see what can be done with them. Your Grace will easily imagine, that this Incident has revived the Project of giving some Assistance from hence to the Elector of Saxony. There has been, this Evening, a Meeting of my Lord Chancellor, my Lord President, my Lord Duke of Newcastle, my Lord Carteret, & Mr Pelham, upon that subject, and I am order'd by my Lord Duke to acquaint your Grace, that the Result of this Deliberation was, not to enter into any onerous Engagements with Saxony, unless the States General, who are so nearly concern'd, consent to take part of the Burthen upon themselves. Orders will be immediately sent to Mr Trevor, to talk to them in a proper manner upon this Point: and, in the mean time, it has been proposed (tho' not yet agreed) that part of the <u>additional</u> Subsidy, lately given by Treaty to the Queen of Hungary, should be advanced, as from her Hungarian Majesty, to the Elector of Saxony, to enable him to put His Troops into Motion, in case it should appear to be absolutely necessary for that purpose: But, (as I said) this is at present only an imperfect Thought, & may, or may not, be carried into execution.

My Lord Duke sends His Compliments to your Grace, & hopes to have the Pleasure of meeting you next week at Lewes.

I am with the greatest Respect My Lord Your Grace's most obedient & most humble servant

Andrew Stone

The Russian Minister at Berlin, join'd with the Saxon Minister there, in dissuading the King of Prussia, in the Czarina's name, from His present Enterprise:- But to no purpose.

220. NEWCASTLE TO RICHMOND

Claremont
Augt 25th, 1744

My Dear Lord,

I intended to thank you by this Post, for your kind and agreable visit at Bishopstone. I am now to add my acknowledgements for your Invitation to Goodwood, which I shall wth the greatest pleasure obey. I have not seen, or heard from old Puff[1] this Month, so

---

1. The Duke of Grafton.

know nothing of Him, and I want no Inducement or other Company to bring me to Goodwood. It will I doubt, be too soon to come next Week, as I have lately been absent for some days, but I hope in the course of next week, to let you know, when I can attend you, & I shall wish, & desire to find you alone, unattended by my very good friends in your Neighbourhood. You may imagine I dont mean literally, for I must beg you would let me wait on you to make a visit to my good friend Sr Ian. As to foreign news, there are two posts due from Holland, So I know little more, than when I saw you at Bishopstone. Things really seem to go well in Holland. They are disposed to come into a Treaty wth us with the Elector of Saxony, to send Ministers to the Czarina, & the several Courts in the Empire to act in concert wth the English Ministers there, upon this great Event of the King of Prussia, & Mr Trevor writes positively that ye Pensionary promises to furnish the artillery, etc, yt we want. If so, I suppose we shall soon hear of a Siege. Lord Stair, has wrote two long replies. I don't understand Military Operations, but Ld Stair's papers tend most to <u>action</u>. His Lordship was set out for Scotland, so I could not make your Excuses to Him. Count Heenning seems very sanguine as to the Conduct of His Court, gives great Hopes that the Prussian Artillery, will not be suffer'd to pass the Elbe. That they shall have an army of 40,000 Men to follow the Prussians into Bohemia & to join the Austrians there, & yt nearly 30,000 Poles will be ready for ye same purpose. They also talk very sanguinely about Russia. On ye other Hand, I much fear, we may soon have an account that Pr Charles, either wth His whole Army, or with a great Detachment has endeavoured to repass the Rhine. If that should be the case, we shall be in a bad condition indeed, but I hope this apprehension will not be well grounded. Whatever situation things may be in abroad, they cannot be worse than they are at home. Ld Harrington has seen the King during our absence. His Majy held the same Language as He did to me six weeks ago, that the <u>King of France was a King etc</u>; that <u>He</u> speaking of <u>Himself</u>, had <u>a parcel of</u> [   ] and then stoped. His Manner, Behaviour, & Looks to me, are as bad as possible, whilst the most gracious accueil, & smiles are every moment bestowed on my Collegue in my presence. Thus things stand, & will stand, as long as we will let them. I wish every Body thought & acted like my dear Duke of Richmond, whose goodness I can never sufficiently acknowledge, but I shall ever be most sincerely and affectly yrs

Holles Newcastle

P.S. Mine and Pickles[2] compliments to my Queen, & Lady Emily.

221. NEWCASTLE TO RICHMOND

Newcastle House
Augt 30th, 1744

My Dear Lord,

I have the favor of both your kind letters, & am extreamly sorry, for your accident, but as the pain is greatly abated, I hope you will soon be about again. You know you are to have the Duke of Grafton's Company on Monday. If His Grace would have gone the latter end of ye week, I should have been proud to have attended Him, But the pleasures of Richmond of a Saturday are not to be withstood. I will however, if your Grace will give me leave wait upon you on Fryday the 7th Sept. if nothing extraordinary happens to prevent me, or if you should choose to have me any other time, when you may be better able to go abroad, if you can let me know it. All times are alike to me. Linky designs Himself the Honor to wait upon you with me. If any extraordinary Business should happen the beginning of next week, I will be sure to let you know it, & in that case I hope you will give me leave to come another week. We are in

---

1. Presumably the Duchess of Newcastle.

great expectation of news from abroad, the Monday post, being not yet come in. However, all the news we have is bad. Pr Charles who was to winter in Alsace, is passed the Rhine with His whole army; but without any loss, as He says; & with ye loss of 5000 men as the French say. There are accounts, yt the whole French army is past after Him. I hope in God that is true, for then we are safe on this side, & they will run great Risk of being destroyed. Poor Ossario, is under great apprehensions, & I doubt with Reason, for their affairs. They seem in a very bad way. At Court things remain as they did. At first we said, Pr Charles' repassing the Rhine was a great thing for the Empire, & Germany. I could not forbear replying, but what is it for Flanders?, where I believe we shall do nothing, tho' every thing seems now preparing for a Siege. Sure as you say, things should be brought to a Decision. It is high time. I was very sorry to hear from, Baron Stronbergh of poor Lady Emily's accident tho' the Baron assured me livelyly, she had no Hurt. Pray my Compliments to my Queen.

I am my Dear Duke Ever Yrs

Holles Newcastle

222. PELHAM TO RICHMOND

Esher
Septr 1st 1744

My Dear Lord,

I am extremely obliged to your Grace for your kind invitation to Goodwood, but as I have long been engaged to Mr Poyntz[1] to go for a day or two to his house in Berkshire, I am afraid I cannot easily manage my affairs so, as to wait upon you both. It is a great mortification to me to think that any of your friends, and servants here, should have the pleasure of being with you, and I not of the party, but I am afraid it must happen so; My Brother proposes coming to you next Friday, the very day I designed my other expedition; and His Grace of Grafton will attend you on Monday. He is to be att Claremont tomorrow night in his way to Goodwood. They will tell you how the publick world goes, but no one can with so great certainty as myself assure you that I am and ever shall be My Lord, your Grace's most affectionate and faithfull servt

H. Pelham.

223. STONE TO RICHMOND

Whitehall
Septr 1st 1744

My Lord,

Your Grace having, in your last Letter to my Lord Duke of Newcastle, desired His Assistance to procure a Student's Place at Christ Church for a young gentleman at Westminster School, (whose name, if I mistake not is Boisdean) His Grace orders me to acquaint you, that, if He is upon the Foundation at Westminster, He will not fail to recommend him to the Dean of Christchurch, when he appears as a Candidate at the Election of Scholars for the two universities; and, in that case, my Lord Duke is persuaded, He may be of service to the young gentleman. But, if He is not upon the Foundation, the only way of procuring Him a Studentship, is to obtain a Nomination from one of the Canons of Christchurch, which he cannot be sure of doing, especially

1. Stephen Poyntz, 1665–1750, of Midgham in Berkshire, was Envoy Extraordinary to Sweden, 1724, and a Privy Councillor, 1735. His family later married into the Browne family, Viscounts Montague of Cowdray.

as Bishop Gilbert[1] has very lately given His Nomination, at my Lord Duke's Request to Dr Russel's son, of Lewes. However, your Grace may be assured of my Lord Duke's doing every thing in his power to obey your Grace's Commands upon this Occasion.

The Dutch Mails, which were due, came in this afternoon. I have not seen the Letters; But, by what I hear, the Accounts they bring are not very favourable. It is to be fear'd, the Prussians will soon be Masters of Bohemia. Prince Charles was at Stuttgart, in his way to the Danube on the 1st Inst. N.S. The French Army follows him pretty close, and, I beleive is superior in Numbers.

We have nothing from the Army in Flanders, which is very astonishing.

I am with the greatest Respect My Lord, Your Grace's most obed, humble servt
Andrew Stone.

224. RICHMOND TO NEWCASTLE

Goodwood
Sunday 2d Septr 1744

My Dear Lord,
I shall be overjoy'd to see you whenever 'tis convenient to you to come, & if you can come on Fryday, I hope you will, for the sooner wee see you the better, & for that reason I wish you could have come with the Duke of Grafton to morrow, however if any thing should happen to hinder your journey on Fryday, I hope it will at least be the week after. I am glad to hear Dear Linky will come with you, & I can tell you, you both flatter your Queen as you call her extreamly, for she looks upon this intended visit as to her. I thanke you for last obliging letter, & cant help saying that somebodys remark upon Prince Charles's repassing the Rhine was extreamly ingenious.

I am My Dear Lord for ever your's
Richmond &c.

225. NEWCASTLE TO RICHMOND

Newcastle House
Sept 4th, 1744

My Dear Lord,
My Lord Lincoln, Jemmy & I, intend ourselves the honor of waiting upon your Grace, & the Dutchess of Richmond on Fryday next. As Jemmy is a sort of an Invalid, He cannot travel without help, & therefore He begs you would send a Chaise for Him to Liphooke on Fryday morning, & we will take care to convey Him hither. Linky and I, young, Hail, strong fellows, ride from Godalming, & propose to be with you by dinner. We conclude you will not dine before three. As I hope to have the pleasure of seeing you so soon, I will defer all political considerations 'till then. We have not much news, there are two Dutch Mails due. Prince Charles is going with the whole army, as some advices say, directly to Bohemia, tho' others mention His going to Bavaria, & the Danube. It is uncertain, what the French intend to do. It is generally believed they are all passed the Rhine, tho' as with what view, is not known; whether to follow Pr Charles; or to beseige the Towns in upper Austria, as Frybourgh, etc; or to detach towards a certain part of Westphalia, where we have sent orders, to do <u>wonders</u>. Nothing new from Italy, & <u>nothing</u> from Flanders. My Duty to my Queen, Compliments to Lady Emily, the D. of Grafton, and Mr. Coulthorpe.

I am my Dear Duke Ever most affectly Yrs
Holles Newcastle

1. John Gilbert, 1693–1761, Bishop of Llandaff, 1740–1749, of Salisbury, 1749, and Archbishop of York, 1757–1761.

226. NEWCASTLE TO RICHMOND

Newcastle House
Sep 13th 1744

My Dear Lord,

I must begin by returning your Grace, & the Dutchess of Richmond my most sincere thanks for your kind & agreable Reception and Entertainment at Goodwood. It is always a Pleasure to me to wait upon you, but never so much, as when I can do it, as I have done this last time. I found things on my Return to Court, much as I left them. The news from Holland rather worse, & from other Parts not better. Mr Trevor has got a little further insight into the <u>Avis</u> of Holland, amongst the powers to be invited by the King & the Dutch to take part with us, in the War. The Elector of Hanover is specifically named, & will be desired to join in the Treaty with the Elector of Saxony, & to furnish either Troops or Money. This shows, what they think in Holland as to the Behaviour, & Conduct of that Electorate. But what is worse, they absolutely refuse to follow any precedents of former wars, either as to the number of Troops, Ships, or Money, that they will furnish in this; & particularly that they will not contribute above one fourth part, to the Subsidy to be granted to the Elector of Saxony, & if they persist in that, that Treaty cannot be made. The Saxons are delatory, & bartering, but I think the Duke of Weissenfeldt will march forthwith with 20m men to join Batterani[1]. Prince Charles makes what haste He can, but I doubt his army will be very much lessen'd by the Troops left to garrison the strong Towns in Bavaria. Seckendorf will be after Him with 40m Men, & Coigny makes the Siege of Nybourgh. I wish I could send you any certain good news from Muscovy. Things are there still in suspence. As you are so good to me, I should be very unwilling to bring you from Goodwood, without an absolute necessity. Lord Chancellor comes on Monday, & tho' I believe, in the course of next week, we may agree to talk strongly upon the necessity of a Plan & sistem, the effectual Concurrence of the Dutch, & even give His Majesty to understand, that there must be an alteration in the Manner, & perhaps the Measure of carrying on the war, or we can't answer for the Success in the next Session of Parliament, yet I despair of such a vigorous <u>Resolution</u>, being taken as to the Cause or Author of our Difficulties, as would alone be an adequate Cure to them, & would make the presence of all our friends, advisable, & indeed necessary next week. I cannot press you to come to Town, if you have no other Occasion for it. I will let you know, every thing that passes. I promise for myself, to do nothing but what I know is agreable to your Opinion.

I am my Dear Duke with the greatest affection Ever yrs
Holles Newcastle

P.S. My compliments to all at Goodwood, & Lavant

227. RICHMOND TO NEWCASTLE

Goodwood
Sunday. 16 Sepr 1744

My Dear Lord,

I thanke your Grace for your most kind & obliging letter of the 13th & now as to my going to town, it will be necessary for me upon my own account to be in town this week or the next, butt if upon other accounts next week will be time enough, I had much rather defer it 'till then, haveing a good deal of business here this week. however it shall be just as you please, & if you desire I should be there this week, I beg you will lett me know it by to morrow night's post, which I shall receive on tuesday, & then I

---

1. Prince Charles Joseph Bathiani, the Austrian Field Marshall.

can be in town on Wednesday night or Thursday morning, which I should thinke might be time enough, butt then I must absollutely return here on Sunday, whereas if I go only next week I can be there on Tuesday night or Wednesday morning, & then I shall not be so absollutely tyed down to a day for my return. So I shall expect your commands & must readyly & cheerfully obey them being My Dear Lord for ever Your's

Richmond &c.

Taw & I joyn in our most sincere thanks for your last kind visit. If I am to go to town this week, I beg you would send a porter with the enclosed order. if you dont expect me this week, you'l burn the letter. Pray forgive this, butt as you are the only judge when I am to go up, you are the only person that can do this I desire you.

228.   NEWCASTLE TO RICHMOND

Newcastle House
Sept 18th 1744

My Dear Lord,

It is now pretty late at Night. My Lord Chancellor, my Lord Harrington, & my Brother; the Duke of Dorset, who came to Town very unexpectedly last night; and the Duke of Grafton, who sets out early tomorrow morning for Euston, are just gone from hence. We are come to a Resolution, (relating to <u>measures</u> only) which I am sure you will approve. It is impossible to acquaint you with the Particulars of it by the Post. But as I have a great mind that you should be acquainted with it, before it is executed, if it would be convenient for you to be in Town on Thursday night, you would certainly be here time enough for that Purpose. I have directed Oakes to be at Godalmin tomorrow night, with a Set of Horses, that you have it in your Power to come to Town if you should chuse to do it. It is very probable, that the thing may not be done, 'till the Beginning of next Week; But I cannot say it will be delay'd so long. If you should come on Thursday, I beg you would let nobody but the Dutchess of Richmond know the Cause of it; and that you would not mention to any one, that you have been sent for by me; for you may easily judge, that that would not be thought proper.

My Compliments to the Dutchess of Richmond, Lady Emily, & all the good Compy at Goodwood.

I am my Dear Lord Ever and unalterably yrs

Holles Newcastle

229.   PELHAM TO RICHMOND

Esher Place
Oct 6th [1744]

My Dear Lord,

I have heard nothing further of the vacancy att Arundel,[1] The Mayor must take the care that proper notice is given of the man's being unable to serve any longer; when that is done, Miles will come in of course. As to the Custom House boats, if any are kept up, I shall have a great disposition to give the preference to Chichester. But the representation of the Commissioners of the Customs is against them all, Whether we

---

1.   The Mayor of Arundel, as returning officer, and the Coporation, were an important influence in the seat. The Government had a certain influence because of the customs service at the port. Sir John Shelley, Newcastle's candidate, had been defeated in 1741, because of a hostile majority in the Corporation and Newcastle and Richmond were trying to prevent this happening again. See G W. Eustace, *Arundel Borough and Castle*, (1922).

have virtue enough to do what is right, I am not sure, If we have, they all go; if we have not, Chichester att least is safe. (I am surprised I have heard nothing, either from his Grace of Bolton, or the gentleman of the Isle of Wight upon the vacancy att Yarmouth upon the death of Gibson.[1] I expect the same attention as my predecessors have had, and if you should see Sr John, possibly a word drop't from your Grace may be of service. I know they are all quarrelling with the Governor, but I should hope that would not extend to the rest of the King's servants; and I believe they are not dissatisfied with me). However, possibly, as Carterets first lady was a Worsley,[2] they may have their eyes to that shop, and if he is to influence, what is commonly called Government Burrough's, as well as <u>Government</u> itself, we shall soon be cyphers indeed. I dare say your are sorry for our County's loss in poor Abergavenny,[3] but by a message I have had from the young Lord, I hope we shall at least keep things upon the foot they have been, with the difference only, of one living constantly in the Country, and the other a Minor without a certainty of where he will live when he comes of age, for your Grace knows, the young men of this age are not much govern'd by the examples of their parents. My compliments to the Dutchess of Richmond, Lady Emily, etc.; and believe me my Dear Lord Your Grace's most obedient and most humble servt

H. Pelham

230. NEWCASTLE TO RICHMOND

Claremont
Oct 6th 1744

My Dear Lord,

As I am always glad to send your Grace, any news, I know will please you, you may believe I am particularly so upon this occasion, when it is to acquaint you, that yesterday I received the King's orders to prepare a Commission for Lord Albemarle for the <u>Coldstream</u>. I would have sent an account immediately to Durham, but the Princess told me, that Lady Albemarle was at Goodwood. I beg your Grace should make my most sincere Compliments & Congratulations to her upon this occasion. I wrote to Lord B. last night to send Him the news, tho' I have my <u>Grievances</u> and my <u>Complaints</u> I can't but feel a most sensible joy & satisfaction. There is very little news since you left us. Things in Holland, go just as they did. In Flanders, after all the late appearances, the Campaign is at an end, as I perceive by a letter just come from Marshall Wade, who lays all the Blame of Inaction, upon d'Strenlugh & the Dutch Generals, & they return the Compliment most strongly. P. Charles has joined Bathiani and ye D. of <u>Weissenfelt</u> with 20m Saxons, entered Bohemia, on the 4th or 5th, Inst. N.S, we shall soon hear of something considerable from thence, if the K. of Prussia, has not extricated Himself so, as not to be attacked. There are Reports yt He is marching to join Seckendorf, who has taken Donauat, & I own I fear will soon retake great part of Bavaria. Things in Russia, remain as they were, except that the Accounts from thence rather mend than otherwise. In Italy, the King of Sardinia acts a truly great Part, & is determined to attack the French, & attempt the Relief of Cony, in which there is great Reason, to hope he will succeed. Your friend V. Admiral Rowley,[4]

1. Thomas Gibson, 1667–1744, MP for Marlborough, 1722–1734, and for Yarmouth in the Isle of Wight, 1736–22 September 1744, was Cashier to the Pay Office until July 1744.
2. John Carteret, 1690–1763, 1st. Earl Granville from 1744, married, as his first wife, Frances, daughter of Sir Robert Worsley.
3. William Nevill, 16th. Lord Abergavenny, died at Bath 21, and was buried at East Grinstead 30 September 1744.
4. William Rowley, 1690–1768, MP for Taunton, 1750–1754, and for Portsmouth, 1754–1761, having distinguished himself in an engagement off Toulon in February 1744, was placed in charge of the Mediterranean Fleet in August. However, as a result of an enquiry into the court martial of Sir John Norris's son, he was relieved of his command, and never went to sea again. He was appointed Admiral in 1747.

154

does admirably well. There is a Loan going on, of 200,000 pds to be lent the King of Sardinia. We all subscribe tho' some of us, don't abound in money. Things at Court are just as they were, sometimes better, sometimes worse, but yesterday our Master made a very ugly Proposition, in which he was much encouraged by my Collegue, viz, to quarter the Hanoverians this winter in Westphalia, to be aparté. I believe that will not go down gently with some of us. Lord Chancellor comes to Town on Tuesday, after which, I hope the finishing stroke, will soon be put to the great work you know of. You shall know every step it takes, & I am sure you will agree wth me in opinion, as to the necessity of that or something stronger. The Ds of Newcastle desires Her Compliments to the Ds. of Richmond, Lady Albemarle, & Lady Emily.

I beg mine, in ye best manner, & am my Dear Lord Ever and unalterably yrs
Holles Newcastle

231.   RICHMOND TO NEWCASTLE

Goodwood
Sunday morn. 7 Octr 1744

My Dear Lord,

I hope & beleive it is very unneccessary for me to assure you that I am ready to go to town whenever my freinds may want me, so I expect your call. As to the affairs in question, you know how very clear my opinion is upon them, & (unless new matter has arisen since I saw you) you may vouch for me, & the representing person make use of my name, insignificant as it is, butt my opinion you know is very determin'd. I own I should be very glad to stay here three weeks longer, & to go up only a few dayes before the birthday: by which time wee may possibly see the event; however, as I have already told you, I am (if I can be of the least service) ready to sett out whenever you thinke it neccessary for the publick good, which I am very sure is the only thing wish'd for by your Grace, all your freinds & very particularly by, your ever faithfull humble servant,
Richmond &c.

If you send for me at any time in a hurry pray send the enclosed to Oakes. I wish to know if the seventeen French ships were really French East India men & not men of warr, for I have heard they were so, & if so, why Daver's[1] squadron, (barr the westerly wind) stayes at Spitthead, where they now are.

232.   STONE TO RICHMOND

Whitehall
Octr 18th 1744

My Lord,

My Lord Duke having refer'd it to me to send your Grace an Account of the publick News, I have the Honour to acquaint you, that a day or two ago, a Messenger arrived from Mr Villiers[2] at Grodno, with the Project of the Treaty between the Maritime Powers, & the Elector of Saxony, in which the Saxon Ministers proposed only some few, and not very material, Alterations: which have been accepted in Holland, and will be so here; so that that Affair may be now look'd upon as concluded. The Subsidy, to be paid to Saxony, is 150,000 £; of which Holland pays one third. The Saxons are so much in earnest, that Count Brühl[3] actually wrote to the Duke of Weissenfeldt, to

1.   Admiral Thomas Davers.
2.   Hon. Thomas Villiers, 1709–1786, MP for Tamworth, 1747–1756, was Envoy to Poland, 1738–1743, and again, 1744–1746. He was Minister to Austria, 1742–1743, and to Prussia in 1746.
3.   Count Brühl was minister to Augustus III King of Poland and Elector of Saxony.

propose to Him his marching with the Saxon troops under His Command, directly to Berlin. But we hope, that the Duke will have pursued his first Resolution of joining Prince Charles, who waits only for that junction, to attack the Prussian Army, which is very near him, and, by its late Motions, seems rather to think of retiring, than advancing. Prince Charles has got between the Prussian Army, & Prague, and, by a Motion that Count Nadasti has made with a Body of the Austrian Troops, it is thought, the Prussians may be put to it for Subsistance; in which case, they may be obliged to attack Prince Charles, at a Disadvantage, He being strongly posted. Things continue to look favourably in Russia, but my Lord Tyrawly[1] complains, & the great Reason, that Business goes on very slowly at that Court. There are likewise good Appearances in the Polish Diet, now assembled at Grodno, & such, as Lord Hyndford says, gives great uneasiness at Berlin. Your Grace will have seen by the publick papers, that the French meet with greater Difficulties, than they imagined, before Fribourg; and the Success of that Siege may possibly be doubtful, notwithstanding the formidable Force that is before it.

In Italy, it is but too true, that the King of Sardinia was unsuccessful in His late Attack of the Enemy, tho' it is acknowledged to have been concerted with great Prudence, and executed with equal Bravery. However, Letters, subsequent to those, which brought an Account of that Action, give great Reason to hope that Coni will not be taken; and some even affirm the Siege to be raised. I have kept the most disagreable Article for the last. I mean, what relates to Flanders. We have no Letters of very fresh Date from Marshal Wade, but Mr Trevor, in his last Dispatch, sends an Account that the Pensionary had assured him, that Mr Wade had withdrawn the Troops under his Command, from the Allied Army; and was sending them into winter quarters; that this was not only done, without any previous Consultation, had with the Austrian & Dutch Generals, but even without giving Notice to them of His Resolution; by which means, the Austrian, & Dutch Troops were left exposed to the Enemy, who were incamp'd at a small Distance from them. This unexpected Step in Mr Wade has given the greatest Surprise, & Alarm to our Friends in Holland, and it has been plainly declared to Mr Trevor that, till some Eclairissement should be given upon this extraordinary Incident, He was not to expect, that the Republic would take any Step of vigour; But that every thing must remain in suspence, till such an Explanation should be given. This Proceeding has occasion'd as much Surprise here, as it did in Holland, Mr Wade having sent no Account of it, as yet, to England: But a copy of Mr Trevor's Letter will be immediately sent to him; that He may see the ill Effects that his Conduct in this Matter had produced, and give the Reasons that he has to alledge in His justification, which, after all, may possibly be good ones; But it is certain that a more untoward Accident could not have happen'd, than this seems to be in our present Circumstances.

I am with the greatest Respect My Lord, Your Grace's most obedient and most humble servant

Andrew Stone

233. PELHAM TO RICHMOND

October ye 20, 1744

My Dear Lord,

I am to acknowledge the favor of two letters from your Grace. As to the first, you know my thoughts of our friend Sr John, he is as friendly and as honest as the day is

---

1.   James O'Hara, 2nd. Lord Tyrawley, 1682–1773, was Ambassador Extraordinary and Plenipotentiary to Russia, 1743–1745. He had been Envoy Extraordinary to Portugal, 1728–1741.

long. His letter to Mr. Holmes[1] shews it, tho' I believe, he is out, in his guess as to the design'd member, for I have had a letter from Coll: Holmes,[2] in which he refers the whole to Bockland,[3] and I have wrote to Bockland, upon the receipt of that letter. That His Grace the Governor is hated, I know, but if his behaviour should be revenged on the Government I should be sorry. It is some time since I heard of the scheme of attacking His Grace, and I plead neutrality. Your last letter conveyed a petition from Chichester to remove the two companys that are quartered there on the smugling duty. I directed the Deputy Secretary att Warr to speak to the Commissioners of the Customs about it; for without their knowledge & approbation, I understand, the Warr Office never changes the quarters of Troops upon smugling Partys. Linky was married last Tuesday;[4] he tells me he thinks himself very happy. I am certain I am so, for I never saw a greater appearance of mutual satisfaction in my whole life. At present I am forc'd to keep terms, and behave myself with great gravity and Respect, by that time your Grace comes to London, I suppose, we may begin to joke, ask questions, and give our own answer to 'em. I conclude the D. of Newcastle furnishes you with Politicks both foreign and domestick. For my part, I think of em as little as I can, for the more I do think of em the less I like 'em. Coni is not taken. The King of Prussia is upon the retreat, and Rowley hopes to meet with the Spanish and French squadrons as he comes to the Straits.

I am my Dear Lord ever Yrs

H. Pelham

234. RICHMOND TO NEWCASTLE

Goodwood
21. Octr. 1744

The Duke of Richmond desires that Mr. Francis Peachy of Bersted or of Chilgrove may be excused serving the Office of Sheriff for the County of Sussex, as he is in low circumstances, the estate which his father had being how divided between him, his mother, & a younger brother.

235. STONE TO RICHMOND

Whitehall
Novembr 8th 1744

My Lord,

Since your Grace left London, some Incidents of great importance have happen'd, of which I am ordered by my Lord Duke of Newcastle to give you an Account. On Saturday last, my Lord Granville call'd upon Mr. Pelham, at his house: & told him, that He had the King's Orders, to acquaint him, that His Majesty had bestow'd upon Mr Edward Finch[5] the Reversion of the place of one of the Auditors of the Imprest, now

---

1. Thomas Holmes, 1699–1764, MP for Newton, Isle of Wight, 1727–1729, and again, 1734–1741, and for Yarmouth, 1747–1764, was Governor of the Isle of Wight, 1763–1764.
2. Henry Holmes, 1703–1762, MP for Newtown, Isle of Wight, 1741–1747, and for Yarmouth, 1747–1762, was Colonel of the 31st. Foot. 1749–1762.
3. Maurice Bocland, 1695 –1765, MP for Yarmouth, Isle of Wight, 1733–1734, and again, 1741–1747, for Lymington, 1734–1741, and for Newtown, Isle of Wight, 1747–1754, served in the campaign in Flanders, 1743–1746.
4. Henry Fiennes Clinton, 9th. Earl of Lincoln, 1720–1794, married his cousin Catherine, daughter of Henry Pelham on 16 October 1744. He was the son of Newcastle's sister.
5. Hon. Edward Finch, 1697–1771, was MP for Cambridge University, 1727–1768. A diplomatist, he spent most of his career in Sweden until he retired in 1742. He was a Groom of the Bedchamber, and, though a supporter of Carteret kept his place on the personal invitation of King George II.

157

held by Mr. Benson,[1] & that the King would have Mr. Pelham give the proper Orders for preparing the Warrant for that purpose. As this Office is under the immediate Direction of the Treasury, and as the Head of that Board has been always thought to have a Right to recommend to it, Mr. Pelham could not but think Himself very much slighted, both in the Matter, & the Manner of this Message, & spoke his thoughts upon it very freely to my Lord Granville, who made Excuses for it's not having been mention'd before to Mr. Pelham, it having been, three Months, at least, in Negotiation.

On Monday, Mr. Pelham waited upon the King, and open'd himself fully, both with regard to the personal Affront offer'd him in this late Instance, & also upon the general situation of Affairs, at home & abroad. His Majesty heard him with great Goodness; as He did my Lord Duke of Newcastle, on Tuesday, who, in a very long Audience, laid before His Majesty all, that your Grace has frequently heard him say, in confidence, to a few friends, with regard to the present State of the Administration, & the Necessity of some Alteration in it. My Lord President was in the Closet yesterday, & my Lord Steward, & the Duke of Devonshire this day; and, as I apprehend, all spoke to the same Effect. My Lord Chancellor is to attend His Majesty tomorrow, on the same Errand. All that has been, or will be, said, with regard to foreign Affairs, is founded upon the paper, deliver'd last Week. Lord Granville, as yet, has taken no Notice of any of these things, of which He cannot be supposed to be entirely ignorant. The King, this day, talk'd to the two Secretaries of State together, of referring the foreign Questions to the Decision of the Cabinet Council. Whether that will take place I am not certain. If it should be necessary for your Grace to come to Town, my Lord Duke will not fail to send you immediate Notice; and will write to your Grace, in all Events, very speedily. It is certain, that every day may produce some great Event.

I am with the greatest Respect My Lord Your Grace's most obedient & most humble servant

Andrew Stone

236. NEWCASTLE TO RICHMOND

Newcastle House
Novr 10, 1744

My Dear Lord,
In the great Hurry, I have been in of late, I was obliged to make use of Mr. Stone to send your Grace an Account of the material Incidents that have happen'd since your Grace left London. You will have been inform'd, by His Letter of last Post, of everything, that passed 'till yesterday morning. Things now ripen so fast, that I thought it necessary to dispatch this Messenger to acquaint you with our present situation. My Lord Chancellor was with the King on Monday last; and, in that Audience, confined his Conversation to General Business, & foreign Affairs. Yesterday, He waited upon His Majesty again; and enter'd very largely, into the present State of the Administration, and the Impracticability of it's continuing any longer upon the present Foot; which He inforced with more Spirit, Weight, and Dignity, than it is possible for me to express. As Part of His Discourse was much to my Honour, I cannot forbear bragging of it to my best Friends, and valuing myself a little upon such an honorable & seasonable Testimony of his Friendship, & good Opinion. The King seem'd very civil to my Lord Chancellor, during the whole Conference; thank'd Him for what he had said; complain'd of his Situation, & the Difficulties he was under; and ended very

---

1. William Benson, 1682–1754, MP for Shaftesbury, 1715–1719, was Auditor of the Imprest, 1735–1754.

remarkably, with saying, that, if He parted with Lord Granville, He should loose the Prince of Wales's, and Lord Bath's, People: But, that if He parted with us, He found He should loose almost his whole Administration, and those, He loved best. This, I conclude, your Grace will look upon, as we do, to be a pretty certain Indication of the Resolution, the King will take at last. We are gone so far, that it is impossible now to go back. In the several Conversations the King has had this Week, He has frequently flung out, that as to His Measures, they should be decided by His Council; and He has, at last (in order, I conclude, to get rid of them) directed them to be laid before the whole Cabinet Council; for which Purpose, (as things now stand) a Cabinet Council is to meet, on Monday Night or Tuesday Morning next, where the two great Points mentioned in our Paper, are to be determined, viz, the Renewing our Instances with the Dutch to Declare War; and, the settling the Proportions of Force, & Expense, to be furnish'd by each of the Allies, for carrying on the War. My Lord Chancellor & the rest of our Friends are very desirous, that your Grace & the Duke of Grafton, should be present at the Cabinet Council. I therefore thought your Grace would not dislike to be acquainted with all these Particulars; and, having, done that, I leave it entirely to you to come or not, as you shall think proper. It is possible that after all, the Cabinet Council may not meet; tho' the King said again yesterday that He would have it. I really do not, myself, know what to advise your Grace upon this Occasion, and therefore barely state the Facts to you. I have wrote just in the same way to the Duke of Grafton, and am quite uncertain, whether He will come or not. I will, in all Events, endeavour not to have the Cabinet Council meet 'till Tuesday Morning, that you may have the more time for your journy if you should determine to come. My Dear Duke, do just as you like as to coming. Our Friends certainly wish to have you all here. I think it possible the great Affair may be decided, before ye Council meets, & in that case, I suppose it will not meet at all. I am sure you will approve all we have done.

I am ever most affectly Yrs

Holles Newcastle

P.S. My best services to ye D. of St. Albans. You may acquaint Him from me, that things are coming to a point, & at present look well.

237. PELHAM TO RICHMOND

December ye 4th 1744

My Dear Lord,

I am now att Linky's, who is in bed with the chicken pox, a youthfull distemper; he looks damnably, but I hope all will end well, and if he will take care of himself afterwards, they tell me, it will do him a great deal of good. I ask a thousand pardons for not ansering your letter yesterday, but we were so taken up till twelve last night, that I realy forgot it. I spoke to the King in behalf of Admiral Townshend[1] the day after I saw you: Winchelsea has retained him for Capt Mostyn,[2] but I beleive he will yeild, and in case Matthews is chosen, or has a probability of success in Glamorganshire, I am determined to be for Townshend, but we cannot in decency set aside Matthews; this is the true state of the case, which nothing can quite determine but a new Admiralty.

I am my Dear Lord ever yr Grace's servt

H. Pelham.

1. George Townshend, 1715–1769, son of the 2nd Viscount Townshend, was present at the action off Toulon in 1744. He was created Admiral in 1765.
2. Savage Mostyn, 1713–1757, a cousin of Lord Winchelsea, and MP for Weobley, 1747–1757, was a captain from 1739, and Comptroller of the Navy, 1749–1755. He became a Vice-Admiral, 1757.

238. NEWCASTLE TO RICHMOND

Claremont
Dec 8th 1744

My Dear Lord,

I was in hopes I should have been able to send you by this Post some Account of things being a little settled, but I am sorry to acquaint you, that they are far from being so in every Respect. The Closet continues pretty much as it was, as to manner. I think rather more civil, but full as displeased, & seemingly as determined as ever. We have had several Meetings with our new friends.[1] In the main, they are very reasonable in their Recommendations, both as to their Numbers, & their Persons. The Tories are but few, & they not at all obnoxious, so that as to that, we might easily agree with them. But they surprised us the other night, by insisting absolutely, that the Duke of Bedford,[2] & Lord Sandwich,[3] should be in the Admiralty. They were so peremptory in this, that we have been forced to yield, & the Admiralty will be, if we agree with them, the Duke of Bedford, Ld Sandwich, Ld Vere Beauclerck,[4] Lord Anson, Ld Baltimore[5] Wm Chetwynd,[6] Ld A. Hamilton[7] or Mr Philipson.[8] The King has been spoke to, & has consented almost to this, but His Majesty has at present absolutely refused, to send Ld Chesterfield to the Hague, or to turn out any of Lord Granville's[9] friends, in order to make room for any in the Opposition. This must ruin us, & effectually do Lord Granville's Business. This will exclude all the Opposition, and it is impossible for us to go on without them. If the King would but give us leave to make a reasonable Bargain with them, I think every thing would go well, but without it, we are in a worse Condition than ever. As things are, in this situation, I desire you would say nothing to your Company, but that you find things are not settled, that we have great Difficulties in the Closet, but that otherwise every thing might easily be adjusted. You may let the Duke of St Albans know, that ye D. of Bedford will probably be at ye head of ye Admiralty, that Ld Vere is acquainted with it, & that the Duke of Bedford, expresses the greatest Regard imaginable for Him. We have not yet determined what to do, but things must be soon brought to a Point, & I am afraid, there will be no way of doing it, but by speaking as plainly as we did before. I beg my Compliments to all the good Company

1. The new members of the administration after the fall of Carteret.
2. John Russell, 4th. Duke of Bedford, 1710–1771, was made 1st. Lord of the Admiralty in December 1744, and a Privy Councillor on 27 December. He retained the office until 1748, when he became Secretary of State for the Southern Department until 1751.
3. John Montagu, 4th. Earl of Sandwich, 1718–1792, was made a Lord of the Admiralty on 27 December 1744. He was 1st. Lord of the Admiralty, 1749–1751, in 1763, and again, 1771–1782. He was Secretary of State for the Northern Department, 1763–1765, and 1770–1771. He was Minister Plenipotentiary at the Conference at Breda, 1746, at Aix-la-Chappelle, 1748, and at the Hague, 1746–1749.
4. Lord Vere Beauclerk, 1699–1781, MP for New Windsor, 1726–1738, and again, 1738–1741, and for Plymouth, 1741–1750, was a Lord of the Admiralty from 1738 to the fall of Walpole, and was reappointed in December 1744 under the Duke of Bedford. He was created Admiral in 1748.
5. Charles Calvert, 5th. Lord Baltimore, 1699–1751, MP for St. Germans, 1734–1741, and for Surrey, 1741–1751, was a Gentleman of the Bedchamber to the Prince of Wales, 1731–1747, and a Lord of the Admiralty, 1742–1744. He was Elder Brother of Trinity House, 1744–1751.
6. William Chetwynd, 1683–1770, MP for Stafford, 1715–1722, and again, 1734–1770, and for Plymouth, 1722–1727, was a Lord of the Admiralty, 1717–1727. He became Master of the Mint in December 1744.
7. Lord Archibald Hamilton had been a Lord of the Admiralty for the second time, since 1742.
8. John Phillipson had been a Lord of the Admiralty since 1743. The Duke of Bedford refused to have him at the Admiralty, as not being of sufficient station, and he was compensated by being made Surveyor of woods and forests north and south of the Trent, 1745–1756.
9. John Carteret became Earl of Granville on his mother's death on 18 October 1744.

at Charlton, I have had the pleasure to drink your Health here this day, with Sr Francis Poole, & Charles Monson.[1]

I am my Dear Lord Ever most affectly yrs

Holles Newcastle

239. RICHMOND TO NEWCASTLE

Charlton
11. Decr. 1744

My Dear Lord,

I thanke you for your most obliging letter, butt am very sorry to find things dont yett go on as they should do. As for His Grace of Bedford's being at the head of the Admiralty, I own I am sorry for it, for I look upon him to be vain, proud & wrong headed, & I fear you will have a great deal of plaque with him. I am very glad to hear 'tho that they are reasonable upon the article of Torys. butt I find the only difficulty is in the Closet, where indeed our Master must be spoke to in the same manner as he has been, & you are all in duty to him obliged to insist upon it. for he will most certanly be undone if he falls back into My Lord Granville's hands again, & that must be, if he wont agree to take in new strength with you. I wish you would be so good as to lett me know when the King goes to the house, & I would go up just for that day. I told the Duke of St Albans just what you bid me, & no more. Wee have had better sport than wee, any of us, ever remember. Old Puff has an account sent him of a most prodigious chase; I am My Dear Lord, Your Grace's ever faithfull & most affectte humble servant,

Richmond &c.

I hope Dear Linky is well of the Chicken pox, which 'tho a Childish distemper is better than the Cock Pox.

240. STONE TO RICHMOND

Whitehall
Dec 17th 1744

My Lord,

I recieved this day the Honour of your Grace's Letter; and am directed by my Lord Duke of Newcastle to dispatch this Messenger, to acquaint you, that the King will certainly go on to the House on Thursday next, so that my Lord Duke concludes he shall have the pleasure of seeing your Grace in Town, or at least hearing that you are arrived, on Wednesday night.

As to the great Affairs now depending, my Lord Duke bids me say, that He beleives, your Grace will find them concluded, in some way or other when you come to Town. Some small Progress has been made in them, since he wrote to you on Saturday night, but his Grace does not think the Appearances quite so agreable at this time, as He did then.

I am with the greatest Respect My Lord Your Grace's most obedient & most humble servant

Andrew Stone

---

1. Charles Monson, 1695–1764, MP for Lincoln, 1734–1754, was Deputy Paymaster of the Army, 1737–1746.

241. RICHMOND TO NEWCASTLE

Charlton
9 Jan 1744/5

My Dear Lord,

I have not heard from your grace since Sunday was sennight, however I dont complain for I am very sure you would have wrote to me if you had had time. I write this purely to know if you thinke there will be any business in the house of Lords next week, or if any thing else will require my attendance in town. for I am inclinable to stay one week longer here. I have wrote to Taw also about it, to know if she has no pressing business for me. however if the frost lasts I shall go whether I have any thing to do or no; butt if it should be open weather, I should chuse to stay one week longer. butt shall be glad to be govern'd by you two. Wee are all here in the greatest concern for poor Honywood, butt as he was alive, 'tho the expression was breathing his last, wee have still some glimmering hopes. if he does dye I assure you it will be a loss to the army as well as his freinds, for his attachment to the service, as well as his courage & spirit, was worthy of imitation. & I am very sorry to say I fear there are not many such left. I am impatient to know what will be done with Bellisle[1] when he comes; surely he will be closely garded 'tho to be sure not confin'd. London would be a bad place for him, because of insults he might meet with from our governors the mob. I should thinke Windsor Castle would be the best, & he is most heartily welcome to my lodgins there, which are pleasant & airy. & I thinke he should have the liberty of riding out with a propper gard attending him. butt if the Castel does not oblige us, for Godsake dont lett us give him up whilst the warr lasts. I cant conclude this letter without telling you that notwithstanding what I have said in the beginning of it, I am some what uneasy at your not writing, fearing that you might take something ill in the private advice I took the liberty to give you in my last, If you knew my heart you could not be angry, for I am most entirely, unfeinedly, & unalterably Your's

Richmond &c.

The Duke of St Albans & Harcourt are much yours. I wish you had spoke to Harcourt about the Troop of Grenadiers, tho he is satisfyd with what you bid me tell him about Ld Petersham.[2] He will be in town next week. Carpenter has a horse here above fifteen hands high, consequently not fitt for you, he is full strong enough to carry me, & I am in great distress for want of a horse, butt he wont lett me have him without your consent, so I beg you would lett me have him.

242. NEWCASTLE TO RICHMOND

Claremont
Jany 12th 1744/5

My Dear Lord,

I will begin with what I am sure you will be the most pleased. Ld Albemarle arrived last night, & was with me this morning in high Spirits, & Health. We were just as when I last saw Him, & I own, I had so much pleasure, in seeing one I so sincerely love, yt I forgot every thing that had passed, which at the time gave me uneasiness. I dined yesterday wth the Dutchess of Richmond & Cheale. You may imagine your Health was

---

1. Marshall Belle-Isle had been captured on Hanoverian soil in December 1744. He was taken to England and detained, but as he had been engaged on a diplomatic mission to Prussia, he could not properly be regarded as a prisoner of war. However, he was released by exchange in August 1745.
2. William Stanhope. Viscount Petersham, 1719–1779, MP for Aylesbury, 1741–1747, and for Bury St. Edmunds, 1747–1756, succeeded his father as 2nd. Earl of Harrington in 1756. He was Colonel of the 2nd. Troop of Horse Grenadiers, 1745–1749.

not forgot. I drank it once to the Duchess of R. in a common glass, & afterwards to Cheale in a Bumper. The same Company dine with me on Wensday with the addition of the <u>Albemarles</u>. I can't say I wish you there, for as I know you like hunting, & I really think it so right for your Health, I never would call you from it, when there is not a real Occasion, and as the Dutchess of Richmond assures me she has <u>no call</u> for you; our insipid political Situation, don't require your presence, till something more particular or material happens, than at present seems likely, for some time. Things go on just as they did, that is to say, they hardly go on at all. The King scarce vouchsafes to speak upon business, wth His Ministers; at least but short. Lord Chesterfield could hardly get an audience, & when he had one, which was yesterday, in ye presence of Lord Harrington, it was a most extra ordinary one; scarce a word, or only <u>one</u>. In short, things are so bad, that it is impossible for them to remain long in this Situation. However, Ld Chesterfield's Instructions, are as good as possible, & must bring things to some precision, as to a Plan of Operations, the appointing a General, & the settling the Proportions. His Majesty seems now to be much inclined to have Ld Stair, to Command, or rather to settle, the Army at Home, & then to go to command in Flanders. If our allies will like it, that may do very well. Our new Admiralty goes on very well. They think in the first place, of having a sufficient strength at home, which is the most necessary Consideration, especially as the French seem to be drawing all their naval strength this way. Capt Honeywood came over wth Albemarle; there was not the least Foundation for the Report about Him. I wonder you would think, I was angry at your most kind advice in your Letter. You know me very little, if you are not sure that such Marks of Friendship, increase the Love & Regard I have for my Friends. Pray my kind Complts to ye D. of St Albans, & Lord Harcourt. I am sorry I did not think mentioning the Grenadiers to Him, It was quite out of my Head, & that being the Truth, must be my Excuse. If he likes Carpenter's Horse, I will not interfere with you.

I am my Dear Duke Ever & unalterably Yrs

Holles Newcastle

P.S. <u>Lord George</u> desired me particularly to send his Duty to his pappa.

243.   RICHMOND TO NEWCASTLE

Charlton
10 Feb 1744/5

My Dear Lord,

Tho I have nothing of any consequence to say, yett I cant help congratulating you upon the birth of an other Arch Duke, & the Queens being well, which next to the Emperor's death[1] has been the best peice of news I have heard this great while. They had kill'd her in the Citty, & had that been true it would have been a most fatal stroke to all affairs at this time. If the King has been at the house I beg you would make my excuse & say I did not know it. This cursed frost has hinder'd us hunting, however I shall persevere one week more & no longer, for then & thereabouts, I hope my Taw will follow the example of the queen of Hungary.

I am My Dear Lord, Your Grace's ever faithfull, & affectionate humble servant

Richmond &c.

---

1.   The Emperor Charles VII died on 27 December 1744, being succeeded as Elector of Bavaria by his son Maximilian Joseph, and as Emperor by Francis of Lorraine, husband of Maria Theresa. Marie Theresa had given birth to a son who founded the line of Lorraine Hapsburgs.

244.   RICHMOND TO NEWCASTLE

Thursday night [14 or 21 Feb. 1745]

My Dear Lord,

I forgott to mention one particular to you which is that the Mareschal[1] said that if the ill usage to him is continued wee must certanly expect a thorough retalliation whenever any officer of ours of any distinction should be taken, which must at last bring the warr to the cruel consequence of no quarter of either side. Indeed I must say to you (tho I did not say any such thing to him) that to refuse the Parolle of honor to such a man as him is I beleive an unheard of thing. his dignity really should be consider'd. a Mareschall Duke & Peer of France, Grandee of Spain, Prince of the Empire, Knight of the Holy Ghost, & Golden Fleece. how such a man's parolle can be refused I can not conceive & is it pollitick to Irritate a man <u>unjustly</u> that one time or other is very likely to be at the head of affairs at Versailles. This is my private opinion, only between you & I, & you will make what use of it you please, I wish you could go on Saturday, you own you are for treating him civilly, therefore the sooner you go the better, dont be angry with me, who am for ever, Your's

Richmond &c.

dont answer this for I am gon as Roper used to say, butt when you have seen the Mareschall I wish Mr. Stone would lett me know what is settled about him. & if you hear of any mischeif that was going forward at the Masquerade, I should be glad to know it.

245.   RICHMOND TO NEWCASTLE

Charlton
Sunday 3d March 1744/5

My Dear Lord,

I thanke your Grace for the letter Mr. Stone wrote to me by your order. I own I cant see why Mareschall Bellisle need be removed from Windsor, for as I suppose you mean he should allways have an officer of trust about him, & as he told me he expected I can not imagine he could do more mischeif at Windsor than at Nottingham, & as to his parolle of honor he told me he was ready to give it that he would not directly or indirectly correspond by letter or otherways with any body whatsoever without the knowledge of the government, so as he offer'd it I suppose you will insist on such a parolle. & after that if he should be detected, a Dungeon should & ought to be his fate; as I dare swear he would freely acknowledge himself. I am glad the Duke's affair is fix'd, is there any thoughts of the Kings going to Hannover or not? surely that would be a most wrong thing. If you, or Mr. Pelham, upon the toppick of Oeconnomy could ask him whether he does not thinke propper to send for his horses home from Antwerpe, I wish you would, for they'l eat there heads off there. you made Harcourt mighty happy with your kind letter; he, the Duke of St Albans, & Linky who plays at Whist from morning 'till night, are all your humble servants, wee have not been able to go out once in the last week, & the snow now is deeper than any I have ever seen in England since the year 1709 I thinke it was. Wee shall however weather it out this week, butt propose to be in town to dine with my Lord Lincoln at all events on Sunday next.

I am, My Dear Lord, for ever & most affectionately Your's

Richmond &c.

---

1.   Marshall Belle-Isle.

246. NEWCASTLE TO RICHMOND

Newcastle House
March 5, 1744/5

My Dear Lord,

I am infinitely obliged to you for your kind letter. I own, I am not so good a Correspondent, as I used to be, but I have nothing agreable to write upon, & seldom anything very new. The only thing that really gives me any satisfaction, is what relates to the Duke, which I am persuaded will more good to the King & His family, than anything that has been done for many years. His R.Hs will be appointed Captain General, & I have no apprehension of inaction in Flanders this Campaign. Lord Chesterfield succeeds beyond expectation in Holland, & says the Dutch are resolved that this shall be their last effort, but it shall be a strong one. Our Army upon the lower Rhine, has made Monsr Maillebois retire, & Prince William begins to think of returning to His old friends.[1] The Court of Vienna according to custom, expects every thing should be done for them, & will do nothing themselves for those whose assistance they want, & in their Desperation, they are wooing Saxony, & urging them into France, if the strong Representations, that will be made from hence & from Holland do not prevent it.

I may in great Confidence acquaint you, tho' I beg it may be ye greatest Secret, that the King of Prussia has sent a Courier here, to offer to make peace, & to separate in effect from France, & to give His Vote to the Duke of Lorraine to be Emperor, on the fair Renewal of the Treaty of Breslaw, & the Offer only to restore to ye Elector of Bavaria His Hereditary Countries, without any De dommagement of any kind. Since, if we could detach Him from France on such Conditions, we might then make a good end of the War. At present no Resolution is taken, but I think, it is too strong to be absolutely rejected. I am a great favourite wh your friend the Marshal Bellisle. I am in constant Correspondence with Him, sending Letters every Day to & from Him. He has given us a Memorial insisting on His being released by virtue of the Cartel, that Cartel certainly subsists, but I think he is not comprehended in it. However that point must be discussed & the Memorial answered. The King will not suffer Him to stay at Windsor, & I find most People think it is too near London, so that I consider Nottingham will be His Habitation.

Albemarle sets out for Holland on Fryday. Bury stays to go wth the Duke. Pray my Compliments to the Duke of St. Albans, Ld Harcourt, & all friends. Linky looks fatigued. I doubt my friend Sir J Miller is angry with me for not answering His Letter. I beg you would make my Excuses. It is impossible for me to obey His Commands. The Living is near 200 per ann., within three miles of Lewes, & I am engaged to pay only Parson Mr Hurdiss[2].

Ever yrs

Holles Newcastle

247. RICHMOND TO NEWCASTLE

Cranburn Lodge
18. May. 1745

My Dear Lord,

I have a thought come into my head, which would please me extreamly if your Grace & Mr. Pelham should approve of it. It is that my Lord Harrington should be desired to

---

1.   Prince William, the Administrator of Hesse Cassel for his brother, who was King of Sweden. Having quarreled with Carteret after the Hanau negotiations, he withdrew his troops from the English service and joined the League of Frankfort.
2.   Rev. Thomas Hurdis, chaplain to Newcastle and a Canon of Windsor, was Prebendary of Middleton in Chichester Cathedral and a Canon Residentiary, 1754–1784.

aply to the King for Huske to have Churchill's Dragoons; His Lordship (if you remember it) was desired some years ago to aske for that regiment for him which is now Duvours, & he was so adroit as to gett it for Duvour, at the time wee all thought he was aplying for Huske, which makes the claim upon him now so much the stronger. Mr. Pelham who is a sort of millitary man, must know that Huske's pretensions are good, for that there is hardly a Genll officer, at least very few, that are older than him, & good for anything, that are not allready on horseback, or equally provided for, whereas he has, besides his regiment of foot, nothing butt the Government of Hurst Castle, which is barely ten shillings a day. I shall see you on tuesday at the Regency, & then you will be so good as to tell me what you thinke of it. I am excessively obliged to you for the accounts you sent me down by the Messager. & am glad to find they turn out something better, or rather less bad than wee expected. I long to hear how our Master takes the misfortune.[1] The Duke of St Albans is much yours, butt nobody living more so, than, My Dear Lord, Your Graces's ever faithfull, & affectte humble servant,

Richmond &c.

248.   RICHMOND TO NEWCASTLE

Goodwood
Fryday. 7. June 1745

I thanke you my Dear Lord for your obliging message by Cheale, butt I cant possibly waite on you on Sunday, for I am engaged to dine that day at Cobham with your neighbour Hamilton.[2] I would lye at Claremount, butt that it would be extreamly inconvenient to me haveing business in town at eight o'clock on Munday morning, so I must lye in town on Sunday night; I am engaged to the Duke of Bedford all Munday, butt Tuesday or Wednesday I shall be at your commands.

I am My Dear Lord Your Grace's ever faithfull

Richmond &c.

Cheale goes up to town with me.

249.   STONE TO RICHMOND

Whitehall
June 8th 1745

My Lord,

A Messenger, last Night, from Hanover, and the Dutch Mail, which came in about the same time, brought a Confirmation of the melancholy news received on Tuesday last, of the Victory gain'd by the King of Prussia over the combined Army in Silesia.[3] The Duke of Weissenfeldt, & Prince Charles, tho' they knew they were near the Enemy, suffer'd themselves to be surprised, at two in the morning, by the Prussians, in such a Position, that they could only fight, Battalion by Battalion. The Loss of the Saxons amounts to 4,000 Men; and that of the Austrians is not less. Of the Saxon Generals, only the Duke of Weissenfeldt, the Chevr de Saxe, & two others, remain unwounded. Of the Austrians, seven General Officers are said to be kill'd. They retired to Reichenau, & afterwards to Landshut. Some Accounts say, they were not pursued by the Enemy; others say, that there has been a second Engagement, and a second Defeat of the Allies: But this is not beleived: But it is thought they are retired into

---

1. The Battle of Fontenoy fought on 10 May 1745.
2. Hon. Charles Hamilton, 1704–1786, of Painshill near Cobham, MP for Truro, 1741–1747, was Clerk of the household of the Prince of Wales, 1738–1747.
3. The Battle of Hohenfriedburg fought on 4 June 1745.

Bohemia. My Lord Harrington says that, the Court of Dresden keep up their Spirits, and talk of reinforcing their Army, & taking their Revenge: But it is to be fear'd, they want the Means. His Lordship has wrote to Sir Thos Robinson, to press the Court of Vienne to reinforce Prince Charles's Army without weakening those on the Rhine, & in Flanders: and, in His Office Letter to my Lord Duke of Newcastle, seems to hope, that this Misfortune may be repair'd. But I am directed by His Grace, in the utmost Confidence, to acquaint you, that my Lord Harrington, in a private Letter to Mr Pelham, expresses great Apprehensions even for the safety of the King's person, and suggests it as his Opinion, that it might be advisable for his Majesty's Servants here to advise Him to return to England. Ld Harrington says, His Majesty has thought of going to the Army on the Rhine: But a Difficulty arises there on account of the Great Duke's being with that Army. No Resolution is yet taken here; nor has this private Letter been as yet communicated to any one, (that I know of) but my Lord Duke. The first Thought that occurs on this Occasion, as your Grace will easily think, is to try the Accommodation with the King of Prussia, which two Months ago was offered by Him, but which will not now be so easy to be had.

Cr Traun, & Duke d'Aremberg, are supposed to be join'd.

We have nothing new from our Army in Flanders: The Citadel of Tourney still holds out. I am afraid (but this is of a most secret nature) Prince Waldeck's Roughness of Temper makes it impossible for that good Agreement to subsist amongst the Generals which is always so necessary; and especially in a time of Difficulty, like this.

I have the honour to be with the greatest Respect My Lord Your Grace's most obedient and most humble servant

Andrew Stone.

250. NEWCASTLE TO RICHMOND

Newcastle House
July 18th 1745

My Dear Lord,

My Lady Albemarle, who was so good as to pass three or four days with us at Claremont, will have acquainted your Grace, that you was to expect a Letter from yr faithful Correspondent. I wish I had any good news to send. Our Army, they say, is safely encamped between Brussels & Antwerp. The French, you know, are in possession of all Flanders, & the good Q. of Hungary's Governor Ct Kaunits[1] has ordered a Stop to be put to the Inundation at Ostend, Wch was actually begun, & the only thing to save the Place. I sent immediately a Courier to Brussels to complain, but to what purpose? The Genoese have declared against us, joined 10,000 Men to ye Spaniards, & have furnished them Artillery. Belislles is dispatched to the Fleet to put the Provisional Order in execution for acting hostilely against Genoa. Poor Rowley is on the Coast of Portugal, & I suppose will now be immediately recalled. Belisle will be relieved, & the Cartel reestablished, which Negotiation is carrying on at the Army. I am soon to have the Marshal at Claremont, & I shall expect you would do the same Honour, as you did the Duke of St Albans from Goodwood upon that Occasion. Our Provisions, & Ordnance, are gone to Ostend. I doubt whether our Troops will go, for I see no Sign of a Reinforcement from the Duke. You know Ingoldsby's[2] affair is over. He is declared to have not followed Orders, but as it was thro' failure of judgement & not want of

---

1. Wenzel Anton Count von Kaunitz, Austrian negotiator with Sandwich, and Governor to the Queen of Hungary.
2. Richard Ingoldsby, died 1759, was courtmartialled for failing to take a French redoubt at Fontenoy. For papers relating to the court martial see Goodwood Ms. 106 ff.453–455.

Courage, He is sentenced only to be suspended, during the Duke's Pleasure. As to our secret Correspondence with Ld Har:n, the Prussian Accommodation goes on very slowly, & is certainly so disliked, that tho' they will not directly oppose it, all possible Difficulties will be flung in our way. This is a terrible thing, when we are in such Circumstances as we are at present, and nothing but that can possibly help us. We write strongly & firmly, & shall declare plainly tomorrow that we do so, neither to reproach ourselves, nor be reproached by Others, for the Consequences. I have picked up all the News, publick & private that I could collect, & have I find forgot the only good Circumstance in our Favour, which is, that the Prince of Conti, has certainly passed the Rhine, with His whole Army, burnt His Bridges, which looks as if He was afraid of Monr de Traun. We shall soon see, what effect this will have, I should hope that, of bringing on the Election immediately. I beg my compliments to all the Ladies and all my good Sussex Friends.

I am my Dear Lord Ever most sincerely and unalterably yrs

Holles Newcastle

251.   RICHMOND TO NEWCASTLE

Goodwood
Tuesday. one o'clock 23 July 1745

My Dear Lord,

Your Grace knows that your commands to me must ever be cheerfully obey'd, & I shall certanly attend you at Claremount on Sunday by dinner, butt can not possibly be with you on Saturday night. butt as for your assizes I must beg to be excused, butt will certanly attend you at Bishopstone on Thursday the 15th. Sr John will attend you at either the assizes or Races, butt will not go to both. I know nothing of Cheale only that he is doing nothing in London. I thanke you for the news that you sent me & both your kind letters, I was just going to answer the first, as your Messager came. I have great hopes from the Rhine, butt not the glimmering of any from Flanders. Prussia is the great point & am glad to find you & our freinds so sett upon it; Il faut pas demandie. say to our Master do this or 'tis impossible to serve you. & if he does not do it make your words good & upon my soul I thinke if his servants dont insist upon it they will & ought to be impeach'd. I beg pardon for taking upon me to dictate, 'tho I beleive I only propose what you mean, butt whilst I am dictating why dont you write a threatening letter to Kaunitz? for it is plain either he or his mistress intend to betray us. I am not so mad as My Lord Stair butt (you'l say it's stupid in me) I can not conceive why the Duke should refuse the reinforcement, for as he has butt 34,000 men he can act butt upon the defensive; can the sparing of two battallions then so much weaken that defense? all this I own is of no use if Ostend is not to be attack'd, butt if it is I really thinke our two Battallions ought to go, & that then the Duke can not answer the not sending two more. & the great inundation ought to be insisted upon directly; & that very likely may prevent the seige, & then the sending of any troops would be unneccesary. The Duchess of Richmond, Lady Albemarle, & Emily, are much obliged to your Grace & the Duchess of Newcastle for your kind remembrance of them. My sister particularly desires me to say that she does not write to thanke you both for your goodness to her at Claremount, because a letter would be only troubling you, butt she desires me to return her most sincere thankes.

I am My Dear Lord, for ever & most affectionately Your's

Richmond &c.

The Duke of St Albans went away on Sunday last.

252.   RICHMOND TO NEWCASTLE

Goodwood
Wed. 31 July 1745

My Dear Lord,

I wish when you have half an hour to spare you would be so good as to look over the enclosed papers, & give me your opinion upon them. I own at first sight it looks to be as wild a project as the conquering of France can be, & upon the first reading I should have thrown it aside, butt when I see the names of Burrell, Bristow, Young, Hume, & Salvador, I own I thinke it may merit some attention; the thing in itself (if Practicable) to be sure would be a great advantage to the nation, in every respect butt one, & that I am allways against, which is that of dispeopling this country. as to the advantage to myself I thinke that very Chimericall, & if ever any, it might be some to March, which would be consideration enough for me, butt lett whatever happen, I shall certanly give into no scheme that will cost me a farthing. nor will I make the people any answer till I hear your opinion on it. & whether you thinke it will look like a job the thing in the world I detest the most. butt if the thing in it self is right, & that somebody of distinction must be at the head of it, & that it will cost no mony, & that some may be gott fairly, honestly, & quite openly, I dont see why I should not have it as soon as any other, butt still I cant help thinking that raising so many thousand familys is a wild scheme, & impossible, however if these people will venture their mony, I thinke it would be hard to refuse them the prayr of their petition. Pray lett me know what you hear of Le Prince Catholique de Galles.

Your's My Dear Lord for ever,

Richmond &c.

253.   NEWCASTLE TO RICHMOND

Claremont
Augt 3d, 1745

My Dear Lord,

I had the Honor of your Grace's Letter, with the enclosed Papers, & tho' I am a very bad judge of such sort of things, yet as you desire my Opinion, I have looked over the Project, & with the sincerity, I shall always use in any thing that concerns yourself, I must freely own, that I do not much approve these Proposals. They have always the air of a Job, which I know you detest of all things, & the desiring one of your Quality & Condition, to be at the Head of it, does not lessen the Appearance of a Job, which perhaps these Gentlemen thought, would go down much better, if they could have your Graces Countenance, who, all the World knows, would not give it them, if you had the least suspicion that it was a Job. I have that real Love & Friendship for your Grace, & know how much you detest those sort of things, if any way liable, to what I now mention, that I have no difficulty in speaking very freely my Opinion to you, & I am sure you will not take it amiss of me. As to this particular Project, I am really no judge of it. To be sure, if it could be done, it would be a good thing for the Publick, but I should much doubt the practicability of it. Burrel, Bristowe, & Hume, are very good Men, but as likely, especially the two last, to be engaged in a sensible Job, as any two Men in England, but this is only to yourself. If you will give me leave, & not otherwise, I will enquire into the Nature of this Project & let you know, what some understanding Men in West Indian Affairs think of it. As to publick News, I conclude you know Ostend has been besieged since last Saturday or Sunday. The fort of Plassendale surrender'd immediately, & yesterday the Lords of the Admiralty had a very bad

169

Account from Commodore Smith,[1] that the Garrison could not hold out long; that the Communication with the sea would be very soon cut off, & Com. Smith proposes the sinking Transports with Stones, in order to make the Harbour useless to the French. I had a Letter yesterday from Consul Hutton, but nothing from Chandos.[2] The Consul does not write so despondingly as the Commodore. Chandos has sent for Water & Vinegar, which is sent Him. As to the Young Pretender, he was, as they say, on board the Elizabeth which was attacked by the Lyon, but He was afterwards put on board the Fregate, which they suppose is gone to Scotland. The Elizabeth is returned to Brest. We have Accounts that there are seventeen large French ships in the Western Ports of France besides three of four Spanish Ships at St Ander, & Ferrol. The French Ships are supposed to be designed to convoy their Trade to America, but some imagine they are intended to support the Young Pretender, & that seems the more probable. At present I am afraid, we have very little to oppose them. However we have at last determined to send for Admiral Martin home, to collect all our Sea Force together, & for them to rendezvous at the Lizard, where Admiral Vernon is to have the Command of the whole. I am afraid the French, will be very soon Masters of Ostend. Where they will go next, God knows. I hope they will not come hither. We have orderd Transports to be taken up for 10,000 Men, & shall send them to Flushing in Zealand, to be ready to bring such a Number from our Flanders Army, & the Duke will have them in readiness. This is the only Scheme for any real Defence, in case we should be attacked, tho' I hope we shall not be obliged to put it in Execution. They talk much of a great Detachment going from the French Army in Flanders to the Rhine, but there is no certainty of it. The whole View of the Austrians is to get the Great Duke elected Emperor, & indeed that would be a great Point. I hope it will succeed, but there are other things also, which we must have a Regard to. There is nothing material from Hanover, since you was here. We have yet no Answer either from the King of Prussia, or the Court of Vienna, upon what I think, the most material Point of all, I mean the Accommodation with Prussia. We have repeated our earnest Advice to His Majesty to return immediately to His kingdoms, which it is generally thought He will do. In our present Circumstances it will be impossible for me to be at the Assizes, but I intend to meet your Grace at the Races at Lewes on Fryday Morning, the 16 inst. I beg you would tell Sr John Miller this, & that therefore I hope He will accompany you to Lewes. I wish you would bring as many of your neighbouring Gentlemen with you, as you can, for I think in these Times, the more of our Friends we see, the better. I propose to go to Bishopstone on Saturday night, where I hope I shall have your Company & Sr John's. I have troubled you with a very long Letter, but you know I always love, that you should know every thing, that I know and do. Marshal Belisle, will set out for France on Monday or Tuesday next. He has signed the Declaration, I prepared for Him. We have order'd a Proclamation offering 30,000 pounds for apprehending the Young Gentleman,[3] landing, or attempting to land. I beg my Compliments to the Ladies, & am my Dearest Lord Ever unalterably Yours

Holles Newcastle

I beg leave to add a line, with Compliments to the Ds of Richmond, and Lady Emily, and should be much oblig'd to yr Grace if you tell my Lady Albemarle that I return her ten thousand thanks, for six, of the prettyest fowles that ever was seen, which came to Claremont this day.

---

1.   Thomas Smith, died 1762, a Commodore in the navy, became Commander-in-Chief in the Downs, 1755, and Admiral of the Blue, 1757.
2.   Henry Brydges, 2nd Duke of Chandos, 1707–1771, MP for Hereford, 1727–1734, for Steyning, 1734–1741, and for Bishop's Castle, 1741–1744, was Groom of the Stole, 1742–1751.
3.   Charles Edward Stuart, 1720–1788, the Young Pretender, the eldest son of the titular James III.

254. RICHMOND TO NEWCASTLE

Goodwood
Wednesday 7 Aug, 1745

My Dear Lord,

I am so used to your goodness to me that I am no longer suprised at it. & I am glad as well as vain to find that you thinke just as I do upon this Nova. Scotia project, yett still I must own there is an appearance of fairness in it, since they propose doing the whole at their own risque & expence. as for the renewall of the Pattent, I suppose that may be refer'd, to the board of trade as to the merchantile part, & to the attorney & Sollicr Genll as to the Law part; if then it is approved by all these, & that they demand neither mony, nor assistance of the publick, I cant see how it can be a job, for by the word job, I understand aplying the Publick mony to private uses; which in my opinion is villany, & job is too soft a term for it. you are very good to say you will enquire into it, I should thinke Peter Burrell would be the propperest man you could talke to about it, & if you would lett one of the proprietors explain the affair to Mr. Stone, it might be of service. if you approve of this & will lett me know it I can desire them to attend; tho without your leave I shall not. butt I own I could wish you to be thoroughly inform'd of the affair before I see you at Lewes, where I shall certanly meet you at the ordnary on Fryday the 16th butt I beleive I must go to London on the 18th. I thanke you for all your news bad as it is, & I approve most excessively of the transports for 10,000 men, butt if it is neccesary to send for them (which I really beleive it will be) where are the remainder to be? I fear the whole of English is not above 16,000 men, so I should thinke transports might be prepared for them all. butt when will they go? & when will our fleet be ready? I declare I am uneasy 'till they are.

The Dss of Richmond, Lady Albemarle & Emily are extreamly obliged to the Duchess of Newcastle for her kind compliments to them, & beg theirs to your Grace & her Grace, to which I must also beg leave to add myne.

I am My Dear Lord, ever faithfully & most affectionately Your's
Richmond &c.

255. NEWCASTLE TO RICHMOND

Claremont
Aug 10th 1745

My Dear Lord,

I had yesterday three Messengers from Hanover, the first of which had been detained some days by contrary winds. He brought orders for the Yachts to go immediately to Helvoet Sluys, & directions for getting Kensington ready, for the King's Reception. I have hasten'd the yachts all I can, but notwithstanding I gave a private Hint some time ago, to the Duke of Bedford, I hear they will not be ready before Wensday next, & they are at a loss to get proper Convoy. We have also received the Answers from the Court of Vienna, & the King of Prussia. The first, is as bad as possible, & the last very good. Nothing but Resolution, and a sort of Compulsion, will do with her Hungarian Majesty, and that Compulsion must be used, & surely we have a right to use it, for it is very unreasonable that we should almost singly support by our Money, etc, the Queen of Hungary, & she employ it only to carry Her own views against the King of Prussia, & sacrifice every thing, that concerns us and her allies, as plainly appears by the Loss of Flanders, & the Danger that Italy is in, of being lost also. There is also another Proposal on foot, from the Court of Saxony, to make Peace with France, on condition that the Elector of Saxony, shall be Emperor, & Don Philip have an Establishment in Italy. All this is refer'd to us here, and I think, the King will at last do, what we advise, or rather, what we have advised these three months. We are very positive in our

Opinion, & shall remain so, so I hope we have a certain Prospect, of making up with Prussia, & then we may be in a Condition to make either a tolerable Peace or a tolerable War. Lord Harrington says, He has talked very seriously to the King, upon the necessity of giving His Ministers, His Confidence, & Authority. His Majesty heard Him with great Coolness & Temper, & said, that upon his Return to England, His Servants should have no reason to complain of Him, upon that Head. The last Letters from Chandos, were not very promising. He does us great justice, for the Assistance sent from hence, but I am afraid, all will not do. I think the Town will not hold out very long, tho' they were to make a Sallée, and had, as was said, by their fire, done much mischief to the Enemy. I have already informed myself about the Nova Scotia Affair, & will get more Intelligence, against I have the pleasure of meeting you at Lewes on Fryday next. I shall bring Linky & Keene with me. The King can't possibly be here in less than a fortnight. It will, and with reason, do Him a great deal of good in the Nation, coming at this time, and in this manner.

I am dear Lord Ever most affectly yrs

Holles Newcastle

The Ds of Nle and I join in Compliments to all the Ladies.

256. RICHMOND TO NEWCASTLE

Goodwood
11 Aug. 1745

My Dear Lord,
If any thing should hinder your journey to Lewes, pray lett me know it by tuesday's post else I shall certanly be there on Fryday, butt without you I should not chuse to go. I must be in town on Sunday next.

Your's my dear Lord, for ever & most affectionately

Richmond &c.

257. NEWCASTLE TO RICHMOND

Newcastle House
Augt 13, 1745

My Dear Lord,
I received this Morning an Express from the Duke of Argyle,[1] with an Account that he had Intelligence from his Steward, that a Vessel was landed in Arisaig, about thirty miles north & by west, from Fort William, with the Pretender's Son, about two or three hundred Men, & 2000 stand of Arms. The Account tallys so exactly, in every particular, with the Description of the Fregate, which had the Pretender's Son on board, that there is little doubt, that it is the same Vessel, & that he is landed somewhere upon that Coast.

Proper Directions are sent down to Scotland: Sr John Cope[2] will march immediately, with such force as He can get together, to the Place, where they shall have their Rendezvous. I shall send a Messenger, this Night, to Hanover, with this Account; which undoubtedly will hasten His Majesty's Departure. I shall also send Advice of it to the Duke of Cumberland, with a Recommendation, to insist more than ever upon defending Antwerp, in order to preserve a Communication with this Country.

---

1. Archibald Campbell, 3rd. Duke of Argyll, 1682–1761, was a Representitive Peer for Scotland, 1707–1713, and for 1715–1761, and was Keeper of the Great Seal of Scotland.
2. Sir John Cope, 1690–1716, MP for Queenborough, 1722–1727, for Liskeard, 1727–1734, and for Orford, 1738–1741. Created Lieutenant General, 1743, he was Commander-in-Chief in Scotland in 1745, and was defeated by the Jacobites at Prestonpans.

Whether, upon this Intelligence, & considering we expect a material Messenger from Hanover, upon the Prussian Affair, which must be answer'd, it will be possible for my Brother, & me to be at the Races, I cannot yet possibly say: But am, at present, rather inclined to hope, we may come to Lewes on Friday Morning: But however, in all events, as soon as anything is determined, your Grace shall know by a Messenger on purpose, time enough, I hope, to prevent your setting out from Goodwood. But, if you should be set out, (as I hope you will, if you do not hear further from me) the Messenger shall be sure to be at Cheal's, on Thursday Evening, (where I conclude you will lie that Night) with Directions to go on to Goodwood if he does not find you there. I expect my Lord Chancellor, & some other Lords here this Evening, in order to consider what may be proper to be done upon this Occasion.
and am My Dear Lord Yrs most affectly and unalterably

Holles Newcastle

P.S. I beg my Compliments to the Ladies.

258.   NEWCASTLE TO RICHMOND

Newcastle House
Aug 14th 1745

My Dear Lord,
Your Grace will probably have been prepared, by my Letter of last Night, for this Messenger, whom I now send to acquaint you, that it will be impossible for me to be at the Lewes Races. We had a Meeting, last Night, to consider, what was proper to be done upon the certain Account of the Pretender's Son's being landed in Scotland. We determined to make use of the most effectual methods for the speedy manning of the Fleet, and to get our Army in as good a Condition as possible. It was the unanimous Opinion, that in these Circumstances, it would have an odd Appearance, for my Brother, & me, to be at any Distance from London; and to be known to be so. Another Reason, that would make it extremely inconvenient for me to go, is, that we have not yet received the Messenger, we expected, from Hanover; which will probably be a very material one, as it will decide upon the great Affair of the Prussian Negotiation. I am very sorry, that it is impossible for me to have the Pleasure of meeting your Grace at Lewes; and more so, that it was not in my Power to send you earlier Notice of it. I hope however, this Messenger will be with you time enough to prevent your setting out from Goodwood. I flatter myself I shall soon have the Pleasure of seeing your Grace in Town; and, as I shall be at Claremont the latter end of the Week, I hope you will call there on your way to London.
I am my Dear Ld Ever most affectly yrs

Holles Newcastle

P.S. Marshal Wade is just gone out of this Room, who does not in the least doubt but as soon as Ostend is taken we shall have an embarcation for England.

259.   RICHMOND TO NEWCASTLE

Goodwood
Fryday 16 Aug. 1745

My Dear Lord,
I shall certanly dine with your Grace on Sunday next at Claremount, unless you countermand me by a Messager on the road. I propose being there at two, & have nobody with me butt Miller, who, I suppose I may bring. butt seriously, if my dining

with you on Sunday is the least troublesome, I beg you would lett me know it.
    Your's most truely

Richmond &c.

I shall enjoy no ease till troops are in England. I have not the least fear of the young Gentn in Scotland, 'tho to be sure his being there ought to be look'd to, butt my great apprehensions are from a french invasion which I look upon as certain, if not timely prevented.

260.   RICHMOND TO NEWCASTLE

Goodwood
Sunday 25 Aug. 1745

My Dear Lord,
    As I came here butt for three dayes indeed I had not time to call at Claremount, for I sett out from London only at half an hour after nine, & did not eate a morcell or drinke a drop 'till I came to Goodwood at near eight o'clock at night. If I hear nothing from you I shall be at the Stables at Hampton Court where I have a great deal of business, on Wednesday morning, shall dine perhaps with Jemmy Brudenell there, & come to town in the afternoon, tho upon recollection I beleive I shall be in town by three o'clock for dinner, butt if I hear of the King's journey being delay'd, I shall delay myne in proportion. I am mighty glad you have taken so much care to recommend the bringing of troops over here, indeed I most sincerely wish they were all here, for the French have enough to cutt them to peices there, & invade us at the same time here; all I wonder at, is that they have not done it already, & I dread the fatal day which I thinke is at hand.
    I am My Dear Lord, Your's most sincerely, & most affecty

Richmond &c.

All here desire their best services to your Grace, & the Dss of Newcastle. Enclosed is a memdm from Lady Albemarle.[1]

261.   STONE TO RICHMOND

Whitehall
Septr 5, 1745

My Lord,
    I conclude, your Grace will have heard that the Rebels had found means to pass by Sr John Cope, who was marching towards Inverness, that they had got, at least two days March of him, & were supposed to be going towards Perth, or Edenburgh. This News was received on Monday Evening, since which there have been no Letters from Scotland. A Messenger was dispatched last Night, with Orders for ten Regiments to be sent immediately to England from our Army in Flanders: Sir John Ligonier is to come to England with them. There are, at this time, Ships at Dunkirk, sufficient to bring over 7 or 8,000 Men. There are also four Men of War there. A. Vernon will remain in the Downs, & Vice.A. Martin is to cruise off the Lizard, with 14 or 15 Men of War.
    I am with great Respect My Lord Your Grace's most obedient and most humble servant

Andrew Stone

---

1.   Lady Albemarle's memorandum recommended Captain Segrave of General Ruth's Regiment, who knew the Pretender's son.

174

262. STONE TO RICHMOND

Whitehall
Sept 7, 1745

My Lord,

I received, this day, the honour of your Grace's Letter. The Pass, your Grace desired for Miss Gifferd, (if I do not mistake the Lady's name) was signed two or three days ago. I will be sure to remind my Lord Duke of the Appointment of the person your Grace is pleased to recommend, to be Consul at Buenos Ayres. It does not occur to me that there can be any Difficulty in it, (if His being a Foreigner none, in point of Law). There are, I am very certain, no Competitors.

My Lord Tweeddale received, this day, an Express from Scotland, with Letters from Sir John Cope, dated at Inverness the 29th past, in which He gives an Account of His Arrival there, with the Troops under his Command, not having been able to continue His March, as he intended, on account of the Rebels having possessed themselves of the strong Pass at Carrick Mount. He repeats his Complaints at not having been joined by any of the Friends of the Government: says, that the Rebels are greatly superior in number, but that he will at all Events attack them, as soon as he can come up with them. The Lord Advocate in a Letter dated from Edenburgh the 3rd inst acquaints Lord Tweeddale, that they suppose the Rebels to be still at Blair, (the Duke of Athol's Estate). He does not apprehend their numbers to be so great as has been represented to Sir John Cope; they can form no judgment, as to their further proceedings.

Major General Blakeney,[1] finding it unsafe to continue His journey to join Sir John Cope, turn'd off to Sterling where there is a Regiment of Dragoons.

The King has, this day, order'd Brigadr Foulks[2] to go down immediately to Scotland; there being, I presume, no Officer of that Rank, there, at present.

There is nothing new from abroad.

I am with the greatest Respect, My Lord Your Grace's most obedient and most humble servant

Andrew Stone

263. RICHMOND TO NEWCASTLE

Goodwood
8th Septr 1745

My Dear Lord,

I have wrote to My Lord Stair to desire him to recommend me to His Majesty to be upon the staff of Genll officers, in case any is appointed, as I am sure there ought to be. I only mention it to you as I never would take any step without communicating it to you, being with the utmost truth & sincerity, My Dear Lord Your Grace's ever faithfull & affectte humble servant

Richmond &c.

I find at last every body is for doing what I humbly advised a month ago.

---

1. William Blakeney, 1672–1761, had been Brigadier General in the expedition to Cartagena in 1741. He was made Major General and Governor of Stirling Castle in 1744.
2. Brigadier Thomas Fowke arrived in Edinburgh on 15 September to take command of two Regiments of Dragoons. He was later to be defeated serving under Sir John Cope at Prestonpans.

264. STONE TO RICHMOND

Whitehall
Sept 12, 1745

My Lord,

My Lord Duke of Newcastle intended to have wrote, Himself, to your Grace, this Evening; but having been prevented by Business, orders me to acquaint you, that by the last Accounts from Scotland, the Rebels were still at Perth; their Number was supposed to be about 4000 Men, tho' some will not allow it to be so large. Lord George Murray,[1] the Duke of Athol's Brother, (who was in the Rebellion of 1715, & pardon'd) has join'd them; and so has Mr Murray,[2] Brother & Heir to the Earl of Dunmore; and, I think, also a Gentleman who is call'd Lord Ogilvie.[3] Sir John Cope, with the King's Troops, was at Aberdeen. It was generally thought in Scotland, that the Rebels would march directly into England, without taking Edenburgh in their way; tho' the good people of that Town are not without Apprehensions of a Visit from them. The Wind having been now, sometime, fair, we conclude, we shall hear tomorrow of the Arrival of the Dutch Troops in the River. One Regiment we hope, is, by this time, at Leith. When the whole Corps is arrived, & our own ten Regiments from Flanders, (which we flatter ourselves will be soon) more Troops will be sent northwards.

It has been thought proper, upon this Occasion, to grant Powers to the Lords Lieutenants of several Counties in England, to form into Troops, or Companies, such persons as shall be willing to associate themselves for the Common Defence against the Rebels; and to appoint Officers to command them. This was done in the year, 1715; and has been now thought fit to be renew'd: and His Mty has accordingly signed Warrants granting such Powers to the Duke of Devonshire, the Earl of Malton,[4] Lord Herbert,[5] & Lord Irwin.[6] My Lord Duke orders me to suggest to your Grace, whether it may not be practicable, (as the Lord Lieutenant of the County of Sussex[7] cannot at present take an active part in raising militia, etc), to raise a Regiment in Sussex, as will probably be done in other Counties, in this time of Danger, and the rather, as it is one of those that lies most open to Invasion from France; and as it is generally supposed, that there is a considerable Number of disorderly people there, who, living in open Defiance of the Laws, may be too likely to countenance and assist such an attempt. My Lord Duke begs your Grace would consider this Point; and favour Him with your Thoughts upon it: and if your Grace should think it practicable & advisable to set it on foot, in what manner you think it should be done: and He leaves it to your Grace whether you would not give so much Countenance to it, (if thought proper to be undertaken) as to suffer the Regiment to be raised in your own name.

1. Lord George Murray, 1700–1760, son of the 1st. Duke of Atholl, having fought in the 1715 Rebellion, was made Lieutenant General by Prince Charles. He defeated Cope at Prestonpans, and successfully beseiged Carlisle; attacked Cumberland on the retreat from Derby; and lead the right wing at Falkirk and Culloden. He then retired to France.
2. John Murray of Broughton, 1718–1777, joined Prince Charles on his arrival in Scotland, and became his secretary.
3. David Lord Ogilvy and titular Earl of Airlie, 1725–1803, joined Prince Charles with 600 men in 1745. He commanded the cavalry during the retreat from Derby and fought at Falkirk and Culloden.
4. Thomas Watson-Wentworth, Earl of Malton, 1693–1750, MP for Malton, 1715–1727, and for Yorkshire, 1727–1728, was Lord Lieutenant of Yorkshire West Riding, 1733–1750. He was later 1st. Marquis of Rockingham.
5. Henry Herbert, Lord Herbert of Cherbury, 1703–1772, MP for Bletchingly, 1724–1727, and for Ludlow, 1727–1743, was Lord Lieutenant of Shropshire, 1734–1761.
6. Henry Ingram, 7th. Viscount Irwin, 1691–1761, MP for Horsham, 1721–1736, was Lord Lieutenant of Yorkshire East Riding, 1736–1761. He commanded a corps of volunteers in the East Riding against the Jacobites in 1745.
7. Charles Seymour, 6th. Duke of Somerset, 1662–1748, Lord Lieutenant of Sussex, was 83 at the time.

I am sorry to acquaint your Grace, (as I am ordered to do) that things at Kensington grow every day worse and that there appears, upon every Occasion the most disagreeable personal prejudices; and the most open & avow'd Predilection for Others. This gives a very unpleasant Prospect and it is impossible to say, what Effects it may produce. But the present distressed situation of publick Affairs must take place of all other Considerations

I am with the greatest Respect My Lord Your Grace's most obedient & most humble servant

Andrew Stone

265.   NEWCASTLE TO RICHMOND

Claremont
Sepr 14, 1745

My Dear Lord,

I desired Mr. Stone to give your Grace an Account of the Progress of the Rebels in Scotland. I had this morning from the Duke of Argyle pretty good news of them. They were still at Perth, had had some Desertion, their numbers were not said to be above 2000. Many of them, Bad men, & ill armed. They were also said to want Money, &c. Sr. J. Cope was at Aberdeen, last Monday night, & the Transports were to bring Him to Edinburgh, on Wensday or Thursday last, in which case, He would probably be before the Rebels, & I conclude one Dutch Regiment is by this time at Edinburgh, & I hope Ld Harrington has this day ordered the whole first Embarcation to Scotland, & indeed, it might not be amiss, if all the Dutch Troops were sent thither, for the Dutch have now declared in form in answer to la Bille, that their Troops are to act against the Rebels, & not against the French. I am afraid they will not be very expeditious in sending our ten Regiments from our Army. We have an Account that they are coming, but they don't seem in haste. I have desired this day, that an Express may be sent to hasten them. Our Fleet is certainly most luckily placed at present, & I think all Parts of the Channel are secured. Admiral Martin is cruizing off the Lizard, with twelve or 15 large Ships. Admiral Vernon, wh a large Squadron in the Downes, & A. Byng,[1] with 8 ships of Dunkirk and Ostend, so that we are really as secure as Ships can make us. But as for Troops we have yet very few. The <u>Closet</u> grows worse than ever. We are now come to bad Language, <u>Incapacity</u>, to my Brother, Spectator of other People's <u>Follies,</u> & <u>Measures</u>, & yesterday <u>Pitiful Fellows</u>. This can not be born, & what is even worse, He yesterday order'd His Name should be struck out of the Orders sent to Sr T. Robinson, upon the Prussian Affair, & said He would tell Wasner[2] that it was not His Measure, but that of the English Ministry. You may imagine, I was not wanting to make the proper Reply's. We have considered, what is to be done. Lord Chancr & I, are of opinion, it is impossible to continue under such Treatment, and such Management of His Business. My Brother is, I think, of that Opinion too. Ld Chancellor has desired, that I would get all our Friends to Town, & particularly that I would write to you. I am sure you will not refuse to come up, in this critical Conjuncture, & give your Opinion to those, who you know love you, & who, I am sure you think, do the best they can for their Country. Ld Chanr will not be in Town 'till next Tuesday night. There will be a Council on Wensday for the Parliament, so I think you

1. John Byng, 1704–1757, MP for Rochester, 1751–1757, was created Rear-Admiral in 1745. He was later court martialed and executed in Portsmouth Harbour after failing to prevent the French taking Minorca in 1756.
2. Ignaz von Wasner was the Austrian minister in London.

may be in Town on Wensday morning to attend the Council, & it need not be known, that you were sent for. My Compliments to all ye good Company at Goodwood.

I am my Dear Lord ever most affectly yrs

Holles Newcastle

266. RICHMOND TO NEWCASTLE

Goodwood
Sunday 15th Septr 1745

My Dear Lord,

I thanke you for the letters Mr. Stone has wrote to me by your orders, & am sorry to find things go so ill every where, as to the raising of a regiment of Volluntiers here, you know I mention'd it to you before I came out of town, & it is what I am sure I could easily do here, butt I beg to know the scheeme, & upon what footing the Duke of Devonshire, Lord Malton, & Lord Irwin undertake it, which I should desire to know as soon as possible, because I shall have a very propper occasion to mention it on Munday sennight when I shall have a great deal of company at the Council house,[1] upon my going out of my Mayoralty;[2] so the sooner I am prepared the better & till I know upon what footing other people undertake it, I can offer nor suggest no scheeme of my own, is it to be horse or foot, is it to have any pay incase 'tis employ'd? is it to be under the command of the Genll of the army to march any where? or only to stop & fight upon our own dunghills incase wee are attack'd here? when, where & how are they to be arm'd–? it is necessary to know all these things before it can be mention'd; I have hitherto hinted it to nobody butt Sr John Miller, who entirely approves of it, & I beleive he must be my Lt Coll.; if it is to be made up of Country Gentn & not real officers, 'tho I am sure some would be very necessary; & God knows where to find them. Sr John is mightily for getting a great many smuglers in, how far that would be propper I cant tell; I have been very busy last night in takeing of affidavits against a man for talking of Treason at a Publick house, & if it turns out strong against him as I beleive it will, upon his examination I shall send them up to your Grace, & shall keep him in prison 'till I hear what you would have done with it; & I hope he will be severely prosecuted, for this is not a time to shew any mercy. I am glad to see the proclamation out against the Papists, butt I have often told you My Dear Lord, & must again repeat it to you, that nothing can be done in this County without Deputy Lieutnts & indeed there ought to be two in each Rape, Sr John Miller & major Battine would be two excellent ones for this Rape of Chichester. pray thinke of this & soon; else I do assure you the Government can have no authority here. another thing I must remind you of, which is what Genll Folliot proposed which is that of makeing the seventys up hundreds in every company, by enlisting only for one year, which would augment your army 14 or 15,000 men with little expence, & great expedition. I have talk'd of it here & I find every body is opinion that now harvest is over, a prodigious number would enlist upon that condition. in short this is a time to sett all the wheels that can go to worke. for every honest man must own that our whole is at stake. My Lord Stair has not thought fitt to answer my letter in which I desired to be upon the staff, as Lt Genll incase any was appointed, as I am sure there ought to be. for I cant bear to sitt <u>avec les bras crossieux</u> at such a time.

Your's My Dearest Lord for ever

Richmond &c.

1. The red-brick Council House in North Street, Chichester, was built in 1731, at a cost of £1,189 to the design of Roger Morris.
2. Richmond had been elected Mayor of Chichester for the ensuing year, on 24 September 1744.

267. RICHMOND TO NEWCASTLE

Goodwood
Munday morning Septr: 16: 1745

My Dear Lord,

You will now be angry with me because, ('tho for the first time of my life) I refuse you to come to town, tho I do not absollutely refuse you, butt demurr. so if you insist upon it, you must send the bearer back to me to morrow tuesday morning, & I will be with you on wednesday evening; butt unless you absollutely insist upon it I beg to be excused, first because I am very sure it is unnecessary; for you all, butt yourself in Particular know my way of thinking, haveing perhaps too often troubled you with my thoughts of late, which I will once more trouble you with again. they are in the first place that <u>wee</u> I mean your self & all of us are bound in duty to our Country to bear with any thing, even with such foul Language that no one Gentleman could take from another, at this criticall time, rather than give up our employments, for this single reason because our Master is so blind to his own interest that he will putt his whole government into the hands of My Lord Granville & others, who I am persuaded will bring about imediate distruction to him & his government, perhaps by rashness of measures, perhaps by design for the pretender's interest, I therefore am of opinion that wee ought to serve the King, & to save him from Destruction whether he will nor no, that is if it is in our Power to do it. butt after I have said this, I here give it you under my hand that, if you, your brother, & My Lord Chancellor quit your employments, I will imediately resign myne, for hitherto I have pin'd my faith upon you three; what you will do after you have quitted I dont know, butt I am very confident you will do what is right, however as it will be a new sceene, I cant in honor tye myself up afterwards, tho I protest to you upon my soul word & honor, that I have no meaning butt to do what is right, & my first principle is & ever shall be, to keep the Hanover family upon the throne, as I am very sure that is all your meaning.

As to my thoughts upon getting what strength wee can at home, the whole world knows them, & I am sure the Dutch refusing to act against the French is the strongest proof of the strength of my argument. butt I must observe that this behaviour of the Dutch is the most treacherous & astonishing thing that ever I heard of, & as it was My Lord Harrington's measure, I thinke he will be torn to peices in Parliament for it, & I am sure you will see the whole nation in a flame about it; & indeed there is no retreiving it, nor any safety to ourselves, without the Duke & our whole army's being sent for home imediately, to defend us against the French, & to send all the Dutch against the Rebells. this has been & still is my advice, butt I am so tired of advising of late, & see so plainly that it has never been listened to, & I beleive laugh'd at, that I do not care to trouble them or myself any more, 'tho in this point I am as positive as a mule, & can never depart from my opinion. & now I am upon this subject I cant help makeing one observation, which is that every one of you singly have always seem'd to be of my opinion, yett when you are all together the advising the King to send for the whole army home, has never been thought expedient. I own it has given me the greatest uneasiness, for I do thinke distruction is at our door. I have troubled you with perhaps a vast deal of nonsense, that is my words may be nonsensical, & I know I express myself very ill, butt I am sure my meaning is right; my all which is not inconsiderable is at stake. you'l say why then dont you come to town? I answer because I know by experience that I can do no good. I therefore beg again to be excused. I have also a good deal of business here, this week. butt I shall certanly be in town the latter end of next. If you dont send my servant back to fetch me up in a hurry, which I hope will not be the case, I should be glad of a line by this nights post from you, & you know any time before twelve o'clock to night will be time enough if you send your letter to the Genll Post office. Pray dont take any thing ill I have said, if you do, it will be

179

unjust, for I never entertained a wrong thought of you, Mr. Pelham, or the Chancellor & you know I hope my particular attachment to you & your brother, which never will fail as long as their is life in your faithfull humble servant

Richmond &c.

I will send you all the affidavits about the treason that has been talk'd in Chichester by to morrow's post. I have committed one man to Jail, & a soldier whose name is Mackintosh is now in irons in the gard room. I assure you wee are very watchfull here, & am very sorry to say I beleive it is very necessary.

I hope by to morrow nights post to have my querys answer'd, & a full account of the scheme for raising a regiment here.

If you have a mind to keep my servant in town a day or two, in order to send me any further commands of yours, he has orders to attend you.

Since I have wrote the above, the enclosed Coppy of the examinations has been brought to me,[1] & I send them to your Grace, to desire to know in what manner it is propper to proceed, for I am sure you will be of opinion that some notice should be taken of such treasonable words, espetially at this time.

What the soldier has said will amount to little or nothing, butt I will send you a Coppy of that examination to morrow.

268. NEWCASTLE TO RICHMOND

Newcastle House
Septr 17, 1745

My Dear Lord,

I received last Night, by your Servant, your very kind Letter: and tho' I am far from being angry with you for not coming to Town, yet I own, in our present Circumstances, I think, we want the Presence, Assistance, & Advice of all our Friends. As to the Hints, you give, of your's not having been follow'd, and that you know by Experience of what little use you are here; I cannot think it meant to me, because I am sure, I don't deserve it. I was always of Opinion that a good Number of Troops should be sent for from Flanders: But I never thought, the whole Army should come, unless it were necessary for the Defence of this Country; which, when the ten Regiments are arrived, I hope, it will not be; especially, as there are not yet any Attempts made from abroad. But, whatever may be my Opinion, & that of my Friends, we are not in a Situation to get any thing done, that is right; and yet must answer for every thing, that is wrong. Things grow, every day, worse; and the means of supporting the Government are taken away from us, whilst our Friends think it necessary, for that very Reason, that we should bear every thing, & continue in our Employments. My Lord Chancellor, my Brother & I, are under greater Difficulties than ever; and we shall continue to be so, if, (as it may easily happen) the thing is not decided for us, whether we will, or no; For we have great Reason to believe, that the Resolution has been taken, to remove my Brother & me, in hopes the rest will stay; But this must be the greatest Secret. When our Friends press us, on account of the Circumstances, to remain in, they do not consider, that the Parliament must open in a very short Time; that the Speech must contain the Scheme of the Session; that the king will probably not let our Scheme be follow'd; and if He should, will certainly not allow us to take those Measures, which alone can

---

1. The examination of Matthew Caffyn of Chichester, cordwainer, Thomas Sanders of Chichester, carpenter and John Ride of Westhampnett, carpenter, in which they stated that in the Eight Bells in Chichester, John Mackentosh, a corporal in Colonel Lowther's Regiment of Marines, quartered in the city, and a Scot, said that the Scotch were ill used and that there ought to be a King in Scotland once every three years according to the Act of Union.

make that Scheme succeed; and yet we must stay in. I am sure I would do nothing, in, or out, that could do any real Hurt to the King or his Family, in this Country. Our all depends upon keeping them here; and keep them here we will, if we can: I had almost said, in spite of themselves. My Lord Chancellor my Brother, & I, are extremely obliged to you for your kind Dependance upon us; we will never deceive you; and, as when in, I flatter myself, I have done very few things, you have disapproved; and none, but what you thought, were well meant; I hope, you will not imagine, that, when I am out, I shall do any thing to forfeit the good Opinion of my old Friends, and especially yours. After what I have said, you may be sure, we shall be glad to see you in Town, as soon as you can conveniently, which I hope will be some time next week, at farthest. I will send the Affidavit you transmitted to me, to the Attorny General; and you shall have His Opinion, what is further to be done upon it; you have done very rightly, in committing the Man. As to the raising the Regiment, I really don't know what Steps will be proper to be taken upon it. As soon as I know what the Duke of Devonshire, Lord Malton, & Lord Irwin have done, I will let you know it. But to be sure, next week, when you come to Town will be time enough. We have a Project on foot about the Smuglers, which, I should think, may take place. However, I shall know more of it against you come to Town. I beg my Compliments to the Duchess of Richmond, Lady Albermarle and all the good Company at Goodwood and am My Dear Lord Ever most affectly yrs

Holles Newcastle

269.   RICHMOND TO NEWCASTLE

Goodwood
17 Septr 1745

My Dear Lord,

I should not trouble you with the enclosed if I had not told you in my last that I should certanly do it, butt there is nothing in it that can be taken hold on; however you may see from his discourse his way of thinking which would be of mighty little consequence, if it was not the same with 99 out of a hundred of his country men.

I am My Dear Lord for ever & unalterably Your's

Richmond &c.

270.   RICHMOND TO NEWCASTLE

Goodwood
Septr 18th 1745

My Dear Lord,

You will dred to see my hand, as I have troubled you so often of late, butt I am pollitick mad at present & cant help troubleing you with another affair quite foreign from any thing I have said to you yett. It is to tell you what Mr. Huske of Boston, brother to the Generall has told me, which is that he is just now arrived from New England, with a great fleet of merchant ships, & he (who lives at Boston & is concern'd in this affair of Cap Breton) & every man that knows those Countrys & seas, say that our transports that are now bound for Louisbourg with the Regiments from Gibralter, can not gett there in this season, nor even to New England butt will in all probability be obliged to go to the West Indias, 'till the frosts are over at Cap Breton, which in all likelyhood will kill 9 out of 10, of our troops. whereas the right time of going from hence is in January or February, & those that go from hence in that season, will certainly gett there sooner than those that sett out now, for they will as surely be obliged to go to the West Indias. Mr. Huske is now with me, & does not know I write to you about this, butt he will be in London in about four or five dayes. I know this whole expedition was Totty's[1] scheeme & directly contrary to the opinion of the whole Regency, however so great a man must be submitted to, butt I should be sorry to loose two good Battallions by his positiveness.

Your's My Dear Lord most sincerely

Richmond &c.

This Huske is Post Master at Boston in New England, & as I have told you one brother to our freind the generall.

271. NEWCASTLE TO RICHMOND

Claremont
Sept 21st 1745

My Dear Lord,

I was in hopes of a Letter from your Grace this day, and am a little afraid you was not pleased with my last. Indeed, our Situation grows every day so much worse, that nothing but a Rebellion, & that a very serious one, could make us stay one Hour.

The Pretender has now got possession of Scotland. The Rebels took possession of Edinburgh on Tuesday last, proclaimed the Pretender, by the King's Heralds, & seized 14 or 1500 Arms in the Town. Sir J. Cope with the Army landed the same day at Dunbar 20 miles of this side of Edinburgh, & was joined by the two Regiments of Dragoons, that were at Edinburgh, but did not think proper to face the Rebels. Sr J. Cope sends word, He would make what Haste He could to Edinburgh. The Rebels were said to be 4000, & were expecting then Reinforcements from the Highlands. All the Dutch Troops are now come. Three Swiss Batallions with ye D. of Montagu's Regt of Horse, St George's Dragoons, & five Companies of Blakeney's march on Monday, under the Command of General Wentworth towards Lancashire, & two Dutch Batallions go by sea, under the Command of our friend Huske to Newcastle, for the security of that Place, & the adjacent Parts. The ten English Regiments were to embark at Williamstadt last Thursday, & as the Wind is so fair, we may expect to hear of them very soon. Ld H. told me he had sent orders to the Duke, to keep some more Regiments in readiness to come over, if necessary. I am very apprehensive, that the Pretender's being in possession of Scotland, may encourage France to try to put him in Possession of England also. The proper Orders & Powers are sent to the several Lord Lieutenants in the north, and the D. of Bedford, D. of Montagu, Ld Gower, Ld Malton, Ld Irwin, Ld Londsdale,[2] &c., have all powers to raise Troops. In short, every thing is done, that can be done, by an Administration, that has no Power, and to whom the King their Master, will hardly vouchsafe to say one Word, about his own Business. The greater the Danger is, the more angry he grows, with those, who alone can help Him out of it, & if He goes on, He may run the risk of loosing another kingdom by the Rashness & Flattery of some, as He has already done one by the Folly & Obstinacy of others. But, however, in or out, we will do our utmost for the Support of the King, & His Family. I wish all our Friends were in Town, to be witnesses of our Treatment, & also of our Constant Endeavours to do the King, & our Country, the best Service we can. I hope we shall have your Company soon in London. My best Compliments to

1. John Russell, 4th. Duke of Bedford.
2. Henry Lowther, 3rd. Viscount Lonsdale, 1694–1751, was Lord Lieutenant of Cumberland and Westmoreland, 1738–1751. He is said to have raised 10,000 men against the Jacobites in 1715. Lowther Hall, his seat, was plundered by some of the Jacobites in 1746.

Dutchess of Richmond, & Lady Albemarle; the Ds of Newcastle desires this also.
I am with the greatest truth My Dear Lord Your most affect and humble servant
Holles Newcastle

272. STONE TO RICHMOND

Whitehall
Sept 21 – 1745

My Lord,
I have the Order to send your Grace inclosed a Letter, that came under my Lord Duke's Cover this day from the Army in Flanders.

Your Grace will have had an Account of the Rebels being in possession of Edenburgh, where the Pretender has been proclaim'd. We are in the utmost Impatience for the next Letters from that part of the world: Sr J. Cope was moving towards Edenburgh on the 18th. The second Embarcation of the Dutch Troops arrived yesterday at Gravesend. Two of those four Regiments are order'd to proceed by sea to Newcastle, under the Command of M. Genl Huske. Orders were sent to His Royal Highness, last night to have some more Regiments in readiness to be transported to England upon the first Notice.

Maj. Genl Wentworth will begin His March from hence, on Monday next, north-ward, with 2 Dutch Regiments, five Companies of Blakeny's Regiment; the Duke of Montagu's Regt of Horse, & one Regt St George's Dragoons
I am with great Respect Your Grace's most obedient, humble servt
Andrew Stone

273. STONE TO RICHMOND

Whitehall
Tuesday night
Sept 24. 1745

My Lord,
I am order'd by my Lord Duke of Newcastle to dispatch this Messenger to your Grace with the melancholy news which we received this morning, of the Rebels having attack'd the King's Troops, under Sir J. Cope, on Saturday morning, last, at break of day, at Preston, between Dunbar & Edenburgh, & having entirely defeated them.[1] The Horse, & Foot, behaved equally ill: the whole Corps was siezed with a Panick, and after the first Fire, fled. We know but few particulars: Sir J. Cope got to Berwick, with 450 Dragoons: the Foot were all either dispersed, or taken. We know nothing of the Motions of the Rebels since this unfortunate Event. 'Tis composed they returned to Edenburgh, where they will, 'tis feard, soon be able to reduce the Castle;[2] and con-sequently be Masters of all the Arms and all the Wealth of that Country.

In this unhappy state of affairs my Lord Duke imagines, your Grace will think it proper to come soon to Town, where He will be extremely glad to see you. It is a happy & providential thing that our Troops are arrived from Flanders. Orders are sent for more to be ready.
I am with great Respect My Lord, your Grace's most Obd and humble sert
Andrew Stone

1. On September 20 at the Battle of Prestonpans, Prince Charles and Murray decisively defeated a British army of about 3,000 men under General Sir John Cope.
2. Prince Charles had occupied the City of Edinburgh, and Holyrood Palace on 17 September, but the English garrison, under General Joshua Guest held Edinburgh Castle.

274. RICHMOND TO NEWCASTLE

Goodwood
Wednesday 25th Septr 1745

My Dear Lord,

I did not answer you letter of the 14th because as I had troubled you with so many I was willing to give you some rest, butt so farr from disapproving of what you say both in that & the other of the 21st which I have received since that I entirely agree with you that your scituation is most cruel & disagreeable. it is also so difficult that it is above me to give advise in it, 'tho your own expression in your last is the very thing I have before said to you. <u>That nothing butt a Rebellion should make you stay one hour</u>. I am glad to find our ten Battallions are arrived safe, & I thinke the disposition that has been made of the troops a very good one; & I am glad that my property at Newcastle is to be garded by Huske, 'tho I could wish he commanded in Scotland, butt I should thinke that there are almost troops enough now for Marshall Wade to go himself. I own my mynd is vastly more easy since the arrival of the ten Battallions, butt I still wish they were all here. I shall be in town on Saturday which I hope will be time enough for any commands you may have for me. I can't help sending you the two enclosed I have had from my old freind Rowley, they are cheifly in regard to yourself so I hope you will read them; & then tell me what I shall say to him.

Your's My Dear Lord for ever,

Richmond &c.

I hope nobody of a superior ranke to Huske may be sent to command him at Newcastle, butt if that should be judged necessary, I should be very glad to be sent & then you may easily imagine Huske would still command in effect.

Pray thinke of this seriously for my heart is sett upon being employ'd on this occasion.

275. RICHMOND TO STONE

Goodwood
25 Septr 1745

Dear Sir,

The enclosed letter which I cant call anonimous, as it is signed <u>Briton</u> came to my hand the last post, it did not come from London, for there was no post marke upon it, butt upon enquiry I found it was left by an unknown person at the post house at Chichester: it is very plainly from a good freind to the government, & I really thinke it a sensible well drawn thing, & as it is undoubtedly well meant, I thinke it would be right to putt it in some of the papers as he desires. however I would not have it done without the Duke of Newcastle's advice & opinion upon it, if he has time to give either. I shall be in town on Saturday so I desire no answer to this 'till I see you. I beg the enclosed may go in the first Packett to His R.H. the Duke.

I am, Dear Sir, most sincerely your's

Richmond &c.

I wish wee could have his Grace's directions what to do with Wm Faith[1] that I have committed to Jayl for treasonable words.

---

1. At the Assizes held at East Grinstead on 24 March 1746, William Faith was charged on the oaths of Thomas Tilley and James Chatfeild, that on the 11th. and 12th. March 1745 "he did at the public house of John Philbrow at the Star Inn, Chichester, wish he had twenty thousand or thirty thousand men to fight for King James III; that George II had no right to the crown, and that James III was the rightful King of England". He was fined 6s. 8d., ordered to remain in gaol for one year without bail or mainprice, and until he found security in himself for £40 and two sureties of £20 each for his good behaviour.

276. RICHMOND TO NEWCASTLE

Whitehall
Munday [21 October 1745]

My Dear Lord,

I don't know whether Sr Hector Macklean[1] is your Grace's Prisoner or My Lord Tweedale's, butt the Messager in whose hands he is, is very negligent, for a servant of myne is ready to make oath that last Saturday night at eleven o'clock he saw a letter or peice of paper lett down by a Pack thred from the garret window of the house where Sr Hector is kept; into the street, & there taken by three men, that had been walking up & down the street the whole day.

I am My Dear Lord most sincerely Your's
Richmond &c.

Would it not be best to seem to know nothing of this butt have a trusty person to watch, & to take up these men if they return. This servant of myne is Mirand the Confectr who lives over against the Messager, & sayes he is ready to take his oath of this.

277. RICHMOND TO NEWCASTLE

Coventry[2]
Thursday morning eleven o'clock
21 Novr 1745

My Dear Lord,

Enclosed is a letter from My Lord Lonsdale to the Duke of Devonshire, which was sent by My Lord Hartington cross the country to me. The conclusion I make from it is, that the Rebells intend to gett as fast as they can to North Wales, or at least that Mareschall Wade will drive them this way, if they dont thinke fitt to stand him, butt at all events they can & certanly will gett to the mercy before us, if they come this way. I therefore (with the advice of Major Genll Bland) have order'd Howard's Regiment that was to have halted here to day, & Semples & Sowles that are now at Litchfield, to march on as far as Stone & the other quarters between that & Litchfeild & the old Battallions that are now in our rear to march up without any halt to Litchfeild, & the neighbouring quarters, & the Cavalry have the same orders, so that wee propose to cantoon our whole army in & about Litchfeild, by which time Sr John Ligonier will I hope be with us; butt I thought on such authentick intelligence, I could do no less than gather the troops together as fast & as forward as possible, still keeping them together. as for the new raised foot they have already orders to move on as fast as they can, & as soon as they have gott their camp equipages, butt indeed wee must not lett them interfere with the marches of our old corps. I am sorry to tell you there is a good deal of sickness among our men, butt great chearfulness among those that are well, & the people of the country hitherto have done all they could to assist them. I go to Litchfeild to morrow, & Majr Genll Bland with me, Majr Genll Skelton[3] is there, & wee propose

1. Sir Hector MacLean, chief of the clan MacLean, had arrived in Edinburgh with a message from Prince Charles to John Murray of Broughton, but he was arrested and imprisoned in Edinburgh Castle.
2. Richmond had joined the troops opposing Prince Charles's march into England, had been entrusted with the command of the cavalry, and on 8 November was promoted to the rank of full general.
3. Major General Skelton was one of the Generals of foot who had fought with the Duke of Cumberland at Fontenoy.

staying there till Sr John Ligonier comes up to us. butt I have order'd Brigdr Lord Semple[1] on to Stone which is the head of our Cantoonment.

I am with the gretest truth & affection, My Dear Lord, Your Grace's ever faithfull humble servant

Richmond &c.

278.   NEWCASTLE TO RICHMOND

Whitehall
Nov. 22nd 1745

My Lord,

I received, this day the honor of your Grace's Letter of yesterday's Date by Express; and immediately laid it before the King; and I have the Pleasure to assure your Grace that His Majty entirely approved the Disposition, you had made, & the care, you had taken, to get the Troops forward, & kept together. As it is yet uncertain which way the Rebels may take, His Majesty thinks, it would be right for the Troops not to advance farther than Stone, except the Cavalry; 'till we hear further, or Sr John Ligonier arrives; who, I am informed, sets out, tomorrow morning.

I have just now recieved Letters from Ml Wade dated from Hexham, the 19th: that upon the news of the Surrender of the Town, & Castle, of Carlisle,[2] and an Account they had received, that the Rebels had sent to provide Quarters for their army at Penrith, on tuesday last; Marshal Wade had, by the advice of a Council of War, determined to return with his Army to Newcastle, in order to be the better able to follow them, whichever way they should take.

There are various Conjectures about the Designs of the Rebels. Some Gentlemen in Yorkshire apprehend, that, knowing the Troops under Sr John Ligonier were going to Lancashire, the Rebels may come across from Penrith, over Stainmoor into Yorkshire.

His Royal Higness, the Duke, sets out, on tuesday next; and as I am inform'd My Lord Albemarle with Him.

I am &c.

Holles Newcastle

279.   RICHMOND TO NEWCASTLE

Litchfeild
Saturday noon 23d Novr 1745

My Dear Lord,

I received your Grace's of the 21st by express, as also one from Sr John Ligonier of the same date containing several orders from His Royall Highness the Duke. my answer to all which your Grace will see in the enclosed coppys of my letter to Sr Everard Fawkener,[3] & the result of the consultation I had with the two Magor Genlls here. I have had no less than three expresses from the north & one from Yorkshire since last night, all which I take for granted you are aprised of, so I do not send them to you not haveing time to take copys of them, butt the principall part of them is that the Rebells are certanly marching forwards, & towards us, that the greatest part of them

---

1.   Hew Semple, 12th. Lord Sempill, 1688–1746, had a long army career. He was Colonel of the 43rd. Highlanders, 1741–1745, of the 25th. Foot from April 1745, fought at Fontenoy on 11 May 1745, and was created Brigadier General in June 1745. He commanded the left wing at Culloden.
2.   Carlisle surrendered to Prince Charles's army on 14 November.
3.   Sir Everard Fawkener, 1684–1758, was a cloth merchant. He was Ambassador in Turkey, 1735–1746, though he returned to England in 1742. He was Secretary to the Duke of Cumberland, and was Postmaster General, 1745–1758.

are at Kendall & are expected at Lancaster as to night. this proves that they avoid fighting Marschall Wade, & intend to take Chester, & gett into North Wales, or to attack us before wee are formed into one corps, which can not be even here before the 29th or 30th instant altho I have done all I can to press forwards the Divisions in our rear butt what gives me great concern is that by our computation the Rebells if they do not amuse themselves in Lancashire may be at Chester by the 27th take that & slip into Wales before wee can possibly come up to them, butt if they thinke fitt to come here wee shall certanly be prepared for them. & if they should move towards Yorkshire wee hope also wee may cut a cross to them. butt you see plainly that the reason why wee can not thinke of advancing towards them is because our artillery, all our cavalry, & severall Battallions are not yett come up. butt when they are you may depend upon it wee shall do our duty. as I want to dispatch this express to you, I will answer the other parts of your most obliging letter by this nights post, & am with the greatest truth My Dear Lord, most faithfully & sincerely Your's

Richmond &c.

280.   RICHMOND TO NEWCASTLE

Litchfeild
Saturday night Novr 23d 1745

My Dear Lord,

I have just received your Grace's of the 22d. by express, & am mighty happy to find that His Majesty approves of what I have done. I own that the quick advance of the Rebells, & our not being strong enough to opose them had wee advanced, gave me great perplexity, butt since the resollution (of which I have this morning sent you a coppy) was taken, to advance our head no farther than Stone, 'till our rear comes up, I am very easy, because I am sure now they can not come upon us 'till wee are thoroughly perpared not only to receive butt meet them, & as Marshall Wade is retired to Newcastle, I hope & beleive wee shall have the honor of defeating, & also destroy-ing these villains; which I really look upon to be certain if wee can butt meet them in a fair field, & that wee keep a good look out for fear of a surprise. not butt that I wish wee had more force with us, for in such a cause I must always wish to be more that morally sure of success & as for the two Battallions of Gardes I fear they cant be up before wee have a brush with the Rebells, that is if they advance. butt now Wade is retired suppose they should, after raising great contributions at Lancaster, Leverpool & other places, retire again to Carlisle; then Ml Wade is quite out of their way, & wee shall be march'd to death, for follow them I take for granted wee must, & in my poor opinion, ought to do it.

Now as to your first kind letter relating to the advice you gave to My Dear Taw, I am vastly obliged to you for it, & am entirely of your opinion that she would have done much better to have stay'd in town, & I have sent a servant a cross the Country to meet her at Grantham, or Stilton, to desire her either to return, or if she does go on to stay butt three or four dayes at Worksopp for that really I should be in very great pain about her if the Rebells should gett into Yorkshire, which by the by, if they make forced marches, I dont see how wee can hinder it, then wee must follow, & Wade meet them; butt if they should march that way as I have said, it would be a most shaking circumstance to me, so as she has all her life taken my advice, I hope she will do so now. nothing now is come in since I wrote this morning to you, 'tho I have had one from the Duke of Devonshire, & one from the Post Master of Yorke, butt they contain nothing butt what wee had accounts of before.

I am, My Dear Lord, most sincerely & affectionately, Your's

Richmond &c.

281. RICHMOND TO NEWCASTLE

[Litchfeild]
[24 November 1745]

To yourself <u>Secret</u>

For Gods sake dont thinke of sending Hawley from us. indeed he is equal to any body, & will speake his mind. Leg is a good man butt in my poor opinion too complaisant, besides that, on of his legs was numb'd the other day, & I dont thinke his life to be depended on. this is only between you & I, butt pray make good use of my hint. I am sorry to say wee are in a strange irregular way, & if the Rebells had attack'd us at Stone on Munday night, as wee thought they would, wee had been undone, & Ligonier said so himself. & it must be so, if they ever attack us in the night, if wee are not encamp'd; & at Stone it was impossible for want of straw.

It is neccessary to hurry on our troops else they'l be in London before us, & yett these dreadfull fattiging marches, will make them incapable of fighting. wee none of us know what rest is. I wish wee could have speedy help from London. if not wee must & will do our best without it. the Duke is not here, so nobody knows of my writing this. pray shew it to nobody butt the Chancellor & Mr. Pelham; & I desire you would shew it to them.

282. NEWCASTLE TO RICHMOND

Whitehall
Nov. 24th 1745

My Dear Lord,

I received this morning, by Express, the Honor of your Grace's Letter of yesterday's Date, with the enclosed Paper; and have laid Them before the King and the Duke, who extremely approve what you have done. His Majesty has this Day encreased your Army by the addition of a Third Battalion of Guards, & Cobham's Dragoons, which will set out to join you as soon as possible. We have nothing new relating to the Motions of the Rebels, or of Marshl Wade; the former seems to be coming into Lancashire; and M Wade will probably follow them by Boroughbridge, Leeds and Manchester.

I am &c.

Holles Newcastle

This Messenger proceeds to Chester to bring up some Prisoners.

283. RICHMOND TO NEWCASTLE

Litchfeild
Monday morning nine o'clock
25th Novr 1745

My Dear Lord,

As I am going to view a place this morning about twelve miles off, near Stafford incase his Royall Higness thinks propper to encamp the troops; I shall not have time to write two letters, so I must beg of your Grace to communicate the contents of this to His Majesty, & also to His R: Hss the Duke, & I hope you will make my excuses for not sending it directly to him. I must begin with greivances, which are so frequent in armys that I fear they are the less regarded, butt I will venture to say that the success of this little handfull of men is of so great importance that if wee are not help'd & attended to, this kingdome may be undone in a fortnight. I could therefore wish that the two Battallions of Gardes might be push'd on with all expedition, & horses press'd

188

for them as they were for Blighs,[1] for I thinke by all appearances the rebells mean to attack us, & I am sure as yett wee have not a sufficient number to defend this Country, & I allways thought so, for I allways recon'd that if wee fight 500 men a Battallion it is all that can be done. I therefore send your Grace the returns of the four only regiments that are yett come up with us, & you will see that those four Battallions make butt 2325 men rank & file fitt for service; & I beleive they are as compleat as any wee shall have, & I question if the Scotch Fusileers & Handasides[2] will both together make more than one battallion, & that not a strong one. I must now inform your Grace that wee have neither paymaster nor hospitall here, wee cant move without the first, & shall be in a most miserable way without the latter. I know the answer to the first will be they are pay'd till Christmass which is true, butt as it has been mostly sent in bank bills, & that there is not specie to be gott in the country, wee dont know who to apply to, for the subsistance of the troops. I know the agents are greatly to blame for not sending the cash down in specie, therefore I could wish there might be some directions given to them about it. I may write very ignorantly as to these mony matters, butt that you know is a detail I never understood in my life, butt the fact is that they are in great distress here for want of specie. now as to an hospitall wee have not seen the face of a Phisician, Surgeon or Apothecary, nor is there an ounce of druggs, or a surgeon's needle, butt what belongs to the regiments, which I do say is a most shamefull thing. I do not know nor do I care who is to blame, butt it is a most cruel thing to thinke that every poor soldier that is sick must be left at best in a barn without help, & our wounded men if wee have action upon the feild. I have sent to look upon a house here for that purpose & every thing that is in my power shall be prepared. I must now lett your Grace know that wee have made a new disposition of a Cantonement, of which enclosed I send you a coppy & you will see that wee have now advanced our Cavalry as farr as Newcastle under Lyne & I have sent major Genll Bland thither to take the command upon him, & Brigdr Lord Sempell will be there with him, & I have order'd Brigdr Bligh to Stafford so you can see our head will be at Newcastle, & our rear here at Litchfeild, & the place I am going to see for a Camp, is by all accounts a very strong one, & in the very center of the Cantonement, it is within a mile of Stafford, & between the two rivers of the Penk, & the Sow, & they say a fine dry peice of ground, & extreamly well garded by these two rivers, that are deep & now overflow'd, & I am not at all asham'd to say that 'till all our troops are assembled, I should be glad of a secure Camp, then when wee are once gott together, I shall be as desirous as any one to march up to the Rebells. I send your Grace coppys of letters I have had from lords Derby[3] & Chomley, & am glad to find they have broke down the bridge at Warrington, & hope they will do the same at Stockport. enclosed is also an extract of all the material intelligence wee have had since my last to your Grace.

I am with the greatest truth & affection, My Dear Lord Your ever faithfull humble servant,

Richmond &c.

Wee all here hope Marschall Wade will have detach'd his Cavalry & a good body of Grenadiers across the country to joyn us, for he must conclude that the scene of action will be here, & if he comes up it must soon be decided.

---

1. General Thomas Bligh, 1685–1775, was Colonel of the 20th. Foot from 1740, and a Brigadier General from 1745.
2. Lieutanant General Roger Handasyde arrived in Edinburgh on 14 November to replace Sir John Cope in the command in Scotland.
3. Edward Stanley, 11th. Earl of Derby, 1689–1776, was MP for Lancashire, 1727–1736. He took little part in national politics, but was Lord Lieutenant for Lancashire, 1742–1757, and again, 1771–1776.

Cantoonment for the Cavalry as order'd the 24 Novembr. 1745

Regiment	Cantoonment	Days of arrival
King's Dragoons	Newcastle	29 & 30 Novembr
Lord Mark Kerrs	Trentham, Stoke & Darliston	26 & 27 ''
Ligonier's	Stone	28 ''
Kingston's	Uttoxeter	24 ''
Montagu's	Burton Upon Trent	When ready to march

Foot

Bligh's	Chester	
Sempills	Newcastle	25 Novembr
Sowle's	Stafford	21 ''
Douglas	Eccleshall	26
Johnson's	Stafford	26 or 27 ''
Howard's	Rugely	27 ''
Skelton's 5 Compy	Litchfeild	24 ''
Fuzileers	Litchfeild	27 ''
Handasydes on their march at Dunstable		24 ''
The Train will be at Litchfeild		27 ''

NB The last Division of Skelton's consisting of 5 Compy is 5 days march behind the first division of that Regiment. It is proposed to move the North British Fuzileers from Litchfeild to Penkridge, & adjacent Places, as soon as the last Division of Skelton's come up.

284. RICHMOND TO NEWCASTLE

Litchfeild
28 Novr 1745

My Dear Lord,
As the Duke dispatches an express to night, it would be ridiculous in me to pretend to give you any account of his disposition so I shall only take this oportunity of assuring you how truely I am, Your ever faithfull
Richmond &c.

285. RICHMOND TO NEWCASTLE

Litchfeild
Fryday night. 29 Novr 1745

My Dear Lord,
I know you would be angry with me if I did not write to you, butt you must consider that the case is now different from what it was in Germany when you had nobody butt your brother Cartaret to write to you. & that he thought it beneath him to correspond with an English Secretary of State, that had nothing butt the good of England of heart. The case thanke God is now different, wee have a brave Generall & a dutifull son to command us, who will certanly be extreamly exact in sending accounts of every step that is taken, to His Majesty, so your Grace of course will be acquainted with it. & all I could say would be butt repetition. I own I have hitherto been a cautious adviser, or

rather an adviser of caution; meerly because the stake is so great, if it was not for that upon my honor I thinke it would be a shame if six old battallions & two Regiments of Dragoons did not drive these rascalls to Hell, which is little worse, butt a more propper place for them than their own Country they came from. however I own that the stake was so great that I was uneasy 'till our whole force came up, & by Sunday I thinke they will pretty near be all here, & then I shall be as desirous as His Royall Higness' young blood can be to march on & attack them wheresoever they are. & if wee do butt meet them wee must & will destroy them. You know I have not generally much bile or choler about me, butt upon this occasion my gall overflows, & I long to be revenged upon these Scotch Rascalls, that dare disturb such a nation as this, & I shall be excessively happy to have an oportunity of doing it, & you may be assured I will make good use of it. I would not say so much of myself to anybody butt you. butt as I know you love me I am sure you will excuse it. The Duke of Devonshire was here to day, as also the Duke of Kingston, who is going to Congleton the advanced post of our army, & by the spirit I see in him, I am sure he & his corps will do well, butt as wee are now so strong, that is as wee shall be so to morrow & next day, I really beleive they will not dare to attack us, I wish to God they may, & then wee certanly shall destroy them, & eate a Turkey & Chine with you at Christmass. I fancy the Duke will send you some food for Tyburn soon, the particulars you will hear from him. I hear My Lady Lincoln is brought to bed of a boy, if true I wish you & Dear Mr. Pelham most sincerely joy of it, if I was sure of it, I would congratulate Linky upon the evident marks of his vigour. Poor dear Taw I find is miserable, I have told her that the Rebells would never face us, which will give her some ease, & I really beleive its true, & am sans aucune gasconade very sorry for it. butt if Wade had been now at Manchester the affair had been over, & if we had march'd sooner the affair would also have been over, butt our eternall misfortunes proceed from our tardy resollutions. this army should have been order'd a fortnight sooner, & the whole Flanders army should have been sent for when I & your Grace first desired it, pardon me for putting myself before you, butt when I first proposed it even you did not quite come in to it, 'tho you did soon after, butt give me leave to be proud of being the first that was for that step, which now (tho late) the whole nation thinks neccessary. I again beg pardon for troubling you so much of myself, butt I must add another thing I am proud of, which is that of being for ever, Dear Duke Your faithfull & affectionate humble servant,

Richmond &c.

286. NEWCASTLE TO RICHMOND

Newcastle House
Nov 30th 1745

My Dear Lord,

I am very much obliged for your kind Letters, & particularly, your note which I had last night. I am so hurried, with Business, & Writing, that you must excuse me, if I don't answer your kind Letters so regularly, as I ought. That, & nothing but that, has prevented my waiting upon the Dutchess of Richmd, which I will often do, if she is in Town, tho' I have heard this afternoon, yt she is not, but I believe my Information was not a good one. I am very happy, you forgave the liberty I took in my visit. It proceeded, from what will ever remain with me, my sincere Love & Affection for you & yours. I should be glad to know, whether the Duke shows you the Letters, for then I would not repeat the Contents of them, which otherwise I would do. Hawley came here last night, & sets out for Litchfield tomorrow morning. I shall send a very voluminous Letter by Him to the Duke. We extreamly approve his R. Highness' Disposition. I send the Advices we have recd, of nine Sail of Transports said to be arrived in Scotland wth

Ld J. Drummond's[1] Regt on board. The Highlanders are getting together again, & are already got to the number of 3,000 to join ye Rebels. This makes it necessary as soon as possible to send a strong Force thither, wch the Duke & M. Wade will be order'd to do as soon as they can be spared from both Armies, under the Command of Wade. But this is not to be done, 'till you are in a Condition, by the junction or approach of the two Armies, to do it. Wade marched from Newcastle last Tuesday, & you must now soon hear of Him. By a Route that has been taken from one of the French Ships, it seems to have been the Design of the Rebels, to come directly from Carlisle to London. There is the greatest reason to think that the second son of the Pretender, is taken in the Soleil & passes for your Cousin Ratcliff's son.[2] We have sent a strong Guard to bring them up to London. Wade is to have what Officers He likes with Him. I wish He would choose Hawley & Huske, for the Duke can do without them. I write four or five lines to Sr Everard, by the Express, to prepare the Duke for Hawley, & my long Dispatches; I must insist with you, that you don't show this Letter to any Body, for it would be indecent in me to write to any Body about H.R.H's Orders before He receives them Himself, but my Letter has not yet been wth the King, so I cannot send it away tonight. I pray God grant you good success, & be assured that I am ever (as I ought to be) Most affectly & unalterably Yrs

Holles Newcastle

P.S. My Compliments to Albemarle & Bury.

287. RICHMOND TO NEWCASTLE

Litchfeild
Saturday night 30th Novr 1745

My Dear Lord,

I never thought I should have had reason of complaining of your unkindness to me, which is in the little notice you have taken of my Poor dear Taw, who has been a most miserable creature ever since I left town., where she hates to stay butt does it merely in obedience to my positive directions, & strong assurances I have ventured to give her that you will as often as you can let her know our scituation, 'tho that I have constantly done myself, butt she was in hopes to have seen you sometimes, & that you would at least have given her notice when you send a Messager or express this way. She sayes she has never seen you once, nor has had any message from you, except a How do you since Thursday last was sennight, nor any news, nor notice of any messager or express either going out or comeing in, & that the only letter she has sent me by express, was by her porter's finding out at your office that one was just then going out, 'tho she had just before sent to newcastle house, & the answer was they knew of none that was to go that day. I acknowledge women are often figgitingly troublesome, butt in this very particular case, I thinke you might excuse the person in the whole world you know I love the best. I beg pardon for saying so much on the subject, I am sorry to do it, because I know it will vex you, butt I could not help telling it you, & you know I have often promis'd you that if ever I am dissatisfy'd with you, I would lett you know my reasons for it.

Now as to our scituation here at present between you & I, I dont much like it, nor shant be quite easy 'till Monday is over, for the whole Rebell army is by our intell-

---

1. Lord John Drummond, died 1747, brother of the Duke of Perth, had arrived from France with 800 men of his own regiment of Royal Scots. He contributed greatly to the Jacobite victory at Falkirk, 1746, and fought at Culloden. He died at Bergen-op-Zoom.
2. James Radcliffe, 4th. Earl of Newburgh, 1725–1786. He and his father, Charles Radcliffe, Earl of Derwentwater, 1693–1746, were captured at Deal in 1746. Derwentwater was beheaded in 1746 under his indictment after the 1715 Rebellion.

igence now at Manchester,[1] & wee are not all yett so cleverly together as I could wish, 'tho much stronger by the first Battallion of gardes comeing in to day, & to morrow the two others & Handasides will be up. butt then there is a great distance between this & our avant parte which is now at Congleton, above forty miles off. however, I hope the disposition now form'd by the Duke will be such as that wee may be all together if they advance towards us, & indeed in my opinion I thinke they will not dare to do it, unless they can attack us en detuil, which must be entirely garded against else wee might be in a bad way. They have their choice of five things to do, one is to attack us, & if wee are together I wish they would, for then I am sure wee may do what wee please with them, an other is to march to Derbyshire, that would be the next thing I could wish, for the Duke of Devonshire has tore up all the roads in the Peake for them, & wee by marching the good road to Derby & Nottingham, may & certanly should gett them between Wade & us. The third they have to do is to March to Chester & beseige it, if so wee can certanly march up & have a brush with them; which would also be to be wish'd, the fourth would be to push for North Wales without attacking Chester at all, & that would be bad indeed, for I am confident wee can not gett up time enough to stop them. then the fifth & last thing which would be the worst of all, would be their going quite back again to the Highlands, which they may do in spight of our teeths, if they take their resollution before Wade getts to Manchester or behind them which he cant do, before the middle of next week. these are my thoughts upon their scituation & ours, so I will trouble you no farther at present than to assure you that I am my Dear Lord, Your Grace's ever faithfull & most affectionate humble servant,

Richmond &c.

The Duke of Bedford's Regiment march'd out here to day & wee are not at all pleas'd with it, the men are pretty good; & mighty well cloth'd, the grenadier compy indeed a very fine one. butt they dont yett know a ranke from a file; & if wee have action, I should be sorry to have them with us, 'tho they may very likely stand their ground, butt if they are ever broke, I am very sure they can never form again, & how should they with not above four or five officers that know any thing at the head of them.

288.   NEWCASTLE TO RICHMOND

Newcastle House
Decr 1st, 1745

My Dear Lord,

Tho' I am in such a Hurry that I have scarce time to dine, I cannot avoid returning you my best thanks for your most kind Letter, where all the Proofs of Zeal for the Government, Detestation for the Rebels, & good judgements in not slighting them too much; & also of Friendship & Affection for me, that words can express, & for which I never can be sufficiently grateful. My Dear Duke, be assured, I most sincerely love you, & esteem those rare Qualities, I know in you. God send you good success, & safe back to us. The Rebels certainly intend to give you the slip, but I hope you will not let them. I have wrote strongly on that head to the Duke. We shall assemble soon our Army about London, in expectation of them. A million of thanks for your goodness to Linky, 'Tis the prettiest little boy I ever saw.[2] I call Him Pigg, for he is just like one. I will tell my Brother how good you are to us.

My Dear Duke, I can never forget it, or cease to be unalterably Yrs

Holles Newcastle

1.   The Jacobite army entered Manchester on 29 November.
2.   George Clinton, styled Lord Clinton, 1745–1752, first son of the Earl of Lincoln, was born, 26 November, and baptised 23 December 1745. He died, 19 August 1752.

P.S. Love to Albemarle & Bury. I don't think Hawley will be with you before Tuesday night, or Wensday morning.

289. NEWCASTLE TO RICHMOND

Newcastle House
Decr 3d, 1745

My Dear Lord,

Your Grace judges very rightly, that your last most kind letter gave me as much Concern, as is possible. Can you my Dear Duke, suggest that any thing but unavoidable Business can prevent my waiting upon ye Ds of Richmond, when I know you desire it. As to the Messenger's going, it is entirely the fault of the people of the Office, who deny it, but that often happens. We must take care, that ye same thing shall not happen again. I have just sent a little note, of the news I have received this day from Ld. Lonsdale, of the March of the Rebels towards Wales. For my part, I can hardly believe it, & for that reason have been very sorry to find your Army was dispersed, by your Horse &c. being advanced too far towards Chester. I still think their Design is to push for London; all the Accounts say so & of Desperate things, that seems the most reasonable. We have an Account, of their getting all sorts of small Craft together at Dunkirk, to throw over a great number of Men, into Kent & Sussex, or Norfolk or Suffolk, & this may encourage the Rebels to come inward. For Godsake don't think it impossible or improbable. Ld Derby says they may very easily give you the slip.

Ever & unalterably Yrs

Holles Newcastle

290. RICHMOND TO NEWCASTLE

Litchfeild
4th Decr 1745

My Dear Lord,

Upon the rebells march to Derbyshire[1] I am order'd here upon the <u>avant garde</u> with the King's & Mark Kerr's[2] dragoons, to morrow to Coventry, & fryday to Northampton. I hope I shall be strengthen'd, as I am sure it is of the utmost consequence, however, I promise you I will fight the Rebells with these two Regiments, if I have not orders to the contrary, & i dont see why they should not be at Northampton as soon as us, as they are certanly at Derby to night. I thought this of consequence enough to acquaint you with it by express, butt as there are no horse here to be gott for an express I shall send it by a servant of myne to Coventry & dispatch it from thence. I have just received your graces of yesterday the 3d & am extreamly obliged to you for it, & have also received two others from you by Messagers. I am very glad Hawley has join'd the Duke at Stafford. H.R. Highss will march his army in here to morrow.

Your's most sincerely

Richmond &c.

Litchfeild
Decr ye 4th [1745]

The avant guard, the King's and Markear's Dragoons, to-morrow at Coventry o' fryday at Northampton. I dont see why they should not be at Northampton as soon as us. His Royal Highness will march his Army in here to-morrow.

1. Prince Charles entered Derby with the Jacobite army on the evening of 4 December.
2. Lord Mark Kerr, died 1752, son of Robert Kerr, 1st. Marquis of Lothian, had been Governor of Guernsey, 1740, and a General since 1743.

291. RICHMOND TO NEWCASTLE

Litchfeild
Thursday morning, nine o'clock
5 Decr 1745

My Dear Lord,

Enclosed are coppys of intelligence I have received from Dr. Taylor, & of my letter to Sr Everard Fawkener upon it both which I thinke right to send to your Grace, as I am a days march nearer to you, than H.R. Higness. I am indeed apprehensive they may gett to London before us. As a Generall I dont presume to advise, butt as one of His Majesty's council, I do advise a Camp to be formed imediately upon Barnet or Finchley Common or some where thereabouts, & imediately else you will be too late, if the rebbells thinke propper to advance, for I know by this short experience that cantoonments, will not do, for you are liable to be destroyed every night, for there is no forming from a cantonement, whereas 'tis done instantly from a Camp.

I am, My Lord, Your Grace's ever faithfull humble servant

Richmond &c.

292. NEWCASTLE TO RICHMOND

Whitehall
Decr 6th 1745

My Lord,

I have received the Honor of your Grace's Letters by two Expresses; and have laid them before the King; who extremly approves your Conduct, in the Execution of the Orders, you had received from His Royal Higness the Duke; and the Zeal, and Concern, your Grace shews for His Majesty's Service.

The King is in great Hopes, that His Royal Highness, by the Expedition He is making, will be able to get between the Rebels, and London. The King has not thought proper to give His Royal Highness any Directions; not doubting, but He will make the greatest Expedition possible.

There is one Letter receiv'd this Afternoon, from the Post Master of Uppingham, that the Rebels were in Possession of Nottingham. If so, it is very possible, the Rebels will take the Stamford, & Huntingdon Road; and never come to Northampton. The King has ordered Col Kingsley, of the Third Regiment of Guards, and Captain Parslow, of the First, the Former to go to Northampton; and the Latter to Huntingdon, and Bugden, in order to procure the most exact Intelligence of the Motions of the Rebels; and to transmit immediately what Accounts, they shall get, to His Royal Highness, and to me.

I am &c,

Holles Newcastle

Ps: By a Letter, which I have just now receiv'd from Marshall Wade, it appears, that his Army will be at Doncaster to morrow. And the Messenger, that comes from him, says, that Ml. Wade Himself will be there this Night. I do not find, that the Report of the Rebels being at Nottingham is confirmed.

293. RICHMOND TO NEWCASTLE

Coventry
Fryday afternoon 7 Decr 1745

My Dear Lord,

I do not know what intelligence the Duke may have sent you, for as he is butt four miles from us, he has it all if there is any, & wee have hardly any here. butt by all I can find you may be easy in London as to any aproach of the Rebells, that way, for as they halted at Derby wee had gott the lead of them here; butt as they are continually altering their motions, wee are obliged to do the same, for this which was the advanced post yesterday, is this morning become the <u>arriere garde</u>. & Bland is gon with the avant garde of the Kings & Kerr's dragoons, & one squadron of the Duke of Montagu's carabinieres to Litchfeild, & I am order'd there to morrow with the remainder of the Cavalry viz, Cobhams Dragoons, Ligoniers, & Kingston's horse. The Duke is at Packington Lord Guernseys,[1] & the foot encamp'd just by it upon Meridan heath. & the artillery is here with Sowl's & Handisides foot, the latter is not half a battallion; & the carryages of the artillery are so disabled in these cursed roads that I am very much afray'd wee shall have butt little or rather no help at all from it. What in the name of wonder is become of Marschall Wade? some say he is now at Newarke, if so I hope he will advance by Derby, & then the rebells retreat that way is stop'd, all I fear is they may still slip back to their own damn'd country by Manchester, & Lancashire, & I dont see how wee can prevent it. butt I really thinke wee can cutt them off from Wales. I dare swear thousands in London now sett upon their arses & say why does not the Duke march up to them. & if it was all hounslow heath between us, it would be a shame if he did not, butt it not to be conceived what a cursed country this is for marching, & wee can move butt so slowly, that I fear they will allways have time to escape. I have just received the Duke's orders, a detail of which I have not time to send you, butt I conceive by them that wee shall make a bold push at them to morrow, & if wee can butt come up with them there can be no doubt of success, this will be only a detachment for it is impossible our whole army can gett on, butt I am sure this detachment can do the business effectually, butt as I am to be upon it, pray say nothing of it to my poor Taw; butt I am persuaded in three or four dayes she will be out of all her fears, for I thinke the business must be done by that time, or not at all. I dont mean that there is any possibility of our haveing any cheque, for I am sure that is absollutely impossible, butt I still apprehend they may escape us; & by all accounts they are most damnably afrai'd of us, & I dont wonder at them. I never pretended, you know, to be a judge of this or any thing else, butt in my opinion wee are now going on quite in a right way, & I am vastly glad Hawley is come up with us. adieu my dearest Lord, Your's most sincerely & for ever,

Richmond &c.

Pray dont mistake me, & thinke what I say of Hawley means in the least to reflect upon Ligonier; for I have the highest opinion of him, butt his health is excessively bad still; & at all times you know two heads is better than one.
Since I wrote the above I have receiv'd your two letters of the 6th yesterday by Jack Parker & am extreamly pleas'd to find that what I have done has been approved of by his Majesty, Jack Parker is gon on to the Head Quarters four computed six measured miles from this place, & at his return, will take this letter. I thanke your Grace for your kind expressions in that which you wrote to me. & as for my discretion you may in generall depend upon it, butt cases may arise where it must be lay'd aside. 1000 voluntaries out of the foot are going upon this command, & they are all mad to go upon it. & I am sure with them & the horse wee shall drive them to the devill.

The Rebells will certanly be two dayes march a head of us,[2] they will be at Manchester when even our advanced party is only at Stafford, so I conclude them gon, & I fear they will secure themselves in Carlisle which wee cant take without Battering peices, 'tho

---

1. Heneage Finch, Lord Guernsey, 1715–1777, eldest son of the 2nd. Earl of Aylesford, was MP for Leicestershire, 1739–1741, and for Maidstone, 1741–1747, and again, 1754–1757, when he succeeded his father.
2. The Jacobite army started the retreat from Derby on the morning of 6 December.

our people surrender'd it so shamefully to them. I make no doubt butt this embarcation will go on at Dunkirke. are ye all mad? that you dont send for ten thousand more foot, by they Hessians, Hanoverians, or Devills, if they will but fight for us. I'l send you a proxy next post which I desire may be given for any motion to bring over more troops of any kind. indeed the whole kindgome is still asleep. our cavalry cant be here before Febry & the Pretender may be crown'd at Westr by that time. dont be angry with me, butt our all is at stake

294. RICHMOND TO NEWCASTLE

Newcastle under Line
Wednesday morning 11th Decr 1745

My Dear Lord,
   Enclosed is a coppy of intelligence from the post mistress at Warrington;[1] I sent the originall away directly to the Duke. His Royall Higness has fairly joky'd me, for he gott last night to Maklesfeild, & I only here by his order, whereas I thought to have been upon the advanced post, butt I fear our pursuite will be vain, for you see they are two dayes march a head of the Duke, for he can only be at Manchester to night, & the rebells will certanly be at Lancaster to night. I thanke you extreamly for your goodness to the Dss of Richmond. I have sent her a coppy of the enclosed, so you need not give yourself that trouble, & am My Dear Lord Your most faithfull humble servant,
   Richmond &c.

This goes by a servant of the Dss of Richmonds which she sent to me taking for granted there would have been an action.

295. NEWCASTLE TO RICHMOND

Whitehall
Decr 12th, 1745

My Dear Lord,
   We are under the greatest Alarms of an immediate Invasion from France.[2] It was even reported, that they were actually landed yesterday in Pevensey Bay. Adl. Vernon expects them every Hour. For Godsake hasten to us, for if they should come before Legonier with His Foot, we shall not have 6,000 men to oppose them. I wanted you extreamly, this day in Council, when I was forced to differ even with my good & valuable friends the Chancellor & Ld Harrington. But the King decided for me, & it is now all agreed. The Question was whether Legonier, or rather the Duke's whole Army should come hither immediately or only six Batallions, or that six old Batallions should be detached to Wade. I was for all coming. London is the great Object, & must be prefer'd to all other Considerations. At last we agreed to let you detach Jack Cambels, & Semples. The six thousand Hessians are ordered over immediately into Scotland. The Dutchess of Richmond will be very happy. I will now go & congratulate Her. I doubt I am ill wth the Duke but I can't help it. I must, if I can, keep out the Pretender.
   Ever Yrs
   Holles Newcastle

1. Sarah Blackburne, the Post Mistress of Warrington wrote announcing that the Jacobite Army would be in Manchester on the night of 10 December.
2. Prince Charles's brother, Henry, was completing preparations to embark French troops at Dunkirk, but the plan was abandoned on the news of the retreat.

296. RICHMOND TO NEWCASTLE

Preston
Sunday 15 Decr 1745

My Dear Lord,

Never was an army so disapointed as this by so positive an order to retire, had the Duke had butt a discretionall pour, he had destroy'd these rebells to morrow, & even this part of the army would have been within three dayes as soon as it now can be in London. I own it makes me mad to thinke of the number of oportunitys this country has lost of destroying its enemys; Ligonier you will have as soon as possible, butt if the invasion really takes place our Cavalry even now will be too late to help you. I am order'd by the Duke to march the second division of Cavalry, & enclosed is our routes that you may know exactly where to direct to me.

I am most truely & sincerely Your's

Richmond &c.

Forgive my enclosing these two letters to you.

First Division	Second Division
King's Dragoons	Ligonier's
Mark Kerr's Dragoons	D. Montagu's Cavalry
	D. Kingston's
Lieut. Genl. Hawley	Lieut. Genl. Duke of Richmond

Decr	From Preston	Miles	Decr	From Preston	Miles
Monday 16	To Wigan	16	Tuesday 17	To Wigan	16
Tuesday 17	Manchester		Wednesd 18	Manchester	
Wednesd 18	Macclesfield	14	Thursday 19	Halt	
Thursday 19	Halt		Fryday 20	Macclesfield	14
Fryday 20	Leake		Saturday 21	Leake	
Saturday 21	Uttoxeter		Sunday 22	Uttoxeter	
Sunday 22	Derby		Monday 23	Halt	
Monday 23	Halt		Tuesday 24	Derby	
Tuesday 24	Loughborough	15	Wednesd 25	Loughborough	15
Wednesd 25	Leicester	8½	Thursday 26	Leicester	8½
Thursday 26	Harberough	14	Fryday 27	Halt	
Fryday 27	Halt		Saturday 28	Harborough	14
Saturday 28	Northampton	17	Sunday 29	Northampton	17

297. RICHMOND TO NEWCASTLE

Penrith
19. Decr. 1745

My Dear Lord,

You will have a full account of the action from the Duke, so I shall trouble you with none, only beg you would send the enclosed packett to the Duchess of Richmond. If you care to see what I have wrote to her, you may if she will give you leave.

I am My Dear Lord, for ever Your's

Richmond &c.

298. RICHMOND TO NEWCASTLE

From my quarters at Uprightby
Tuesday 24th Decr 1745

My Dear Lord,

I am sorry you are so angry with us, butt ('tho I dont nor never did say it was your fault) it so hapned that if the order had not come, wee should certanly have been up with their whole corps. however tis too late to thinke of it now, the Duke has done all that could be done, & at least he has cleared this part of the kingdome of the vermin, 'tho it would have been much better to have destroy'd them. no mortal shall ever see your letter to me; & in answer to it I must say there was one days halt at Macklesfeild, that I never could account for, which I also desire you would never mention, for the very same reasons you desired secrecy of me. our scituation here is a very disagreeable one. for the Duke certanly cant treate with these rebellious wretches,[1] & yett I dont see how he can reduce them by force without looseing more men than the object is worth. there are miners indeed that are to blow up even the Castle, & they are to do it if they can, butt I can give no credit to that, & as for battering them <u>en breche</u>, it will be a long peice of worke, & our amunition is scanty, & I dont beleive one real gunner amongst us. Storming & scaling the walls indeed might & I really beleive would do, butt it would cost us at least 200 of our best grenadiers, & I am very sure that would not be worth while, for 300 such lowly scoundrells. starving them may also be a long & difficult taske, & opening trenches impossible as they would fill with water. so you see what reall difficultys the Duke lyes under, & upon my word if he was to aske my advice I do not know what I should give him. I spoke to Hawley as you desired; butt I assure you it was not necessary for I know both he & Huske have allways had a great opinion of one an other. every body here is extreamly pleased with their being sent to Scotland, & as for myself, I assure you I never had the least thought or desire of going there;[2] & am sure it is in much better hands. & now I really thinke all must & will be quiet between the Tweed & the Thames, butt if an invasion happens, I shall beg & desire to be employ'd. I am glad the Hessians are order'd to Scotland, butt for God's sake why are not the remainder of our Cavalry sent for home? that I am sure can not be answer'd for, since the Hessians are to come, which I also thinke extreamly right.

I am My Dear Dear Lord, for ever & most faithfully Your's
Richmond &c.

299. RICHMOND TO NEWCASTLE

Upperby near Carlisle
Mund 30th Decr 1745

My Dear Lord,

Our six gun battery has been playing these two dayes upon the Castle, 'tho butt gently yesterday, for wee were short of amunition, however enough came up last night from Whitehaven, & wee erected an other three gun battery last night, & as the engineer reports not a shott fired at them by the Rebells during the whole time they were at worke, & some of our artillery officers say they are sure they fired three times yesterday from the Castle without shott; so their amunition certanly fails them; & as there is a good deal of their wall beat down, & a great crack made in it, I thinke the breach will certanly be made by tonight or to morrow, & then the whole is our own. You will hear of a very odd letter the Duke has received from A French officer of Artillery, <u>ne sujet de France</u> as he sayes, butt his name is Geoghahagen, which is Irish

---

1. Cumberland was beseiging the Jacobite garrison left behind at Carlisle.
2. Richmond took no further part in the campaign after the main Jacobite Army had retreated to Scotland.

enough. they want extreamly to capitulate, butt to be sure the Duke can not treat with them, yett if they putt out the White flag, I really cant see how he can putt them to the sword after it, 'tho to be sure they ought all to be hanged. This letter I mention'd shews how useless these damn'd Dutch troops are; I actually thinke they should not be pay'd, butt transport themselves home again; for it will be very odd to pay troops, that wee know will not fight for us. I wish you joy of this Prussian Treaty, if it is well follow'd it will sett every thing to right again.

I am My Dear Lord, for ever, Your's

Richmond &c.

The Rebells have just hung out the White flagg.
Munday night. Our troops are now marching into the town. Pray send the enclosed quick to my dearest Taw.

300. STONE TO RICHMOND

Whitehall
Tuesday night 11 o'clock
[17 Jan 1746 (*in pencil*)]

My Lord,
An Express is arrived from Edenburgh, with Letters from L. G. Hawley, dated at Lithgow the 17th, to which place he was retreated, after an unsuccessful Action with the Rebels which happen'd that day, near Falkirk.[1] The Account, He gives of it, is very short. M. G. Huske with our right wing beat the Rebels' left; and the Rebels right beat our left, which was Commanded by Mr Hawley. He does not suppose, we have lost more than 300 men: Some Officers are kill'd. We have lost 7 Cannon out of ten: the Artillery Horses having run away, at the Beginning of the Action. Mr Hawley is gone back to Edenburgh; & the Rebels to Sterling

301. RICHMOND TO NEWCASTLE

Goodwood
Tuesd 28th Jany 1745/6

My Dear Lord,
Tho I had a long examination, for twas rather I that gave audience on Saturday I had nothing material to trouble your Grace with, else I certanly should have staid in town on purpose to have communicated it to you; which I could safely do without the impu-tation of a Spy, since I told the Great Lord Granville at Haneau that I allways did & ever would communicate every thing to you, that I thought had the least shadow of Polliticks in it; that it was my inclination butt I also thought it my duty. I only went into the Closet on Saturday to tell His Majesty that I had again offer'd myself to His Royall Highness, & came to do the same to His Majesty, in which he cutt me short with a No, No & some personall compliments which I dont know I deserv'd. butt to speake truth to you, I thinke it look'd as if your Grace had bespoke that no, no, I wish he would shew his complyance to you, in much more essential things. our whole discourse was millitary, & bewailing the want of discipline which God knows is enough to be lamented, butt how it is to be brought about in this nation, the wisest I am sure can not tell.

---

1. The Battle of Falkirk, 17 January 1746, in which General Hawley was defeated by Prince Charles and Murray, while advancing to try to raise the siege of Stirling, after he had captured Edinburgh.

Give me leave now My Dear Lord to lay a thing before you which gives me some concern, 'tho no difficulty, as my word is given & must consequently be kept. Poor Charles Feilding is dying, or most likely dead by this time. My first engagement you know is to your Godson Jack Boscawen,[1] butt in the first place I beleive the King will putt his third <u>no</u> upon him, for he has given me two for him already, & besides that as he is about the Duke, I am in some doubt if he would accept of it. Then the next I am engaged to recommend, you know is Phill Meados, at your request; & I thinke, 'tho perhaps with some difficulty, I might succeed for him, when I could not for Jack Boscawen, butt now I must tell you the thing that gives me no small concern, which is that Sr Thomas Prendergast, who you must consider is one of the nighest relations the Duchess of Richmond has, thinkes himself entitled to my recommendation preferable to any one else. & yett four have been made since I have been Master of the Horse, viz, Mordaunt, Feilding, Elliot, & Worsley, & the only reason why I have not recommended him before is that you know I have been these ten years solliciting something better for him without success, yett have often thought I had been upon the brinke of succeeding. butt still <u>nous voila</u> in <u>statu quo</u>. he has often formerly asked me to recommend him for Equerry, & my answer has constantly been, I hope to get you something better; butt supposing he should now renew his request to me, which I beleive he will; what shall I, or what can I then say to him? that I am engaged, 'tis true, butt why did I engage? is a question that will puzzle me. 'tho really & truely the reason is because I thought I should have gott something better for him, butt as that has not been the case, the excuse will be butt a poor one. So you see my dilemma is no small one, & I see no way of getting out of it, butt getting either Sr Thomas, or Phill Meados, a thing that will please either of them better, & God knows neither is in power, & very likely may not be in yours & even all this is in case Jack Boscawen can not succeed or does not care for it. I really dont say all this by way of plaguing you for employments, butt meerly for your advice what I am to say, for I know what I am to do, as I have promis'd. forgive all this My Dear Duke, & be assured that I am, eternally & most affectly Your's

Richmond &c.

The enclosed memorandum is from Hughes,[2] who is the only Sussex Parson that I have ask'd any thing of value for. he is a very honest man, a most zealous hearty freind to the common cause. & an unexceptionable man as to his character, except only in one small instance which our good Bishop poked out, or rather was officiously & in an ill natured manner was told him by Williams, which was that twelve years ago he hapned to gett his maid with child. & it was hush'd up in so private a manner that it was never known till Williams fish'd it out, & then told the Bishop of it meerly I beleive because the poor man was a freind of myne. His life, conversation, & behaviour has really been thoroughly modest & good, so it would really be hard that, because a man gott his maid with child at 22 years old, he should never have any preferment dureing his whole life, 'tho an unexceptionable one ever after. he was nevew to Bisp Waddington[3] who would have provided for him had he lived.

1. Hon. John Boscawen, 1714–1767, MP for Truro, 1747–1767, Captain in the 3rd. Horse Guards, 1742–1746, was Master of the Horse to the Duke of Cumberland, 1747–1757. He rose to the rank of Major General in 1761.
2. Rev. Simon Hughes asked for the living of Copford near Colchester, or Methley near Wakefield, both worth £200 per annum.
3. Edward Waddington, 1670–1731, was Bishop of Chichester, 1724–1731.

302. RICHMOND TO STONE

Goodwood
29. Janry 1745/6

Dear Sir,

I beg the enclosed may go in your very first packett to H.R. Higness, & you will oblige, Your faithfull humble servant,

Richmond &c.

The Smugglers have been hereabouts lately & wherever they go they declare themselves Rebells, I thinke it a much more serious thing than people seem to apprehend in London.

303. RICHMOND TO NEWCASTLE

Goodwood
31. Janry. 1745/6

My Dear Lord,

I should not trouble you so soon again if it was not to transcribe a very odd papagraff in a letter I have received from an officer of Cholmondleys who was at the battle at Falkirke. viz.

"Our Majr Lockyart march'd with the Regiment from the feild of battle to this side of Falkirke, & soon after wee miss'd him and he never has been with us since. There is various opinions of him, which I fear will turn out to his disadvantage for all the Officers of our Regiment were examin'd this day on his affair by the Genlls order".

You know I suppose tis the Huzzaring Lockyart, recommended by Ld Petersham. surely he & his father have had very bad luck in their favourites. pray if there is any more particulars about it lett Mr. Stone write me word of it. & if any very very good news should come from Scotland which I dont at all despair of, dont grudge me a Messager, espetially if it should arrive upon a no post day.

I am My Dearest Lord, for ever & most affectly Your's

Richmond &c.

304. STONE TO RICHMOND

Whitehall
Febry 1st 1745/6

My Lord,

I received the honour of your Grace's Letter, inclosing one for H.R.H. the Duke, which I will take particular care to forward by the first Express to Scotland. We had Letters, this day, from Mr Hawley, of the 28th. He expresses the greatest joy upon the Duke's going to Scotland:[1] and says, the Army would be ready to march at an Hour's warning, after His R.H.'s arrival at Edenburgh, which we conclude was on Wednesday night: so that, in all probability, He will have moved towards the Rebels, yesterday, or this day. Mr Hawley had Intelligence from M. Genl Blakeney, on Monday last. He had not then lost a Man, by the fire of the Rebels, (which at that time, had been only Musketry) and had kill'd a considerable number of them, some Accounts say, not less than 700, but that seems improbable. However, it is certain they have lost many men, both by the Fire of the Castle, and by Desertion: they are also in great want of provisions: which, I conclude, will make them take the first Opportunity of coming to an Action: unless they should repass the Forth, which I can hardly beleive. Sir William

1.   The Duke of Cumberland was given the supreme command in Scotland after Hawley's defeat at Falkirk.

Yonge received this day the proceedings of the Court Martial at Edenburgh, containing the Trials of three or four of the Officers. I have not seen those papers; nor so much as heard the names of the Officers. But, I know, they are all acquitted from the Charge of Cowardice; and censured, for some misconduct, to be suspended, during the pleasure of the General. My Lord Duke bids me tell your Grace, that he knows nothing of Major Lockhart's Behaviour; but that it was said, in general, that there was an odd Story about him, but no particulars mention'd. My Lord Duke would have wrote to your Grace by this post, but was obliged to go to a Meeting of Business. He will not fail to write by the next post.

I am with the greatest respect My Lord Your Grace's most obedt humble Serv.

Andrew Stone

305. NEWCASTLE TO RICHMOND

Newcastle House
Feby 5th 1745/6

My Dear Lord,

I have only time to congratulate your Grace upon the great News arrived this day from Scotland, all the Particulars of which, you will have in the enclosed printed Letters, which contain every word I have received from thence. Our young Hero has outdone Himself,[1] & it is a double pleasure to consider, that this Country will probably owe its Deliverance entirely to the King's Son, as far as Human Means could contribute to it. I wish I could send you as good an Account of the Closet as of the Feild, of the Father as of the Son. On Saturday last we thought, our Affair was settled, tho' in a very awkward way, but yet with tolerable Temper towards us. But on Monday last, Lord Bath got into the Closet, exclaimed against the King's being forced to take Mr. P_____[2] contrary to his will, promised to stand by Him, if He would resist it, that He would act with us, &c. & the Consequence of that has been, that Lord Granville has sent His Emissaries to endeavour to detach some of our old Corps, & His Majesty has taken a bold Resolution, not to make P. Secretary at War, but on Condition of the King's not seeing Him, on which foot P. cannot take it, nor the Office be executed, so that the whole Scheme is blowed up. The D. of Bedford & Gower will infallibly quitt; we, I suppose, shall follow, & Ld Bath, & Ld Granville govern, or rather, destroy the King's Affairs.

I am in vast haste Yrs

Holles Newcastle

As to the Equerry's Place, you are really good in thinking of P. Meadows. But other People are made like me, I never think of insisting upon a Friend performing a particular Promise, when I see evidently He intends to do it, but that there is a most reasonable Cause for His not doing it. This I take to be the Case of Sr T. Pendergrass, & as such, I will represent it, if you desire I should, to ye D: of Kingston. My Dear Duke, it is always my Inclination & Study to make you easy, & Happy for I have not many such Friends.

---

1.   Cumberland, having relieved Stirling Castle, set off on 4 February in pursuit of the Jacobites, who had crossed the Forth on 1 February.
2.   William Pitt, 1708–1778, MP for Old Sarum, 1735–1747, for Seaford, 1747–1754, for Aldborough, 1754–1756, for Buckingham, 1756, for Oakhampton, 1756–1757, and for Bath, 1757–1766, when he was created Earl of Chatham, was successively Groom of the Bedchamber to the Prince of Wales, 1737–1745; Joint Vice-Treasurer for Ireland, 1746; Paymaster General, 1746–1755, Secretary of State for the Southern Department, 1756–1757, and again, 1757–1761; and Lord Privy Seal, 1766–1768. He had remained out of office until 1746 because of the King's personal objection to him, but his appointment, 'into some honourable employment' was one of the Pelhams' conditions for their return to office in February 1746.

306. RICHMOND TO NEWCASTLE

Goodwood
Wed. 5 Feb. 1745/6

My Dear Lord,

Twelve miles is too farr & the weather too cold for me to go last night to Parham, & by the enclosed you see Sr Cecyll very rightly thinkes the same reason good for not comeing here to day. So I dispatch'd a servant with the papers, & a letter I wrote to him myself last night at seven o'clock & enclosed is his answer that I have just received. Buckner told me three dayes ago that the country had suspected Ibbotson was gon off, he was steward to the Duke of Norfolke,[1] & rents some large farms now. If this damn'd weather lasts, I shall be in town on Saturday night, butt if you have any commands for me shall be here on Fryday. Mr. Pelham has recommended Captn Denny to me for Equerry, butt if your Grace should have leasure enough to tell him the story I troubled you with, he will see how impossible 'tis for me to obey his commands.

I am, My Dear Lord, Your Grace's ever faithfull, & most affectionate slave
Richmond &c.

307. RICHMOND TO NEWCASTLE

Goodwood
Thursday noon 6 Feb. 1745/6

I am excessively obliged to you My Dearest Lord for the very good news you sent me; 'tho to have heard that these Villains were totally destroy'd would have been still better. however 'tis all I expected, tho you used to scold me for despising them, butt I allways did & allways shall despise them as the scum of Scotland which is certanly the sinke of the Earth. & I allways said that it was butt only looking these rascalls in the face, & I was sure they would never stand their ground; this the late Lord Cadogan[2] allways said & I have since been an eyewitness of it. butt indeed if our people run away at the sight of them, they must be beat even by the Westminster schollars; & what did that pannick come from, butt their hearing that these were desperate fellows with Broad Swords, Targetts, Lochaberax's, & the Devill knoes what, that was eternally preach'd up by the Scotch Jacobites, even at White's & St. James's, stuff actually fit to frighten nothing butt old women & Children.

I am very sorry to find things go so ill in the Closett. between you & I, for I never said it to any mortall, dont you thinke it wrong of Totty, Gour, & Pitt himself to insist so much upon it. I wish it could be decided one way or other for it is not only a disagreeable butt horrid scituation. Wee certanly can not go on without Totty, Gowr & Pitt, I own I wish wee could, tho I love the two first very well particularly Gowr, butt as to ever joining those two honest men Lds Bath & Granville, I beleive you never will; I am sure I never can.

You are excessively kind in what you say about the Equerrys place, butt I dont apprehend the Duke of Kingston, will be quite so reasonable nor indeed can I expect it of him.

I am, My Dear Lord Your Grace's ever faithfull & most affectionate
Richmond &c.

The weather looks as if it was going to breake. if it does, I stay here. You say nothing about poor Hughes.

---

1. Edward Howard, 9th. Duke of Norfolk, 1686–1777.
2. William Cadogan, 1st. Earl Cadogan, 1675–1726, who succeeded the Duke of Marlborough as Master General of the Ordnance and Commander-in-Chief in 1726, served as second-in-command under the Duke of Argyll in the 1715 Rebellion. He was Richmond's father-in-law.

Captn Nash was here when the Messager came, so I dispatch'd him back to the Court of Pettworth, with the printed account I enclosed in a letter to the Sovereign there, telling him how pleasing I knew such a peice of news must be to him. So I thinke I shall be well again there. 'tho I am pretty indifferent about it.

308. NEWCASTLE TO RICHMOND

Lord Harrington's House
Monday, 3 o'clock
[10 Feb. 1746]

My Dearest Lord,
Lord Harrington & I are just come from leaving our Seals with the King.[1] My Brother goes tomorrow, the Chancellor in a day or two; that depends on the Term. I am perswaded, when your Grace knows all that has passed ye last Week, you will think, that in Duty to the King, in regard to our Country, & in Justice to ourselves, we could not do otherwise. The Resolution was taken last Fryday night. We met again on Saturday, where I expected you would be. Afterwards, I thought it unnecessary to send a Messenger, 'till I could send you Word, that His Majesty had accepted our Resignations. It is plain He was prepared for it, & if we had gone on, we must have run the Risk of our Heads every Day, with the certain Loss of our Honour. Our Enemies put it upon Mr. Pitt's not being Secretary at War. That is not the Case; that was over. The Reason is, the King in the strongest Manner almost publickly declares his Dissatisfaction wth us, & our Conduct both at home, & abroad, & consequently does not, & will not, give us his Countenance, without which nobody but Fools or knaves could go on.
My Dearest Duke every Yrs
Holles Newcastle

309. RICHMOND TO NEWCASTLE

Charlton
Tuesday Morn 11 Feb 1745/6

My Dear Lord,
You have acted like men of honor in every respect, & I should be as bad as I desire to be thought good, if I did not follow so good an example & I am impatient to be in town for that purpose, butt am really so much out of order that I am not able to go through in a day, & shall hardly as the roads are be in town time enough to resign to morrow. however on Thursday I certanly shall. butt I desire you would not speake of it to any body butt my two ever dear & estimable freinds Mr. Pelham & the Chancellor, for this single reason only, that I thinke it indecent to the King, to publish an intention of that kind, before he is acquainted with it. I certanly can serve him no longer for two reasons, the first because the only honest sett of men I know are out, & secondly because I know a sett of thorough paced rogues will come in, butt I am determin'd as long as I have a tongue to vote with & an arm to fight with, to keep him & his familly, such as it is, upon this throne. butt I wish 'tis not all in vain. My Lord Granville must have a new Parliament, & that I fear will be a Jacobite one, and then adieu Pannier &c. Pray send the enclosed to Taw who is the only one in my secret.
adieu My Dear Lord, I am for ever & unalterably Your's
Richmond &c.

---

1. Newcastle and Harrington had resigned their offices on 10 February and the rest of the cabinet was to follow on the 11th. The Earl of Bath became 1st. Lord of the Treasury on 10 February, with Earl Granville as sole Secretary of State. Four days later, the King was forced to recall the Pelhams, when it was found that Bath and Granville could not 'depend upon more than 31 Lords and 80 Commoners'.

Where & at what hour may I see you to morrow in the evening. I shall be in town by two, butt I must dine with my dear Taw.

I am curious about old Puff. & cant help laughing a little to myself. butt for god's sake dont tell him. & if you please you may communicate my intentions to him for I most sincerely love & <u>value him</u>.

310. RICHMOND TO STONE

Godalming
18 Feb. 1745/6

Dear Sir,

I forgott to aske you this morning what became of the examination of Mr. Bishopp,[1] I fancy his designs must have been treasonable because My Lord Gage[2] assured me they were not. so pray lett me know it & you will oblige, Your's most sincerely
Richmond &c.

Pray direct to me at Charlton in Sussex.

311. RICHMOND TO NEWCASTLE

Charlton
26 Feb. 1745/6

My Dear Lord,

I have received a letter from Jack Boscawen, who, as he is in the Duke's service, resigns all pretensions of comeing into the Kings as Equerry. what then may I do? & have you spoke to the Duke of Kingston? you know how I am tyed by promis to him as well as to you. so unless I am entirely, & willing released I stand bound to him, 'tho you are so good as to release me. butt even if you do God knows if I shall succeed, for Taw is hardly spoke to yett. butt if he knew how great Philosophers wee are both upon that head, he would not pique himself so much upon taciturnity. Mr. Pelham has expres'd himself very kindly to me upon my application to him for Tom Hill. you have been so good to him already that I can ask nothing more of you for him. Linky arrived here yesterday & brought you message to me. I own I like things as they are, & am not too apprehensive of that snake in the grass you & Mr. Pelham seem to suspect.

I am My Dear Lord, for ever, & most affectionately Your's
Richmond &c.

312. RICHMOND TO STONE

Charlton
28th Feb. 1745/6

Dr Sir,

I received your of the 25th with that from His Royall Highness enclosed,[3] & I take the liberty of encloseing an other to him, which I beg you would send by the first oportunity. I own I am so vain & proud of that which the Duke has wrote to me that I

---

1. James Bishopp, younger brother of Sir Cecil Bishopp, was arrested at Pevensey in January 1746 as a Jacobite, on trying to cross over to France.
2. Thomas Gage, 1st. Viscount Gage, 1695–1754, MP for Minehead, 1717, and for Tewkesbury, 1721–1754, succeeded to Firle on the death of Sir William Gage in 1744. He was a member of the Opposition until the death of the Prince of Wales.
3. Presumably the letter from Cumberland to Richmond dated 20 February, congratulating Richmond on the Pelhams' return to power, printed in The Earl of March, *A Duke and His Friends*, (1911), vol. 2, pp. 486, 487.

cant help desireing you to shew it to the Duke of Newcastle, for which purpose I have enclosed it to you. & when his Grace has read it you will be so good as to return it to me. for vain as I am of it, none butt those concerned should see it, as his goodness to us, might be a disadvantage to him.

I am Dear Sir most sincerely Your's

Richmond &c.

313.   STONE TO RICHMOND

Whitehall
March 4th, 1745/6

My Lord,

I return your Grace inclosed His Royal Highness's Letter, and am directed by my Lord Duke of Newcastle to return you His thanks for the Communication of it, and to acquaint you that He had the Honour to receive one from His. R.H. to the same effect, and feels an equal satisfaction with your Grace, in this Proof of His R.H.'s Goodness & Friendship. Your Grace will have heard, that when the Rebels having possess'd themselves of Inverness, and Lord Loudon's Retreat from it, His R.H. has thought proper to detain the Hessian Troops in Scotland, and to send the Transports away with the Dutch. The Hessians are advancing towards Perth by Cantoonments, in order to stop the Passage, should the Rebels attempt to return into the Low Lands by the Blair of Athol, &c. Count FitzJames,[1] the Major Generals Tyrconnel;[2] & Rooth, and the Brigadiers, Nugent & Cook, and a Colonel Nugent, are returned to France, on giving their Parole, not to serve, against the King or His Allies 'till they are exchanged.

As to foreign Affairs; there is great Reason to apprehend; that the King of Sardinia has actually sign'd, or is on the point of signing, a separate Treaty with France, which they say, Spain protests against. The Queen of Hungary is marching strong Bodies of Troops into Italy, & the Low Countries where Bathiani is to command. There is no Appearance of the Dutch having any Design to make a separate Accommodation, but on the contrary they seem disposed to do their utmost to make a Stand. The Situation at Court is pretty much the same as when your Grace left London. The Prejudice against Lord H____[3] seems rather to abate.

My Lord Duke bids me acquaint your Grace, that He spoke this day, to the Duke of Kingston about the Equery's Place, who seem'd to take it very rightly, and to be disposed to make the thing easy. He will speak to Mr. Meadows tomorrow, & acquaint my Lord Duke with what passes; so that He will be able to write something positive to your Grace by Thursday's post. My Lord Duke is far from being able, at present, to say that it will do; But he thinks the Duke of Kingston wishes that it may. My Lord Duke talked to Him, in the way, He thought your Grace would like, without pushing it too strongly, as He well knows your Grace's scrupulousness not to recede, if (contrary to what my Lord Duke hopes) it should be insisted upon.

I am with great truth & respect My Lord your Grace's most obedient & humble sert

Andrew Stone

1.   James Stuart Fitzjames, but for the attainder of his father, 3rd. Duke of Berwick and 12th. Count of Gelves, 1718–1785, had a career in the service of the Spanish Army.
2.   Richard Talbot, styled Earl of Tyrconnel, 1710–1752, was a Major General in the French Army, because of the attainder of his family. He was taken prisoner by Commodore Knowles while attempting to join Prince Charles in Scotland, 21 February 1746, and was soon exchanged.
3.   Lord Harrington.

314. RICHMOND TO NEWCASTLE

Whitehall
Tuesday night. [4 March 1746]

My Dear Lord,

Enclosed is Cheale's memoriall,[1] which you have certanly no time to consider at present, butt in my opinion it would be right to referr it to the Attorney Genll, as it is really a matter of right if Garter has any; if not I'm sure you will continue your favor to Cheale.

Your's most sincerely

Richmond &c.

Cheale goes into Sussex with me for a week or ten dayes.

315. NEWCASTLE TO RICHMOND

Newcastle House
March 6, 1745/6

My Dear Lord,

The continual Hurry, I am in, will, I hope, be my excuse for not having sooner returned you my thanks for your kind Letter. Mr. Stone however, has given you some Account, how things go here. The Duke of Kingston was with me this morning; and has behaved most extremely handsomely, & politely. He is Himself very desirous to release you from your Promise; and has tried to make His Brother Meadows easy: But He told me today, that Phil Meadows had so set his heart upon it, that if it should not be done, He thinks, He would suspect Him, the Duke of Kingston. I never saw a man more reasonable. He sees the Force of the Arguments in favour of Sr Thomas Prendergast; and yet, at the same time, He is afraid of disobliging His Brother-in-Law, whose Circumstances, He says, want this Assistance. He is extremely apprehensive of doing any thing to displease you; which I have assured Him would not be the Case. In short, we must find out some way to serve Sr Tho. Prendergast: He deserves it from you, and I am sure, you deserve ten thousand times more from us. As to Tom Hill; whenever I can give Him a Lift, He & you may depend upon it. Our Affairs at Court rub on, as much as they did. We have not much to complain of, and less to brag of; and my Opinion is, that, if we determine to serve the King, & the Publick, with the same Integrity, that we have always done, and with more Resolution, & more Union amongst ourselves than has sometimes been the Case, we shall either carry on the King's Affairs, with ease and success, in Employment; or go out of it with the Approbation of our Friends, & with Satisfaction to Ourselves, and I own I am now for laying aside Complaints, & making the best of it, whilst we are in : and that we shall do, if we are all equally well, & equally in, at Court.

Our Accounts from Scotland are very bad. The Rebels are certainly reassembling; and it was thought, they will have more real Highlanders, than ever. The Rebels have got Inverness, & the Castle. Lord Loudon is retreated further north. The Duke complains extremely of the Country, and I am afraid with the greatest Reason. H.R.H. is afraid the Rebels will also get Fort Augustus, But He has taken care to secure, I hope, Fort William. H.R.H. deserves His Statue in Gold, for having stop'd the Hessians,[2] But you & I must be partial to Him for His Goodness to us upon our late great Event. Our foreign Affairs go as ill as ever. The King of Sardinia, I fear, has made His Peace with

---

1. John Cheale had petitioned to be able to carry the Ensign of the Garter to the Duke of Saxe-Weissenfels.
2. The Dutch had been promised that the Hessians should return to the Netherlands.

France, tho' Spain, they say, is enraged at it. The Queen of Hungary is certainly marching between 30 & 40,000 Men in to Flanders, & more into Italy. The Dutch are losing their Towns, & their Troops, but yet show no Inclination to make a separate Peace.

Sr John Barnard[1] &c. are to attack our Money Matters on Monday next. I hope we shall beat them by a great Majority. If there is such a thing as a Member of the House of Commons near you; pray take care to send him up to Town. My kindest Compliments to the Duke of St. Albans, & Linky, Old Puff killed a Fox yesterday, after the finest Chace of six hours & a half. Can we say as much in Sussex.

I am my Dearest Lord Ever & unalterably yrs

Holles Newcastle

316.   RICHMOND TO NEWCASTLE

Charlton
9. March 1745/6

My Dear Lord,

Linky is gon off this morning in high health, spirits, & vigor, so woe be to your neice to night. I thanke your Grace for your kind letter of the 6th. & particularly for your endeavours to make things easy about Sr Thos Prendergast, butt since Phil Medos insists upon my promis, I shall certanly recommend him the first day I find my Master in good temper, which I am glad to find by you rather begins to mend. I am also extreamly obliged to you for your kind intentions for Tom Hill. 'Tho neither he nor I ought to aske them considering how good you have been to him already. You seem not to like the accounts from Scotland, I own I had always much rather the Duke should destroy the rebells, than that they should lay down their arms, the dread & example of a great many of them being putt to the sword, & I hope a great many hanged, may strike a terror in them & keep them quiet, butt depend upon it nothing butt force can do it, for 'tis vain thinke any Government can ever root out Jacobitism there. Is it true that my Lord Louden's men refuse to take the oaths ? & to fight against the Highland rebells? if it's true & wee suffer it, wee are a most despicable government. I hope & beleive the Duke will paint that whole nation in their right colors when they come home; & he will certanly find now, what he has often call'd nationall prejudice in me, to be pure naked truth. I agree wee two cant help being partial to him for he has been most excessively good to us. here is no member of Parliament hereabouts, not even Sr John Peachy, & if he was, I should not chuse to send him up. I shall be in town on Fryday next at farthest. the Duke of St Albans is much yours, you know I suppose our master will not speake to him. & I am very sure his suspicions were better founded than yours. as for Harcourt he made his declaration to Linky the day you went in.

Before I conclude this letter I must tell you how wee are all in love with my Lord Dalkeith,[2] Linky will give you a full account of him. he is as honest as any of us & vastly desirous to be in Parliament, now surely it would be a credit to a ministry to bring him in. wee jokeingly sayd the P— could do it, upon he swore he would never come in upon that interest, he as eldest son you know cant be chose in Scotland, so his brother will be chose for the County of Tweedale. he sayes he is ready to spend a thousand, & would be glad to be chose by the interest of this administration. so indeed I thinke it worth while to talke to Mr. Pelham about it, for the haveing, & encouraging

1. Sir John Barnard, 1685–1764, MP for London 1722–1764, had been a supporter of Carteret's administration. On 10 March 1746, he attacked Henry Pelham's proposals for a new war loan.
2. Francis Scott, Lord Dalkeith, 1721–1750, son of the 2nd. Duke of Buccleuch, was returned by Newcastle as MP for Boroughbridge at a bye-election on 22 April 1746.

a man of his quality, property, & good character is an honor to a party, & 'tis upon that footing meerly I mention it. he is gon up with Linky & without reflecting upon any body, I fancy my Lady Dalkeith, will be almost as well pleas'd as other Ladys may be to morrow morning.

 I am My Dear Lord, for ever & most affectionately, Your's
Richmond &c.

317. STONE TO RICHMOND

[20 March 1746]

My Lord,
 An Express came in this Morning with the Letters from His R. Highness dated the 19th at Aberdeen. M. Genl Bland was never near surprising, & cutting off, a party of about 1000 of the Rebels. They fled, upon His Approach, with the utmost Precipitation. There was some Skirmishing, and Roy Stewart,[1] a Colonel, & a noted man amongst them, is said to have been kill'd. On the other side, the Rebels have surprised some very small parties of our Highlanders (I think) in Athol; which has occasion'd a kind of Alarm at Perth, but without any Foundation. A Council of War was held there, & some Resolutions taken, which H.R.H. to whom they were transmitted, did not altogether approve, & sent Colonel Yorke[2] to Prince Frederick,[3] & Lord Cranford, at Perth, to prevent the making any Motion in consequence of them.
 The Duke is fully persuaded, the Rebels do not exceed 7,000 Men, in their whole Number. H.R.H. very much commends the Duke of Kingston's Regiment of Horse. He was preparing to go on to Inverness; but does not mention any certain Time for His March. He sends a Return of the Troops, with Him, which are as follows

Foot	Fit to serve	Cavalry
Effective		Fit for service
9,400	6,500	between 6 & 7,00
		Effective – more than
		500

and this is exclusive of Bligh's Regiment, & about 700 recovered Men that were daily expected to join him from Edenburgh. No mention is made of Fort William. Lord Loudon with his Highlanders, is to remain where He now is, which I think, is in the Shire of Sutherland.

318. STONE TO RICHMOND

Whitehall
April 23rd 1746

My Lord,
 This day at noon an Express arrived from the Lord Justice Clerk at Edenburgh, with the Account,[4] which your Grace will find in the inclosed Gazette, which my Lord Duke

1. John Roy Stewart, 1700–1752, fought in the French army at Fontenoy and then joined Prince Charles in Scotland. He survived, and accompanied Prince Charles into exile.
2. Hon Joseph Yorke, 1724–1792, a colonel in the Foot Guards, was ADC to the Duke of Cumberland, 1745–1749. He was later MP for East Grinstead, 1751–1761, for Dover, 1761–1774, and for Grampound, 1774–1780. He was Minister at the Hague for 30 years.
3. Frederick, Prince of Hesse, had landed at Leith with 5,000 Hessian soldiers on 6 February 1746.
4. The Account of the Battle of Culloden fought on 15 April 1746.

of Newcastle orders me to forward to your Grace by Express, and to congratulate you in His Name, upon this great & glorious News. We wait with great Impatience for Letters from his Royal Highness with further Particulars. The Lord Justice Clerk thinks, some Accident must have befaln the Messenger, who, He concludes was dispatched from the Army, with an Account of this Action. Some Letters say, that the Pretender's son has escaped with only twelve Men in his Company; others, that He retired too soon: But all agree that his Royal Highness's Victory was complete.

My Lord Duke sends his Compliments to your Grace, my Lord Lincoln, & all the good Company with you; & desires Lord Lincoln may be acquainted that He shall send for Him & his Friends to come to Town in a few Days, a Motion having been made yesterday by my Lord Oxford[1] in the House of Lords, for the Papers, relating to the Hanover Troops, &c. to be laid before that House, which will occasion a Day of Business there.

I am with the greatest Respect My Lord Your Grace's most obedient & most humble servt

Andrew Stone

Poor Mr. Winnington[2] died, this morning.

319. STONE TO RICHMOND

Whitehall
April 24th 1746

My Lord,

Lord Bury arrived this morning, with a full Confirmation of good News, that I had the honour to send your Grace last night. He was dispatched by His Royal Highness, immediately after the Action; But, as He came by Sea, & met with contrary Winds, & bad Weather, He was glad to be able to land, on Monday last, at North Berwick, from whence he came post to London. He brought only a short Letter from His R. Highness to the King, which confirms the particulars, received yesterday from Edenburgh; with very little variation, or addition. One thousand of the Rebels were left dead on the Field of Battle; and I don't find that many were kill'd in the pursuit. Ld Strathallan[3] is said to be kill'd. Secretary Murray of Broughton[4] is among the Prisoners. The Rebels made their Attack, in two Columns, and, at first, made some little Impression on Barrel's Regiment, where Lord Robert Kerr[5] was kill'd, & Lt Colo Rich[6] lost his hand. Captain Grossette of Price's was kill'd; as were about 130 private men. General Hawley; & Kingston's Horse; are extremely commended, & all the Troops in general behaved perfectly well; tho' I apprehend they could not all be engaged. Three piquets of French surrenderd themselves prisoners, amounting to about 300 Men. John

1. Edward Harley, 3rd. Earl of Oxford, 1699–1755, had been MP for Herefordshire, 1727–1741. He was a Tory, and a supporter of the House of Stuart.
2. Thomas Winnington, 1696–1746, MP for Droitwich, 1726–1741, and for Worcester, 1741–1746, had been successively a Lord of the Admiralty, 1730–1736; a Lord of the Treasury, 1736–1741; Cofferer of the Household, 1741–1743; and Paymaster General from 1743. He bled to death in the hands of a quack after a bout of rheumatic fever on 23 April 1746.
3. William Drummond, 4th. Viscount Strathallan, 1690–1746. A Jacobite commander, he was taken prisoner at Sheriffmuir in 1715, but released in 1717. He was killed at Culloden.
4. Sir John Murray of Broughton had been ill and had not fought at Culloden, but he remained in Scotland after the battle, and was betrayed.
5. Lord Robert Kerr, a captain in the Grenadier Guards, was the only brother of William Kerr, Earl of Ancram. He was killed at Culloden.
6. Possibly Lieutenant Colonel Sir Robert Rich, 1685–1768, MP for Dunwich, 1715–1722, for Bere Alston, 1724–1727, and for St Ives, 1727–1741, who was Groom of the Bedchamber to King George II, 1718–1759, and who fought at Culloden.

Drummond is escaped. The Duke of Perth[1] is said to be kill'd, but without any Certainty. The Rebels were upwards of 8,000. Lord Ancram[2] was upon the point of killing Ld Kilmarnock,[3] his near relation, without knowing him; but upon his telling his name, made him prisoner. The inclosed Letter, is just now brought me, from Lord Albemarle to your Grace, I dare say, contains more particulars than I have told your Grace, & than are yet known here; but we expect further Accounts every Hour.

My Lord Duke bids me acquaint your Grace, that the Day of Business in the House of Lords will certainly be in the course of next Week; & He therefore hopes, your Grace & the Lords with you, will be ready to come to Town, when He shall send you notice of the time.

I am with the greatest Respect Your Grace's most obedient & most humble servt
Andrew Stone

320.   RICHMOND TO NEWCASTLE

Bolderwood
25 April 1746

Joy to you My Dear Lord upon this great event; I shall certanly attend with my Lords Lincoln & Dell, at the house of Lords, butt wee have petitions to you for which I refer you to my letter to Mr. Stone, who will be so good as to order my relays when the day of business is fix'd. Enclosed is a letter from Albemarle about Dear Bury,[4] surely Bury might stay for a regiment which is much more substantial than the ranke without it. 'tis true Bury is a young Lt Coll but I was made aid de Camp from a Captn; I will speake myself to the King when i come to town; if you have no objection, & tell him truth that except only the Duke he has not an officer in his army under forty years old that knows more than Bury. I suppose I shall be huff'd butt nimporte. I'l speake if you give me leave & thinke I shall not do more harm than good.

I am My Dear Lord, for ever & most affectly Your's
Richmond &c.

321.   RICHMOND TO STONE

Bolderwood Lodge
Fryday morning. 25th April 1746

Dear Sir,

A thousand thankes to the Duke of Newcastle & yourself for the exceeding good news I received from you last night, & the confirmation I had of it this morning. it has given us all the greatest pleasure, butt not the least suprise to me, 'tho I know the Duke of Newcastle thinkes I am as wrong headed as others in despiseing these rebells too much. butt I do maintain it from what I have myself seen of them, they will always be beat if our people will butt fight. which I fear is not always the case with other enemys. Lord Lincoln Lord Delawarr & myself, will certanly attend the house of Lords if wee have timely notice, butt wee hope & beg of all things that it may not be before

1.   James Drummond, 6th. Earl and 3rd. titular Duke of Perth, 1713–1747, commanded the Jacobite left wing at Culloden. He retreated to Ruthven in Badenoch after the battle.
2.   William Kerr, Earl of Ancram, 1710–1775, MP for Richmond, 1747–1763, was ADC to the Duke of Cumberland, 1745–1746. He was wounded at Fontenoy, and commanded the cavalry on the left wing at Culloden.
3.   William Boyd, 4th. Earl of Kilmarnock, 1704–1746, Privy Councillor to Prince Charles, colonel of Guards and subsequently General, fought at Falkirk, and was captured at Culloden by Lord Ancram. He was executed at Tower Hill.
4.   Albemarle's letter asked that Lord Bury should be made ADC to the King in succession to Lord George Sackville, who had been given Monroe's Regiment.

Thursday, butt if it should be Tuesday, you will order the landau to be at Twyford on Sunday night, & the other sett to be at Egham on Munday night. butt as I shall chuse to be in town by Thursday, if the business should stand for that day, or even be putt off for a week, you will still be so good as to send the enclosed order to the mews as it stands, butt acquaint my Lord De Lawarr with it's being putt off that he may stay here this week incase it is. I send the enclosed directions to the Coachman open that you may read them, & alter them incase wee are to be in town sooner than Thursday, if not you may depend upon our being there by Thursday noon. I find by My Lord Albemarle's letter that twas wrote before the battle for it is dated from Nairn the 15th. I write this & direct it to you for fear His Grace should be gon this fine weather to Claremount. I have however wrote also to him & you'l be so good as to send it by the first oportunity. I must also beg you to send the other enclosed as directed, I am, Dear Sir, most truely & sincerely, Your's

Richmond &c.

322. STONE TO RICHMOND

Whitehall
April 26, 1746

My Lord,
I have my Lord Duke's Orders to dispatch this Messenger, with the inclosed Letters, which were received this day by an Express that arrived from Scotland. By these last Accounts, the Loss of the Rebels in the late Action appears to be much greater; & consequently His Royal Highness's Victory, more considerable, than was at first thought. The Duke's Relation makes 2000 of the Rebels kill'd; other Letters say 2,500; & it is certain the Rebels themselves say, they have lost from 3, to 4,000 Men: amongst which there are many Heads of Clans; viz, Ld Strathallon, Ld Balermino,[1] Cameron of Lochiel,[2] Appin, Kinloch, & many others. There are also many considerable men among the prisoners. The Rebels seem to be in a manner quite dispersed. His R.H. not having had any Intelligence since the Action, of any considerable Number of them being any where together, so that He was at a Loss which way to pursue them. The night after the Action, the Pretender's Son, (who ran away at the beginning of it) lay at Ld Lovat's[3] House. The next day, Brigr Mordaunt[4] was sent with a Detachment into that part of the Country, which caled at Lord Lovat's House, & finding it empty, set fire to it, & burned it to the Ground. The Earl of Cromarty,[5] with his Son the Ld McLeod, & 150 private men are brought prisoners to Inverness from Sutherland. Of the King's Troops, there were about 50 kill'd, (officers included) and 250 wounded. All the Troops behaved to Admiration.

As Friday next is appointed for the great day of Debate in the House of Lords, my Lord Duke hopes to have the Pleasure of seeing your Grace, my Lord Lincoln, my Lord Delawar, & all the Lords that are with you, in Town, before that time.

My Lord Duke desires your Grace would be so good as to make His Compliments to

---

1.   Arthur Elphinstone, 6th. Lord Balmerino, 1688–1746, had fought for the Jacobites at Sheriffmuir in 1715 and then escaped to the Continent. He was Colonel and Captain of the Guards to Prince Charles, and fought at Falkirk. He was delivered up by the Grants after Culloden and executed.
2.   Donald Cameron of Lochiel, 1695–1748, Chief of the clan Cameron from 1719 was wounded at Falkirk and Culloden. He was attainted but escaped to France with Prince Charles.
3.   Simon Fraser, 12th. Lord Lovat, 1677–1747. Prince Charles actually rested at Gortuleg, the house of Lord Lovat's steward. Lovat was beheaded in 1747.
4.   Brigadier General John Mordaunt, 1697–1780, MP for Pontefract, 1730–1734, for Whitchurch, 1735–1741, and for Cockermouth, 1741–1768, commanded a brigade at Culloden.
5.   George Mackenzie, 3rd. Earl of Cromarty, died 1766, was taken prisoner, tried and sentenced to death after Culloden, but was pardoned in 1749.

those Lords, who, He hopes will excuse him for not writing to them separately on this Occasion. His Grace sends his best Respects & Congratulations, to your Grace & all the good Company, upon this glorious Success in Scotland.

I am with great respect My Lord Your Grace's most obedient & most humble servant
Andrew Stone

323. RICHMOND TO STONE

Bolderwood Lodge
Sunday. 27th April 1746

A thousand thankes Dear Sir to the Duke of Newcastle & yourself for this augmentation of good news & most joyfull it is to thinke that so many of those villains are destroy'd, & indeed the Rope must finish those that have escaped with their lives & are taken, else wee shall all deserve to have all this over again. I shall certanly be in town on Thursday, & the other two Lords the same day or Fryday at farthest. & My Lord De Lawarr & I beg our services to the Duke of Newcastle. Lord Lincoln went to Salisbury yesterday, & will return here after seeing Wilton to night. I am astonish'd you had not received my letter which I sent you back by express & ought to have in London by yesterday noon.

I am, Dear Sir, for ever Your's
Richmond &c.

324. NEWCASTLE TO RICHMOND

Newcastle House
May 6th, 1746

My Dear Lord,

I am perswaded your Grace knows me too well, to doubt of my real Friendship & Regard to you, or that any thing that I can say upon your own Subject, can proceed from any other Cause. Ever since you left London, I have been endeavouring to obey your Commands about the War Office in the best manner I could. Sr Wm Yonge is laid up, & will not probably be able to go abroad in some days. I understand that the King has given Him the Choice either to remain Secretary at War, or to be Paymaster in Ireland. His Intention was, & is, to choose Ireland. I have talked fully to my Brother upon this Matter and have also mentioned it to Lord Harrington who is Yonge's cheif Friend. As He can't go abroad, He has not yet made His Choice in form, & I will prevent its being done till I receive your Answer, but I hear Yonge is very impatient on Account of his Re-election. I find it is generally thought by all your Friends, that Sr Wm Yonge's Health, & Infirmities are such, as will make it impracticable for Him to continue in the War Office, and that, if He should not go out now, He will be obliged to resign it in 5 or six months, when the same Question will arise again. It is also thought, that as our Affairs stand now in the H. of Commons, Nobody, but Mr Fox,[1] can succeed Sr Wm Yonge. I know how disagreable it must be to you, but at the same time, I don't know what you would have me do in it. I have endeavoured to see, whether Yonge could not continue, & no notice be taken, but to let Mr Fox have the Irish Place, which I am told, He would like better; but as it is thought, that the Business will suffer extreamly, if Yonge should continue at the War Office both from His want of Health, & other Circumstances, which you are no stranger to, I desire you

1. Henry Fox succeeded Sir William Yonge at the War Office in April 1746, but had hoped to succeed Winnington at the Pay Office, instead of Pitt. Richmond was still not speaking to him after his elopement with Richmond's daughter.

would let me know by the Return of this Messenger, what upon the whole you would wish, I should do, & I shall most certainly do what you desire. Sr Wm Yonge's wishes should be moved for, on Thursday by which time the Messenger may be back. If Mr Fox should be Secretary at War, care must be taken to prevent the disagreableness of being in ye same Rooms at Court, which I should hope, might be done, & as to the Affairs of the War Office, Nobody would imagine that you could transmit them with Mr Fox, the Duke, or in His absence, my Brother would, I am sure, make that easy. I can think of nothing but this Affair for this Letter. My Dear Duke, you know my Mind & in this Matter, you are Master of it. It is a most disagreable, but difficult Point to get over. I beg you would not show this Letter to any Body, but let me have your Thoughts as soon as possible. My Compliments to the Ds of Richmond & Lady Louise.

I am ever yrs

Holles Newcastle

325.   RICHMOND TO NEWCASTLE

Goodwood
Wednesday noon. 7 May 1746

My Dear Lord,

If Mr. Fox is Secretary of Warr, the world will never beleive I am so well with your Grace & Mr. Pelham, as you both are so good to say, & I know I am. by which you see at least my vanity will be hurt, & indeed it will be very disagreeable to me, however I must & will submitt to it rather than distress either of you, tho I would not putt it upon that foot neither, for I will never allow myself to thinke that either of you love Mr. Fox better than me, butt that this present difficulty arises purely from Young's incapacity of holding the place, & Fox being the only man that can succeed to it, because 'tis necessary he should have something better than Lord of the Treasury. As to the first I entirely agree with you, & your Grace & Mr. Pelham are the best judges of the last, 'tho still I should thinke Arundell[1] (if he liked it) or Harry Legge, would either of them make as good a Secretary of Warr. butt then Mr. Fox's pride will not lett him submitt to that, & in plain English his pride must be flattered preferable to myne, because he can & would speake against you & I never can nor never will vote against my princ-iples, which I am farr from being asham'd of, butt that must allways make Mr. Fox a man of much greater consequence than myself 'tho I beg you would not misunderstand me, for upon my honor I dont mean that either of you would personally preferr him to me, butt that you are really obliged to do it for the King's service, & for that reason I do submitt, however disagreeable it is to me. butt if Young should dye soon, or Donington[2] be turn'd out, which every good Whig in England thinkes ought to be, would you recommend Fox for either of their places ? & would he accept of it ? & give up the Warr office. I thinke he ought, & it would make me very easy. however I submitt the whole to you & I most sincerely am, & really beleive I shall allways have reason to be, my Dear Lord, Your Grace's ever faithfull affectionate, & most obliged humble servant,

Richmond &c.

have you heard that Fox himself sayes that he thinkes the Duke will not like him.

1.   Edward Howard, Earl of Arundel, died 1767, was the son of Lord Philip Howard, the younger brother of the 9th. Duke of Norfolk.
2.   George Bubb Dodington, 1691–1762, MP for Winchelsea, 1715–1722, for Bridgewater, 1722–1754, and for Weymouth, 1754–1761, was a supporter of the Opposition, but was made Treasurer of the Navy on the dismissal of Bath and Granville in 1744.

326. NEWCASTLE TO RICHMOND

Newcastle House
May 8th 1746

My Dear Lord,

I received last night your Grace's Letter of the 7th, which indeed concerned, & surprised me more, than any I ever received. I did not imagine, that after the long Friendship, which I have professed, and I hope shewed your Grace, and the Attention I have ever had, to do what lies in my Power, to deserve your Favour, and particularly, after I had ceased any Correspondence with Mr Fox, and had never seen Him, but at Court, or in the House of Lords, and then had seldom had any Conversation with Him, I could be accused by your Grace of any Partiality, or Preference to Mr Fox; especially, when, I am the only one, of all your acquaintance, that I know; that has made any, the least alteration towards Him, in His having offended your Grace. You can't think well of me, if you are not sensible, that this Imputation must set very hard upon me. When you left London and gave me your Commands upon this Affair, you was then so sensible of my Inclination to do any thing, that was agreable to you, that you only desired, it might not create any uneasiness between my Brother & I. Little did I think to find myself so soon put at the Head of those, who would do a disagreable thing to you, in favour of Mr Fox. I did not sleep, without sending to Sr Wm Yonge, and found, that He was so laid up, that there was no possibility of His going to Court, to make His Choice. I spoke fully to my Brother, and as I thought, in the rightest way for your Grace and myself. I also talked in a proper Manner to Lord Harrington, and I found by them, it was impracticable, to make any other Disposition, since Sr Wm Yonge, Lord Harrington said, could not on acct of His Health remain Secretary at War, and it was not thought right for other Reasons that he should. When this was the Case, I truly, and as a Friend & Servant acquainted your Grace with it, and engaged that nothing should be done 'till the Return of the Messenger. I offered you twice in my Letter, to do what you should desire me, tho' at the same time, were I worthy to advise, I am too sincere, not to own, I would not advise your Grace to do otherwise, than you have done. I am sure nobody meant either disrespectfully, or unkindly to your Grace. But as to myself, I am amazed your Grace should charge me, with any Part in this Transaction, except with my Endeavour to adjust to your satisfaction, if it could have been done conveniently with the Publick Service, in the H. of Commons. I hope I have sufficiently cleared myself of the Imputation, of doing any thing that could give you any Offence, or of having omitted anything, that was practicable in the present Situation, to bring about what you desired. I believe Mr Fox, does not think me partial to Him, or that He is Secretary at War by my means. I shall conclude with begging one Favour of your Grace, that for the future whenever you have any particular Commands in any thing that relates immediately to my Brother, you would yourself apply directly to Him, which would avoid many Mistakes and I think would be the most likely way to succeed, or at least for me not to incur your Displeasure. I must beg, & indeed very earnestly, that you would burn this Letter & show it nobody. I hope I have proved to you that if you had any Jealousies they were without Foundation, for I am incapable of being in any degree defective in my Friendship to you, being, as I have ever been my Dear Lord, unalterably

Holles Newcastle

327. PELHAM TO RICHMOND

May ye 10th 1746

My Dear Lord,

My Brother tells me that your Grace has some uneasiness att the necessary and indeed unavoidable measure of Mr. Fox's coming into the War Office. You know my gratitude and friendship for you Grace, would with me prevail more than any other personal considerations. But as things now stand, I don't see how it is possible to avoid taking this step. Yonge has already accepted the vice treasurership of Ireland, and had he not, his health, with many other unsurmountable objections, must soon have remov'd him; that being so, who have we in the House of Commons capable and of a rank in business to supply his place. It is not what Mr Fox desires for himself, and I can assure your Grace, had it been possible to have made any other disposition, I would on your account, have avoided any disagreable incident that could have happened to you. My wishes were rather to have heald the sore, than by irritation, to have provok'd it. I doubt not but Mr Fox's good understanding will make him avoid all unnecessary inter-course with your Grace, and if so, I can't but think it pretty indifferent to your Grace what particular office he has in the King's service. My Dear Lord, believe me there is no want of friendship, regard, and attention to you in this affair; it grieves me to think you can ask yourself that question. I must do my Brother the justice to say, I never saw more uneasiness in him than when he shew'd me you letter, for I can truly say, if there is one man in the world he loves better than another, it is, without exception, your Grace. I am not apt to make passion but I hope I am sensible of what is due to an open heart, and a constant uninterrupted series of friendship and goodness, that I have found in your Grace for many years, and I should be extremely concern'd if an event of this nature could make any variation in your Grace, towards whom I shall never vary; being with the greatest truth, affection, and esteem My Dear Lord Your Graces most obedient, humble servt

H. Pelham

328.   RICHMOND TO NEWCASTLE

Goodwood
Sunday 11 May 1746

My Dear Lord,

That my letter of the 7th gave you concern I dont wonder at, because, as I know you love me, you must feel for my distress, but I am astonish'd you say it suprised you by my accusing your Grace of partiallity or preferance to Mr. Fox. I beg my Dearest Lord that you would recollect my letter, & I am very sure you can not accuse me of any expression that tended towards that, so far from it, & for fear you should mistake me, I declared upon my honor in it, that I did not mean, that either you or your brother would personally prefer Mr. Fox to me, butt that you were really obliged to do the thing for the King's service. What could i say or thinke more ? I wish I had the talent of explaining myself better; butt upon my word I can not say more, at the time I am endeavouring to express what I am sure you would wish me to say & thinke upon the occasion. You see I give the point up, & declare I am convinced you have had no hand in it, further than is absollutely necessary for the King's service; & is not that the meaning of what you say yourself. I dont complain of your doing it, butt of my mis-fortune that it is necessary to be done. it affects me perhaps too much butt that is the unhappiness of my temper, which I cant help, & truth I ever have, & ever will tell you, 'tho it is to my own disadvantage, as it may give you a worse opinion of me; butt pray dont thinke I take any thing ill of you or Mr. Pelham, for upon my honor I do not, knowing the necessity of this measure. butt now I must tell you that I have not comply'd with your request of not shewing you letter to any body, for I have shewn them both to the Duchess of Richmond; for such a wife as she is, has a right to know every thing that personally relates to me or my familly, & I as truelly tell you that whenever your Grace, or any Minister have ever trusted me with a State or politicall

217

secret, I have thought myself as strictly tyed up in honor to keep it from her as from My Lord Gage, not butt I am so sure of her fidellity, that she might be entrusted with any thing, butt still I should be guilty of the highest breach of trust, as well as oath, if I was to divulge any thing you say to me of that kind to anybody. butt I have constantly told you that I as certanly will allways tell her what relates to myself. & now I am upon this toppick, I will as fairly tell you that these difficultys of myne have not arrisen from her, butt myself; so farr from it that when I told her last Sunday morning at Hampton Court that I beleived I had putt a stop to Mr. Fox's being Secretary of Warr, she blamed me for it, 'till I told her, I was in hopes that the consequence of it would be his haveing a more serviceable thing for his family, the Vice Treasurership of Ireland, & I must also tell you that when I shew'd her my last letter to you, she thought it too strong, 'tho she was as sensible as I was, that I did not mean to blame you. I hope my Dear Lord that I have fully explain'd myself to you in this letter, & that you can not have an reason to thinke I can entertain an unkind thought of you. indeed it is impossible, for I am for ever, most truely, & most affectionly Your's

Richmond &c.

I beg you would send me both Hawley's letters to me, & tell me what I shall answer to the last.

329.   RICHMOND TO PELHAM

Goodwood
Wed: 14th May 1746

Dear Sir,

I was in hopes that my first letter of the 7th & I am morally sure that my last of the 11th instant, to the Duke of Newcastle, must have convinced both him & you that I never took any thinke ill of either of you in my life not even the promotion of Mr Fox because (tho' it was & certainly will be every day excessively disagreeable to me) yett I was sure it was a necessary measure for the King's service, & that it was not by choice that either you proposed it or the Duke of Newcastle was inclinable to consent to it, & it was the necessity of the measure that concerned me & not your doing of it, but now I am upon that subject I will tell you plainly Dear Sir that if I was inclinable to take any thing, ill of any body it would be of you for not haveing ever once mention'd this affair to me, which I can't help thinking I had a claim to, both from the friendship I know you have for me & from that I may say it personally regarded me. However, I do not nor will not take it unkindly because I am very sure you did not mean it so, & it proceeded from your not thinking of it, having seen me butt seldom of late from my being so much out of town. I am vastly obliged to you for the many kind expressions in your letter. I am sure they are very sincere both from the honesty of your heart & the many years experience I have had of your's as well as of the Duke of Newcastle's friendship for me, & I do assure you that I am with the utmost truth & sincerity, now as much as ever dear Sir Your faithfull & affectionate humble servant

Richmond, etc

I fear this will draw some trouble upon yourself for you must give me leave to apply to you, in the Duke's absence, upon many little military affairs, with which I only troubled the Secretary of War formerly. One thing I do assure you gives me pleasure is that I hope & believe now, that the business of the army will go on much better than it has done of late.

330. RICHMOND TO STONE

Goodwood, near Midhurst
18. May. 1746

Dear Sir,

There can be no objection to Mr. Amyand,[1] butt that he does not live in the Country, butt as for Mr. <u>Hamilton</u> not <u>Hambleton</u> of Binderton, he is certanly a man of great property, tho butt little in this County, he is also in very high ranke at the barr, & lives a good deal in the Country here, within two miles of this place. he is also a very gentleman like man, & I recon him one of the best neighbors I have, & when he talkes to me he always talkes like a Whig; butt he is a Scotch man, & as such I would venture to say a hundred to one he is a Jacobite, butt I assure you even the Scotch themselves call him so, & I beleive there is no doubt about it, & that is the only reason why I did not name him; however if this is no objection to the Duke of Newcastle & Mr. Pelham, it is none to me, for I thinke the man has too good sense to act like a Jacobite in this Country espetially, 'tho he may thinke like one.

I desire you would send me the list of Justices of the whole County when tis settled, & a marke upon the new ones. I thinke my Lord Berkeley & my Lord Tankerville are not in the old list, if not, they should certanly be in this.

I am, dear Sir, Your faithfull humble servant

Richmond &c.

My love to Coll: Pelham.

331. STONE TO RICHMOND

Whitehall
May 20th 1746

My Lord,

I am charged by my Lord Duke of Newcastle to make His Excuses to your Grace for not having return'd you his thanks for your last kind Letter. He will not fail to do it soon, Himself; but, in the mean time, hopes, your Grace will accept them, thro' my Canal.

As to Mr Hawley's Letters to your Grace, which are in my Lord Duke's Hands, relating to His Recall from Scotland; my Lord Duke has received one from him to the same Purpose, which has been laid before the King; and Mr Hawley will have His Majesty's Leave to come away from Scotland, when his Royal Highness leaves that Country. But as no time is, as yet, fix'd for that, and as no person is pitched upon, to Command there, my Lord Duke has not yet wrote to Mr Hawley upon that Subject, but proposes to do it, by the next Express; and He will send your Grace Mr Hawley's Letters, when He writes to you.

My Lord Duke orders me to acquaint your Grace, in the utmost Confidence, that there is at present an Affair, of the greatest Consequence, under Consideration. A few days ago, Mr Trevor transmitted a paper, delivered by Mr D'Argenson to the Dutch plenipotentiaries at Brussels, containing the Conditions, upon which the French Court would come to an immediate Accommodation, which, all things consider'd, seem'd more moderate, than could well have been expected. They agree to restore all they have taken in Flanders, & Brabant; to renounce the Pretender, & His Posterity; to put Dunkirk into the Condition, it was in, in the year 1740; to acknowledge the Emperor,

---

1. Claudius Amyand, 1718–1774, MP for Tregony, 1747–1754, and for Sandwich, 1754–1756, Keeper of the King's Library, and later, Newcastle's junior under-Secretary.

& ce. But they propose that a perpetual neutrality shall be stipulated for the Low Countries; that we should restore Cap Breton; and that Tuscany should be given to D. Philip, to be possessed by Him, till He shall succeed to Naples & Sicily, which will happen, if the Prince of Asturias should die without Children. There are other Articles, But these are the most material. My Lord Harrington, my Lord Chesterfield, & Mr Pelham, are of Opinion, that these Conditions were such, as, in our present Situation, should be accepted, and that Mr Trevor should be empower'd to conclude upon that Foot, rather than run the hazard of the Dutch making up separately. But my Lord Chancellor, & my Lord Duke of Newcastle, (and I might add a greater Name), think the Article of the perpetual neutrality for the Netherlands so exceptionable, and the giving up of Cap Breton so great a Sacrifice, that they should not be yielded to, without some Negotiation; and they are also extremely unwilling, absolutely to conclude an Affair of such importance to our Allies without their Consent or knowledge; and are therefore for making a previous Communication of the whole to the Courts of Vienna & Turin. This is the present State of this great Question. How it will be determined, I cannot say; and I can as little say, whether every Day may not produce some Event, that may put it out of our power to obtain even these Conditions however liable they may be to just Objections. As soon as any thing is determined, my Lord Duke will not fail to acquaint your Grace with it.

Your Grace will see by the Gazette the position of the Armies in the Netherlands. The Hanoverians, it is hoped, will join the Army about the 28th O.S. We have nothing new from Scotland.

I am with the greatest Respect my Lord your Graces most obedient & most humble Servant

Andrew Stone

332. RICHMOND TO NEWCASTLE

Goodwood
25th May 1746

My Dear Lord,

I thanke you for your obliging letter by Mr. Stone, the contents of which I assume shall ever be a profound secret, & an affair of great consequence indeed it is; it convinces me of what I always thought, that the makeing of peace was a more difficult thing than the carrying on the warr. & since you have been so good as to communicate this affair to me, I'l venture to give you my, (very likely weake) thoughts upon it. The French restoring of all they have taken in Flanders & Brabant, is not in their power now, that is the restoring it in <u>statu quo</u> because they have demolish'd all those places that might annoy them hereafter. their renouncing the Pretender & his posterity is easily promis'd & as easily broke whenever they please. the putting Dunkirke into the condition it was in in the year 1740, is to be sure a good article, & would be a popular one. the acknowledgeing the Emperor &c, is also good, butt they know it must be a <u>sine qua non</u> of what powers there are against them. As for the perpetuall neutrality of the Low Countries, I am asham'd of my dullness butt I dont comprehend it. surely they dont mean that the States should agree to a perpetuall neutrallity, lett whatever disputes happen between France & England, if it is, it would be anulling that old treaty between the States & us by which they are obliged ever to assist us incase of invasions or rebellions. butt by Mr. Stone's saying <u>a perpetuall neutrallity for the Low Countrys</u> he can't mean what I have said, & then I own I dont understand it, so I beg to have it explained. As to the restoring of Cap Breton, it seems the strongest demand of all, & such as an administration will be less able to stand than any other. I own I dread the consequences of it. I thinke it would be attended with the worst here, & a rebellion in the plantations. for which reasons, I do actually thinke it should be the last possession

220

out of this Island that wee should ever give up. yett God knows as Mr. Stone sayes events may every day happen that may putt it out of our power to obtain even these conditions. however I own fairly the risque of agreeing to them seems to me greater, & more imediate, than any event that may happen after wee have refused them. I also thinke it would be wrong to conclude any thing without previously acquainting the Court of Vienna with it, & infamous to do it unknown to so faithfull an ally as the King of Sardinia. these are my thoughts upon the great affair, & such as they are I thought it my duty to lett you have them.

I must now trouble your Grace with an affair of not quite so much conseqence. Princess Emily[1] it seems likes the bay gelding I sent her & has order'd me to name my price which putts me under great difficulty. I do sincerely assure you I wish she would accept of it, butt that I dare not offer & saying she shall pay me what she will is saying nothing. I thinke he cost me threescore guineas, & I told Ligonier & Alt that if Prince William of Hesse had him he should certanly pay me fourscore, for he is certanly a twenty pounds better horse now than when I bought him, & Alt told me I should have what I asked. yett I really thinke tis too much for Her.R.H. to give for any horse. so I wish you would settle it, & not thinke it a hard taske, since you are very sure you will please us both by settling it entirely to her satisfaction.

I am, My Dear Lord, for ever, & most affectionately Your's
Richmond &c.

Dear Bury arrived here yesterday, & I shall keep him till Tuesday. I wish I had the letters Hawley sent to me that I might answer them.

As the Princess did me the honor to write to me about the horse & to send a very kind compliment to Taw, I am in doubt whether 'tis right to make an answer or not. so I send one with a flying seal for your perusall. if 'tis right I beg you to give it, if wrong, I hope you make the same use of it, as I hope you'l do of all Scotch petittions at present.

333.   NEWCASTLE TO RICHMOND

Claremont
May 31 1746

My Lord,

If you knew the constant Hurry, I am in, you would, I am sure, forgive my not having oftener troubled you with my Letters. I desired Mr Stone to acquaint you, with the important Consideration, that is now depending, relating to Peace, & War, and with the Difference of Opinion there was between us, relating to the Answer to be return'd to the Pensionary, upon the Counter project, given by Mr D'Argenson to the Dutch Ambassadors, & transmitted hither from Holland. I am persuaded by the Contents of your Letter of the 25th, that, had your Grace been here, you would have agreed in Opinion with my Lord Chancellor, & me, which was, not immediately to send Orders to Mr Trevor to conclude; to make our Objections to the Terms proposed; to endeavour to get more advantageous Conditions; to communicate the proposals to our Allies, the Queen of Hungary, & the King of Sardinia; and to be at Liberty to determine upon the Whole, according to the Answers, we should receive, and the then Situation of our Affairs : whereas what my Lord Harrington, and those, who agreed with Him, contended for, was, that Mr Trevor should have an absolute power to conclude, without the Communication, or knowledge of our Allies; and to give up Cap Breton; to consent to the perpetual neutrality of the Low Countries; to give Tuscany to

1.   Princess Amelia, daughter of King George II. Her letter to Richmond about the gelding on 20 May 1746, is Goodwood Ms. 1427 f.43.

Don Philip; for the restitution of Flanders, & the restoring Dunkirk to the Condition, it ought to be in, by the Treaty of Utrecht. The King was extremely of Opinion with my Lord Chancellor, & me, tho' Lord Harrington omitted no Arguments, to induce Him to agree with Him, by shewing the immediate Danger, to which Hanover might be exposed, by not consenting to these proposals. Had I time to explain the Consequences of a perpetual neutrality, I am persuaded, you would agree with me entirely relating to it. It is, in my Apprehension, the most prejudicial Engagement of them all; for, when once France, & Holland agree that the Low Countries shall not be attack'd, tho' the powers are at war, in other places, Holland will think, they have nothing to fear from France; & will never concern themselves in the Affairs of Europe; and without Holland, England can never do any thing upon the Continent; so that France will be absolutely Master of the House of Austria, the Empire, & Italy, and possibly, at last, of England also. These Reasons weigh'd so much with the King; and my Lord Chancellor, & I, were so firm in our Opinion; that my Lord Harrington thought proper to write an awkward Letter to Mr Trevor, in our way of thinking, to which we are now impatiently expecting the Answer.

By our last Accounts the French seem'd to be turning towards Mons, & Namur, rather than thinking to attack Marshal Bathiani. The ten thousand Hanoverians will join the Army in a few days; and it is said, that fifteen thousand Austrians more are far advanced on their March from Germany towards Flanders. By our last Letters from Scotland, the Hessians waited only for a fair wind to embark; The Prince of Hesse is expected in London, tomorrow night. I have been very desirious to send six, or seven Regiments to Flanders; which with the Hessians, might make up a Reinforcement of ten thousand Men; and in order to enable us to do it, I would have kept up the fifteen noble Regiments for some time longer. Nothing is yet determined; but I apprehend those Regiments will be immediately broke; and possibly some regiments may be sent to Flanders; But that is yet uncertain. The Duke is determined to see every thing finish'd in Scotland; He is march'd to Fort Augustus; & I suppose, will go from thence to Fort William. There are Accounts, that the Rebels are got together in or near Lochhaber to the number of about four thousand; that the Pretender is in the Isle of Lewis; intends to return to Scotland; & expects great Succours from France. I own, I am far from thinking it clear, that the Brest Squadron, which is now at Rochfort, may not be design'd for either Scotland, or Ireland. Admiral Martin has now a great Force with Him, & is order'd to go to Rochfort, to watch their Motions. He had eighteen Ships of the Line actually with Him, & four more very large ones are sent after him.

I am now to acquaint you with a Secret of the greatest Consequences. The Duke has had the good Fortune to sieze, in Sullivan's[1] or Sheridan's[2] Baggage, Papers of the greatest Importance. There is the Treaty between France & the Pretender's Son, sign'd by D'Argenson, & O'Bryan.[3] There is an Account of the whole Transaction with France; & also of the Offers made by the Jacobites in England to the Court of France, in August last; the Names of the Persons who were sent from England; and also the Names of the great persons in England with whom the Correspondence was held, which I may, in the greatest Confidence, acquaint you, were, the Duke of Beaufort,[4]

1. John O'Sullivan, died 1747, was Adjutant General to Prince Charles. Having fought in the French Army in the War of Austrian Succession, he assisted Lochiel in the capture of Edinburgh, 1745, and drew up the Jacobite army at Culloden. He escaped to France after the battle.
2. Thomas Sheridan, died 1746,, was tutor to Prince Charles and accompanied him throughout the campaign of 1745 and 1746.
3. Colonel Daniel O'Brien, titular Earl of Lismore, had been appointed by James, 'The Old Pretender', his Envoy and Representative to the Court of France in 1745.
4. Charles Somerset, 4th. Duke of Beaufort, 1709–1756, MP for Monmouthshire, 1731–1734, and for Monmouth, 1734–1745. A leader of the Tory party, he had expressed support for Prince Charles in 1745, but the Government took no action against him.

my Lord Barrymore,[1] my Lord Ossery,[2] Sr Watkin Williams,[3] & Sr John Hynde Cotton.[4] You may imagine, that this is the greatest Secret, of which however, great & good use must be made. The Duke has sent Brigadier Mordaunt, with the Royal, Pulteney's & Sempil's Regiments to Perth; & I think with a Design, that they should go to Flanders; which in all probability, will be the Case. Some time ago, His Royal Highness in a private Letter to me mention'd the Command in Scotland, after He should leave it. Hawley, he said, desired to be excused. He thought, it would be either Lord Albemarle, Lord Tyrawly, or Wentworth; tho' he had some Objections to them all, and that He would write further to me upon the Subject, but He has said nothing of it in his late Letters, and I have said nothing, but that the King would give Leave to General Hawley, to come away with His Royal Highness, and would be thinking of a proper person for that Command.

I must now acquaint you with my having executed your agreeable Commission to the Princess Emely; in which I have done for you, as I shall always do in every thing that relates to you, just as I would have done for myself. I told Her Royal Highness, that, since she liked the Horse, your Grace was too happy if she would accept it; that you had no Notion of making any price, or taking any thing from Her for it. Her Rl Highness accepted it very readily; & was extremely obliged to you for it, and has order'd me to return you a million of Thanks, which she will do Herself, and I am sure, in the most agreeable manner, when she sees you. The King comes to the House, on Tuesday or Wednesday next, to pass the Duke's Bill.

My Compliments to both the Duchess of Richmond & all good Company at Goodwood

Ever yrs, my dear Ld

Holles Newcastle

334. RICHMOND TO NEWCASTLE

Goodwood
Wednesday 4th June 1746

My Dear Lord,

I am most extreamly obliged to your Grace for your last most kind & obliging letter of the 31st of May, & I assure you I was farr from expecting so long & circumstantiall a one at such a busy time as this. as for my opinion of this important consideration now depending relating to Peace or Warr, you already know it by my last letter. & now you have explain'd the perpetuall neutrallity proposed by France, I am stronger than ever of your opinion, 'tho I should be glad to know if Luxembourg is included in this neutrallity. I am exceedingly glad that our Master, (who certanly when he divests himself of Partiallitys, knows the affairs of Europe better than most people) the Chancellor & Yourself have carry'd this very important point, & I long impatiently for the Pensionarys answer, & also what the Court of France say to it, for no man living wishes more sincerely for a tollerable peace than myself. butt indeed upon these terms I fear

1.   James Barry, 4th. Earl of Barrymore, MP for Stockbridge, 1710–1713, and again, 1714–1715, and for Wigan, 1715–1727, and again, 1734–1747, was one of the leaders of the Jacobites in England. His treasonable correspondence was made public at Lord Lovat's Trial, but no action was taken against him.
2.   Charles Butler, Earl of Ossory, 1671–1758, later 3rd. Marquis of Ormonde.
3.   Sir Watkin Williams, 1693–1749, MP for Denbighshire, 1716–1741, and again, 1742–1749, and for Montgomeryshire, 1741–1742, was a long time supporter of the House of Stuart, but no action was taken against him.
4.   Sir John Hynde Cotton, 1688–1752, MP for Cambridge, 1708–1722, and again, 1727–1741, for Cambridgeshire, 1722–1727, and for Marlborough, 1741–1752, was Treasurer of the Chamber, 1744–1746. A long time supporter of the House of Stuart, he was dismissed in May 1746, but no action was taken against him, after Murray of Broughton's disclosures at Lord Lovat's Trial.

this would be ever call'd a shamefull one, 'tho at the same time I own I fear that wee are not at present likely to gett better terms. I dont love <u>If's</u> tho God knows in time of warr most things depend upon them, butt <u>if</u> upon the reinforcement of the army in Flanders, a lucky stroke should happen on our side, every body must agree that a much more honorable & profitable peace may & would be obtain'd. I must now differ with you upon sending six or seven regiments to Flanders, as it is plain that this rebellion 'tho stop'd for a while is not yett over. consider if seven regiments were sent to Flanders, as many upon the american expedition, & all the Hessians gon, what wee have left in England ? even with the new raised Regiments, butt if they should be broke also; wee actually should not have enough left to quell a Westminster mob, & then depend upon it the moment the Duke leaves Scotland the rebellion breaks out again. & so it will at any time if wee have ever less than eight thousand men in that country. for it is now evident beyond contradiction that nothing butt force will ever keep that stinking corner of the Kingdome quiet; & since I am upon that Toppick I wonder to hear nothing of the Tyralls of those Peers or of any of the rebells. I hope that untimely compassionate argument of their haveing still some of our people prisoners does not prevail, for if it did all these villains would escape unpunish'd which I am sure every honest English subject would have butt too much reason to cry out loudely upon. & now as to the discoverys you have made by the papers seized in Scotland, it does not in the least surprise me, & I am glad to hear you say they are circumstantial enough to have great & good use made of them, which I hope you will all stick to, else indeed wee should deserve to be plagued with an other rebellion. I can easily conceive how secret this must be, butt I hope before it is blown (which at last all secrets are & will be) you will take care to secure those great English Jacobites. & now as to the command in Scotland I cant help saying something upon that head, I find H.R.H. has named three, the first viz Albemarle to be sure a very propper one I should thinke in every respect; butt I should doubt if he would like it, & whether it would be worth his while espetially if there is any chance of going to Flanders, butt he is the best judge of that himself, & I am very sure no objection can be made to him. Tyrawley also would certanly be a good man for the purpose, butt as most people only consider themselves I am persuaded he would decline it. butt begging the Duke's pardon I thinke Wentworth the most impropper man in the world. 'tho he certanly does not want sense, & has more military method than any man in the army; butt if you was to enquire into his character as to courage, I fear you will find people that will say as bad things of him as ever you heard say of Cope, & added to that he is reccon'd the most covetous wretch, & thorough Skin fleaer. I am sorry to say so much of man that never did me any injury, butt to you upon such an occasion I really thinke it my duty. I am very glad the Duke did not name me for I should certanly be very sorry to go, unless I had a chance of giveing them an other drubbing. which I own would give me vast pleasure. butt I do assure you I do not thinke myself fitt for it, & I beleive for that reason H:R:Hss very rightly did not name me. & I at the same time assure you that if I was fitt for it, & could do my King & Country any service, I would certanly accept of it, if offerd me, however disagreeable it would be to me. I am ashamed to trouble you with so long a letter, butt I could not help saying something upon that subject, & before I conclude I must tell you that Her R:Hss has made me very happy in accepting of my horse. all I beg is that your Grace in particular would keep clear of his heels, else I do assure you he may breake your leg, & perhaps her neck, neither of which you would like. I own between you & I, I should have gon up to have attended my Master to day to the house, for which I beg you to invent some excuse, & the Duke of Grafton has also hinted that I should come up for Prince Frederick,[1] butt that I am sure would

1. Frederick, Prince of Hesse.

be useless for I have not a servant in town, so can not entertain him in my house, & I dont know I could do any thing for him butt attend him to Mother Douglass or to a Lodge of Freemasons, which I assure you are his two highest pleasures, butt I had rather be excused, & consider that I have only this month of June to stay here, for I must be with Taw by the first of July in town, so I beg you would gett me excused any attendance if possible till then. Adieu my Dearest Lord, excuse the enormous length of this letter & be assured that I am & ever shall be most unalterably & affectionately Your's

Richmond &c.

Taw is much your's

335. RICHMOND TO NEWCASTLE

Goodwood
8 June 1746

My Dear Lord,
   Enclosed is a letter I have received from Sr Tho Robinson. & really what he desires in it, is so just & reasonable, that I could not help sending it to you. & I am sure you will grant his request which is only that of being heard before he is condemn'd, which I am sure is reasonable 'tho I know nothing of the affair.
   I am for ever, Your's

Richmond &c.

I am vastly impatient to hear from Holland.

336. STONE TO RICHMOND

Whitehall
June 17, 1746

My Lord,
   I am directed by my Lord Duke of Newcastle to acquaint your Grace, that he yesterday obtained His Majesty's Consent, (tho' not without some Difficulty) for the Irish Pension to my Lord Jersey;[1] which makes way for my Lord Halifax,[2] and the other intended Promotions, with which your Grace is acquainted, and which, I conclude will now immediately take place. My Lord Duke, at the same time, acquainted His Majesty with my Lord Gower's Desire to be made an Earl; which the King agreed to with the greatest Chearfulness, and in the most gracious Manner imaginable. My Lord Duke orders me to mention one Circumstance, which passed in this Audience, which He desires your Grace would communicate to no one, but my Lord Lincoln. His Majesty, talking of the necessity of sending some Minister of Rank to the Hague at this time, proposed to my Lord Duke, that He should go Himself, and upon His Grace's declining it, and in the course of the Conversation, mentioning Mr Villiers, as a person, He thought fit for the Employment, the King ask'd Him, whether He was sure Villiers would be govern'd by Him (the Duke of Newcastle) and not by Ld H——. Your Grace will judge by this, of the present Situation of things in the Closet. Mr Puiszeux,[3] the French Minister, is gone from the Hague, without either breaking off the

1. William Villiers, 3rd. Earl of Jersey, died 1769.
2. George Montagu, 2nd. Earl of Halifax, 1716–1771, a Colonel in 1745, was President of the Board of Trade, 1748–1761; Viceroy of Ireland, 1761–1763; 1st. Lord or the Admiralty, 1762; Secretary of State for the Northern Department, 1762–1763, and again, 1771: and Secretary of State for the Southern Department, 1763–1765.
3. Louis Philoxene Brulart, Marquis de Puysieulx, the French Secretary of State.

Negotiation, or having brought it to a final Conclusion. The French Court has proposed, that a Minister should be sent from hence, fully authorised, & instructed to treat: which I believe will be done, as soon as a proper person can be found. Mons. Wasner received, this morning, an Express, with the good News, which your Grace will find in the inclosed Gazette, from Italy.[1] This Victory of the Austrians is certainly of the utmost Importance, and there is the greatest Reason to hope, may be attended with the most happy Consequences.

I am with the greatest Respect My Lord your Graces most obedient & most humble servant

Andrew Stone

337. RICHMOND TO NEWCASTLE

Goodwood Carne's Seat[2]
24 June 1746

My Dear Lord,

I thanke you extreamly for the letter Mr. Stone wrote to me of the 17th past of which I communicated to nobody butt Linky as you desired. & I wish you joy of being so well in the Clossett butt I do suspect a snake in the grass. however whether there is one or no I am very glad of it, as I am sure it pleases you, & certanly (while it lasts) makes business go on the pleasanter. Surely this success in Ittaly will alter the tone of France, as it ought allso to alter the tone of our Minister whosoever he is that is to treat at the Hague. I own (inform'd as I am, & considering our good scituation at home as to the rebellion, & this great news from Ittaly,) I dont approve of treating at all at present, at least yett a while; till wee see a little what turn things will take in Flanders, 'tho to be sure the prospect there is butt a bad one. I am now at Carne's seat where wee have the whole american fleet & embarcation in full view; they gott all under sail this morning, the wind at S:E: which is the fairest that can blow & will be out of sight by the afternoon. Its a most beautifull prospect to the eye; butt a shocking one to my heart, for the reasons I gave you in my last letter, for I am sure they are too late to do any thing.

I troubled you last year about an affair which you promis'd to consider of, & give me your opinion upon, butt as I know the constant hurry of business you are in, I have avoided askeing you about it. however you will excuse me if I do now, it is about that Nova Scotia affair. I sent you all their papers, & you have them still in your hands, & their proposalls to me; you know I hate a job as much as you do yourself. therefore if the thing, that is the scheme in itself is not a reasonable one, & a right one I am sure I would have nothing to do with it. butt if it is right, reasonable, & practicable, I really dont see why I should not have the advantage as well as any other, & as it would be publick, for I do assure you I would not upon any account enter into any private or secret bargain, or agreement, which from its privacy allways denotes a job, & a dirty thing. so all I beg is that whenever you can spare half an hour, you would consider those papers & give me your opinion of it. The petition of <u>Beawes & Waldo</u> upon it now hangs in Council, for want of somebody to support it, which I would not do if it was wrong. & your opinion singly upon that is all I desire.

I am My Dear Dear Lord for ever & most affectionately Your's

Richmond &c.

1. The Battle of Piacenza on 16 June 1746 at which the combined French and Spanish army under Infante Don Philip fought an inconclusive engagement with the Austrians and Sardinians. The French and Spanish armies were separated and forced to retreat.
2. Carné's Seat, a house on the Goodwood Estate, and Richmond's favourite spot. The family were engaged in rebuilding it throughout the 1740s. It was built in the place where Monsieur de Carne, a faithfull retainer, had occupied a wooden cottage. It affords a fine view of the sea.

338. RICHMOND TO NEWCASTLE

Goodwood
25 June 1746

My Dear Lord,

I received by the last nights post the enclosed letter, from one who you see stiles himself <u>Comte de Tyrconnell</u> & claims acquaintance with me butt I am very sure I never knew him by that name; nor have I the least idea who he is, & as the letter is not dated I dont know where he is. by the seal he should be a Talbot, & as to the contents of his letter all I can say is that if he is not a natural born subject of the Kings, his request is a reasonable one, butt if he is a natural born subject of His Majesty's I should certanly hope he as well as all the rest of them in the same case would be hang'd. In which I cant help saying the government have been, or at least seem to have been somewhat dilatory as yett. The fleet strech'd out to sea yesterday in the afternoon & gott quite out of sight by half an hour after six in the evening. pray lett Mr. Stone tell me who this <u>Comte de Tyrconnell</u> is, Your's my Dearest Lord for ever

Richmond &c.

Since I wrote the above the whole Cap Breton Fleet are return'd to St Helens, being drove there by a very strong wind at S:W:

339. NEWCASTLE TO RICHMOND

Claremont
June 28th 1746

My Dear Lord,

Even your Grace, must excuse me in the great & disagreable Hurry, that I am in, that I am not so regular a Correspondent as, I wish to be. I have order'd Stone to send on the material Intelligence and Occurrences, that we have had. As to your Comte de Tyrconnel, I suppose He is a Descendant of the famous Lord Tyrconnel. He was taken wh the Comte de Fitz James, coming from Dunkirk & was with Him released on His Parole. He now wants to be discharged His Parole, paying His <u>Ransom</u>. That Affair is not yet settled. We know nothing of this Monsr Seigneur's coming, so I don't know what can be done in it. My Lady Fitzwilliam in France has wrote to me on ye same Subject. As to your Nova Scotia Affair, when you come to town, which I hear will be on Monday or Tuesday next, your Grace, Stone, & I will consider it, & then consider what it may be proper for you to do in it. As to Politicks, & public Affairs, Admiral Martin having not prevented the French Fleet from going out, we suppose they are gone to America, & probably to Cap Breton. The Lords of the Admiralty have therefore advised that Sinclair's Expedition[1] should be countermanded, which accordingly is done; or otherwise they apprehend, it would inevitably fall into the Enemy's Hands, who is so much superior to them. We hope Cap Breton is not in much Danger. If it should be taken, it would be the most unfortunate thing, that could happen, as it would both take from us the Means of making Peace, and of carrying on the War with the Approbation & Satisfaction of this Country. Our Difference of Opinion with regard to Peace, & War, or rather, to the Terms of Peace, & time of putting an end to the War, remains as it did. The great Turn in Italy, and the near Prospect of Marshal Bathiani's having an Army sufficient at least to defend itself, & the Republick of Holland, should, I should have hoped, have convinced every Body both here, & in Holland, that this is just not the Time, when we should accept those disadvantageous Conditions which France offer'd, when they thought themselves Masters every where, & able to overrun

---

1. The Hon. James St Clair's expedition intended against Canada in 1746.

all Europe, which is certainly not now the Case. But notwithstanding this, the Pacifick, or rather the submissive Disposition still prevails in the same Persons both here or in Holland. The Pensionary is running away to Spa for six weeks. Boys is to operate in His Room & your friend Trevor (who has been strangely mistaken of late) supposes the separate Peace will be made during the Pensionary's absence. If it is, I think we may at any time have as good Terms, as those now offer'd, (if we don't loose Cap Breton), & not have the Blame & Shame of making that —— Peace our own Act & Choice. My best Compliments to ye Ds of Richmond & Lady Emily.

I am my dear Duke Ever Yrs

Holles Newcastle

340. RICHMOND TO NEWCASTLE

Goodwood
29 June 1746

My Dear Lord,

I cant help sending you the enclosed from poor Albemarle. indeed his case is a particular one; I find he has wrote to you about it. I am well assured you will do what lyes in your power to help him, so I'l say no more to you about it. butt beg you would shew his letter to none butt those you may thinke it's necessary should see it, & then send it me back again. I have not heard from you this age. I shall be in town in a week, & am My Dear Lord Your Grace's ever faithfull & most affectte

Richmond &c.

your answer to Van Hoe[1] is a good one, pray keep up to it. When are our Scotch peers to be try'd.

341. PELHAM TO RICHMOND

Arlington Street
July 1 1746

My Dear Lord,

I understand by Lady Lincoln that we shall soon have the pleasure of seeing your Grace in London; it will be time enough then, I conclude, to settle the affair of Norton's son. I have some thing to say to you on that head, but if you think it not material, I shall obey your commands in your own way. As to Mr Rowley, I dare say, he was very well satisfied with my reception of him. Jack Hill[2] had told me the case before I received your Grace's letter, and as I knew him to be a friend of yours, I was very ready with an answer for him. Gordon has further leave of absence for the present, and if any alteration is made, your Grace may be assured Mr Rowley shall be taken good care of. I can't help repeating my thanks to you Grace and the Dutchess of Richmond for your kindness to Lady Lincoln. I hope and believe she will always deserve it; as to the Noble Earl, his merit is so conspicuous, that it would be injuring him to put the question. But to be serious, I am sure it will make you happy, when I tell you, that in my retired way from pleasurable life, they both give me as much comfort, as they do themselves in the more publick enjoyment of it. The French fleet is sailed; whither we don't know; but a resolution was immediately taken upon it, to stop

---

1. Abraham van Hoey, Dutch Ambassador to France. The Marquis d'Argenson had sent a letter to Newcastle via M. van Hoey, giving the French King's warning against excessive severity against the defeated Jacobites. Newcastle replied deploring the tone and content of the letter. See Goodwood Ms. 109 ff.866–870.
2. John Hill, 1716–1775, author and medical man, who conducted the *British Magazine,* 1746–1750, worked for both Richmond and Newcastle. He was a personal friend of Richmond, and a fellow mason.

Sinclair let the motions be what they will. I am sure your Grace was glad to hear that I have been out of order for a day or two; in the interim Totty is arrived, blames the measure, has startled some of our friends, and att present every thing remains doubtful. I hate contradicting measures every other day. Our last letters from Holland promise not well; the Pensionary is going to Spa and old Bugs is to transact the affairs of Holland with the Union during his absence. Greffier Gilles[1] is gone to Paris. As I dread a separation of the maratime powers, this forbodes ill. I conclude you have more sanguine accounts from another quarter, who, as he is better informed, I hope judges righter than I do. I must trouble your Grace with my compliments to the Dutchess of Richmond, and am with great truth and affection My Lord Your Grace's most obedient, humble servt

H. Pelham

342. RICHMOND TO NEWCASTLE

Whitehall
Thursday night [29 July 1746]

My Dear Lord,
Tho this is a busy time I must trouble you in favor of Mr. Hughes, as the thing may be gone if wee dont apply soon. I gave you some memorandums six months ago for him, & you was so good as to promis me you would try with the Chancellor to do something for him, & by the enclosed letter which I have just received from him, you'l see there is now an oportunity, if it is not gone. so pray Dear Duke lett me beg of you to do it if you can.
Your's for ever

Richmond &c.

343. RICHMOND TO NEWCASTLE

Whitehall
12 Aug 1746

My Dear Lord,
Enclosed is the petition of Ensign Barbier[2] for a Poor Knight of Windsor's place, which I spoke to you for the other day. I listed him myself 22 years ago, & should be excessively glad to provide for the poor old fellow, so I beg he may be putt upon the list, to come in as soon as possible.
Your's my Dear Lord most sincerely,

Richmond &c.

I beg you will not forgett Parson Hughes. indeed I have it at heart, & I dont know what I shall or can say to him, & severall of his freinds at Chichester if something is not done. so pray dont forgett it.

344. RICHMOND TO NEWCASTLE

Goodwood
Wed 20 Aug 1746

My Dear Lord,
Ld Bury was chose yesterday[3] not only without oposition, butt nem. con. for when

---

1. Jacob Gilles, the Dutch Ambassador in Paris.
2. Ensign Abraham Barbier had served with Richmond in the Horse Guards at Dettingen and at Fontenoy.
3. George Keppel, Viscount Bury, 1724–1772, Richmond's nephew was elected MP for Chichester on 19 August 1746. The vacancy was caused by the death of James Brudenell, Richmond's uncle.

he went round the town, he actually did not meet with one negative, & only three that said they would not promis him. even Lisbon Peckham told him, not only now butt at the next Genll Election he might depend upon his vote, & what interest he could make for him, & indeed the Tory interest at Chichester is as low as possible. I thought this account would please you, & now I must wish you joy of this great news from Ittaly,[1] & I should be obliged to you if you would lett either Mr. Stone or Mr. Ramsden,[2] send me the account, when you receive it, of the farther consequences of this Victory, which ought to be great & good, if the Austrian wrongheadedness, does not spoil it all, which I am eternally in dread of.

I shall be at Horsham on Munday, when I hope to meet either your Grace or Mr. Pelham, or both, & from thence I shall go to Lewes; I propose to have Mr. Steel for our Recorder,[3] it being absolutely necessary to have a lawyer, & I hear he has a good caracter, & am sure he is & ought to be a freind of your's, however I shant absolutely determine without your aprobation. so pray lett me have your answer to that particular, only yes or no by the return of the post. they are all most extreamly desirous of him at Chichester, & have a notion that he has a mind to settle there.

I am My Dear Lord, most sincerely & affectly Your's

Richmond &c.

Bury's respects to you

345. NEWCASTLE TO RICHMOND

Newcastle House
Augt 21, 1746

My Dear Lord,

I rejoice to hear that my friend Bury has been so unanimously chose at Chichester. It is a great Pleasure to me, & Honor to our County, to have Him chose for the first Town in it. You may imagine, the great & decisive Victory in Italy has given me the greatest Pleasure. We have no other Particulars, than those that were printed in the Gazette extraordinary, which I conclude you have had. I hope soon to send you word, that the best use has been made of it; for the King of Sardinia, & the Austrians, seem determined to follow their Blow, pursue the poor Remains of the French & Spanish Army, which are gone into the Riviera of Genoa, & are said not to amount to 20,000 Men; & from thence to make an Irruption into France, on the side of Provence. I send a Messenger tomorrow, with the strongest Instances to the King of Sardinia, to pursue this Scheme; & Orders to our Ships in the Mediterranean, to assist them on the Coast of Provence. Our Army in Flanders, I am afraid, will find itself under some Difficulties, by the taking of Huy, & the French thus possessing themselves of the Lower Meuse. Sandwich has begun admirably well in Holland and has had His Majesty's Approbation.

I am now to acquaint you with a Secret, that you will like; But I am sure you will keep it a Secret. It seems to be the Opinion of every Body that St. Clair's Expedition can go no further than Boston this year, and therefore I beleive, it will be thought improper to send it so far. I shall send Directions to Lestock, & St. Clair tomorrow to send their Opinion whether this whole Expedition might not be immediately employ'd to make a Descent upon some part of the Western Coast of France, viz, Bordeaux,

1. The Battle of Rottofreddo on 12 August 1746 in which the French army escaped from the pursuing Austrians and found refuge in Genoa.
2. Thomas Ramsden, Collector and Transmitter of State papers in the Secretary of State's Office.
3. Thomas Steele of Chichester became Recorder of the City after the death of James Brudenell on 9 August 1746.

Port l'Orient, Rochelle, Rochfort, &c., and they will be directed to sail no further than Plymouth, till further Orders. But this, as I said before must be kept a great Secret.

I am glad, you think of Steele for your Recorder. You cannot have a better Man, or a better Friend: and I hope he is a good Lawyer.

I am afraid I shall not be able to meet you at Horsham; but I hope to attend you at Lewes. There, & every where else, I hope, you know how much I am My Dearest Lord Ever most unalterably Yrs.

Holles Newcastle

My most affect Respect to our new Members.

346. RICHMOND TO NEWCASTLE

Wednesday night [10 Sept. 1746]

My Dear Lord,

I am sorry, I have engaged company for to morrow, butt so it is, & they are as follows

> Lady Albemarle[1]
> Miss Macartney
> Count Rosenberg[2]
> Monsr Wasnaar
> Lord Duncannon[3]
> Young Horace Walpole[4]
> Coll Lloyd

which with Taw, Em, & I, makes ten, & wee have a table of twelve so there is not only room butt youl be heartily welcome, if you care for it. butt do as you like, & yes or no upon a card will be a sufficient answer. I wish I could see you before I go to Kensington. or if you would carry me or lett me carry you. & apoint your time & place I should be obliged to you, for I am sorely hurt about this affair of Gentn of the horse, & I really can not bear such personall ill usage. to you & you only I open my heart, knowing it is to the best & dearest freind I have in the world, Your's for ever

Richmond &c.

347. RICHMOND TO NEWCASTLE

Whitehall
Fryday 12 Septr 1746

My Dear Lord,

Enclosed is Henry Berkeley's original warrant sign'd by My Lord Scarborough,[5] & also that for Jemmy Brudenell signed by myself. & from this circumstance alone it is plain that it is in my gift. The warrants for the avenar, Equerrys, Pages of honor, & Equerrys of the Crown Staple, being all in the King's gift are sign'd by the King, & only countersign'd by the Master of the Horse, whereas the King signs none for the Gentlemen of the horse. & I also send you a true coppy of the establishment, (the

---

1. Anne Keppel, wife of the 2nd. Earl of Albemarle, and daughter of the 1st. Duke of Richmond.
2. Philip Joseph Orsini, Count Rosenburg, the Imperial Envoy to the Hague.
3. William Ponsonby, Viscount Duncannon, 1704–1793, MP for Derby, 1742–1754, for Saltash, 1754–1756, and for Harwich, 1756–1758, when he became 2nd. Earl of Bessborough.
4. Hon. Horace Walpole, 1717–1797, MP for Callington, 1741–1754, for Castle Rising, 1754–1757, and for Kings Lynn, 1757–1768, was the third son of Sir Robert Walpole, and the famous memorialist and letter writer.
5. Thomas Lumley, 3rd. Earl of Scarbrough, 1691–1752, MP for Arundel, 1722–1727, and for Lincolnshire, 1727–1740, was Treasurer to the Prince of Wales, 1738–1751.

original being in the Green Cloth Office) & there His Majesty may see that the place of Gentlemen of the horse is plac'd after all those that are in his majesty's gift, & at the head of those that are in my gift, as all are that follow it. Enclosed is also a paper that Mr. Adams, the Clerke of the Stable, sent me, which is an account of what was done in this affair in the late King's reign. I hope all this will convince his Majesty that this employment is in my gift, & then that Sr Thomas Prendergast is in no ways an impropper person for it, for in the first place he is a gentleman, of a good tho' not a noble family, & as he is the nearest relation the Duchess of Richmond has except her unkle my Lord Cadogan, I thinke I cant be blamed for recommending him. I beg therefore you would lay all this before his Majesty to day & that I may know his answer, for I have it most extreamly at heart. I shall stay at home all day haveing taken a dose of phisick.

Your's my Dear Lord most affectly

Richmond &c.

Pray forgive all this trouble I give you. I am sure I am very much vex'd at the ocassion of it, & thinke it a little hard after nineteen years faithfull service.

Pray dont loose the Warrants, as they are originalls, & must be kept in the office.

I give you my honor there are no fees nor perquisites belonging to the place, nor no allowance butt when they travell with the King. so I do assure you the value is no more than the meer sallery which is £256 per annum, & four shillings in the pound out of that, & seven quarters in arrears.

348.   RICHMOND TO NEWCASTLE

Goodwood
19 Septr 1746

My Dear Lord,

Enclosed are two letters which I beg you would read, & shew to His Majesty if you thinke propper espetially that from the Duke of Somerset, which is really so plain & strong that I should be the dirtyest of men if I ever gave that point up. I am very very sorry to give you so much trouble butt I hope you will forgive it nay I am sure you will, for I know you love me, & I beleive you know I am & ever shall be My Dear Lord, Your faithfull humble servant,

Richmond &c.

I have received two most pressing letters from the Bp of Worster[1] & Arch Deacon Ball, about the Deanery of Worster, & I cant help thinking that it will look very odd for you to refuse the Bishop's recommendation of a Dean, when it is certanly, for one of the most zealous freinds you & all of us have in the County of Sussex, & a man of irreproachable life & character. I cant butt remember both you & your brother said it was too high a step for a Country parson; butt consider he is archdeacon & might have been Dean of Chichester. I beg pardon for saying so much as it looks like giveing you advice, which may be impertinent in me, butt, I own the thing strikes me so much that I cant help it.

If his Majesty insists upon giveing it to one of his own Chaplains, I hope it will be to Blomer who is the oldest he has; & I thinke it a little hard that he has never had any thing, if it was butt upon my account.

Pray dont be angry with me, for I have your freindship much more at heart than the Church of England.

---

1. Isaac Maddox.

349. RICHMOND TO NEWCASTLE

Goodwood
21st Septr 1746

My Dear Lord,

In the letter I wrote to you last post I forgott to send you the enclosed[1] which is an authentick coppy, butt I am upon honor not to tell the name of the writer of the letter nor the person writ to, butt I know enough of them to beleive the contents true, & very melancholy ones they are. I shall be in town on tuesday night, shall sett very long at the board of Genll officers on Wednesday, butt shall be glad to dine with you on Thursday, either at newcastle house, the Duke of Grafton's, or at my house, which you like best, only be so good as to lett me know on Tuesday night.

Your's for ever,

Richmond &c.

350. RICHMOND TO STONE

Tuesday night [?23 Sept 1746]

Dear Sir,

I beg pardon for being so often troublesome to you in one day, butt upon looking over some papers I found the enclosed from my cousin the Countess of Newburgh[2] who is Radcliffe's wife. it is about a servant whose name is <u>Vaughler</u>,[3] I beg you would acquaint the Duke of Newcastle with it, & (if it is right) that he may be sent back to France as a servant; & I beg (if it is right to grant it) that it may not be forgott,

Your's most sincerely

Richmond &c.

If you have any materiall news, be so good as to direct to me, at Robt Nugents, Esqr[4] at Gossefield near Braintree in Essex. & pray putt the Duke of Newcastle in mind of Monsr Le Comte de Mirabell.

351. RICHMOND TO NEWCASTLE

Goodwood
12 Octr 1746

My Dear Lord,

You was in such a hurry when I saw you last that you would not give me time to tell you what the Bishop of Worster say'd of <u>my</u> freind, & I assure you, <u>your</u> good freind, Archdeacon Ball, which in justice to him I must inform you of, it is since you was so good as to putt him in the list you lay'd before the King as reccommended by the Bishop of Worster, he wish'd you would inform his Majesty of the reasons of his recommending him, which to save myself the trouble of repeating you will find in the second page of the enclosed letter from the Bisp to me, & I earnestly beg you would read it, & I hope you will not thinke it impropper to repeat to the King, at least from the Bishop, & I beg then you would return me the letter, & tell me what answer I should make to it.

I am my Dear Lord, for ever, Your's

Richmond &c.

---

1. An anonymous letter from the army in Maestrick complaining about the English Army's ill-treatment at the hands of the Austrians.
2. Charlotte Radcliffe, Countess of Newburgh, 1694–1755, married Charles Radcliffe, Earl of Derwentwater, like Richmond, a grandson of King Charles II.
3. Vaugler, a prisoner, was formerly Valet de Chambre to the Countess of Newburgh.
4. Robert Nugent, 1709–1778, of Gosfield in Essex, was MP for St Mawes, 1741–1754, and again, 1774–1784, and for Bristol, 1754–1774.

352.   NEWCASTLE TO RICHMOND

Claremont
Nov. 8th 1746

My Dear Lord,

Tho' I have desired Stone to write to you, to lett you know that the King comes to London on Tuesday, and the Birthday is to be kept on Thursday, I could not however forbear giving you myself some Account of what has passed since you left London. I have had several Conversations with our Master upon the Lieutenancy of Ireland, and on Thursday got him to consent to Lord Harrington, tho' with some difficulty. I put it, upon the single Point, which indeed weighed with me: the necessity of making my Brother easy, which could be done no other way, but by making Ld Harrington Lord Lieutenant. At last, I succeeded, & never was more pleased in my life, for I think I have, by this, and by refusing to take the Northern Province, tho' pressed to it in the strongest Manner, convinced my Brother that I have no views, but in conjunction with Him, and that I will refuse the most flattering offers, if they are any way disagreable to Him. Give me leave my Dear Duke, to say, I can do no more. I am not sure, that every Body, would have done so much. However, I have the satisfaction to tell you, that I have all, that I expected from it. My Brother is thoroughly sensible of my regard to Him, & I beleive in better humour with me, than He has been these four or five years last past. My new Collegue[1] goes on well, supports in every thing, the Measures I have advised, is complaisant in the Closet, and reasonable and submissive out of it. I really beleive He will do nothing wrong. I have at present one Advantage; all my old Friends will be partial to me, which in Lord Harrington's time, was not the Case. I have this day had in a trifeling Instance, a great Mark of the King's steadiness & Predelection to me. My Brother has His doubts about my new Collegue, & that will in the main contribute to his doing right, & indeed at present I see no sign of the Contrary. Lord Greenville talks much of the Impossibility of Chesterfield's, & my, agreeing long. I have told Chesd of it, & I hope we shall Both resolve to disappoint Him. We met last night about the Speech. We all agreed, & it will be a very good one. I think <u>Linky</u> should move the Address. Pray tell Him so & shew Him this Letter. You will forgive me if I beg you would be in Town, to go on Tuesday with the King from Kensington to St. James'. May I trouble you wh my Compliments to the Dutchess of Richmond, & Lady Amely, not forgetting Harcourt & Linky.

I am with the truest affection My Dearest Lord ever Yrs
Holles Newcastle

P.S. If Bury is with you, remember me to Him.

353.   STONE TO RICHMOND

Whitehall
Novr 8th 1746

My Lord,

I am order'd by my Lord Duke of Newcastle, to acquaint your Grace, that His Majesty has declared His Intention to return to St James's on Tuesday next, the 11th, and that the Birthday is to be kept on Thursday next, the 13th. My Lord Duke con-

---

1.   Philip Dormer Stanhope, Earl of Chesterfield, 1694–1773, became Secretary of State for the Northern Department in October 1746, in succession to Lord Harrington, who became Lord Lieutenant of Ireland.

cludes he shall have the Pleasure of seeing your Grace in Town, on Tuesday next, as He supposes your Grace will be at Kensington to attend His Majesty to St James's.

My Lord Harrington is to kiss the King's Hand on Monday next, for the Lieutenancy of Ireland.

I am with great Respect My Lord Your Grace's most obedient & most humble servant

Andrew Stone

354. RICHMOND TO NEWCASTLE

Goodwood
30th Novr 1746

My Dear Lord,
  You will not take it amiss I hope that I have wrote to the Duke, to thanke him for his goodness to Dear Bury, & at the same time to beg his protection for Albemarle that he may go with him & not remain in that sinke of the Earth Scotland. I could have added one thing butt thought it was not propper 'tho I fear too true, which is that the only reason he is liked in Scotland, is because his hands are tyed up from doing what they would not like him so well for, if they were free. you may fancy him in an agreeable way there butt indeed it is farr from it, & you know I allways was of opinion that if the Commander there had not as full power as the law would admit of, & if he had not the attention as well as the confidence of the administration here, I mean perferable to the Duke of Argile, the President, & the Justice Clerke, every thing in that cursed countrey would be in as bad (nay, after such a rebellion) in a worse way than ever. you will have nothing butt Jacobites encouraged, the very few freinds to the government there discouraged, & your troops ill treated, all which, with the very great lenity, & in my opinion ill timed mercy, to so many notorious rebells, will certanly bring about an other rebellion. I know you will be angry with me, butt I cant help it, 'tis the spirit of true patriotism that workes upon me, so you must forgive me. besides that I thinke the sincere & mutuall freindship that is between us, obliges us both to speake our minds freely to one another. my heart was full & it has now had its vent, so I shall conclude with assureing you that I am with the truest, esteem, affection & unalterable freindship my Dear Lord, Your ever faithfull humble servant
Richmond &c.

As you have forgott to speake to the Chancellor for a Prebend of Rochester for Mr. Hughes, which I gave you a memorandum of six months ago, I have ventured to write to him myself, so pray add one word for it. he is really a good man, & you can not imagine how many people of the best sort in Chichester, I shall oblige in it.
Dr. Bayley of Havant,[1] has just been here & tells me that Dr. Brady chaplain to the garrison at Portsmouth is dying, & I have recommended Dr. Bayley, really as a good phisician, & with no other view, to Sr Philip Honywood, 'tho it is in the King's gift, yett I suppose I really thinke the Governors recommendation should be taken, so I hope you will be so good as to give way to it.

---

1. Dr. George Bayley, was the father of Dr. John Bayley of Chichester, and brother in law to John Carter, five times Mayor of Portsmouth. He was Richmond's candidate to succeed Samuel Brady as Physician to the Garrison at Portsmouth and the Hospital at Forton. In fact, when Brady died in April 1747, he was succeeded by Dr. George Cuthbert, 1693–1771.

355. NEWCASTLE TO RICHMOND

Newcastle House
Dec 4th, 1746

My Dear Lord,

I sent your letter to the Duke last Tuesday, which I extreamly approved, & was as all yours are, very proper, & full of Goodness & Sincerity to your Friends. Bury has all, He can wish, & I hope Albemarle will succeed in every thing that He can desire. The Point of his going to Flanders is over; the King has consented to it. I hinder'd Wentworth's being sent there, as I thought it would prevent Ld Albels going. The Duke tells me, Ld Albemle wants to go to Flanders, & remain Comr in Chief in Scotland, & Huske to be ye Commanding Officer. That I doubt is impossible. I find the Duke intends Wentworth for Scotland, But nothing is to be done 'till the Duke comes back. I hope you will always write to me, in the same kind, & confidential Manner, that you did in your last letter. I really love to be told kindly of my Faults by my Friends. As to Scotland, I am as little Partial to it, as any man alive. I believe they are not better pleased with me, than wth other people but however, we must consider that they are within our Island, & have the Benefit of our Laws, & I hope they will soon have the benefit of no other. Albemarle has all the powers any Commander-in-Chief ever had, & if He desires more, He shall have them. I do believe, it is the use He makes of the Power He has, & not the want of more Power makes Him so beloved. But enough of that; our Affairs abroad go well every where. The Queen of Hungary aproves of our Plan & engages to have 60,000 Men in Flanders, & as many in Provence, where we expect to hear every hour, that the Combined Army is. The Dutch I think will furnish 40,000 Men. If so, we shall have in March, I hope, the Duke of Cumberland at the head of 140,000 Men, & with that Force He will be able to talk to Messieurs les Francois. We have a little dispute amongst ourselves, about the North American Expedition. If it does not go, all the Zeal & Warmth for the War will, I am afraid, cool, if not vanish quite. In this, I know you are against me. I had a long & good Conversation <u>alone</u> this day wth His Majesty. I think He is not at all alter'd towards me. He asked me several Questions about my new Collegue, which I answered very freely, & in general, very satisfactorily. I had an Opportunity of speaking about Mr. Fox's being put, & His children into Ld Ilchester's Remainder. The King opposed it very much at first. I told Him, I knew it would not be disagreable to you, and at last upon my pressing Him, He consented to it. Dr. Bayley was wth me this morning. I spoke to Honeywood for him. He said He had thoughts of another, but I hope He will be for our Man. I suppose you know two Troops of Horse Guards are to be broke & all the Regts of Horse except <u>The Blues</u> sent to Ireland or made Dragoons, a saving of 62 thousand pounds per ann, for ever, according to what has been practised ever since ye Revolution.

My Compliments to ye Ds of R. Ever Yrs.

Holles Newcastle

356. RICHMOND TO NEWCASTLE

Goodwood
16th Decr 1746

How can you thinke My Dear Lord that I could ever take any thing ill of you, particularly your first letter of the 8th which as well as the last of the 13th was most excessively kind, as indeed every letter you have ever wrot to me in your whole life has ever been. wee now & then may differ a little in our home polliticks, butt essentially to disagee is impossible as wee most certanly mean exactly the same thing. I am glad you aproved of my letter to the Duke, & I agree with you that Dear Bury who is now with me & presents his respects to you has all he can wish, & I am sure both he & his father

236

as well as my self have the highest obligations to you. I am glad Albemarle is to go to Flanders, & I hope Wentworth will do well in Scotland, tho I doubt it, for you know he is no favourite of myne, butt indeed he or whoever is there must be supported by the administration here, for consider what a nest of rogues such a man is sent to. The execution of Radcliffe[1] I am sure must be aproved of by every freind to this government. I wish the Att Genll had not forgott him & that it had been done imediately upon the receit of Van Hoe's letter, however better late than never. I hear Old Puff and the master are in mourning for him, surely that's ridiculous. I fancy my relations would not mourn for me if I was to be hanged which I am vain enough to thinke I certanly should be if the Pretender came in.

& now as to any american expedition you know how averse I am to it, for this single reason that wee certanly have not troops enough for that, Flanders & our security at home, for I am convinced that the french will most certanly repay our last visit, if wee have not a force at home to prevent it. & I thinke an army here is of much more consequence than in Flanders, & surely an american expedition is the last of these three services, 'tho I certanly should like it, if you had wherewithall, butt I am very sure you have not & pray recollect this was last year your own way of thinking; & surely as to an invasion things are not so very much alter'd, 'tho it may be a little, butt I am sure t'would be wrong to tempt them to it, after the provocation has been given.

Mr. Pelham's reduction of the cavalry I thinke must be aproved of by every body butt those that are imediately affected by it, & his scheme of raising four millions meeting with no oposition is greatly for his honor. So much for home polliticks: & as for your foreign affairs they are certanly in a good way, & you know I never differ'd with you in them. God knows my aproving or disaproving is of very little consequence, butt as you are so good as to write to me so fully upon these things, I should be to blame if I did not tell you my sentiments poor as they maybe.

I am glad Dear Linkys affair goes on to his satisfaction, I wish it was done & that he was here, for wee have glorious sport. I am also mightily pleased to hear things go on well with you in the Clossett, I am sure it does so in the house of Commons, & indeed you must forgive me for saying if it goes well between you & your brother, it will go well every where. I am glad the King has consented to Fox & his children being putt in to Ld Ilchester's[2] remainder. & now My Dear Duke I must acquaint you, & you are the first that I have acquainted with it, that I thinke wee have agreed with Ld Kildare,[3] & our Lawyers are going to worke directly. he settles 3000 a year jointure. butt as I have not yett acquainted my relations with it, I would not yett have it mention'd, & indeed it is my duty to acquaint the King with it before the Publick, besides as nothing in this world is absollutely sure 'till done, I hate to publish these sort of things.

I thanke you for your goodness to Dr. Bayley, & little Hughes, & I have received the most polite, freindly, & truely kind letter that's possible from the Chancellor upon it, 'tho he can not do the thing I imediately desire for Hughes, yett he is so kindely disposed that I flatter myself he will when he has an oportunity. I am actually ashamed for the length of this letter, butt your reproaches in your last to me have drawn it upon yourself. Taw & all the company here are much your Grace's humble servants, butt no one living more truely & affectionately so, than My Dear Lord, Your ever faithfull slave

Richmond &c.

---

1. The Earl of Derwentwater was beheaded on 8 December 1746 on his 1715 conviction.
2. Stephen Fox, 1st. Lord Ilchester, 1704–1776, MP for Shaftsbury, 1726–1734, and again, 1735–1741, and for Hindon, 1734–1735, was the elder brother of Henry Fox.
3. James Fitzgerald, 20th. Earl of Kildare, 1722–1773, had proposed to Richmond's daughter, Lady Emily Lennox, in November 1746.

357. NEWCASTLE TO RICHMOND

Newcastle House
Jany 1st 1746/7

My Dear Lord,

I am really ashamed for not having sooner returned you thanks for your last kind letter, and congratulated you upon every thing being agree'd for Lady Amaly's Marriage. I beg you would make my Compliments to the Dutchess of Richmond upon it, & that you would be Both assured that nobody can more sincerely wish all sorts of Happiness and Prosperity, to you, & yours than myself. We are in hourly Expectation of His Royal Highness, who was to leave Holland as yesterday, after having finished every thing to His satisfaction. The Dutch agree to furnish 40m. Men. Their <u>Resultat</u> was to be settled as last Monday, & our Convention ready to be signed by all Parties. Every thing goes on in Provence in the most successful manner. General Brown does not doubt being able to support & maintain himself there. Belisle, at present retired before Him & we suppose is now under the Cannon of Toulon. We are assured that the Commotions at Genoa, shall not obstruct or retard our Operations in France, & indeed I believe they will soon turn upon themselves, for the Austrians are marching from the Milanese, &c. to Genoa, which I suppose, they will soon be Masters of again. We are very impatient to hear what the Alteration of the Ministry in Spain, will produce. Keene was very sanguine about it, tho' the French still give out that they are promised 25m. Men from Spain to join Belisle's Army. By all our Accounts the King of Prussia will not engage against us, but remain quiet, so that, I really think the next Campaign has a most prosperous look, & I cannot but be a little vain that things are in this Situation. You will be glad to hear, that in all probability the Expedition to N. America, as designed last year, will not go forward. I am far from opiniating any thing that does not appear to me to be right for the Publick, taking all Considerations together. I had last night Admiral Warren[1] & the Duke of Bedford with me. We talked the whole Affair over, & Ad Warren is strongly of Opinion, that except we can have a force of Regular Troops, & North Americans amounting to 30,000 Men, it will be in vain to attempt the Conquest of Quebeck & Canada, & such a Force I doubt is impracticable to be got at present. If this comes out so, we shall probably only send two or three Regiments to fortifie & secure Nova Scotia, and Cape Breton. But as nothing is yet determined I beg you would say nothing of it. My best wishes of Happy years, etc. to all the good Company at Goodwood & Charlton. My humble respects to the Cofferer. I lament the Frost which is come so unluckily. Could the King have foreseen the Frost, He certainly would have finished the Cofferer's Affairs long ago, that he might have hunted all December. I drank your Health at Tankey's today, wth my good Lady & old Puff.

I am my dear Lord most affectly & unalterably Yrs.

Holles Newcastle

358. RICHMOND TO NEWCASTLE

Goodwood
2d Janry 1746/7

My Dear Lord,

It is now my turn to complain, for it is now a fortnight since I wrote last to you, butt I know you have so much business that I can easyly conceive you have not had time.

---

1. Admiral Sir Peter Warren, 1703–1752, MP for Westminster, 1747–1752, commanded the fleet at the Capture of Louisbourg, 1745. He was second-in-command to Anson at the victory off Cape Finisterre, 1747, and succeeded him in command of the Channel Fleet.

yett I wish I could have had your answer about Orme, for he presses most prodigiously to declare & engage the government interest at Arundell for him,[1] & to which as I told you before I could not nor would not make any answer without you. had it been a common house of Commons affair, I should only have troubled Mr. Pelham about it, butt as it is a Sussex affair your Grace must decide it. & now I am upon Sussex affairs I must indeed putt you in mind of one in which I thinke all our honors as well as our credit in this part of the County is engaged, I mean for Arch Deacon Ball, who you know has been more serviceable to our interrest here than any one Clergyman in the County, & I wont reproach you that a man has been prefer'd to him for serving a half Whig interest in oposition to an old establish'd one. however Ball is extreamly reasonable & I assure you does not complain, butt askes in my opinion a most reasonable thing, which I thinke you can easyly do, & I beg you would. it is to recommend him to the Bishop of Winchester[2] for a Prebend in his Cathedrall. The Bishop he sayes has a great many there, & surely so much has been done ('tho I really thinke not too much) for the Hoadley family, that he can not refuse it.

& now I am so deep in the Church, I must aske an other thing of you, which is not a favor, for I do not aske it, butt an answer, it is whether you ever spoke to the Duke of Grafton for Dr. Dayley[3] to be a King's Chaplain. The Bishop of Chichester sayes that he spoke to you & you promis'd him you would. & the good man is shy of speaking to you again for Dr. Dayley who you know marry'd his niece for fear of being troublesome to you, so the Dr. has beg'd me to aske you only if you have spoke, & if he is to flatter himself with any hopes. So I beg an ostensible answer. I am sorry to give you so much trouble butt there is no avoiding it whilst an interest is to be kept up in the Country.

Wee are all lock'd up here with a confounded hard frost, the Cofferer is extreamly well, butt I thinke a little tired of our company last night for all Goodwood dined & sup'd yesterday at Charlton. & he'l have more of us, for they all dine here to day; I propose being in town about the latter end of next week, & am My Dear Duke, with the greatest truth & affection, for ever & unalterably Your's

Richmond &c.

I wrote you an account of our agreement with my Lord Kildare, near a fortnight ago, which was two posts before I had acquainted any body with it, even before the Dss of Richmond had wrote to her mother. butt as I told you then, I shall not publickly own it 'till I have myself acquainted our Master with it, which is decent to do before wee sign & seal.

359. NEWCASTLE TO RICHMOND

Newcastle House
Jany 3rd 1746

My Dear Lord,

Tho' I troubled your Grace with a very long letter last post, yet I would not omit the first Opportunity, of making up for my neglect in forgetting to give you an answer about Orme. I spoke immediately to my Brother upon it, who begs you would not give Him any encouragement or Assistance, for Reasons you may easily guess. As to Ball, I

---

1. The chief interest at Arundel was that of the Lumley family, Earls of Scarbrough, and it had always returned government supporters until the election of Garton Orme in 1741. He continued to sit for Arundel until 1754, in spite of Richmond's attempt to unseat him in 1747.
2. Benjamin Hoadley, 1676–1761, was Bishop of Winchester, 1734–1761.
3. Rev. Thomas D'Oyley, Prebendary of Selsey, 1743–1744, and of Bishophurst, 1744–1770, was Chancellor of the Diocese of Chichester, 1747–1770, and Archdeacon of Lewes, 1751–1770.

wish Him most exceedingly well, provided a promise from the Bishop for Him of the Chancellorship which was the thing He then asked, & would in conjunction with you, have made Him Dean of Chichester had He liked it, so that I don't think he has any reason to complain, tho' He has yet had nothing directly from us. I will with all my heart, join with you in recommending him to the Bishop of Winchester. Alone I despair of success. I never asked but one favour of Him in my life, which was only a Living of 70l pr ann., which He not only refused me, but told me He was engaged for those Livings, that would probably fall in His time. As to Dr. Doyley, the Bishop of Chichester spoke to me that he might be King's Chaplain. I advised Him to speak to ye Duke of Grafton, knowing that was the likely way to succeed. I did tell Him, I should be glad to assist, & join wth Him, which I am very ready to do, but cannot take it singly upon myself. I am now pressing my Ld Duke, for Dr. Hume,[1] who educated the Cofferer & that was a Service to the State, as well as to me. He will tell you, how necessary it is that Hume should be made Chaplain immediately, but as to Dr. Doyley, I did not press the Bishop of Chichester to perform a Promise He had actually given me, of the Living of Rodmel, near Lewes, which He has given to Dr. Doyley. So I think, He has no reason, to be dissatisfied wh me, tho' I own I have not spoke to the D. of Grafton, nor did I understand, that I was to move first in it, or at least, not without being again spoke to, by the Bishop. You will think that I am much upon the Defence & Justification. I don't mean by that that I am not ready, always to do what you would have me, but only to state those Cases as they really are. The Duke arrived yesterday morning in the highest Spirits imaginable, having succeeded in every thing. The convention is signed & Dutch, He says, forwarder & _warmer_ than _most_ of us, are here. In short things can't go better there. And, who was always of opinion, to say, at least, what they would do? We have no News from Provence, Genoa or Italy. The French I think have got ye better of a trifling party, in Provence, of no consequence. My best Compliments to the Ds of Rd & best wishes to Lady Emily, _&c._ My Respect to the Double Place Man, the Cofferer. I am sorry, Bury was not in Town yesterday, to receive the Master.

I am my Dear Duke, every Day, more than other. Yrs most affectly
Holles Newcastle

360.   RICHMOND TO NEWCASTLE

Charlton
1st Febry 1746/7

My Dear Lord,

When any thing is upon my spirits you know I must out with it, I am uneasy about my nephew Berkeley, & I beg pardon for saying upon your account as well as my own, for I told him by your express direction that you would do what you could to help him; 'tho certanly the King would dispose of the bedchamber as he pleased; he also asked my assistance which God knows is nothing, however I told him that he might depend upon what was in my poor power, for which reason you see I could by no means mention the bedchamber to My Lord Cardigan, altho I thinke as you do that the King will not give it to Lord Berkeley. & you'l forgive me, my Dear Lord for saying it, how can you propose Cardigan ? & much less my Lord Ashburnham, after what you bid me say to my Lord Berkeley, before you have mention'd his name to the King. If then you have a positive negative, I wish you would lett him know it, & then certanly you are at liberty to help who you please; butt indeed I wish you would mention him first, & mention it in the right true way, which is that (at least I understand it so) he is desirous

---

1.   Dr. John Hume, successively Bishop of Bristol, Oxford and Salisbury.

of getting quit of the Prince's party, & he can mean nothing else by asking it. So I wish his Majesty would consider whether it would be prudent at this time to reject the offers of a man that can certanly do him some service, & in effect the refusing him is makeing the Prince of Wales a present of him & Glostershire; & I assure you that hurts me much more than the young man's disapointment, 'tho I assure you that neither is no small concern to me. Pray thinke of it, & if you see it in the same light as I do, I am sure you will mention it in the manner I propose, whatever you thinke the event may be. I know your difficultys at this time; & am sorry there are so many, butt lett me putt one thing to you, supposeing you should succeed for my Lord Ashburnham, what will Berkeley thinke, after he told me that he suspected you intended to recommend Ld Ashburnham prefereable to himself, & that I assured him, you did not, butt would help him Lord Berkeley preferable to any body, 'tho you thought it was not in your power. I beg a thousand pardons for saying so much upon this, butt I could not help it as you employ'd me as your Messager, & that I am very sure I only repeated your own words to him; so as I am personally concern'd you must forgive me.

I am my Dear Dear Lord, for ever & most affectly Your's
Richmond &c.

I have wrote about Arundell affairs to Mr. Pelham, haveing troubled you enough with this long letter already.

361.   RICHMOND TO NEWCASTLE

Charlton
13 Feb. 1746–7

My Dear Lord,

Now My Lord Kildare has has His Majesty's consent for the peerage[1] from his own mouth, I must again & again thanke you for your great goodness to me, Taw, & all of us, in this affair, which does indeed touch us most nearly. I find he wants to be a Viscount, which surely is most reasonable, & I take for granted will not be refused him. Did he mention the Irish Dukedome to you ? I know it is what he has sett his heart upon. yett I am sure he will be govern'd by you in it, & not desire it to be asked if you thinke it improper at present, butt as you thought it not improper when I first spoke to you about it, I wish you may still thinke it adviseable, because I know it will make him most compleatly happy.

Now as to our Charlton affairs which you know are of no small consequence. The Puff hounds, & myne have each had a good Chace, butt to both our shame, have been baffled by a true gallant Sussex fox, that seems to despise us both. however old Puff is sett upon his death, & the first time wee attack him, either he or all our hounds are to dye. wee are now twenty inhabitants of Charlton besides chance commers, & a jolly sett wee are.

Your's my Dear Lord, for ever & most affectly
Richmond &c.

362.   RICHMOND TO NEWCASTLE

Charlton
Sunday night 15 Febry 1746

My Dear Lord,

I am extreamly obliged to you for your very kind answer about my Lord Kildare, & for what you have done for him, which is doing for me. & now as to the Duke of

---

1.   James Fitzgerald, 20th. Earl of Kildare, was created Viscount Leinster of Taplow on 21 February 1747. He was later created Marquis and finally 1st. Duke of Leinster.

Graftons & my going up, I thinke neither of us need say, wee are ready to serve the King, nor need we say wee are ready to help the Pelhams, if they want help, butt what help can wee give you this week that wee cant do next; as for the Scotch bill, on Tuesday, it will have too much Law for me to understand, & my proxy is in the house, & ('tho in the Duke of St Albans's hands) you know at your commands. so all the help I can give you is there already. As to anything relating to the government of Scotland, you know that you & I have as often differ'd as agreed, & you also know that it is the only point wee ever did, or I beleive ever shall differ upon. butt when you & the Pelhams, as they call it, are personally attack'd, I hope you know how clear I shall be. butt what my Dear Lord can I do at present ? you aske for advice, it is impossible that I can give you any, or could give you any, if in London, butt to go on in your own honest way, & to fear neither the Prince of Wales, nor the Pretender; 'tho the first I thinke is doing all he can for the last: if any thing of consequence that will meet with a serious oposition should come into our house, I shall certanly attend you, butt really if there is nothing butt talking over this oposition together, I neither conceive or comprehend that I can be of any service to you, that is not of so imediate service to you, as to require my quitting this place, 'tho I am only here for divertion. you who are in real business know how difficult it always is for you to give up Claremont even for a day, 'tho you may enjoy it the next, allow this then to be my Claremont & judge by yourself. I shall again add, & repeat, if you really want us, & wee can be of reall service to you, wee will come, butt pray dont send for us only to talke over such misfortunes as will certanly not happen. before I conclude I must greatly applaud one expression in your letter viz; <u>a thorough Concert, union, & agreement amongst us, will defeat &c &c</u>, indeed you are right, & I most ardently wish that that <u>concert, union & agreement</u>, may be kept up, where it is so essential, & so absollutely necessary for the whole. that is the only <u>concert &c</u>, that is of consequence; all the rest is trifling, & if Brothers that both mean right, & exactly the same thing differ when the father & son are at open warr, the whole is undone. dont be angry, butt (au contraire) be assured I am & ever shall be, eternally yours my Dear Lord,

Richmond &c.

Enclosed is Lord Harcourt's proxy which he sends with his kind compliments to you, to be fill'd up as you please.

363. RICHMOND TO NEWCASTLE

Whitehall
Munday night

My Dear Lord,

My nevew Berkeley has just been with me, & I told him what you had said about him to the King, with which he is extreamly pleased, & he has lay'd open his heart entirely to me; for upon my saying to him that I (in my own opinion) look'd upon his askeing the bedchamber of the King as a declaration that he had a mind to detach himself from the Prince, he told me honestly & plainly that had possitively no attachment to the Prince, nor never would have any, even if he was disapointed of what he has ask'd of the King, altho he should be extreamly hurt & piqued at it. he exclaims loudly against the Prince's measures, & swears he will never have any thing to do with them, & to my great surprise he assured me that his father Drax[1] is entirely left out of what he calls H.R.H.s's cabinet, & is not at all consulted in his measures, & that Drax has declared his dislike of the violent measures they are pursuing; which he aprehends

---

1. Henry Drax of Ellerton Abbas in Yorkshire was the father in law of the 4th. Earl of Berkeley, Richmond's nephew.

is the reason he is left out of his Councill. butt as to himself he declares Drax nor nobody else shall govern him; & at the same time complimented me so far as to say he should take my advice sooner than anybody's. butt that his inclination as well as his conscience lead him to serve the King & his cause, & that he would do it whether he was obliged or not. upon this I beg'd him to go to you & to tell you all this himself. & I am sure you will thinke it right to make a report of it to the King.

Your's my Dear Lord most affectly

Richmond &c.

364. RICHMOND TO NEWCASTLE

Whitehall
Munday night. March

My Dear Lord,

Sr Henry Liddell or Admll Anson has done a most unreasonable thing for they have gott the hospitall for Doctr Cuthbert who is the same person Sr Harry recommended for the Garrison & for whom I gave up Doctor Bayley, so that Cuthbert getts both, & Bayley nothing. however I hope & beg you will putt a stop to Cuthbert haveing the Physiciansp of the Garrison, for that is in your power; at least till he gives up the hospitall; & if he won't do it, I then must beg of you notwithstanding my freind Sr Phillip,[1] to gett the Garrison for Bayley. I go to morrow for Goodwood.

Your's most affectly

Richmond &c.

365. RICHMOND TO NEWCASTLE

Bolderwood
7. April. 1747

My Dear Lord,

Le vray Chien anglois ne demorde jamais. & Totty will not give up his point, 'tho Dr Cuthbert who he has apointed Phisician to the hospitall, is extreamly desirous to give it up himself. So the Doctor is drove to give up the Garrison, & Sr Harry Liddell as you may see by the enclosed gives it up also. & I have wrote in answer to Sr Harry that I thinke 'tho the Duke of Bedford wont take a resignation, I thinke Sr Phillip Honywood might. I hope therefore when Dr Cuthbert does resign you will be so good as to desire his Majesty to give the place of Phisician of the Garrison to Dr Bayley, which will extreamly oblige, my Dear Lord Your Grace's ever faithfull

Richmond &c.

366. NEWCASTLE TO RICHMOND

Newcastle House
April 11th 1747

My Dear Lord,

I have been in such constant hurry this whole week, by Business of the utmost Importance, that I have not been able to attend to the Surgeon of Portsmouth & indeed I don't well know what to do in it. Your Grace yourself told me, it was hard upon poor old Honeywood to disoblige Him, & therefore I should hope if it can be delay'd, which I will endeavour to do, It may at last be settled with Honeywood's Consent. But to come to our Business. We have received letters from Lord Sandwich,

---

1. Sir Philip Honywood, the Governor of Portsmouth, 1741–1752.

that Macanas[1] is now disposed to come to a separate Peace with us, without insisting either upon Gibraltar, or an Establishment for Don Philip, and there is some reason to think, that Lord Sandwich has already signed a Treaty with him for that purpose. I have been employed all this Week in drawing Preliminary Articles, which are this day sent to Lord Sandwich, in case He should not have signed. If this succeeds, it is the greatest national Advantage, that could happen: to detach Spain from France, in a Manner most probable to fix the Separation for ever, & to unite them for us, for no Consideration except perhaps the Assiento Contract & Annual Ship. This I say, is doing material service to this Country. I hope it will be thought so. The French have given in a threatening Declaration of ye Dutch, & in consequence of it, have actually invested, L'Ecluse, Sas bas Ghent, Philippins, & Isenach. The whole Province of Zealand, is in the utmost Consternation. We have sent Comr Mitchel[2] with a good Force thither, & have ordered M.G. Fuller with His three Batallions to Flushing, if Fuller is still at sea. We have heard nothing from Sandwich. This News comes directly from Flushing. We are very impatient to see, what Effect this will have in Holland, whether it will intimidate them to take separate Measures, or as I hope, exasperate them, & give them new Vigour, & Courage to depend upon the Assistance & Protection of the superior Army, which they have now in their Countrey. There are good Letters from Italy: at least the King of Sardinia will have his 30,000 Men ready the end of this Month, or beginning of the next. Wentworth is gone, & we shall soon know what they will do. But now I shall surprise you as to our home Affairs. The Scotch Bill, which was loudly, & universally called for by our Friends, & indeed by all Friends to England, & this Government, had like not to have had a second reading in the House of Commons. It was carried but by 25, & nobody spoke one Word for it, but my Brother, the Attorney, & Solicitor genl & Advocate of Scotland, every one Friend of the D of Argyle against it, except one or two who were away. The P. who was so loud last year, it is said will be against it. Ld Doneraille[3] voted against it the other day. In short, this Battle for our Constitution comes on again on Tuesday next. It is too much to ask Mr. Conolly[4] to come up on purpose. Pray my Complimts to him and all ye Company.

Ever Yrs

Holles Newcastle

P.S. You must not open your Mouth about Spain.

367. RICHMOND TO NEWCASTLE

Goodwood
12th May 1747

My Dear Lord,

It seems the Ladys have a sort of engagement to dine at Oatlands on Sunday next, & your Grace knows that the Lord of Oatlands[5] is not a nobleman to be trifled with. so I have wrote to him to tell him if he insists upon it wee shall certanly pay our Duty to him on Sunday next & then from London wee will waite on your Grace at Claremount

---

1. Melchior Macanas was the Spanish Plenipotentiary to the Conference at Breda.
2. Matthew Michell, 1705–1752, MP for Westbury, 1748–1752, circumnavigated the world with Anson. Commodore of a squadron in the Downs during the Jacobite Rebellion, he was Commodore of a fleet stationed off the Scheldt to assist the Dutch, 1747–1748.
3. Arthur St. Leger, 3rd. Viscount Doneraile, 1718–1750, MP for Winchelsea, 1741–1747, and for Old Sarum, 1747–1750, was Lord of the Bedchamber to the Prince of Wales, 1747–1750.
4. William Conolly, died 1754, was MP for Aldeburgh, 1734–1747, and for Petersfield, 1747–1754.
5. Oatlands was the seat of the Earl of Lincoln in Weybridge. He extended the park and laid out the grounds in 1747.

on Sunday, the 24th or any other time you shall appoint; butt if his Lordp should not care to have us on Sunday next which is not at all impossible, wee would then attend your Grace at Claremount, so I have left him to settle it with you, & he is to lett me know it on Sunday morning at Godalming; & wee shall steer our course accordingly.

I hear the Dutch have behaved ill at Hulst, is it true? I do not at all like the Duke's situation, which is as disadvantageous, as the French is advantageous, which is a cruel circumstance as he has now so glorious an army. When I saw you last I spoke to you about poor Bury, who knows & feels not only his own personall obligations to you, as he ought, butt also the high obligations wee all really have to you, & tho myne are greater to you than any man living, yett Ld Albemarle's are I may say still greater as he owes his salvation from Ruin to you. All this I say that dear good boy is perfectly sensible of, as he ought to be, therefore is unhappy to thinke he should ever give you reason to be displeased with him, I mean only about his writing, as you positively insisted he should so often, his expression in his letter to me is <u>what can I do about writing to the Duke of Newcastle? he wants news & says I must write him every thing I know. & if ever it happens I do know anything, it is in such a way that it is not in my power to repeat it, & any thing else that is common in the army, I am sure it is not worth His Grace reading.</u> Indeed My Dear Lord there is both sense & honesty in what he sayes, so pray consider of it, & don't be angry with him. you will say & very truely I wrote every thing I knew without reserve to you, butt his scituation & myne are very different, he has a master he entirely depends upon, & owes almost all to him. I, thanke God, depend upon nobody, & have <u>managements</u> only for those I love, & that I loved you better than anybody was no secret to my Master nor his then Secretary of State.

& I am now as much as ever, & I can't be more most truely & affectly Your's
Richmond &c.

368.   STONE TO RICHMOND

Whitehall
May 16, 1747
My Lord,

Captain Dennis, of the Centurion, arrived early this morning, with Letters from Admiral Anson, giving an Account of His having met with the French Fleet, bound partly to the East Indies, & partly to North America, and that He had taken six Men of War, & four large East India Men, fitted as Men of War, and was in great Hopes, that the Ships, which He had detached after the Merchant Ships, that were under the Convoy of the Men of War, would be able to give a good Account of most, if not all of them.[1] The Particulars are contained in the inclosed Copy of a Letter from Mr Anson to my Lord Duke of Newcastle, which I send by his Grace's Order, and beg leave to congratulate with your Grace upon this very great & important Success. My Lord Duke went to Claremont, this morning, where, He bids me say, He depends upon having the Honour of seeing your Grace, and all the Company with you tomorrow at Dinner. The inclosed is from the Earl of Lincoln, who desired me to forward it to your Grace.

I am with the greatest Respect My Lord your Grace's most obedient & most humble servant

Andrew Stone

Two mails arrived this morning from Holland. Our Army continued at Schield on Tuesday last; but they were soon to make a Motion. The French were not, at that time, incamped.

---

1.   The first Battle of Finisterre was fought on 3 May 1747, in which Anson intercepted a convoy escorted by a squadron led by Admiral de la Jonquiere, and captured the warships and several of the convoy.

369. RICHMOND TO NEWCASTLE

Goodwood
3d June 1747

My Dear Lord,

It is so long since I have seen your Grace, that I am quite in the darke as to the last ten dayes polliticks, even Anson[1] & Warren's[2] honors, I heard for the first time at My Lord Leister's[3] at dinner. & very right & really justly due honors I thinke them. butt what I want mostly to know at present, is if the Parliament is certanly to be dissolved, & if it is when the generall elections particularly in this County will be, for I am to attend his Majesty on Saturday sennight to Windsor, & then that is when the house is up, I would go to Harcourts in Oxfordshire, & our water expedition which would carry us to the end of this month of June. butt if the elections should be soon, & that you or Mr. Pelham thinke of comeing into Sussex in June, I would then defer our party, & if you dont come 'till July, it would be most convenient to me to have the party over first; so I only waite your commands & the sooner I have them the better. & I beg to know when the dissolution of the Parliament is no longer a secret, for every soul I meet with has it, & I look like a fool when I lye, which I am not used to. I mean to lye. & I also beg to know what day is fix'd for the King's going to the house, which I take for granted cant be 'till after the hollydays. all this Mr. Stone may answer me if you will order him, for I would not have you give yourself the trouble. I have been with Sr Thos Ridge,[4] according to Mr. Pelham's directions, & he is to be with me on Fryday & will go with Leeves to try his fortune at Arundell on Saturday, & when I know how he is received I will acquaint your Grace & Mr. Pelham with it.

I am, My Dear Lord, for ever & most affectly Your's,

Richmond &c.

Shall you be at Claremount on Fryday sennight ? tho upon recollection I beleive I shall not have time to call.

370. RICHMOND TO NEWCASTLE

Goodwood
7. June. 1747

My Dear Lord,

I thanke you for your Stone, & your Grace's commands to me must allways be a Law, so I shall certanly putt of the water expedition. I shall certanly be in town on Fryday next in order to attend my Master to Windsor, & shall then stay in town till the breaking up of both houses. & I wish wee could dine together on Tuesday, the 16th for I am engaged to the Duke of Bedford on the munday. if you care to dine with me then on Tuesday, you'l lett me know it. the company I suppose your brother, old Puff, Linky, Arundell, & Jemmy Pelham, or any body else you please. Sr Thomas Ridge goes to morrow to declare at Arundell, & I have wrote for him to the Duke of Norfolk, & so indeed should your Grace & Mr. Pelham. what do you do about Sr John Shelley there ? & do you care to ask his interest for Ridge ?

1. George Anson was created Baron Anson on 15 July 1747 for his victory off Cape Finisterre.
2. Peter Warren, Anson's second-in-Command, was knighted on 29 May 1747.
3. Thomas Coke, 1st. Earl of Leicester, 1697–1759, creator of Holkham, was MP for Norfolk, 1722–1728, and Postmaster General, 1733–1759.
4. Sir Thomas Ridge was Richmond's original candidate for Arundel at the 1747 Election with William Leaves. Richmond hoped to gain control of the seat in the absence of any candidate put up by the Lumleys, who held the predominant interest. In fact, Ridge was replaced by Robert Brudenell, and both Richmond's candidates were defeated.

Anson's being a Peer will please every body butt poor old Norris, butt I fear Sr H. Liddell will not go down so well, among our old freinds, as he has certanly been a wavering freind. I hope in God Jack Campbell[1] is not to be one, if he is you can not imagine how all English man kind will cry out; & tho I love you so much, I could not command my tongue upon such an occasion; dont be angry with me, butt indeed it would be so wrong a thing that I thinke I am sure you would not do it, & indeed Linky told me there was no thoughts of it, for I desired him to speake to you from me upon it. upon my honor I have no meaning in what I say butt the King's service, for if there is a Scotchman, that I am more acquainted with than an other 'tis Jack Campbell. The Dissolution of the Parliament is known to every soul here, & every letter from London is full of it, yett 'till I have your leave I shall deny it.

I am My Dear Lord, for ever & most affectly Your's

Richmond &c.

371. RICHMOND TO NEWCASTLE

Whitehall
20 [June 1747]

I am just going to Goodwood & so to Arundell to try for Geo. Brudenell, & if that wont do, for Leeves, & one or the other I thinke will. Pray lett a letter be wrote imediately to Sawyer of Lewis to write to his son Edwd Sawyer of Arundell, & also to Charles Verrall of do to be for Mr. Brudenell if he stands, if not for Mr. Leeves. Pray lett me know the hour you will be at Lewes on Tuesday, & I will be there punctually, & a good many freinds will go with me for the West.

Your's My Dear Lord in a Great hurry

Richmond &c.

372. NEWCASTLE TO RICHMOND

Claremont,
June 20th 9 at night, 1747

My Dear Lord,

I am very sorry I did not see you when you was in Town. I will be sure to obey yr Commands as to Sawyer, & Verrall, & most heartily wish you success at Arundel. Ld Gage was to be this day at Lewes, to declare His Son for the Town.[2] He gave notice of it yesterday. We despise the Opposition extreamly. I hope we are not mistaken. Ld Middlesex & the whole Clan are to be at the Meeting, therefore pray bring Sr John & all considerable Friends. I have insisted upon Sr Cecil's being there, & He comes. My Brother has had the most impertinent Letter from the Duke of Somerset, with the highest Enconiums of Ld Middlesex, & recommending Him for the County. We should have a warm Meeting, on Tuesday, but thank God we have Honor, Honesty & Numbers of our Side. I hear Mr. Boone[3] stands at Shoreham. I suppose he is to be at

1. James Campbell, 1719–1788, MP for Stirlingshire, 1747–1768, fought under Cumberland at Fontenoy and Culloden. He served at Lauffeld in June 1747.
2. Hon. William Hall Gage, 1718–1791, had been MP for Seaford, 1744–1747, and his family had filled one of the seats there since 1722, due to the proximity of their estates at Firle, but Gage had followed the Prince of Wales into opposition and Newcastle refused to support him, and he and the Earl of Middlesex were defeated by Newcastle's candidates.
3. Daniel Boone, 1710–1770, MP for Ludgershall, 1731–1741, for Grampound, 1741–1747, for Stockbridge, 1747–1754, and for Minehead, 1754–1761, was a Groom of the Bedchamber to the Prince of Wales. He was a possible opposition candidate for New Shoreham, but Charles Frederick and Robert Bristow were returned unopposed.

our Meeting. Ld Donnerail, is, I hope, quite routed at Winchelsea, & Jemmy[1] & Mr. Stone will have no Opposition at Hastings, & Mr. Pitt & Mr. Hay[2] as little at Seaford. We all lie at John's at Sheffield on Monday Night. I wish you would come there that Night, for we shall have several things to settle in the Meeting. If you cannot, we will certainly be at Lewes on Tuesday before twelve o'clock.

Ever Yrs

Holles Newcastle

373. RICHMOND TO NEWCASTLE

Godalming
Sunday 4 O'clock in the evening [21 June 1747]

My Dear Lord,

I will certanly be at Lewis before twelve with Sr John Miller &c; if he is in the County. the County oposition is as trifling as that at Lewis. I wish I was as sure at Arundell; & I doubt much if Orme can be thrown out. I'l send to Crawley at Shoreham to be against Boon.

Your's most affectly & for ever

Richmond &c.

374. PELHAM TO RICHMOND

July ye 2nd, 1747

My Dear Lord,

I think you judg'd very right in setting up Mr. Brudenel and Leeves against the bribery of Orme and Taaff.[3] I will take care to secure you two good councill. As we shall meet so soon as next Sunday I will not trouble your Grace to send any bills by letter or otherways. I can take them myself when I come to Goodwood. As to Peck William's opposition for the County[4] it is a joke, if intended, but I presume he will not think of it. However, I agree with you we should be prepared, and have accordingly desired my Brother to collect some friends from the East, which I trust he will execute most punctually. Tom Hill's verses please me much, but if I can judge, instead of turning them into Latin for the use of Lord March he turned them into English for the sake of your Grace. Politicks are at present melancholy subjects; but by all we hear the English and Hannoverians behaved like Heros. Lord George Manners[5] is come to London, who tells the young Keppel is well, tho' a Prisoner, most damndly bruised but not wounded, as is his own brother Lord Robert Sutton.[6] We may say with the Roman Hero, thanks to the Gods our boys have done their duty. I will not fail to attend your

1. James Pelham, Newcastle's second cousin, who shared the representation of Hastings with Andrew Stone.
2. William Pitt and William Hay of Glyndebourne, 1695–1755, were Newcastle's successful candidates at Seaford. Hay was MP for Seaford, 1734–1755, and Keeper of the records in the Tower of London, 1754–1755.
3. Thomas Taaffe, 1708–1780, with Garton Orme, the sitting member, defeated Richmond's candidates at Arundel. Taaffe, who bought an estate near Midhurst, was MP for Arundel, 1747–1754.
4. Peckham Williams did not contest the county seat, and Henry Pelham and John Butler were returned unopposed.
5. Lord George Manners, 1723–1783, MP for Grantham, 1754–1780, and for Newark, 1780–1783. He was the younger brother of Lord Robert Manners Sutton, whom he succeeded in 1762, taking the additional name of Sutton.
6. Lord Robert Manners Sutton, 1722–1762, MP for Nottinghamshire, 1747–1762, and a Lieutenant Colonel in Cumberland's Dragoons, was taken prisoner at the Battle of Lauffeld in 1747, and exchanged the next day.

Grace att time and place appointed, when I shall, as in duty bound, thank for ye repeated instances of your goodness and friendship to your faithfull and obedient servant.

H. Pelham

My Compliments to the Dutchesse of Richmond, and recommend from me to Tom Hill to read a Pamphlet intitled a Dialogue between a gentleman and an Alderman.
Alteration to the two last lines of the Dutchesse of Richmond's advice to Ld March.
As bad fortune to good is oft tacked, let me tell you.
Hereafter beware, how you mount a Girl's belly.

375. NEWCASTLE TO RICHMOND

Newcastle House
July 16th, 1747

My Dear Lord,
I have received all your Grace's Commands, and will obey them as well as I can. I will enquire into Consul Allen's[1] Demands, I am afraid they are not very regular, tho' they may be very just, for I doubt He never had any Order, for making those expenses. Poor Cheale, I really think deserves some immediate provision. I will speak to my Brother, for I know of no Office but the Treasury, that can do any thing of that sort. I send ye Duke of Lennox[2] enclosed, the List of the 16 Scotch Lords, which I wish may be elected. I send them only to a Friend, for as Secretary of State, I must not appear in it.
I come now to acquaint you wth a very great Secret, for I keep nothing from you. Soon after the Battle,[3] Marshal Saxe sent the enclosed Message N1 by Sr J. Legonier[4] to the Duke. His. R.Hs returned immediately the Answer N2 & upon Consideration we determined to send the Answer N3 as the King's Answer to ye M. Saxe's Overture. We shall soon see, what the Court of France will do upon it; whether they will explain themselves further, or drop the whole Affair. The Prince of Orange[5] has wrote in the strongest Manner to protest against this Negotiation, & to propose vigorous Measures for carrying on the War. But considering our present Situation; the Danger Bergen opp Zoom & all the Republick is in (which by the by must, & ought to be more the Business of the Statholder than ours) It has been agreed & I think rightly, not to put a Negative upon the proposal, but to hear what France has to say. The great Point is to act in concert with our Allies, & especially the Statholder of Holland, and for that purpose we shall have Lord Sandwich in Holland, & wherever the Negotiation is to be carried on. Some of our Friends are not much inclined to Lord Sandwich's going to the Army, imagining He would not promote the Success of this Negotiation, but that the Duke might alone convey the Proposals & Answers. For my part I dread the Duke's being concerned in making what will be called a bad Peace. He will be severely attacked, or reproached for it & we shall be thought to have employed Him to save Ourselves. What will be done, I know not, but as things advance, I will take care, you shall be constantly informed. This is the time when Men of Art will have the advantage of plain dealers, & plain Speakers. I believe Ld Sandwich will go soon to Holland to quiet

1. Edward Allen was Consul at Naples.
2. Richmond was Duke of Richmond and Lennox.
3. The Battle of Lauffeld near Maastricht fought on 2 July, in which Marshall Maurice de Saxe defeated the Allied Army.
4. Sir John Ligonier had been captured in the battle.
5. William IV, Prince of Orange, son in law to King George II, had been elected Stadholder in April and May 1747, and replaced the pacific republicans.

the P. of Orange, & put things in some Method, tho' the jealously there is of Him, may hinder his doing all the Good, he might do. I most sincerely congratulate you, upon the Account received this day, which may be depended upon, that poor Kepple is safe in France, the Ship is lost, but they say all the Crew are saved. I was at great pains for Him, both on publick, & private Accounts.

I beg my Compliments to the Ds of Richmond & thanks for all her Goodness.

I am my Dear Duke Ever and unalterably Yrs

Holles Newcastle

376. PELHAM TO RICHMOND

July ye 16, 1747

My Dear Lord,

I have just time to thank your Grace for your letter, and should not, for form's sake only, do that, did I not imagine that your Grace would be uneasy upon poor Keppel's account, when you read in the papers that his ship and crew were lost, but I hear from what I think good hands, that tho' his ship is certainly lost, he and his whole crew are sav'd. The King this day gave publick directions to Lord Anson that he would have Keppel immediately exchanged, which shewd a regard to him and his family; that I thought would be a pleasure to you. Old Puff is now happy, upon reflection, but at first was much affected upon the news of Ld Euston's[1] death. We none of us know what the impressions of nature are, even for the most unworthy, 'till we are tryed. I think however he was in the wrong, and is now in the right, to recommend an Agent to you, upon the affair of Arundel, I don't know how to name. If Leeves, who is upon the spot can't or won't bring it to bear, no one else can. We have retained Courvill, and if we do no more, there is little lost. My compliments as due, and believe me my Dear Duke Your Grace's most obedient humble servt

H. Pelham

377. RICHMOND TO NEWCASTLE

Goodwood
17 July 1747

My Dear Lord,

You may easyly conceive my anxiety for those two Dear boys my nevews, tho I have great hopes that Keppell is safe tho his ship I fear is lost. Adair the Surgeon also writes word that he has good hopes of Wm butt as the cutt is in the joynt of the shoulder it will not surprise him if he does not recover. I sincerely pitty my poor Dear Sister[2] in this cruel state of uncertainty, & beg most earnestly that you will constantly send her what news you know of them. Adair the agent has promis'd to send me what account he can gett, even by a Messager, so I will not trouble your Grace, only beg you will transmit what accounts you have of either of them to Adair, who will acquaint both my Sister & me with it. I make no apology to you for giving you this trouble, as I know your good nature & compassion for every body & particularly for your freinds.

I am My Dear Dear Lord, for ever & most affectionately Your's

Richmond &c.

---

1. George Fitzroy, Lord Euston, 1715–1747, son and heir of the Duke of Grafton. He was on the worst possible terms with his father. He was MP for Coventry, 1737–1747.
2. Lady Anne Lennox, Richmond's sister, was the wife of William Keppel, 2nd. Earl of Albemarle.

378. NEWCASTLE TO RICHMOND

From the cottage at Claremont
July 18th 1747

My Dearest Lord,

Tho' I troubled you with a long, & very important Letter by last post, I can't forbear returning you thanks, for the best natur'd letter, that ever was wrote, which I received this day. I sent you an Account of the poor General by the last. Since that, my Lord Anson has assured me, He is a safe Prisoner in France. The only Account I had, was from Adair which Will Rogers brought me, & carried immediately to <u>Durhams.</u> Since that, Dick the Messenger is arrived from the Army. He tells me, poor Kepple's wound is not dangerous, & that He will do well. He spoke so sensibly, & seemingly so knowingly about it, that I really believe Him. You may be assured, whenever I know any thing relating to yr Family, you & yr Sister shall know it. There is little new since my last. Lord Sandwich goes on Monday Morning. His Instructions are settled, as I could wish. Our Master is sometimes a little startled, but if He knew me as well as I hope you do, He would not be so; especially if He knew others as we do. In the <u>main</u> all is well here. I wish I could say the same abroad, for I think I see, a very unfortunate Difference arising between the Duke, & the Prince of Orange. The latter is entirely to blame. I have given Sandwich a Hint about it. By the last Letters, Bergen opp Zoom is like to defend itself well. Old Cromstiom[1] does well there but He is the cause of the Misunderstanding. I hunt at Little Carpenters & I have drank yr Health in a Bumper. You see that great Man Ld Gage is to demolish me.

Ever Yrs

Holles Newcastle

379. RICHMOND TO NEWCASTLE

Goodwood
Sund. 19 July 1747

My Dear Lord,

I thanke you for your last most obliging letter, & the great confidence you putt in me, by trusting me with a secret of such very great consequence to this kingdome, & as you have trusted me with it, I take for granted you will not think me officious or impertinent in telling you my thoughts upon it. which are in the first place that the King's answer no. 3 which Ligonier is to read to the Marrle Saxe, is a wise & a cautious paper, & a very honorable one, particularly in the last line of it, in which His Majesty sayes he shall do as much as <u>les Interests de ses alliez</u> will permit him. I own that the first paper no. 1, is in my opinion as fair a one as could be offer'd that is for what it contains, & considering our situation, butt it does not mention one word of Ittaly, which is a point of the greatest consequence. Furnes may to them be an equivalent for Dunkerke, & they admit it, butt then wee have none for the restitution of Cap Breton, & as they have certanly at present the better end of the staff I fear they mean to give us none, unless they would call the disavowing the Pretender & his familly so, butt as that must necessaryly be a <u>sine qua non</u> of ours, it really can not in justice be call'd an equivalent for any thing. 'tho (if they mean to be reasonable in Ittaly) this would not be quite so bad a peace in the eyes of reasonable men. yett I fear by some, it will be call'd a bad one & loudly too, & I dread the thought of it's being negotiated by the Duke, & your honest scruples in that are (without compliment) vastly for your honor, & he ought to be highly obliged to you for it. butt I entirely agree with you that the admin-

---

1. M. Cronstrom the Governor of Furnes.

251

istration could not answer, the putting a negative upon the offer, butt still they can not, nor in my poor opinion <u>should not</u> make a peace without the entire concurrence of <u>all</u> our allys, common prudence forbids it without the Stadtboulder, & <u>Justice</u> will not allow it without the King of Sardinia. & as for the Empress, as they offer to restore her the Low Countreys, (tho they are not as they were) her husband's being Emperor is some <u>dedomagement</u> for Silesia, tho she wont thinke so, nor can I say it would be enough, if she had not as aparent a disadvantage in the feild, as wee have. my polliticks may be confused butt no opinion can be quite clear till the proposals from France are so.

I must now thanke you for your good intentions for poor Cheale, the accomplishment of which I wish extreamly. I also thanke you for thinking of Consull Allan, 'tho I am sorry his demands are irregular, however when you enquire into it, you may not perhaps find them so much so. if they are, twill be a great favor, if they are not, twill be butt justice.

You see how many things I have constantly to thanke you for, butt now above all for the good news you sent me of Dear Keppell's safety. I wish I could hear as much of poor Willm. I beg pardon for troubling you with so long a letter & am My Dear Dear Lord, for ever & most unalterably Your's

Richmond &c.

380. STONE TO RICHMOND

Whitehall
July 22d, 1747

My Lord,

I have the Honour to acquaint your Grace, by my Lord Duke of Newcastle's Order, that M. Ossorio has received a Courier from his Court, with the good News of a Victory gain'd by the Piedmontese & Austrian Troops over the French, at <u>Assiete</u>, near Exiles. The French attack'd the Intrenchments with forty Battalions, supported by a Corps de Reserve of eight Battalions; and nine Pieces of Canon. There were in the Intrenchments only fourteen Battalions, ten Piedmontese, & four Austrian, (of which only eight of the former, & two of the latter could act) and not one piece of Canon. The Enemy attack'd four different times; but was repulsed each time with great Loss, & at last, was obliged to retire towards Sestrieres. They were pursued in their Retreat by the Grenadiers, & suffer'd some loss. The whole Loss of the Enemy is acknowledged by themselves to amount to between five & six thousand Men. The Chevalier de Belleisle was kill'd upon the Spot. The Allies did not lose more than 120 Men. I most heartily congratulate your Grace upon this most happy & seasonable Event, & am with the greatest Respect My Lord your Grace's most obedient, humble servant

Andrew Stone

The last Accounts from Berg-op-Zoom are more favourable than the preceding ones. The Enemy, (as it is said) having made no Progress in the Siege; & the Reinforcement being arrived in the Line.

381. NEWCASTLE TO RICHMOND

Newcastle House
July 30th 1747

My Dear Lord,

Your Grace will excuse my not having returned my thanks sooner for your several kind letters. Indeed I have had so much Business that I have not had time to write, & nothing from abroad has been material enough for A. <u>Stone</u>. Our Victory in Italy is rather greater, than we at first represented it, & Bergen-op-Zoom, holds out yet, & I hope will do so. The Detachment formerly under P. Waldeck is arrived in the Neighbourhood, but it is resolved that only three Batallions should go into the Lines & the rest with the Horse endeavour to attack one Part of Löwendall's[1] Army, whilst a strong Sally from the Town is to attack the other part of it. This seems a pretty bold Stroke. I wish we are strong enough within the Lines for such attempts. Our Negotiation with M: Saxe goes on but odly. I send you a Copy of M: Saxe's Letter to Legonier,[2] as extraordinary in the substance as it is in its form & writing. The Marshal seems to write quite in His Correspondent Legonier's style. We have had several Deliberations on the Answer to be returned. Lord Chancellor, & I have been strongly of Opinion that the best Answer to be returned, would be the sending Lord Sandwich immediately to the Army, there to treat under the Inspection & Direction of the Duke, with M: Saxe or any other person appointed by the King of France. Lord Ches. & my Brother have strongly opposed this, & would have the Duke authorised to make some general Overtures, tending to show the King's Disposition to Peace, even at the Expense of <u>C.B.</u>[3] if necessary. Lord Chancellor & I have very much opposed the employing the Duke in this manner as what may bring difficulties upon H.R.Hs, & an Imputation upon us Ministers, as if we exposed the King's Son to secure ourselves from Danger. That has so far prevailed that the Answer to be returned tomorrow will be to the following purport : that in answer to M: Saxe's Question, it is not to be presumed that H.R.Hs has any such power to treat & conclude; that as soon as France has explained itself, the King will send a Minister to treat, under the Inspection & Direction of the Duke. This may probably break off the Negotiation which I should be sorry for, but it is the fault of those, who would not take the middle way, & have encouraged, & rather drove, the King into this Measure contrary to their own Inclinations. In short, our present Situation is most disagreable; a good deal of Suspicion amongst ourselves, & an endeavour to lay hold of any particular Irresolution in a certain place, which will always confound Business, & has lately turned upon the very Persons, who have brought it about. As to Ireland, Lady Kildare must be contented with an old Spanish King, who sets out for His kingdom very soon, as I am informed. I have not time to answer your Observations about our Scotch List, But they surprise me a little. If you will not (which I am sure your Grace, of all Men, desires not to do) make <u>one Man</u> every thing there, you must take all the considerable Men you can get, who are Friends to ye Government & not the Dependancy & <u>Portmore</u>,[4] must make way for them. Twedale was <u>somebody's</u> own.

I am ever Yrs

Holles Newcastle

I thank you for your Chichester Freeman.

382. NEWCASTLE TO RICHMOND

Newcastle House
Augt 12th 1747

My Dear Lord,

Your Grace, I am persuaded, will neither be concerned, nor surprised that

1.   General Count Ulrich de Lowendahl, had been sent with a corps by Marshal de Saxe to beseige Bergen-op-Zoom, which he eventually captured on 18 September 1747.

2.   A Memorandum of a conversation between Sir John Ligonier and the Marechal de Saxe, and copy letters about the treaty to be concluded through negotiations between de Saxe and the Duke of Cumberland, 7 July to 5 August 1747, are to be found in Goodwood Ms. 109 ff.866–870.

3.   Charles John Bentinck, Count Bentinck of Nieuhays, second son of William, 1st. Earl of Portland.

4.   Charles Colyear, 2nd. Earl of Portmore, 1700–1785, MP for Chipping Wyecombe, 1726 and for Andover, 1727–1730.

Benteniks[1] unexpected arrival, and short stay here, makes it impossible for my Brother & I, to be at the Races or Assizes. I have therefore sent our Excuses by Coll. Pelham & Mr. Sergison. I conclude you will not think of going. I would by no means have you give yourself that trouble, tho' I hope some of our Friends will be there. My best Compliments & thanks to Sr John Miller for his kind Intention. I really hope to be at Goodwood before the summer is quite over. As to publick Affairs I saw B. the first, who said, He was come to follow my <u>directions</u>. I acted, I am sure, like an honest Man, told him the Truth; how necessary, it was thought, to put an end to the War, if it could be done in any tolerable Manner; that therefore this Negotiation must be pursued in earnest, but with the Connivance & Approbation of our Allies & especially the Prince of Orange; that I must own freely to Him His Highness present way of talking of <u>being abandon'd by the King, of protesting in form against the present Negotiation for Peace, etc</u>, had greatly offended the King; that my Advice was, that if He could, He should talk in a quite different Style; that He should assure the King, that the P of W had that deference for the King; that Dependance upon His Majesty; that whatever his own private opinion may be, He should always submit it to the King's. This Frankness had so much Effect upon this Honest Man, that He had in every respect followed my advice. <u>Every Body</u> is pleased with Him, and I really think all Jealousies & Misunderstanding will be over, and we shall send Him away thoroughly satisfied. The Plan agreid upon between B & me is, that the P of O should heartily concur with us in bringing this Negotiation with the Marshal Saxe to a happy Conclusion, if possible; and on the other side, that we should <u>in time</u>, join with Him in takeing proper Measures to shew France, that we may be in a condition to carry on the War another year, if they will not consent to reasonable Terms of Peace. This I really think right, and this in some shape or other, every Body will agree to. I am sorry to tell you, that things go ill at Berg-op-Zoom. It is the greatest Secret, but there is an unhappy Misunderstanding between the <u>D</u> & the P. of O., & the Dutch Generals, & there has not been an agreable Correspondance between the Army, & B.op.Zoom; and what is worse, Cromstiom writes word, that it must fall, and that no <u>Reinforcement</u> from the Army can save it, so that <u>they</u> press extreamly for the March of the whole Army from Mastreicht to save Holland. I am no Military Man, but I own, that strikes me as a necessary Measure, but this I am sure you will not drop to any Body. You will be surprised to hear, that we have certain Proofs of a Negotiation & some suspicions of a secret Treaty signed between the Q. of Hungary & the King of Spain, wholly at the Expense of the King of Sardinia. It is most abominable Treachery, but I think if there is such a Treaty, it is not ratified, & will not be proceeded upon. I have ordered Stone to send, you, any Material papers that have passed since my last, that you may not have seen. My Compliments to the Dutchess of R & all Western Friends.

I am as you know most sincerely & affectly Yrs

Holles Newcastle

383. PELHAM TO RICHMOND

Greenwich
Augt 14 1747

My Dear Lord,

I spoke to the Secretary att War,[2] upon the receipt of your letter. He will do his part,

---

1. Count Willian Bentinck, first son of the 1st. Earl of Portland, and chief adviser to the Orangist party. He was a relative of Richmond, having married Lady Margaret Cadogan, younger sister of the Duchess of Richmond.
2. Henry Fox.

but what stands in our way is a personal application of George Bridges[1] to the King for one Major Sewel. How we shall get rid of that I dont know. George has most earnestly press'd for him a great while. I know the man; he was Aid du Camp to Sr Robert Rich, and is an excellent sollicitor. Bentinck's arrival, and the hourly expectation of hearing some fatal event from abroad, prevented His Grace and of course your humble servant from going to Lewes. My Brother said he would send you word, which I conclude sav'd your Grace the trouble of a hot journey. You had Politicks, I presume, enough from him; pleasanter than you could have had from me, tho' I am of opinion His Grace now sees our affairs in a most desperate situation. The Gentleman, that is come from the Stadtholder, is an honest man, partial, as we all are, to our own particular cause. But what is the worst of all, as he is a man of truth and honour, he cannot hide the nakedness of his country, even att a time he wishes to represent it, as in a condition of spirit and resolution to give fresh vigour and force to the Alliance. I am as much for saving the Republick as any man. I know where we shall be when they are subdued, but I cannot flatter myself, that an inferior Army, can with any degree of certainty retain a country that has lost, or will soon loose its best fortress, and where the people are enervated and lost their own antient force and power. I wont detain you longer on this melancholy subject; a few days I will explain matters further. Bergen-op-Zoom holds out well, the garrison do their duty, but the luigers gain around every post, which makes me say what I do in this letter. The warrants were sign'd for Pelham and Stone before your Grace's last came to hand. I desire you will tell Norton I should have been glad to have obliged him, but it was not in my power this time.

I am with all truth and affection My Lord, Your Grace's most obliged and faithfull servant

H. Pelham

P.S. My best respects to the Ds of Richmond.

384. NEWCASTLE TO RICHMOND

Claremont
Augt 29th 1747

My Dear Lord,

I beg your Graces pardon for having being so long writeing to you, & I own I begin to fear I am not so well with you as usual, not having had the pleasure of hearing from you, as I used to do. I fully intended last week to write a letter of thanks to Lord March, for having done the honors so well at Lewes, supplied your Grace's place, & mine, & made Lord Gage appear, as insignificant as He is. I desired Stone to give you an Account of our News about Bergen-op-Zoom. We are all in great Spirits about it. The Letters come in this day, are very good; the Ennemy make no great Progress, & every Body is now as sanguine, that the Siege must be raised as they were at first sure the Place could not hold out a Week. M. Saxe has sent an Answer to our last Reply, & the Ministers, Ld Sandwich, & Monr Puyseux, are to meet at Liege, so we shall soon see, whether any good is to be expected from thence. M. Saxe's Letter seems sincere, but I will never Answer for them. If the Siege of Berg-op-Zoom is raised, and the K. of Sardinia, who is now at the Head of the Army, drives M. Belisle back into France, & follows them thither, France may think it is in their Business, to make Peace. Our friend Bentinck is not so well satisfied with us as He was at first. He wants we should be a little more explicit, as to what we would do, if this Negotiation should miscarry, & that He would immediately set about it. I think He has reason for his uneasiness, but

---

1. George Brydges, 1679–1751, MP for Whitchurch, 1708–1710, and for Winchester, 1714–1751, was cousin to the 1st. Duke of Chandos.

we are so afraid of engaging too far, that I doubt we shall discourage our Friends & particularly the Statholder. My little Collegue goes on as usual. He is extreamly ill with Bentinck. I am told Ld Ashburnham, Ld. Montfort,[1] &c., go to Goodwood the next week, & that they return hither tomorrow sennight. I suppose you will not think of making a visit to these parts so soon. The <u>Peace</u> & the <u>War</u> will necessarily keep me in Town, so that I am afraid I shall not be able to perform my Promise to the Dutchess of Richmond and wait upon Her at Goodwood. I am sure you will not think, it proceeds from want of Inclination, for I can truly say, no one living is more an Humble Servant to Goodwood than myself. I beg my best Respects to the Ds of Richmond, & kind Compliments to Lord March, who I know, is now to be counted, as a considerable young Nobleman of Sussex. Whenever you can spare a Saturday, & Sunday from Goodwood, Claremont will always be glad of your Company & Sr Johns.

I am my Dear Duke ever Yrs

Holles Newcastle

385. NEWCASTLE TO RICHMOND

Claremont
Sept 5th, 1747

My Dear Lord,

Lord Ashburnham, Ld Montfort, etc dine here tomorrow. They go to <u>Oatland</u> at night, & to Goodwood on Tuesday. I hear they talk of staying 'till Sunday, but I am not sure. You will be surprised, to hear, that I will not let your Grace come to Claremont, except you can pay a visit at the same time to your Master. Old <u>Puff</u>, & <u>somebody else</u> who are your very good friends were blaming you extreamly for having been two Months in the Country, & during that time, not come up one Saturday to attend the King at Richmd. Old <u>Puff</u> comes ever Saturday from Northamptonshire & returns on Monday. Your coming here cannot be a Secret, & I had rather punish myself with your absence, than be any ways instrumental to your doing any thing that can be blamed, as I really fear this would be, & with some sort of Reason. And to be serious: why can't you come to London of a Fryday, leave Sr John at Claremont, wait upon the King on Saturday to Richmond, & come hither at night. You see what liberty I take with you, but when I think, anything for your service, I can't help saying it, tho' as in this Instance I may suffer by it, & after this, do as you will. You know I shall be very glad to see you, but I wish you to go, a few miles further. Bentinck will be going back next week. He has replied to the Answer Lord Chesd made Him, & I think <u>with my help</u>, He has now got one, that he is tolerably satisfied with. This Dissatisfaction wh ye Secretary of the Province is very great. As to News, our late Accounts from Berg-op-Zoom are not good. They seem to fear, they shall not hold out long, & they say, they have no Assistance from Chandos. Your friend Huske is sent over by the Duke, to explain His Conduct, & H.R.H has received most ample Approbation. Huske returns to the Army on Monday or Tuesday next. He is wiser, & better than ever, & in high favor with our Master. By our last Letters from Italy, the King of Sardinia had taken the Command of the Army, which was not a numerous one. However, He intends to make incursions into France, oblige, if possible, Belisle to repass the bar, & then begin again the siege of Genoa. Lord Sandwich has had a Conference with Monr Puyisseux. I have not seen the Letters, they came in this morning, but, I hear it is not very promising & particularly that Puyisseux makes difficulties of extending the Guaranty of

---

1. Henry Bromley, 1st. Lord Montfort, 1705–1755, MP for Cambridgeshire, 1727–1741, was Lord Lieutenant of Cambridgeshire, 1730–1742.

our Succession against the Pretenders Children which is monstrous. I hear there is a person coming over hither from Spain. That, if so, is a very good thing but these are great Secrets. I wrote shortly every thing that is stirring here, that I have never wrote you word of Nutcracker & the Chancellor. I should not be so easy, as I am, about Politicks if there was any Foundation for that. I beg my Compliments to my Queen & my Schoolfellow & Country Man, & am my Dearest Lord Ever most unalterably Yrs

Holles Newcastle

386. STONE TO RICHMOND

Whitehall
Septr 10th, 1747

My Lord,

On Tuesday last, the Admiralty receiv'd an Account from Cre Michel; that Bergen-op-Zoom was taken by Assault, early on Saturday morning. By Letters that arrived this afternoon from Mr. Stewart at Flushing, we are told, that the Place was surprised; that there was no Breach; But that the Enemy enter'd the Town, by a Port in the Ditch, which was not guarded, & where they found no Resistance. When the Alarm was given, the Soldiers ran to their Arms and a great Slaughter was made. The two Scotch – Dutch Regiments, which made Part of the Garrison, behaved with the greatest Bravery imaginable; and a very small number, (They say not above twenty or thirty out of Both Regiments) escaped with their Lives. The Prince of Hesse Philipsdale is said to be kill'd; tho' some Accounts say, that He was carried off wounded. Cronstrom escaped (with the Remains of some of the Battalions) to Steenberg. Lt General Lelie got into the Island of Tholen, with six Battalions. He has Orders (as Mr. Stewart says) to listen to no Offers of Terms, if attack'd; but to defend himself, to the last Extremity, and when He shall be obliged to leave the Island, to lay it under Water. These are the Accounts, we have, by the way of Flushing, of this most unhappy Event; the Consequences of which are to be so much apprehended. What Effects it has produced at the Hague; we do not yet hear.

From the Army, we have an Account, that Lord Sandwich has had his Conference with Monsr Puisieux, at Liège, in which, tho' it was not imagined, or intended, that anything should be finally agreed, Lord Sandwich had an Opportunity of hearing the French Minister's Sentiments upon most of the material Points. Mr. Puisieux declared, that the Paper, sent by Marshal Saxe to Sr John Legonier, in the Beginning of this Negotiation (which Paper I beleive your Grace has seen) was, what France would insist upon. Upon Ld Sandwich's mentioning, that the King would expect, that the Engagements they are under by former Treaties, with regard to the person of the Pretender, should be extended to His Descendants & Posterity, M. Puisieux seemed to make a Difficulty of it; & said, if they consented to it, it deserved some Concession on the part of England. Upon the whole, He did not talk in such a Manner as shew'd a real Disposition for Peace. However, it was proposed, & agreed, (as far as they could agree it), that Conferences should be open'd at Aix la Chapelle, which will probably be done; & the Ministers of the Allies be admitted to them. His Royal Highness writes, that He has received His Reinforcements from Hanover, & is now as strong as Marsl Saxe. It is generally supposed Lowendal will go to Breda; towards which place Gen Chandos is probably retir'd; but we have no particular Account of it.

There is now in London an Emissary from the Court of Spain. He has Instructions to treat upon the foot, that Macanas treated in the Spring, with Lord Sandwich; so that I fear, much is not to be expected from his Negotiation.

I have nothing to add to this tedious Letter, but to make my Lord Duke of Newcastle's Compliments to your Grace, & to acquaint you, that He shall depend upon the Pleasure of seeing you at Claremont, at the time you have appointed, & that He hopes, your Grace will not fail to bring Sr John Miller with you.

I am with the greatest respect My Lord, Your Grace's most obedt Humble servt

Andrew Stone

387.   NEWCASTLE TO RICHMOND

Claremont
Sept 12th 1747

My Dear Lord,

I am extreamly sorry I prevented your coming to Claremont tomorrow, where you would have met Charles Bentinck. He arrived very unexpectedly on Thursday last. I knew nothing of it 'till yesterday. His cheif Business was to keep up our Spirits here, & to assure us, that they were not frightened by the scandalous Surrender of Berg-op-Zoom. He says, the French Army is not in a Condition to make any further Progress, & that Chandos' Corps, will hinder it, if they attempt it. There was either the grossest Neglect & Ignorance, or Treachery in our loss of Berg-op-Zoom. I have had a most obliging Letter from the Duke, full of Resentment to the French, for their extravagant proposals, made by Puyisseux to Lord Sandwich. H.R.H's was then in Spirits, thinking B. might hold out. Mr. Bentinck returns tomorrow to Holland, very well satisfied with your Humble Servant. My Brother told Charles B. your Grace would be here tomorrow, which was the reason that He first thought of coming here. I shall expect you next week, but insist upon your bringing Sr John. Cronstom with part of the Garison & all the Troops in the Line got off safe.

I am my dear Lord ever Yrs

Holles Newcastle

P.S. My Compliments to the Dutchess of Richmond.

388.   RICHMOND TO NEWCASTLE

Goodwood
2d Octr 1747

My Dear Lord,

Since I saw your Grace I have had nothing to make a letter of, & this is of no great consequence, only to tell you, you owe me £8. 7. 4 for two Alderney Cows that I have by your own commands gott for you, butt by His Majesty's commands in his last pro-clamation they are & must be prisoners in the feild they are now in, for three months. however, they are in good pasture below Chichester, at a farm of our freind Sr John Miller, & the best care will be taken of them. & when the time of their quarantaine is out, you shall have them paying for their keeping. I cant finish my letter without a bitt of Sussex polliticks, viz: that I have (by operation) gott the Corporation of Arundell fill'd up with four of my freinds, by which I shall have it sure for the future.[1] I am sorry to find Mr. Pelham so cool about the petition, 'tho he expresses himself as kindly as possible to me about it.

I am My Dear Lord, your Grace's ever faithfull & most affectte Humble servant

Richmond &c.

---

1.   In spite of which the Mayor of Arundel reported to the 3rd. Duke of Richmond after his father's death in 1750, that 'one half or something more of the voters will go to the best bidder'.

389. RICHMOND TO NEWCASTLE

Goodwood
18th Octr 1747

My Dear Lord,

I am extreamly obliged to your Grace for the letter I have had from Mr. Stone. I thinke the Archbishop[1] dyed in good time, for I beleive he was growing an old Rogue. Sherlock[2] will fill that see with dignity, butt he'l not last long in it, for I take him to be in a bad way as to his health. I wish our Dean Ashburnham may now come in for a Bishoprick; & surely now there will be so many removes, I should hope my quondam & His Majestys now eldest Chaplain Poor Blomer will come in for a Deanery somewhere. indeed his case is a hard one, & the forty last years of his life irreprochable, he is now seventy years old, so if he has not something soon, twill be too late. & I own his having been my Chaplain, & recommended for King's Chaplain by me, makes me more than commonly anxious for his preferment. so pray thinke of him now, & I shall be vastly obliged to you.

The Duchess of Richmond & I have a scheme of dining next Sunday at Claremount, that is if it is entirely convenient to you, so you will be so good as to lett me know it. you have not told me whether you will have the two Alderney Cows, & if you want a pretty little bull there is also one, who I assure you will not submit to My Lord Lincoln's in point of Vigor. I assure you they are curiositys as there are very few now to be gott, & that these are true Alderney bred, butt you know that by His Majesty's proclamation, they cant be moved these three months, butt when they can, I'l send them you, if you will have them.

I am My Dear Lord Your ever faithfull & most affectte servant
Richmond &c.

You'l give the Dss of Richmond leave to bring Miss Folkes[3] with her, if you allow her to dine at Claremount herself on Sunday. I shall have nobody else with me to trouble you with.

390. NEWCASTLE TO RICHMOND

Newcastle House
Oct 20th 1747

My Dear Lord,

I had yesterday your most kind letter, and shall be extreamly glad to have the honor of your good Company & the Ds of Rds wh Miss Folkes at Claremont next Sunday. I also beg to have the Alderney Cows with the Linky <u>Bull</u>, which, I hope need not to be tied up, as my Lord has been since the last <u>accident</u>. I will pay for them, when I see you, but beg they may stay where they are, till they can be removed. The Bishop of Salisbury, to my great Concern, has again refused the Archbishoprick, so it will be the A.B. York,[4] & I hope, Bishop Hutton[5] who is the fittest Man, will go to York. As to

---

1. John Potter, 1674–1747, who had been successively, Regius Professor of Divinity at Oxford, 1707–1715; Bishop of Oxford, 1715–1737; and Archbishop of Canterbury, 1737–1747.
2. Thomas Sherlock, 1678–1761, Dean of Chichester, 1715–1727, was successively Bishop of Bangor, 1728–1734; Bishop of Salisbury, 1734–1748; and Bishop of London, 1748–1761. He declined the see of York in 1743, and Canterbury in 1747.
3. Presumably the daughter of Martin Folkes, 1690–1754, President of the Royal Society, and a friend and correspondent of Richmond.
4. Thomas Herring, 1693–1757, Archbishop of York, 1743–1747, and Archbishop of Canterbury, 1747–1757.
5. Matthew Hutton, 1693–1758, was successively Bishop of Bangor, 1743–1747; Archbishop of York, 1747–1757; and Archbishop of Canterbury, 1757–1758.

Politicks, they are very bad, both at home & abroad, & Differences in opinion will destroy things in both Places. We shall have neither Peace nor War. The first we can't have, I am afraid, tolerable at present. The last we won't make, because we have not the time. We have no Scheme, & content ourselves, that is some of us — with being <u>witty, ridiculing</u> & expressing what is, without pretending, or venturing, to say what should be, in a way to bring it to any Maturity. A few days ago, I had great hopes, we should make our separate Peace with Spain. I don't yet despair of it, but things do not look so well as they did. When I see you, I will explain myself upon all these Topicks, & am more than I can express Yrs

Holles Newcastle

My Compliments, &c.

P.S. By the cahier of yesterday poor Bentinck is much better, which is great good news to all who wish things may go well there

391. STONE TO RICHMOND

Whitehall
Octobr 26th 1747

My Lord,
  I dispatch this Messenger, by Order of my Lord Duke of Newcastle, to acquaint your Grace that Captain Moor arrived this day, having been sent express by Rear Admiral Hawke, with the following Account; viz.

  that, on the 14th Inst. R.A. Hawke[1] fell in with the French Squadron which sail'd from Rochelle, on the 7th, consisting of eight Ships of the Line, some Fregats; and about 250 Sail of Merchant Ships bound to Martinico. The Engagement began between 12 & 1, at noon; and lasted 'till night. Two of the French Men of War escaped; But the other six (of which two were of 74 Guns, one of 68; two of 64; & one of 52) were taken, and probably by this time are arrived at Plymouth. Our Ships are much shatter'd, the French having fought with great Bravery; but we have lost none. The Enemy lost a great many Men in the Engagement; and there are upwards of 3,000 Prisoners. The Behaviour of our Officers, & Men, is much commended; excepting only that of Captain Fox of the Kent, who is to be tried by a Court Martial, &, it is thought, will be condemned for Cowardice. Captain Saumare was kill'd in the Engagement; His Loss is much lamented.

  All the French Merchant Ships escaped, having been order'd to make the best of their way before the Engagement began. Mr. Hawke sent a Sloop to Cre Legge at the Leward Islands, with an Account of His having intercepted this Squadron; so that it is very possible, many of the trading Ships may fall into the Hands of our Cruisers in those Seas.

  Your Grace will easily imagine the great Joy occasioned by this happy Event; upon which my Lord Duke desires your Grace, & the Company at Weybridge, would accept his most hearty Congratulations.

  I am with the greatest Respect My Lord Your Grace's most obedient & most humble servant

Andrew Stone

1. Sir Edward Hawke, 1710–1781, MP for Portsmouth, 1747–1776, was appointed Rear Admiral in 1747. His first great naval success was this capture of seven out of nine ships off Belle Isle at the second Battle of Finisterre. He was later 1st. Lord of the Admiralty, 1766–1771, and Admiral of the Fleet in 1768.

392. NEWCASTLE TO RICHMOND

Claremont
Novr 21st 1747

My Dear Lord,

I am sure you will be glad to hear that the Personal Attack, that was made yesterday upon me in the House of Commons by my Lord Gage and —— was received in the manner I could wish, & ended much to the mortification of those, who brought it on. Lord Gage brought in the Petition, signed by Lord Middlesex, & Mr. Gage, & as it contained only a Complaint of the Interposition of a Peer, by His Presence at the Election, entertaining the Voters at His House, &c.,[1] Mr. Pitt (as had been agreed) desired the Sense of the House, whether, it should be received, & whether He or Mr. Hay were affected by it. Pitt turned Gage, greatly with Ridicule, & spoke admirably well. Murray[2] in an excellent Speech, moved to reject the Petition, My Brother gave an account of the whole Election extreamly well, & I must do justice to Harry Fox who, spoke more for me, & my Honor than any of them. All the Speakers against us, viz, Nugent, Dr Lee,[3] &c., spoke decently enough; except Mr. Potter,[4] the late Archbishop's worthy Son, who in a long Speech, was pleased to say all the reflecting things, upon your Humble Servant that the Malice & Impudence of a Hot headed Fool could invent. Our Majority was surprising, we rejected the Petition 247 against 96, a Majority hardly ever heard of before, in such a Case, and this notwithstanding all Force & Endeavours used to the contrary by ——. However I have this Comfort; that I have stood by my Friends & they have steadily stood by me. Had I, (which I hope I never shall) consented even to treat, this Attack had never been made upon me & I should not have had an opportunity, of knowing the Goodness & Steadiness of this House of Commons in personal Points. The only thing that concerns me & indeed surprises me is; Bethel[5] the City Member and Sr Wm Codrington,[6] voted against me. I doubt the last is gained by ——.

I have not troubled you a great while wh news, & shall only now tell you that the Duke is come, without vanity, just in the same way of thinking, with regard to our Measures, that I have long been in. My Lord Chancellor, Ld Chesterfield, my Brother, & I had a Conference of near five Hours with his R.Hs last Monday night, upon the proposed augmentation of our Contingent to 70,000 Men, at the earnest Request of the Statholder. H.R.Hs & I were zealously for it; Ld Chancellor, not against it, Ld Chesterfield silent, & my Brother, at last yeilded to the Duke. Pray let me know a little of your Motions, whether you think of coming to Town, or commanding Linky, & your Followers to attend you at Charlton. My Compliments to the Ds of Richmond, & believe me my Dear Duke most affectly Yrs

Holles Newcastle

---

1. William Hall Gage and the Earl of Middlesex, who had been defeated by William Pitt and William Hay at Seaford, presented a petition to Parliament based on Newcastle's contravention of the standing House of Commons resolution against interference by peers in elections.
2. Hon William Murray.
3. George Lee, 1700–1758, MP for Brackly, 1733–1742, for Devizes, 1742–1747, for Liskeard, 1747–1754, and for Launceston, 1754–1758, was Chairman of the Committee of Elections and Privileges. He was Treasurer of the Household to the Prince of Wales, 1751–1757.
4. Thomas Potter, 1718–1759, MP for St. Germans, 1747–1754, for Aylesbury, 1754–1757, and for Oakhampton, 1757–1759, was Secretary to the Princess of Wales, 1748–1751.
5. Slingsby Bethell, 1695–1758, MP for London, 1747–1758, was Lord Mayor of London, 1755–1756.
6. Sir William Codrington, 1719–1792, Bethell's nephew, was MP for Beverley, 1747–1761, and for Tewkesbury, 1761–1792.

393. NEWCASTLE TO RICHMOND

Newcastle House
Jany 1st 1747/8

My Dear Lord,

I believe your Grace will wonder, that you have been so long without a Letter from me, and indeed you may. But as I always write to you in the greatest Confidence, and without any Reserve, the State of our Affairs abroad has been, & is, so unpleasant, and perplexing that I did not know well, where to begin, but as I see no immediate Amendment, or Decision, I will give a short Sketch of our most disagreable Situation. Abroad, the Queen of Hungary, & the King of Sara are quarreling about the Command in Italy, the Statholder insisting upon a new Article obliging our Troops to take their turn in Garrison Duty, & our several Allies, flinging such difficulties in ye way of our Convention, which is to determine the Troops to be furnished by each power, so that every one, will have some Pretence, not to have their Contingents ready in time. The States are by degrees, tho' slowly augmenting their Army, & the Prussians, by the most unjustifiable Delay in sending the Dutch Minister full power to conclude the Treaty, will not be with our Army before the end of May at soonest, if a Quickener which I prevailed to have sent five weeks ago, does not encourage them to begin their March, without waiting for the Ratifications of the Treaty. But what is worst of all, we have some Accounts that his Prussian Majesty will be soon in Motion, but this is, and must be kept the greatest Secret. In these Circumstances, what is to be done? The only thing thoroughly to be depended upon, & on no Account to be neglected, is to get all the Force you can possibly, at any Rate, & at any Expense, both in Flanders & Italy, for it is a jest to think of 1 or 200,000li more or less at this critical & dangerous Conjuncture. But that Reasoning will not prevail; The next thing is to make Peace. I agree in it if it can be upon any tolerable Terms, but what appearance is there of that? However, it should & must be tried. But I think it is but reasonable, that those who have been the most clamorous for Peace, & I suppose think it the most practicable, and in whose Department particularly it is, should propose the Conditions, & the Manner of bringing it about. No, that is not to be done. Who will expose themselves to be the first Proposers?

In short this necessary Work, nobody cares, or dares to set about. To come more closely to the Point. It has been represented to the Duke by H——— W———le,[1] entre nous, that there is but one Person in the Closet of a different Opinion, & that one Person differs from all his Friends, Confidents, & Relations, & this particularly as to the gaining Prussia. The D of Devonshire, has been with the Chancellor, with the knowledge of my Brother, & the D of Grafton, to express His great uneasiness at the State of Affairs, tho' in a very civil Manner, & that the King & the Duke of Newcastle are for continuing the War & flinging out Hints, of His Design to resign His Employment, and all this, without any previous Notice to me, or saying what particular thing, they would have done. I can talk as loud for Peace, as any Body, but talking without setting about it, or shewing upon what Terms, it is to be had, is nothing but Talk, & very unkind & very unjust Talk.

As to Prussia, I was till yesterday the only Minister about the King, that has of late dared to open his Mouth upon it, & yesterday my Brother only, sounded upon what I had said to the King the day before. Some time ago, I stated the Affair of Prussia so; represented the universal Opinion to be such; that I prevailed to have a Minister

---

1. Horace Walpole.

named, which Minister then was, <u>Sr Everard</u>. I knew Sr Everard, as well as any body, & am afraid have not a higher Opinion of Him, than those, who knew Him best; but I knew also He depends absolutely upon <u>one</u> who I think will make Him do right, & that is no small advantage in this Case. I renewed my Application the day before yesterday. I talked very freely, & <u>honestly</u>, so that if other People will, I will take it upon me, to say, that any Proper Person may be sent, & what is more, with any proper Instructions, or I am much mistaken, & yet the D. of N. is the only one, who differs with all His <u>Friends</u> & <u>Relations</u> upon this Point, or in other words, who is a <u>Stinking Dirty Courtier</u>. I don't deserve this to be said by my Enemies, who don't know it. It is unjust if said or believed, by my Friends, <u>who know the Contrary</u>. I have not seen the King alone but three or four times, these two <u>Months</u>, & then I have always talked upon Prussia. Seeing him in Company, is not seeing Him at all. The only Person, that I have Obligations to, is the <u>Duke</u> who has been present at all our Meetings; seen my Behaviour, & that <u>of Others</u>; knows all that I have said, & done; the injustice of this Charge, or Suggestion in every Respect; & has declared so, to those, who have talked to Him upon it. I have wrote to my Lord Sandwich, & to Bentinck, as becomes an honest Man, as you will see by the two enclosed Letters. I have had a sort of an Answer to some former Letters, in the like strain, but not a satisfactory one. I have declared to the King, & the Duke, & they know it, or may know it, that if they produce, what they would have done for Peace, if I think, it can be accepted, or followed, I will co-operate to my utmost, to bring it about; that, if on the Contrary, I cannot in Conscience approve it, I will however, not obstruct it, and I will keep my Word. I think, upon the whole, we shall at last have a Meeting on Monday or Tuesday next, & I suppose these Gentlemen, will then speak out. I have formed my Thoughts, so at least, I know what to say; but my Dear Lord, we are led away by <u>generals</u>, & our good Friends, who won't or can't enter into <u>particulars</u> run away with <u>generals</u> artfully suggested by designing Men, or a <u>Designing Man</u>, & so blame their best <u>Friends</u>. This is the Case. I wish your Grace was here, to see & judge for yourself. I should not fear, your or any impartial Determination. I have worked hard to get our separate Peace with Spain. I have at times hoped to succeed, but by the last Answer given us by <u>Wall</u>,[1] I begin to dispair of it. I have thus stated to you the present state of our Publick & Private Affairs. that of the Publick is certainly bad, tho' I really hope not so desperate, as is represented, but bad enough, to require all the Care & Attention possible to amend it either by a tolerable Peace, if that can be procured this Winter, or by assembling all the Force we can get, to prevent things from going worse in Flanders, & Italy; and that I should hope might be done, if we can but escape some fatal Stroke on the Republic this Winter, & the beginning of Spring, I should hope, things would mend upon us. As to our private Situations at home, we have all of us just Credit enough to hurt each other if we have a mind to it, and to obstruct any Measure, that is proposed. I should make a great many Excuses, for this long Letter, but as the Frost will keep you at home, you may perhaps have nothing much better to do, than to read this Account of your Friends. I desire you would say nothing of this Letter, to any Body but my Lord Lincoln, to whom you may read it, <u>if you can</u>. I don't know whether Lady Lincoln's Illness has not called Him away. She is I hope in God, in no Danger at all. If He is with you, I beg you would give him the enclosed Letter. Pray send back my Letters to Ld Sandwich & Bentinck. I wish you & yours all the Compliments of the Season, & am with my best Respects to the Dutchess of Richmond ever most unalterably & sincerely yrs.

Holles Newcastle

---

1. General Ricardo Wall, Spanish Minister in England, and Minister of State.

394. RICHMOND TO NEWCASTLE

Goodwood
Sunday, 3d Jany 1747/8

My Dear Lord,

You are very good to give yourself so much trouble as to inform me so fully of the situation wee are in. which I am sorry to say I thinke allmost desperate; the Duke of Devonshire's opening himself in the manner he did to the Chancellor, I own allarms me, for I am very sure it proceeded from the honesty of his heart, & I have the greatest defference for his judgment. yett I do thinke whatever his opinion is, he ought to have open'd himself to you first, & particularly because it differ'd from yours. it is what I really thinke is due from one freind to an other. & whenever I have the misfortune to differ from your Grace you may depend upon it, you will be the first person that shall know it, butt essentially I am sure wee never can differ, as our principals are the same.

& now I will tell you what I have said before to you, that in my poor opinion your behaviour in the whole course of this most important consideration of Peace or Warr, has been, not only fair honest & clear butt your opinion of makeing the utmost efforts to carry on the Warr, is the most likely way to obtain a tollerable peace. Yett I must plainly tell you there is one & only one point in which I do thinke you have been deficient, I have not sayed so to any body else so I have a right to say it to you, which is that I do not thinke you have push'd enough in the Closset, for the means to gain Prussia. you say you have done it lately, butt indeed it ought to have been done long ago, & it is a point of such consequence, that no fear of Clossett favors ought intimidate. My polliticks are in a very narrow compass. If wee could gain Prussia, or make a seperate peace with Spain, wee might still have a good chance. if both could be done, all might be retreived; butt without either wee are absollutely undone. for then wee must be drove to make a peace upon France's terms, & that must end in sure destruction. I am persuaded you have done all that man could do with Wall, & am very sorry to find it has not suceeded. & for that very reason every engine ought to be sett to worke to gain Prussia, for I see no salvation without it. & surely the sending of that poor creature, 'tho very honest man, Sr Everard, is declaring to the world that you mean nothing. I hear Marchmont[1] offer'd to go, & 'tho I look upon him as entirely Chesterfeild's man & consequently dislike him, yett I thinke the stake is so great, I would employ him, or the great Devil himself, if he was butt capable of bringing about a worke so absollutely necessary for the very beeing of this Country. Holland you see is resolv'd upon its own ruin, & your letter to Bentinck proves it. I wish to know if My Lord Sandwich delivered it, & what was his answer to it. I could say a thousand things more to your letter, butt fear to tire you, whilst the consideration of this grand affair is in the hands of few, (which is certanly right provided you give it dispatch) My being in town would be of no service, butt if you should come to take the opinions of more, I shall attend you upon the first call, & (tho you know I cant deliver it well), I shall be ready to speake my poor thoughts without reserve or fear of any body, for I assure I have no fear butt that for my Country about me. dont imagine that I thinke you have, for I know you will have none, when it comes to the push. butt I own in the point of Prussia, I wish & now hope you will have no <u>menagement</u> in the Clossett.

adieu My Dear Dear Lord, Your's for ever & most affectionately

Richmond &c.

I tremble for Zealand this weather, & look upon Bevelandt as gon. I dont return you the Coppys of the letters not knowing whether it is propper to trust them by the common post, so you will order Mr. Stone to lett me know how I shall return them to you. or if you have other coppys whether I shall burn them.

---

1. Hugh Hume Campbell, 3rd. Earl of Marchmont, 1708–1794, MP for Berwick, 1734–1740.

395. RICHMOND TO NEWCASTLE

Charlton
Sunday night 3d Janry 1747/8

My Dear Lord,

As I am sure my Lord Harcourt is a safe conveyance, I send you the enclosed coppys, which I thought you might not so well like I should send by the post. I have read your long letter over again with great attention, & am pleased to find that you have of late push'd this affair of Prussia, only I am not at all pleased that poor Sr Everard should be the man. for tho he will do what the Duke bids him & I am sure the Duke will bid him do right, yett at that distance, I fear he is not capable of doing what a man of superior parts might do. I observe also in your letter that you say you wish I was in town, that I might judge impartially, butt whilst this very important question is only before four or five of you, as it is certanly right it sould be, I can not conceive what use my being in town could be of, butt if you thinke it may, I certanly will attend you upon the first call as I told you in my letter this morning; tho if it thaws I shall be sorry to leave the Country.

Your's my Dear Lord, for ever

Richmond &c.

I wish the person whosoever he is that is to go to Berlin, was there now. half our bad success has proceeded from delays somewhere or other.

396. RICHMOND TO NEWCASTLE

Findon
Tuesday 26 Janry 1747/8

My Dear Lord,

You know how long I have been earnestly solliciting you for my good freind Mr. Hughes, & I formerly aply'd to you for the living of <u>Methley near Wakefeild in Yorkshire</u>. The present incumbent Mr. Goodwin father to our Goodwin of Petworth, fourscore years old & now as you may imagine in a declining way; it is imediately in his Majesty's gift being upwards of £20 a year in the Kings books. the real value is 210: now you know I have been so long a solicitor for Mr. Hughes that I really thinke it will be hard if I do not succeed in this for him, as I aply before the present incumbent's death; & that I hope I shall meet with no powerfull Yorkshire antagonist, espetially as you know how many things of this kind you have done for My Lord Rockingham,[1] so that really he can not in decency aske for any more. I therefore flatter my self you will oblige me in it, it being the only favor of consequence I have to aske for my Clergy man in this County, & you know what assurances you was so good as to make him yourself, when I presented him last to you at Chichester. I therefore beg you would thinke of it seriously, & you will highly oblige My Dear Lord, Your Grace's ever faithfull & most affectte humble servant

Richmond &c.

397. RICHMOND TO NEWCASTLE

Goodwood
2d Febry 1747/8

My Dear Lord,

I have a gossiping affair to trouble you with, for which you must excuse me, butt as

---

1. Thomas Watson-Wentworth, 3rd. Earl of Rockingham, 1693–1750, MP for Malton, 1715–1727, and for Yorkshire, 1727–1728, was Lord Lieutenant of Yorkshire West Riding, 1733–1750. He was created 1st. Marquis of Rockingham, 1746.

the Duchess of Richmond is not in town, I actually know nobody to employ in it butt yourself. you must know then that before I left London, I waited on the King in My Lord Kildare's name to ask the honor of His Majesty to be Godfather to his son,[1] which His Majesty consented to really in a most kind & obliging manner. butt it seems I should have ask'd him to apoint his deputy, & at the same time leave for me to be the other Godfather, & My Lady Dowager Kildare the Godmother; all which I have actually neglected not haveing consulted Grantham as I certanly ought to have done. So now Grandmother Taw & I beg of you to aske His Majesty on Thursday these questions, & who he pleases to apoint his proxy, which I take for granted will be his own Lieutenant My Lord Harrington; if so you will I suppose acquaint his Lordship with it, & I beg you would gett His Majesty's orders on Thursday that you may write My Lord Kildare word of it by Thursday night's post, for they are in a great hurry to Christen their Child, & that will be saveing time; so I want no answer at all, & desire you would spare your self that trouble, butt wee both beg you would write to My Lord Kildare on Thursday which will give him great pleasure, & oblige us extreamly. Taw thought My Lord Kildare should have wrote to the King to have asked this favor, & indeed he asked me if he should not, butt I was of opinion that my askeing it as I did in his name was most propper, so if it is wrong I take the whole blame to myself, butt the Princess will tell you if you aske her, which Taw wishes you would do, as she is in some fidgetts about it. I must again beg pardon for giveing you so much trouble.

    & am, My Dear Lord, for ever & most affectly Your's
Richmond &c.

I am very uneasy to hear how great affairs go on, butt as I shall see Linky on Sunday, I shall not expect any letter from you.

A glorious chase to day. Found after a drag of an hour & half by Mitchell grove, & kill'd this side of Houghton Bridge.

Your direction, <u>to My Lord Kildare at Dublin</u>, is sufficient.

398. NEWCASTLE TO RICHMOND

Claremont
Feby 6th, 1747/8

My Dear Lord,

    As no Hurry of Business can ever make me neglect your Commands, I spoke to the King on Thursday, & wrote two Letters in my own hand to my Lord Kildare, & my Lord Lieutenant,[2] just as you order'd me. I beg you would make my Compliments to the Dutchess of Richmond, with my best wishes, for whatever concerns your Grace & your Family. I was this evening surprised with an Account, that Lord Chesterfield resigned the Seals this day. I can't quite say surprised, for by some Appearances, I thought, it might be so, tho' my Brother, had no Notion that it would happen so soon. Everything has been done, that could be, to prevent it, but He was determined. Lord Gower seems thoroughly vexed with Him, & has thrice expressed to me His great Satisfaction at my Disposition, to do everything, that could be expected from me, to make him easy, but to no purpose. He promises very fairly, but one that quitts in this Manner, will hardly be Master of Himself. The D, of Bedford, is what we could wish Him, but I fear my Brother will feel it, and not enter into any Measures, or Scheme to supply the Vacancy, and that is the worst thing, that can happen. Who it will be, I know not. I fancy Nobody, for some days. I go to Town tomorrow morning. His

---

1. George Fitzgerald, Lord Offaly, 1748–1765.
2. Lord Harrington was Lord Lieutenant of Ireland, 1746–1751.

Majesty was very gracious, to me upon the Subject some days ago, but since, He has been more reserved. If ye Frost lasts, I hope you will come to London, for I want the Advice, & Assistance of my best Friends. I say of you, "of my best Friend".

I am ever most gratefully & cordially Yrs

Holles Newcastle

399. RICHMOND TO NEWCASTLE

Goodwood
7. Feb. 1747/8

My Dear Lord,

You are vastly good to have giving yourself so much trouble to oblige the Duchess of Richmond, Ld & Lady Kildare & myself in this affair, which 'tho trifling was necessary. Mr. Stone writes me word that the living of Meathly is in the gift of the Chancellor of the Duchy of Lancaster, which I thinke is old Edgecumb,[1] & if you remember at Chichester you told Hughes that you would speake to Ld Edgecumb for him, incase he should have any thing that would do, so I wish you would speake to him, which you have a right to as he has obligations to you, & I have not for he has none to me. I assure you I have Hughes's preferrment vastly at heart. I long to see Linky who I hope will be here to day 'tho it freezes hard, that I may hear something how things go.

Your's My Dearest Lord, at all events & in all circumstances,

Richmond &c.

400. RICHMOND TO NEWCASTLE

Goodwood
9. Febry. 1747/8

My Dear Lord,

I again return you our most sincere thankes from the whole familly for the trouble you have been at to write to Ld Kildare &c. My Lord Chesterfeild's resignation displeases me very much, for (as I dont love him) I fear it will give him eclat, & even credit among severall people wee do love. butt my cheif concern is for his successor,[2] which I fear will bring you in to great difficultys; for I know you are in your heart for a man disliked by most people. he has flattered you & will continue to do so, butt depend upon it he is no more to be trusted than the last, & in the eye of the world is a much worse man. yett how Totty & his father in Law will take his being refused I dont know. 'twould be pitty to loose them, yett, the takeing in this man, who is only their freind, will be the ruin of you.

You see how freely I write, for I have no menagements for any body hardly at any time, butt espetially when I thinke your good is concern'd, & I am sure it is in this point more than you may perhaps be aware of, & an other very great objection I have to him is that your brother does not like him, & I am sure that singly ought to be an objection to you, & I hope will be so. Surely there can be no objection to Sr T:R:[3] & he would be glad to act as you would have him; & as such I should like him prefereable to any body. butt I hope you have by this time taken the first essentiall step, which is to

1. Richard Edgcumbe, 1st. Lord Edgcumbe, 1680–1758, MP for Cornwall, 1701, for St. Germans, 1701–1702, for Plympton Erle, 1702–1734, and again, 1741–1742, and for Lostwithiel, 1734–1741, was Chancellor of the Duchy of Lancaster, 1743–1758.
2. When Chesterfield resigned as Secretary of State for the Northern Department in February 1748, Newcastle wanted to replace him with Sandwich, but was persuaded against it by the rest of the Ministry, and himself took the vacant Northern Department while the Duke of Bedford took the Southern Department.
3. Sir Thomas Robinson.

desire the King to give you the Northern Province. I am very glad to hear what you say of the Duke of Bedford & Lord Gowr; they are certanly both honest, & good men, so I dont doubt of their continuing to be reasonable.

If the frost lasts I will go to town; not that I can be of any service. I can't help giving my advice by letter, 'tho I am very diffident of my capacity in giving it. butt, I know that when I give advice that is liked it will be taken, & when I offer such as is disliked it will not be taken, which is a very good reason for not giving my self the trouble of a journey, whereas paper advice may be used in a water Clossett. dont thinke I am testy now, tho you know you made me damnably so last time I was at Newcastle house. & be sure I never can be so with you butt when I thinke you are hurting yourself, for I am, My Dear Lord, most affectionately & unfeindedly Your's
Richmond &c.

I am prodigiously concern'd to hear of Henry Legge's illness. I thinke his life is of great consequence to the publick, & extreamly so to me, as I most sincerely love & value him.

401. RICHMOND TO NEWCASTLE

Goodwood
12 Febry 1747/8

My Dear Lord,
I have butt one word to trouble you with, which is to tell you that if Henry Fox should be Secretary of State, the Duchess of Richmond & I should be vastly Happy, tho wee still wish him the Paymaster's place as it is less precarious, & a better thing, for his familly's sake.
I am, My Dear Lord, for ever & most affectly Your's
Richmond &c.

402. NEWCASTLE TO RICHMOND

Whitehall
Fryday, 4 o'clock [? 13 Feb 1748]

My Dear Lord,
I am infinitely obliged for your most kind letter; these Marks of Friendship always make the right Impression upon me. The great Strain is now over. The D. of Bedford has kissed the King's hands this day for Secretary of State, of the Southern Province, & Lord Sandwich succeeds him at the Head of the Admiralty. Every thing passed as well as possible. The Duke of Bd told me this morning, He would take it for six months, if the King thought it for His Service. I went in, & did it immediately. I hope every Body will be pleased, & that my good <u>Friends</u> will no longer lament their late great Loss. I write this night a Pacifick Letter to Sandwich, which I am in hopes will please. It is upon my principle of not continuing the War another year.
Ever Yrs
Holles Newcastle

My best Love to Dear Linky.
Compliments to the Dutchess.

403. RICHMOND TO NEWCASTLE

Goodwood
Sat 13 Febry 1747/8

My Dear Lord,
Since I find it is all your own doing, I will strive to like what is done, & I wish it may

268

last, butt I can't help thinking it looks like a tottering scheme. not butt that you know I have allways stood up for the Duke of Bedford's being as honest, & as well meaning a man as ever was born. I am obliged to you for letting me know it, & am, My Dear Lord, Your ever faithfull & most affectte humble servant,

Richmond &c.

I suppose My Ld Sandwich will not be sent for home upon this, for nobody can do better abroad, and any body may do as well as him at the admiralty board.
The Duke of Grafton is now at breakfast with Taw, & says that the express was to me, so he need not write.

404. RICHMOND TO NEWCASTLE

Goodwood
Wednesday 17th Febry 1747/8

My Dear Lord,
   You do me great injustice if you thinke me capable of joyning in any cry against you, & indeed you explain yourself in your letter, & say you do not mean any part of your letter to me, butt I must explain myself also to you, which is to tell you that my only objection against your new Colleague, is, that if you do not agree together, you can not gett rid of him, so easyly as the last; in whom I am fully persuaded there is no loss, only by the difficulty it caused in the choice of a successor, & since your only view was to proove to the world that you did not mean to be sole Secretary, you certanly have pitch'd upon the most propper man in England. butt I own fairly & declare that I am not that Cabinett Counsellor who wont bear your having one entirely your Commis, for I most sincerely wish you had such a one, & Fox or Robinson would have been so, butt all my argument is stop'd at once by nobody in the house of Commons could have it. I have then done, & the Duke of Bedford then is Hobson's choice. butt I must disagree with you about Sandwich, indeed the run against him is not so unjust as you imagine. you have say'd a great deale about yourself which to me was very unnecessary, for I know you to be an honest man, & it is for that I love you, as you very justly observe. & it is for that I ever shall be my dear Lord, your ever faithfull, sincere freind, & affectionate humble servant,

Richmond &c.

I had thoughts of going to town to day butt the snow is so deep that I dare not carry up the Duchess of Richmond, 'till the roads are a little beate. butt Saturday, or Sunday at farthest I beleive wee shall be in town if this weather lasts.
Is there any thing in Albermarle's coming over ?

405. RICHMOND TO NEWCASTLE

Charlton
2d March 1747/8

My Dear Lord,
   Carpenter told me that you say'd you had receiv'd my letter, & read the paper contain'd in it, so I hope you have given it to Mr. Pelham, & that you will both be of opinion that it is a call of great compassion, & I beg also that My Lord Chancellor may see it, & I am persuaded he will be of the same opinion.
Sir John Miller has been with me & has again renew'd his request about the reversion of Robert's place. I own I wish most extreamly that Mr. Pelham would do it, for tho to give Sr John his due he can not be more hearty than he is, such a thing as this would pin down his whole familly as well as himself for ever, & you know how considerable a familly it is, haveing now four boys, & such a number of relations in this part of the Country. & tho he has a good fortune, yett as he has God knows how many

girls besides his four boys, he certanly wants the help of his freinds, & you know you have often ask'd him, what you could do to serve him; & that not <u>parmaniere de parler</u> butt I am sure with your own naturall sincerity, so I really thinke he has a just claim to your freindship.

Wee are now kept at home by the rain which is better than by frost, for as soon as it hold up wee are now sure of sport. Old Puff is finer than ever he was in his life, & Linky is a comicall, & as testy.

Adieu My Dearest Lord. I am for ever, & unalterably, Your's

Richmond &c.

406. STONE TO RICHMOND

Whitehall
April 16, 1748

My Lord,

A Messenger arrived, last night, from the Army, with Letters from H.R.H. the Duke, of so late a Date, as Tuesday last, & H.R.H. had then received the important Dispatch which your Grace (if I remember rightly) read, at Newcastle House, on Friday the 8th inst, & which was sent away that night; so that the very next mail may probably bring some Accounts of what my Lord Sandwich may have done, in consequence of those Orders. In the mean time His Lp has had some further Conference, with St Severin,[1] who continues to talk with great seeming fairness, & moderation; and even pretends to enter into Ld Sandwich's Notion of finding out an Equivalent, for the King of Sardinia, for Final; But what looks very suspicious is, that he has found out a most frivolous Pretence to delay the Opening of the Conference, so that it is fear'd, nothing will be done, till the Fate of Maestricht is determined: and then, no one can say, what their Demands may be. Your Grace will see the State of that Siege, in this night's publick papers; with an Account of the successful Sally that that has been made by the Garrison. We hope, it may hold out, for some time; But, as it cannot be relieved, it must fall at last. H.R.H. has proposed to the Prince of Orange, that the two Corps should join, near Bois-le-Duc, & Weyndhoven. When that junction shall be made, the Duke hopes to be able to cover the Meuse from Grave, to Zeland; and to remain upon the Defensive, till it is seen, what turn the Negotiation takes at Aix-la-Chapelle; but as this Scheme is not yet finally adjusted, & perhaps may be varied; it is necessary, that it should be kept an entire Secret.

H.R.H. is not yet perfectly recover'd from the ill Effects of his late Indisposition. His chief Complaint is a great Weakness & Rheumatick Pains in his Limbs.

I am with great Respect My Lord your Grace's most obedient & most humble servant

Andrew Stone

407. RICHMOND TO NEWCASTLE

Bolderwood
20: April: 1748

My Dr Lord,

I am most extreamly obliged to your Grace, for the letter Mr. Stone wrote to me by your orders of the 16, & indeed I am more than uneasy, for I am vastly unhappy with the thoughts of the dreadfull situation wee are in, for I thinke it extreamly plain that St Severin is only amusing Ld Sandwich 'till Maestrick is taken, & that must happen, & then it is as plain to me that he will not consent even to the utmost of Ld Sandwich's

---

1. Alphonse Marie Louise, Comte de St. Severin d'Aragon was French Minister of State.

instructions in their favor, & then I fear wee shall have reason to repent of not haveing jump'd at Mareschall Saxe's proposals last year, Tho I own I was of your opinion then, to which I was induced by the vain hopes of what our ally's would do, tho you may remember that all along I told you that I suspected both their power, & will, to perform what they had promis'd, & from the beginning I never thought these Russians would be time enough to be of any service & what affects me as much as the publick concern is your own situation in these lamentable circumstances. I, that know the uprightness of your heart, know that arises from you being deceived by the Prince of Orange, Willm Bentick, & Lord Sandwich, the last was perhaps was deceived himself, Bentick may also have been deceived by his Master, however his business might be to flatter his Master, butt I do thinke it impardonable in Sandwich, all the time allmost upon the spott to have suffer'd himself to be so imposed upon. butt notwithstanding all this the unreasonable part of the world & the rage of party will be for throwing the whole upon you. dont be angry at what I say. I never did nor never will talke in this stile to any one else upon earth, butt it would be unfreindly in me if I did not tell you my apprehensions, which besides the publick good, are founded upon my love & freindship for you, & ever shall remain as I have been, most affectionately & unalterably, Your's,

Richmond &c.

Tho I have as much diversion here as foxhunting can possibly afford me; I shall at any time return to town upon the first summons from you, & if the King should go to the house, or the Parliament be up soon, I beg you would lett me know it. butt if I hear nothing from you, that requires my going up, I propose staying here all next week, & then going for two or three dayes only to Goodwood & to be in town about the 5th or 6th of May.

I should be glad to hear again from Mr. Stone how affairs go on abroad, I mean at Aix la Chapelle, for the Gazette will inform me from the army.

408.   RICHMOND TO NEWCASTLE

Bolderwood Lodge
Mund 25th April 1748

My Dear Lord,

Enclosed, is a letter I have had from my brother Grand Ecuyer, Prince Charles of Lorraine, which I beg you would lay before His Majesty, you will see it is for forty horses for the King of France, & he desires some may be added for himself, so an order for fifty would be sufficient. I take for granted his Majesty will grant it, butt shall I, in answer to this letter, lett him know that Monsr Butler he formerly sent here was not Welcome & that wee knew him to be a rascally Jacobite agent for the pretender ? Prince Charles is my old freind & I long to give it him, butt will not, unless you thinke it propper, & if you aprove of it, will shew you my letter before I send it.

I am, My Dear Lord, for ever & most affecty Your's
Richmond &c.

lett me have Prince Charles's letter back again. I go Sunday to Goodwood if I hear no more from you & shall be about the middle of the week in London.

409.   RICHMOND TO NEWCASTLE

Bolderwood Lodge
26: April: 1748

My Dear Lord,

I am vastly obliged to your Grace for the news you sent me, & it is so far good, that it is better than imediate distruction, which I thinke wee were upon the brink of, & yett

I fear I may live long enough to see it still. I own I pitty the King of Sardinia, & thinke his not haveing Finall is a hard case, yett 'twas plain it could not be, butt Kaunitz's protest I own provokes me, & 'twould be a short answer to him that His Mistress's never haveing perform'd her engagements to us is one of the chief arguments that have drove us to this very bad peace, for very bad surely it is, butt better could certanly not be procured now. I look upon their being so bent on the takeing of Maestrick, to be in order to destroy the works there, as I see by the foreign papers they are now doing at Bergen op Zoom, so as not to leave one place of defence to the Duch. these are shocking circumstances, & I look on time to come with horor. I wish that Spanish old debt might be in a private article, for the honor of one wee all wish so well to. adieu My Dear Lord, If you have any commands for me on Thursday, direct them to me here, if on Saturday to Goodwood, & if I hear nothing from you, I shall be in town the midle of next week.

I am, My Dear Lord, for ever & most affectionately, Your's

Richmond &c.

I am excessively obliged to you for sending me this news by a Messager.

410. STONE TO RICHMOND

Whitehall
May 2d 1748

My Lord,

The inclosed Paper will inform your Grace of the Success of R. Adml. Knowle's Expedition in the West Indies; which may possibly have a great good effect in keeping the French in their present pacifick Disposition.

The Dutch mail arrived this morning. Maestricht has capitulated, upon honorable Conditions for the Dutch Garrison. The Capitulation was not quite concluded for the Austrian Garrison: But it was thought, it would be done immediately. The Cessation of Hostilities in Flanders, was to commence, as on Saturday last the 30th of April. O.S. Mos St Severin's Conduct has been approved by His Court, &, by his last Conversation, with Lord Sandwich, His Lordship thinks, their Intentions are sincere. St Severin hinted the sending of a Minister from hence immediately to Paris, as what would have a very good Effect.

If the Parliament can make an end of the Business before then, so as to rise the latter end of next week; the King would set out for Hanover on Monday the 16, or Tuesday the 17th inst.

I am with great Respect My Lord your Grace's most obt humble serv.

Andrew Stone

411. NEWCASTLE TO RICHMOND

Newcastle House
Saturday morning [May 1748]

My Dear Lord,

I hope you will come to Claremont tomorrow morning early. There is no sort of Reasson for going to the P. of W. Ld Chancellor rides out. Pray send me word, when, & in what temper you left our Master, & if you had any discourse about my Hanover Journey.[1] I am afraid some tricks have been play'd me upon that.

Ever yrs

Holles Newcastle

How is the Ds of Richmond?

1. King George II determined to visit Hanover as usual during the summer, despite the danger of slowing down the peacemaking. Remembering how Carteret had used a similar opportunity in 1743, Newcastle accompanied the King.

412. RAMSDEN TO RICHMOND

Whitehall
May 24, 1748

My Lord,

Ward, the Messenger, being arrived this afternoon with an Account that his Majesty landed at Helvoetsluys on Sunday last between 5 & 6 o'clock in the morning, in perfect Health. I am commanded by my Lord Duke of Newcastle to acquaint your Grace therewith, and to desire you will be pleased to meet the other Lords Justices at His Grace's Office at the Cockpit tomorrow, being Wednesday, at 12 o'clock at noon, in order to open their Commission.[1]

I am with the greatest Respect My Lord your Grace's most obedient, humble servant
Thos Ramsden

413. RICHMOND TO NEWCASTLE

Whitehall
17/28 June 1748

My Dear Lord,

I am vastly happy to hear of your safe landing, & shall long to know how you like Holland, the army, &c; & when you come to Hanover, I hope to hear from you.

It will allways be a pleasure to me to do what you like, butt you know what I dislike, so pray consider of what I say'd upon a certain affair the last time I saw you.

I am, My Dear Lord, for ever & most affectionately. Your's
Richmond &c.

414. RICHMOND TO NEWCASTLE

Whitehall
21. June 1748

My Dear Lord,

I hope this will find your Grace safely arrived at Hanover after a pleasant journey, through that charming country of Westphalia.

Last Thursday My Lord Kenaird's[2] petition was read at the Regency, & I never saw so thorough a good natured disposition as was shewn by every Lord there. My Lord Chancellor sett forth the difficultys in his usuall clear & candid way, & Mr. Pelham as well as every body else entirely agreed with him in the enclosed minute[3] which was drawn up by My Lord Chancellor himself, & I hope His Majesty will aprove of it, & I do assure you that wee were unanimous upon it. so if wee are so happy as to have His Majesty's aprobation, I hope you will be so good as to signify it to us, & then I will gett a sketch of a bill prepared, or more propperly a petition first to Parliament, for the opening of next sessions, to be first examin'd & aproved of by such persons as His Majesty shall thinke propper, which I suppose will be the attorney & Sollicitor Genll. so I thinke this affair is in as good a way, as the difficult circumstances of it will admit.

I hope, when you have a leasure minute, that you will just lett me know how you do.

I am My Dear Lord, for ever, & most affectionately Your's
Richmond &c.

1. Richmond was one of the Lords Justices of the Realm during the King's absence in 1748, as he had been in 1740 and 1745, and was to be again in 1750.
2. James Radcliffe, Viscount Kinnaird, 1725–1786, was imprisoned during the 1745 Rising. In November 1749, he married Barbara, daughter of Anthony Kempe of Slindon. He was 4th. Earl of Newburgh from 1755.
3. The Minute stated that the Meeting of the Lords Justices declared that the King ought to petition Parliament because it would be a precedent.

415: RICHMOND TO NEWCASTLE

Goodwood
28 Aug. 1748

My Dear Lord,

As I have not heard from your Grace since I wrote to you last, I have butt little to say only that I have received a most kind & obligeing letter from the Chancellor, in answer to one I had wrote to him, in which I express'd the sincere pleasure I had in Coll. York's being likely to go with me to Paris.[1] I find they are in hourly expectation of the Duke in London, & I shall go there as soon as I shall know if you have mention'd any thing of my going to France to the Duke of Bedford, for till I know that I shall be excessive awkward before him, for it should certanly come to him from your Grace & not from me. So I own I am impatient to hear from you. & now in the midst of your business you must forgive me for troubling you with things that are trifles to you, butt not at all so to the people concern'd. The Chancellor has been so good as to say that if Hughes can pitch upon a propper living, he will give it him; & you know you have promis'd Hughes to help him when in your power, so I beg to know if you have any objection to my askeing the living of Barcombe near Lewes for him. I assure you I should not aske this of you for any other Parson butt Hughes, butt as you are equally engaged with me to help him, for which I am obliged to you; I thinke it butt reasonable, unless you have already engaged to speake for somebody else. & I am pretty well assured the Chancellor will oblige me in it, if your Grace has no objection, & very sure of it if you will joyn in the recommendation. I beg you won't forgett my memorandum about Hibbins for the living of St. Mary Woolnoth in the Citty, which Mr. Stone, by your direction told him two years ago was not engaged, & I have been plaguing you ever since about him. & now I know you will curse me for troubling you about so many parsons, butt I can't help it, & I assure you if I can help it, these shall be the last.

Wee have all been allarm'd here with Mr. Pelham's illness, butt are now rejoyc'd to hear he is quite well again. the Duchess of Richmond & I joyn in our most sincere compliments to the Duchess of Newcastle, who wee hope is perfectly recovered by this time, & I am my Dear Lord for ever & most affectionately Your's

Richmond &c.

416. RICHMOND TO NEWCASTLE

Whitehall
Tuesday 6 Septr 1748

My Dear Lord,

I received Mr. Stone's of the 30th. Aug/10th. Sept & will punctually obey your Grace's orders in <u>takeing no step</u> in consequence of your former letter to me upon <u>that subject</u>. butt it is very lucky that I have taken none already as in that former letter you was pleased to say, The King said I should go &c; & that I was to <u>prepare accordingly</u>. butt finding the Duke of Bedford had not been inform'd of it, I did nothing, butt come to town to receive H:R:Hss commands, & talke to My Lord Chancellor & Coll. Yorke, & I found them in the same awkward situation with myself, as they found the Duke of Bedford had had no account of it, at least none that he has communicated to any body. This being the case I shall go to Goodwood as soon as the Duke goes abroad, or sooner if he does not go soon. & 'till I receive your further commands, I shall take <u>no step</u> of any kind whatever, butt wish to be soon releived by your Grace from this uncertain situation.

I am My Dear Lord, Your Grace's ever faithfull humble servant,

Richmond &c.

---

1. Lord Hardwicke's son, Hon Joseph Yorke, was to be Secretary to the proposed Paris Embassy of the Duke of Richmond.

417. NEWCASTLE TO RICHMOND

Hanover
Sept 21st/Oct 2d 1748

My Dear Lord,
   I am in such a hurry, as indeed I always am, when the Messenger is going away, who plagues me about missing the Paquet, that I have never time to write to my best Friends. Which must be my excuse. I hope you constantly hear how things go, from Ministers in England. You know I never conceal any thing from you; but I am so employ'd, that I have scarce time to write necessary letters with orders. I suppose you will see Dutheil's[1] project of Peace, which is so reasonable a one, that I am apt to hope, all parties will agree to it or very soon accede. We were going on in a strange separate way but Dutheil, Sr T. Robinson, & myself, have prevented it, & I hope set all things right. Your Embassy will probably be now soon declared. Till then you can't take a House, or make any Step in France, but I do not see why you may not be preparing things in England, if you, & my Brother think the Peace as sure, as I really think it now, & I own I am a little vain upon it. I wrote to the Duke of Bedford, as I remember, the same time I wrote you, & my Brother. I wonder He has not mentioned it. I will mention it again by this Messenger. I don't propose <u>Joe</u> should go as Secretary. You may take who you please. I would have Joe as second Minister, to remain when my Lord Ambassador comes away. I love Hughes, & would have Him, but Barcomb within half a mile of Lewes, can't go to a Chichester man. What would poor Hurdiss say? My love to my Queen. I thank God, the Ds of N. is at times pure well. She will set out, I hope, on her return next week.
   Ever yrs
Holles Newcastle

418. RICHMOND TO NEWCASTLE

Goodwood
12th Octr 1748

My Dear Lord,
   I received your Grace's most kind & obligeing letter of the 21 Sept/2 Oct from Hanover, & soon after it, went to town where the Duke of Bedford spoke to me about my going to Paris as an affair absollutely setled, & told me I might prepare accordingly, saying at the same time that he had made no secret of it, so I need not, as indeed I can not, as soon as I begin to make any preparations, in which no time should be lost, as I take for granted your Grace will be hurrying me over as soon as His Majesty pleases to declare me. tho I would not have you think by this that I am at all impatient to go, on the contrary I do assure you, for the longer it is putt off, the better I shall be pleased, butt all I mean is that when the time of my going is fix'd I may have the earlyest notice. As to any preparations in France such as takeing a house &c I shall certanly not do it 'till I hear again from you. butt there are severall other things that must be thought of in time, & you'l forgive me for troubling you with one of them now, it is about getting a foreign sett of horses, which can't be had in a day, butt better where you are than in any other part of the world, for which reason I have wrote the enclosed for Monsieur de Freechapelle, which I send open for your Grace to read, & then beg you would according to your own discretion, give it him or burn it. & now I must inform you of what pass'd between the Duke of Bedford & myself. he said he supposed I knew that it was proposed that Coll. Yorke should go with me, as <u>secretaire d'Ambassade</u>. & he

---

1. Jean Gabriel de la Porte Du Theil, French agent at Vienna.

asked me if I liked it. to which I reply'd that as I knew him extreamly well, & had a sincere freindship for him, I should be very happy in haveing him with me, & that even if I had not known him at all, I could certanly have had no objection to a servant of the Duke's, who was also a son of one of my best freinds. now upon this I must beg an explanation of one part of your Grace's last letter to me, where your words are <u>I dont propose Joe should goe as secretary, you may take who you please I would have Joe as second minister, to remain when my Lord Ambassador comes away.</u> Now do you mean that Coll. Yorke should have the character of envoy ? I wish you may for then I may take the liberty to recommend Mr. Hill for secretary to the embassy, butt you see the Duke of Bedford means that for Coll. Yorke. If you mean only my own secretary when you say <u>take who you please</u>, it is no great favor, for it would be hard I should not chuse my own servants; butt if you mean the secretary to the Embassy, t'would indeed be a very great favor, & I should be infinitely obliged to you, as well as to His Majesty for it, & Coll. Yorke would certanly be better pleased to go at once with the title of Envoy, as Trevor, was in Holland, when Horace [Walpole] & afterwards Chesterfeild was Ambassador there. & as to Tom Hill's capacity, you know it as well as myself. I own it would make me extreamly happy, & I then should with some pleasure.

As I was butt half a day in town, I did not read Monsr Dutheil's project, butt heard that the material points it differed in from the others, is leaving more to the Empress Queens interest, which as it facillitates the whole is sure to meet with aprobation at the Cock Pitt. butt how you will be able to satisfy the Court of France upon the two hostage peers[1] I don't know, nor do I conceive you can by law agree to it; if you could I should fancy a couple of Scotch peers might be found that would not be sorry to go. As I have troubled you butt seldome, I'l make no excuses for the length of this, butt conclude as I ever shall with assureing you of the truth & freindship, with which I am, My Dear Lord, your Grace's ever faithfull & most affectionate humble servant,

Richmond &c.

419.   PELHAM TO RICHMOND

Esher
November 12, 1748

My Dear Lord,

I have read over Steel's examination[2] and such a scene of villainy and barbarity I never before heard or read of. I conclude the Attorney General[3] has seen it, for sure something may be done with those persons that seem concerned in this shocking act, tho' possibly not immediate partys in the murder. What are become of the women, and are not the Public Houses marked out, somehow or other, as harbourers of these villains? I ask these questions, not as I in the least doubt, that your Grace and the other gentlemen, who have acted the honest and brave part in detecting these murders, can have omitted any thing that the law can do against their accomplices. I shall in my sphere pursue these villains to the utmost, and will take care that the officers of the revenues shall either do their duty in looking after them, or suffer if they do not. I

1.   George Yelverton, 2nd. Earl of Sussex, and Charles Cathcart, 9th. Lord Cathcart were hostages to the French court for the due performance of the articles in the Treaty of Aix-la-Chapelle for the restoration of Louisburg to France.
2.   The examination of William Steele, a King's witness in the smuggling trials, in which he described the torture and murder of William Galley and Daniel Chater. See A Gentleman of Chichester, *A Full and Genuine History of the Inhuman and Unparalleled Murders of Mr. William Galley a Custom-House Officer, and Mr. Daniel Chater, a Shoemaker, by fourteen Notorious Smugglers, with the Trial and Execution of seven of the bloody criminals at Chichester.* (1749). The examination is Goodwood Ms. 155 f.16.
3.   Dudley Ryder, 1691–1756, MP for St. Germans, 1733–1734, and for Tiverton, 1734–1754, was Attorney General, 1737–1754.

think we are all obliged to your Grace for the spirit you have shewn on this occasion, the next best thing is to use our endeavours to suppress the practice of smuggling, for it is that profession that breeds up the young idle fellows to these villainys. We had yesterday a messenger come from Hannover. His Grace in his publick letter says nothing of the King's setting out, nor of their having heard of the arrival of the yatchts. He says indeed he shall himself leave Hanover as on Tuesday last. But in his letter to me, he says the King talks of leaving the place on Monday or Tuesday next, in order to be att Helveot Sluys on Satturday the 19th, our style. My Brother stays at the Hague, 'till he is sure of the time the King will be at Helveot, and then will meet his Majesty in order to come over together. I must own they have stayed to the last hour, so hope contrary winds will not make it much longer.

This is all I know, or I believe any one else with certainty, of the time the King will be here.

I am with ever greatest truth and Respect Yr Grace's slave

H. Pelham

420.   RICHMOND TO PELHAM

[November 1748]

Memorandums for Mr. Pelham

As the taking of Carter[1] Jackson[2] Mills[3] Curtis[4] & the others cheifly concern'd in the murders in Sussex, is attended with so much difficulty, from the whole county being intimidated, would it not be right for the government to offer pardon to any person or persons who have offended against the Laws of Custom & Excise (even to outlaws) who have not been concern'd in any murders or in breaking open the custom house at Poole, who shall apprehend, or by giving Private notice or information, cause to be apprehended, so as they be brought to justice, any one or more of the persons concern'd in the murders of Gallay Chater,[5] or Hawkins,[6] or in breaking open the custom house at Poole ? If so the names of the murderers must be publish'd.

One Mr. Wakeford of Hampshire has been lately attack'd, his house broke open, Robbed & Plunder'd by a sett of these desperate villains, many of them outlaws, as they suppose; he is afraid to move towards justice least a greater evil should fall upon him, & does not complain of it even to his neighbors. Butt notwithstanding that, should such open violence of all laws pass over uninquired into ? would it not therefore be

1. William Carter of Rowlands Castle, thatcher, the son of William Carter of East Meon in Hampshire, was one of the gang of smugglers who broke open the Customs House at Poole, and was executed for the murder of Galley and Chater.
2. William Jackson of Aldsworth, a labourer of about 50. He was probably the leader of the gang of smugglers who murdered Galley and Chater. He was ill at the time of his trial, and died in prison the night before he was due to be executed with the other smugglers.
3. Richard Mills senior, a coltbreaker from Trotton, and Richard Mills, junior, his son, a coltbreaker from Stedham, aged 68 and 37 respectively, were both members of the gang of smugglers, and were executed for the murder of Galley and Chater.
4. Jeremiah Curtis of Hawkhurst in Kent, labourer, one of the infamous Hawkhurst gang of smugglers, was wanted for the murder of Richard Hawkins of Yapton, labourer, who was suspected of having concealed a small bag of tea from the gang.
5. William Galley and Daniel Chater, a witness at Fordingbridge to the return of the gang of smugglers from breaking open the Customs House at Poole, were tortured and cruelly murdered by the smugglers in February 1747, their bodies being found in Ladyholt Park. See Cal Winslow, 'Sussex Smugglers', in D. Hay, P. Linebaugh and E.P. Thompson, *Albion's Fatal Tree. Crime and Society in Eighteenth Century England*, (1975), pp. 119–166.
6. Richard Hawkins of Yapton, labourer, himself a smuggler, was murdered by two of the Hawkhurst Gang on suspicion of concealing a small bag of tea. Like Galley and Chater he was killed with extreme barbarity. His body was found in a pond in Parham Park.

right to send some propper person from London to enquire into the circumstances of this fact, & to have it publish'd with the shocking circumstances attending it in the Gazette & pardon & reward offer'd to those concern'd in it (altho outlaws) who shall discover their accomplices, so as they shall be brought to justice.

Indeed nothing butt an active zeal in the Government, manifested by publick acts, can give a cheque to these dangerous outrages, & barbarous & inhumane murders, with which our part of the Country is so justly terryfy'd.

Mr. Wicker of Horsham, & Mr. Mitford & Mr. Goodwin of Petworth, have, (as I have heard) declared they would act in nothing relating to smuglers. If this is true, & I beleive it is, is it not a shame ? & should not Mr. Pelham give them some intimation of it ? tis particularly scandalous in Mr. Mitford who is a servant of the Government.

Mr. Pelham is desired to order a propper letter to be wrote to the Jaylor of Horsham to be very carefull that their prisoners make no escape, & to threaten him with the severest punishments that the law can inflict in case any thing of that kind should happen.

As the marines that are there now, & who keep a strong gard within call of the prison, will soon be broke may I aply to Mr. Fox, for a company of Bocklands to be sent there ?

421.   RICHMOND TO NEWCASTLE

Goodwood
13th Novr 1748

My Dear Lord,

I dare not complain of your silence for I know you will be angry with me if I did. butt may I not complain of your not ordering Mr. Ramsden or somebody to write two words to me in answer to some questions I ask'd in my last? which I should not have known you had received butt from an answer I had from Monsr de Freechappell. I am sorry to see the peevish expressions in your last letter to me about your freinds here as if suspecting they either dont aprove of what you have done, or that they claim some share of the honor of it themselves, indeed both suspitions are groundless. every body here is satisfy'd (as far as I can see) with what you have done, & dont pretend to dispute the honor of it with you. so for God's sake be easy, & dont plague yourself with suspecting things that never had existance. & dont be angry with me, you know I have no attachment to any body butt yourself & your brother, & your interests ought to be inseperable.

I must now complain of your never haveing answerd me one word about poor Lord Kenairds affair. I suppose you laid the minute of the Regency before the King. did His Majesty then agree in consequence of that minute, to his aplying to Parliament? for nothing can be done 'til His Majesty's pleasure is known, which (tho I dont in the least doubt of it) wee should have had. & I beg wee may, authentically from your Grace. I wish you a safe & pleasant voyage home, where indeed you will find all your freinds glad to see you, butt none more so, than My Dear Lord, Your Grace's ever faithfull, & most affectionate humble servant

Richmond &c.

422.   RICHMOND TO NEWCASTLE

Goodwood
Sunday 11th Decr 1748

My Dear Lord,

I wrote to your Grace for Godalming to beg you to press the Chancellor upon the

point of getting these murderers try'd at Horsham directly by a special commission[1]. & I hope you will do it as the thing in the world that will do most good in this country, & I am sure nothing butt treason can be a stronger claim for such a commission, for this is not only murders of the deepest dye attended with the most shocking circumstances of cruelty, butt also committed by whole gangs of these villains in open defyance of the Laws, & all government whatever. So tho it maynt be treason in Law, I am sure it is so in common sence. I had no answer to that letter & I own I have been impatient for one ever since, for at present I am under a good many difficultys. your Grace told me I should prepare as fast as I could to go to France, butt then at the same time told me that if the Court of France did not send one of equall ranke with myself here, the King would not send me, upon which I can not with any decency make any preparations at Paris. Such as takeing a house there, orderieng my equipages there, & my sett of horses from Hanover. these are necessary steps, which must be taken some considerable time before I can sett out, I therefore beg to have the earlyest notice when it is determin'd whether I am positively to go; or not. & from that time I hope you will gett me into pay; & that Mr. Pelham would immediately advance me a summe of about £2000, to begin with; for I hope & beleive you are too much my freind to thinke that I should begin by laying out my own money; for that would really be very hard, as this honor is none of my own seeking, & what nothing butt my duty to my Master, & the desire of my freinds, would ever have persuaded me to undertake. I would not have you thinke that I am in a hurry to go, butt it is necessary I should have a propper time allow'd me to prepare, & when I know that, & have received the advance I mention, I assure you I will loose no time in preparing every thing for it. I have wrote the enclosed in a seperate letter that you may shew it to his Majesty if you thinke propper, I own it will be a strong mortification to me to be deny'd the Royall Livery; & really I thinke a very strong reason for my desiring to be excused from going on this Embassary, which I dont thinke at all a greater honor than that of apearing as well as being his Majesty's Master of the horse.
    I am my Dear Lord Your Grace's most affectte
Richmond &c.

423.   RICHMOND TO NEWCASTLE

Goodwood
11th Decr 1748

My Dear Lord,
    Before I am apointed to go to the Court of France, I must beg your Grace to lay me at His Majesty's feet for an explanation upon one point, which will be necessary for me to know his pleasure in, that is what number of his liverys his Majesty will allow me to take. When I was last in France, as I had the honor then to be his Master of the horse, I had my four foot men as usual in the Royall livery & some few stable people; & all the Duchess of Richmond's servants in my own livery as usuall, my haveing therefore the Character of His Majesty's ambassador now will not to be sure barr me of haveing the same, butt I then had only <u>a Carosse de homage</u> whereas now I must have Voitures of my own. I should be glad to know then if his Majesty will allow me to have two Voitures, as I have here with his Royall Arms, & if the Coachman that drives those two Voitures only, & solely for my use, should not also have the Royall livery, all others to

---

1. Richmond devoted the last three years of his life to a campaign to stop smuggling in Sussex altogether. The relevant papers will be found in Goodwood Ms. 154–156. As part of the campaign he successfully petitioned for a Special Commission of Oyer and Terminer for the County of Sussex, which was held in Chichester, and at which seven of the smugglers — Jackson, Tapner, Carter, the two Mills, Cobby and Hammond were tried and found guilty.

be sure must be in myne. I dont mean by this to putt his Majesty to the expence of one Voiture, or livery extraordinary; as I can make what Royall liverys I want out of my allowance here; & that the Voitures must be at my own expence. I therefore hope his Majesty will be gratiously pleas'd to allow it in the way I propose, else it would be takeing an honor from his Master of the horse that was allways attach'd to it. there can be no ceremoniall where the Royall livery can be committed, for even Ambassadors liverys have the <u>entree du Louvre</u>; & have all the same entrees that the French Kings own liverys have. & if His Majesty is pleas'd to allow me this, I would have the Coach-man that Monsr de Freechappelle is to send me from Hanover in the Royall livery. I am, My Dear Lord Your Grace's most truelly affectionate servant,

Richmond &c.

I own, in my way of thinkeing, the honor of apearing, as well as being His Majesty's Master of the Horse, is as great to me, as being apointed his Ambassader.

424. RICHMOND TO NEWCASTLE

Goodwood
Sunday 18th Decr 1748

My Dear Lord,

I am extreamly sorry you thinke I am angry with you, indeed I am not, because I am very sure you had never the least thought of proposing any thing to me that would prejudice my familly, & make me uneasy as long as I live. I am very sure that was farr from your thoughts, & I am very sure you thought my allowance would be 12000ll a year when you proposed to me to go to France. butt then give me leave to say it was upon that I consented & even then you know with difficulty, & great diffidence of myself. You told me t'was to be an Embassy of Eclat, if so I am sure I ought to have an allowance suitable to it, if not, I am the most impropper person you can send, you can easly find out men much more conversant in business, & far better managers by way of oeconomy than myself, therefore give me leave to say, that 'tis ridiculous to send me. I assure you for ten thousand reasons I had rather not go; if I must 'twill be with a heavy heart, & I shall do the business sadly, for I plainly see that it must end in distressing my self and familly, or makeing a most scandalous figure, in an Embassy of Eclat as you call'd it, & as I know very well 'tis expected at Paris. Indeed my Dear Lord my situation is to be pitty'd, & I thinke no man can be call'd unreasonable who after having served his King & Master faithfully dureing a reign of upwards of 21 years, desires only to remain in the employment he is in.

butt in answer to the particulars, the whole allowance of the first year comes 8300ll including 1500ll for equipage, which equipage cant cost me less than 3000ll, nay the expence of buying equipages setts of horses &c & keeping them a year will stand me in 4000ll then I have only 4300ll for my table house rent & all other expences, to which I would willingly add 6000ll of my own, butt then I know that even 10,000ll will not do by a great deal, & your Grace that is the only man in England that lives greatly, knows that what I say is true. as for the mony that comes to me for the plate, I really can not look upon that as the least help to me, for tho I have a great deal of plate of my own it is so old fashion'd & would to my knowledge make so scrub a figure at Paris that it must be all new made, & severall pieces will be wanting to it, so that my whole allowance I'l answer for it will, & indeed must be lay'd out, if I am to have a service suitable to the character I go in. The Duke of Shrewsbury's[1] Embassy I find is to be a president

---

1. Charles Talbot, 1st. Duke of Shrewsbury, 1660–1718, was Ambassador Extraordinary in Paris, 1712–1713.

280

for myne, I am sorry for it for he hurt himself very much by it, butt he had no children. Lord Stair's[1] I know was extravagant, so perhaps myne would be call'd if I had what I desired. tho if i had which is only to make my allowance up to 12,000ll, which is only an adittion of 4000ll more, it would be short of what Lord Stair's had, & would satisfy me, & without it, I shall be with great reason extreamly disatisfy'd. yett lett whatever happen, I know you love me, & I shall allways be My Dear Lord, Your Grace's ever faithfull & most affectte humble servant,

Richmond &c.

Surely I may be allow'd to stay here dureing the Holydays when no mortall will be in town, & that really I have been employ'd severall hours most days & severall whole days, & shall be so for ten days longer, in makeing enquirys into these horrid murders, & preparing evidences for the Tryalls. The Assizes can not be at Horsham, unless the Judges ride there on horseback, so they must be at East Grinsted or at Chichester. & in either case the prisoners must be removed butt by military helpe. I'l answer the Prisoners shall not escape. — I beg it may be at Chichester.

425. RICHMOND TO NEWCASTLE

Charlton
21. Feb. 1748/9

My Dear Lord,
   Pray lett Mr. Ramsden or any of your people write me word by next post, on what day you intend to entertain the University of Cambridge, that I may settle my hunting in the new forrest so as to be able to waite on your Grace.
   I am My Dear Lord, your Grace's ever faithfull, & most affectionate humble servant,
Richmond &c.

426. PELHAM TO RICHMOND

Feb 21st 1748/9

My Dear Lord,
   I must return your Grace my hearty thanks, as a citizen of this country, for the unwearied and successful pains you have taken in detecting all sorts of villains and rogues in any shape. I have seen Mr. Chetwynd,[2] and every thing is settled between us, as your Grace can wish, and indeed nothing further can be done, 'till he sees the honorable and beautiful young Lady you mention. I will send your letter to my Brother this evening, but I believe I may venture to say, any hopes of pardon you think fit to give to these execrable wretches, will be fully made good. It is impossible to discover and convict such a gang of Rogues without some of the accomplices in the wickedness being partners in the discovery. I hope good may come from the encouragement you intend to give Mrs. Jackson, and if she should wipe off her guilt in any degree by the justice she shall do her country in detecting such a set villains, as your Grace speaks of, I should then be curious to know a little of her amours with our friend in her younger and more innocent days. I shall hardly look upon Tankey[3] without laughing, and if your Grace was present, I would venture his Lordships displeasure rather than loose my joke.

---

1.   John Dalrymple, 2nd. Earl of Stair, 1673–1747, general and diplomatist, was British Minister in Paris, 1714–1715, Envoy Extraordinary in 1715, and Ambassador Extraordinary, 1715–1720.
2.   William Chetwynd was Under-Secretary of State, 1745–1748.
3.   Charles Bennett, 2nd. Earl of Tankerville was suspected of having a romantic entanglement with Mrs. Jackson, the wife of William Jackson, the leader of the smugglers.

The sea and land are both in a meeting, but I hope we shall soon pass bills for quieting 'em. There is a talk as if Albemarle was to go to Paris. Since your Grace don't like to go, I see no one so proper, but I would not have you understand from me that I take it as a thing done. There can be but one objection and I fear that objection would have equal force wherever he goes. My Duty to the Earl of Lincoln, and compliments to all other friends. God bless you; you are born to do good to mankind, and for that as well as a thousand other reasons, I shall ever be with the greatest truth and affection My dear Lord Your Grace's faithfull slave and servant

H. Pelham

427. RICHMOND TO NEWCASTLE

Charlton
26. Febry. 1748/9

My Dear Lord,
Your letter of the 23rd gave me pleasure, comfort & ease; & you will do me the justice to say that I told you long ago that Lord Albemarle was the fittest man in all England for a French Embassy, in every particular butt one; I dont mean his extravagance butt his inabillity in point of fortune, & considering his situation, of being able to make that figure abroad he ought, & I am sure would wish to do. Linky seems quite easy about it. & as to myself I am extreamly happy in being quitt of an employment I never liked, <u>with honor</u>, for after I had once undertaken it, I would not have receded on any account myself, for I am old enough to know my own mind, & am pretty much determined when I have taken a resollution & I expect as a peice of justice that the true cause of my not going should be known, for I should be to blame if I was not vain of my Royall Masters distinquishing goodness to me upon this occasion. & I can assure you it is very well known at Paris, so makeing a mistery of it here, would in my opinion be takeing off of the dignity I thinke the King has justly shewn; tho I know there are a great many that are not of my opinion. & the reason why they are not of my opinion is that they dont know French Punctillos so well as I do. I return your Grace ten thousand thankes for the very freindly part you have taken for me in this whole affair, & you may be very well assured you will never have an ungratefull return, from, My Dear Lord, Your Grace's ever faithfull & most affectionate humble servant

Richmond &c.

May I dine, & lye at Claremount next sunday.

428. RICHMOND TO NEWCASTLE

East Grinsted
Thursday 16 March 1748/9

My Dear Lord,
Our honest country men the Sussex jurys continue to do their duty, haveing Capitally convicted six notorious smuglers, viz: John Mills for the murder of Hawkins, Henry Sheerman for the murder of Galley, & Rob Fuller, Jocky Brown & the two Kemps for severall robberys committed in this county, & they are all to be executed, & the two murderers hung in Chains.[1] Mr. Justice Dennison[2] has done extreamly well, & greatly to the satisfaction of all our Gentlemen. I am sorry Sharpe just pitch'd upon Gilbert for solliciter of the crown side, because I hear he is an inveterate enemy to your Grace's

1. John Mills and Henry Sheerman were sentenced to death at the Assizes at East Grinstead in March 1749. Mills was hanged in chains near the Dog and Partridge on Slindon Common, where he had tortured Richard Hawkins, and Sheerman, known as 'Little Harry', was executed and hanged in chains near Rake.
2. Sir Thomas Denison, Justice of the Kings Bench, presided at the East Grinstead Assizes.

interest here. tho I must do him the justice to say he has behaved well in this affair. tis dreadfull to thinke of the sceenes of villany, & number of Robberys & Burglarys that have been lay'd open, in these proceedings. there is a bad sett of villans amongst us that must be clear'd, & wee are in a good way for it, butt pray dont hearken to representations of what is falsly call'd mercy. I shall be in town to morrow noon, for all will hardly be over today.

I am, My Dear Lord, for ever & most affectly Yours

Richmond &c.

429. RICHMOND TO NEWCASTLE

Bolderwood
17th April 1749

My Dear Lord,

Tho you frequently give me hints that I write to you too often, espetailly when it is not upon polliticks, yett I cant help being troublesome at present out of meer compassion for a poor unhappy man who is now in great distress. I know you will start at his name, because you formerly took a bad impression of him, give me leave to say a little without reason, tis Mr. Hibbins, for whose character at present I refer your Grace to all the inhabitants of your own parish of Esher, where he has long been a Curate; you promis'd me near two years ago the living of St. Mary Woolnoth for him, butt Mr. Stone now tells me tis not in the gift of the King butt of my Lord Chancellor, so the poor man is quite drove to despair, unless you will out of compassion to him, & freindship to me, recommend him for some other living, for I take for granted this of St. Mary Woolnoth is to good a thing for him to expect of My Lord Chancellor, & I must not nor can not aply for him or any body to My Lord Chancellor, as I have made repeated applications to his Lordship for Mr. Hughes, who has gott nothing yett. pray excuse my plaguing you about this, butt I beg an answer not by letter, butt by word of mouth when I see you next week in town.

I told My Lord Kildare that I mention'd his former request of being created an Irish Duke, to you, so I wish you would speake to him upon it, & I surely thinke His Majesty will be so good as to grant it.

I am, My Dear Lord, Your Grace's ever faithfull & most affectionate servant,

Richmond &c.

430. NEWCASTLE TO RICHMOND

Claremont
June 18th, 1749

My Dear Lord,

I thought your Grace would not dislike to know, that the Chapter for the disposal of some of the vacant Garters is at last fixed for Thursday next at Kensington. Possibly you may think it right to be there; in all events, it is not amiss to know it in time. I have had a great deal of disagreable Altercation about Lord G ————. It has ended as well as I could expect. The K. thought His Honor so much concerned to keep His Word, that He ordered me to tell the Servants that he would not give it to Lord G. if they were all against it, but that if He was thought to break His word in this instance He should be authorised, to break His word to <u>us</u> hereafter. I think He spoke very wisely, and very honestly. Upon this every body, (tho' a little awkwardly) has acquiesced & I shall acquaint Ld G. with it on Tuesday. I own I never was so clear in a Measure, in my whole life. I think it does the King Honor, and Honor to his Ministers. I think it shows plainly our Security & I am perswaded is rather to be looked upon, as a final Discharge than as an earnest, or promise of future Favor, & never believe me more, if it has not this effect, provided we don't talk & act sillyly upon it. If we had obstructed it, what would have been the Consequences: a Continuation, for nothing, of all ye disagreable Reproaches, &c that we had four years ago, & this is the way, to have them all forgot. The new Knights will be, the Margrave of Anspach, the Duke of Bedford (If He will take it, which I think He will not), the Duke of Leeds,[1] the Earl of Albemarle, and the Earl of Granville,[2] (If He will take it, which I now think He will). Two of my best Friends will be much mistified, but I can't help it: poor Linky & Harcourt. As for Linky, He is sorely hurt, but it was impossible. If He is quiet, He will come the next promotion. As for Harcourt, I have wrote Him the truth, in the most friendly, & affect: Manner I could. I attempted to speak abt Prince G. but my mouth was stopd. I know what you intend to say, But ———————. I think I have no other News. The King is in the best Humour, I ever saw Him. We have ten thousand Winters today & yesterday. I dined yesterday at Boder's Pond. I beg my best Compliments to my Queen. I hope the young Ladies are Both quite well.

Ever & unalterably Yrs

Holles Newcastle

431.   RICHMOND TO NEWCASTLE

Goodwood
Fryday. 14th July 1749

My Dear Lord,

I am very impatient to hear the result of what wee was talking of the night before I left you, I sincerely wish it may succeed as I am in hopes it may be a means to establish that harmony, which I am very sure every man that wishes well to this government, must be very desirous of seeing, for without it, tis impossible to go on. so it is really a publick consideration, butt abstracted from that, my personall love & attachment to you & your brother, makes me wish it with more than common zeal.

I forgott when I saw you to tell you that Linky, Tanky, & numbers of your humble servants will joyn with me in a request for Brice Fisher,[3] which is that whenever the Wardrobe is fix'd he may be recommended by your Grace & all us your humble servants, & his freinds to the Person that has that employment, for what they call Packer to the Wardrobe. tis allways a man in trade, & the last person that had it was employ'd by the Duke of Montagu because no other was at that time recommended to him. Tho afterwards I did recommend Fisher for it, butt it was too late.

I am My Dear Lord, for ever & most affectionately yours

Richmond &c.

I own I should like the great mastership of the Bath, for sans vanitez my haveing it would be keeping up the dignity of it better than Ld. Pomfrett or De Lawarr's having it.

432.   RICHMOND TO NEWCASTLE

Goodwood
16. July. 1749

My Dear Lord,

My Lord Clanricarde[4] has wrote to me to desire me to interceed for one Henry

---

1. Thomas Osborne, 4th. Duke of Leeds, 1713–1789, was created a Knight of the Garter on 22 June 1749, and installed on 12 July 1749.
2. John Carteret, Earl Granville, 1690–1763, was made a Knight of the Garter, in 1750.
3. Brice Fisher, died 1767, MP for Malmesbury, 1754–1761, and for Boroughbridge, 1761–1767, was a Director of the South Sea Company.
4. John de Burgh, 11th. Earl of Clanricarde, 1720–1782.

Aburrow who is condemn'd to dye at the Winton Assizes for most notorious & horrid crimes as your Grace will see in the enclosed account, which as you may easyly imagine I absollutely refused & I hope your Grace has done the same, for I hear he has aply'd to you. Mr. Foxcraft who is the prosecutor, who has been extreamly injured by this villain, & who has carry'd on the prosecution at a vast expence, besides paying fifty pounds reward upon his conviction, is extreamly desirous the Law should take its course. 'tis certain that the fellow is a most notorious villain, a poacher, & a smugler, & so are his whole familly, one of his brothers was evidence against him to save himself, & an other of his brothers who is a famous bowler at Crickett & goes by the name of Curry[1] I committed some time ago to Horsham jayle for smugling with fire arms, 'tho he has made a full confession of the whole affair, & for want of better I beleive he will be admitted an evidence, butt your Grace sees what a family they are. & indeed if cutting down plantations, heads of ponds, & burning houses are not punish'd to the utmost vigour of the Law, there will be no living in the country, so I hope there will be no mittigation of the sentence. The enclosed is a very full & authentick account of the whole affair. Baron Legge try'd him, & I am persuaded will say nothing in his favor.
I am, My Dear Lord, Your Grace's ever faithfull humble servant
Richmond &c.

I hope to meet your Grace at our assizes at Lewis on Munday morning the 31st. July, 'tho I beleive I shall be there on the Sunday, for there are a terrible number to be try'd for murder, & other crimes, & our jayle is also full of smuglers that wee have committed for carrying fire arms, butt I beleive the Comissrs of the Customs will chuse to try them at the old Bayly. I long to hear from you.
I hear Mr. Foxcraft has not pay'd the 50ll butt that is no ways materiall

433. RICHMOND TO NEWCASTLE

Goodwood
19 July 1749

My Dear Lord,
I thanke your Grace for your last kind letter, & am mighty glad to hear things are better where I so much wish them. I dont like the scheme of the Ordnance, I mean as you all do, for the Duke's sake, for the way you mention, he will still be at the head of it, & indeed I fear it will not be liked in the house of Commons. I cant conceive why His & Her R:Hss should dislike so much your mentioning the garter, I am sure it would be a healing salve, & as such I am sure they ought to wish it as much as all your other freinds do. I burnt your letter as you directed me. & no soul shall know one word of the contents of it, & for the same reason you should burn this.
The Duchess of Richmond & I beg our services to the Duchess of Newcastle & are overjoy'd to hear she is so well as to be at Claremount.
I am, My Dear Lord, for ever, & most affectionately Your's
Richmond &c.

Pray tear of the next sheet & keep it as a memorandum. & I seriously hope that the villain will be hang'd. it really would be a shame even to transport him, & I assure you Jack Butler will beshitt himself. now you see tis necessary to burn this side of the sheet.

---

1. Edward Aburrow alias Curry or Cuddy, the Slindon Cricketer. See Timothy J. McCann, 'Edward Aburrow, Cricketer and Smuggler: another link between Slindon and Hambledon', in *Journal of the Cricket Society*, vol. 10, no. 2, (1982), pp. 17–19.

434. RICHMOND TO NEWCASTLE

Goodwood
19. July 1749

My Lord,

I hear intercession has been made for Maplerden[1] the outlaw, that also broke open the Custom house at Pool, & has since threatened Mr. Butler our worthy representitive with nothing less than murdering him, & even, as Mr. Butler assures me, lay wait for him. so I really hope no application, whoever it comes from, will be listened to, for if it is, it will be such a discouragement both to Mr. Butler, my self, & all the Western Justices that I beleive wee shall give ourselves no further trouble about these villains.

I am your Grace's ever faithfull humble servant
Richmond &c.

435. RICHMOND TO NEWCASTLE

Goodwood
Sunday. 23rd July 1749

My Dear Lord,

I am an eternall correspondent & am really asham'd of it. Sometimes tis in favor of a parson or a Sussex freeholder, sometimes tis to hang a smugler or house burner, sometimes you give me leave to trouble you upon your own affairs, butt now I write to you in favor of a Popish Preist, namely Grossea Testa,[2] tho Jacquemar[3] calls him Labbe de la grosse Couille. he is now here with Wall, Haslang,[4] & Chevr de St George, & wee want to keep them all here till Wednesday. butt the Abbe sayes your Grace has apointed him on Wednesday morning at Newcastle house, so I have boldly taken upon me to say that I am sure upon this occasion you would excuse him, butt that alone will not do, for he insists that I should use all my interest with you that you should give him audience, et bonne Audience on Thursday, insted of Wednesday. he sayes you have promis'd to depeches un courier a Vienne pour les affaires de son Pauvre et cher Maitre, & that he must speake to you upon it. So if you dont see him on Thursday, he will conclude that I have brag'd of my interest with you without foundation. so my vanity makes me really wish you would see him on Thursday morning.

Now as to myself, you will excuse me waiting on you on Sunday at Halland, because I know I can be of some publick utillity at Lewes that evening, to keep things quiet between our active Country justices, & the Custom house sollicitors, for like Welsh justices they allways quarell, when they meet to carry on the prosecutions against the smuglers, & in that particular they do me the honor to shew some regard to my opinion, for 'tho 'tis the Crown that prosecutes by the Customs, yett our freinds Wicker, Sergison, Jack Fuller & others, will be giving their advice where 'tis very often not necessary, & I know in that I can keep them quiet, & every thing relating to the tryalls is to be setled that night, & I have promis'd Simon[5] to meet him there.

I am My Dear Lord, Your Grace's ever affectionate slave
Richmond &c.

---

1. William Fairall alias Shepherd alias Maplerden, aged 25, of Horsendown Green in Kent, had a particular grudge against Jack Butler, who had sent him to London for trial. He escaped and tried to burn down Butler's house at Worminghurst. He was eventually executed at Tyburn.
2. The Abbe Grossa Testa, the Modenese Minister in London.
3. Thomas Jacquemar was one of Richmond's servants.
4. Count Haslang, the Bavarian Minister in London.
5. Henry Simon of the Customs House in London.

436. RICHMOND TO NEWCASTLE

Catherine Yacht in the Peer of Calais
Thursday 31 Aug/11 Sept 1749

My Dear Lord,

In obedience to your Grace's commands I shall trouble you with a letter, tho I have nothing agreable to acquaint you with from the Country I come from. I left Helveot Sluyce on Tuesday, & am just arrived here by sea.[1] the first person I had any talke with about publick affairs there was the Elder Bentinck, who I accompany'd some few miles from the Hague, when he sett out on his journey to Vienna, & dined with him in the road. I told him how earnestly your Grace & every body in England wish'd to see the interior affairs of the republick better settled than they seem'd to be at present, & also that some generall scheme for our mutual security might be thought of & be begun upon, butt he said every thing was in so bad a way as to the first, that the last would meet with great difficultys, & would be impracticable without the old recourse of the purse of England. I told him that both ministry & parliament would be most extreamly averse to any thing of that kind, as I beleived, butt he said without it he despaired.

I had afterwards pretty near the same discourse with the Greffier, with the Pensionary I had none as I am very little acquainted with him, butt the Prince of Orange, when I took leave of him, sent for me into his Closet, & held the following discourse to me, which I thinke my duty to acquaint you with. he began by lamenting extreamly the unhappy situation of the republick, caused as he said by forty years total neglect of every thing that was necessary to carry on government within themselves, as well as their affairs abroad; that he found every thing in so desperate a situation as to both, that he almost despaired of being able to sett it right. that the finances were in so bad a way, & the remedy so difficult to putt in practice, the army in so scandalous a condition, tho he hopes he has putt that on a better footing, butt in short every thing in so bad a way that he saw nothing but a most melancholy prospect before him, so much that he assured me that altho his birth, his situation, his duty to his Country & every thing call'd him to the Stadtholdership, yett if he had known beforehand the plague, trouble & vexation that he has since mett with, & the great uncertainty he still meets with of putting their affairs in a right way, he thinkes he should not have accepted of it, & that if he consider'd himself only he certainly would have refused it. butt he said he told me this in great confidence, so I only mention it to your Grace. however he said the cheif point at present as to foreign affairs was the settlement of the Barrier which with a strong emphasis he said concern'd England as well as the republick, that it was therefore absollutely necessary that wee should bear our share of the expence of repairing it. I told His Higness that was a point I had no authority to say any thing upon, butt that in my own private opinion, our country was so drain'd by the last warr it would be very difficult to bring them to consent to fresh expences, butt then I did aske him leave to putt one question, which was whether he thought, (if all he could wish was granted from England & the barrier towns even in the condition he desired) they would be absollutely secure against the power of France, to which he answered with some quickness, I know your meaning, you thinke that our places might be as ill defended as they were in the last warr. I thanked him for the explanation, & acknowledged that it was partly my meaning, & that I beleived more people in England would be of the same opinion till they saw more examples made of those officers that they thought behaved so shamefully. he then talk'd of the severe sentence against La Rogue; that that ought to satisfy every body; & that the prosecution against Cromstrom

---

1. The Duke and Duchess of Richmond left England for Paris at the end of August 1749, and paid a visit to Lady Cadogan at the Hague on their way.

was going on, tho he own'd butt slowly from the difficulty he said of getting proofs, & particularly because Chandos would say nothing without possitive orders from the Empress Queen, which he had not yet received. then he talk'd a great deal about the affair of Bergen op Zoom, said it had been greatly misrepresented to the King, that a thousand lyes had been told about it, & that, 'tho bad, not near so bad as the world imagin'd. which latter part of his discourse I own gave me great concern, to see that the Stadtholder who should be desirous to bring such offenders to justice was doing all he could to palliate their offences, & at that time it gave me some suspitions, which, I am almost afraid to say it, & 'tis to my sorrow that I do say it, I heard in a manner veryfy'd in a private conversation I had with a gentleman the very next morning, who said he beleived that the enquiry would be drop'd, because he had heard that Cromstrom had produced such orders, as clear'd himself, & lay'd the blame too high to admit of any further enquiry. I hope this is not true, if it is, it's shoking to thinke of. butt to return to my discourse with His Higness, I told him there were toppicks that I should not have presumed to have talk'd of, had not he began them himself, that I was a private person, had no authority for any thing I said, & only spoke my own private opinion. butt that I could venture to say that you wish'd extreamly that some generall plan & practicable scheme could be hitt upon for our mutual preservation, by strengthening our alliances. I thinke those were your Grace's words to me, & so ended our conversation.

& now I am sorry to tell you, tho you have heard it before that the P: of O. is entirely govern'd by the Princess, & that her Pride, mix'd with his obstinacy, have made them generally disliked, so that they have lost their credit with their best freinds, & are now reduced to that low servillity of courting their enemys. from which you see what little dependeance you can have upon a country that has no head nor no government in it. the Pensionary & greffier are both good men, butt the two Benticks, have more power & credit than any body else, butt for want of the Prince's confidence, they have not power enough to do that service to their country, & the liberty of Europe, that their honest hearts desire. the eldest shew'd me your letter to him, & beg'd me to assure you that he not only had the highest regard & freindship for you, butt that his greatest dependance was upon you. I do assure you it hurts me to say what I have of the Prince & Princess, as they have both been so civil to me, & I shall ever thinke my self personally obliged to them, butt your situation, & the confidence you are pleased to place in me, are such; that I should not act an honest part to my Country, & yourself, if I did not write to you so fully as I have. butt I could wish that the greatest part of this letter might be a secret, as it can do no good & may do harm. I shall write to you from Paris, if any messager goes: this goes by the Captain of the Yacht, Captain William, who is a good man, so 'tis safe in his hands.

I am, My Dear Lord, your Grace's ever faithfull, & most affectionate humble servant,

Richmond &c.

437. NEWCASTLE TO RICHMOND

Newcastle House
Sept 7th 1749

My Dear Lord,

I received your Graces most kind letter from Calais, and take the Opportunity of a Messenger that is going to Albemarle,[1] to thank you for it. It contained so clear, so sensible an Account of the melancholy State of the Republick of Holland, & was wrote with so much Judgement, and Impartiality, that I could not avoid showing it to the

1. William Keppel, 2nd. Earl of Albemarle was Ambassador Extraordinary and Plenipotentiary to France, 1749–1754, and had arrived in Paris on 25 July 1749.

King & the Duke, in the greatest Confidence. I have not seen the Duke since, but the King said it was a very sensible letter. He doubted, it was all true, & was extreamly pleased with the manner, tho' greatly mortified with the matter contained in the letter, and yet, Bad as things are there, & almost every where else, we must not give up the Game. What the Prince of Orange says about the Barrier is very true, but if we postpone all other Considerations 'till that Barrier is refortified, France will put it out of our power ever to fortifie it again. Your Reply to the P. of Orange was admirable, & indeed your whole Conduct in Holland, as right and prudent as possible. As to the Barrier, I see the P. of Oranges little view. He wants the Queen of Hungary to pay them the Subsidy of 1,250,000 florins, to keep a number of Dutch Troops. If that was done, it would only maintain a number of perhaps very bad Troops, but that would not restore the Barrier, & its Fortifications. My Notion with regard to the Demolished Barrier, is this; I look upon Flanders as a sort of Common Country between the Empress-Queen, England & Holland, in which we are all interested; I think the whole Revenue of the Country, should be put upon the best Foot it could, and then all applied to the present Security of it, & to the putting the several Strong Towns again in a proper state of Defence. This would be doing something, & by this Means the Fortifications may by degrees be restored. I am afraid I shall soon receive a letter from you, with a quite different Account of the present State of France. Where, tho' they have suffered greatly by the War, they have ressources, & are making use of them, for establishing a Marine, restoring their Commerce, & gaining all the powers of Europe on their Side, by which means they will hope, & that with reason to be able to impose what Conditions they please upon the rest of the World, without running the Risk of a War, and that is what I would prevent, & I think it might be yet done, & at little expense. We are now invited by the two Empresses to accede to a Defensive Treaty they made in 1746. That I would do, & as the Treaty is purely defensive, & should contain no new engagements for us, France cannot pretend to say any thing against it, after what they acknowledge they have done in renewing their Subsidiary Treaties with <u>Denmark</u>, & <u>Sweden</u>. To this Treaty other powers may accede, no Subsidies will be at present asked, & there will by this means be a Foundation of a Considerable Alliance, which will have its weight, both with France & Prussia. I think Holland cannot avoid acceding. There our friends the Bentinks must assist us. I have a suspicion, that the Greffier, who, by the by, is one of the best, & ablest man amongst them, is not quite well, or in the first Confidence with Bentinck. Groensfeldd[1] is the great Favourite. I hear He is a very able Man & well intentioned. I doubt not but I shall have the same confidential Account of the State of things in France from you, their Views their Intrigues, the State of their Finances, their Manners, their Administration &c. I dare say they are for Peace, but during that Peace they will establish such a power in Europe, as will not be to be controuled hereafter. They have pulled off the Mask a little too soon, by a very haughty letter wrote to Mirepoix, wth orders to communicate it to us, of which Alble will give you an account.

   I am my Dear Duke ever & unalterably yrs
                                    Holles Newcastle

438. RICHMOND TO NEWCASTLE

Paris
Tuesday 12/23 Septr 1749

My Dear Lord,
   I had the favor of your very kind letter of the 7th & have not time to answer it as I would, because I am butt just come from Versailes, where I met with more than a

---

1. Count Bertram Gronsfeld-Diepenbroek, the Dutch Ambassador at Berlin.

common gracious reception; & to morrow morning early I sett out for Aubigny;[1] it is impossible for me to give you the informations you require, for I am not in the way of being inform'd myself, & it is Lord Albemarle's duty to do it, & I am sure he will as far as lyes in his power, butt to be so fully instructed as you require, I am very sure he never can be without a very considerable expence & your intelligence must be in proportion to what is allow'd for it.

As for the intrigues of the court there seems to be some upon the tapis at present, <u>La Marquise</u> as they call Madame de Pompadour governs every thing at present, butt she is generally hated, & upon the least coolness from the King, she will soon be demolish'd. & so extraordinary a thing hapned to me to day that I cant help acquainting you with it, butt it is in the utmost confidence, else I shall be very justly accused of betraying the private conversation of a very old acquaintance of myne who sayes he loves me, I mean Monsr de Puysieulx. I told him that when I went at Aubigny, I should have an inclination to go to Bourges, & had indeed some business there with the Cardinal de La Roche foucauld & Monsr Dodart the Intendent du Roy, about things relating to my tenants at Aubigny, that they were both old freinds & acquaintances of myne & that they had always been extreamly civil to me, & had formerly visited me at Aubigny. butt that I had some difficulty about Monsr de Maurepas[2] who was in the Cardinall's house, that I had received great civillitys & really had obligations formerly to him, so it would be mean, & pittifull in me to go to Bourges & not see him, yett on the other hand I should be sorry to do anything that might displease the King. so I beg'd his advice, saying at the same time that if he thought it would be taken ill; I would not go at all to Bourges, for that I could not go there without seeing Monsr de Maurepas. he heard me very attentively & then said <u>allez y et allez chez Monsieur de Maurepas, on ne le prendra pas mall, au contraire, on sera bien aise que vous allier chez lui. J'eu repond, et j'eu parlerai au Roy, cependant je vous prie de ne dire mot a personne que vous m'en avez parlez.</u> I own this struck me as a very odd speech from a minister in favor, his saying that the King would even be glad I should go, for that was the meaning of what he said, shews plainly that the King loves Monsr de Maurepas, & that the Marquise had teased him into the banishment of that minister, & it also shew'd Puysieulx friendship for him. & to this I must add that Madame de Florentin[3] has gott leave to go & see him, so I see that intrigues are going on. all which I thinke right to lett you know, tho I dont see that it is of any sort of consequence to us whether Maurepas, or the Marquise is in or out. by the by the Marquise is a most glorious fine peice, so his Majesty must love change, or she behave like a fool if she is turn'd off soon.

In answer to one part of your letter I must tell you why the Greffier is not quite so well as he was with the Bentincks, tho I know they love & value him; butt I beleive he is too good, & pliant with the Prince, & does not preserve that firmness that they wish all good people about him to have; butt he is certainly an able & a good man. Gronsfeldt is as you observe a great favorite of theirs, & has a generall good character both as a sensible & an honest man, butt I must tell you that they thinke some whispers have sett him in a bad light at our court, & that thinke it is Grovestin that has done it, & begging Pietys pardon his son in Law is the dirtyest & most misceivious rascall that ever was born, & corrupt to a most infamous degree.

Now whether you will shew this letter as you did my last I leave to your Grace's better judgement, my only objection is that it is sadly writ & very likely nonsense, & so

1. Aubigny was Richmond's estate in France as Duke of Aubigny. King Louis XIV of France had granted the fief of Aubigny to the Duchess of Portsmouth, Richmond's grandmother, in 1673, and, in 1684, at the persuasion of King Charles II, he created her Duchess of Aubigny.
2. Jean Frederic Phelypeaux, Comte de Maurepas, French Secretary of State.
3. Madame de Florentin, the wife of Louis Phelypeaux, Comte de Florentin, French Secretary of State.

far from haveing time to write it over again, that I have scarce time to read it over. butt indeed I am very sorry you shew'd my last letter, my writing freely of a mistress, a minister, or a pimp, is of no consequence, butt in that letter I remember I made too free mention of persons of a higher ranke, whose birth I respect, & was sorry to say what I did of them; & heartily wish that what I had said had been a lye. butt indeed I did not mean that it should go any farther than your own ears or rather eyes. familly quarells or even dislikes are allways disagreeable, & cursed is he that foments them. & it vexes me excessively to thinke that I may inocently have been guilty of what my heart abhors. the taske you sett me of writing to you upon these subjects is indeed too hard, & I assure you I am not equal to it. I leave this letter with Lord Albemarle, to send by the first Messager that goes, for I have begged him not to trust it by the post.

Before I conclude I must putt in one word for myself. I own I expected to hear some thing from you about the Grand Mastership of the Bath. have you ever spoke to the King about it? tho I would not have you if H:R:H: the Duke thinkes of it. butt surely it is beneath his dignity. the words of the institution of the order are, <u>it shall be composed of the Sovereign, a Prince of the Royall Blood, a Grand Master, & thirty five knights.</u> by which I conceive it incompatible with His Royall Highness's dignity. I should there-fore be glad to know what is decided about it, & I own it would hurt me excessively to have any body of an inferior ranke prefer'd to me, & if I am to have it, I wish it may be soon. I beg pardon for saying so much about myself, & am My Dear Lord, for ever & most affectionately Your's

Richmond &c.

439. RICHMOND TO STONE

Aubigny
Sunday 24th Septr/5th Octr 1749

Dear Sir,

I will not trouble his Grace with a letter now as I have nothing particular to say to him. so I write this to you only to beg of you to remind him of poor Doctor Hibbins, whose preferment I really have much at heart, for he is necessitous, & I am asham'd to say how long I have been very earnestly solliciting the best freind I have in the world for him. I am just return'd here from Bourges where I went to see two old freinds & acquaintances of myne. the Cardinall de La Rochefoucauld who is nevew to late Lord Lifford,[1] & Monsr Dodard the intendant there. & I there also saw two other old acquaintances of myne, Monsr & Madame de Maurepas. I could have imagin'd that even a French minister out of Employment, should have been gay & easy in a retire-ment upon his own estate, butt I own I was astonish'd at not only his aparent content-ment butt gaiety, banish'd as he is to the worst town in France, in the center of the Kingdome, at a vast distance from his own Estate & all his freinds butt a very few that are permitted to be with him. & it really gives me a great opinion of the man. I beg my sincere service to his Grace & am Dear Sir, Your faithfull humble servant

Richmond &c.

I have had a hint that Little Blew[2] who was the villain that murderd Michael Bath the dragoon with his own hand, is at Flushing. & Lord Holderness & Mr. Charles Bentinck say that they are sure if a propper letter was wrote to the Prince of Orange about it the government would secure him & give him up. butt as yet wee have not gott a sufficient description of the man, to be sure of takeing the right person. however I have wrote

1. Frederic De Roye de la Rochefoucauld, 1st. Earl of Lifford, 1666–1749, a minor figure at the Court of King George II.
2. Isaak Adrian, alias Little Blue, the smuggler.

to Lord Bury who will aply to the man that gave me the first account of him, & if Lord Bury can gett such an account, as will be sufficient to find the man, He will give it to the Duke of Newcastle or yourself, & then I hope his Grace will send it to Lord Holderness who is already aprised of it, & at the same time a propper requisitioriall letter to the Stadthoulder & that orders may be given if he is taken, that he should be sent home in irons on board a packett, & the master of the packett to have the cheif Barons warrant by which he may be sent up to London & secured in Newgate 'till removed by Habeas Corpus to Sussex. & for this purpose I have had Mr. Simons wrote to, to gett such a warrant of the Lord Cheif Barons. butt all this must be done with the utmost secrecy else it will certainly fail.

440.   RICHMOND TO STONE

Paris
7/18 Octr 1749

Dear Sir,

I have had a letter from Doctor Hibbins, who mentions the living or rather vicarage of St. Austell in Cornwall, it's a £160 a year, & the incumbent 80 years old, is in a cursed country, & a vast distance from London. so I desire the favor of you to tell the Duke of Newcastle that I earnestly beg of him to order Dr. Hibbins to be minuted down for that living when it shall become vacant, which will extreamly oblige, dear Sir, His Grace's & your faithfull humble servant,

Richmond &c.

My porter knows how to direct to me.
I shall be at Bruxelles on tuesday the 17/28 Octr & at Calais on Munday the 23 Octr/3 Novr.

441.   NEWCASTLE TO DUCHESS OF RICHMOND

Lady Lincoln's
Thursday, past three [? 8 Nov 1749]

Madam,

I have been so ill of a Cold, that I have not stird out in the Evening, & shall not venture to do it this night, or I would do myself the honor to wait upon your Grace. I am now at Lady Lincoln's, who is to be my Lady Mayoress to entertain the French Ambassadress at my House on Tuesday next. May I beg the honor of your Grace's Company at dinner. I shall write to my Friend to night, tho' I despair of this sad pen & ink.

I am ever Yr Grace's most faithful servt
Holles Newcastle

P.S. Be so good as to send me Word if I can have the honr of yr Company.

442.   NEWCASTLE TO RICHMOND

Newcastle House
Novr 9th 1749

My Dear Lord,

I received your Grace's letter, & am myself much for your friend Bolten. Nothing is yet done in it, but I hope soon to get it over. Mr. Nicolas Turner[1] has insisted upon being excused. I wish you could get Peck Williams to appoint [?] & Rideout[2] Under

1. Nicholas Turner of Bignor Park.
2. Richard Rideout was the officer at Lewes Gaol.

Sheriffs, & then little <u>Peck</u> would be a very pretty <u>High</u> Sheriff. I dare say you may bring it about. I am forced at last to have their Exeys the French Ambs & Ambss to dinner & Cards on Tuesday next. Lady Lincoln is <u>Lady Mayeress</u> for the Day. The Ds of Richmond comes. Stone writes to Dayrolle to be here in the Evening. If you come to Town, I hope you will dine with us. Tell my Lord Lincoln from me, He <u>must</u> be here at dinner on Tuesday. You will be glad to hear yr Friend Stone succeeds Sr T. Rob. in ye Board of Trade.[1]

Ever Yrs

Holles Newcastle

443. RICHMOND TO NEWCASTLE

Goodwood
Sunday 24 Decr 1749

My Dear Lord,

I know you will be angry with me for troubleing you with what you will call trifles, butt I cant thinke them so, when the very existance I may say, of two good creatures depend you; I am sure my term is propper for without your speedy releif they actually neither of them can exist. I mean Sr Thos Robinson[2] & Hibbins; you know how long I have spoke for them both; & how often you have promis'd me for both. the first has often lay'd his scheeme before you, & I am assured it is not only a very practicable one, butt what you might gett for him for speaking to the King. & give me leave (as I am used to take liberty with you) to say you ought to do it, consideraing the manner you recall'd him in, for you gave butt one reason for it, which was an accusation of a thing that never hapned. I, that know your heart, know you to be incapable of dong an ill natured action knowingly; butt indeed if you dont speedily releive him, you will do one, without excuse. I know you will not like this stile, espetially upon such a subject as this, butt as you know my heart & love for you, you will be extreamly in the wrong to take it ill of me.

so much for poor Sr Thomas, now as to the other which is poor Hibbins, I must apply to you in quite a different stile, for him I aske, I beg, I entreat you, to gett him a living speedily, for he is actually starving, so much so that by this post I send him something out of my own pocket, for immediate releif. I am not asham'd to own I have a heart that feels for the distress'd, & when I cant help them, & my best freind in the world can, & does not, it gives me double concern. forgive me, I am now what I hardly ever am without great reason in very low spirits, for my poor Dear little boy George, is extreamly ill of the meazles, & a most shocking cough.

I am, My Dear Lord, most sincerely, & most affectionately Your's
Richmond &c.

I wrote the above last night, butt this morning wee find the dear boy much better, haveing considerably mended since bleeding. so wee hope he is out of danger.

444. NEWCASTLE TO RICHMOND

Claremont
Decr 25th 1749

My Dear Lord,

I have received this afternoon the favour of your letter, which I really take very

1. Andrew Stone was a Lord of Trade, 1749–1754, in succession to Sir Thomas Robinson, 1695–1770, who became Master of the Great Wardrobe.
2. Sir Thomas Robinson, 1702–1777, MP for Morpeth, 1727–1734, was Governor of Barbados, 1742–1747, when he was recalled on suspicion of diverting defence funds for rebuilding Government House. He was never employed again. In 1750 he received a pension of £500 a year.

kindly, tho' yr Grace imagined I would not. I must begin with the latter parts of it, which relates to Dear Lord George. The P.S set me at ease. I know the Measles very well. If there is Bleeding & purging enough, there is seldom any Danger, especially in Children of His age, and He was relieved by Bleeding. I hope the Danger is over. However, I shall expect an acct by next post, wth a Confirmation of it. As to the two unhappy Men you mention, were it in my power to relieve them, I should be very much to blame if I did it not, as you, my best Friend, so earnestly desire it. However, I will immediately do my best. What is proposed to Sr T. Robinson is an Allowance out of the 4 & half pr cent, which is, in other words, out of the King's Pocket, and I don't know any Body who can make His Majesty give <u>any thing,</u> but His Treasurer, & therefore if Mr. Pelham was disposed to do it, He might bring it about. I can get a Negative, & I will venture one, rather than one moment be suspected of Want of Attention to your Requests. But a Line to Mr. Pelham would really do more, than all I can say, <u>powerful as I am</u>. As to poor Hibbins, His Case is unfortunate, but nothing has fallen, that could be done conveniently for Him. I thought you had fixed upon something, which I suppose has not fallen. If you could let me know the particular Living or Preferment you wish for Him, He shall have my Assistance against all the World, if it has not been previously engaged. I can't agree that Sr. T. Robinson was wrongly removed. The Complaints against Him were so strong, that it was scarce possible to stand it. However, He is a good natured Man. You interest yourself for Him, & I will set seriously to work to serve Him, if possibly I can, & I will do the same for Hibbins. I have been in great pain about <u>Blew</u>. I really thought He had made his escape, or had bribed the Captain of the Packet to carry him off. Three Packets came in, & no Notice of Him, but this Evening, I have received the enclosed Bland Account of Him. I think however, He is safe, & will soon be brought safe to London, so I beg your Orders what to do wh Him. As to our Ministerial Situation, things remain just as they did, & worse they cannot well be. Nobody can tell what I go thro' except they were to be as happily coupled as I am, and their agreable Collegue, for His Significance or Insignificance supported by those who should be their best Friends. But I will trouble you no longer upon that disagreable Subject. I can never think of it with ease to myself, but amongst the many who do not act kindly by me, I must ever acknowledge my Obligation to yr Grace whose Friendship appears upon every occasion wherein I am concerned. Genl Luchesi, Harcourt, Linky & Sussex made a good Meat Breakfast here this Morning, I hope they are safely arrived. My Compliments to the Ds of Richmond.

I am my Dear Lord Ever most affectly Yrs

Holles Newcastle

445. RICHMOND TO NEWCASTLE

Whitehall
Thursday morning [22 March 1749/50]

Haveing a bougie of seven inches & a half in me[1] at this time prevents my waiting on your Grace this morning, tho as it will be out by three or four I hope to meet you at the Duke of Grafton's. I send you the sessions paper & am asham'd to say that I did not attend as I should have done to the report, for if I had known as much as I now do by

---

1. The first mention of urethral dilation to treat Richmond's cancer of the bladder, which was to kill him in the following year. The process of the disease can be traced in Richmond's letters to Henry Fox. I am grateful to Dr. Howard Smedley for diagnosing Richmond's condition from the autopsy performed on him after his death. For the autopsy, see B.L. Add. Ms. 51, 424 f.103. I am grateful to Professor Mary Margaret Stewart for bringing it to my attention.

the sessions paper <u>Page 47</u>. I certainly should have spoke for William Fry the Dog horse stealer; for he actually sold him for 10s & 6, the price of a Dog horse to a collar maker, so really as there will be eleven hangued without him, I wish you would speake for him to the King that he may be transported; I know nothing of the Wretch, butt from the sessions paper, nor has he made the least application to me, or any body that I know of; so it is really nothing butt propper compassion that moves me to aske this, & what confirms me in it is that you yourself seem to be of my opinion. so for God's sake dont lett this poor Wretch be hangued for want of speaking, for him.

The Duchess of Richmond & I have a boon to aske of your Grace, which is that you would be Godfather to our little Girl.[1] & I wish it had been a boy that his name might have been Thomas. & you'l tell me to day whether next Wednesday evening will suite you.

Lady Lincoln, & a little Kreuningen as proxy for Lady Margaret Bentinck are to be Gossips, neither of them bad kisses, so I hope you wont object to them.

Your's my Dear Lord, most affectionately
Richmond &c.

quoque vous me bonde quelque fois.

446. RICHMOND TO NEWCASTLE

Whitehall
Saturday 31 March 1750

My Dear Lord,
If there is a vacancy of Reader to the Charter house, I beg you would be for young Norton[2] the Alderman's son. he is a good & sober lad, is in orders, & was bred at the Charter house, & elected off from thence to Peter house in Cambridge. I recommended him last year butt the vacancy did not then happen, so if it should now I hope he will succeed. The Arch Bishop is for him, & so is every officer in the Charter, except Man who has gott I beleive a freind of his own. I beg you would not forgett this, I am, My Dear Lord, most affectionately your's
Richmond &c.

447. RICHMOND TO STONE

Whitehall
April 9 1750

The Duke of Richmond's Compliments to Mr. Stone and encloses a Letter he has just wrote to the Duke of Newcastle, relating to Holman Trower and Gearing,[3] which he desires Mr. Stone to read; he will see by it, that his Grace is of Opinion that Mercy may very properly be extended to Trower and Gearing.

His Grace desires Mr. Stone to deliver the Letter to the Duke of Newcastle as soon as he arrives — Lady Yarmouth[4] and most of the Company being engaged on wednesday, the Duke of Richmond is obliged to put off his dinner to thursday next, when he hopes to have the favour of Mr. Stone's Company.

1. Lady Cecilia Margaret Lennox, Richmond's youngest daughter, was born on 27 February 1750.
2. Robert Norton, son of Robert Norton, Mayor of Chichester in 1734 and 1747, after taking his degree at Peterhouse was Rector of Southwick and Hangleton, 1751–1756.
3. Thomas Holman, William Trower and John Geering, smugglers, were convicted of the murder of Michael Bath, a dragoon in Lord Mark Kerr's Regiment, near Sea Place, Goring, in January 1744. The relevant papers are in Goodwood Ms. 156.
4. Amalia Walmoden, Countess of Yarmouth, 1704–1765, mistress of King George II.

448. RICHMOND TO NEWCASTLE

Whitehall
Fryday 27th April 1750

My Dear Lord,

I am overjoy'd at hearing by Mr. Ramsden that your Grace & the Duchess of Newcastle arrived safe at Calais yesterday, & I thanke you most extreamly for your goodness to me in ordering Mr. Ramsden to send me word of it immediately, which he did very punctually. & I hope the rest of your journey will be as agreeable. I suppose your stay at the Hague wont be long, I dont envy you the audience you must have there. I hope in God our Master has arrived in good health at Hanover, I own I am uneasy till I hear of it, for he was not well when he went, nor when he landed; 'tis a life of too much importance to be indifferent about. God send him safe there & back again. I take the liberty of enclosing a letter to my old friend Monsieur Hardenberg.[1] I wish you would bring him back with you, for I should be excessively glad to see him particularly at Goodwood, for he is a brother gardiner, & I really love him extreamly. Mr. Fox has wrote to you about poor Major Sowle, wee wish to have Keppell succeed him, & the Duke has been exceedingly good in it, butt hitherto without success; however if his Majesty absollutely refuses poor Keppell, which I shall be excessively sorry for, yett I must beg of you then to gett his Majesty to do it as first proposed & to let it go in the Regiment. it is indeed a case of Charity & great compassion to poor Sowle, who has served not only without reproach butt with great honor, & has been in every respect as good a man as ever was born. butt in reality the poor man is now out of his senses & his unhapiness for fear of his family starving (which it must do if he is not permitted to sell) has brought him to such a low degree of spirit, that he is actually one of the greatest objects of compassion that I ever saw, so for pitty's sake recommend his case. I long to hear of your safe arrival at Hanover, & the Duchess of Richmond & I joyn in our best compliments to the Duchess of Newcastle.

I am, My Dear Lord, for ever, & most affectionately, Your's
Richmond &c.

449. RICHMOND TO NEWCASTLE

Cockpitt
3d May 1750

My Lord,

I find all the papers relating to Holman, Geering & Trower here in Mr. Aldworth's hands, butt no referece at all to the Regency, without which nothing can be done upon it here. & when the time of their repreive is out I shall be in Ireland, so I wish this reference could be sent soon.

I am My Lord, Your Grace's most faithfull humble servant
Richmond &c.

450. RICHMOND TO NEWCASTLE

Whitehall
Thursday 10th May 1750

My Dear Lord,

Your Grace will receive a letter at the same time with this from the Duke of Bedford, relating to some exchange in His Majesty's Royall regiment of Horse Guards.

---

1. Friedrich Carl Baron von Hardenburg, was the Hanoverian Minister of State.

butt in case his Majesty should thinke by this scheeme that Cornet Keyt[1] is too well provided for by comeing into nine shillings a day, I must beg you to inform His Majesty that this method was thought of to gett rid of him, without a Court Martial, for wee were all here of opinion that 'tho he is known to be a scoundrell, yett he would certainly have been acquitted for want of legall prooffs. The enclosed is the scheme which was aproved of by His Royall Highness the Duke. & I hope His Majesty will be gratiously pleased to give his orders upon it. & if His Majesty is pleased to aprove of it, I hope the Comission, & warrant will be sign'd & sent here soon; for I own I am impatient to gett rid of Keyt, as I really beleive he is the only bad man in the regiment. besides he belongs to the King's troop, so there is nobody to do duty with it, butt the Captn Lieutnt & Quarter Master.

I am, My Dear Lord, Your Grace's most faithfull & affectionate humble servant
Richmond &c.

The following scheme is humbly submitted to His Majesty, Viz:

	li	d	
That Cornet Keyt be placed on the			
half pay of Lord Rutherford	2	6	a day
On the <u>En Second</u> pay of ditto	2	6	
and also on the <u>En Second</u> pay of Lieutnt Merrick	4	0	
		in all 9 shillings a day	

That Lord Rutherford should succeed Cornet Keyt in the Cornetcy. and that five shillings a day be made good to him on the Contingencies of the Army till provided with Cornet's pay from the Regiment.

Lieutenant Merrick, has now no pay from the Regiment, because of His Majesty haveing some time ago given leave to Sir John Bennett to retire upon his pay. butt by this method Lieutnt Merrick will come into Cornet Keyt's pay. & his half pay of Brigadier in the horse Guards, will cease, & be a saveing to the half pay establishment. NB: Cornett Keyt bought first an ensignery in the foot gards, then this cornetcy, which in all cost him 1800

451. RICHMOND TO NEWCASTLE

Goodwood
18th May 1750

My Dear Lord,
You know how long I have sollicited both your Grace & the Chancellor in favor of Mr. Hughes, & you know how often you have promis'd, & I am very sure with great sincerity, that you would either recommend him or give him a good King's living when an oportunity offer'd. I know at the same time your engagements, to Mr. Hurdress, who I thinke as much as you can, ought to be well provided for, for which reason I take the liberty of laying the following scheeme before you, which would provide well for Mr. Hurdress, & my freind Mr. Hughes also. & I assure you it would extreamly oblige me, as I have the preferment of the latter most extreamly at heart. The living of Bexhill, now is the Deans, & that of Barcombe is likely to be soon vacant, as the incumbent is 80 years of age. Now what I have to propose is that Mr. Hughes should have Bexhill, if our Dean is promoted to a Bishoprick which I sincerely wish may be soon. butt if you should design that for Mr. Hurdress then that I may have an absollute promis, not of my Lord Chanceller because I know he wont give it, butt of your Grace

---

1. Cornet Robert Keyt was removed from the Royal Regiment of Horse Guards owing to his bad behaviour after quarrels with Captain Francis Wheeler, Mr. Stubbs and Major Sowle. The papers relating to the case are now Goodwood Ms. 91.

that you will strongly joyn with me in recommending Mr. Hughes for it. I beg therefor that you would thinke of this, & lett me have your answer upon it; that I may give some comfort to poor Hughes, who really has waited a great deal too long already.

I am, My Dear Lord, Your ever faithfull, & most affectte slave

Richmond &c.

452.   RICHMOND TO NEWCASTLE

Whitehall
31st May 1750

My Dear Lord,

I am vastly in arrear of correspondence with you, butt I really have not had time to write, as I have according to my duty been severall dayes with my regiment,[1] & have made a thorough examination both of men & horses, & as thorough an inspection into the whole detail of it. As to clothing, arms, sadles, accoutrements, & every thing belonging to a trooper or his horse. & have the peasure to tell you that I found every thing far beyond my expectation, in the best order that's possible. a most glorious body of men, & very few horses that any exception could be made to. all which is for the honor of the late Duke of Somersett, & my feild officers, who have in their severall stations taken all the care that's possible of the regiment, so that all that lyes upon me is to keep it where it is, for really there is hardly room for improvement. this is what few Colls that come to a regiment would own, butt you'l do me the justice to own that I have allways loved truth. & I should be a sad dog if I pretended to take to my self any honor that belongs to other people, which I thinke I have no more right to, than their mony. butt if it is kept up to the high perfection it is in, I shall have some merit, & I shall certainly spare neither trouble nor expense to attain that end. I am extreamly obliged to you for haveing gott the Comission & warrants sign'd; & (thankes to His Majesty now this Keyt is out) I dont know one officer in the regiment that the least exception can be made to. I am sorry you say nothing to me about poor Major Sowle. I am sure if the King knew how thoroughly incapable of service the poor man is now, his affair would not have been delay'd so long, for nobody is better appraised of his former services than his Majesty. I am extreamly glad to find your Grace & My Lady Duchess have had so pleasant a journey, & that her Grace enjoys so good a state of health. I have also the pleasure to tell you that Lord Clinton is a great deal better, the Earl is gon to <u>Veiller a ses interests</u> in the Fenns, in which his Lordship will not give way to any subject, be he never so great. I hope I shall hear from you sometimes, & am with the most perfect truth & affection My Dear Lord, Your Grace's ever faithfull humble servant,

Richmond.

I have heard nothing of the refference to the Lords Justices of the cases of Holman, Trower, & Geering, butt perhaps it may be come, butt the Duke of Bedford is out of town, so I know nothing of it.

You may easyly guess My Dear Lord why this & my other letter are seperately wrote. you may shew the other if you thinke propper, if not burn it; or do as you please with it. I thanke you in the first place for your very kind letter of the 11/22 from the Hague; & for your good intentions in regard to poor Keppell, over whose head you know young Harry came. I mention this only as a fact, not by way of complaint I assure you; for I know you could not do otherways, butt it makes poor Keppell's pretensions the stronger. As to your Hague conferences, I had no doubt of your being well pleased

---

1. Richmond had been appointed to the command of the Royal Horse Guards in place of the Duke of Somerset, who had died on 7 February 1750.

with the Greffier, Charles Bentinck, & the pensionary, because they are honest men & in your own way of thinking as to Publick affairs. & I had no doubt of your being politely received by the great persons there, who really to do them justice never fail in that point. & I am very glad the Pss Rll is in so good a way. as to Publick affairs, I am happy in hearing that my freind Dayrolle is so well with you; he is damn'd passionate, butt as honest a fellow as ever was born. I should have shewn your letter as you desired to the Chancr D. of Grafton & Mr. Pelham, butt I was with the Regiment when I received it. Every thing here goes on <u>humdrum</u> not a soul in town, butt I am confined here with Pegs[1] who is not well yett, tho in a good way, butt fear I shant be well enough to go to Ireland this month yett. I suppose you know there has been a grand party at Wooburn, the Duke & Princess Emily &c. I had not the honor to be invited; so it's no merit to say I should have excused my self. butt I am to call there in my way to Ireland. I had a great deal of discourse with your brother the other day at Oatlands, who talked as to Publick affairs I really thinke as well as <u>you</u> could wish & as to you personally as well as <u>I</u> could wish; & he was so good as to shew me your letter to him, which as it was very kind pleased both him & me. I pleaded ignorance to one part of your letter, as I promis'd you never to own I knew any thing of it. I mean the French affair. I must tell you that when Totty ask'd me to call on him in my way to Ireland he press'd your brother extreamly to be of the party; butt he with great civillity fended off, & at last said it was impossible. I have now troubled you with a long letter butt before I conclude I must beg of you to read the enclosed letter to me with attention. Tis from Mr. Knollys[2] of Hampshire. he has two thousand pounds a year now; and is heir to Mr Flemings estate which is above three thousand a year more so you see he is a man of consequence & I assure you he is as good a Whig as you, or I, which I can answer for as I know him intimately well. you may perhaps know him yourself, his mother was only daughter to Old Gibson of Lethbury. now I thinke this is the very living you wanted for Jack Fuller's brother; butt pray consider twice before you disoblige such a man as I have described to you, & consider also, the justice of his request, for after Flemin's death the living comes to him with the estate; so it really would be hard to take the advantage of Fleming's lunacy. I beg your answer to this, that if you thinke as I do upon it, Mr. Knollis may make his aplication to you. as for it's being disposed of by the Regency, I am in no aprehension about it, for I dont imagine wee have a power to do it.

adieu My Dear Lord, Your's for ever, & most affectionately
Richmond &c.

Webster the Meassager refused to take a letter of myne directed to you, & scurrilously abused my footman tho he had the King's livery on. I wish you would rate him for it, for he is a most impertinent rascal.

453.   RICHMOND TO NEWCASTLE

Goodwood
6th June 1750

My Dear Lord,
Your Grace was so good as to tell me in your last letter that the commission & warrant for my regiment were sign'd. butt I fear they were forgott to be sent for when I came out of town last munday they knew nothing of them at the office, nor do I find that the King's refference to the regency of the affair of Holman, Trower & Geering is received, so if they are not already sent, I beg you would be so good as to give your

---

1.   Lady Cecilia Margaret Lennox.
2.   Thomas Knollys of Grove Place, Nursling in Hampshire, died 1751, the son and heir of Henry Knollys, MP for St. Ives, 1722–1734.

orders about it. I wrote to you about three weeks ago about our Dean, & Hughes, & I should be obliged to you for your answer to that. You will wonder to hear that Mr. Webber[1] has got the living of Selsea, which you know has allways been recon'd the finest thing in the Bishop of Chichester's gift, & of course what I never thought of for Mr. Webber; butt the Bishop told me he would give Selsea to Mr. Adams,[2] & Mr. Adams's two livings of Walburton & Yapton to Mr. Webber, which two livings were worth 140ll per annum, which would have fully satisfy'd Mr. Webber, butt upon Dr. Manningham's death,[3] Sr Hutching Williams, & Parson Adams came to me, & beg'd that I would relinquish the Bishop's promis as to the living of Walburton worth 80ll a year, that he might keep that with Selsea, which he assured me was not 140ll per annum, by the great mischeif the sea had done by breaking the dams there. to which, as you may imagine I told him, I certainly should not, nor as an honest man, could not compliment him, at poor Webber's expence, who instead of 140, that the Bishop was so good as to promis him, would then have butt a poor living of 60ll a year. then Mr. Adams said he could not part with Walburton & Yapton, as Selsea was under their value. upon which our good Bishop, who I shall ever love & honor for it, at once said that Mr. Webber should have Selsea, which at present bad as it is, is worth 150ll for Adams had undervalued it, & will with a little expence, & what he will recover from delapidations, be soon worth 200ll a year. so you see wee have had some luck, & shall profit from other people's wrongheadedness.

I should not have troubled you with so long a story, butt as it is a peice of Sussex history, I need make no excuse for it; & as it pleases me extreamly I have vanity enough to thinke it will not displease your Grace. & now I have butt one Sussex parson left upon my hands, which is poor Hughes, & you must lett me apply to you for him, when any thing propper for him falls. & now before I conclude I shall say two words about myself, which is that I have putt off my Irish journey[4] for some time, as I would be perfectle cured of my disorders in the <u>urethra</u> before I go. & the cure has gon on much slower that I at first thought, which proceeds from the cheif disorder being at the neck of the bladder. however, I find a sensible alteration for the better; & am sure it will do at last. butt in this as well as in most things patience is required.

adieu My Dear Lord, I am for ever, most truely, & most affectionately Your's
Richmond &c.

My two little girls Louisa & Sarah have been innoculated, & are thanke God perfectly well; & neither of their pretty faces hurt. I was glad to hear before I left London that Lord Clinton was much better.

454.   RICHMOND TO NEWCASTLE

Whitehall
Fryday 15th June 1750

I thanke you, My Dear Lord, for your letter of May 30th/June 10 butt how can you be so peevish with me about only reminding you of poor Hughes, & only offering a scheeme which I thought not only practicable butt agreeable to you, butt I suppose

---

1.   William Webber was instituted as Rector of Selsey on 13 June 1750, on the death of Thomas Manningham, and continued to hold the living until 1790.
2.   George Adams had been Vicar of Yapton since June 1732, and Vicar of Walberton since August 1732. He died in November 1750.
3.   Thomas Manningham, Prebendary of Ipthorne in Chichester Cathedral, 1711–1750, and Treasurer of the Cathedral, 1712–1750, died on 4 May 1750.
4.   The Duke and Duchess of Richmond were planning to go to Cartown in Ireland to stay with Lady Emily Lennox, and her husband the Earl of Kildare.

twas a bad day with you, 'tho your letter began peevishly yett it ended kindly to me, & I am sure your heart dictated. & I thanke you for assuring me that when anything reasonable is proposed for poor Hughes, you will allow me to apply for it. I thanke you again for the care you took to gett the Commission & warrant for my regiments sign'd; butt by some mistake or other they are not yett come to either office. You desired me to send you some news, butt I really have none being butt just arrived from Sussex. I wrote a long letter & a double one to you some dayes ago which I hope you received. adieu My Dear Lord, my best respects attend the Duchess of Newcastle,

    Your's most affectionately

Richmond &c.

What is become of poor major Sowles affair? it makes my heart bleed to see so good & gallant a man; in such distress.

455. RICHMOND TO NEWCASTLE

Hampton Court
18th June 1750

My Dear Lord,

    I have now a scheme for Mr. Hughes, which I thinke & hope is a very practicable one. Dr Gardiner is just dying, or dead, & he has the following preferments, viz:

    St. Olaves Southwarke. clear money only 84ll – 7 – 6 a year, it is in the King's gift.

    Walton upon Thames. In the Chancellrs gift 29

    Moulsea only a curacy, of the Bishp of Winchester's 28 – 10 – 0 in all, butt 141 – 17 – 6 Now if your Grace would gett his Majesty's nomination, or rather apointment for St Olaves, I would aske the Chancellor for Walton, which I am persuaded he would give, & Mr. Hughes sayes he can by his own interest gett Moulsea of the Bishop of Winchester for these three thing have always gon together. butt now I must beg of you not to thinke me unreasonable in what I am going to aske still farther, butt before I mention it, I will tell you my reasons. what I have allways sollicited for Mr. Hughes has been to make up his preferment to about two hundred a year. the living of Donington near Chichester which he now has is a clear 80ll a year, for which he now letts it, therefore if I could have gott him 120ll tenable with that, I should have been satisfy'd, or 200ll if he was obliged to quit it; as he will be now if he succeeds in what I have here allready ask'd for him, butt then you'l see that his whole preferment will be under 150ll, which however he will be happy with if he could have some hopes given him of the living of St. Johns Southwarke, which is near 200ll & in the King's gift, or of Bexhill in case the Dean should ever be promoted to a Bishoprick, which indeed you have already been so good as to say you would be for him preferable to any other. Neither of these are likely to be soon vacant, however the hopes of either of them would make him happy; & 'tis upon this condition that he asks it which is giving up St Olaves & the other two little preferments, when the other happens. So in fact all I aske for Mr. Hughes now is in value butt an adition of 61 – 11 – 6, & a promis as far as depends upon your Grace of 50ll a year more. all which I hope & beg you wont thinke unreasonable, as in fact, if the whole was completed 'tis no more that what I ask'd at first.

    I am My Dear Lord Your Grace's, most affectionate humble servant,

Richmond &c.

456. RICHMOND TO NEWCASTLE

Whitehall
21st June 1750

My Dear Lord,

    I must now inform your Grace that Dr. Gardiner is dead, & that My Lord

Chancellor has been so good as to promiss the living of Walton to Mr. Hughes if his Majesty gives him that of St. Olaves, which I hope with your kind intercession will now be the case. & if it is; Mr. Hughes does not desire it, that is would not chuse to have it before Michealmass, because if he had he would loose a whole year's income at Donington, so a promiss of haveing St. Olaves by Michaelmass would make him happy & extreamly oblige My Dear Lord, Your ever faithfull & affectionate humble servant

Richmond &c.

The Duchess of Richmond & I joyn in our best compliments to the Duchess of Newcastle. wee are to dine on Sunday with Jemmy at Claremount.

457.   PELHAM TO RICHMOND

July ye 17, 1750

My Dear Lord,

It is with great pleasure that I hear your Grace intends to be in town on thursday, for I hope that intention will facilitate what I am now going to desire of you, and for which I send this Messenger on purpose to Goodwood. The Duke and Princess Amelia design me the honour of dining att Esher next friday. I insist on your being of the Party, and if the Dutchess of Richmond comes this way, I shall be extremely proud if Her Grace would honour me with her company also. It is in your way home, you may take a bed, without ceremony att Esher, go away in the morning as early, or as late as you please, no crowd, no Lady nor Master of the house but yourselves. Our freind <u>Puff</u> and Waldegrave will be there. I shall with prudence and choice avoid any jealousies from abroad, but notwithstanding all I can do or say, that will now and then arise, but your presence and the Dutchess of Richmond's will be my protection. <u>Linky</u> is a great Prince & a great <u>fool</u>. He demurrs about coming even to my house on this occasion, but I shall putt on the Parent, and command him; I hope you will tell him to behave himself well, for in that respect I have no influence; forgive my Dear Duke, the liberty I take, & let me have the pleasure of knowing that I shall see you, and give me hopes att least of the Ds of Richmond. I write with the knowledge and approbation of my <u>Lord Chamberlain</u>.[1]

I am my Dear Lord your Grace's faithfull slave

H. Pelham

458.   RICHMOND TO NEWCASTLE

Goodwood
18th July 1750

My Dear Lord,

I have a great deal to say to your Grace, butt will begin with Hughes about whom I have already plagued you a great deal, butt the only way to putt a stop to it is to do what is now in your power, that is give him the living of St. Olaves. & since you dont care to make any future promis for him, I shall wave that, & he must be satisfy'd with St. Olaves, & the other two little things, which will be a tollerable good provision for him 'tho very short of what I first ask'd for him, & as you are not engaged I hope you will recommend him to the King for it, notwithstanding the very good natured objection you have to it upon the account of Dr. Gardiner's son. butt what you propose that is the getting of the living of Donnington for him, will never do, for I must inform you that our Bishop has promis'd that living to a very good man that you know & I beleive have a value for, Mr. Smelt,[2] who was recommended to the Bishop by Mr. Page, who

1. Charles Fitzroy, 2nd. Duke of Grafton was Lord Chamberlain, 1724–1757.
2. Maurice Smelt succeeded Simon Hughes as Vicar of Donnington on 29 January 1751.

is not only Lord of the Manner, butt allmost the whole propperty of the Parish of Donnington belongs to him; so you see that scheme is not practicable. butt surely your Grace will have it in your power to gett some other living of that value for Mr. Gardiner; I pitty the poor man & by your accounts he has merit. butt putt yourself in my place, & say whether I can give up poor Hughes when such an opportunity offers, & after so many years sollicitation for him. & that now the whole depends upon yourself, for the Chancellor has promis'd him Walton & he has also gott the promis of Molsea which is only a donative, & the two together dont make above 57ll a year, & what he could not take without St. Olaves, which I am assured is not near 200ll a year, & the outgoings reduce it to under 100ll for it is so populous a Parish that even when he resides there, he is obliged to have a curate at 70ll a year to help do the duty. I have troubled you too much about this already so I shall say no more only that I hope your answer will be that you have gott it for him.

& now as to our Poor Good Bishop,[1] who I find you are damn'd angry with. he is indeed as you own a good man in the main, 'tho to be sure he has broke his word with you, butt he certainly forgott, as he did to button his cod peice, butt last week when he received the Duchess of Richmond, & shew'd her a <u>Yard</u> of his shirt, when she went to pay him a visit. As to my interest with him 'twas sufficient to gett the livings of Walburton & Yapton. 140ll a year for Webber if they had been vacant, butt his getting of Selsea, was an accident owing to the stupidity of Adams, & his wise Counsellor Sr Hutchins Williams, & not to my interest with the Bishop., for I assure you I never thought of asking him for Selsea.

I must now thanke you for your reprimand of Webster, & for his paper you sent me, butt till I see my footman Thorpe who is in London, I can say nothing as to the truth of it. I also thanke you for doing your best for my nevew Keppell, butt am very well satisfy'd that poor Sowls affair was done at last, which I assure you I had more at heart in this instance than Keppell's preferment, for Sowle's life, & his familly's bread depended upon it, & he has been as good an officer, & as gallant, & as honest a man as ever lived.

I am vastly obliged to you for your severall letters of June 17/28 – June 24/July 5 & June 29/July 10 all which I have now answered except the Polliticall parts, of which you know I never sett up for a judge, butt am glad to find things in a good way abroad, & am excessively happy to see, the good correspondence between you & your brother, as you are the two men I love the best. I attended the installation where I own I had no small divertion, from some excessive ridiculous figures that would have delighted our poor deceased freind the Duke of Montagu;[2] I shall not however describe them to you only My Lord Granville who look'd wretchedly, & really was ill from the excessive fatigue, & a most monstrous full bottom Wigg, & Sr Clement had exactly the fellow to it. They both dranke a good deal of Wine, in the Chapter house, & two vast glasses of brandy before dinner; notwithstanding all which, & the courage that I have heard My Lord Granville brag of when he was with the baggage behind the wood at Dettingen, I never saw two people run more nimbly than his Lordship & His Grace of Portland[3] did out of the Hall when the mob broke in at the end of the Table, dureing which time the other two new Knights stood up very quietly & had their Titles proclaimed by Garter. butt when he was to proclaim the Titles of the Earl of Granville, his Lordp was fled, & Garter assured us all that there was no instance in the history of the order that the Titles of an absent Knight was ever proclaimed; & unless, I who presided as senior Knight possitively commanded him, he would not proclaim him. butt I would not take upon me to give any order contrary to our old customs, so wee stay'd there, till the

---

1. Matthias Mawson, 1683–1770, was Bishop of Chichester, 1740–1754, when he was translated to Ely.
2. John Montagu, 2nd. Duke of Montagu had died on 6 July 1749.
3. William Bentinck, 2nd. Duke of Portland, 1709–1762.

Valliant corps of Beefeaters had repuls'd the mob, & then I sent <u>Norroy</u>[1] & a Herald to bring back our fugitive Knight, which with some difficulty they did, & then (he being present) Garter proclaim'd his Titles. The Duke of Bedford's breeches came down in the scuffle, & these I thinke are the most remarkable occurences that hapned at this ceremony. forgive this long letter & allow me to be, My Dear Lord, your ever faithfull, & most affectionate humble servant

Richmond &c.

Wee are all vastly happy in hearing His Majesty is so well. God in heaven bless & preserve him.

I grow better, butt not well yett, yett I am in a sure way of being well. you are very good to be uneasy about me, butt I assure you, you need not. Hawkins[2] & Ranby I know can do me no good, & if Tomkyns cant cure me, I'l go to Daran himself at Paris, butt I have no doubt butt Tomkyns will do it at last. butt it requires patience, which is a virtue I am proud of haveing a considerable share of.

The Duchess of Richmond & I joyn in our best compliments to the Duchess of Newcastle. wee dined about a fortnight ago with Jemmy at Claremount; he did the honors admirably, & wee dranke your Grace's, & My Lady Duchess's health. Claremount in great beauty.

459. RICHMOND TO NEWCASTLE

Whitehall
Fryday 27th July 1750

My Dear Lord,

I thanke you extreamly for your very obligeing letter of the 18/29 instt & kind concern for my health. as for your uneasiness from not hearing from me, that must have been removed by the time almost you sent away your letter, for I had long before that wrote to you from Goodwood; & for God's sake my Dear Lord dont imagine that a trifle from you could ever disoblige me, indeed it must be extraordinary ill usage, that could even stagger the love & freindship I have for you. As to my health, I have had two fitts of an ague, & Mr. Pelham was taken at the same time & in the same manner. however I am better & hope I shall have no return, & I hope he is better tho I have not heard from him this morning. as to my operations they certainly now not only go on better, butt apace; which I attribute to a better that is a more propper Bougie that Daran has lately made up on purpose for me. & now I begin to thinke seriously on my journey to Ireland.

butt before I go I hope to hear from you that poor Hughes has the living of St. Olaves, & if it turns out near what you imagine it is, I shall certainly never give you any more trouble about him & am very sorry I have given you so much. butt I must tell you that I beleive Mr. Gardiner has putt his circumstances upon a lower footing than they really are; for I have been inform'd that the Doctor dyed rather rich, however as what I say is only report, I would not hurt the poor man by it, & if he wants it, hope you will find some other provision for him; butt I hope you wont do it at poor Hughes's expence, espetially as wee have secured the other little thing for him. & I assure you the Great Earl of Lincoln, & of course the rich Mr. Dicker, the two chiefs of Walton Parish will be pleased to have Mr. Hughes. Mr. Pelham & I were to have mett the Earl to day at Dicker's, butt Doctor Wilmott has lay'd an Embargo upon us both. the Dr. sayes Mr. Pelham is better, tho not so much so as I am, & I should certainly have gon, butt that the Dr. call'd in a powerfull alliance, Taw, & stopp'd me.

1. John Cheale.
2. Sir Caesar Hawkins, 1711–1786, Sergeant Surgeon to King George II and King George III, was Surgeon to St. George's Hospital, 1735–1774.

I suppose you have had an account of the entertainment of the Royall Guests at Esher, however I know you'l be testy with me if I dont say something upon it. it was last fryday the 20th & the company were

The Duke		Mr. Pelham	
Princess Emily		Duke of Grafton	
Dss of Richmond	at one table in the	Duke of Richmond	at another table in
Lady H: Campbell	Library	Ld Lincoln	the old dining
Ldy: B: Levson		Ld Waldegrave	room
		Ld Ancram	

I thinke you cant dislike the company, for I am very sure all the invited are very entirely your humble servants. it went off extreamly well, only I lost 250ll so was the only one that had any reason to be out of humour, butt I certainly was not so. Puff was admirable, & would not lett Mr. Pelham give the Royall Guests any supper, tho the Princess wanted it extreamly; butt then he & all the rest of us satt down to a very good one after they were gon. they were in exceeding good humour, & I assure you exceedingly civil to Linky, & ask'd very kindly after my Lady who at that time was a good deal out of order. I love Dear Linky for a thousand reasons, butt not a little for his affectionate attachment to you. I dont know if you have heard it, butt if you have not I beg you would not betray me. twas actually with difficulty that Mr. Pelham persuaded him to be of the party. butt indeed I took the liberty to say that however commendable a difficulty of that kind in any other Place might be, it really would be inexcusable at Esher. however he was there, and behaved well.

The Discourse all day was generall, and the chief toppicks were the place & the improvements that are & may be made, not a word drop'd that could in the least offend your sincerest freinds; not was there ever mention'd even the names of any one that you thinke are not your freinds. so really every thing went just as I could have wish'd it; & I am sure it pleased your brother who by the way is not a little offended at this beating up for voluntaires for Huntington Races, & told me if Sandwich provokes I can give him a kick in that County, for all his vain pretended popularity. butt pray dont say I told you this. & he spoke so freely upon this meeting before old Wall, that he has declared off & does not go to them. & I have heard that even Ld Gower himself has hinted his disaprobation of it to the Duke of Beford who's answer as I hear was, Good God what can I do? Sandwich is so poppular that I cant help it. people will crowd in upon us whether we will or no. Now I must own this is the first time I ever heard of Sandwich's popularity, & it is my firm opinion that the two people in England now the most unpoppular are Sandwich & his freind. butt I cant help throwing in a maxim I have heard that the Greenland Fishery have, when the Wale is struck give loose to the rope & they are sure to catch him, for he will at last throw himself on the shore. butt if they pull at the rope it most likely oversetts the Vessell, or at least the rope breaks, & the Whale certainly escapes & if the Whale may be allowed to laugh he certainly does at the too hasty fishermen. – butt to return to our Esher Party, it went on, & ended well. the Duchess of Richmond & I lay there (not together) & tho wee were both engaged on business in London the next day, yett as it was the 21st July wee could not refuse going to Oatlands to join in a health that is dear to us all. I hear the messager is ready so I must conclude. tho it had perhaps been better for you that he had been ready an hour ago. so adieu my Dearest Lord. Taw is gon to dine at Dickers, butt if she had been here I am sure she would have joyned with me in my most sincere compliments to the Duchess of Newcastle.

Your's most affectionately & for ever,

Richmond &c.

460. RICHMOND TO NEWCASTLE

Whitehall
27th July 1750

My Dear Lord,

I suppose his Majesty knows of the death of Lt Coll. Jenkinson,[1] which was a very great loss to the Regiment consequently to me. it hapned some time ago & I imediately acquainted His Royall Highness the Duke with it, butt I thought it was impropper to trouble his Majesty with any recommendation before he return'd to England, so did not mention it sooner to you. My Major Sr James Chamberlayn is as good an officer as any of his ranke in the army; & he was a Captain of foot in 1706. butt I will say no more for fear I should break in upon what I was avoiding. all I shall therefore add is that till his Majesty is pleased to appoint a Lieutenant Coll: to the Regiment, I will do my best to see it shant suffer for the want of one. for I really thinke I need not assure you that I have the good of the Corps most extreamly at heart.

I am, My Dear Lord, Your Grace's most faithfull humble servant

Richmond &c.

461. NEWCASTLE TO RICHMOND

Hanover
Augt 3/14 1750

My Dear Lord,

I have receiv'd both your Letters; and will obey your Commands about you Lieut. Colonel; and endeavour to do so, about the Living of St. Olav's for little Hughes. There has happen'd here a most melancholy Accident. Your friend Mor Freechappel, has kill'd poor Schwicheldt, the Elder, in a Duel. Everybody is concern'd for Him. I am sure, I have Reason to be so; having lost one of the best Friends, I had, in this Country. The King is extremely concern'd for Him. Mor Freechappel is gone off. The Duel was, immediately, occasion'd by Something, that pass'd at Court, the night before. Schwicheldt was as Honest, and as good natur'd a Man, as ever was born. I am much oblig'd to you, for all your kindeness in your long Letter – But it is only a Continuance of your Goodness. I hope, I am well with the Earl of Lincoln. The Duchess of Newcastle sends Her best Service to you, and the Duchess of Richmond; to whom I beg mine.

I am, Ever Your's

Holles Newcastle[2]

462. STONE TO RICHMOND

Privy Garden
Monday afternoon near 5 o'clock

My Lord,

My Lord Duke of Newcastle received yesterday, the honour of your Graces two Letters, by Brettle. He depends upon seeing you at Newcastle House, this Evening, at eight o'clock, where your Grace will meet my Lord Chancellor, Mr Pelham, &c. I have

---

1. Lieutenant Colonel Charles Jenkinson, an officer of the Royal Horse Guards, and one of Richmond's squadron commanders at Dettingen.

2. Richmond died on 8 August 1750 at Godalming, where he kept an establishment as a half way house, and a place for changing horses, on his journeys to London. He had been there a week, having been taken ill on the journey from London. The Duchess of Richmond was with him when he died.

my Lord Duke's Orders to relate many very material things to your Grace, before you go to Newcastle House and I therefore beg to receive your Orders, whether I should wait upon you, at your House, & at what time; or whether I am to expect the honour of seeing your Grace here, as you mentioned your Intention to be.

I am with the greatest Respect My Lord your Graces most obed, humble servt
Andrew Stone

The Correspondence of
the Dukes of
Richmond and Newcastle
1724–1750

INDEX

by Ann Hudson

INDEX

An asterisk denotes a footnote with biographical details. Place-names are given their modern locations where possible.

311

Fauquiere, William, 25*
Fawkener, Sir Everard, 186*, 192, 195, 263–5
Felpham (W. Sussex), 43, 99
Fens, 298
Fenton, Lavinia, 58n
Fermor, Thomas, 1st Earl of Pomfret, 284
Fernhurst (W. Sussex), 43–4
Ferrol (Spain), 35, 39–40, 42, 44, 170
Fielding, Hon. Charles, 17*, 19, 201
Fielding, Henry, xxxii, xxxvi
Finale (Italy), 270, 272
Finch, Daniel, 8th Earl of Winchelsea and 3rd Earl of Nottingham, 112*, 115–16, 159
Finch, Hon. Edward, 157*
Finch, Heneage, 2nd Earl of Aylesford, 196n
Finch, Heneage, Lord Guernsey, 196*
Finchley Common (Greater London), 195
Findon (W. Sussex), 10n, 51, 81
Finisterre (France), 30n; Battles of (1747), 245n, 246n, 260n
Finland, 74
Firle (E. Sussex), 10n, 51, 206n, 247n
Fisher, Brice, 284*
Fittleworth (W. Sussex), 33n
Fitzgerald, Emily, Countess of Kildare, see Lennox, Lady Emily
Fitzgerald, George, Lord Offaly, 266*
Fitzgerald, James, 20th Earl of Kildare (later 1st Duke of Leinster), xxxvi, 101n, 237*, 239, 241, 266–7, 283, 300n
Fitzgerald, Mary, Countess of Kildare, 266
Fitzgerald, Sir Thomas, 19*–20
Fitzjames, James Stuart, 'Count', 207*, 227
Fitzroy, Lady, 67
Fitzroy, Lord Augustus, 67*, 69
Fitzroy, Charles, 2nd Duke of Grafton, 23*, 36, 55–6, 69, 82, 91, 98, 101, 104, 109, 113, 115, 146–53 passim, 159, 161, 206, 209, 224, 233, 237–42, 246, 250, 256, 262, 269–70, 294, 299, 302, 305
Fitzroy, George, Lord Euston, 250*
Fitzwilliam, Lady, 227
Fitzwilliam, Richard, 5th Viscount, 69
Fitzwilliam, William, 2nd Earl (Baron Milton), 83*, 122
Flanders, see Netherlands, Austrian
Fleming, _____, 299
Fleury, Cardinal André Hercule de, 21*, 28, 30, 34, 42, 45, 87, 135n
Florence (Italy), 18n, 19, 21n
Flushing (Netherlands), 170, 244, 257, 291
Foliot, _____, 147
Folkes, Miss, 259
Folkes, Martin, xxxiv, 259n
Folliot, _____, 9
Folliott, General, 99, 178
Fontenoy (Belgium), Battle of (1745), xxiv, 166n, 167n
Fordingbridge (Hants.), 277n
Fort Augustus (Highland), 208, 222
Fort William (Highland), 208, 210, 222
Forth, river, 202, 203n
Forton, Gosport (Hants.), 235n
Foster, Henry, xxix
Foster, William, 10, 13

Fouquet, Marshal Charles Louis Auguste de, Duc de Belle-Isle, 85n, 87*, 97, 162–7 passim, 170, 238, 252, 255–6
Fowke, Brigadier Thomas, 175*
Fowler, _____, 37
Fox, Capt., 260
Fox, Lady Caroline, see Lennox, Lady Caroline
Fox, Henry, xxiv, xxxvi, 136n, 137*, 138n, 214–18, 236–7, 254, 261, 268–9, 278, 294n, 296
Fox, Stephen, 1st Lord Ilchester, xxxvi, 236–7*
Foxcraft, Henry, 285
Foxhall, Charlton (W. Sussex), xxviii, xxxiv
Frampton, Rev. Thomas, 63n
France, xxxv, 14, 18, 21n, 28, 30–1, 34, 42–50 passim, 58–9, 68, 75–87 passim, 93–157 passim, 163–71 passim, 192, 207–11 passim, 219–64 passim, 270–82 passim, 287–9, 292–3, 299; fear of invasion from (1745–6), xxv, 174–82 passim, 194, 197, 237; see also Paris
Francis I, Holy Roman Emperor, 78*, 85, 87, 163n, 165, 167, 170, 219–20, 252
Frankfurt (W. Germany), 102–3, 107
Frankland, Mary, 37n
Fraser, Simon, 12th Lord Lovat, 213*, 223n
Frederick II, 'The Great', King of Prussia, 48, 50, 53, 59n, 85, 87, 143, 148–9, 154, 157, 165–7, 170–1, 238, 262
Frederick, Prince, see Hesse, Prince Frederick of
Frederick, Prince of Wales, see Wales, Frederick, Prince of
Frederick, Charles, 247n
Frederick, John?, 53
Frederick, Thomas, 10*, 13
Freechappell, _____, 103*, 116–17, 275, 278, 280, 306
Freemasons of the Grand Lodge of England, xxxv, xxxvii, 23n
Freiburg (W. Germany), 117, 151, 156
Frisi, Paolo, xxxiv
Froubert, _____, 87–8
Fuller, Maj.-Gen., 244
Fuller, John, of Brightling, 7*, 8, 9, 32n, 37, 286, 299
Fuller, John, of Uckfield, xxxv
Fuller, Rob, 282
Funtington (W. Sussex), 37
Furnes (Veurne) (Belgium), 251
Furnese, Henry, 86*

Gage, Thomas, 1st Viscount, 206*, 218, 247, 251, 255, 261
Gage, Sir William, xxxv, 10*, 13, 25–6, 51, 69n, 206n
Gage, Hon. William Hall, 247*, 261
Galilei, Alessandro, xxvii
Galley, William, xxxi, 276n, 277, 282
Galway (Ireland), 73, 78–9
Gardiner, _____, 302–4
Gardiner, Dr., 301–2, 304
Garland, _____, 126
Garland, Nathaniel, 5*, 126
Gashry, Francis, 21*, 78
Geering, John, 295–6, 298–9
Gelves, Count of, see Fitzjames, James Stuart
Genoa (Italy), 167, 230, 238, 256
Geoghahagen, _____, 199–200

316

317

and '45 Rebellion, 187–98; foreign travel, 13n, 14, 106, 111–12, 287n; indispositions, 38–9, 70

Lennox, Lady Sarah, xxxviii, 300

Lequis, ———— de, 99

Lestock, Commodore Richard, 81*, 230

Lethbury, 299

Leveson-Gower, John, 1st Earl Gower, 86*, 91, 182, 203–4, 225, 266–8, 305

Levis, Pierre Louis de, Marquis de Mirepoix, 289

Levson, Lady B., 305

Lewes (E. Sussex), xxvi, 4–8, 10, 18, 29, 51, 60, 67, 170–3, 230–1, 247–8, 255, 285–6, 292; election of 1742, 77, 80–1; election of 1743, 121, 123, 126, 128, 130, 132

Lewis, Thomas, 38, 43

Lewis, Isle of (Western Isles), 222

Lewkenor family, 15n

Leyden (Netherlands), University of, xxxiv

Lichfield (Staffs.), 185–96

Liddell, Sir Henry, 25*, 82, 243, 247

Lidsey (W. Sussex), 37

Liège (Belgium), 255, 257

Lifford, 1st Earl of, see La Rochefoucauld, Frederic de Roye de

Ligonier, John, 65*, 88, 120–1, 147, 174, 185–90 passim, 196–8, 221, 249–53 passim, 257

Lille (France), 147

Lima (Peru), 83

Limerick, Viscount, see Hamilton, James

Lincoln, 9th Earl of, see Clinton, Henry Fiennes; Countess of, see Clinton, Catherine

Lindsay, John, 20th Earl of Crawford, 29*

'Linky', see Clinton, Henry Fiennes

Linlithgow (Lothian), 200

Liphook (Hants.), 151

Lisbon (Portugal), 81

Lismore, Earl of, see O'Brien, Col. Daniel

'Little Blue', see Adrian, Issak

'Little Rock', 25

Littlegreen, in Compton (W. Sussex), 7n

Liverpool (Merseyside), 187

Lizard, The (Cornwall), 168, 174, 177

Lloyd, Col., 231

Lobkowitz, Prince Johann G., 97*

Lochaber (Highland), 222

Lochiel, see Cameron, Donald

Lockhart/Lockyart, Major, 202–3

London: cricket matches in, xxxv; 2nd Duke of Richmond's houses in, xxvii–viii; threatened by rebel army (1745), xxv, 192, 194–7; and passim

London Hospital, xxxiii, xxxviii

Lonsdale, 3rd Viscount, see Lowther, Henry

Lorraine, 119, 133; Prince Charles of, 85, 104–5, 107, 111, 114–22 passim, 125–8, 142–56 passim, 166–7, 271; Grand Duke Francis of, see Francis I, Holy Roman Emperor

Lothian, 1st Marquis of, see Kerr, Robert

Loudoun, 4th Earl of, see Campbell, John

Loudun, 120

Loughborough (Leics.), 198

Louis XIV, King of France, 290n

Louis XV, King of France, 21n, 30, 45, 145, 149, 271, 290

Louisburg (Canada), 181, 276n

Lovat, 12th Lord, see Fraser, Simon

Lovell, Sir Nathaniel, 22*

Low Countries, see Netherlands, Austrian

Lowendahl, General Count Ulrich de, 253*, 257

Lowther, Col., 64, 180n

Lowther, Henry, 3rd Viscount Lonsdale, 182*, 185, 194

Lowther Hall (Cumbria), 182n

Luchesi, General, 294

Ludgater, ————, 63

Lumley family (Earls of Scarbrough), xxx, 239

Lumley, James, 32n, 48, 57*, 67, 80, 101

Lumley, Richard, 2nd Earl of Scarbrough, 18*, 20, 32, 57

Lumley, Thomas, 3rd Earl of Scarbrough, 231*

Lunenberg, Baron, 117

Luxembourg, 223

Lys, river, 148

Maastricht (Netherlands), 233n, 249n, 254, 270, 272

Macanas, Melchior, 244*, 257

Macartney, Miss, 231

Macclesfield (Cheshire), 197–9

Mackentosh, John, 180*

Mackenzie, George, 3rd Earl of Cromarty, 213*

Mackenzie, John, Lord Macleod, 213

MacLean, Sir Hector, 185*

MacLeod, Lord see Mackenzie, John

MacSwiney, Owen, xxxii–iii, 40, 73*, 101

Maddox, Isaac, 101*, 232–3

Madeira Islands, 31

Madrid (Spain), 28n, 43, 96

Magdalen Hill fair, 67

Maillebois, Jean Baptiste François Desmarets, Marquis de, 75*, 87, 165

Mainz (Mayence) (W. Germany), 114, 117, 119, 128–9

Malaga (Spain), 44

Malton, Earl of, see Watson-Wentworth, Thomas

Manchester, 188, 191–3, 196–8

Manhood, Hundred of (W. Sussex), 62

Mann, Sir Horace, xxxvi, 21*

Mann, Nicholas, 23*, 295

Manners, Lord George, 248*

Manners, John, 2nd Duke of Rutland, xxvi, 3n

Manners, Lady Katherine, see Pelham, Lady Katherine

Manningham, Thomas, 77*, 300*

Mansfield, 1st Earl of, see Murray, William

Mantua (Italy), 84

Maplerden, William, 286*

March, Earl of, see Lennox, Charles, Earl of March

Marchmont, 3rd Earl of, see Campbell, Hugh Hume

Maria Theresa, Queen of Hungary, later Empress, 31n, 48, 56n, 59, 68, 75, 78n, 83–99 passim, 105, 118, 126, 132–3, 139, 148, 163, 167, 171, 207, 209, 221, 236, 252, 254, 262, 272, 276, 288–9

Market Harborough (Leics.), 198

Marlborough, 1st Duke of, see Churchill, John; 3rd Duke of, see Spencer, Charles

Martin, Edmund, 10*

Martin, Admiral William, 142*, 170, 174, 177, 222, 227

Martinique (West Indies), 260

Matthews, Thomas, 85*, 87, 159

North Berwick (Lothian), 211
Northampton, 5th Earl of, *see* Compton, James
Northampton, 194–5, 198
Northumberland, 9th Earl of, *see* Percy, Henry
Norton, Robert, 228, 295*
Norton, Robert (junior), 228, 255?, 295*
Norton, in Aldingbourne (W. Sussex), 37, 43
Nottingham, 3rd Earl of, *see* Finch, Daniel
Nottingham, 23, 164–5, 193, 195
Nova Scotia (Canada), 169, 171–2, 181–2, 226–7, 238
Nugent, Brigadier, 207
Nugent, Col., 207
Nugent, Robert, 233*, 261
Nursling (Hants.), 299n
Nyton, in Aldingbourne (W. Sussex), 43, 144

Oakes, ———, 153, 155
Oatlands, in Weybridge (Surrey), 244, 256, 260, 299, 305
O'Brien, Col. Daniel, titular Earl of Lismore, 222*
Offaly, Lord, *see* Fitzgerald, George
Ogilvy, David, Lord, titular Earl of Airlie, 176*
Oglander, George, 31
Ogle, Sir Chaloner, 34*–5, 40, 42, 44, 46–7, 58, 68, 142
O'Hara, James, 2nd Lord Tyrawley, 156*, 223–4
Old Pretender, *see* Stuart, James
'Old Puff', *see* Fitzroy, Charles
Old Warden (Beds.)
Oneglia (Italy), 143
Ongley, Sir Samuel, 5n
Ongley, Samuel, 5*
Onslow, Richard, 102*
Opdam, ———, 14
Opero, ———, 136
Oppenheim (W. Germany), 107
Orange, Anne, Princess of, 14, 288, 299; William Charles Henry, Prince of, 14, 249*–52, 254–6, 261–2, 270–1, 287–92
Orford, 1st Earl of, *see* Walpole, Sir Robert
Orme, Garton, xxxi, 14–15*, 16, 32n, 37–8, 47, 76, 90, 145, 239, 248
Ormonde, 3rd Marquis, *see* Butler, Charles
Orsini, Philip Joseph, Count of Rosenburg, 231*
Orten, Comte d', 48
Osborne, Thomas, 4th Duke of Leeds, 284*
Ossorio, Chevalier Giuseppe d', 30*, 41, 43, 85, 88?, 96–7, 150, 252
Ossory, Earl of, *see* Butler, Charles
Ostend (Belgium), 129, 142–3, 167–70, 172–3, 177
O'Sullivan, John, 222*
Over, ———, 108–9, 112–13, 115, 119
Oving (W. Sussex), 8n
Oxford, 3rd Earl of, *see* Harley, Edward
Oxford, Christchurch, 150–1

Packington Hall (Warwicks.), 196
Page, John, xxx, 4*–8, 11, 36, 38, 52–6, 302–3
Pagham (W. Sussex), 43, 62
Painshill, nr. Cobham (Surrey), 166n
Palatinate, Upper, 97
Palfi, ———, 59
Palmer, ———, 48–9
Panama, 32, 34, 41n, 67, 83, 85

Pardo, Convention of, 21n
Parham (W. Sussex), 5n, 204, 277n
Paris (France), xxxiii, xxxv, 30n, 31, 43, 75, 229, 272, 282, 287n, 288–9, 292, 304; 2nd Duke of Richmond's proposed embassy to, xxx, xxxv, 274–5, 279, 280–2
Parke, John, 94*
Parker, George, 8
Parker, Jack, 100, 110, 115, 118, 128–9, 196
Parslow, Capt., 195
Passarowitz, Treaty of (1718), 31n
Paulet, Charles, 3rd Duke of Bolton, xxxiv, 58*–9, 154, 157
Pauncefort, Edward, 25*, 51, 68, 88
Paxton, ———, 11
Payne, George, 91–2*
Peachey, Bulstrode, *see* Knight, Bulstrode Peachey
Peachey, Francis, 37*, 91, 157
Peachey, Sir John (of West Dean), 19*, 21, 35n, 36, 41, 44, 47, 62, 64, 69, 209
Peachey, John (of Eartham), 6n
Peachey, William, 37n, 90–1
Peckham, Henry ('Lisbon'), 31–2*, 62–3, 77, 78, 230
Peckham, Mary, 7n
Peckham, Richard, 144n
Peckham, Sir Thomas, 144n
Peckham, William, 144*
Pelham, Col., 219, 254
Pelham, Catherine, *see* Clinton, Catherine
Pelham, Frances, 126n
Pelham, Henrietta, Duchess of Newcastle, xxv, 44, 71–4, 89, 138–40, 149, 296; indispositions, 90, 274–5, 285, 298
Pelham, Henry, xxv–vi, xxxvii–ix, 22, 30, 33, 35, 49–50, 71–2, 80, 94, 101–13 *passim*, 129–59 *passim*, 166–7, 177, 179–81, 188, 191, 209, 215–20, 228–30, 234, 237, 241, 244–62 *passim*, 266–7, 273–82 *passim*, 299, 302–6, Plate 3; and 1734 election, 4, 6–8, 10–11, 14; and 1741 election, 40–1, 43–7, 52, 54, 60; and 1742 election, 64, 66–8, 76, 81; and 1743 election, 23; appointed 1st Lord of the Treasury, xxiv–v, 106–7, 109–10, 114–16, 118–21, 124–5, 127; patronage, 32, 49, 77–9, 92–5, 98, 123, 125–6, 129, 159, 204–6, 239, 249, 269, 294
Pelham, James, 19*–20, 25, 46, 60, 114, 151, 246, 248, 302, 304
Pelham, Lady Katherine, xxvi, 3*
Pelham, Thomas, 1st Lord, xxv
Pelham, Thomas (of Lewes), 5n
Pelham, Thomas (of Lewes, junior), 11, 30, 121
Pelham, Thomas (of Stanmer), 5n
'Pem', *see* Herbert, Henry
Pembroke, 9th Earl of, *see* Herbert, Henry; Countess of, *see* Herbert, Mary
Penkridge (Staffs.), 190
Penn, William, 4n
Penrith (Cumbria), 186, 198
Peper Harrow (Surrey), xxxv
Percy, Henry, 9th Earl of Northumberland, xxvii
Perkins, ———, 88
Perth, Duke of, *see* Drummond, James
Perth (Tayside), 174, 176–7, 207, 210n, 223
Peter the Great, Tsar of Russia, 48n

Peter, ———, 57
Peterborough, 3rd Earl of, *see* Mordaunt, Charles
Peterborough, Deanery of, 118, 122
Petersfield (Hants.), 66
Petersham, Viscount, *see* Stanhope, William
Petre, Robert, 8th Lord, xxix
Petworth (W. Sussex), 18, 37n, 38, 46–7, 63, 66–7, 80, 265, 278
Pevensey (E. Sussex), 46, 206n
Pevensey Bay, 197
Phelypeaux, la Comtesse de St. Florentin, 290
Phelypeaux, Jean Frederic, Comte de Maurepas, 290–1
Phelypeaux, Louis, Comte de St. Florentin, 290n
Philbrow, John, 184n
Philip, Infante Don, 171, 220, 222, 226n, 244
Philippins (Belgium), 244
Philippsburg (W. Germany), 143
Phillipson, John, 13*, 49, 160*
Piacenza (Italy), Battle of (1746), 226
Piazzetta, Giovanni Battista, xxxii
Piedmont, 252; *see also* Savoy
Pierrepoint, Evelyn, 2nd Duke of Kingston, 58*, 190–1, 196, 198, 203–4, 206–8, 210–11
Piosassque, Charles, le Comte, 102*
Pitshill, in Tillington (W. Sussex), 46n
Pitt, William, the Elder (later Earl of Chatham), 95n, 203*–5, 214n, 248, 261
Pizaro, ———, 83
Plassendaal, nr. Ostend (Belgium), 169
Plymouth (Devon), 133, 231, 260
Pococke, Dr. Richard, xxix
Poland, 149, 155–6; King of, *see* Augustus III
Pomfret, 1st Earl of, *see* Fermor, Thomas
Pompadour, Madame de, 290
Ponsonby, William, Viscount Duncannon (later 2nd Earl of Bessborough), 231*
Pont à Tressine, 147
Poole, Sir Francis, 26, 33, 126*, 130n, 161
Poole (Dorset), 277, 286
Pope Benedict XIV, 97
Port l'Orient (France), 231
Port Mahon (Minorca), 34, 81
Portland, 2nd Duke of, *see* Bentinck, William
Portland, 1st Earl of, *see* Bentinck, William
Portmore, 1st Earl of, *see* Colyear, David
Porto Bello (Panama), 32, 34, 41n, 83, 85
Portsdown Fair, 67
Portslade (E. Sussex), 69
Portsmouth, Duchess of, *see* Keroualle, Louise de
Portsmouth (Hants.), 35, 44, 62–5, 72, 75, 134, 136, 235, 243; dockyard, 34, 49, 70; *see also* Spithead
Portugal, 167
Potter, John, Archbishop of Canterbury, 28*, 99, 101, 106, 259*, 261
Potter, Thomas, 261*
Poyntz, Stephen, 150*
Prague (Czechoslovakia), 85–8, 93, 97, 156
Prattin, ———, 21
Preddon, John, 43*
Prendergast, Lady, 32
Prendergast, Sir Thomas, xxviii, xxx, 3*–5, 8–9, 16n, 20, 24, 52n, 63, 73–4, 78, 86, 99, 101–2, 106, 123, 201, 203, 208–9, 232
Preston (Lancs.), 198

Prestonpans (Lothian), Battle of (1745), 183
Princess Royal, *see* Orange, Anne, Princess of
Provence (France), 230, 236, 238, 240
Prussia, 58–9, 68, 78, 83, 87, 130–1, 148–9, 151, 156, 166–73 *passim*, 177, 200, 262–5, 289; King of, *see* Frederick II
Pulborough (W. Suss.), 38
Pulteney, Harry, 102*, 223
Pulteney, William, 1st Earl of Bath, xxv, xxxii, xxxvi, 12n, 86*, 106, 109, 112–27 *passim*, 159, 203–5n
Puysieulx, Marquis de, *see* Brulart, Louis Philoxene

Quebec (Canada), 238
'Quimp, Old' *see* Fleury, Cardinal de

Radcliffe, Charles, Earl of Derwentwater, 192n, 233n, 237
Radcliffe, Charlotte, Countess of Newburgh, 233
Radcliffe, James, Viscount Kinnaird (later 4th Earl of Newburgh), 192*, 273*, 278
Raddon, ———, 31
Rake (W. Sussex), 282n
Ramsden, Thomas, 230*, 273, 278, 281, 296
Ranby, John, 103*, 117, 304
Rastat (W. Germany), 114
Ravensworth Castle, 25n
Rawlinson, Robert, 77*
Read, Maj.-Gen., 142–3
Réaumur, René Antoine, xxxiv
Reichenau (W. Germany), 166
Reid, David (the Bristol Buggerer), 22*
Reigate (Surrey), 22
Renewoode, Lord, 14
Rentone, Capt., 32
Rhine, river, 99, 107–17 *passim*, 122, 125–6, 129, 142–51 *passim*, 165–70 *passim*
Rhineweiller (W. Germany), 122
Ricci, Marco, xxxii
Ricci, Sebastiano, xxxii
Rich, Lt.-Col. Sir Robert, 211?*, 255
Richardson, Samuel, xxxii
Richelieu, Duc de, *see* Vignerot du Plessis, Louis François Armand de
Richmond, Ann, Duchess of, *see* Lennox, Ann; Sarah, Duchess of, *see* Lennox, Sarah; Dukes of, *see* Lennox, Charles
Richmond House, Whitehall (London), xxvii-viii, xxxiii, 17n, 57n
Ride, John, 180n
Rideout, Richard, 292
Ridge, Sir Thomas, 144, 246
Riggs, Ogle, 44*
Robert, ———, 269
Robinson, Sir Thomas (1695–1770; later 1st Lord Grantham), 28*–9, 31, 75, 167, 177, 267, 269, 275, 293
Robinson, Sir Thomas (1702–77), 225, 293*–4
Rochalart, Admiral, 34*
Rochefort (France), 222, 231
Rockingham, 3rd Earl and 1st Marquis of, *see* Watson-Wentworth, Thomas; 2nd Marquis of, *see* Watson-Wentworth, Charles
Rodmell (E. Sussex), 240

322

Simon, Henry, 286, 292
Singleton (W. Sussex), xxvii, 37
Skelton, Maj.-Gen., 185*, 190
Slindon (W. Sussex), 43, 60, 93–4, 282; cricket team, xxxv, 37n, 62–3, 69, 73, 285n
Slingelandt, M. Simon van, 14*
Sloane, Sir Hans, xxxiv
Smelt, Maurice, 302
Smith, _____, xxxiii
Smith, Capt., 8
Smith, Edward, 58n–9
Smith, Joseph, xxxiii, 35–6, 40*, 43, 63
Smith, Robert/Robin, 9, 11
Smith, Commodore Thomas, 170*
Smith, Thomas, 140*
Smythe, Robert, 15n
Soane family, 4n
Soane, Francis, 8*, 14, 36–7, 54, 56
Society of Antiquaries, xxxiv, xxxviii–ix
Soissons, see Pelham, Thomas (of Lewes, junior)
Somerset, 6th Duke of, see Seymour, Charles
Somerset, Charles, 4th Duke of Beaufort, 222*
Sorgvliet, The Hague (Netherlands), xxxiii
South Beveland (Netherlands), 264
South Seas, 42–3, 83, 85
Southby, _____, 107
Southwark (Greater London), 301–4, 306
Sowle, Major, 296–8, 301, 303
Spa (Belgium), 228–9
Spain, 19n, 20, 170, 207, 209, 230, 238, 244, 254–64 passim; and Central America, 27–35 passim, 42–4, 61, 80–7 passim; and Italy, 58, 84, 96–7, 133, 142–3, 157, 167, 226, 230
Spence, Mrs., 43
Spencer, Charles, 3rd Duke of Marlborough, 99*, 116, 119, 122, 125–6
Spencer, Charles, 4th Earl of Sunderland, xxv
Spencer, Tom, 16
Speyer (W. Germany), 119–20, 122, 126, 128
Spithead, 47, 76, 78, 134, 155; see also Portsmouth
Stafford, 188–90, 194, 196
Stainmoor (Durham), 186
Stair, 2nd Earl of, see Dalrymple, John
Stanhope, Philip, 4th Earl of Chesterfield, xxxii, xxxvi, 49*, 51n, 95n, 160, 163, 165, 220, 234*, 236, 253, 256, 261–7 passim, 276
Stanhope, William, 1st Earl of Harrington, 22n, 57*, 75, 141, 146, 148–9, 153, 158, 163, 165–8, 172, 177, 179, 182, 197, 202, 205, 207, 214, 216, 220–2, 225, 234–5, 266
Stanhope, William, Viscount Petersham (later 2nd Earl of Harrington), 162*, 202
Stanley, Edward, 11th Earl of Derby, 189*, 194
Stanley, James, 10th Earl of Derby, 40n
Stanley, Mary, Countess of Derby, 40*–1, 43, 70
Stanmer (E. Sussex), 5n
Stansted (W. Sussex) 18n, 62–3
Stedham (W. Sussex), 277n
Steele, Thomas, 230*–1
Steele, William, 276
Steenbergen (Netherlands), 257
Steep (Hants.), 41n
Stewart, see also Stuart
Stewart, _____, 257
Stewart, John Roy, 210*

Steyning (W. Sussex), 7, 47
Stilton (Cambs.), 187
Stirling (Central), 175, 200, 203n
Stockport (Greater Manchester), 189
Stoke-on-Trent (Staffs.), 190
Stokes, _____, 33
Stone, Andrew, xxiv, xxvi, 19*, 43, 70, 73, 88, 171, 184, 248, 274, 293, 295, and passim
Stone (Staffs.), 185–8, 190
Strange, John, 94*
Strasbourg (France), 111, 119
Strathallan, 4th Viscount, see Drummond, William
Strenlugh, _____ d', 154
Strickland, Tom, 37
Stronbergh, Baron, 150
Stuart, Charles Edward, xxiv–v, xxxi, 133–5n, 140, 169–70*, 172–4, 179, 182–3, 185–6, 194n, 197, 200, 210n–11, 213, 219–20, 222, 242, 257
Stuart, Henry, Cardinal of York, 192, 197n
Stuart, James, 12n, 40n, 95
Stubbs, _____, 297n
Sturt, _____, 37
Stuttgart (W. Germany), 151
Sunderland, 4th Earl of, see Spencer, Charles
Sunninghill (Berks.), 58n
Surrey, cricket team, 73
Sussex, 2nd Earl of, see Yelverton, George
Sutherland (Highland), 210–13
Sutton, Lord George Manners, 248*
Sutton, Lord Robert Manners, 248*
Sweden, 74, 93, 95, 165n, 289
Swiss, _____, 57
Switzerland, 147, 182

Taaffe, Thomas, xxxi, 248*
Talbot, Charles, 1st Duke of Shrewsbury, 280
Talbot, Richard, styled Earl of Tyrconnel, 207*, 227
Tallard, Marshal Count Camille de, 101
Tankerville, 2nd Earl of, see Bennett, Charles
'Tanky', see Bennett, Charles
Tapner, Benjamin, 279n
'Taw', see Lennox, Sarah, Duchess of Richmond
Taylor, Dr., 195
Temple, Richard, Viscount Cobham, 86*, 91
Tencin, Cardinal Pierre Guerin, 135*
Tholen, Island of (Netherlands), 257
Thompson, Lt.-Col. 64
Thompson, Anthony, 135
Thorndon (Essex), xxix
Thorpe, _____, 303
Thynne, Thomas, 2nd Viscount Weymouth, 23*
Till, Tom, 19*, 21
Tilley, Thomas, 184n
Tillington (W. Sussex), 46n
Tomkyns, _____, 304
Torbay (Devon), 39
Torres, Admiral, 142
Tortington (W. Sussex), 32
'Totty', see Russell, John
Toulon (France), 34, 42–3, 45, 59, 79, 154n, 238
Tournai (Belgium), 167
Townshend, Charles, 2nd Viscount, xxv, xxxvi, 22, 57n, 159n
Townshend, George, 159*

325

PALLANT HOUSE GALLERY

9 North Pallant Chichester

A Finely-Restored
**Queen Anne
Town House**

**The Walter Hussey
Collection**
Paintings, Drawings,
Prints, Sculpture

**The
Geoffrey Freeman
Collection of
Bow Porcelain**

**The Shippams
Edwardian Kitchen**

18th century
**English
Drinking Glasses**

Period Furniture
in Historically-Decorated Rooms

Open Tuesday to Saturday
10.00 a.m. to 5.30 p.m.
Further enquiries telephone Chichester (0243) 774557